# 100

# Fastest-Growing

# CAREERS

Your Complete Guidebook to Major Jobs with the Most Growth and Openings

TENTH EDITION

jist Works
America's Career Publisher®

Michael Farr

# 100 Fastest-Growing Careers, Tenth Edition
*Your Complete Guidebook to Major Jobs with the Most Growth and Openings*

© 2009 by JIST Publishing

Published by JIST Works, an imprint of JIST Publishing
7321 Shadeland Station, Suite 200
Indianapolis, IN 46256
Phone: 800-648-JIST          Fax: 877-454-7839
E-mail: info@jist.com        Web site: www.jist.com

Some books by Michael Farr:
*Best Jobs for the 21st Century*
*Overnight Career Choice*
*Next-Day Job Interview*
*Same-Day Resume*
*The Quick Resume & Cover Letter Book*
*The Very Quick Job Search*

JIST's Top Careers™ Series:
*Top 300 Careers*
*Top 100 Health-Care Careers*
*Top 100 Careers Without a Four-Year Degree*
*Top 100 Careers for College Graduates*
*Top 100 Computer and Technical Careers*

Visit www.jist.com for free job search information, tables of contents and sample pages, and ordering information on our many products.

Quantity discounts are available for JIST products. Please call 800-648-JIST or visit www.jist.com for a free catalog and more information.

Acquisitions Editor: Susan Pines
Development Editor: Stephanie Koutek
Database Work: Laurence Shatkin
Cover Layout: Alan Evans
Interior Design: Marie Kristine Parial-Leonardo
Interior Layout: Aleata Halbig
Proofreaders: Linda Seifert, Jeanne Clark

Printed in the United States of America

10 09     9 8 7 6 5 4 3 2

We have been careful to provide accurate information throughout this book, but it is possible that errors and omissions have been introduced. Please consider this in making any career plans or other important decisions. Trust your own judgment above all else and in all things.

ISBN 978-1-59357-601-1

# Relax. You Don't Have to Read This Whole Book!

You don't need to read this entire book. I've organized it into easy-to-use sections so you can get just the information you want. You will find everything you need to

★ Learn about the 100 fastest-growing jobs, including their daily tasks, pay, outlook, and required education and skills.

★ Match your personal skills to the jobs.

★ Take seven steps to land a good job in less time.

To get started, simply scan the table of contents to learn more about these sections and to see a list of the jobs described in this book. Really, this book is easy to use, and I hope it helps you.

## Who Should Use This Book?

This is more than a book of job descriptions. I've spent quite a bit of time thinking about how to make its contents useful for a variety of situations, including

★ **Exploring career options.** The job descriptions in Part II give a wealth of information on many of the most desirable jobs in the labor market. The assessment in Part I can help you focus your career options.

★ **Considering more education or training.** The information helps you avoid costly mistakes in choosing a career or deciding on additional training or education—and it increases your chances of planning a bright future.

★ **Job seeking.** This book helps you identify new job targets, prepare for interviews, and write targeted resumes. The advice in Part III has been proven to cut job search time in half.

★ **Career planning.** The job descriptions help you explore your options, and Parts III and IV provide career planning advice and other useful information.

## Source of Information

The job descriptions come from the good people at the U.S. Department of Labor, as published in the most recent edition of the *Occupational Outlook Handbook*. The *OOH* is the best source of career information available, and the descriptions include the most current, accurate data on jobs. Thank you to all the people at the Department of Labor who gather, compile, analyze, and make sense of this information. It's good stuff, and I hope you can make good use of it.

*Mike Farr*

Mike Farr

# Contents

## Summary of Major Sections

**Introduction.** Provides an explanation of the job descriptions, how best to use the book, and other details. *Begins on page 1.*

**Part I: Using the Job-Match Grid to Choose a Career.** Match your skills and preferences to the jobs in this book. *Begins on page 15.*

**Part II: Descriptions of the 100 Fastest-Growing Careers.** Presents thorough descriptions of the 100 fastest-growing jobs. Education and training requirements for these jobs vary from on-the-job training to a four-year college degree or more. Each description gives information on the nature of the work, work environment, employment, training, other qualifications, advancement, job outlook, earnings, related occupations, and sources of additional information. The jobs are presented in alphabetical order. The page numbers where specific descriptions begin are listed in the detailed contents. *Begins on page 31.*

**Part III: Quick Job Search—Seven Steps to Getting a Good Job in Less Time.** This relatively brief but important section offers results-oriented career planning and job search techniques. It includes tips on identifying your key skills, defining your ideal job, using effective job search methods, writing resumes, organizing your time, improving your interviewing skills, and following up on leads. The last part of this section features professionally written and designed resumes for some of the fastest-growing jobs. *Begins on page 331.*

**Part IV: Important Trends in Jobs and Industries.** This section includes two well-written articles and two charts on labor market trends. The articles and charts are worth your time. Titles of the articles are "Tomorrow's Jobs" and "Employment Trends in Major Industries." Titles of the charts are "High-Paying Occupations with Many Openings, Projected 2006–2016" and "Large Metropolitan Areas That Had the Fastest Employment Growth, 2006." *Begins on page 397.*

## Detailed Contents

# Introduction

This book is about improving your life, not just about selecting and getting a fast-growing job. The career you choose will have an enormous impact on how you live.

A huge amount of information is available on occupations, but most people don't know where to find accurate, reliable facts to help them make good career decisions—or they don't take the time to look. Important choices such as what to do with your career or whether to get additional training or education deserve your time.

If you are considering more training or education, this book will help with solid information. The education and training needed for the jobs described in this book vary enormously. You will notice that many of the better-paying jobs may require more training or education than you now have. Some require brief training or on-the-job experience. Many better-paying jobs, however, call for technical training lasting from a few months to a few years. Others require a four-year college degree or more. But some jobs, such as certain sales and management occupations, have high pay but do not always involve advanced education. This book is designed to give you facts to help you explore your options.

A certain type of work or workplace may interest you as much as a certain type of job. If your interests and values lead you to work in health care, for example, you can choose from a variety of work environments and a variety of industries. This book includes details to help you weigh your options.

The time you spend in career planning can pay off in higher earnings, but being satisfied with your work—and your life—is often more important than the amount you earn. For this reason, I suggest that you begin to explore alternatives by following your interests and finding a career path that allows you to use your skills and talents. This book can help you find the work that suits you best and that offers a promising future.

## The 100 Fastest-Growing Careers List

I think it's important for you to understand how I developed the list of the fastest-growing careers for this book. I used the most recent data from the U.S. Department of Labor, which provides growth projections through 2016 for 269 major jobs that encompass 90 percent of the workforce. I started by sorting all of those jobs based on their percent of projected growth through 2016, from highest to lowest. I then sorted the jobs based on the projected number of annual new job openings, also from highest to lowest. For these 269 jobs, the average (mean) growth rate is 10.7 percent, and the average number of openings annually is 89,944.

From these two lists I created a third list based on the relative position of each job on the first two lists. I did this by adding the score for each job's position on the lists. For example, a job with a high percentage of growth and a high number of new job openings appears toward the top.

Perhaps you're wondering why I use figures for both job growth and number of openings. Aren't these two ways of saying the same thing? Actually, both are important. A job may have a fast growth rate overall, but it may be a relatively small occupation with not many people employed in it. So jobs with both a high rate of growth *and* many openings offer the best opportunity.

The 100 jobs with the most favorable combined scores for projected percent increase and annual number of job openings through 2016 appear in the following table. As you can see, the list includes a variety of jobs at all levels of education, training, and interest.

Notice that four of the top 10 fastest-growing jobs are in the health-care area, the most rapidly growing field of all. Another point to notice is that most of the fastest-growing jobs require training or education beyond high school. While job opportunities at all levels of education and training are listed in the table, many better-paying jobs require postsecondary education or training. If you want more information on important labor market trends, consider reading the excellent and brief review of labor market trends in Part IV.

Note that you can find a complete description for each job listed below in Part II. You will also find these jobs listed in the table of contents along with the page number where each job description begins.

# The 100 Fastest-Growing Careers

|  | Percent Growth Through 2016 | Annual Job Openings |
|---|---|---|
| 1. Personal and Home Care Aides | 51 | 255,301 |
| 2. Nursing, Psychiatric, and Home Health Aides | 28 | 553,632 |
| 3. Customer Service Representatives | 25 | 600,937 |
| 4. Registered Nurses | 23 | 233,499 |
| 5. Computer Software Engineers | 38 | 91,829 |
| 6. Medical Assistants | 35 | 92,977 |
| 7. Teachers—Postsecondary | 23 | 237,478 |
| 8. Social and Human Service Assistants | 34 | 80,142 |
| 9. Child Care Workers | 18 | 471,956 |
| 10. Counter and Rental Clerks | 23 | 123,769 |
| 11. Bill and Account Collectors | 23 | 118,709 |
| 12. Computer Scientists and Database Administrators | 37 | 60,619 |
| 13. Counselors | 21 | 142,874 |
| 14. Computer Systems Analysts | 29 | 63,166 |
| 15. Grounds Maintenance Workers | 18 | 350,089 |
| 16. Management Analysts | 22 | 125,669 |
| 17. Receptionists and Information Clerks | 17 | 334,124 |
| 18. Pharmacy Technicians | 32 | 54,453 |
| 19. Security Guards and Gaming Surveillance Officers | 17 | 224,209 |
| 20. Financial Analysts and Personal Financial Advisors | 37 | 46,431 |
| 21. Teachers—Self-Enrichment Education | 23 | 64,449 |
| 22. Computer Support Specialists and Systems Administrators | 18 | 134,344 |
| 23. Social Workers | 22 | 77,292 |
| 24. Fitness Workers | 27 | 51,235 |
| 25. Accountants and Auditors | 18 | 134,463 |
| 26. Building Cleaning Workers | 14 | 885,403 |
| 27. Food and Beverage Serving and Related Workers | 13 | 2,734,108 |
| 28. Human Resources, Training, and Labor Relations Managers and Specialists | 16 | 158,266 |
| 29. Securities, Commodities, and Financial Services Sales Agents | 25 | 47,750 |
| 30. Retail Salespersons | 12 | 1,367,480 |

| | Percent Growth Through 2016 | Annual Job Openings |
|---|---|---|
| 31. Office Clerks, General | 13 | 765,803 |
| 32. Hotel, Motel, and Resort Desk Clerks | 17 | 75,502 |
| 33. Teachers—Preschool, Kindergarten, Elementary, Middle, and Secondary | 12 | 464,967 |
| 34. Bookkeeping, Accounting, and Auditing Clerks | 12 | 286,854 |
| 35. Dental Assistants | 29 | 29,482 |
| 36. Tellers | 13 | 146,077 |
| 37. Market and Survey Researchers | 20 | 49,974 |
| 38. Chefs, Cooks, and Food Preparation Workers | 11 | 882,881 |
| 39. Automotive Service Technicians and Mechanics | 14 | 97,350 |
| 40. Barbers, Cosmetologists, and Other Personal Appearance Workers | 14 | 99,695 |
| 41. Correctional Officers | 16 | 62,982 |
| 42. Animal Care and Service Workers | 19 | 42,539 |
| 43. Public Relations Specialists | 18 | 51,216 |
| 44. Veterinary Technologists and Technicians | 41 | 14,674 |
| 45. Construction Laborers | 11 | 257,407 |
| 46. Licensed Practical and Licensed Vocational Nurses | 14 | 70,610 |
| 47. Athletes, Coaches, Umpires, and Related Workers | 15 | 59,854 |
| 48. Cost Estimators | 19 | 38,379 |
| 49. Advertising Sales Agents | 20 | 29,233 |
| 50. Medical Records and Health Information Technicians | 18 | 39,048 |
| 51. Gaming Services Occupations | 23 | 22,197 |
| 52. Paralegals and Legal Assistants | 22 | 22,756 |
| 53. Demonstrators, Product Promoters, and Models | 18 | 33,367 |
| 54. Instructional Coordinators | 22 | 21,294 |
| 55. Surveyors, Cartographers, Photogrammetrists, and Surveying and Mapping Technicians | 21 | 25,427 |
| 56. Insurance Sales Agents | 13 | 64,162 |
| 57. Property, Real Estate, and Community Association Managers | 15 | 49,916 |
| 58. Teacher Assistants | 10 | 193,986 |
| 59. Construction Managers | 16 | 44,158 |
| 60. Health Educators | 26 | 13,707 |
| 61. Carpenters | 10 | 223,225 |
| 62. Surgical Technologists | 24 | 15,365 |
| 63. Recreation Workers | 13 | 61,454 |
| 64. Painters and Paperhangers | 11 | 102,967 |
| 65. Secretaries and Administrative Assistants | 9 | 574,285 |
| 66. Physical Therapists | 27 | 12,072 |
| 67. Maintenance and Repair Workers, General | 10 | 165,502 |
| 68. Financial Managers | 13 | 57,589 |
| 69. Teachers—Special Education | 15 | 39,496 |
| 70. Medical and Health Services Managers | 16 | 31,877 |
| 71. Advertising, Marketing, Promotions, Public Relations, and Sales Managers | 12 | 65,317 |
| 72. Dental Hygienists | 30 | 10,433 |
| 73. Sales Representatives, Wholesale and Manufacturing | 9 | 199,684 |
| 74. Computer and Information Systems Managers | 16 | 30,887 |
| 75. Emergency Medical Technicians and Paramedics | 19 | 19,513 |

*(continued)*

*(continued)*

## The 100 Fastest-Growing Careers

|  | Percent Growth Through 2016 | Annual Job Openings |
|---|---|---|
| 76. Pharmacists | 22 | 16,358 |
| 77. Physical Therapist Assistants and Aides | 29 | 10,049 |
| 78. Truck Drivers and Driver/Sales Workers | 8 | 490,877 |
| 79. Engineers | 11 | 92,700 |
| 80. Roofers | 14 | 38,398 |
| 81. Education Administrators | 12 | 56,178 |
| 82. Real Estate Brokers and Sales Agents | 11 | 79,921 |
| 83. Science Technicians | 12 | 56,749 |
| 84. Artists and Related Workers | 16 | 29,527 |
| 85. Physicians and Surgeons | 14 | 38,027 |
| 86. Police and Detectives | 11 | 62,829 |
| 87. Bus Drivers | 10 | 86,909 |
| 88. Loan Officers | 11 | 54,237 |
| 89. Pipelayers, Plumbers, Pipefitters, and Steamfitters | 10 | 77,545 |
| 90. Automotive Body and Related Repairers | 12 | 40,926 |
| 91. Taxi Drivers and Chauffeurs | 13 | 35,954 |
| 92. Environmental Scientists and Hydrologists | 25 | 7,648 |
| 93. Physician Assistants | 27 | 7,147 |
| 94. Construction and Building Inspectors | 18 | 12,606 |
| 95. Food Processing Occupations | 8 | 115,379 |
| 96. Medical Scientists | 20 | 11,099 |
| 97. Brokerage Clerks | 20 | 10,826 |
| 98. Occupational Therapists | 23 | 8,338 |
| 99. Lawyers | 11 | 49,445 |
| 100. Sales Worker Supervisors | 4 | 270,124 |

# Some Advice for Reviewing the Fastest-Growing Careers

Major changes are occurring in our labor market, and Part IV describes these changes. Rapidly growing jobs will often be more attractive career options than jobs that are not growing quickly. Rapidly growing jobs often offer better-than-average opportunities for employment and job security. For this reason, you should pay attention to jobs that are projected to grow rapidly.

But there most likely will be openings for new people in slower-growing or declining jobs. Some slower-growing jobs employ large numbers of people and will create many openings due to retirement, people leaving the field, and other reasons. Considering jobs that are generating large numbers of openings but that may not have high percentage growth rates will give you more options to consider. Information on all major occupational and industry groups is provided in Part IV, including those that are growing more slowly than average or even declining.

# Keep in Mind That Your Situation Is Probably Not "Average"

Although the employment growth and earnings trends for many occupations and industries are quite positive, the averages in this book will not be true for many individuals. Earnings and job opportunities vary enormously in different parts of the country, in different occupations, and in different industries. My point is that your situation is probably not average. But this book's solid information is a great place to start. Good information will give you a strong foundation for good decisions.

# Four Important Labor Market Trends That Will Affect Your Career

Our economy has changed over the past years, with profound effects on how we work and live. Here are four trends that you must consider in making your career plans.

## 1. Education Pays

I'm sure you won't be surprised to learn that people with higher levels of education and training have higher average earnings. The data that follows comes from the U.S. Department of Labor. I've selected data to show you the median earnings for people with various levels of education. (The median is the point where half earn more and half earn less.) Based on this information, I computed the earnings advantage of people at various education levels over those who did not graduate from high school. I've also included information showing the average percentage of people at that educational level who are unemployed.

**Earnings for Year-Round, Full-Time Workers Age 25 and Over, by Educational Attainment**

| Level of Education | Median Annual Earnings | Premium Over High School Dropouts | Unemployment Rate |
|---|---|---|---|
| Professional degree | $76,648 | $54,860 | 1.1 |
| Doctoral degree | $74,932 | $53,144 | 1.4 |
| Master's degree | $59,280 | $37,492 | 1.7 |
| Bachelor's degree | $50,024 | $28,236 | 2.3 |
| Associate degree | $37,492 | $15,704 | 3 |
| Some college, no degree | $35,048 | $13,260 | 3.9 |
| High-school graduate | $30,940 | $9,152 | 4.3 |
| High school dropout | $21,788 | | 6.8 |

*Source: Bureau of Labor Statistics*

As you can see in the table, the earnings difference between a college graduate and someone with a high school education is $19,000 a year—enough to buy a nice car, make a down payment on a house, or even take a few months' vacation for two to Europe. As you see, over a lifetime, this earnings difference will make an enormous difference in lifestyle.

The table makes it very clear that those with more training and education earn more than those with less and experience lower levels of unemployment. Jobs that require education and training beyond high school are projected to grow significantly faster than jobs that do not. People with higher levels of education and training are less likely to be unemployed and, when they are, they tend to remain unemployed for shorter periods of time. There are always exceptions, but it is quite clear that a college education results in higher earnings and lower rates of unemployment.

## 2. Knowledge of Computer and Other Technologies Is Increasingly Important

As you look over the jobs in this book, you may notice that many require computer or technical skills. Even jobs that do not appear to be technical often call for computer literacy. Managers, for example, are often expected to understand and use spreadsheet, word-processing, and database software.

In most fields, people without job-related technical and computer skills will have a more difficult time finding good opportunities because they are often competing with those who have these skills. Employers tend to hire people with the skills they need, and people without these abilities won't get the best jobs. So, no matter what your age, consider upgrading your job-related computer and technology skills if you need to—and plan to stay up to date.

## 3. Ongoing Education and Training Are Essential

School and work once were separate activities, and most people did not go back to school after they began working. But with rapid changes in technology, most people are now required to learn throughout their work lives. Jobs are constantly upgraded, and today's jobs often cannot be handled by people who have only the knowledge and skills that were adequate for workers a few years ago.

To remain competitive, you will need to constantly upgrade your technology and other job-related skills. This may include taking formal courses, reading work-related materials and Web sites, signing up for on-the-job training, or participating in other forms of education. Upgrading your work skills on an ongoing basis is no longer optional for most jobs.

## 4. Good Career Planning Is More Important Than Ever

Most people spend more time watching TV in a week than they spend on career planning during an entire year. Yet most people will change their jobs many times and make major career changes five to seven times. For this reason, it is important to spend time considering your career options and preparing to advance.

While you probably picked up this book for its information on jobs, it also provides a great deal of information on career planning. For example, Part I offers an assessment to match your skills to the fastest-growing jobs. Part III gives good career and job search advice. Part IV has useful information on labor market trends. I urge you to read these and related materials because career-planning and job-seeking skills are the keys to surviving in this economy.

# Tips on Using This Book

This book is based on information from a variety of government sources and includes the most up-to-date and accurate data available. The job descriptions are well written and pack a lot of information into a brief format. *100 Fastest-Growing Careers* can be used in many ways, and this discussion provides tips for the following individuals:

- ★ Students and others exploring career, education, or training alternatives

- ★ Job seekers

- ★ Employers and business people

- ★ Counselors, instructors, career specialists, librarians, and other professionals

# Tips for People Exploring Career, Education, or Training Alternatives

*100 Fastest-Growing Careers* is an excellent resource for anyone exploring career, education, or training alternatives. Many people do not have a good idea of what they want to do in their careers. Others may be considering additional training or education but may not know what sort of training they should get. If you are one of these people, this book can help in several ways.

**Review the list of jobs.** Trust yourself. Research studies indicate that most people have a good sense of their interests. Your interests can be used to guide you to career options you should consider in more detail.

Begin by looking over the occupations listed in the table of contents. Look at all the jobs, because you may identify previously overlooked possibilities. If other people will be using this book, please don't mark in it. Instead, on a separate sheet of paper, list the jobs that interest you. Or make a photocopy of the table of contents and use it to mark the jobs that interest you.

Next, look up and carefully read the descriptions of the jobs that most interest you in Part II. A quick review will often eliminate one or more of these jobs based on pay, working conditions, education required, or other considerations. After you have identified the three or four jobs that seem most interesting, research each one more thoroughly before making any important decisions.

**Match your skills to the jobs in this book using the Job-Match Grid.** Another way to identify possible job options is to answer questions about your skills and job preferences in Part I, "Using the Job-Match Grid to Choose a Career." This section will help you focus your job options and concentrate your research on a handful of job descriptions.

**Study the jobs and their training and education requirements.** Too many people decide to obtain additional training or education without knowing much about the jobs the training will lead to. Reviewing the descriptions in this book is one way to learn more about an occupation before you enroll in an education or training program. If you are currently a student, the job descriptions in this book can help you decide on a major course of study or learn more about the jobs for which your studies are preparing you.

Do not be too quick to eliminate a job that interests you. If a job requires more education or training than you currently have, you can obtain this training in many ways.

**Don't abandon your past experience and education too quickly.** If you have significant work experience, training, or education, do not abandon it too quickly. Many people have changed careers after carefully considering what they wanted to do and found that the skills they already had could still be used.

*100 Fastest-Growing Careers* can help you explore career options in several ways. First, on a separate sheet of paper, list the skills needed in the jobs you have held in the past. Then, using the descriptions in this book as a reference, do the same for jobs that interest you now. By comparing the lists, you will be able to identify skills you used in previous jobs that you could also use in jobs that interest you for the future. These "transferable" skills form the basis for moving to a new career.

You can also identify skills you have developed or used in nonwork activities, such as hobbies, family responsibilities, volunteer work, school, the military, and extracurricular involvements.

If you want to stay with your current employer, the job descriptions can also help. For example, you may identify jobs within your organization that offer more rewarding work, higher pay, or other advantages over your present job. Read the descriptions related to these jobs, because you may be able to transfer into another job rather than leave the organization.

## Tips for Job Seekers

You can use the job descriptions in this book to give you an edge in finding job openings and in getting job offers—even when you are competing with people who have better credentials. Here are some ways *100 Fastest-Growing Careers* can help you in the job search.

**Identify related job targets.** You may be limiting your job search to a small number of jobs for which you feel qualified, but by doing so you eliminate many jobs you could do and enjoy. Your search for a new job should be broadened to include more possibilities.

Go through the entire list of jobs in the table of contents and check any that require skills similar to those you have. Look at all the jobs, since doing so sometimes helps you identify targets you would otherwise overlook.

You may wish to answer questions about your skills and job preferences in Part I, "Using the Job-Match Grid to Choose a Career." Your results can help you identify career options that may suit you.

Many people are not aware of the many specialized jobs related to their training or experience. The descriptions in *100 Fastest-Growing Careers* are for major job titles, but a variety of more-specialized jobs may require similar skills. Reference books that list more-specialized job titles include the *Enhanced Occupational Outlook Handbook* and the *O*NET Dictionary of Occupational Titles*. Both are published by JIST.

The descriptions can also point out jobs that interest you but that have higher responsibility or compensation levels. While you may not consider yourself qualified for such jobs now, you should think about seeking jobs that are above your previous levels but within your ability to handle.

**Prepare for interviews.** This book's job descriptions are an essential source of information to help you prepare for interviews. If you carefully review the description of a job before an interview, you will be much better prepared to emphasize your key skills.

**Negotiate pay.** The job descriptions in this book will help you know what pay range to expect. Note that local pay and other details can differ substantially from the national averages in the descriptions.

## Tips for Employers and Business People

Employers, human resource professionals, and other business users can use this book's information to write job descriptions, study pay ranges, and set criteria for new employees. The information can also help you conduct more-effective interviews by providing a list of key skills needed by new hires. You and your employees can consult the job descriptions when planning lateral moves and promotions.

## Tips for Counselors, Instructors, Career Specialists, Librarians, and Other Professionals

Counselors, instructors, librarians, and other professionals will find this book helpful to clients and students who are exploring career options or job targets. You can help clients and job seekers by encouraging them to review the table of contents to find jobs of interest. You may wish to familiarize them with the structure of the job descriptions so that they can find the information they need easily.

My best suggestion to professionals is to get this book off the shelf and into the hands of the people who need it. Leave it on a table or desk and show people how the information can help them. Wear this book out. Its real value is as a tool used often and well.

# Information on the Major Parts of This Book

This book is designed for easy use. The table of contents provides brief comments on each part, and that may be all you need to understand its contents. Here are some additional details for getting the most out of *100 Fastest-Growing Careers*.

## Part I: Using the Job-Match Grid to Choose a Career

Part I features an assessment with checklists and questions to match your skills and preferences to the jobs in this book. The seven skills covered in the assessment include artistic, communication, interpersonal, managerial, mathematics, mechanical, and science. The five job characteristics covered in the assessment are economically sensitive, geographically concentrated, hazardous conditions, outdoor work, and physically demanding.

## Part II: Descriptions of the 100 Fastest-Growing Careers

Part II is the main section of the book and probably the reason you picked it up. It contains well-written descriptions for the 100 fastest-growing jobs in alphabetical order. The content for these job descriptions comes from the U.S. Department of Labor and is considered by many to be the most accurate and up-to-date available. The jobs provide an enormous variety at many levels of earnings and interest.

To explore career options, do the assessment in Part I or go to the table of contents and identify those jobs that seem interesting. If you are interested in medical jobs, for example, you can quickly spot those that you want to learn more about. You may also see other jobs that look interesting, and you should consider these as well. Your next step would be to read the descriptions for the jobs that interest you and, based on what you learn, identify those that *most* interest you.

Each occupational description follows a standard format, making it easy for you to compare jobs. The following overview describes the information found in each description and offers tips on how to interpret it.

### Job Title

This is the title used for the job in the *Occupational Outlook Handbook,* published by the U.S. Department of Labor.

### O*NET Codes

The numbers in parentheses that appear just below the title of every job description are from the Occupational Information Network (O*NET)—a system used by state employment service offices to classify applicants and job openings, and by some career information centers and libraries to file occupational information.

O*NET codes are based on the Standard Occupational Classification (SOC) system. You can access O*NET on the Internet at http://www.online.onetcenter.org. The *O*NET Dictionary of Occupational Titles* offers the information in a reader-friendly book and is published by JIST.

### Significant Points

This section highlights key occupational characteristics discussed in the job description.

### Nature of the Work

This section discusses what workers do on the job, what tools and equipment they use, and how closely they are supervised. Individual job duties may vary by industry or employer. For instance, workers in larger firms tend to be more specialized, whereas those in smaller firms often have a wider variety of duties. Most occupations have several levels of skills and responsibilities through which workers may progress. Beginners may start as trainees, performing routine tasks under close supervision. Experienced workers usually undertake more difficult tasks and are expected to perform with less supervision.

Some job descriptions mention common alternative job titles or occupational specialties. For example, the job description on accountants and auditors discusses a few specialties, such as public accountants, management accountants, and internal auditors.

Information in this section may be updated from earlier editions for several reasons. One is the emergence of occupational specialties. Information also may be updated due to changing technology that affects the way in which a job is performed. Or job duties may be affected by modifications to business practices, such as restructuring or changes in response to government regulations. An example is paralegals and legal assistants, who are increasingly being utilized by law firms in order to lower costs and increase the efficiency and quality of legal services.

Many sources are consulted in researching the nature of the work section or any other section of a job description. Usual sources include articles in newspapers, magazines, and professional journals. Useful information also appears on the Web sites of professional associations, unions, and trade groups. Information found on the Internet or in periodicals is verified through interviews with individuals employed in the occupation; professional associations; unions; and others with occupational knowledge, such as university professors and counselors in career centers.

The Work Environment subsection identifies the typical hours worked, the workplace environment, physical activities, susceptibility to injury, special equipment, and the extent of travel required. In many occupations, people work regular business hours—40 hours a week, Monday through Friday—but many do not. The work setting can range from a hospital to a mall to an outdoor site. Truck drivers might be susceptible to injury, while paramedics have high job-related stress. Some workers may wear protective clothing or equipment, do physically demanding work, or travel frequently.

Information on various worker characteristics, such as the average number of hours worked per week, is obtained from the Current Population Survey (CPS)—a survey of households conducted by the U.S. Census Bureau for the Bureau of Labor Statistics.

## Training, Other Qualifications, and Advancement

After knowing what a job is all about, it is important to understand how to prepare for it. This section describes the most significant sources of education and training, including the education or training preferred by employers, the typical length of training, and the possibilities for advancement. Job skills sometimes are acquired through high school, informal on-the-job training, formal training (including apprenticeships), the U.S. Armed Forces, home study, hobbies, or previous work experience. For example, sales experience is particularly important for many sales jobs. Many professional jobs, on the other hand, require formal postsecondary education—postsecondary vocational or technical training, or college, postgraduate, or professional education.

In addition to training requirements, this book mentions desirable skills, aptitudes, and personal characteristics. For some entry-level jobs, personal characteristics are more important than formal training. Employers generally seek people who read, write, and speak well; compute accurately; think logically; learn quickly; get along with others; and demonstrate dependability.

Some occupations require certification or licensing for entry, advancement, or independent practice. Certification or licensing usually requires completing courses and passing examinations. Some occupations have numerous professional credentials granted by different organizations. In this case, the most widely recognized organizations are listed in this book.

Many occupations increasingly are requiring workers to participate in continuing education or training in relevant skills, either to keep up with the changes in their occupation or to improve their advancement opportunities.

Some job descriptions list the number of training programs. For example, the job description on pharmacists indicates the number of colleges of pharmacy accredited by the American Council on Pharmaceutical Education. The minimum requirements for federal government employment cited in some job descriptions are based on standards set by the U.S. Office of Personnel Management.

The training section may focus on changes in educational, certification, or licensing requirements, such as an increase in the number of hours of required training or in the number of states requiring a license.

## Employment

This section reports the number of jobs that the occupation provides, the key industries in which those jobs were found, and the number or proportion of self-employed workers in the occupation, if significant. When significant, the geographic distribution of jobs and the proportion of part-time workers (those working less than 35 hours a week) are mentioned.

## Job Outlook

In planning for the future, you need to consider potential job opportunities. This section describes the factors that will result in employment growth or decline.

*Employment change.* This subsection reflects the occupational projections in the National Employment Matrix. Each occupation is assigned a descriptive phrase based on its projected percent change in employment over the 2006–2016 period. This phrase describes the occupation's projected employment change relative to the projected average employment change for all occupations combined.

Many factors are examined in projecting the employment change for each occupation. One such factor is changes in technology. New technology can either create new job opportunities or eliminate jobs by making workers obsolete. Another factor that influences employment trends is demographic change. By affecting the services demanded, demographic change can influence occupational growth or decline.

Another factor affecting job growth or decline is changes in business practices, such as restructuring businesses or outsourcing (contracting out) work. Corporate restructuring has made many organizations "flatter," resulting in fewer middle management positions. Also, in the past few years, jobs in some occupations have been "off-shored"— moved to low-wage foreign countries. The substitution of one product or service for another can also affect employment projections. Competition from foreign trade usually has a negative effect on employment. Often, foreign manufacturers can produce goods more cheaply than they can be produced in the United States, and the cost savings can be passed on in the form of lower prices with which U.S. manufacturers cannot compete. Another factor is job growth or decline in key industries. If an occupation is concentrated in an industry that is growing rapidly, it is likely that that occupation will grow rapidly as well.

*Job prospects.* In some cases, this book mentions that an occupation is likely to provide numerous or relatively few job openings. This information reflects the projected change in employment, as well as replacement needs. Large occupations in which workers frequently enter and leave generally provide the most job openings—reflecting the need to replace workers who transfer to other occupations or who stop working.

---

## Key Phrases Used in the Job Descriptions

This table explains how to interpret the key phrases that describe projected changes in employment. It also explains the terms for the relationship between the number of job openings and the number of job seekers.

**Changing Employment Between 2006 and 2016**

| If the statement reads | Employment is projected to |
| --- | --- |
| Grow much faster than average | Increase 21 percent or more |
| Grow faster than average | Increase 14 to 20 percent |
| Grow about as fast as average | Increase 7 to 13 percent |
| Grow more slowly than average | Increase 3 to 6 percent |
| Little or no change | Decrease 2 percent to increase 2 percent |
| Decline slowly or moderately | Decrease 3 to 9 percent |
| Decline rapidly | Decrease 10 percent or more |

**Opportunities and Competition for Jobs**

| If the statement reads | Job openings compared to job seekers may be |
| --- | --- |
| Very good to excellent opportunities | More numerous |
| Good or favorable opportunities | In rough balance |
| May face or can expect keen competition | Fewer |

---

## Projections Data

The employment projections table lists employment statistics from the National Employment Matrix. It includes 2006 employment, projected 2016 employment, and the 2006–2016 change in employment in both numerical and percentage terms. Numbers below 10,000 are rounded to the nearest hundred, numbers above 10,000 are rounded to the nearest thousand, and percentages are rounded to the nearest whole number. Numerical and percentage changes are calculated using non-rounded 2006 and 2016 employment figures and then are rounded for presentation in the employment projections table.

## Earnings

This section discusses typical earnings and how workers are compensated—by annual salaries, hourly wages, commissions, piece rates, tips, or bonuses. Within every occupation, earnings vary by experience, responsibility, performance, tenure, and geographic area. Almost every job description contains earnings data for wage and salary workers. Information on earnings in the major industries in which the occupation is employed may be given as well.

In addition to presenting earnings data from Bureau of Labor Statistics sources, some job descriptions contain additional earnings data from non-BLS sources. Starting and average salaries of federal workers are based on 2007 data from the U.S. Office of Personnel Management. The National Association of Colleges and Employers supplies information on average salary offers in 2007 for students graduating with a bachelor's, master's, or Ph.D. degree in certain fields. A few job descriptions contain additional earnings information from other sources, such as unions, professional associations, and private companies.

Benefits account for a significant portion of total compensation costs to employers. Benefits such as paid vacation, health insurance, and sick leave may not be mentioned, because they are so widespread. In some job descriptions, the absence of these traditional benefits is pointed out. Although not as common as traditional benefits, flexible hours and profit-sharing plans may be offered to attract and retain highly qualified workers. Less common benefits also include childcare, tuition for dependents, housing assistance, summers off, and free or discounted merchandise or services. For certain occupations, the percentage of workers affiliated with a union is listed.

## Related Occupations

Occupations involving similar duties, skills, interests, education, and training are listed.

## Sources of Additional Information

No single publication can describe all aspects of an occupation. Thus, this book lists the mailing addresses of associations, government agencies, unions, and other organizations that can provide occupational information. In some cases, toll-free telephone numbers and Internet addresses also are listed. Free or relatively inexpensive publications offering more information may be mentioned; some of these publications also may be available in libraries, in school career centers, in guidance offices, or on the Internet.

# Part III: Quick Job Search—Seven Steps to Getting a Good Job in Less Time

For more than 25 years, I've been helping people find better jobs in less time. If you have ever experienced unemployment, you know that it is not pleasant. Unemployment is something most people want to get over quickly—in fact, the quicker the better. Part III will give you some techniques to help.

I know that most of you who read this book want to improve yourselves. You want to consider career and training options that lead to a better job and life in whatever way you define this—better pay, more flexibility, more-enjoyable or more-meaningful work, proving to your mom that you really can do anything you set your mind to, and other reasons. That is why I include advice on career planning and job search in Part III. It includes the basics that are most important in planning your career and in reducing the time it takes to get a job. I hope it will make you think about what is important to you in the long run.

Part III showcases professionally written resumes for some of America's fastest-growing jobs. Use these as examples when creating your own resume. I know you will resist completing the activities in Part III, but consider this: It is often not the best person who gets the job, but the best job seeker. People who do their career planning and job search homework often get jobs over those with better credentials because they have these distinct advantages:

1. **They get more interviews,** including many for jobs that will never be advertised.

2. **They do better in interviews.**

People who understand what they want and what they have to offer employers present their skills more convincingly and are much better at answering problem questions. And, because they have learned more about job search techniques, they are likely to get more interviews with employers who need the skills they have.

Doing better in interviews often makes the difference between getting a job offer and sitting at home. And spending time planning your career can make an enormous difference to your happiness and lifestyle over time. So please consider reading Part III and completing its activities. I suggest you schedule a time right now to at least read it. An hour or so spent there can help you do just enough better in your career planning, job seeking, and interviewing to make the difference.

# Part IV: Important Trends in Jobs and Industries

This part is made up of very good articles and charts on labor market trends. These articles come directly from U.S. Department of Labor sources and are interesting, well written, and short. They will give you a good idea of factors that will impact your career in the years to come.

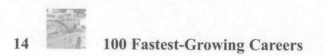

# Other Major Career Information Sources

The information in this book will be very useful, but you may want or need additional facts and guidance. Keep in mind that the job descriptions here cover major jobs and not the many more-specialized jobs that are often related to them. Each job description in this book provides some sources of information related to that job, but here are additional resources to consider. All are available through JIST Publishing.

*Occupational Outlook Handbook* (or the *OOH*): Updated every two years by the U.S. Department of Labor, this book provides descriptions of 270 major jobs covering more than 90 percent of the workforce. The *OOH* is the source of the job descriptions used in this book.

*Enhanced Occupational Outlook Handbook:* This resource includes all descriptions in the *OOH* plus descriptions of more than 5,800 more-specialized jobs that are related to them.

*O\*NET Dictionary of Occupational Titles:* This book is the only printed source of the jobs described in the U.S. Department of Labor's Occupational Information Network (O\*NET) database.

*New Guide for Occupational Exploration:* This important reference features an intuitive system based on extensive research to organize more than 900 jobs into 16 major interest areas and 117 more-specific work groups. The interest areas are based on U.S. Department of Education career clusters to closely link interests, learning, and occupations.

*Best Jobs for the 21st Century:* This best-selling book includes descriptions for the 500 jobs with the best combination of earnings, growth, and number of openings. Useful lists make jobs easy to explore (examples: highest-paying jobs by level of education or training; best jobs overall; and best jobs for different ages, personality types, interests, and more). Other books in the series include *200 Best Jobs for College Graduates, 300 Best Jobs Without a Four-Year Degree, 50 Best Jobs for Your Personality, 250 Best Jobs Through Apprenticeships, 40 Best Fields for Your Career, 225 Best Jobs for Baby Boomers, 250 Best-Paying Jobs, 10 Best College Majors for Your Personality, 150 Best Jobs for a Better World, 150 Best Jobs for Your Skills, 150 Best Jobs Through Military Training, 150 Best Low-Stress Jobs, 175 Best Jobs Not Behind a Desk, 200 Best Jobs for Introverts,* and *150 Best Recession-Proof Jobs.*

*Exploring Careers—A Young Person's Guide to 1,000 Jobs:* For youth in grades 7–12 exploring career and education opportunities, this book covers 1,000 job options in an interesting and useful format. Featured are profiles of real people at work, "skill samplers" that help youths better understand whether they have the skills required for certain jobs, and brief descriptions of jobs in logical groups.

*Young Person's Occupational Outlook Handbook:* This popular resource offers age-appropriate descriptions for each job in the *Occupational Outlook Handbook.* Very easy to use and understand, for grades 4 on.

# Using the Job-Match Grid to Choose a Career

*By the Editors at JIST*

This book describes so many occupations—how can you choose the best job for you? This section is your answer! It can help you to identify the jobs where your abilities will be valued, and you can rule out jobs that have certain characteristics you'd rather avoid. You will respond to a series of statements and use the Job-Match Grid to match your skills and preferences to the most appropriate jobs in this book.

So grab a pencil and get ready to mark up the following sections. Or, if someone else will be using this book, find a sheet of paper and get ready to take notes.

## Thinking About Your Skills

Everybody knows that skills are important for getting and keeping a job. Employers expect you to list relevant skills on your resume. They ask about your skills in interviews. And they expect you to develop skills on the job so that you will remain productive as new technologies and new work situations emerge.

But maybe you haven't thought about how closely skills are related to job satisfaction. For example, let's say you have enough communication skills to hold a certain job where these skills are used heavily, but you wouldn't really *enjoy* using them. In that case, this job probably would be a bad choice for you. You need to identify a job that will use the skills that you *do* enjoy using.

That's why you need to take a few minutes to think about your skills: the ones you're good at and the ones you like using. The checklists that follow can help you do this. On each of the seven skills checklists that follow, use numbers to indicate how much you agree with each statement:

3 = I strongly agree

2 = I agree

1 = There's some truth to this

0 = This doesn't apply to me

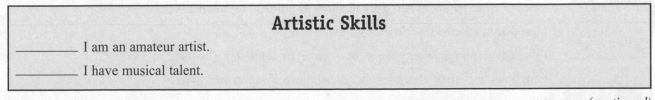

### Artistic Skills

_____ I am an amateur artist.

_____ I have musical talent.

*(continued)*

*(continued)*

_____ I enjoy planning home makeovers.

_____ I am good at performing onstage.

_____ I enjoy taking photos or shooting videos.

_____ I am good at writing stories, poems, articles, or essays.

_____ I have enjoyed taking ballet or other dance lessons.

_____ I like to cook and plan meals.

_____ I can sketch a good likeness of something or somebody.

_____ Playing music or singing is a hobby of mine.

_____ I have a good sense of visual style.

_____ I have participated in amateur theater.

_____ I like to express myself through writing.

_____ I can prepare tasty meals better than most people.

_____ I have a flair for creating attractive designs.

_____ I learn new dance steps or routines easily.

_____ **Total for Artistic Skills**

**A note for those determined to work in the arts:** Before you move on to the next skill, take a moment to decide whether working in some form of art is essential to you. Some people have exceptional talent and interest in a certain art form and are unhappy unless they are working in that art form—or until they have given their best shot at trying to break into it. If you are that kind of person, the total score shown above doesn't really matter. In fact, you may have given a 3 to just *one* of the statements above, but if you care passionately about your art form, you should toss out ordinary arithmetic and change the total to 100.

## Communication Skills

_____ I am good at explaining complicated things to people.

_____ I like to take notes and write up minutes for meetings.

_____ I have a flair for public speaking.

_____ I am good at writing directions for using a computer or machine.

_____ I enjoy investigating facts and showing other people what they indicate.

_____ People consider me a good listener.

_____ I like to write letters to newspaper editors or political representatives.

_____ I have been an effective debater.

_____ I like developing publicity fliers for a school or community event.

_____ I am good at making diagrams that break down complex processes.

_____ I like teaching people how to drive a car or play a sport.

_____ I have been successful as the secretary of a club.

_____ I enjoy speaking at group meetings or worship services.

_____ I have a knack for choosing the most effective word.

_____ I enjoy tutoring young people.

_____ Technical manuals are not hard for me to understand.

_____ **Total for Communication Skills**

# Interpersonal Skills

_____ I am able to make people feel that I understand their point of view.

_____ I enjoy working collaboratively.

_____ I often can make suggestions to people without sounding critical of them.

_____ I enjoy soliciting clothes, food, and other supplies for needy people.

_____ I am good at "reading" people to tell what's on their minds.

_____ I have a lot of patience with people who are doing something for the first time.

_____ People consider me outgoing.

_____ I enjoy taking care of sick relatives, friends, or neighbors.

_____ I am good at working out conflicts between friends or family members.

_____ I enjoy serving as a host or hostess for houseguests.

_____ People consider me a team player.

_____ I enjoy meeting new people and finding common interests.

_____ I am good at fundraising for school groups, teams, or community organizations.

_____ I like to train or care for animals.

_____ I often know what to say to defuse a tense situation.

_____ I have enjoyed being an officer or advisor for a youth group.

_____ **Total for Interpersonal Skills**

# Managerial Skills

_____ I am good at inspiring people to work together toward a goal.

_____ I tend to use time wisely and not procrastinate.

_____ I usually know when I have enough information to make a decision.

_____ I enjoy planning and arranging programs for school or a community organization.

_____ I am not reluctant to take responsibility when things turn out wrong.

_____ I have enjoyed being a leader of a scout troop or other such group.

_____ I often can figure out what motivates somebody.

_____ People trust me to speak on their behalf and represent them fairly.

_____ I like to help organize things at home, such as shopping lists and budgets.

*(continued)*

*(continued)*

_____ I have been successful at recruiting members for a club or other organization.

_____ I have enjoyed helping run a school or community fair or carnival.

_____ People find me persuasive.

_____ I enjoy buying large quantities of food or other products for an organization.

_____ I have a knack for identifying abilities in other people.

_____ I am able to get past details and look at the big picture.

_____ I am good at delegating authority rather than trying to do everything myself.

_____ **Total for Managerial Skills**

# Mathematics Skills

_____ I have always done well in math classes.

_____ I enjoy balancing checkbooks for family members.

_____ I can make mental calculations quickly.

_____ I enjoy calculating sports statistics or keeping score.

_____ Preparing family income tax returns is not hard for me.

_____ I like to tutor young people in math.

_____ I have taken or plan to take courses in statistics or calculus.

_____ I enjoy budgeting the family expenditures.

_____ **Subtotal for Mathematics Skills**

x 2    **Multiply by 2**

_____ **Total for Mathematics Skills**

# Mechanical Skills

_____ I have a good sense of how mechanical devices work.

_____ I like to tinker with my car or motorcycle.

_____ I can understand diagrams of machinery or electrical wiring.

_____ I enjoy installing and repairing home stereo or computer equipment.

_____ I like looking at the merchandise in a building-supply warehouse store.

_____ I can sometimes fix household appliances when they break down.

_____ I have enjoyed building model airplanes, automobiles, or boats.

_____ I can do minor plumbing and electrical installations in the home.

_____ **Subtotal for Mechanical Skills**

x 2    **Multiply by 2**

_____ **Total for Mechanical Skills**

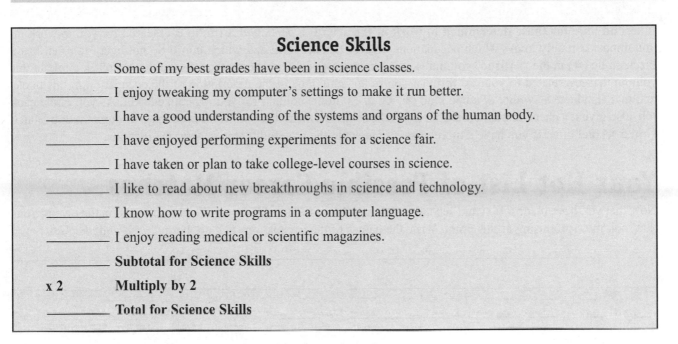

**Science Skills**

_____ Some of my best grades have been in science classes.

_____ I enjoy tweaking my computer's settings to make it run better.

_____ I have a good understanding of the systems and organs of the human body.

_____ I have enjoyed performing experiments for a science fair.

_____ I have taken or plan to take college-level courses in science.

_____ I like to read about new breakthroughs in science and technology.

_____ I know how to write programs in a computer language.

_____ I enjoy reading medical or scientific magazines.

_____ **Subtotal for Science Skills**

x 2     **Multiply by 2**

_____ **Total for Science Skills**

## Finding Your Skills on the Job-Match Grid

Okay, you've made a lot of progress so far. Now it's time to review what you've said about skills so you can use these insights to sort through the jobs listed on the Job-Match Grid.

Look at your totals for the seven skills listed previously. Enter your totals in the left column on this scorecard:

| Total | Skill | Rank |
|---|---|---|
| _____ | Artistic | _____ |
| _____ | Communication | _____ |
| _____ | Interpersonal | _____ |
| _____ | Managerial | _____ |
| _____ | Mathematics | _____ |
| _____ | Mechanical | _____ |
| _____ | Science | _____ |

Next, enter the rank of each skill in the right column—that is, the highest-scored skill gets ranked #1, the next-highest #2, and so forth. **Important:** Keep in mind that *the numbers in the Total column are only a rough guideline*. If you feel that a skill should be ranked higher or lower than its numerical total would suggest, *go by your impressions rather than just by the numbers*.

Now turn to the Job-Match Grid and find the columns for your #1-ranked and #2-ranked skills. Move down through the grid, going from page to page, and notice what symbols appear in those columns. If a row of the grid has a black circle (●) in *both* columns, circle the occupation name—or, if someone else will be using this book, jot down the name on a piece of paper. These occupations use a high level of both skills, or the skills are essential to these jobs.

Go through the Job-Match Grid a second time, looking at the column for your #3-ranked skill. If a *job you have already circled* has a black circle (●) or a bull's-eye (◉) in the column for your #3-ranked skill, put a check mark next to the occupation name. If none of your selected jobs has a black circle or a bull's-eye in this column, look for a white circle (○) and mark these jobs with check marks.

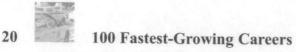

**A second note for those determined to work in the arts:** If a *particular* art form is essential for you to work in, you almost certainly know which occupations involve that art form and which don't. So not every job that has a black circle (●) in the "Artistic" column is going to interest you. Circle only the jobs that have a black circle in this column that *are* related to your art form (if you're not sure, look at the description of the occupation in this book) and that also have a symbol of some kind (●, ◐, or ○) in the column for your #2-ranked skill. As you circle each job, also give it a check mark, because there will be so few of them that you won't need to go through the Job-Match Grid a second time. If you have a more general interest in the arts, follow the general instructions.

# Your Hot List of Possible Career Matches

Now that you have made a first and second cut of the jobs on the Job-Match Grid, you can focus on the occupations that look most promising at this point. Write the names of the occupations that are both *circled* and *checked*:

_____        _____

_____        _____

_____        _____

_____        _____

_____        _____

_____        _____

This is your Hot List of occupations that you are going to explore in detail *if* they are not eliminated by certain important job-related factors that you'll consider next.

# Thinking About Other Job-Related Factors

Next, you need to consider four other job-related factors:

- ★ Economic sensitivity
- ★ Outdoor work

- ★ Physically demanding work
- ★ Hazardous conditions

## Economic Sensitivity

You've read about how our nation's economy has gone up and down over the years. When the economy is on an upswing, there are more job openings, but when it veers downward toward recession, jobs are harder to find.

Are you aware that these trends affect some occupations more than others? For example, during an economic upswing, people do more vacation traveling and businesses send more workers on business trips. This keeps travel agencies very busy, so they need to hire more travel agents. When the economy is going down, people cut back on their vacation travel, businesses tell their workers to use teleconferencing instead of business trips, and travel agents are not in demand. Some may be laid off, and people who want to enter this field may find very few openings. By contrast, most jobs in the health-care field are not sensitive to the economy, and automotive mechanics are just as busy as ever during economic slowdowns because people want to keep their old cars running.

So this issue of economic sensitivity (and its opposite, job security) is one that may affect which occupation you choose. Some people want to avoid economically sensitive occupations because they don't want to risk losing their job (or having difficulty finding a job) during times of recession. Other people are willing to risk being in an economically sensitive occupation because they want to profit from the periods when both the economy and the occupation are booming.

> How important is it to you to be in an occupation that *doesn't* go through periods of boom and bust along with the nation's economy? Check one:
>
> _____ It doesn't matter to me.
>
> _____ It's not important, but I'd consider it.
>
> _____ It's somewhat important to me.
>
> _____ It's very important to me.

If you answered "It doesn't matter to me," skip to the next section, "Outdoor Work." Otherwise, turn back to the Job-Match Grid and find the column for "Economically Sensitive."

If you answered "It's not important, but I'd consider it," see whether any of the jobs on your Hot List have a black circle (●) in this column. If so, cross them off and write an "E" next to them.

If you answered "It's somewhat important to me," see whether any of the jobs on your Hot List have a black circle (●) or a bull's-eye (◉) in this column. If so, cross them off and write an "E" next to them.

If you answered "It's very important to me," see whether any of the jobs on your Hot List have *any* symbol (●, ◉, or ○) in this column. If so, cross them off and write an "E" next to them.

# Outdoor Work

Some people prefer to work indoors in a climate-controlled setting, such as an office, a classroom, a factory floor, a laboratory, or a hospital room. Other people would rather work primarily in an outdoor setting, such as a forest, an athletic field, or a city street. And some would enjoy a job that alternates between indoor and outdoor activities.

> What is *your* preference for working indoors or outdoors? Check one:
>
> _____ It's very important to me to work **indoors.**
>
> _____ I'd prefer to work mostly **indoors.**
>
> _____ Either indoors or outdoors is okay with me.
>
> _____ I'd prefer to work mostly **outdoors.**
>
> _____ It's very important to me to work **outdoors.**

If you answered "Either indoors or outdoors is okay with me," skip to the next section, "Physically Demanding Work." Otherwise, turn to the Job-Match Grid and find the column for "Outdoor Work."

If you answered "It's very important to me to work **indoors,**" see whether any of the jobs on your Hot List have *any* symbol (●, ◉, or ○) in this column. If so, cross them off and write an "O" next to them.

If you answered "I'd prefer to work mostly **indoors,**" see whether any of the jobs on your Hot List have a black circle (●) in this column. If so, cross them off and write an "O" next to them.

If you answered "I'd prefer to work mostly **outdoors,**" see whether any of the jobs on your Hot List have *no* symbol—just a blank—in this column. If so, cross them off and write an "O" next to them. All the jobs remaining on your Hot List should have some kind of symbol (●, ◉, or ○) in this column.

If you answered "It's very important to me to work **outdoors,**" see whether any of the jobs on your Hot List have either *no* symbol or just a white circle (○) in this column. If so, cross them off and write an "O" next to them. All the jobs remaining on your Hot List should have either a black circle (●) or a bull's-eye (◉) in this column.

## Physically Demanding Work

Jobs vary by how much muscle power they require you to use. Some jobs require a lot of lifting heavy loads, standing for long times, climbing, or stooping. On other jobs, the heaviest thing you lift is a notebook or telephone handset, and most of the time you are sitting. Still other jobs require only a moderate amount of physical exertion.

---

What is *your* preference for the physical demands of work? Check one:

_____ I don't care whether my work requires heavy or light physical exertion.

_____ I want my work to require only light physical exertion.

_____ I want my work to require no more than occasional moderate physical exertion.

_____ I want my work to require moderate physical exertion, with occasional heavy exertion.

_____ I want my work to require a lot of heavy physical exertion.

---

If you answered "I don't care whether my work requires heavy or light physical exertion," skip to the next section, "Hazardous Conditions." Otherwise, turn to the Job-Match Grid and find the column for "Physically Demanding Work."

If you answered "I want my work to require only light physical exertion," see whether any of the jobs on your Hot List have *any* symbol (●, ◉, or ○) in this column. If so, cross them off and write a "P" next to them.

If you answered "I want my work to require no more than occasional moderate physical exertion," see whether any of the jobs on your Hot List have either a black circle (●) or a bull's-eye (◉) in this column. If so, cross them off and write a "P" next to them.

If you answered "I want my work to require moderate physical exertion, with occasional heavy exertion," see whether any of the jobs on your Hot List have either a black circle (●), a white circle (○), or *no* symbol in this column. If so, cross them off and write a "P" next to them. All the jobs remaining on your Hot List should have a bull's-eye (◉) in this column.

If you answered "I want my work to require a lot of heavy physical exertion," see whether any of the jobs on your Hot List have either *no* symbol or just a white circle (○) or a bull's-eye (◉) in this column. If so, cross them off and write a "P" next to them. All the jobs remaining on your Hot List should have a black circle (●) in this column.

## Hazardous Conditions

Every day about 9,000 Americans sustain a disabling injury on the job. Many workers have jobs that require them to deal with hazardous conditions, such as heat, noise, radiation, germs, toxins, or dangerous machinery. These workers need to wear protective clothing or follow safety procedures to avoid injury.

---

What is *your* preference regarding hazardous conditions on the job? Check one:

_____ I want hazardous workplace conditions to be very unlikely.

_____ I want hazardous conditions to be unlikely or minor.

_____ I am willing to accept some major workplace hazards.

---

If you answered "I am willing to accept some major workplace hazards," skip to the section "Geographically Concentrated Jobs." Otherwise, turn to the Job-Match Grid and find the column for "Hazardous Conditions."

If you answered "I want hazardous workplace conditions to be very unlikely," see whether any of the jobs on your Hot List have *any* symbol (●, ◐, or ○) in this column. If so, cross them off and write an "H" next to them.

If you answered "I want hazardous conditions to be unlikely or minor," see whether any of the jobs on your Hot List have a black circle (●) in this column. If so, cross them off and write an "H" next to them.

# If Every Job on Your Hot List Is Now Crossed Off

It's possible that you have crossed off *all* the occupations on your Hot List. If so, consider these two options:

★ You may want to relax some of your requirements. Maybe you were too hasty in crossing off some of the jobs. Take another look at the four job-related factors and decide whether you could accept work that doesn't meet the requirements you set previously—for example, work that is not as much indoors or outdoors as you specified. If you change your mind now, you can tell by the letters in the margin which jobs you crossed off for which reasons.

★ You may want to add to your Hot List by considering additional skills. So far you have considered only occupations that involve your top three skills. You may want to add jobs that have a black circle (●) or a bull's-eye (◐) in the column for your #4-ranked skill and possibly for your #5-ranked skill. If you do add any jobs, be sure to repeat your review of the four job-related factors.

# Evaluating Occupations Described in This Book

You are now ready to make the jump from the checklists to the detailed information about jobs in this book. The first detailed issue you need to consider is whether you will be able to find work in your area or have to relocate.

## Geographically Concentrated Jobs

Turn to the Job-Match Grid one more time and find the column for "Geographically Concentrated." Look at all the occupations on your Hot List that haven't been crossed off. If there is a symbol in this column, especially a bull's-eye (◐) or a black circle (●), it means that employment for this occupation tends to be concentrated in certain geographic areas. For example, most acting jobs are found in big cities because that's where you'll find most theaters, TV studios, and movie studios. Most water transportation jobs are found on the coasts and beside major lakes and rivers.

If a symbol shows that a Hot List occupation *is* geographically concentrated, the location of the jobs may be obvious, as in the examples of acting and water transportation. If it's not clear to you where the jobs may be found, find the occupation in "The Job Descriptions" section and look for the facts under the heading "Employment" in the description. Once you understand where most of the jobs are, you have to make some decisions:

★ **Are most of the job openings in a geographic location where I am now or would enjoy living?** If you answered "yes" to this question, repeat this exercise for all the other occupations still on your Hot List. Then jump to the next heading, "Nature of the Work." If you answered "no," proceed to the next bulleted question.

★ **If most of the job openings are in a distant place where I don't want to relocate, am I willing to take a chance and hope to be one of the few workers who get hired in an *uncommon* location?** If you answered "yes," take a good look at the Job Outlook information in the job description. If the outlook for the occupation is very good and if you expect to have some of the advantages mentioned there (such as the right degree, in some cases), taking a chance on being hired in an unusual location may be a reasonable decision. On the other hand, if the outlook is only so-so or not good and if you have no special qualifications, you probably are setting yourself up for disappointment. You should seriously consider changing your mind about this decision. At least speak to people in your area who are knowledgeable about the occupation to determine whether you have any chance of success. If you answered "no"—you are not willing to take a chance—cross off this occupation and write a "G" next to it. (If you now have no jobs left on your Hot List, see the previous section titled "If Every Job on Your Hot List Is Now Crossed Off.")

# Nature of the Work

When you read the job description for an occupation on your Hot List, you will see that the "Nature of the Work" section discusses what workers do on the job, what tools and equipment they use, and how closely they are supervised. Keep in mind that this is an overview of a diverse collection of workers, and in fact few workers perform the full set of tasks itemized here. In fact, in many cases the work force covered by the job description is so diverse that it actually divides into several occupational specialties, which are italicized.

Here are some things to think about as you read this section:

★ Note the kinds of problems, materials, and tools you will encounter on the job. Are these are a good match for your interests?

★ Also note the work activities mentioned here. Do you think they will be rewarding? Are there many that stand out as unpleasant or boring?

The Work Environment section identifies the typical hours worked, the workplace environment (both physical and psychological), physical activities and susceptibility to injury, special equipment, and the extent of travel required. If conditions vary between the occupational specialties, that is mentioned here. Here are some things to look for in the Work Environment section:

★ If you have a disability, note the physical requirements that are mentioned here and consider whether you can meet these requirements with or without suitable accommodations.

★ If you're bothered by conditions such as heights, stress, or a cramped workspace, see whether this section mentions any conditions that would discourage you.

★ Note what this section says about the work schedule and the need for travel, if any. This information may be good to know if you have pressing family responsibilities or, on the other hand, a desire for unusual hours or travel.

★ If you find a working condition that bothers you, be sure to check the wording to see whether it *always* applies to the occupation or whether it only *may* apply. Even if it seems to be a condition that you cannot avoid, find out for sure by talking to people in the occupation or educators who teach related courses. Maybe you can carve out a niche that avoids the unappealing working condition.

# Training, Other Qualifications, and Advancement

In the "Training, Other Qualifications, and Advancement" section, you can see how to prepare for the occupation and how to advance in it. It identifies the significant entry routes—those that are most popular and that are preferred by employers. It mentions any licensure or certification that may be necessary for entry or advancement. It also identifies the particular skills, aptitudes, and work habits that employers value. Look for these topics in this section:

★ Compare the entry requirements to your background and to the educational and training opportunities that are available to you. Be sure to consider nontraditional and informal entry routes, if any are possible, as well as the formal routes. Ask yourself, Am I willing to get the additional education or training that will be necessary? Do I have the time, money, ability, interest, and commitment?

★ Maybe you're already partway down the road to job entry. In general, you should try to use your previous education, training, and work experience rather than abandon it. Look for specifics that are already on your resume—educational accomplishments, skills, work habits—that will meet employers' expectations. If you have some of these qualifications already, this occupation may be a better career choice than some others.

## Employment

The "Employment" section in the job description reports how many jobs the occupation currently provides, the industries that provide the most jobs, and the number or proportion of self-employed or part-time workers in the occupation, if significant. In this section, you'll want to pay attention to these facts:

★ Note the industries that provide most of the employment for the occupation. This knowledge can help you identify contacts who can tell you more about the work, and later it can help in your job hunting.

★ If you're interested in self-employment or part-time work, see whether these work arrangements are mentioned here.

## Job Outlook

The "Job Outlook" section describes the economic forces that will affect future employment in the occupation. Here are some things to look for in this section:

★ The information here can help you identify occupations with a good job outlook so that you will have a better-than-average chance of finding work. Be alert for any mention of an advantage that you may have over other job seekers (for example, a college degree) or any other factor that might make your chances better or worse.

★ If you are highly motivated and highly qualified for a particular occupation, don't be discouraged by a bad employment outlook. Job openings occur even in shrinking or overcrowded occupations, and with exceptional talent or good personal connections, you may go on to great success.

★ These projections are the most definitive ones available, but they are not foolproof and apply only to a 10-year time span. No matter what occupation you choose, you will need to adapt to changes.

## Earnings

The "Earnings" section discusses the wages for the occupation. Here are some things to keep in mind:

★ The wage figures are national averages. Actual wages in your geographic region may be considerably higher or lower. Also, an average figure means that half of the workers earn more and half earn less, and the actual salary any one worker earns can vary greatly from that average.

★ Remember to consider *all* the pluses and minuses of the job. Not every day of the work week is payday, so make your choice based on the whole occupation, not just the paycheck.

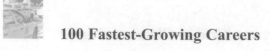

## Related Occupations

The "Related Occupations" section identifies occupations that are similar to the one featured in the job description in terms of tasks, interests, skills, education, or training. You may find this section interesting for these reasons:

★ If you're interested in an occupation but not strongly committed to pursuing it, this section may suggest another occupation with similar rewards that may turn out to be a better fit. Try to research these related occupations, but keep in mind that they may not all be included in this book.

★ You may want to choose one of these occupations as your Plan B goal if your original goal should not work out. In that case, it helps to identify an occupation that involves similar kinds of problems and work settings but requires *less* education or training.

## Sources of Additional Information

This section in each job description lists several sources and resources you can turn to for more information about the occupation. Try to consult at least some of these sources. This book should be only the beginning of your career decision-making process. You need more detailed information from several viewpoints to make an informed decision.

Don't rely entirely on the Web sites listed here. You especially need to talk to and observe individual workers to learn what their workdays are like, what the workers enjoy and dislike about the job, how they got hired, and what effects the job has had on other aspects of their lives. Maybe you can make contact with local workers through the local chapter of an organization listed here.

# Narrowing Down Your Choices

The information in the job descriptions should help you cross more jobs off your Hot List. And what you learn by turning to other resources should help you narrow down your Hot List jobs to a few promising choices and maybe one best bet. Here are some final considerations: Have I talked to people who are actually doing this work? Am I fully aware of the pluses and minuses of this job? If there are aspects of the job that I don't like, how do I expect to avoid them or overcome them? If the odds of finding a job opening are not good, why do I expect to beat the odds? What is my Plan B goal if I lose interest in my original goal or don't succeed at it?

# The Job-Match Grid

The grid on the following pages provides information about the personal skills and job characteristics for occupations covered in this book. Use the directions and questions that start at the beginning of this section to help you get the most from this grid.

Below is what the symbols on the grid represent. If a job has no symbol in a column, it means that the skill or job characteristic is not important or relevant to the job.

**Personal Skills**

● Essential or high-skill level

◉ Somewhat essential or moderate-skill level

○ Basic-skill level

**Job Characteristics**

● Highly likely

◉ Somewhat likely

○ A little likely

# Job-Match Grid

| | Personal Skills | | | | | | | Job Characteristics | | | | |
| --- | :---: | :---: | :---: | :---: | :---: | :---: | :---: | :---: | :---: | :---: | :---: | :---: |
| | Artistic | Communication | Interpersonal | Managerial | Mathematics | Mechanical | Science | Economically Sensitive | Outdoor Work | Physically Demanding Work | Hazardous Conditions | Geographically Concentrated |
| Accountants and auditors | | ○ | ○ | ◉ | ● | | | ○ | | | | |
| Advertising Sales Agents | ◉ | ● | ● | | ○ | | | ● | | | | |
| Advertising, marketing, promotions, public relations, and sales managers | ● | ● | ● | ● | ● | ◉ | | ● | | | | |
| Animal care and service workers | | ○ | ○ | | ○ | ◉ | ○ | ◉ | ◉ | ● | ● | |
| Artists and related workers | ● | ○ | ○ | ○ | ○ | | ○ | ◉ | ○ | ○ | | |
| Athletes, coaches, umpires, and related workers | ◉ | ◉ | ◉ | ● | | ○ | ○ | | | ● | ● | ○ |
| Automotive body and related repairers | ○ | ○ | ○ | | ○ | ● | ○ | | ○ | ◉ | ○ | |
| Automotive service technicians and mechanics | | ○ | ○ | | ○ | ◉ | ◉ | | ○ | ◉ | ○ | |
| Barbers, cosmetologists, and other personal appearance workers | ● | ◉ | ○ | | ○ | ◉ | ○ | ◉ | | | ○ | ○ |
| Bill and account collectors | | ○ | ◉ | | ◉ | | | ◉ | | | | |
| Bookkeeping, accounting, and auditing clerks | | ○ | ○ | | ● | | | ○ | | | | |
| Brokerage clerks | | ○ | ○ | | ◉ | | | ○ | | | | ● |
| Building cleaning workers | ○ | ○ | | | ○ | ● | | ○ | | ● | ○ | |
| Bus drivers | | ○ | ○ | | | ○ | | | ○ | ◉ | ● | |
| Carpenters | ◉ | ○ | ○ | | ○ | ● | ○ | ● | ◉ | ● | ● | |
| Chefs, cooks, and food preparation workers | ● | ◉ | ◉ | ● | ○ | ◉ | ○ | ● | | ◉ | ○ | |
| Child care workers | ○ | ◉ | ● | ○ | ○ | ○ | | | ○ | ◉ | | |
| Computer and information systems managers | | ● | ● | ● | ● | ● | ● | ● | | | | |
| Computer scientists and database administrators | | ◉ | ○ | ○ | ● | | ● | ○ | | | | |
| Computer software engineers | | ◉ | ◉ | ◉ | ● | ● | ● | ○ | | | | |
| Computer support specialists and systems administrators | | ◉ | ◉ | ○ | ◉ | ● | ◉ | ○ | | | | |
| Computer systems analysts | | ◉ | ○ | ○ | | | ● | ○ | | | | |
| Construction and building inspectors | | ○ | ○ | ○ | ○ | ● | ◉ | ○ | ◉ | ○ | ○ | |
| Construction laborers | ○ | ○ | ○ | | ○ | ● | ○ | ● | ◉ | ● | ● | |
| Construction managers | ○ | ● | ● | ● | ● | ● | ● | ● | ● | ○ | ◉ | |
| Correctional officers | | ◉ | ○ | ○ | ○ | ○ | | | | | ◉ | ● |
| Cost estimators | | ○ | ○ | ○ | ● | | ○ | ◉ | ◉ | | | |
| Counselors | | ● | ● | ○ | ○ | | ○ | | | | | |
| Counter and rental clerks | | ○ | ◉ | | ◉ | | | ◉ | | ◉ | | |
| Customer service representatives | | ● | ● | | ◉ | | ○ | ○ | | | | |
| Demonstrators, product promoters, and models | ● | ● | ● | | ○ | ○ | | ◉ | | ◉ | | |
| Dental assistants | | ◉ | ◉ | ○ | ○ | ● | ◉ | | | ◉ | ◉ | |

*(continued)*

**Personal Skills:** ●—Essential or high-skill level; ◉—Somewhat essential or moderate-skill level; ○—Basic-skill level
**Job Characteristics:** ●—Highly likely; ◉—Somewhat likely; ○—A little likely

© JIST Works

(continued)

| | Artistic | Communication | Interpersonal | Managerial | Mathematics | Mechanical | Science | Economically Sensitive | Outdoor Work | Physically Demanding Work | Hazardous Conditions | Geographically Concentrated |
|---|---|---|---|---|---|---|---|---|---|---|---|---|
| | **Personal Skills** | | | | | | | **Job Characteristics** | | | | |
| Dental hygienists | | ◉ | ◉ | ○ | ◉ | ● | ◉ | | | ○ | ◉ | |
| Education administrators | | ● | ● | ● | ◉ | | ○ | | | | | |
| Emergency medical technicians and paramedics | | ● | ● | ● | ○ | ● | ● | | ● | ● | ● | |
| Engineers | ◉ | ◉ | ○ | ◉ | ● | ● | ● | ◉ | ○ | ○ | ○ | ◉ |
| Environmental scientists and hydrologists | ○ | ◉ | ○ | ◉ | ● | ● | ● | ○ | | | ○ | ● |
| Financial analysts and personal financial advisors | | ● | ● | ○ | ● | | ○ | ● | | | | |
| Financial managers | | ● | ● | ● | ● | | ○ | ◉ | | | | |
| Fitness workers | ○ | ● | ● | ○ | ○ | ○ | ○ | ◉ | ◉ | ● | | |
| Food and beverage serving and related workers | ○ | ◉ | ● | | ○ | | | ● | ○ | ● | | |
| Food processing occupations | | ○ | | | ○ | ● | | | | ● | ● | |
| Gaming services occupations | ○ | ◉ | ● | ● | ○ | ○ | | ◉ | | ● | | ● |
| Grounds maintenance workers | ● | ○ | | | ○ | ● | ○ | ○ | ● | ● | ◉ | |
| Health educators | | ● | ● | ◉ | | | ○ | | | | | |
| Hotel, motel, and resort desk clerks | ○ | ◉ | ● | ○ | ○ | | | ● | | ◉ | | |
| Human resources, training, and labor relations managers and specialists | | ● | ● | ● | ○ | | | ○ | | | | |
| Instructional coordinators | ○ | ● | ● | ◉ | ◉ | ◉ | ◉ | | | | | |
| Insurance sales agents | | ● | ● | | ◉ | | | ◉ | | | | |
| Lawyers | | ● | ● | ● | ○ | | ○ | ◉ | | | | |
| Licensed practical and licensed vocational nurses | | ◉ | ● | ○ | ○ | ● | ● | | | ◉ | ◉ | |
| Loan officers | | ◉ | ● | ○ | ◉ | | | ◉ | | | | |
| Maintenance and repair workers, general | | ○ | ○ | | ○ | ● | ○ | | ◉ | ◉ | ◉ | |
| Management analysts | | ● | ◉ | ○ | ● | | | ○ | | | | |
| Market and survey researchers | | ● | ● | ○ | ● | | | ◉ | | | | |
| Medical and health services managers | | ● | ● | ● | ◉ | ◉ | ◉ | | | | | |
| Medical assistants | | ◉ | ◉ | ○ | ◉ | ● | ● | | | ◉ | ◉ | |
| Medical records and health information technicians | | ◉ | ○ | ○ | ◉ | | ◉ | | | | | |
| Medical scientists | | ◉ | ○ | ◉ | ● | ● | ● | ○ | | | ○ | |
| Nursing, psychiatric, and home health aides | | ◉ | ◉ | ○ | ○ | ◉ | ○ | | | ● | ● | |
| Occupational therapists | | ● | ● | ◉ | ◉ | ◉ | ◉ | | | | ○ | ◉ |
| Office clerks, general | | ○ | ◉ | | ○ | | | ◉ | | | | |
| Painters and paperhangers | ◉ | ○ | ○ | | ○ | ● | ○ | ● | ● | ● | ○ | |
| Paralegals and legal assistants | | ● | ● | ○ | ○ | | ○ | ◉ | | | | |
| Personal and home care aides | | ◉ | ● | ○ | ○ | | ○ | | | ● | ◉ | |
| Pharmacists | | ● | ◉ | ◉ | ● | ○ | ● | | | | ○ | |

**Personal Skills:** ●—Essential or high-skill level; ◉—Somewhat essential or moderate-skill level; ○—Basic-skill level
**Job Characteristics:** ●—Highly likely; ◉—Somewhat likely; ○—A little likely

| | Artistic | Communication | Interpersonal | Managerial | Mathematics | Mechanical | Science | Economically Sensitive | Outdoor Work | Physically Demanding Work | Hazardous Conditions | Geographically Concentrated |
|---|---|---|---|---|---|---|---|---|---|---|---|---|
| | | **Personal Skills** | | | | | | **Job Characteristics** | | | | |
| Pharmacy technicians | | ◉ | ◉ | ○ | ◉ | ◉ | ◉ | | | ○ | | |
| Physical therapist assistants and aides | | ◉ | ◉ | ○ | ○ | ◉ | ◉ | | | ● | ◉ | |
| Physical therapists | | ● | ● | ○ | ◉ | ○ | ● | | | ● | ◉ | |
| Physician assistants | | ● | ● | ○ | ● | ◉ | ● | | | ◉ | ◉ | |
| Physicians and surgeons | ◉ | ● | ● | ● | ◉ | ● | ● | | | ◉ | ◉ | |
| Pipelayers, plumbers, pipefitters, and steamfitters | | ○ | ○ | | ○ | ● | ◉ | ● | ○ | ● | ○ | |
| Police and detectives | | ● | ○ | ◉ | ○ | ● | ○ | | | ● | ● | ● |
| Property, real estate, and community association managers | ○ | ● | ● | ● | ○ | ○ | | ○ | ○ | | | |
| Public relations specialists | ◉ | ● | ● | ○ | ○ | | | | | | | ◉ |
| Real estate brokers and sales agents | ○ | ● | ● | ◉ | ◉ | | | ◉ | ○ | | | |
| Receptionists and information clerks | | ● | ● | | ◉ | ◉ | | ○ | | | | |
| Recreation workers | ○ | ● | ● | ○ | ○ | ○ | ○ | ◉ | ◉ | ● | | |
| Registered nurses | | ● | ● | ◉ | ● | ● | ● | | | ◉ | ◉ | |
| Retail salespersons | ○ | ◉ | ● | | ○ | | | ◉ | | | | |
| Roofers | ○ | ○ | ○ | | | ● | ○ | ○ | ● | ● | ● | |
| Sales representatives, wholesale and manufacturing | ○ | ● | ● | | ◉ | | ○ | ● | | | | |
| Sales worker supervisors | ○ | ● | ● | ● | ◉ | ○ | ○ | ◉ | | | | |
| Science technicians | ○ | ◉ | ○ | | ● | ● | ● | ◉ | ○ | ○ | ○ | |
| Secretaries and administrative assistants | ○ | ● | ● | ○ | ○ | ● | ○ | ○ | | | | |
| Securities, commodities, and financial services sales agents | | ● | ● | ● | ● | | | ● | | | | ● |
| Security guards and gaming surveillance officers | | ○ | ○ | ○ | | ○ | | ○ | ◉ | ○ | ● | |
| Social and human service assistants | | ◉ | ● | | | | ○ | | | | | |
| Social workers | | ● | ● | ○ | ○ | | ○ | | | | | |
| Surveyors, cartographers, photogrammetrists, and surveying and mapping technicians | ◉ | ◉ | ◉ | ○ | ◉ | ◉ | ◉ | ◉ | ◉ | ◉ | | |
| Surgical technologists | | ◉ | ◉ | ○ | ● | ● | ● | | | ◉ | ◉ | |
| Taxi drivers and chauffeurs | | ○ | ○ | | | ○ | | | ○ | ◉ | ● | ◉ |
| Teacher assistants | ◉ | ● | ● | ◉ | ○ | | ◉ | | | | | |
| Teachers—postsecondary | ◉ | ● | ● | ● | ● | | ◉ | | | | | |
| Teachers—preschool, kindergarten, elementary, middle, and secondary | ◉ | ● | ● | ● | ◉ | ○ | ◉ | | | | | |
| Teachers—self-enrichment education | ◉ | ● | ● | ● | ◉ | | ◉ | | | | | |
| Teachers—special education | ◉ | ● | ● | ● | ◉ | ○ | ◉ | | | | | |
| Tellers | | ◉ | ● | | ● | | | ○ | | | | |
| Truck drivers and driver/sales workers | | ○ | | | | ○ | | ● | ○ | ● | ● | |
| Veterinary technologists and technicians | | ◉ | ◉ | ◉ | ◉ | ● | ◉ | ○ | ○ | ● | ● | |

**Personal Skills:** ●—Essential or high-skill level; ◉—Somewhat essential or moderate-skill level; ○—Basic-skill level
**Job Characteristics:** ●—Highly likely; ◉—Somewhat likely; ○—A little likely

# Descriptions of the 100 Fastest-Growing Careers

This is the book's main section. It contains helpful descriptions of the 100 major occupations that have the most-favorable combined scores for projected percent increase and number of job openings through 2016. To learn a job's ranking, see the introduction.

The jobs are arranged in alphabetical order. Refer to the table of contents for a list of the jobs and the page numbers where their descriptions begin. Review the table of contents to discover occupations that interest you, and then find out more about them in this section. If you are interested in medical careers, for example, you can go through the list and quickly pinpoint those you want to learn more about. Or use the assessment in Part I to identify several possible career matches.

While the job descriptions in this part are easy to understand, the introduction provides additional information for interpreting them. Keep in mind that the descriptions present information that is average for the country. Conditions in your area and with specific employers may be quite different.

Also, you may come across jobs that sound interesting but require more education and training than you have or are considering. Don't eliminate them too soon. There are many ways to obtain education and training, and most people change careers many times. You probably have more skills than you realize that can transfer to new jobs. People often have more opportunities than barriers. Use the descriptions to learn more about possible jobs and look into the suggested resources to help you take the next step.

## Accountants and Auditors

(O*NET 13-2011.00, 13-2011.01, and 13-2011.02)

### Significant Points

- Most jobs require at least a bachelor's degree in accounting or a related field.
- Opportunities will be best for jobseekers who have a master's degree, obtain certification or licensure, or are proficient in the use of accounting and auditing computer software.
- Faster-than-average growth of accountant and auditor jobs will result from an increase in the number of businesses, changing financial laws and regulations, and greater scrutiny of company finances.

### Nature of the Work

Accountants and auditors help to ensure that the nation's firms are run efficiently, its public records kept accurately, and its taxes paid properly and on time. They analyze and communicate financial information for various entities such as companies, individual clients, and government. Beyond carrying out the fundamental tasks of the occupation—preparing, analyzing, and verifying financial documents in order to provide information to clients—many accountants also offer budget analysis, financial and investment planning, information technology consulting, and limited legal services.

Specific job duties vary widely among the four major fields of accounting and auditing: *public, management, and government accounting,* and *internal auditing.*

*Public accountants* perform a broad range of accounting, auditing, tax, and consulting activities for their clients, which may be corporations, governments, nonprofit organizations, or individuals. For example, some public accountants concentrate on tax matters, such as advising companies about the tax advantages and disadvantages of certain business decisions and preparing individual income tax returns. Others offer advice in areas such as compensation or employee health-care benefits, the design of accounting and data-processing systems, and the selection of controls to safeguard assets. Still others audit clients' financial statements and inform investors and authorities that the statements have been correctly prepared and reported. These accountants are also referred to as *external auditors.* Public accountants, many of whom are Certified Public Accountants (CPAs), generally have their own businesses or work for public accounting firms.

Some public accountants specialize in forensic accounting—investigating and interpreting white-collar crimes such as securities fraud and embezzlement, bankruptcies and contract disputes, and other complex and possibly criminal financial transactions, including money laundering by organized criminals. Forensic accountants combine their knowledge of accounting and finance with law and investigative techniques to determine whether an activity is illegal. Many forensic accountants work closely with law enforcement personnel and lawyers during investigations and often appear as expert witnesses during trials.

In response to recent accounting scandals, new federal legislation restricts the nonauditing services that public accountants can provide to clients. If an accounting firm audits a client's financial statements, that same firm cannot provide advice on human resources, technology, investment banking, or legal matters, although accountants may still advise on tax issues. Accountants may also advise other clients in these areas and may provide advice within their own firm.

*Management accountants*—also called cost, managerial, industrial, corporate, or private accountants—record and analyze the financial information of the companies for which they work. Among their other responsibilities are budgeting, performance evaluation, cost management, and asset management. Usually, management accountants are part of executive teams involved in strategic planning or the development of new products. They analyze and interpret the financial information that corporate executives need in order to make sound business decisions. They also prepare financial reports for other groups, including stockholders, creditors, regulatory agencies, and tax authorities. Within accounting departments, management accountants may work in various areas, including financial analysis, planning and budgeting, and cost accounting.

*Government accountants and auditors* work in the public sector, maintaining and examining the records of government agencies and auditing private businesses and individuals whose activities are subject to government regulations or taxation. Accountants employed by federal, state, and local governments ensure that revenues are received and expenditures are made in accordance with laws and regulations. Those employed by the federal government may work as Internal Revenue Service agents or in financial management, financial institution examination, or budget analysis and administration.

*Internal auditors* verify the effectiveness of their organization's internal controls and check for mismanagement, waste, or fraud. They examine and evaluate their firms' financial and information systems, management procedures, and internal controls to ensure that records are accurate and controls are adequate. They also review company operations, evaluating their efficiency, effectiveness, and compliance with corporate policies and government regulations. Because computer systems commonly automate transactions and make information readily available, internal auditors may also help management evaluate the effectiveness of their controls based on real-time data rather than personal observation. They may recommend and review controls for their organization's computer systems to ensure the reliability and integrity of the data.

Internal auditors may also have specialty titles, such as information technology auditors, environmental auditors, and compliance auditors.

Technology is rapidly changing the nature of the work of most accountants and auditors. With the aid of special software packages, accountants summarize transactions in the standard formats of financial records and organize data in special formats employed in financial analysis. These accounting packages greatly reduce the tedious work associated with data management and recordkeeping. Computers enable accountants and auditors to be more mobile and to use their clients' computer systems to extract information from databases and the Internet. As a result, a growing number of accountants and auditors with extensive computer skills specialize in correcting problems with software or in developing software to meet unique data management and analytical needs. Accountants also are beginning to perform more technical duties, such as implementing, controlling, and auditing computer systems and networks and developing a business's technology plans.

Accountants also act as personal advisors. They not only provide clients with accounting and tax help, but also help them develop personal budgets, manage assets and investments, plan for retirement, and recognize and reduce their exposure to risks. This role is in response to clients' demands for a single trustworthy individual or firm to meet all of their financial needs. However, accountants are restricted from providing these services to clients whose financial statements they also prepare.

*Work environment.* Most accountants and auditors work in a typical office setting. Some may be able to do part of their work at home. Accountants and auditors employed by public accounting firms, government agencies, and organizations with multiple locations may travel frequently to perform audits at branches, clients' places of business, or government facilities.

Most accountants and auditors usually work a standard 40-hour week, but many work longer hours, particularly if they are self-employed and have numerous clients. Tax specialists often work long hours during the tax season.

## Training, Other Qualifications, and Advancement

Most accountants and auditors need at least a bachelor's degree in business, accounting, or a related field. Many accountants and auditors choose to obtain certification to help advance their careers, such as becoming a Certified Public Accountant (CPA).

*Education and training.* Most accountant and auditor positions require at least a bachelor's degree in accounting or a related field. Beginning accounting and auditing positions in the federal government, for example, usually require four years of college (including 24 semester hours in accounting or auditing) or an equivalent combination of education and experience. Some employers prefer applicants with a master's degree in accounting or with a master's degree in business administration with a concentration in accounting. Some universities and colleges are now offering programs to prepare students to work in growing specialty professions such as internal auditing. Many professional associations offer continuing professional education courses, conferences, and seminars.

Some graduates of junior colleges or business or correspondence schools, as well as bookkeepers and accounting clerks who meet the education and experience requirements set by their employers, can obtain junior accounting positions and advance to accountant positions by demonstrating their accounting skills on the job.

Most beginning accountants and auditors may work under supervision or closely with an experienced accountant or auditor before gaining more independence and responsibility.

*Licensure and certification.* Any accountant filing a report with the Securities and Exchange Commission (SEC) is required by law to be a Certified Public Accountant (CPA). This may include senior-level accountants working for or on behalf of public companies that are registered with the SEC. CPAs are licensed by their State Board of Accountancy. Any accountant who passes a national exam and meets the other requirements of the state where they practice can become a CPA. The vast majority of states require CPA candidates to be college graduates, but a few states will substitute a number of years of public accounting experience for a college degree.

As of 2007, 42 states and the District of Columbia required CPA candidates to complete 10 semester hours of college coursework—an additional 30 hours beyond the usual four-year bachelor's degree. Several other states have adopted similar legislation that will become effective before 2009. Colorado, Delaware, New Hampshire, and Vermont are the only states that do not have any immediate plans to require the 150 semester hours. In response to this trend, many schools have altered their curricula accordingly, with most programs offering master's degrees as part of the 150 hours. Prospective accounting majors should carefully research accounting curricula and the requirements of any states in which they hope to become licensed.

All states use the four-part Uniform CPA Examination prepared by the American Institute of Certified Public Accountants (AICPA). The CPA examination is rigorous, and less than one-half of those who take it each year pass every part they attempt on the first try. Candidates are not required to pass all four parts at once, but most states require candidates to pass all four sections within 18 months of passing their first section. The CPA exam is now computerized and is offered two months out of every quarter at various testing centers throughout the United States. Most states also require applicants for a CPA certificate to have some accounting experience; however, requirements vary by state or jurisdiction.

Nearly all states require CPAs and other public accountants to complete a certain number of hours of continuing professional education before their licenses can be renewed. The professional associations representing accountants sponsor numerous courses, seminars, group study programs, and other forms of continuing education.

*Other qualifications.* Previous experience in accounting or auditing can help an applicant get a job. Many colleges offer students the opportunity to gain experience through summer or part-time internship programs conducted by public accounting or business firms. In addition, as many business processes are now automated, practical knowledge of computers and their applications is a great asset for jobseekers in the accounting and auditing fields.

People planning a career in accounting and auditing should have an aptitude for mathematics and be able to analyze, compare, and interpret facts and figures quickly. They must be able to clearly communicate the results of their work to clients and managers both verbally and in writing. Accountants and auditors must be good at working with people, business systems, and computers. At a minimum, accountants and auditors should be familiar with basic accounting and computer software packages. Because financial decisions are made on the basis of their statements and services, accountants and auditors should have high standards of integrity.

*Certification and advancement.* Professional recognition through certification, or a designation other than the CPA, provides a distinct advantage in the job market. Certification can attest to professional competence in a specialized field of accounting and auditing. Accountants and auditors can seek credentials from a wide variety of professional societies.

The Institute of Management Accountants confers the Certified Management Accountant (CMA) designation upon applicants who complete a bachelor's degree or who attain a minimum score or higher on specified graduate school entrance exams. Applicants must have worked at least two years in management accounting, pass a four-part examination, agree to meet continuing education requirements, and comply with standards of professional conduct. The exam covers areas such as financial statement analysis, working-capital policy, capital structure, valuation issues, and risk management.

The Institute of Internal Auditors offers the Certified Internal Auditor (CIA) designation to graduates from accredited colleges and universities who have worked for two years as internal auditors and have passed a four-part examination. The IIA also offers the designations of Certified in Control Self-Assessment (CCSA), Certified Government Auditing Professional (CGAP), and Certified Financial Services Auditor (CFSA) to those who pass the exams and meet educational and experience requirements.

The ISACA, formerly known as the Information Systems Audit and Control Association, confers the Certified Information Systems Auditor (CISA) designation upon candidates who pass an examination and have five years of experience auditing information systems. Information systems experience, financial or operational auditing experience, or related college credit hours can be substituted for up to two years of information systems auditing, control or security experience.

The Accreditation Council for Accountancy and Taxation, a satellite organization of the National Society of Accountants, confers four designations—Accredited Business Accountant (ABA), Accredited Tax Advisor (ATA), Accredited Tax Preparer (ATP), and Elder Care Specialist (ECS)—on accountants specializing in tax preparation for small and medium-sized businesses. Candidates for the ABA must pass an exam; candidates for the other designations must complete the required coursework and in some cases pass an exam.

The Association of Certified Fraud Examiners offers the Certified Fraud Examiner (CFE) designation for forensic or public accountants involved in fraud prevention, detection, deterrence, and investigation. To obtain the designation, individuals must have a bachelor's degree and two years of relevant experience, pass a four-part examination, and abide by a code of professional ethics. Related work experience may be substituted for the educational requirement.

The Association of Government Accountants grants the Certified Government Financial Manager (CGFM) designation for accountants, auditors, and other government financial workers at the federal, state, and local levels. Candidates must have a minimum of a bachelor's degree, 24 hours of study in financial management, two years of experience in government, and passing scores on a series of three exams. The exams cover topics in governmental environment; governmental accounting, financial reporting, and budgeting; and financial management and control.

For those accountants with their CPA, the AICPA offers the option to receive any or all of the Accredited in Business Valuation (ABV), Certified Information Technology Professional (CITP), or Personal Financial Specialist (PFS) designations. CPAs with these designations demonstrate a level of expertise in these areas in which accountants practice ever more frequently. The business valuation designation requires a written exam and the completion of a minimum of 10 business valuation projects that demonstrate a candidate's experience and competence. The technology designation requires the achievement of a set number of points awarded for business technology experience and education. Candidates for the personal financial specialist designation also must achieve a certain level of points based on experience and education, pass a written exam, and submit references.

Many senior corporation executives have a background in accounting, internal auditing, or finance. Beginning public accountants often advance to positions with more responsibility in one or two years and to senior positions within another few years. Those who excel may become supervisors, managers, or partners; open their own public accounting firm; or transfer to executive positions in management accounting or internal auditing in private firms.

Management accountants often start as cost accountants, junior internal auditors, or trainees for other accounting positions. As they rise through the organization, they may advance to accounting manager, chief cost accountant, budget director, or manager of internal auditing. Some become controllers, treasurers, financial vice presidents, chief financial officers, or corporation presidents.

Public accountants, management accountants, and internal auditors usually have much occupational mobility. Practitioners often shift into management accounting or internal auditing from public accounting or between internal auditing and management accounting. It is less common for accountants and auditors to move from either management accounting or internal auditing into public accounting. Additionally, because they learn about and review the internal controls of various business units within a company, internal auditors often gain the experience needed to become upper-level managers.

## Employment

Accountants and auditors held about 1.3 million jobs in 2006. They worked throughout private industry and government, but 21 percent of wage and salary accountants worked for accounting, tax preparation, bookkeeping, and payroll services firms. Approximately 10 percent of accountants and auditors were self-employed.

Many management accountants, internal auditors, and government accountants and auditors are not CPAs; however, a large number are licensed CPAs. Most accountants and auditors work in urban areas, where public accounting firms and central or regional offices of businesses are concentrated.

Some individuals with backgrounds in accounting and auditing are full-time college and university faculty; others teach part time while working as self-employed accountants or as accountants for private industry or government.

## Job Outlook

Strong growth of accountants and auditor jobs over the 2006–2016 decade is expected to result from stricter accounting and auditing regulations, along with an expanding economy. The best job prospects will be for accountants and auditors who have a college degree or any certification, but especially a CPA.

**Projections data from the National Employment Matrix**

| Occupational Title | SOC Code | Employment, 2006 | Projected employment, 2016 | Change, 2006-16 | |
|---|---|---|---|---|---|
| | | | | Number | Percent |
| Accountants and auditors ................................................... | 13-2011 | 1,274,000 | 1,500,000 | 226,000 | 18 |

NOTE: Data in this table are rounded.

*Employment change.* Employment of accountants and auditors is expected to grow by 18 percent between 2006 and 2016, which is faster than the average for all occupations. This occupation will have a very large number of new jobs arise, almost 226,000 over the projections decade. An increase in the number of businesses, changing financial laws, and corporate governance regulations and increased accountability for protecting an organization's stakeholders will drive growth.

As the economy grows, the number of business establishments will increase, requiring more accountants and auditors to set up books, prepare taxes, and provide management advice. As these businesses grow, the volume and complexity of information reviewed by accountants and auditors regarding costs, expenditures, taxes, and internal controls will expand as well. The globalization of business also has led to more demand for accounting expertise and services related to international trade and accounting rules and international mergers and acquisitions.

An increased need for accountants and auditors also will arise from changes in legislation related to taxes, financial reporting standards, business investments, mergers, and other financial events. As a result of accounting scandals at several large corporations, Congress passed the Sarbanes-Oxley Act of 2002 in an effort to curb corporate accounting fraud. This legislation requires public companies to maintain well-functioning internal controls to ensure the accuracy and reliability of their financial reporting. It also holds the company's chief executive personally responsible for falsely reporting financial information.

These changes are expected to lead to increased scrutiny of company finances and accounting procedures and should create opportunities for accountants and auditors, particularly CPAs, to audit financial records more thoroughly. Management accountants and internal auditors increasingly will also be needed to discover and eliminate fraud before audits and ensure that important processes and procedures are documented accurately and thoroughly. Also, efforts to make government agencies more efficient and accountable will increase demand for government accountants.

Increased focus on and numbers of financial crimes such as embezzlement, bribery, and securities fraud will increase the demand for forensic accountants to detect illegal financial activity by individuals, companies, and organized crime rings. Computer technology has made these crimes easier to commit, and they are on the rise. At the same time, the development of new computer software and electronic surveillance technology has made tracking down financial criminals easier, thus increasing the ease and likelihood of discovery. As success rates of investigations grow, demand for forensic accountants will increase.

The changing role of accountants and auditors also will spur job growth, although this will be slower than in the past because of changes in the law. Federal legislation now prohibits accountants from providing many types of management and consulting services to clients whose books they audit. However, accountants will still be able to advise clients that are not publicly traded companies and those they do not audit.

Also, the increasing popularity of tax preparation firms and computer software will shift accountants away from tax preparation. As computer programs continue to simplify some accounting-related tasks, clerical staff will increasingly handle many routine calculations.

*Job prospects.* Overall, job opportunities for accountants and auditors should be favorable. Those who earn a CPA should have excellent job prospects. After most states instituted the 150-hour rule for CPAs, enrollment in accounting programs declined. However, enrollment is again growing as more students have become attracted to the profession by the attention from the accounting scandals.

In the aftermath of the accounting scandals, professional certification is even more important to ensure that accountants' credentials and knowledge of ethics are sound. Regardless of specialty, accountants and auditors who have earned professional recognition through certification or licensure should have the best job prospects. Applicants with a master's degree in accounting or a master's degree in business administration with a concentration in accounting also will have an advantage.

Individuals who are proficient in accounting and auditing computer software or have expertise in specialized areas—such as international business, specific industries, or current legislation—may have an advantage in getting some accounting and auditing jobs. In addition, employers increasingly seek applicants with strong interpersonal and communication skills. Many accountants work on teams with others who have different backgrounds, so they must be able to communicate accounting and financial information clearly and concisely. Regardless of qualifications, however, competition will remain keen for the most prestigious jobs in major accounting and business firms.

In addition to openings from job growth, the need to replace accountants and auditors who retire or transfer to other occupations will produce numerous job openings in this large occupation.

# Earnings

Median annual earnings of wage and salary accountants and auditors were $54,630 in May 2006. The middle half of the occupation earned between $42,520 and $71,960. The top 10 percent earned more than $94,050, and the bottom 10 percent earned less than

$34,470. Median annual earnings in the industries employing the largest numbers of accountants and auditors were as follows:

Accounting, tax preparation, bookkeeping,
    and payroll services .........................................$57,020
Management of companies and enterprises ............55,560
Local government ...............................................50,120
Depository credit intermediation ..........................49,380
State government ...............................................47,200

According to a salary survey conducted by the National Association of Colleges and Employers, bachelor's degree candidates in accounting received starting offers averaging $46,718 a year in 2006; master's degree candidates in accounting were offered $49,277 initially.

According to a 2007 salary survey conducted by Robert Half International, a staffing services firm specializing in accounting and finance, general accountants and internal auditors with up to one year of experience earned between $31,500 and $48,250 a year. Those with one to three years of experience earned between $36,000 and $60,000. Senior accountants and auditors earned between $43,250 and $79,250, managers between $51,250 and $101,500, and directors of accounting and internal auditing between $68,000 and $208,000. The variation in salaries reflects differences in size of firm, location, level of education, and professional credentials.

In the federal government, the starting annual salary for junior accountants and auditors was $28,862 in 2007. Candidates who had a superior academic record might start at $35,752, while applicants with a master's degree or two years of professional experience usually began at $43,731. Beginning salaries were slightly higher in selected geographic areas where the prevailing local pay level was higher. Accountants employed by the federal government in non-supervisory, supervisory, and managerial positions averaged $78,665 a year in 2007; auditors averaged $83,322.

Wage and salary accountants and auditors usually receive standard benefits, including health and medical insurance, life insurance, a 401(k) plan, and paid annual leave. High-level senior accountants may receive additional benefits, such as the use of a company car and an expense account.

## Related Occupations

Accountants and auditors design internal control systems and analyze financial data. Others for whom training in accounting is valuable include budget analysts; cost estimators; loan officers; financial analysts and personal financial advisors; tax examiners, collectors, and revenue agents; bill and account collectors; and bookkeeping, accounting, and auditing clerks. Recently, some accountants have assumed the role of management analysts and are involved in the design, implementation, and maintenance of accounting software systems. Others who perform similar work include computer programmers, computer software engineers, and computer support specialists and systems administrators.

## Sources of Additional Information

Information on accredited accounting programs can be obtained from

▸ AACSB International—Association to Advance Collegiate Schools of Business, 777 South Harbour Island Blvd., Suite 750, Tampa FL 33602-5730. Internet: http://www.aacsb.edu/accreditation/AccreditedMembers.asp

Information about careers in certified public accounting and CPA standards and examinations may be obtained from

▸ American Institute of Certified Public Accountants, 1211 Avenue of the Americas, New York, NY 10036. Internet: http://www.aicpa.org

▸ The Uniform CPA Examination, 1211 Avenue of the Americas, New York, NY 10036. Internet: http://www.cpa-exam.org

Information on CPA licensure requirements by state may be obtained from

▸ National Association of State Boards of Accountancy, 150 Fourth Ave. North, Suite 700, Nashville, TN 37219-2417. Internet: http://www.nasba.org

Information on careers in management accounting and the CMA designation may be obtained from

▸ Institute of Management Accountants, 10 Paragon Dr., Montvale, NJ 07645-1718. Internet: http://www.imanet.org

Information on the Accredited in Accountancy, Accredited Business Accountant, Accredited Tax Advisor, or Accredited Tax Preparer designation may be obtained from

▸ Accreditation Council for Accountancy and Taxation, 1010 North Fairfax St., Alexandria, VA 22314-1574. Internet: http://www.acatcredentials.org

Information on the Certified Fraud Examiner designation may be obtained from

▸ Association of Certified Fraud Examiners, 716 West Ave, Austin, TX 78701-2727.

Information on careers in internal auditing and the CIA designation may be obtained from

▸ The Institute of Internal Auditors, 247 Maitland Ave., Altamonte Springs, FL 32701-4201. Internet: http://www.theiia.org

Information on careers in information systems auditing and the CISA designation may be obtained from

▸ ISACA, 3701 Algonquin Rd., Suite 1010, Rolling Meadows, IL 60008. Internet: http://www.isaca.org

Information on careers in government accounting and the CGFM designation may be obtained from

▸ Association of Government Accountants, 2208 Mount Vernon Ave., Alexandria, VA 22301. Internet: http://www.agacgfm.org

Information on obtaining positions as an accountant or auditor with the federal government is available from the Office of Personnel Management through USAJOBS, the federal government's official employment information system. This resource for locating and applying for job opportunities can be accessed through the Internet at http://www.usajobs.opm.gov or through an interactive voice response telephone system at (703) 724-1850 or TDD (978) 461-8404. These numbers are not toll free, and charges may result. For advice on how to find and apply for federal jobs, see the *Occupational Outlook Quarterly* article "How to get a job in the federal government," online at http://www.bls.gov/opub/ooq/2004/summer/art01.pdf.

# Advertising Sales Agents

(O*NET 41-3011.00)

## Significant Points

- Overall earnings are higher than average but vary considerably because they usually are based on a salary plus performance-based commissions and bonuses.

- Pressure to meet monthly sales quotas can be stressful.

## Nature of the Work

Advertising sales agents—often referred to as *account executives* or *advertising sales representatives*—sell or solicit advertising primarily for newspapers and periodicals, television and radio, websites, telephone directories, and direct mail and outdoor advertisers. Because such a large share of revenue for many of these media outlets is generated from advertising, advertising sales agents play an important role in their success.

More than half of all advertising sales agents work in the information sector, mostly for media firms including television and radio broadcasters, print and Internet publishers, and cable program distributors. Firms that are regionally based often need the help of two types of advertising sales agents, one to handle local clients and one to solicit advertising from national advertisers. Print publications and radio and television stations employ local sales agents who are responsible for sales in an immediate territory, while separate companies known as media representative firms sell advertising space or time for media owners at the national level with their own teams of advertising sales agents. Sales agents employed in media representation work exclusively through executives at advertising agencies, called media buyers, who purchase advertising space for their clients that want to initiate national advertising campaigns. When a local television broadcaster, radio station, print, or online publisher is working with a media representative firm, the media company normally employs a national sales manager to coordinate efforts with the media representative.

Local sales agents are often referred to as outside sales agents or inside sales agents. *Outside sales agents* call on clients and prospects at their places of business. They may have an appointment, or they may practice cold calling—arriving without an appointment. For these sales agents, obtaining new accounts is an important part of the job, and they may spend much of their time traveling to and visiting prospective advertisers and current clients. *Inside sales agents* work on their employer's premises and handle sales for customers who walk in or telephone the firm to inquire about advertising. Some may also make telephone sales calls—calling prospects, attempting to sell the media firm's advertising space or time, and arranging follow-up appointments between interested prospects and outside sales agents.

A critical part of building a relationship with a client is to find out as much as possible about the client. Before the first meeting with a client, sales agents gather background information on the client's products, current customers, prospective customers, and the geographic area of the target market. They then meet with the clients to explain how specific types of advertising will help promote the client's products or services most effectively. If a client wishes to proceed, the advertising sales agent prepares an advertising proposal to present to the client. This entails determining the advertising medium to be used, preparing sample advertisements, and providing clients with cost estimates for the proposal. Because consolidation among media industries has brought the sales of different types of advertising under one roof, advertising sales are increasingly in the form of integrated packages. This means that advertising sales agents may sell packages that include print and online ad space and time slots with a broadcast subsidiary.

After a contract has been established, advertising sales agents serve as the main contact between the advertiser or ad agency and the media firm. They handle communication between the parties and assist in developing sample artwork or radio and television spots, if needed. For radio and television advertisements, they may also arrange for commercial taping sessions and accompany clients to these sessions.

In addition to maintaining sales and overseeing clients' accounts, advertising sales agents' other duties include analyzing sales statistics and audience demographics, preparing reports on client's accounts, and scheduling and keeping their appointments and work hours. They read about new and existing products and monitor the sales, prices, and products of their competitors. In many firms, the advertising sales agent handles the drafting of contracts specifying the advertising work to be performed and its cost, and may undertake customer service responsibilities such as answering questions or addressing any problems the client may have with the proposal. Sales agents are also responsible for developing sales tools, promotional plans, and media kits, which they use to help make the sale.

*Work environment.* Selling can be stressful work because income and job security depend directly on the agent's ability to maintain and expand clientele. Companies generally set monthly sales quotas and place considerable pressure on advertising sales agents to meet those quotas. The added stress of rejection places more pressure on the agent.

Although agents work long and often irregular hours, most have the freedom to determine their own schedule. The Internet and other electronic tools allow agents to do more work from home or while on the road, enabling them to send messages and documents to clients and coworkers, keep up with industry news, and access databases that help them target potential customers. Advertising sales agents use e-mail to conduct much of the business with their clients.

Many advertising sales agents work more than 40 hours per week. This frequently involves irregular hours and may also include working on weekends and holidays. However, most advertising sales agents are able to set their own schedule. Eleven percent of advertising sales agents were employed part time in 2006.

## Training, Other Qualifications, and Advancement

For sales positions that require meeting with clients, large employers prefer applicants with a college degree. Smaller companies generally are more willing to hire individuals with a high school degree. Successful sales experience and the ability to communicate effectively become more important than educational attainment once hired. Most training for advertising sales agents takes place informally on the job.

***Education and training.*** Some employers, large companies in particular, prefer applicants with a college degree, particularly for sales positions that require meeting with clients. Courses in marketing, leadership, communication, business, and advertising are helpful. For those who sell over the telephone or who have a proven record of successfully selling other products, a high school degree may be sufficient. In 2006, the highest level of educational attainment for advertising sales agents was as follows.

High school graduate or less .....................................20%
Some college, no degree ..........................................19
Associate's degree ...................................................10
Bachelor's degree or higher .....................................52

Most training, however, takes place on the job, and can be formal or informal in nature. In most cases, an experienced sales manager instructs a newly hired advertising sales agent who lacks sales experience. In this one-on-one environment, supervisors typically coach new hires and observe as they make sales calls and contact clients. Supervisors then advise new hires on ways to improve their interaction with clients. Employers may bring in consultants to lead formal training sessions when agents sell to a specialized market segment. This practice is common when advertising sales agents sell space to automotive dealers and real estate professionals.

***Other qualifications.*** Employers look for applicants who are honest and possess a pleasant personality and neat professional appearance. After gaining entry into the occupation, successful sales experience and the ability to communicate effectively become more important than educational attainment. In fact, when selling or soliciting ad space, personality traits are equally, if not more, important than academic background. In general, smaller companies are more willing to hire unproven individuals.

Because they represent their employers to the executives of client organizations, advertising sales agents must have excellent interpersonal and written communication skills. Being multi-lingual, particularly in English and Spanish, is another trait that will benefit prospective advertising agents as media increasingly seek to market to Hispanics and other foreign-born persons. Self-motivation, organization, persistence, independence, and the ability to multitask are required because advertising sales agents set their own schedules and perform their duties without much supervision.

***Advancement.*** Advancement in the occupation means taking on bigger, more important clients. Agents with proven leadership ability and a strong sales record may advance to supervisory and managerial positions such as sales supervisor, sales manager, or vice president of sales. Frequent contact with managers of other departments and people in other firms provides sales agents with leads about job openings, enhancing advancement opportunities. In small firms, where the number of supervisory and management positions is limited, advancement may come slowly. Promotion may occur more quickly in larger media firms and in media representative firms.

## Employment

Advertising sales agents held over 170,000 jobs in 2006. Workers were concentrated in three industries: More than 3 in 10 jobs were in newspaper, periodical, book, and directory publishers; 3 in 10 in advertising and related services; and nearly 2 in 10 in radio and television broadcasting. Media representative firms are in the advertising and related services industry. A relatively small number of jobs were found in specialized design services, including industrial and graphic designers; printing and related support activities; computer systems design and related services; business support services; and cable and other program distribution.

Employment is spread around the country, but jobs in radio and television stations and large, well-known publications are concentrated in big metropolitan areas. Media representative firms are also concentrated in large cities with many advertising agencies, such as New York City.

## Job Outlook

Employment growth of advertising sales agents is expected to grow faster than average for all occupations for the 2006–2016 period. Because of growth in new media outlets, such as the Internet, advertising agents with an ability to sell, should see good job opportunities.

***Employment change.*** Employment of advertising sales agents is expected to increase by 20 percent from 2006 to 2016, which is faster than the average for all occupations. Fast growth in the number of cable channels, online advertisers, and other advertising mediums will create many new opportunities for advertisers. These opportunities, along with increased efforts by media outlets to market to the growing Hispanic population, will lead to the growth of advertising sales agents.

The industries employing advertising sales agents, particularly the newspaper, periodical, radio, and television industries, have experienced considerable consolidation in recent years, which created efficiencies in the sale of advertising and reduced the need for more sales agents. While this trend is expected to continue over the next decade, it should do so at a slower pace and not affect employment of advertising sales agents significantly.

While advances in technology have made advertising sales agents more productive, allowing agents to take on additional duties and improve the quality of the services they provide, technological advances have not substantially decreased overall demand for these workers. Productivity gains have had the largest effect on miscellaneous services that workers provide, such as accounting, proposal creation, and customer service responsibilities, allowing them to provide faster, improved services to their clients. For example, the use of e-mail has considerably shortened the time it takes to negotiate a sale and place an ad. Sales agents may accomplish more in less time, but many work more hours than in the past, spending additional time on follow-up and service calls. Thus, while productivity gains will temper the growth of advertising sales agents, who can now manage more accounts, the increasing growth in advertising across all industries will ensure that new advertising sales agents will continue to be needed in the future.

**Projections data from the National Employment Matrix**

| Occupational Title | SOC Code | Employment, 2006 | Projected employment, 2016 | Change, 2006-16 | |
|---|---|---|---|---|---|
| | | | | Number | Percent |
| Advertising sales agents............................................................... | 41-3011 | 170,000 | 205,000 | 35,000 | 20 |

NOTE: Data in this table are rounded.

*Job prospects.* Those interested in ad sales positions can expect good job opportunities. This is particularly true for sales people with experience and those with a college degree. For those with a proven sales record in advertising sales, opportunities should be excellent. In addition to the job openings generated by employment growth, openings will occur each year because of the need to replace sales representatives who transfer to other occupations or leave the labor force. Each year, many advertising sales agents discover they are unable to earn enough money and leave the occupation.

Advertising revenues are sensitive to economic downturns, which cause the industries and companies that advertise to reduce both the frequency of campaigns and the overall level of spending on advertising. Advertising sales agents must work hard to get the most out of every dollar spent on advertising under these conditions. Therefore, the number of opportunities for advertising sales agents fluctuates with the business cycle. So while advertising sales candidates can expect good opportunities, applicants can expect keen competition for job openings during downturns in advertising spending.

## Earnings

Including commissions, median annual earnings for all advertising sales agents were $42,750 in May 2006. The middle 50 percent earned between $29,450 and $63,120 a year. The lowest 10 percent earned less than $21,460, and the highest 10 percent earned more than $91,280 a year. Median annual earnings for sales agents in the industries in which they were concentrated were

| | |
|---|---|
| Motion picture and video industries | $55,340 |
| Cable and other subscription programming | 50,260 |
| Advertising and related services | 47,640 |
| Radio and television broadcasting | 41,110 |
| Newspaper, periodical, book, and directory publishers | 36,880 |

Performance-based pay, including bonuses and commissions, can make up a large portion of advertising sales agents' earnings. Most employers pay some combination of salaries, commissions, and bonuses. Commissions are usually based on individual sales numbers, whereas bonuses may depend on individual performance, on the performance of all sales workers in a group or district, or on the performance of the entire company. For agents covering multiple areas or regions, commissions also may be based on the difficulty in making a sale in that particular area. Sales revenue is affected by the economic conditions and business expectations facing the industries that tend to advertise. Earnings from commissions are likely to be high when these industries are doing well and low when companies decide not to advertise as frequently.

In addition to their earnings, advertising sales agents are usually reimbursed for entertaining clients and for other business expenses such as transportation costs, meals, and hotel stays. They often receive benefits such as health and life insurance, pension plans, vacation and sick leave, personal use of a company car, and frequent flier mileage. Some companies offer incentives such as free vacation trips or gifts for outstanding sales workers.

## Related Occupations

Advertising sales agents must have sales ability and knowledge of their clients' business and personal needs. Workers in other occupations requiring these skills include telemarketers; advertising, marketing, promotions, public relations, and sales managers; insurance sales agents; purchasing managers, buyers, and purchasing agents; real estate brokers and sales agents; sales engineers; sales representatives, wholesale and manufacturing; and securities, commodities, and financial services sales agents.

## Sources of Additional Information

To learn about opportunities for employment as an advertising sales agent, contact local broadcasters, radio stations, and publishers for advertising sales representative positions, or look for media representative firms in your area.

For information about advertising sales careers in newspaper publishing, contact

▸ The Newspaper Association of America, 1921 Gallows Rd., Suite 600, Vienna, VA 22182. Internet: http://www.naa.org

# Advertising, Marketing, Promotions, Public Relations, and Sales Managers

(O*NET 11-2011.00, 11-2021.00, 11-2022.00, and 11-2031.00)

## Significant Points

- Keen competition is expected for these highly coveted jobs.
- College graduates with related experience, a high level of creativity, strong communication skills, and computer skills should have the best job opportunities.
- High earnings; substantial travel; and long hours, including evenings and weekends, are common.
- Because of the importance and high visibility of their jobs, these managers often are prime candidates for advancement to the highest ranks.

## Nature of the Work

Advertising, marketing, promotions, public relations, and sales managers coordinate their companies' market research, marketing strategy, sales, advertising, promotion, pricing, product development, and public relations activities. In small firms, the owner or chief executive officer might assume all advertising, promotions, marketing, sales, and public relations responsibilities. In large firms, which may offer numerous products and services nationally or even worldwide, an executive vice president directs overall advertising, marketing, promotions, sales, and public relations policies.

*Advertising managers.* Advertising managers oversee advertising and promotion staffs, which usually are small, except in the largest firms. In a small firm, managers may serve as liaisons between the firm and the advertising or promotion agency to which many advertising or promotional functions are contracted out. In larger firms, advertising managers oversee in-house account, creative, and media services departments. The *account executive* manages the account services department; assesses the need for advertising; and, in advertising agencies, maintains the accounts of clients. The creative services department develops the subject matter and presentation of advertising. The *creative director* oversees the copy chief, art director, and associated staff. The *media director* oversees planning groups that select the communication media—for example, radio, television, newspapers, magazines, the Internet, or outdoor signs—to disseminate the advertising.

*Marketing managers.* Marketing managers develop the firm's marketing strategy in detail. With the help of subordinates, including *product development managers* and *market research managers,* they estimate the demand for products and services offered by the firm and its competitors. In addition, they identify potential markets—for example, business firms, wholesalers, retailers, government, or the general public. Marketing managers develop pricing strategy to help firms maximize profits and market share while ensuring that the firm's customers are satisfied. In collaboration with sales, product development, and other managers, they monitor trends that indicate the need for new products and services, and they oversee product development. Marketing managers work with advertising and promotion managers to promote the firm's products and services and to attract potential users.

*Promotions managers.* Promotions managers supervise staffs of promotions specialists. These managers direct promotions programs that combine advertising with purchase incentives to increase sales. In an effort to establish closer contact with purchasers—dealers, distributors, or consumers—promotions programs may use direct mail, telemarketing, television or radio advertising, catalogs, exhibits, inserts in newspapers, Internet advertisements or Web sites, in-store displays or product endorsements, and special events. Purchasing incentives may include discounts, samples, gifts, rebates, coupons, sweepstakes, and contests.

*Public relations managers.* Public relations managers supervise public relations specialists. These managers direct publicity programs to a targeted audience. They often specialize in a specific area, such as crisis management, or in a specific industry, such as health care. They use every available communication medium to maintain the support of the specific group upon whom their organization's success depends, such as consumers, stockholders, or the general public. For example, public relations managers may clarify or justify the firm's point of view on health or environmental issues to community or special-interest groups.

Public relations managers also evaluate advertising and promotions programs for compatibility with public relations efforts and serve as the eyes and ears of top management. They observe social, economic, and political trends that might ultimately affect the firm, and they make recommendations to enhance the firm's image on the basis of those trends.

Public relations managers may confer with labor relations managers to produce internal company communications—such as newsletters about employee-management relations—and with financial managers to produce company reports. They assist company executives in drafting speeches, arranging interviews, and maintaining other forms of public contact; oversee company archives; and respond to requests for information. In addition, some of these managers handle special events, such as the sponsorship of races, parties introducing new products, or other activities that the firm supports in order to gain public attention through the press without advertising directly.

*Sales managers.* Sales managers direct the firm's sales program. They assign sales territories, set goals, and establish training programs for the sales representatives. Sales managers advise the sales representatives on ways to improve their sales performance. In large, multi-product firms, they oversee regional and local sales managers and their staffs. Sales managers maintain contact with dealers and distributors. They analyze sales statistics gathered by their staffs to determine sales potential and inventory requirements and to monitor customers' preferences. Such information is vital in the development of products and the maximization of profits.

**Work environment.** Advertising, marketing, promotions, public relations, and sales managers work in offices close to those of top managers. Working under pressure is unavoidable when schedules change and problems arise, but deadlines and goals must still be met.

Substantial travel may be involved. For example, attendance at meetings sponsored by associations or industries often is mandatory. Sales managers travel to national, regional, and local offices and to the offices of various dealers and distributors. Advertising and promotions managers may travel to meet with clients or representatives of communications media. At times, public relations managers travel to meet with special-interest groups or government officials. Job transfers between headquarters and regional offices are common, particularly among sales managers.

Long hours, including evenings and weekends, are common. In 2006, about two-thirds of advertising, marketing, and public relations managers worked more than 40 hours a week.

## Training, Other Qualifications, and Advancement

A wide range of educational backgrounds is suitable for entry into advertising, marketing, promotions, public relations, and sales managerial jobs, but many employers prefer those with experience in related occupations.

*Education and training.* For marketing, sales, and promotions management positions, some employers prefer a bachelor's or master's degree in business administration with an emphasis on marketing. Courses in business law, management, economics, accounting, finance, mathematics, and statistics are advantageous. Additionally, the completion of an internship while the candidate is in school is highly recommended. In highly technical industries, such as computer and electronics manufacturing, a bachelor's degree in engineering or science, combined with a master's degree in business administration, is preferred.

For advertising management positions, some employers prefer a bachelor's degree in advertising or journalism. A course of study should include, for example, marketing, consumer behavior, market research, sales, communication methods and technology, visual arts, and art history and photography.

For public relations management positions, some employers prefer a bachelor's or master's degree in public relations or journalism. The applicant's curriculum should include courses in advertising, business administration, public affairs, public speaking, political science, and creative and technical writing.

Most advertising, marketing, promotions, public relations, and sales management positions are filled by promoting experienced staff or related professional personnel. For example, many managers are former sales representatives, purchasing agents, buyers; or product, advertising, promotions, or public relations specialists. In small firms, where the number of positions is limited, advancement to a management position usually comes slowly. In large firms, promotion may occur more quickly.

*Other qualifications.* Familiarity with word-processing and database applications is important for most positions. Computer skills are vital because marketing, product promotion, and advertising on the Internet are increasingly common. Also, the ability to communicate in a foreign language may open up employment opportunities in many rapidly growing areas around the country, especially cities with large Spanish-speaking populations.

Persons interested in becoming advertising, marketing, promotions, public relations, and sales managers should be mature, creative, highly motivated, resistant to stress, flexible, and decisive. The ability to communicate persuasively, both orally and in writing, with other managers, staff, and the public is vital. These managers also need tact, good judgment, and exceptional ability to establish and maintain effective personal relationships with supervisory and professional staff members and client firms.

*Certification and advancement.* Some associations offer certification programs for these managers. Certification—an indication of competence and achievement—is particularly important in a competitive job market. While relatively few advertising, marketing, promotions, public relations, and sales managers currently are certified, the number of managers who seek certification is expected to grow. Today, there are numerous management certification programs based on education and job performance. In addition, The Public Relations Society of America offers a certification program for public relations practitioners based on years of experience and performance on an examination.

Although experience, ability, and leadership are emphasized for promotion, advancement can be accelerated by participation in management training programs conducted by larger firms. Many firms also provide their employees with continuing education opportunities—either in-house or at local colleges and universities—and encourage employee participation in seminars and conferences, often held by professional societies. In collaboration with colleges and universities, numerous marketing and related associations sponsor national or local management training programs. Course subjects include brand and product management, international marketing, sales management evaluation, telemarketing and direct sales, interactive marketing, promotion, marketing communication, market research, organizational communication, and data processing systems procedures and management. Many firms pay all or part of the cost for employees who successfully complete courses.

Because of the importance and high visibility of their jobs, advertising, marketing, promotions, public relations, and sales managers often are prime candidates for advancement to the highest ranks. Well-trained, experienced, and successful managers may be promoted to higher positions in their own or another firm; some become top executives. Managers with extensive experience and sufficient capital may open their own businesses.

## Employment

Advertising, marketing, promotions, public relations, and sales managers held about 583,000 jobs in 2006. The following tabulation shows the distribution of jobs by occupational specialty:

| | |
|---|---|
| Sales managers | 318,000 |
| Marketing managers | 167,000 |
| Public relations managers | 50,000 |
| Advertising and promotions managers | 47,000 |

These managers were found in virtually every industry. Sales managers held more than half of the jobs; most were employed in wholesale trade, retail trade, manufacturing, and finance and insurance industries. Marketing managers held more than a fourth of the jobs; the professional, scientific, and technical services and the finance and insurance industries employed almost one-third of marketing managers. About one-fourth of advertising and promotions managers worked in the professional, scientific, and technical services industries and the wholesale trade. Most public relations managers were employed in service-providing industries, such as professional, scientific, and technical services; educational services, public and private; finance and insurance; and health care and social assistance.

## Job Outlook

Average job growth is projected, but keen competition is expected for these highly coveted jobs.

*Employment change.* Employment of advertising, marketing, promotions, public relations, and sales managers is expected to increase by 12 percent through 2016—about as fast as the average for all occupations. Job growth will be spurred by intense domestic and global competition in products and services offered to consumers and increasing activity in television, radio, and outdoor advertising.

**Projections data from the National Employment Matrix**

| Occupational Title | SOC Code | Employment, 2006 | Projected employment, 2016 | Change, 2006-16 | |
|---|---|---|---|---|---|
| | | | | Number | Percent |
| Advertising, marketing, promotions, public relations, and sales managers .......... | 11-2000 | 583,000 | 651,000 | 68,000 | 12 |
| Advertising and promotions managers ..................... | 11-2011 | 47,000 | 50,000 | 3,000 | 6 |
| Marketing and sales managers ................................. | 11-2020 | 486,000 | 542,000 | 57,000 | 12 |
| Marketing managers................................. | 11-2021 | 167,000 | 192,000 | 24,000 | 14 |
| Sales managers.................................. | 11-2022 | 318,000 | 351,000 | 33,000 | 10 |
| Public relations managers ............................. | 11-2031 | 50,000 | 58,000 | 8,400 | 17 |

NOTE: Data in this table are rounded.

Projected employment growth varies by industry. For example, employment is projected to grow much faster than average in scientific, professional, and related services—such as computer systems design and related services and advertising and related services—as businesses increasingly hire contractors for these services instead of additional full-time staff. By contrast, a decline in employment is expected in many manufacturing industries.

*Job prospects.* Advertising, marketing, promotions, public relations, and sales manager jobs are highly coveted and will be sought by other managers or highly experienced professionals, resulting in keen competition. College graduates with related experience, a high level of creativity, and strong communication skills should have the best job opportunities. In particular, employers will seek those who have the computer skills to conduct advertising, marketing, promotions, public relations, and sales activities on the Internet.

## Earnings

Median annual earnings in May 2006 were $73,060 for advertising and promotions managers, $98,720 for marketing managers, $91,560 for sales managers, and $82,180 for public relations managers.

Median annual earnings of wage and salary advertising and promotions managers in May 2006 in the advertising and related services industry were $97,540.

Median annual earnings in the industries employing the largest numbers of marketing managers were

Computer systems design and related services ....$119,540

Management of companies and enterprises ..........103,070

Management, scientific, and technical
    consulting services .......................................100,200

Architectural, engineering, and related services ......92,480

Depository credit intermediation ..........................91,420

Median annual earnings in the industries employing the largest numbers of sales managers were

Professional and commercial equipment
    and supplies merchant wholesalers ..................$112,810

Wholesale electronic markets and agents
    and brokers ...............................................107,420

Automobile dealers .......................................101,110

Management of companies and enterprises ............98,240

Machinery, equipment, and supplies
    merchant wholesalers........................................93,450

Salary levels vary substantially, depending upon the level of managerial responsibility, length of service, education, size of firm, location, and industry. For example, manufacturing firms usually pay these managers higher salaries than nonmanufacturing firms. For sales managers, the size of their sales territory is another important determinant of salary. Many managers earn bonuses equal to 10 percent or more of their salaries.

According to a survey by the National Association of Colleges and Employers, starting salaries for marketing majors graduating in 2007 averaged $40,161 and those for advertising majors averaged $33,831.

## Related Occupations

Advertising, marketing, promotions, public relations, and sales managers direct the sale of products and services offered by their firms and the communication of information about their firms' activities. Other workers involved with advertising, marketing, promotions, public relations, and sales include actors, producers, and directors; advertising sales agents; artists and related workers; demonstrators, product promoters, and models; market and survey researchers; public relations specialists; sales representatives, wholesale and manufacturing; and writers and editors.

## Sources of Additional Information

For information about careers in advertising management, contact

▶ American Association of Advertising Agencies, 405 Lexington Ave., New York, NY 10174-1801. Internet: http://www.aaaa.org

Information about careers and professional certification in public relations management is available from

▶ Public Relations Society of America, 33 Maiden Lane, New York, NY 10038-5150. Internet: http://www.prsa.org

# Animal Care and Service Workers

(O*NET 39-2011.00 and 39-2021.00)

## Significant Points

- Animal lovers get satisfaction in this occupation, but the work can be unpleasant, physically and emotionally demanding, and sometimes dangerous.

- Most workers are trained on the job, but employers generally prefer to hire people who have experience with animals; some jobs require a bachelor's degree in biology, animal science, or a related field.

- Most positions will present good employment opportunities; however, keen competition is expected for jobs as zookeepers and marine mammal trainers.

- Earnings are relatively low.

## Nature of the Work

Many people like animals. But, as pet owners can attest, taking care of them is hard work. Animal care and service workers—who include animal caretakers and animal trainers—train, feed, water, groom, bathe, and exercise animals and clean, disinfect, and repair their cages. They also play with the animals, provide companionship, and observe behavioral changes that could indicate illness or injury. Boarding kennels, pet stores, animal shelters, veterinary hospitals and clinics, stables, laboratories, aquariums and natural aquatic habitats, and zoological parks all house animals and employ animal care and service workers. Job titles and duties vary by employment setting.

*Kennel attendants* care for pets while their owners are working or traveling out of town. Beginning attendants perform basic tasks, such as cleaning cages and dog runs, filling food and water dishes, and exercising animals. Experienced attendants may provide basic animal healthcare, as well as bathe animals, trim nails, and attend to other grooming needs. Attendants who work in kennels also may sell pet food and supplies, assist in obedience training, help with breeding, or prepare animals for shipping.

*Groomers* are animal caretakers who specialize in grooming or maintaining a pet's appearance. Most groom dogs and a few groom cats. Some groomers work in kennels, veterinary clinics, animal shelters, or pet-supply stores. Others operate their own grooming business, typically at a salon, or increasingly, by making house calls. Such mobile services are growing rapidly as they offer convenience for pet owners, flexibility of schedules for groomers, and minimal trauma for pets resulting from their being in unfamiliar surroundings. Groomers clean and sanitize equipment to prevent the spread of disease, maintain grooming equipment, and maintain a clean and safe environment for the animals. Groomers also schedule appointments, discuss pets' grooming needs with clients, and collect information on the pet's disposition and its veterinarian. Groomers often are the first to notice a medical problem, such as an ear or skin infection that requires veterinary care.

Grooming the pet involves several steps: an initial brush-out is followed by a first clipping of hair or fur using electric clippers, combs, and grooming shears; the groomer then cuts the nails, cleans the ears, bathes, and blow-dries the animal, and ends with a final clipping and styling.

Animal caretakers in animal shelters perform a variety of duties and work with a wide variety of animals. In addition to attending to the basic needs of the animals, caretakers at shelters also must keep records of the animals received and discharged and any tests or treatments done. Some vaccinate newly admitted animals under the direction of a veterinarian or veterinary technician, and euthanize (painlessly put to death) seriously ill, severely injured, or unwanted animals. Animal caretakers in animal shelters also interact with the public, answering telephone inquiries, screening applicants for animal adoption, or educating visitors on neutering and other animal health issues.

*Grooms*, or caretakers, care for horses in stables. They saddle and unsaddle horses, give them rubdowns, and walk them to cool them off after a ride. They also feed, groom, and exercise the horses; clean out stalls and replenish bedding; polish saddles; clean and organize the tack (harness, saddle, and bridle) room; and store supplies and feed. Experienced grooms may help train horses.

In zoos, animal care and service workers, called *keepers*, prepare the diets and clean the enclosures of animals, and sometimes assist in raising them when they are very young. They watch for any signs of illness or injury, monitor eating patterns or any changes in behavior, and record their observations. Keepers also may answer questions and ensure that the visiting public behaves responsibly toward the exhibited animals. Depending on the zoo, keepers may be assigned to work with a broad group of animals such as mammals, birds, or reptiles, or they may work with a limited collection of animals such as primates, large cats, or small mammals.

*Animal trainers* train animals for riding, security, performance, obedience, or assisting people with disabilities. Animal trainers do this by accustoming the animal to human voice and contact and conditioning the animal to respond to commands. The three most commonly trained animals are dogs, horses, and marine mammals, including dolphins. Trainers use several techniques to help them train animals. One technique, known as a bridge, is a stimulus that a trainer uses to communicate the precise moment an animal does something correctly. When the animal responds correctly, the trainer gives positive reinforcement in a variety of ways: food, toys, play, rubdowns, or speaking the word "good." Animal training takes place in small steps and often takes months and even years of repetition. During the conditioning process, trainers provide animals with mental stimulation, physical exercise, and husbandry care. A relatively new form of training teaches animals to cooperate with workers giving medical care. Animals learn "veterinary" behaviors, such as allowing and even cooperating with the collection of blood samples; physical, x-ray, ultrasonic, and dental exams; physical therapy; and the administration of medicines and replacement fluids.

Training also can be a good tool for facilitating the relocation of animals from one habitat to another, easing, for example, the process of loading horses on trailers. Trainers often work in competitions or shows, such as circuses or marine parks, aquariums, animal shelters, dog kennels and salons, or horse farms. Trainers in shows work to display the talent and ability of an animal, such as a dolphin, through interactive programs to educate and entertain the public.

In addition to their hands-on work with the animals, trainers often oversee other aspects of animals' care, such as preparing their diet and providing a safe and clean environment and habitat.

*Work environment.* People who love animals get satisfaction from working with and helping them. However, some of the work may be unpleasant, physically and emotionally demanding, and sometimes dangerous. Most animal caretakers and service workers have to clean animal cages and lift, hold, or restrain animals, risking exposure to bites or scratches. Their work often involves kneeling, crawling, repeated bending, and lifting heavy supplies like bales of hay or bags of feed. Animal caretakers must take precautions when treating animals with germicides or insecticides. They may work outdoors in all kinds of weather, and the work setting can be noisy. Caretakers of show and sports animals travel to competitions.

Animal caretaker and service workers who witness abused animals or who assist in euthanizing unwanted, aged, or hopelessly injured animals may experience emotional distress. Those working for private humane societies and municipal animal shelters often deal with the public, some of whom might react with hostility to the implication that they are neglecting or abusing their pets. Such workers must maintain a calm and professional demeanor while helping to enforce the laws regarding animal care.

Animal care and service workers often work irregular hours. Most animals are fed every day, so caretakers often work weekend and holiday shifts. Some zoo animals skip one meal a week to mimic their lives in the wild. In some animal hospitals, research facilities, and animal shelters, an attendant is on duty 24 hours a day, which means night shifts.

## Training, Other Qualifications, and Advancement

On-the-job training is the most common way animal caretakers and service workers learn their work; however, employers generally prefer to hire people who have experience with animals. Some preparatory programs are available for specific types of caretakers, such as groomers.

*Education and training.* Animal trainers often need a high school diploma or GED equivalent. Some animal training jobs may require a bachelor's degree and additional skills. For example, marine mammal trainers usually need a bachelor's degree in biology, marine biology, animal science, psychology, or a related field. An animal health technician degree also may qualify trainers for some jobs.

Most equine trainers learn their trade by working as a groom at a stable. Some study at an accredited private training school. Because large animals are involved, most horse-training jobs have minimum weight requirements for candidates.

Many dog trainers attend workshops and courses at community colleges and vocational schools. Topics include basic study of canines, learning theory of animals, teaching obedience cues, problem solving methods, and safety. Many also offer business training.

Many zoos require their caretakers to have a bachelor's degree in biology, animal science, or a related field. Most require experience with animals, preferably as a volunteer or paid keeper in a zoo.

Most pet groomers learn their trade by completing an informal apprenticeship, usually lasting six to 10 weeks, under the guidance of an experienced groomer. Prospective groomers also may attend one of the 52 state-licensed grooming schools throughout the country, with programs varying in length from 2 to 18 weeks. Beginning groomers often start by taking on one duty, such as bathing and drying the pet. They eventually assume responsibility for the entire grooming process, from the initial brush-out to the final clipping.

Animal caretakers in animal shelters are not required to have any specialized training, but training programs and workshops are available through the Humane Society of the United States, the American Humane Association, and the National Animal Control Association. Workshop topics include cruelty investigations, appropriate methods of euthanasia for shelter animals, proper guidelines for capturing animals, techniques for preventing problems with wildlife, and dealing with the public.

Beginning animal caretakers in kennels learn on the job and usually start by cleaning cages and feeding and watering animals.

*Certification and other qualifications.* Certifications are available in many animal service occupations. For dog trainers, certification by a professional association or one of the hundreds of private vocational or state-approved trade schools can be advantageous. The National Dog Groomers Association of America offers certification for master status as a groomer. The American Boarding Kennels Association offers a three-stage, home-study program for individuals interested in pet care. Those who complete the third stage and pass oral and written examinations become Certified Kennel Operators (CKO).

All animal caretakers and service workers need patience, sensitivity, and problem solving ability. They also need tact and communication skills. This is particularly true for those in shelters, who often deal with individuals who abandon their pets. The ability to handle emotional people is vital for workers at shelters.

Animal trainers especially need problem-solving skills and experience in animal obedience. Successful marine mammal trainers should also have good public speaking skills as seminars and presentations are a large part of the job. Usually four to five trainers work with a group of animals at one time, therefore, each trainer should be able to work as part of a team. Marine mammal trainers must also be good swimmers; certification in SCUBA is a plus.

*Advancement.* With experience and additional training, caretakers in animal shelters may become adoption coordinators, animal control officers, emergency rescue drivers, assistant shelter managers, or shelter directors. Pet groomers who work in large retail establishments or kennels may, with experience, move into supervisory or managerial positions. Experienced groomers often choose to open their own salons. Advancement for kennel caretakers takes the form of promotion to kennel supervisor, assistant manager, and manager; those with enough capital and experience may open up their own kennels. Zookeepers may advance to senior keeper, assistant head keeper, head keeper, and assistant curator, but very few openings occur, especially for the higher-level positions.

**Projections data from the National Employment Matrix**

| Occupational Title | SOC Code | Employment, 2006 | Projected employment, 2016 | Change, 2006-16 | |
|---|---|---|---|---|---|
| | | | | Number | Percent |
| Animal care and service workers ..................................................... | 39-2000 | 200,000 | 238,000 | 39,000 | 19 |
|   Animal trainers......................................................................... | 39-2011 | 43,000 | 53,000 | 9,800 | 23 |
|   Nonfarm animal caretakers ......................................................... | 39-2021 | 157,000 | 185,000 | 29,000 | 18 |

NOTE: Data in this table are rounded.

## Employment

Animal caretakers and service workers held 200,000 jobs in 2006. Over 3 out of 4 worked as nonfarm animal caretakers; the remainder worked as animal trainers. Nonfarm animal caretakers often worked in boarding kennels, animal shelters, stables, grooming shops, pet stores, animal hospitals, and veterinary offices. A significant number of caretakers worked for animal humane societies, racing stables, dog and horse racetrack operators, zoos, theme parks, circuses, and other amusement and recreations services.

Employment of animal trainers is concentrated in animal services that specialize in training and in commercial sports, where they train racehorses and dogs. About 57 percent of animal trainers were self-employed.

## Job Outlook

Because many workers leave this occupation each year, there will be good job opportunities for most positions. Faster-than-average employment growth also will add to job openings, in addition to replacement needs.

*Employment change.* Employment of animal care and service workers is expected to grow 19 percent over the 2006–2016 decade, faster than the average for all occupations. The companion pet population, which drives employment of animal caretakers in kennels, grooming shops, animal shelters, and veterinary clinics and hospitals, is expected to increase. Pet owners—including a large number of baby boomers, whose disposable income is expected to increase as they age—are expected to increasingly purchase grooming services, daily and overnight boarding services, training services, and veterinary services, resulting in more jobs for animal care and service workers. As more pet owners consider their pets part of the family, demand for luxury animal services and the willingness to spend greater amounts of money on pets should continue to grow. Demand for marine mammal trainers, on the other hand, should grow slowly.

Demand for animal care and service workers in animal shelters is expected to grow as communities increasingly recognize the connection between animal abuse and abuse toward humans, and continue to commit private funds to animal shelters, many of which are working hand-in-hand with social service agencies and law enforcement teams.

*Job prospects.* Due to employment growth and the need to replace workers who leave the occupation, job opportunities for most positions should be good. The need to replace workers leaving the field will create the overwhelming majority of job openings. Many animal caretaker jobs require little or no training and have flexible work schedules, making them suitable for people seeking a first job or for temporary or part-time work. The outlook for caretakers in

zoos and aquariums, however, is not favorable due to slow job growth and keen competition for the few positions.

Prospective mammal trainers will face keen competition as the number of applicants greatly exceeds the number of available positions. Prospective horse trainers should anticipate an equally challenging labor market as the number of entry-level positions is limited. Dog trainers, however, should experience conditions that are more favorable. Opportunities for dog trainers should be best in large metropolitan areas.

Job opportunities for animal care and service workers may vary from year to year because the strength of the economy affects demand for these workers. Pet owners tend to spend more on animal services when the economy is strong.

## Earnings

Earnings are relatively low. Median hourly earnings of nonfarm animal caretakers were $8.72 in May 2006. The middle 50 percent earned between $7.50 and $10.95. The bottom 10 percent earned less than $6.56, and the top 10 percent earned more than $14.64. Median hourly earnings in the industries employing the largest numbers of nonfarm animal caretakers in May 2006 were

  Spectator sports ....................................................$9.38
  Other personal services ...........................................8.78
  Social advocacy organizations...................................8.31
  Other professional, scientific, and technical services ..8.23
  Veterinary services ................................................8.23
  Other miscellaneous store retailers .........................8.22

Median hourly earnings of animal trainers were $12.65 in May 2006. The middle 50 percent earned between $9.11 and $17.39. The lowest 10 percent earned less than $7.66, and the top 10 percent earned more than $22.42.

## Related Occupations

Others who work extensively with animals include farmers, ranchers, and agricultural managers; agricultural workers; veterinarians; veterinary technologists and technicians; veterinary assistants; and biological scientists.

## Sources of Additional Information

For career information and information on training, certification, and earnings of the related occupation of animal control officers, contact

▸ National Animal Control Association, P.O. Box 1480851, Kansas City, MO 64148-0851. Internet: http://www.nacanet.org

For information on becoming an advanced pet care technician at a kennel, contact

▸ American Boarding Kennels Association, 1702 East Pikes Peak Ave., Colorado Springs, CO 80909. Internet: http://www.abka.com/abka

For general information on pet grooming careers, including certification information, contact

▸ National Dog Groomers Association of America, P.O. Box 101, Clark, PA 16113. Internet: http://www.nationaldoggroomers.com

# Artists and Related Workers

(O*NET 27-1011.00, 27-1012.00, 27-1013.00, 27-1014.00, and 27-1019.99)

## Significant Points

■ About 62 percent of artists and related workers are self-employed.

■ Keen competition is expected for both salaried jobs and freelance work because the arts attract many talented people with creative ability.

■ Artists usually develop their skills through a bachelor's degree program or other postsecondary training in art or design.

■ Earnings for self-employed artists vary widely; some well-established artists earn more than salaried artists, while others find it difficult to rely solely on income earned from selling art.

## Nature of the Work

Artists create art to communicate ideas, thoughts, or feelings. They use a variety of methods—painting, sculpting, or illustration—and an assortment of materials, including oils, watercolors, acrylics, pastels, pencils, pen and ink, plaster, clay, and computers. Artists' works may be realistic, stylized, or abstract and may depict objects, people, nature, or events.

Artists generally fall into one of four categories. Art directors formulate design concepts and presentation approaches for visual communications. Craft artists create or reproduce handmade objects for sale or exhibition. Fine artists, including painters, sculptors, and illustrators, create original artwork, using a variety of media and techniques. Multi-media artists and animators create special effects, animation, or other visual images on film, on video, or with computers or other electronic media.

*Art directors* develop design concepts and review material that is to appear in periodicals, newspapers, and other printed or digital media. They decide how best to present information visually, so that it is eye catching, appealing, and organized. Art directors decide which photographs or artwork to use and oversee the design, layout, and production of material to be published. They may direct workers engaged in artwork, design, layout, and copywriting.

*Craft artists* make a wide variety of objects, mostly by hand, that are sold either in their own studios, in retail outlets, or at arts-and-crafts shows. Some craft artists display their works in galleries and museums. Craft artists work with many different materials, including ceramics, glass, textiles, wood, metal, and paper, to create unique pieces of art, such as pottery, stained glass, quilts, tapestries, lace, candles, and clothing. Many craft artists also use fine-art techniques—for example, painting, sketching, and printing—to add finishing touches to their art.

*Fine artists* typically display their work in museums, commercial art galleries, corporate collections, and private homes. Some of their artwork may be commissioned (done on request from clients), but most is sold by the artist or through private art galleries or dealers. The gallery and the artist predetermine how much each will earn from the sale. Only the most successful fine artists are able to support themselves solely through the sale of their works. Most fine artists have at least one other job to support their art careers. Some work in museums or art galleries as fine-arts directors or as curators, planning and setting up art exhibits. A few artists work as art critics for newspapers or magazines or as consultants to foundations or institutional collectors. Other artists teach art classes or conduct workshops in schools or in their own studios. Some artists also hold full-time or part-time jobs unrelated to art and pursue fine art as a hobby or second career.

Usually, fine artists specialize in one or two art forms, such as painting, illustrating, sketching, sculpting, printmaking, and restoring. Painters, illustrators, cartoonists, and sketch artists work with two-dimensional art forms, using shading, perspective, and color to produce realistic scenes or abstractions.

*Illustrators* usually create pictures for books, magazines, and other publications and for commercial products such as textiles, wrapping paper, stationery, greeting cards, and calendars. Increasingly, illustrators are working in digital format, preparing work directly on a computer. This has created new opportunities for illustrators to work with animators and in broadcast media.

*Medical* and *scientific illustrators* combine drawing skills with knowledge of biology or other sciences. Medical illustrators work digitally or traditionally to create images of human anatomy and surgical procedures as well as 3-dimensional models and animations. Scientific illustrators draw animal and plant life, atomic and molecular structures, and geologic and planetary formations. These illustrations are used in medical and scientific publications and in audiovisual presentations for teaching purposes. Illustrators also work for lawyers, producing exhibits for court cases.

*Cartoonists* draw political, advertising, social, and sports cartoons. Some cartoonists work with others who create the idea or story and write captions. Some cartoonists write captions themselves. Most cartoonists have comic, critical, or dramatic talents in addition to drawing skills.

*Sketch artists* create likenesses of subjects with pencil, charcoal, or pastels. Sketches are used by law enforcement agencies to assist in identifying suspects, by the news media to depict courtroom scenes, and by individual patrons for their own enjoyment.

*Sculptors* design three-dimensional artworks, either by molding and joining materials such as clay, glass, wire, plastic, fabric, or metal or by cutting and carving forms from a block of plaster, wood, or stone. Some sculptors combine various materials to create mixed-media installations. Some incorporate light, sound, and motion into their works.

*Printmakers* create printed images from designs cut or etched into wood, stone, or metal. After creating the design, the artist inks the surface of the woodblock, stone, or plate and uses a printing press to roll the image onto paper or fabric. Some make prints by pressing the inked surface onto paper by hand or by graphically encoding and processing data, using a computer. The digitized images are then printed on paper with the use of a computer printer.

*Painting restorers* preserve and restore damaged and faded paintings. They apply solvents and cleaning agents to clean the surfaces of the paintings, they reconstruct or retouch damaged areas, and they apply preservatives to protect the paintings. Restoration is highly detailed work and usually is reserved for experts in the field.

*Multi-media artists and animators* work primarily in motion picture and video industries, advertising, and computer systems design services. They draw by hand and use computers to create the series of pictures that form the animated images or special effects seen in movies, television programs, and computer games. Some draw storyboards for television commercials, movies, and animated features. Storyboards present television commercials in a series of scenes similar to a comic strip and allow an advertising agency to evaluate commercials proposed by advertising companies. Storyboards also serve as guides to placing actors and cameras on the television or motion picture set and to other production details. Many multimedia artists model objects in three dimensions by computer and work with programmers to make those images move.

*Work environment.* Many artists work in fine art or commercial art studios located in office buildings, warehouses, or lofts. Others work in private studios in their homes. Some fine artists share studio space, where they also may exhibit their work. Studio surroundings usually are well lighted and ventilated; however, fine artists may be exposed to fumes from glue, paint, ink, and other materials and to dust or other residue from filings, splattered paint, or spilled cleaners and other fluids. Artists who sit at drafting tables or who use computers for extended periods may experience back pain, eyestrain, or fatigue.

Artists employed by publishing companies, advertising agencies, and design firms generally work a standard work week. During busy periods, they may work overtime to meet deadlines. Self-employed artists can set their own hours. They may spend much time and effort selling their artwork to potential customers or clients and building a reputation.

## Training, Other Qualifications, and Advancement

Artists usually develop their skills through a bachelor's degree program or other postsecondary training in art or design. Although formal schooling is not strictly required for craft and fine artists, it is very difficult to become skilled enough to make a living without some training. Art directors usually have years of work experience and generally need at least a bachelor's degree. Due to the level of technical expertise demanded, multimedia artists and animators generally also need a bachelor's degree.

*Education and training.* Many colleges and universities offer programs leading to a bachelor's or master's degree in fine arts. Courses usually include core subjects such as English, social science, and natural science, in addition to art history and studio art. Independent schools of art and design also offer postsecondary studio training in the craft, fine, and multi-media arts leading to certificates in the specialties or to an associate or bachelor's degree in fine arts. Typically, these programs focus more intensively on studio work than do the academic programs in a university setting. In 2007 the National Association of Schools of Art and Design accredited 282 postsecondary institutions with programs in art and design; most of these schools award a degree in art.

Many educational programs in art also provide training in computer techniques. Computers are used widely in the visual arts, and knowledge and training in computer graphics and other visual display software are critical elements of many jobs in these fields.

Medical illustrators must have both a demonstrated artistic ability and a detailed knowledge of living organisms, surgical and medical procedures, and human and animal anatomy. A bachelor's degree combining art and premedical courses usually is required. However, most medical illustrators also choose to pursue a master's degree in medical illustration. This degree is offered in four accredited schools in the United States.

Art directors usually begin as entry-level artists in advertising, publishing, design, and motion picture production firms. Artists are promoted to art director after demonstrating artistic and leadership abilities. Some art schools offer coursework in art direction as part of their curricula. Depending on the scope of their responsibilities, some art directors also may pursue a degree in art administration, which teaches non-artistic skills such as project management and finance.

Those who want to teach fine arts at public elementary or secondary schools usually must have a teaching certificate in addition to a bachelor's degree. An advanced degree in fine arts or arts administration is usually necessary for management or administrative positions in government or in foundations or for teaching in colleges and universities.

*Other qualifications.* Evidence of appropriate talent and skill, displayed in an artist's portfolio, is an important factor used by art directors, clients, and others in deciding whether to hire an individual or contract for their work. A portfolio is a collection of handmade, computer-generated, photographic, or printed samples of the artist's best work. Assembling a successful portfolio requires skills usually developed through postsecondary training in art or visual communications. Internships also provide excellent opportunities for artists to develop and enhance their portfolios.

*Advancement.* Artists hired by firms often start with relatively routine work. While doing this work, however, they may observe other artists and practice their own skills.

Craft and fine artists advance professionally as their work circulates and as they establish a reputation for a particular style. Many of the most successful artists continually develop new ideas, and their work often evolves over time.

Many artists freelance part-time while continuing to hold a full-time job until they are established. Others freelance part time while still in school, to develop experience and to build a portfolio of published work.

Freelance artists try to develop a set of clients who regularly contract for work. Some freelance artists are widely recognized for their skill in specialties such as cartooning or children's book illustration. These artists may earn high incomes and can choose the type of work they do.

## Employment

Artists held about 218,000 jobs in 2006. About 62 percent were self-employed. Employment was distributed as follows:

Multimedia artists and animators ..........................87,000

Art directors .....................................................78,000

Fine artists, including painters, sculptors,
   and illustrators ..............................................30,000

Craft artists .......................................................8,800

Artists and related workers, all other ...................14,000

Of the artists who were not self-employed, many worked for advertising and related services; newspaper, periodical, book, and software publishers; motion picture and video industries; specialized design services; and computer systems design and related services. Some self-employed artists offered their services to advertising agencies, design firms, publishing houses, and other businesses.

## Job Outlook

Employment of artists is projected to grow faster than average. Competition for jobs is expected to be keen for both salaried and freelance jobs in all specialties because the number of people with creative ability and an interest in this career is expected to continue to exceed the number of available openings. Despite the competition, employers and individual clients are always on the lookout for talented and creative artists.

*Employment change.* Employment of artists and related workers is expected to grow 16 percent through 2016, faster than the average for all occupations.

Demand for illustrators who work on a computer will increase as Web sites use more detailed images and backgrounds in their designs. Many cartoonists, in particular, opt to post their work on political Web sites and online publications. Cartoonists often create animated or interactive images to satisfy readers' demands for more sophisticated images. The small number of medical illustrators will also be in greater demand as medical research continues to grow.

Demand for multimedia artists and animators will increase as consumers continue to demand more realistic video games, movie and television special effects, and 3D animated movies. Additional job openings will arise from an increasing demand for Web site development and for computer graphics adaptation from the growing number of mobile technologies. Animators are also increasingly finding work in alternative areas such as scientific research or design services.

*Job prospects.* Competition for jobs as artists and related workers will be keen because there are more qualified candidates than available jobs. Employers in all industries should be able to choose from among the most qualified candidates.

Despite the competition, studios, galleries, and individual clients are always on the lookout for artists who display outstanding talent, creativity, and style. Among craft and fine artists, talented individuals who have developed a mastery of artistic techniques and skills will have the best job prospects. Multi-media artists and animators should have better job opportunities than other artists, but still will experience competition. Job opportunities for animators of lower-technology cartoons could be hampered as these jobs continue to be outsourced overseas.

Despite an expanding number of opportunities, art directors should experience keen competition for the available openings. Craft and fine artists work mostly on a freelance or commission basis and may find it difficult to earn a living solely by selling their artwork. Only the most successful craft and fine artists receive major commissions for their work. Competition among artists for the privilege of being shown in galleries is expected to remain acute, as will competition for grants from sponsors such as private foundations, state and local arts councils, and the National Endowment for the Arts.

The growth in computer graphics packages and stock art Web sites is making it easier for writers, publishers, and art directors to create their own illustrations. As the use of this technology grows, there will be fewer opportunities for illustrators. However, it also has opened up new opportunities for illustrators who prefer to work digitally. Salaried cartoonists will have fewer job opportunities because many newspapers and magazines increasingly rely on freelance work.

## Earnings

Median annual earnings of salaried art directors were $68,100 in May 2006. The middle 50 percent earned between $49,480 and $94,920. The lowest 10 percent earned less than $37,920, and the highest 10 percent earned more than $135,090. Median annual earnings were $70,630 in advertising and related services.

Median annual earnings of salaried craft artists were $24,090. The middle 50 percent earned between $18,860 and $35,840. The lowest 10 percent earned less than $14,130, and the highest 10 percent earned more than $46,700. Earnings data for the many self-employed craft artists were not available.

**Projections data from the National Employment Matrix**

| Occupational Title | SOC Code | Employment, 2006 | Projected employment, 2016 | Change, 2006-2016 | |
|---|---|---|---|---|---|
| | | | | Number | Percent |
| Artists and related workers ................................................. | 27-1010 | 218,000 | 253,000 | 34,000 | 16 |
| Art directors ................................................................. | 27-1011 | 78,000 | 85,000 | 7,000 | 9 |
| Craft artists................................................................. | 27-1012 | 8,800 | 9,500 | 700 | 8 |
| Fine artists, including painters, sculptors, and illustrators............ | 27-1013 | 30,000 | 33,000 | 3,000 | 10 |
| Multi-media artists and animators ................................................. | 27-1014 | 87,000 | 110,000 | 23,000 | 26 |
| Artists and related workers, all other ......................................... | 27-1019 | 14,000 | 15,000 | 1,200 | 8 |

NOTE: Data in this table are rounded.

Median annual earnings of salaried fine artists, including painters, sculptors, and illustrators were $41,970. The middle 50 percent earned between $28,500 and $58,550. The lowest 10 percent earned less than $18,350, and the highest 10 percent earned more than $79,390. Earnings data for the many self-employed fine artists were not available.

Median annual earnings of salaried multi-media artists and animators were $51,350, not including the earnings of the self-employed. The middle 50 percent earned between $38,980 and $70,050. The lowest 10 percent earned less than $30,390, and the highest 10 percent earned more than $92,720. Median annual earnings were $57,310 in motion picture and video industries and $48,860 in advertising and related services.

Earnings for self-employed artists vary widely. Some charge only a nominal fee while they gain experience and build a reputation for their work. Others, such as well-established freelance fine artists and illustrators, can earn more than salaried artists. Many, however, find it difficult to rely solely on income earned from selling paintings or other works of art. Like other self-employed workers, freelance artists must provide their own benefits.

## Related Occupations

Other workers who apply artistic skills include architects, except landscape and naval; archivists, curators, and museum technicians; commercial and industrial designers; fashion designers; floral designers; graphic designers; interior designers; jewelers and precious stone and metal workers; landscape architects; photographers; and woodworkers. Some workers who use computers extensively, including computer software engineers and desktop publishers, may require art skills.

## Sources of Additional Information

For general information about art and design and a list of accredited college-level programs, contact

▸ National Association of Schools of Art and Design, 11250 Roger Bacon Dr., Suite 21, Reston, VA 20190. Internet: http://nasad.arts-accredit.org

For information on careers in the craft arts and for a list of schools and workshops, contact

▸ American Craft Council Library, 72 Spring St., 6th Floor, New York, NY 10012. Internet: http://www.craftcouncil.org

For information on careers in illustration, contact

▸ Society of Illustrators, 128 E. 63rd St., New York, NY 10021. Internet: http://www.societyillustrators.org

For information on careers in medical illustration, contact

▸ Association of Medical Illustrators, 245 First St., Suite 1800, Cambridge, MA 02142. Internet: http://www.ami.org

For information on workshops, scholarships, internships, and competitions for art students interested in advertising careers, contact

▸ Art Directors Club, 106 W. 29th St., New York, NY 10001. Internet: http://www.adcglobal.org

# Athletes, Coaches, Umpires, and Related Workers

(O*NET 27-2021.00, 27-2022.00, and 27-2023.00)

## Significant Points

■ Work hours are often irregular and extensive travel may be required.

■ Career-ending injuries are always a risk for athletes.

■ Job opportunities will be best for part-time coaches, sports instructors, umpires, referees, and sports officials in high schools, sports clubs, and other settings.

■ Competition to become a professional athlete will continue to be extremely intense; athletes who seek to compete professionally must have extraordinary talent, desire, and dedication to training.

## Nature of the Work

We are a nation of sports fans and sports players. Some of those who participate in amateur sports dream of becoming paid professional athletes, coaches, or sports officials, but very few beat the long and daunting odds of making a full-time living from professional athletics. Those athletes who make it to the professional level find that careers are short and jobs are insecure. Even though the chances of employment as a professional athlete are slim, there are many opportunities for at least a part-time job as a coach, instructor, referee, or umpire in amateur athletics or in high school, college, or university sports.

*Athletes* and *sports competitors* compete in organized, officiated sports events to entertain spectators. When playing a game, athletes are required to understand the strategies of their game while obeying the rules and regulations of the sport. The events in which they compete include both team sports, such as baseball, basketball, football, hockey, and soccer, and individual sports, such as golf, tennis, and bowling. The level of play varies from unpaid high school athletics to professional sports, in which the best from around the world compete in events broadcast on international television.

Being an athlete involves more than competing in athletic events. Athletes spend many hours each day practicing skills and improving teamwork under the guidance of a coach or a sports instructor. They view videotapes to critique their own performances and techniques and to learn their opponents' tendencies and weaknesses to gain a competitive advantage. Some athletes work regularly with strength trainers to gain muscle and stamina and to prevent injury. Many athletes push their bodies to the limit during both practice and play, so career-ending injury always is a risk; even minor injuries may put a player at risk of replacement. Because competition at all levels is extremely intense and job security is always precarious, many athletes train year round to maintain excellent form and technique and peak physical condition. Very little downtime from the sport exists at the professional level. Athletes also must conform to regimented diets during their sports season to supplement any physical training program.

*Coaches* organize amateur and professional athletes and teach them the fundamentals of individual and team sports. (In individual sports, *instructors* sometimes may fill this role.) Coaches train athletes for competition by holding practice sessions to perform drills that improve the athletes' form, technique, skills, and stamina. Along with refining athletes' individual skills, coaches are responsible for instilling good sportsmanship, a competitive spirit, and teamwork and for managing their teams during both practice sessions and competitions. Before competition, coaches evaluate or scout the opposing team to determine game strategies and practice specific plays. During competition, coaches may call specific plays intended to surprise or overpower the opponent, and they may substitute players for optimum team chemistry and success. Coaches' additional tasks may include selecting, storing, issuing, and taking inventory of equipment, materials, and supplies.

Many coaches in high schools are primarily teachers of academic subjects who supplement their income by coaching part time. College coaches consider coaching a full-time discipline and may be away from home frequently as they travel to scout and recruit prospective players.

*Sports instructors* teach professional and nonprofessional athletes individually. They organize, instruct, train, and lead athletes in indoor and outdoor sports such as bowling, tennis, golf, and swimming. Because activities are as diverse as weight lifting, gymnastics, scuba diving, and karate, instructors tend to specialize in one or a few activities. Like coaches, sports instructors also may hold daily practice sessions and be responsible for any needed equipment and supplies. Using their knowledge of their sport and of physiology, they determine the type and level of difficulty of exercises, prescribe specific drills, and correct athletes' techniques. Some instructors also teach and demonstrate the use of training apparatus, such as trampolines or weights, for correcting athletes' weaknesses and enhancing their conditioning. Like coaches, sports instructors evaluate the athlete and the athlete's opponents to devise a competitive game strategy.

Coaches and sports instructors sometimes differ in their approaches to athletes because of the focus of their work. For example, while coaches manage the team during a game to optimize its chance for victory, sports instructors—such as those who work for professional tennis players—often are not permitted to instruct their athletes during competition. Sports instructors spend more of their time with athletes working one-on-one, which permits them to design customized training programs for each individual. Motivating athletes to play hard challenges most coaches and sports instructors but is vital for the athlete's success. Many coaches and instructors derive great satisfaction working with children or young adults, helping them to learn new physical and social skills, improve their physical condition, and achieve success in their sport.

*Umpires, referees, and other sports officials* officiate at competitive athletic and sporting events. They observe the play, detect infractions of rules, and impose penalties established by the rules and regulations of the various sports. Umpires, referees, and sports officials anticipate play and position themselves to best see the action, assess the situation, and determine any violations. Some sports officials, such as boxing referees, may work independently, while others such as umpires work in groups. Regardless of the sport, the job is highly stressful because officials are often required to make a decision in a split second, sometimes resulting in strong disagreement among competitors, coaches, and spectators.

Professional *scouts* evaluate the skills of both amateur and professional athletes to determine talent and potential. As a sports intelligence agent, the scout's primary duty is to seek out top athletic candidates for the team he or she represents. At the professional level, scouts typically work for scouting organizations or as freelance scouts. In locating new talent, scouts perform their work in secrecy so as not to "tip off" their opponents about their interest in certain players. At the college level, the head scout often is an assistant coach, although freelance scouts may aid colleges by reporting to coaches about exceptional players. Scouts at this level seek talented high school athletes by reading newspapers, contacting high school coaches and alumni, attending high school games, and studying videotapes of prospects' performances. They also evaluate potential players' background and personal characteristics, such as motivation and discipline, by talking to the players' coaches, parents, and teachers.

***Work environment.*** Irregular work hours are the trademark of the athlete. They also are common for coaches, umpires, referees, and other sports officials. Athletes and others in sports related occupations often work Saturdays, Sundays, evenings, and holidays. Athletes and full-time coaches usually work more than 40 hours a week for several months during the sports season, if not most of the year. Some coaches in educational institutions may coach more than one sport, particularly in high schools.

Athletes, coaches, and sports officials who participate in competitions that are held outdoors may be exposed to all weather conditions of the season. Those involved in events that are held indoors tend to work in climate-controlled comfort, often in arenas, enclosed stadiums, or gymnasiums. Athletes, coaches, and some sports officials frequently travel to sporting events by bus or airplane. Scouts also travel extensively in locating talent, often by automobile.

Umpires, referees, and other sports officials regularly encounter verbal abuse by fans, coaches, and athletes. The officials also face possible physical assault and, increasingly, lawsuits from injured athletes based on their officiating decisions.

## Training, Other Qualifications, and Advancement

Education and training requirements for athletes, coaches, umpires, and related workers vary greatly by the level and type of sport. Regardless of the sport or occupation, these jobs require immense overall knowledge of the game, usually acquired through years of experience at lower levels.

***Education and training.*** Becoming a professional athlete is the culmination of years of effort. Athletes usually begin competing in their sports while in elementary or middle school, and continue through high school and sometimes college. They play in amateur tournaments and on high school and college teams, where the best attract the attention of professional scouts. Most schools require that participating athletes maintain specific academic standards to remain eligible to play. Athletes who seek to compete professionally must have extraordinary talent, desire, and dedication to training.

Head coaches at public secondary schools and sports instructors at all levels usually must have a bachelor's degree. For high school coaching and sports instructor jobs, schools usually prefer to hire teachers willing to take on the jobs part time. If no suitable teacher is found, schools hire someone from outside. Some entry-level positions for coaches or instructors require only experience derived as a participant in the sport or activity. Those who are not teachers must meet state requirements for certification to become a head coach. Certification, however, may not be required for coaching and sports instructor jobs in private schools. Degree programs specifically related to coaching include exercise and sports science, physiology, kinesiology, nutrition and fitness, physical education, and sports medicine.

Each sport has specific requirements for umpires, referees, and other sports officials. Umpires, referees, and other sports officials often begin their careers by volunteering for intramural, community, and recreational league competitions.

Scouting jobs require experience playing a sport at the college or professional level that makes it possible to spot young players who possess extraordinary athletic ability and skills. Most beginning scouting jobs are as part-time talent spotters in a particular area or region. Hard work and a record of success often lead to full-time jobs responsible for bigger territories. Some scouts advance to scouting director jobs or various administrative positions in sports.

*Certification and other qualifications.* Athletes, coaches, umpires, and related workers must relate well to others and possess good communication and leadership skills. Coaches also must be resourceful and flexible to successfully instruct and motivate individuals and groups of athletes.

To officiate at high school athletic events, officials must register with the state agency that oversees high school athletics and pass an exam on the rules of the particular game. For college refereeing, candidates must be certified by an officiating school and be evaluated during a probationary period. Some larger college sports conferences require officials to have certification and other qualifications, such as residence in or near the conference boundaries, along with several years of experience officiating at high school, community college, or other college conference games.

For those interested in becoming a tennis, golf, karate, or other kind of instructor, certification is highly desirable. Often, one must be at least 18 years old and certified in cardiopulmonary resuscitation (CPR). There are many certifying organizations specific to the various sports, and their training requirements vary. Participation in a clinic, camp, or school usually is required for certification. Part-time workers and those in smaller facilities are less likely to need formal education or training.

Standards for officials become more stringent as the level of competition advances. Whereas umpires for high school baseball need a high school diploma or its equivalent, 20/20 vision, and quick reflexes, those seeking to officiate at minor or major league games must attend professional umpire training school. Top graduates are selected for further evaluation while officiating in a rookie minor league. Umpires then usually need seven to 10 years of experience in various minor leagues before being considered for major league jobs. Becoming an official for professional football also is competitive, as candidates must have at least 10 years of officiating experience, with five of them at a collegiate varsity or minor professional

level. For the National Football League (NFL), prospective trainees are interviewed by clinical psychologists to determine levels of intelligence and ability to handle extremely stressful situations. In addition, the NFL's security department conducts thorough background checks. Potential candidates are likely to be interviewed by a panel from the NFL officiating department and are given a comprehensive examination on the rules of the sport.

*Advancement.* Many coaches begin their careers as assistant coaches to gain the knowledge and experience needed to become a head coach. Head coaches at large schools that strive to compete at the highest levels of a sport require substantial experience as a head coach at another school or as an assistant coach. To reach the ranks of professional coaching, a person usually needs years of coaching experience and a winning record in the lower ranks.

## Employment

Athletes, coaches, umpires, and related workers held about 253,000 jobs in 2006. Coaches and scouts held 217,000 jobs; athletes, 18,000; and umpires, referees, and other sports officials, 19,000. Nearly 42 percent of athletes, coaches, umpires, and related workers worked part time, while 15 percent maintained variable schedules. Many sports officials and coaches receive such small and irregular payments for their services—occasional officiating at club games, for example—that they may not consider themselves employed in these occupations, even part time.

Among those employed in wage and salary jobs, 47 percent held jobs in public and private educational services. About 13 percent worked in amusement, gambling, and recreation industries, including golf and tennis clubs, gymnasiums, health clubs, judo and karate schools, riding stables, swim clubs, and other sports and recreation facilities. Another six percent worked in the spectator sports industry.

About 1 out of 5 workers in this occupation was self-employed, earning prize money or fees for lessons, scouting, or officiating assignments. Many other coaches and sports officials, although technically not self-employed, have such irregular or tenuous working arrangements that their working conditions resemble those of self-employment.

## Job Outlook

Employment of athletes, coaches, umpires, and related workers is expected to grow faster than the average for all occupations through 2016. Very keen competition is expected for jobs at the highest levels of sports.

*Employment change.* Employment of athletes, coaches, umpires, and related workers is expected to increase by 15 percent from 2006 to 2016, which is faster than the average for all occupations. Employment will grow as the general public continues to participate in organized sports for entertainment, recreation, and physical conditioning. Increasing participation in organized sports by girls and women will boost demand for coaches, umpires, and related workers. Job growth also will be driven by the increasing number of baby boomers approaching retirement, during which they are expected to participate more in leisure activities such as golf and tennis which require instruction.

**Projections data from the National Employment Matrix**

| Occupational Title | SOC Code | Employment, 2006 | Projected employment, 2016 | Change, 2006-2016 | |
|---|---|---|---|---|---|
| | | | | Number | Percent |
| Athletes, coaches, umpires, and related workers ............................. | 27-2020 | 253,000 | 291,000 | 38,000 | 15 |
| Athletes and sports competitors .................................................. | 27-2021 | 18,000 | 21,000 | 3,400 | 19 |
| Coaches and scouts ...................................................................... | 27-2022 | 217,000 | 249,000 | 32,000 | 15 |
| Umpires, referees, and other sports officials................................ | 27-2023 | 19,000 | 22,000 | 3,000 | 16 |

NOTE: Data in this table are rounded.

Employment of coaches and instructors also will increase with expansion of school and college athletic programs and growing demand for private sports instruction. Sports-related job growth within education also will be driven by the decisions of local school boards. Population growth dictates the construction of additional schools, particularly in the expanding suburbs, but funding for athletic programs often is cut first when budgets become tight. Still, the popularity of team sports often enables shortfalls to be offset somewhat by assistance from fundraisers, booster clubs, and parents.

*Job prospects.* Persons who are state-certified to teach academic subjects in addition to physical education are likely to have the best prospects for obtaining coaching and instructor jobs. The need to replace the many high school coaches who change occupations or leave the labor force entirely also will provide some coaching opportunities.

Competition for professional athlete jobs will continue to be extremely intense. Opportunities to make a living as a professional in individual sports such as golf or tennis may grow as new tournaments are established and as prize money distributed to participants increases. Because most professional athletes' careers last only a few years due to debilitating injuries and age, annual replacement needs for these jobs is high, creating some job opportunities. However, the talented young men and women who dream of becoming sports superstars greatly outnumber the number of openings.

Opportunities should be best for persons seeking part-time umpire, referee, and other sports official jobs at the high school level. Competition is expected for higher paying jobs at the college level and will be even greater for jobs in professional sports. Competition should be keen for jobs as scouts, particularly for professional teams, because the number of available positions is limited.

## Earnings

Median annual wage and salary earnings of athletes were $41,060 in May 2006. However, the highest paid professional athletes earn much more.

Median annual wage and salary earnings of umpires and related workers were $22,880 in May 2006. The middle 50 percent earned between $17,090 and $33,840. The lowest-paid 10 percent earned less than $14,120, and the highest-paid 10 percent earned more than $45,430.

In May 2006, median annual wage and salary earnings of coaches and scouts were $26,950. The middle 50 percent earned between $17,510 and $40,850. The lowest-paid 10 percent earned less than $13,990, and the highest-paid 10 percent earned more than $58,890. However, the highest paid professional coaches earn much more.

Median annual earnings in the industries employing the largest numbers of coaches and scouts in May 2006 are shown below:

Colleges, universities, and professional schools ....$37,530

Other amusement and recreation industries ...........27,180

Fitness and recreational sports centers ..................26,150

Other schools and instruction ..............................23,840

Elementary and secondary schools ......................21,960

Earnings vary by level of education, certification, and geographic region. Some instructors and coaches are paid a salary, while others may be paid by the hour, per session, or based on the number of participants.

## Related Occupations

Athletes and coaches use their extensive knowledge of physiology and sports to instruct, inform, and encourage sports participants. Other workers with similar duties include dietitians and nutritionists; physical therapists; recreation workers; fitness workers; recreational therapists; and teachers—preschool, kindergarten, elementary, middle, and secondary.

## Sources of Additional Information

For information about sports officiating for team and individual sports, contact

▸ National Association of Sports Officials, 2017 Lathrop Ave., Racine, WI 53405. Internet: http://www.naso.org

For more information about certification of tennis instructors and coaches, contact

▸ Professional Tennis Registry, P.O. Box 4739, Hilton Head Island, SC 29938. Internet: http://www.ptrtennis.org

▸ U.S. Professional Tennis Association, 3535 Briarpark Dr., Suite One, Houston, TX 77042. Internet: http://www.uspta.org

# Automotive Body and Related Repairers

(O*NET 49-3021.00 and 49-3022.00)

## Significant Points

- To become a fully skilled automotive body repairer, formal training followed by on-the-job instruction is recommended because fixing newer automobiles requires advanced skills.

- Excellent job opportunities are projected because of the large number of older workers who are expected to retire in the next 10 to 15 years.

- Repairers need good reading ability and basic mathematics and computer skills to use print and digital technical manuals.

## Nature of the Work

Most of the damage resulting from everyday vehicle collisions can be repaired, and vehicles can be refinished to look and drive like new. *Automotive body repairers,* often called collision repair technicians, straighten bent bodies, remove dents, and replace crumpled parts that cannot be fixed. They repair all types of vehicles, and although some work on large trucks, buses, or tractor-trailers, most work on cars and small trucks. They can work alone, with only general direction from supervisors, or as specialists on a repair team. In some shops, helpers or apprentices assist experienced repairers.

Each damaged vehicle presents different challenges for repairers. Using their broad knowledge of automotive construction and repair techniques, automotive body repairers must decide how to handle each job based on what the vehicle is made of and what needs to be fixed. They must first determine the extent of the damage and order any needed parts.

If the car is heavily damaged, an automotive body repairer might start by realigning the frame of the vehicle. Repairers chain or clamp frames and sections to alignment machines that use hydraulic pressure to align damaged components. "Unibody" vehicles—designs built without frames—must be restored to precise factory specifications for the vehicle to operate correctly. For these vehicles, repairers use benchmark systems to accurately measure how much each section is out of alignment, and hydraulic machinery to return the vehicle to its original shape.

Once the frame is aligned, repairers can begin to fix or replace damaged body parts. If the vehicle or part is made of metal, body repairers will use a pneumatic metal-cutting gun or other tools to remove badly damaged sections of body panels and then weld in replacement sections. Less serious dents are pulled out with a hydraulic jack or hand prying bar or knocked out with hand tools or pneumatic hammers. Small dents and creases in the metal are smoothed by holding a small anvil against one side of the damaged area while hammering the opposite side. Repairers also remove very small pits and dimples with pick hammers and punches in a process called metal finishing. Body repairers use plastic or solder to fill small dents that cannot be worked out of plastic or metal panels. On metal panels, they file or grind the hardened filler to the original shape and

clean the surface with a media blaster—similar to a sand blaster—before repainting the damaged portion of the vehicle.

Body repairers also repair or replace the plastic body parts that are increasingly used on new vehicles. They remove damaged panels and identify the type and properties of the plastic used. With most types of plastic, repairers can apply heat from a hot-air welding gun or immerse the panel in hot water and press the softened section back into shape by hand. Repairers replace plastic parts that are badly damaged or very difficult to fix. A few body repairers specialize in fixing fiberglass car bodies.

Some body repairers specialize in installing and repairing glass in automobiles and other vehicles. *Automotive glass installers and repairers* remove broken, cracked, or pitted windshields and window glass. Glass installers apply a moisture-proofing compound along the edges of the glass, place the glass in the vehicle, and install rubber strips around the sides of the windshield or window to make it secure and weatherproof.

Many large shops make repairs using an assembly-line approach where vehicles are fixed by a team of repairers who each specialize in one type of repair. One worker might straighten frames while another repairs doors and fenders, for example. In most shops, automotive painters do the painting and refinishing, but in small shops, workers often do both body repairing and painting.

*Work environment.* Repairers work indoors in body shops that are noisy with the clatter of hammers against metal and the whine of power tools. Most shops are well ventilated to disperse dust and paint fumes. Body repairers often work in awkward or cramped positions, and much of their work is strenuous and dirty. Hazards include cuts from sharp metal edges, burns from torches and heated metal, injuries from power tools, and fumes from paint. However, serious accidents usually are avoided when the shop is kept clean and orderly and safety practices are observed. Automotive repair and maintenance shops averaged 4 cases of work-related injuries and illnesses per 100 full-time workers in 2005, compared to 4.6 per 100 workers in all private industry.

Most automotive body repairers work a standard 40-hour week. More than 40 hours a week may be required when there is a backlog of repair work to be completed. This may include working on weekends.

## Training, Other Qualifications, and Advancement

Automotive technology is rapidly becoming more sophisticated, and most employers prefer applicants who have completed a formal training program in automotive body repair or refinishing. Most new repairers complete at least part of this training on the job. Many repairers, particularly in urban areas, need a national certification to advance past entry-level work.

*Education and training.* A high school diploma or GED is often all that is required to enter this occupation, but more specific education and training is needed to learn how to repair newer automobiles. Collision repair programs may be offered in high school or in post-secondary vocational schools and community colleges. Courses in electronics, physics, chemistry, English, computers, and mathematics provide a good background for a career as an automotive body repairer. Most training programs combine classroom instruction and hands-on practice.

Trade and technical school programs typically award certificates to graduates after six months to a year of collision repair study. Some community colleges offer two-year programs in collision repair. Many of these schools also offer certificates for individual courses, so that students are able to take classes incrementally or as needed.

New repairers begin by assisting experienced body repairers in tasks such as removing damaged parts, sanding body panels, and installing repaired parts. Novices learn to remove small dents and make other minor repairs. They then progress to more difficult tasks, such as straightening body parts and returning them to their correct alignment. Generally, it takes three to four years of hands-on training to become skilled in all aspects of body repair, some of which may be completed as part of a formal education program. Basic automotive glass installation and repair can be learned in as little as six months, but becoming fully qualified can take several years.

Continuing education and training are needed throughout a career in automotive body repair. Automotive parts, body materials, and electronics continue to change and to become more complex. To keep up with these technological advances, repairers must continue to gain new skills by reading technical manuals and furthering their education with classes and seminars. Many companies within the automotive body repair industry send employees to advanced training programs to brush up on skills or to learn new techniques.

*Other qualifications.* Fully skilled automotive body repairers must have good reading ability and basic mathematics and computer skills. Restoring unibody automobiles to their original form requires repairers to follow instructions and diagrams in technical manuals and to make precise three-dimensional measurements of the position of one body section relative to another. In addition, repairers should enjoy working with their hands and be able to pay attention to detail while they work.

*Certification and advancement.* Certification by the National Institute for Automotive Service Excellence (ASE), although voluntary, is the pervasive industry credential for non entry-level automotive body repairers. This is especially true in large, urban areas. Repairers may take up to four ASE Master Collision Repair and Refinish Exams. Repairers who pass at least one exam and have two years of hands-on work experience earn ASE certification. The completion of a postsecondary program in automotive body repair may be substituted for one year of work experience. Those who pass all four exams become ASE Master Collision Repair and Refinish Technicians. Automotive body repairers must retake the examination at least every five years to retain their certification. Many vehicle manufacturers and paint manufacturers also have product certification programs that can advance a repairer's career.

As beginners increase their skills, learn new techniques, earn certifications, and complete work more rapidly, their pay increases. An experienced automotive body repairer with managerial ability may advance to shop supervisor, and some workers open their own body repair shops. Other repairers become automobile damage appraisers for insurance companies.

## Employment

Automotive body and related repairers held about 206,000 jobs in 2006; about 13 percent specialized in automotive glass installation and repair. Fifty-eight percent of repairers worked for automotive repair and maintenance shops in 2006, while 20 percent worked for automobile dealers. Others worked for organizations, such as trucking companies, that maintain their own motor vehicles. A small number of repairers worked for wholesalers of motor vehicles, parts, and supplies. More than 15 percent of automotive body repairers were self-employed, roughly double the number for all installation, maintenance, and repair occupations.

## Job Outlook

Employment of automotive body and related repairers is expected to grow about as fast as average through the year 2016, and job opportunities are projected to be excellent due to a growing number of retirements in this occupation.

*Employment change.* Employment of automotive body repairers is expected to grow 12 percent over the 2006–2016 decade, as compared to 10 percent for all occupations. Demand for qualified body repairers will increase as the number of vehicles on the road continues to grow. With more motor vehicles in use, more vehicles will be damaged in accidents. In addition, new automotive designs of lighter weight are prone to greater collision damage than are older, heavier designs, so more repairs are needed. Employment growth will continue to be concentrated in automotive body, paint, interior, and glass repair shops, with little or no change in automotive dealerships.

Despite the anticipated increase in the number of auto accidents, the increasing demand for automotive body repairers will be tempered by improvements in the quality of vehicles. Also, technological innovations that enhance safety will reduce the likelihood of accidents.

Demand for automotive body repair services will similarly be constrained as more vehicles are declared a total loss after accidents. In many such cases, the vehicles are not repaired because of the high cost of replacing the increasingly complex parts and electronic components and because of the extensive damage that results when airbags deploy. Also, higher insurance premiums and deductibles mean that minor damage is more often going unrepaired. Larger shops are instituting productivity enhancements, such as employing a team approach to repairs, which may limit employment growth by reducing the time it takes to make repairs.

*Job prospects.* Employment growth will create some opportunities, but the need to replace experienced repairers who transfer to other occupations or who retire or stop working for other reasons will account for the majority of job openings over the next 10 years. Opportunities will be excellent for people with formal training in automotive body repair and refinishing. Those without any training or experience in automotive body refinishing or collision repair—before or after high school—will face competition for these jobs.

**Projections data from the National Employment Matrix**

| Occupational Title | SOC Code | Employment, 2006 | Projected employment, 2016 | Change, 2006-16 | |
|---|---|---|---|---|---|
| | | | | Number | Percent |
| Automotive body and related repairers ............................................... | — | 206,000 | 232,000 | 26,000 | 12 |
|    Automotive body and related repairers ......................................... | 49-3021 | 183,000 | 204,000 | 21,000 | 12 |
|    Automotive glass installers and repairers ................................... | 49-3022 | 24,000 | 28,000 | 4,400 | 19 |

NOTE: Data in this table are rounded.

Experienced body repairers are rarely laid off during a general slowdown in the economy as the automotive repair business is not very sensitive to changes in economic conditions. Although repair of minor dents and crumpled fenders is often put off when drivers have less money, major body damage must be repaired before a vehicle can be driven safely.

## Earnings

Median hourly wage-and-salary earnings of automotive body and related repairers, including incentive pay, were $16.92 in May 2006. The middle 50 percent earned between $13.00 and $22.33 an hour. The lowest 10 percent earned less than $10.10, and the highest 10 percent earned more than $28.71 an hour. Median hourly earnings of automotive body and related repairers were $17.85 in automobile dealers and $16.66 in automotive repair and maintenance.

Median hourly wage-and-salary earnings of automotive glass installers and repairers, including incentive pay, were $14.77. The middle 50 percent earned between $11.44 and $18.42 an hour. The lowest 10 percent earned less than $9.19, and the highest 10 percent earned more than $22.22 an hour. Median hourly earnings in automotive repair and maintenance shops, the industry employing most automotive glass installers and repairers, were $14.80.

The majority of body repairers employed by independent repair shops and automotive dealers are paid on an incentive basis. Under this system, body repairers are paid a set amount for various tasks, and earnings depend on both the amount of work assigned and how fast it is completed. Employers frequently guarantee workers a minimum weekly salary. Body repairers who work for trucking companies, bus lines, and other organizations that maintain their own vehicles usually receive an hourly wage.

Helpers and trainees typically earn between 30 percent and 60 percent of the earnings of skilled workers. They are paid by the hour until they are skilled enough to be paid on an incentive basis.

Employee benefits vary widely from business to business. However, industry sources report that benefits such as paid leave, health insurance, and retirement assistance are increasingly common in the collision repair industry. Automotive dealerships are the most likely to offer such incentives.

## Related Occupations

Repairing damaged motor vehicles often involves working on mechanical components, as well as vehicle bodies. Automotive body repairers often work closely with individuals in several related occupations, including automotive service technicians and mechanics, diesel service technicians and mechanics, auto damage appraisers, and painting and coating workers, except construction and

maintenance. Automotive glass installers and repairers complete tasks very similar to those of glaziers.

## Sources of Additional Information

Additional details about work opportunities may be obtained from automotive body repair shops, automobile dealers, or local offices of your state employment service. state employment service offices also are a source of information about training programs.

For general information about automotive body repairer careers, contact any of the following sources:

▶ Automotive Careers Today, 8400 Westpark Dr., MS #2, McLean, VA 22102. Internet: http://www.autocareerstoday.org

▶ Automotive Service Association, P.O. Box 929, Bedford, Texas 76095. Internet: http://www.asashop.org

▶ Inter-Industry Conference On Auto Collision Repair Education Foundation (I-CAR), 5125 Trillium Blvd., Hoffman Estates, IL 60192. Internet: http://www.collisioncareers.org

▶ National Automobile Dealers Association, 8400 Westpark Dr., McLean, VA 22102. Internet: http://www.nada.org

For general information about careers in automotive glass installation and repair, contact

▶ National Glass Association. 8200 Greensboro Dr., Suite 302, McLean, VA 22102. Internet: http://www.glass.org

For information on how to become a certified automotive body repairer, write to

▶ National Institute for Automotive Service Excellence (ASE), 101 Blue Seal Dr. SE, Suite 101, Leesburg, VA 20175. Internet: http://www.asecert.org

For a directory of certified automotive body repairer programs, contact

▶ National Automotive Technician Education Foundation, 101 Blue Seal Dr. SE, Suite 101, Leesburg, VA 20175. Internet: http://www.natef.org

For a directory of accredited private trade and technical schools that offer training programs in automotive body repair, contact

▶ Accrediting Commission of Career Schools and Colleges of Technology, 2101 Wilson Blvd., Suite 302, Arlington, VA 22201. Internet: http://www.accsct.org

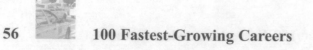

# Automotive Service Technicians and Mechanics

(O*NET 49-3023.00, 49-3023.01, and 49-3023.02)

## Significant Points

■ Automotive service technicians and mechanics must continually adapt to changing technology and repair techniques as vehicle components and systems become increasingly sophisticated.

■ Formal automotive technician training is the best preparation for these challenging technology-based jobs.

■ Opportunities should be very good for automotive service technicians and mechanics with diagnostic and problem-solving skills, knowledge of electronics and mathematics, and mechanical aptitude.

## Nature of the Work

Automotive service technicians inspect, maintain, and repair automobiles and light trucks that run on gasoline, electricity, or alternative fuels such as ethanol. Automotive service technicians' and mechanics' responsibilities have evolved from simple mechanical repairs to high-level technology-related work. The increasing sophistication of automobiles requires workers who can use computerized shop equipment and work with electronic components while maintaining their skills with traditional hand tools. As a result, automotive service workers are now usually called technicians rather than mechanics.

Today, integrated electronic systems and complex computers regulate vehicles and their performance while on the road. Technicians must have an increasingly broad knowledge of how vehicles' complex components work and interact. They also must be able to work with electronic diagnostic equipment and digital manuals and reference materials.

When mechanical or electrical troubles occur, technicians first get a description of the problem from the owner or, in a large shop, from the repair service estimator or service advisor who wrote the repair order. To locate the problem, technicians use a diagnostic approach. First, they test to see whether components and systems are secure and working properly. Then, they isolate the components or systems that might be the cause of the problem. For example, if an air conditioner malfunctions, the technician might check for a simple problem, such as a low coolant level, or a more complex issue, such as a bad drive-train connection that has shorted out the air conditioner. As part of their investigation, technicians may test drive the vehicle or use a variety of testing equipment, including onboard and handheld diagnostic computers or compression gauges. These tests may indicate whether a component is salvageable or whether a new one is required.

During routine service inspections, technicians test and lubricate engines and other major components. Sometimes technicians repair or replace worn parts before they cause breakdowns or damage the vehicle. Technicians usually follow a checklist to ensure that they examine every critical part. Belts, hoses, plugs, brake and fuel systems, and other potentially troublesome items are watched closely.

Service technicians use a variety of tools in their work. They use power tools, such as pneumatic wrenches to remove bolts quickly; machine tools like lathes and grinding machines to rebuild brakes; welding and flame-cutting equipment to remove and repair exhaust systems, and jacks and hoists to lift cars and engines. They also use common hand tools, such as screwdrivers, pliers, and wrenches, to work on small parts and in hard-to-reach places. Technicians usually provide their own hand tools, and many experienced workers have thousands of dollars invested in them. Employers furnish expensive power tools, engine analyzers, and other diagnostic equipment.

Computers are also commonplace in modern repair shops. Service technicians compare the readouts from computerized diagnostic testing devices with benchmarked standards given by the manufacturer. Deviations outside of acceptable levels tell the technician to investigate that part of the vehicle more closely. Through the Internet or from software packages, most shops receive automatic updates to technical manuals and access to manufacturers' service information, technical service bulletins, and other databases that allow technicians to keep up with common problems and learn new procedures.

High technology tools are needed to fix the computer equipment that operates everything from the engine to the radio in many cars. In fact, today most automotive systems, such as braking, transmission, and steering systems, are controlled primarily by computers and electronic components. Additionally, luxury vehicles often have integrated global positioning systems, Internet access, and other new features with which technicians will need to become familiar. Also, as more alternate-fuel vehicles are purchased, more automotive service technicians will need to learn the science behind these automobiles and how to repair them.

Automotive service technicians in large shops often specialize in certain types of repairs. For example, *transmission technicians and rebuilders* work on gear trains, couplings, hydraulic pumps, and other parts of transmissions. Extensive knowledge of computer controls, the ability to diagnose electrical and hydraulic problems, and other specialized skills are needed to work on these complex components, which employ some of the most sophisticated technology used in vehicles. *Tune-up technicians* adjust ignition timing and valves and adjust or replace spark plugs and other parts to ensure efficient engine performance. They often use electronic testing equipment to isolate and adjust malfunctions in fuel, ignition, and emissions control systems.

*Automotive air-conditioning repairers* install and repair air-conditioners and service their components, such as compressors, condensers, and controls. These workers require special training in federal and state regulations governing the handling and disposal of refrigerants. *Front-end mechanics* align and balance wheels and repair steering mechanisms and suspension systems. They frequently use special alignment equipment and wheel-balancing machines. *Brake repairers* adjust brakes, replace brake linings and pads, and make other repairs on brake systems. Some technicians specialize in both brake and front-end work.

***Work environment.*** While most automotive service technicians worked a standard 40 hour week in 2006, 30 percent worked longer hours. Some may work evenings and weekends to satisfy customer service needs. Generally, service technicians work indoors in well-ventilated and -lighted repair shops. However, some shops are drafty and noisy. Although many problems can be fixed with simple computerized adjustments, technicians frequently work with dirty and greasy parts, and in awkward positions. They often lift heavy parts and tools. Minor cuts, burns, and bruises are common, but technicians can usually avoid serious accidents if safe practices are observed.

## Training, Other Qualifications, and Advancement

Automotive technology is rapidly increasing in sophistication, and most training authorities strongly recommend that people seeking work in automotive service complete a formal training program in high school or in a postsecondary vocational school or community college. However, some service technicians still learn the trade solely by assisting and learning from experienced workers. Acquiring National Institute for Automotive Service Excellence (ASE) certification is important for those seeking work in large, urban areas.

*Education and training.* Most employers regard the successful completion of a vocational training program in automotive service technology as the best preparation for trainee positions. High school programs, while an asset, vary greatly in scope. Graduates of these programs may need further training to become qualified. Some of the more extensive high school programs participate in Automotive Youth Education Service (AYES), a partnership between high school automotive repair programs, automotive manufacturers, and franchised automotive dealers. All AYES high school programs are certified by the National Institute for Automotive Service Excellence. Students who complete these programs are well prepared to enter entry-level technician positions or to advance their technical education. Courses in automotive repair, electronics, physics, chemistry, English, computers, and mathematics provide a good educational background for a career as a service technician.

Postsecondary automotive technician training programs usually provide intensive career preparation through a combination of classroom instruction and hands-on practice. Schools update their curriculums frequently to reflect changing technology and equipment. Some trade and technical school programs provide concentrated training for six months to a year, depending on how many hours the student attends each week, and award a certificate. Community college programs usually award a certificate or an associate degree. Some students earn repair certificates in a particular skill and leave to begin their careers. Associate degree programs, however, usually take two years to complete and include classes in English, basic mathematics, computers, and other subjects, as well as automotive repair. Recently, some programs have added classes on customer service, stress management, and other employability skills. Some formal training programs have alliances with tool manufacturers that help entry-level technicians accumulate tools during their training period.

Various automobile manufacturers and participating franchised dealers also sponsor two-year associate degree programs at postsecondary schools across the nation. Students in these programs typically spend alternate six- to 12-week periods attending classes full time and working full time in the service departments of sponsoring dealers. At these dealerships, students work with an experienced worker who provides hands-on instruction and timesaving tips.

Those new to automotive service usually start as trainee technicians, technicians' helpers, or lubrication workers, and gradually acquire and practice their skills by working with experienced mechanics and technicians. In many cases, on-the-job training may be a part of a formal education program. With a few months' experience, beginners perform many routine service tasks and make simple repairs. While some graduates of postsecondary automotive training programs are often able to earn promotion to the journey level after only a few months on the job, it typically takes two to five years of experience to become a fully qualified service technician, who is expected to quickly perform the more difficult types of routine service and repairs. An additional one to two years of experience familiarizes technicians with all types of repairs. Complex specialties, such as transmission repair, require another year or two of training and experience. In contrast, brake specialists may learn their jobs in considerably less time because they do not need complete knowledge of automotive repair.

Employers increasingly send experienced automotive service technicians to manufacturer training centers to learn to repair new models or to receive special training in the repair of components, such as electronic fuel injection or air conditioners. Motor vehicle dealers and other automotive service providers may send promising beginners or experienced technicians to manufacturer-sponsored technician training programs to upgrade or maintain employees' skills. Factory representatives also visit many shops to conduct short training sessions.

*Other qualifications.* The ability to diagnose the source of a problem quickly and accurately requires good reasoning ability and a thorough knowledge of automobiles. Many technicians consider diagnosing hard-to-find troubles one of their most challenging and satisfying duties. For trainee automotive service technician jobs, employers look for people with strong communication and analytical skills. Technicians need good reading, mathematics, and computer skills to study technical manuals. They must also read to keep up with new technology and learn new service and repair procedures and specifications.

Training in electronics is vital because electrical components, or a series of related components, account for nearly all malfunctions in modern vehicles. Trainees must possess mechanical aptitude and knowledge of how automobiles work. Experience working on motor vehicles in the Armed Forces or as a hobby can be very valuable.

*Certification and advancement.* ASE certification has become a standard credential for automotive service technicians. While not mandatory for work in automotive service, certification is common for all non entry-level technicians in large, urban areas. Certification is available in one or more of eight different areas of automotive service, such as electrical systems, engine repair, brake systems, suspension and steering, and heating and air-conditioning. For certification in each area, technicians must have at least two years of experience and pass the examination. Completion of an automotive training program in high school, vocational or trade school, or community or junior college may be substituted for one year of experience. For ASE certification as a Master Automobile Technician, technicians must be certified in all eight areas.

**Projections data from the National Employment Matrix**

| Occupational Title | SOC Code | Employment, 2006 | Projected employment, 2016 | Change, 2006-16 | |
|---|---|---|---|---|---|
| | | | | Number | Percent |
| Automotive service technicians and mechanics............................. | 49-3023 | 773,000 | 883,000 | 110,000 | 14 |

NOTE: Data in this table are rounded.

By becoming skilled in multiple auto repair services, technicians can increase their value to their employer and their pay. Experienced technicians who have administrative ability sometimes advance to shop supervisor or service manager. Those with sufficient funds many times open independent automotive repair shops. Technicians who work well with customers may become automotive repair service estimators.

## Employment

Automotive service technicians and mechanics held about 773,000 jobs in 2006. Automotive repair and maintenance shops and automotive dealers employed the majority of these workers—29 percent each. In addition, automotive parts, accessories, and tire stores employed 7 percent of automotive service technicians. Others worked in gasoline stations; general merchandise stores; automotive equipment rental and leasing companies; federal, state, and local governments; and other organizations. Almost 17 percent of service technicians were self-employed, more than twice the proportion for all installation, maintenance, and repair occupations.

## Job Outlook

The number of jobs for automotive service technicians and mechanics is projected to grow faster than average for all occupations over the next decade. Employment growth will create many new jobs, but total job openings will be significantly larger because many skilled technicians are expected to retire and will need to be replaced.

*Employment change.* Employment of automotive service technicians and mechanics is expected to increase 14 percent between 2006 and 2016, compared to 10 percent for all occupations. It will add a large number of new jobs, about 110,000, over the decade. Demand for technicians will grow as the number of vehicles in operation increases, reflecting continued growth in the driving age population and in the number of multi-car families. Growth in demand will be offset somewhat by continuing improvements in the quality and durability of automobiles, which will require less frequent service.

Employment growth will continue to be concentrated in automobile dealerships and independent automotive repair shops. Many new jobs also will be created in small retail operations that offer after-warranty repairs, such as oil changes, brake repair, air-conditioner service, and other minor repairs generally taking less than 4 hours to complete. Employment of automotive service technicians and mechanics in gasoline service stations will continue to decline, as fewer stations offer repair services.

*Job prospects.* In addition to openings from growth, many job openings will be created by the need to replace a growing number of retiring technicians. Job opportunities in this occupation are expected to be very good for those who complete high school or postsecondary automotive training programs and who earn ASE certification. Some employers report difficulty in finding workers with the right skills. People with good diagnostic and problem-solving abilities, and training in basic electronics and computer courses are expected to have the best opportunities. Those without formal automotive training are likely to face competition for entry-level jobs.

Most people who enter the occupation can expect steady work, even during downturns in the economy. Although car owners tend to postpone maintenance and repair on their vehicles when their budgets are strained, employers usually cut back on hiring new workers during economic downturns instead of letting experienced workers go.

## Earnings

Median hourly wage-and-salary earnings of automotive service technicians and mechanics, including commission, were $16.24 in May 2006. The middle 50 percent earned between $11.96 and $21.56 per hour. The lowest 10 percent earned less than $9.17, and the highest 10 percent earned more than $27.22 per hour. Median annual earnings in the industries employing the largest numbers of service technicians were as follows:

Local government, excluding schools ....................$19.07
Automobile dealers ..............................................18.85
Automotive repair and maintenance........................14.55
Gasoline stations ...............................................14.51
Automotive parts, accessories, and tire stores ..........14.38

Many experienced technicians employed by automobile dealers and independent repair shops receive a commission related to the labor cost charged to the customer. Under this system, weekly earnings depend on the amount of work completed. Employers frequently guarantee commissioned technicians a minimum weekly salary.

Automotive service technicians who are members of labor unions, such as the International Association of Machinists and Aerospace Workers; the International Union, United Automobile, Aerospace, and Agricultural Implement Workers of America; the Sheet Metal Workers' International Association; and the International Brotherhood of Teamsters, may enjoy more benefits than non-union workers do.

## Related Occupations

Other workers who repair and service motor vehicles include automotive body and related repairers, diesel service technicians and mechanics, and small engine mechanics.

## Sources of Additional Information

For more details about work opportunities, contact local automobile dealers and repair shops or local offices of the state employment service. The state employment service also may have information about training programs.

For general information about a career as an automotive service technician, contact

▸ Automotive Careers Today, 8400 Westpark Dr., MS #2, McLean, VA 22102. Internet: http://www.autocareerstoday.org

▸ Career Voyages, U.S. Department of Labor, 200 Constitution Ave. NW, Washington, DC 20210. Internet: http://www.careervoyages.gov/automotive-main.cfm

▸ National Automobile Dealers Association, 8400 Westpark Dr., McLean, VA 22102. Internet: http://www.nada.org

A list of certified automotive service technician training programs can be obtained from

▸ National Automotive Technicians Education Foundation, 101 Blue Seal Dr. SE, Suite 101, Leesburg, VA 20175. Internet: http://www.natef.org

For a directory of accredited private trade and technical schools that offer programs in automotive service technician training, contact

▸ Accrediting Commission of Career Schools and Colleges of Technology, 2101 Wilson Blvd., Suite 302, Arlington, VA 22201. Internet: http://www.accsct.org

Information on automobile manufacturer-sponsored programs in automotive service technology can be obtained from

▸ Automotive Youth Educational Systems (AYES), 100 W. Big Beaver, Suite 300, Troy, MI 48084. Internet: http://www.ayes.org

Information on how to become a certified automotive service technician is available from

▸ National Institute for Automotive Service Excellence (ASE), 101 Blue Seal Dr. SE, Suite 101, Leesburg, VA 20175. Internet: http://www.asecert.org

# Barbers, Cosmetologists, and Other Personal Appearance Workers

(O*NET 39-5011.00, 39-5012.00, 39-5091.00, 39-5092.00, 39-5093.00, and 39-5094.00)

## Significant Points

■ A state license is required for barbers, cosmetologists, and most other personal appearance workers, although qualifications vary by state.

■ About 46 percent of workers are self employed; many also work flexible schedules.

## Nature of the Work

Barbers and cosmetologists focus on providing hair care services to enhance the appearance of consumers. Other personal appearance workers, such as manicurists and pedicurists, shampooers, theatrical and performance makeup artists, and skin care specialists provide specialized beauty services that help clients look and feel their best.

*Barbers* cut, trim, shampoo, and style hair mostly for male clients. They also may fit hairpieces and offer scalp treatments and facial

shaving. In many states, barbers are licensed to color, bleach, or highlight hair and to offer permanent-wave services. Barbers also may provide skin care and nail treatments.

*Hairdressers, hairstylists, and cosmetologists* offer a wide range of beauty services, such as shampooing, cutting, coloring, and styling of hair. They may advise clients on how to care for their hair at home. In addition, cosmetologists may be trained to give manicures, pedicures, and scalp and facial treatments; provide makeup analysis; and clean and style wigs and hairpieces.

A number of workers offer specialized services. *Manicurists and pedicurists,* called *nail technicians* in some states, work exclusively on nails and provide manicures, pedicures, polishing, and nail extensions to clients. Another group of specialists is *skin care specialists,* or *estheticians,* who cleanse and beautify the skin by giving facials, full-body treatments, and head and neck massages as well as apply makeup. They also may remove hair through waxing or, if properly trained, laser treatments. *Theatrical and performance makeup artists,* apply makeup to enhance performing artists' appearance for movie, television, or stage performances. Finally, in larger salons, *shampooers* specialize in shampooing and conditioning hair.

In addition to working with clients, personal appearance workers may keep records of hair color or skin care regimens used by their regular clients. A growing number actively sell hair, skin, and nail care products. Barbers, cosmetologists, and other personal appearance workers who operate their own salons have managerial duties that may include hiring, supervising, and firing workers, as well as keeping business and inventory records, ordering supplies, and arranging for advertising.

*Work environment.* Most full-time barbers, cosmetologists, and other personal appearance workers put in a 40-hour week, but longer hours are common, especially among self-employed workers. Work schedules may include evenings and weekends, the times when beauty salons and barbershops are busiest. In 2006, about 31 percent of cosmetologists and 19 percent of barbers worked part time, and 16 percent of cosmetologists and 11 percent of barbers had variable schedules.

Barbers, cosmetologists, and other personal appearance workers usually work in clean, pleasant surroundings with good lighting and ventilation. Good health and stamina are important, because these workers are on their feet for most of their shift. Prolonged exposure to some hair and nail chemicals may cause irritation, so protective clothing, such as plastic gloves or aprons, may be worn.

## Training, Other Qualifications, and Advancement

All states require barbers, cosmetologists, and other personal appearance workers to be licensed, with the exceptions of shampooers and makeup artists. To qualify for a license, most job seekers are required to graduate from a state-licensed barber or cosmetology school.

*Education and training.* A high school diploma or GED is required for some personal appearance workers in some states. In addition, most states require that barbers and cosmetologists complete a program in a state-licensed barber or cosmetology school. Programs in hairstyling, skin care, and other personal appearance services can be

**Projections data from the National Employment Matrix**

| Occupational Title | SOC Code | Employment, 2006 | Projected employment, 2016 | Change, 2006-16 | |
|---|---|---|---|---|---|
| | | | | Number | Percent |
| Personal appearance workers ............................................................ | 39-5000 | 825,000 | 942,000 | 117,000 | 14 |
| Barbers and cosmetologists............................................................. | 39-5010 | 677,000 | 755,000 | 77,000 | 11 |
| Barbers ...................................................................................... | 39-5011 | 60,000 | 61,000 | 600 | 1 |
| Hairdressers, hairstylists, and cosmetologists.......................... | 39-5012 | 617,000 | 694,000 | 77,000 | 12 |
| Miscellaneous personal appearance workers ................................ | 39-5090 | 148,000 | 187,000 | 39,000 | 27 |
| Makeup artists, theatrical and performance ........................... | 39-5091 | 2,100 | 3,000 | 900 | 40 |
| Manicurists and pedicurists................................................... | 39-5092 | 78,000 | 100,000 | 22,000 | 28 |
| Shampooers................................................................................ | 39-5093 | 29,000 | 33,000 | 3,900 | 13 |
| Skin care specialists ................................................................ | 39-5094 | 38,000 | 51,000 | 13,000 | 34 |

NOTE: Data in this table are rounded.

found in both high schools and in public or private postsecondary vocational schools.

Full-time programs in barbering and cosmetology usually last nine months and may lead to an associate degree, but training for manicurists and pedicurists and skin care specialists requires significantly less time. Makeup artists can attend schools that specialize in this subject, but it is not required. Shampooers generally do not need formal training. Most professionals take advanced courses in hairstyling or other personal appearance services to keep up with the latest trends. They also may take courses in sales and marketing.

During their first weeks on the job, new workers may be given relatively simple tasks. Once they have demonstrated their skills, they are gradually permitted to perform more complicated procedures, such as coloring hair. As they continue to work in the field, more training usually is required to help workers learn the techniques particular to each salon and to build on the basics learned in cosmetology school. Personal appearance workers attend training at salons, cosmetology schools, or industry trade shows throughout their careers.

*Licensure.* All states require barbers, cosmetologists, and other personal appearance workers to be licensed, with the exceptions of shampooers and makeup artists. Qualifications for a license vary by state, but generally a person must have a high school diploma or GED, be at least 16 years old, and have graduated from a state-licensed barber or cosmetology school. After graduating from a state approved training program, students take a state licensing examination. The exam consists of a written test and, in some cases, a practical test of styling skills or an oral examination. In many states, cosmetology training may be credited toward a barbering license, and vice versa, and a few states combine the two licenses. Most states require separate licensing examinations for manicurists, pedicurists, and skin care specialists.

Some states have reciprocity agreements that allow licensed barbers and cosmetologists to obtain a license in a different state without additional formal training, but such agreements are uncommon. Consequently, persons who wish to work in a particular state should review the laws of that state before entering a training program.

*Other qualifications.* Successful personal appearance workers should have an understanding of fashion, art, and technical design. They also must keep a neat personal appearance and a clean work area. Interpersonal skills, image, and attitude play an important role in career success. As client retention and retail sales become an

increasingly important part of salons' revenue, the ability to be an effective salesperson becomes ever more vital for salon workers. Some cosmetology schools consider "people skills" to be such an integral part of the job that they require coursework in that area. Business skills are important for those who plan to operate their own salons.

*Advancement.* Advancement usually takes the form of higher earnings as barbers and cosmetologists gain experience and build a steady clientele. Some barbers and cosmetologists manage salons, lease booth space in salons, or open their own salons after several years of experience. Others teach in barber or cosmetology schools or provide training through vocational schools. Still others advance to become sales representatives, image or fashion consultants, or examiners for state licensing boards.

## Employment

Barbers, cosmetologists, and other personal appearance workers held about 825,000 jobs in 2006. Of these, barbers and cosmetologists held 677,000 jobs, manicurists and pedicurists 78,000, skin care specialists 38,000, and shampooers 29,000. Theatrical and performance makeup artists held 2,100 jobs.

Most of these workers are employed in beauty salons or barber shops, but they also are found in nail salons, day and resort spas, and nursing and other residential care homes. Nearly every town has a barbershop or beauty salon, but employment in this occupation is concentrated in the most populous cities and states. Theatrical and performance makeup artists work for movie and television studios, performing arts companies, and event promoters. Some apply makeup in retail stores.

About 46 percent of all barbers, cosmetologists, and other personal appearance workers are self-employed. Many of these workers own their own salon, but a growing number of the self-employed lease booth space or a chair from the salon's owner.

## Job Outlook

Overall employment of barbers, cosmetologists, and other personal appearance workers is projected to grow slightly faster than the average for all occupations. Opportunities for entry level workers should be favorable, while job candidates at high-end establishments will face keen competition.

*Employment change.* Personal appearance workers will grow by 14 percent from 2006 to 2016, which is faster than the average for all occupations. This growth primarily will be a result of an increasing population and from the growing demand for personal appearance services, particularly skin care services.

Employment trends are expected to vary among the different occupational specialties. Employment of hairdressers, hairstylists, and cosmetologists should increase by 12 percent because many now cut and style both men's and women's hair and because the demand for hair treatment by teens and aging baby boomers is expected to remain steady or even grow. As a result, fewer people are expected to go to barber shops and employment of barbers is expected to see relatively little change in employment.

Continued growth in the number of nail salons and full-service day spas will generate numerous job openings for manicurists, pedicurists, and skin care specialists. Employment of manicurists and pedicurists will grow by 28 percent, while employment of shampooers will increase by 13 percent. Estheticians and other skin care specialists will see large gains in employment, and are expected to grow 34 percent as more facial procedures to improve one's complexion become available and become more popular in spas and some medical settings. Makeup artists are expected to grow by 40 percent, but because of its relatively small size, the occupation will only add a few hundred jobs over the decade.

*Job prospects.* Job opportunities generally should be good. However, competition is expected for jobs and clients at higher paying salons as applicants compete with a large pool of licensed and experienced cosmetologists for these positions. More numerous than those arising from job growth, an abundance of job openings will come about from the need to replace workers who transfer to other occupations, retire, or leave the labor force for other reasons. Opportunities will be best for those with previous experience and for those licensed to provide a broad range of services.

## Earnings

Median hourly earnings in May 2006 for salaried hairdressers, hairstylists, and cosmetologists, including tips and commission, were $10.25. The middle 50 percent earned between $7.92 and $13.75. The lowest 10 percent earned less than $6.68, and the highest 10 percent earned more than $18.78.

Median hourly earnings in May 2006 for salaried barbers, including tips, were $11.13. The middle 50 percent earned between $8.71 and $14.25. The lowest 10 percent earned less than $7.12, and the highest 10 percent earned more than $20.56.

Among skin care specialists, median hourly earnings, including tips, were $12.58, for manicurists and pedicurists $9.23, and for shampooers $7.78.

While earnings for entry-level workers usually are low, earnings can be considerably higher for those with experience. A number of factors, such as the size and location of the salon, determine the total income of personal appearance workers. They may receive commissions based on the price of the service, or a salary based on the number of hours worked, and many receive commissions on the products they sell. In addition, some salons pay bonuses to employees who bring in new business. For many personal appearance workers the

ability to attract and hold regular clients are key factors in determining earnings.

Although some salons offer paid vacations and medical benefits, many self-employed and part-time workers in this occupation do not enjoy such benefits. Some personal appearance workers receive free trail products from manufacturers in the hope that they will recommend the products to clients.

## Related Occupations

Other workers who provide a personal service to clients and are usually professionally licensed or certified include massage therapists and fitness workers.

## Sources of Additional Information

For details on state licensing requirements and approved barber or cosmetology schools, contact your state boards of barber or cosmetology examiners.

State licensing board requirements and a list of licensed training schools for cosmetologists may be obtained from

▸ National Accrediting Commission of Cosmetology Arts and Sciences, 4401 Ford Ave., Suite 1300, Alexandria, VA 22302. Internet: http://www.naccas.orq

Information about a career in cosmetology is available from

▸ National Cosmetology Association, 401 N. Michigan Ave., 22nd floor, Chicago, IL 60611. Internet: http://www.ncacares.org

For information on a career as a barber, contact

▸ National Association of Barber Boards of America, 2703 Pine Street, Arkadelphia, AR 71923. Internet: http://www.nationalbarberboards.com

An additional list of private schools for several different types of personal appearance workers is available from

▸ Beauty Schools Directory. Internet. http://www.beautyschoolsdirectory.com

## Bill and Account Collectors

(O*NET 43-3011.00)

## Significant Points

■ Almost 1 in 4 collectors works for a collection agency; others work in banks, retail stores, government, physicians' offices, hospitals, and other institutions that lend money and extend credit.

■ Most jobs in this occupation require only a high school diploma, though many employers prefer workers with some postsecondary training.

■ Much faster than average employment growth is expected as companies focus more efforts on collecting unpaid debts.

## Nature of the Work

Bill and account collectors, often called simply *collectors*, keep track of accounts that are overdue and attempt to collect payment on

**Projections data from the National Employment Matrix**

| Occupational Title | SOC Code | Employment, 2006 | Projected employment, 2016 | Change, 2006-16 | |
|---|---|---|---|---|---|
| | | | | Number | Percent |
| Bill and account collectors............................................. | 43-3011 | 434,000 | 534,000 | 99,000 | 23 |

NOTE: Data in this table are rounded.

them. Some are employed by third-party collection agencies, while others—known as "in-house collectors"—work directly for the original creditors, such as department stores, hospitals, or banks.

The duties of bill and account collectors are similar across the many different organizations in which they work. First, collectors are called upon to locate and notify customers of delinquent accounts, usually over the telephone, but sometimes by letter. When customers move without leaving a forwarding address, collectors may check with the post office, telephone companies, credit bureaus, or former neighbors to obtain the new address. The attempt to find the new address is called "skip tracing." New computer systems assist in tracing by automatically tracking when customers change their address or contact information on any of their open accounts.

Once collectors find the debtor, they inform him or her of the overdue account and solicit payment. If necessary, they review the terms of the sale, service, or credit contract with the customer. Collectors also may attempt to learn the cause of the delay in payment. Where feasible, they offer the customer advice on how to pay off the debts, such as taking out a bill consolidation loan. However, the collector's prime objective is always to ensure that the customer pays the debt in question.

If a customer agrees to pay, collectors record this commitment and check later to verify that the payment was made. Collectors may have authority to grant an extension of time if customers ask for one. If a customer fails to pay, collectors prepare a statement indicating the customer's action for the credit department of the establishment. In more extreme cases, collectors may initiate repossession proceedings, disconnect the customer's service, or hand the account over to an attorney for legal action. Most collectors handle other administrative functions for the accounts assigned to them, including recording changes of address and purging the records of the deceased.

Collectors use computers and a variety of automated systems to keep track of overdue accounts. In sophisticated predictive dialer systems, a computer dials the telephone automatically, and the collector speaks only when a connection has been made. Such systems eliminate time spent calling busy or nonanswering numbers. Many collectors use regular telephones, but others wear headsets like those used by telephone operators.

*Work environment.* In-house bill and account collectors typically are employed in an office environment, and those who work for third-party collection agencies may work in a call-center environment. Workers spend most of their time on the phone tracking down and contacting people with debts. The work can be stressful as some customers are confrontational when pressed about their debts. Still, some appreciate assistance in resolving their outstanding debt. Collectors may also feel pressured to meet targets for debt recovered in a certain period.

Bill and account collectors often have to work evenings and weekends, when it is easier to reach people. Many collectors work part time or on flexible work schedules, though the majority work 40 hours per week.

## Training, Other Qualifications, and Advancement

Most employers require collectors to have at a least a high school diploma and prefer some customer service experience. Employers usually provide on-the-job training to new employees.

*Education and training.* Most bill and account collectors are required to have at least a high school diploma. However, employers prefer workers who have completed some college or who have experience in other occupations that involve contact with the public.

Once hired, workers usually receive on-the-job training. Under the guidance of a supervisor or some other senior worker, new employees learn company procedures. Some formal classroom training also may be necessary, such as training in specific computer software. Additional training topics usually include telephone techniques and negotiation skills. Workers are also instructed in the laws governing the collection of debt as mandated by the Fair Debt Collection Practices Act, which applies to all third party and some in-house collectors.

*Other qualifications.* Workers should have good communication and people skills because they need to speak to customers daily, some of whom may be in stressful financial situations. In addition, collectors should be computer literate, and experience with advanced telecommunications equipment is also useful.

*Advancement.* Collectors most often advance by taking on more complex cases. Some might become team leaders or supervisors. Workers who acquire additional skills, experience, and training improve their advancement opportunities.

## Employment

Bill and account collectors held about 434,000 jobs in 2006. About 24 percent of collectors work in the business support services industries, which includes collection agencies. Many others work in banks, retail stores, government, physician's offices, hospitals, and other institutions that lend money and extend credit.

## Job Outlook

Employment of bill and account collectors is expected to grow much faster than the average for all occupations through 2016. Job prospects are expected to be favorable because growth in the occupation and the many people who leave the occupation are expected to create plentiful openings.

*Employment change.* Over the 2006–2016 decade, employment of bill and account collectors is expected to grow by 23 percent, which is much faster than the average for all occupations. Cash flow is becoming increasingly important to companies, which are now placing greater emphasis on collecting unpaid debts sooner. Thus, the workload for collectors is expected to continue to increase as they seek to collect not only debts that are relatively old, but also ones that are more recent. In addition, as more companies in a wide range of industries get involved in lending money and issuing credit cards, they will need to hire collectors because debt levels will likely continue to rise.

Hospitals and physicians' offices are two of the fastest growing industries requiring collectors. With insurance reimbursements not keeping up with cost increases, the health care industry is seeking to recover more money from patients. Government agencies also are making more use of collectors to collect on everything from parking tickets to child-support payments and past-due taxes. In addition, the Internal Revenue Service (IRS) has begun outsourcing the collection of overdue federal taxes to third-party collection agencies, adding to the need for workers in this occupation.

Despite the increasing demand for bill collectors, employment growth may be somewhat constrained by the increased use of third-party debt collectors, who are generally more efficient than in-house collectors. Also, some firms are beginning to use offshore collection agencies, whose lower cost structures allow them to collect debts that are too small for domestic collection agencies.

*Job prospects.* Job openings will not be created from employment growth alone. A significant number of openings will result from the many people who leave the occupation and must be replaced. As a result, job opportunities should be favorable.

Contrary to the pattern in most occupations, employment of bill and account collectors tends to rise during recessions, reflecting the difficulty that many people have in meeting their financial obligations. However, collectors usually have more success at getting people to repay their debts when the economy is good.

## Earnings

Median hourly earnings of bill and account collectors were $13.97 in May 2006. The middle 50 percent earned between $11.49 and $17.14. The lowest 10 percent earned less than $9.61, and the highest 10 percent earned more than $21.12. Many bill and account collectors earn commissions based on the amount of debt they recover.

## Related Occupations

Bill and account collectors review and collect information on accounts. Other occupations with similar responsibilities include credit authorizers, checkers, and clerks; loan officers; and interviewers.

## Sources of Additional Information

Career information on bill and account collectors is available from

▸ ACA International, The Association of Credit and Collection Professionals, P.O. Box 390106, Minneapolis, MN 55439. Internet: http://www.acainternational.org

# Bookkeeping, Accounting, and Auditing Clerks

(O*NET 43-3031.00)

## Significant Points

■ Bookkeeping, accounting, and auditing clerks held more than 2.1 million jobs in 2006 and are employed in every industry.

■ Employment is projected to grow as fast as the average due to a growing economy.

■ The large size of this occupation ensures plentiful job openings, including many opportunities for temporary and part-time work.

## Nature of the Work

Bookkeeping, accounting, and auditing clerks are financial record-keepers. They update and maintain accounting records, including those which calculate expenditures, receipts, accounts payable and receivable, and profit and loss. These workers have a wide range of skills from full-charge bookkeepers who can maintain an entire company's books to accounting clerks who handle specific tasks. All of these clerks make numerous computations each day and increasingly must be comfortable using computers to calculate and record data.

In small businesses, *bookkeepers and bookkeeping clerks* often have responsibility for some or all of the accounts, known as the general ledger. They record all transactions and post debits (costs) and credits (income). They also produce financial statements and prepare reports and summaries for supervisors and managers. Bookkeepers also prepare bank deposits by compiling data from cashiers, verifying and balancing receipts, and sending cash, checks, or other forms of payment to the bank. They also may handle payroll, make purchases, prepare invoices, and keep track of overdue accounts.

In large-companies' accounting departments, *accounting clerks* have more specialized tasks. Their titles, such as accounts payable clerk or accounts receivable clerk, often reflect the type of accounting they do. In addition, their responsibilities vary by level of experience. Entry-level accounting clerks post details of transactions, total accounts, and compute interest charges. They also may monitor loans and accounts to ensure that payments are up to date. More advanced accounting clerks may total, balance, and reconcile billing vouchers; ensure the completeness and accuracy of data on accounts; and code documents according to company procedures.

Accounting clerks post transactions in journals and on computer files and update the files when needed. Senior clerks also review computer printouts against regularly maintained journals and make necessary corrections. They may review invoices and statements to ensure that all the information appearing on them is accurate and complete, and they may reconcile computer reports with operating reports.

**Projections data from the National Employment Matrix**

| Occupational Title | SOC Code | Employment, 2006 | Projected employment, 2016 | Change, 2006-16 | |
|---|---|---|---|---|---|
| | | | | Number | Percent |
| Bookkeeping, accounting, and auditing clerks ................................ | 43-3031 | 2,114,000 | 2,377,000 | 264,000 | 12 |

NOTE: Data in this table are rounded.

*Auditing clerks* verify records of transactions posted by other workers. They check figures, postings, and documents to ensure that they are correct, mathematically accurate, and properly coded. They also correct or note errors for accountants or other workers to fix.

As organizations continue to computerize their financial records, many bookkeeping, accounting, and auditing clerks use specialized accounting software, spreadsheets, and databases. Most clerks now enter information from receipts or bills into computers, and the information is then stored either electronically or as computer printouts, or both. The widespread use of computers also has enabled bookkeeping, accounting, and auditing clerks to take on additional responsibilities, such as payroll, procurement, and billing. Many of these functions require these clerks to write letters and make phone calls to customers or clients.

*Work environment.* Bookkeeping, accounting, and auditing clerks work in an office environment. They may experience eye and muscle strain, backaches, headaches, and repetitive motion injuries from using computers on a daily basis. Clerks may have to sit for extended periods while reviewing detailed data.

Many bookkeeping, accounting, and auditing clerks work regular business hours and a standard 40-hour week, although some may work occasional evenings and weekends. About 24 percent of these clerks worked part time in 2006.

Bookkeeping, accounting, and auditing clerks may work longer hours to meet deadlines at the end of the fiscal year, during tax time, or when monthly or yearly accounting audits are performed. Additionally, those who work in hotels, restaurants, and stores may put in overtime during peak holiday and vacation seasons.

## Training, Other Qualifications, and Advancement

Employers usually prefer bookkeeping, accounting, and auditing clerks to have at least a high school diploma and some accounting coursework or relevant work experience. Clerks should also have good communication skills, be detail-oriented, and trustworthy.

*Education and training.* Most bookkeeping, accounting, and auditing clerks are required to have a high school degree at a minimum. However, having some college is increasingly important and an associate degree in business or accounting is required for some positions. Although a bachelor's degree is rarely required, graduates may accept bookkeeping, accounting, and auditing clerk positions to get into a particular company or to enter the accounting or finance field with the hope of eventually being promoted.

Once hired, bookkeeping, accounting, and auditing clerks usually receive on-the-job training. Under the guidance of a supervisor or another more experienced employee, new clerks learn company procedures. Some formal classroom training also may be necessary, such as training in specialized computer software.

*Other qualifications.* Experience in a related job and working in an office environment also is recommended. Employers prefer workers who can use computers; knowledge of word processing and spreadsheet software is especially valuable.

Bookkeeping, accounting, and auditing clerks must be careful, orderly, and detail-oriented in order to avoid making errors and to recognize errors made by others. These workers also should be discreet and trustworthy because they frequently come in contact with confidential material. They should also have good communication skills because they increasingly work with customers. In addition, all bookkeeping, accounting, and auditing clerks should have a strong aptitude for numbers.

*Certification and advancement.* Bookkeeping, accounting, and auditing clerks, particularly those who handle all the recordkeeping for a company, may find it beneficial to become certified. The Certified Bookkeeper (CB) designation, awarded by the American Institute of Professional Bookkeepers, demonstrates that individuals have the skills and knowledge needed to carry out all bookkeeping functions, including overseeing payroll and balancing accounts according to accepted accounting procedures. For certification, candidates must have at least two years of bookkeeping experience, pass a four-part examination, and adhere to a code of ethics. Several colleges and universities offer a preparatory course for certification; some offer courses online.

Bookkeeping, accounting, and auditing clerks usually advance by taking on more duties for higher pay or by transferring to a closely related occupation. Most companies fill office and administrative support supervisory and managerial positions by promoting individuals from within their organizations, so clerks who acquire additional skills, experience, and training improve their advancement opportunities. With appropriate experience and education, some bookkeeping, accounting, and auditing clerks may become accountants or auditors.

## Employment

Bookkeeping, accounting, and auditing clerks held more than 2.1 million jobs in 2006. They work in all industries and at all levels of government. Local government and the accounting, tax preparation, bookkeeping, and payroll services industry are among the individual industries employing the largest numbers of these clerks.

## Job Outlook

Job growth is projected to be average through 2016, and job prospects should be good as a large number of bookkeeping, accounting, and auditing clerks are expected to retire or transfer to other occupations.

*Employment change.* Employment of bookkeeping, accounting, and auditing clerks is projected to grow by 12 percent during the

2006–2016 decade, which is as fast as the average for all occupations. Due its size, this occupation will have among the largest numbers of new jobs arise, about 264,000 over the projections decade.

A growing economy will result in more financial transactions and other activities that require recordkeeping by these workers. Additionally, the Sarbanes-Oxley Act of 2002 calls for more accuracy and transparency in the reporting of financial data for public companies, which will increase the demand for these workers. Moreover, companies will continue to outsource their bookkeeping and accounting departments to independent accounting, tax preparation, bookkeeping, and payroll services firms. However, at the same time, the increasing use of tax preparation software in place of the services of tax professionals will hinder growth somewhat.

Clerks who can carry out a wider range of bookkeeping and accounting activities will be in greater demand than specialized clerks. Demand for full-charge bookkeepers is expected to increase, for example, because they do much of the work of accountants and perform a wider variety of financial transactions, from payroll to billing. Technological advances will continue to change the way these workers perform their daily tasks, such as using computer software programs to maintain records, but will not decrease the demand for these workers, especially in smaller establishments.

*Job prospects.* Some job openings are expected to result from job growth, but even more openings will stem from the need to replace existing workers who leave. Each year, numerous jobs will become available as clerks transfer to other occupations or leave the labor force. The large size of this occupation ensures plentiful job openings, including many opportunities for temporary and part-time work. Certified Bookkeepers (CBs) and those with several years of accounting or bookkeeping experience will have the best job prospects.

## Earnings

In May 2006, the median wage and salary earnings of bookkeeping, accounting, and auditing clerks were $30,560. The middle half of the occupation earned between $24,540 and $37,780. The top 10 percent of bookkeeping, accounting, and auditing clerks more than $46,020, and the bottom 10 percent earned less than $19,760.

Benefits offered by employers may vary by the type and size of establishment, but health insurance and paid leave are common.

## Related Occupations

Bookkeeping, accounting, and auditing clerks work with financial records. Other workers who perform similar duties include accountants and auditors; bill and account collectors; billing and posting clerks and machine operators; brokerage clerks; credit authorizers, checkers, and clerks; payroll and timekeeping clerks; procurement clerks; and tellers.

## Sources of Additional Information

For information on the Certified Bookkeeper designation, contact

▸ American Institute of Professional Bookkeepers, 6001 Montrose Rd., Suite 500, Rockville, MD 20852. Internet: http://www.aipb.org

# Brokerage Clerks

(O*NET 43-4011.00)

## Significant Points

■ More than 9 out of 10 brokerage clerks work for securities and commodities firms, banks, and other establishments in the financial services industry.

■ High school graduates qualify for many of these positions, but many workers now hold associate or bachelor's degrees.

■ Good prospects are expected for qualified jobseekers as employment grows and as existing brokerage clerks advance to other occupations.

## Nature of the Work

For a typical investor, buying and selling stock is a simple process. Often, it is as easy as calling a broker on the phone or entering the trade into a computer. Behind the scenes, however, buying and selling stock is more complicated, involving trade execution and a fair amount of paperwork. While brokers do some of this work themselves, much of it is delegated to brokerage clerks.

Brokerage clerks perform a number of different tasks with a wide range of responsibilities. Most involve computing and recording data pertaining to securities transactions. Brokerage clerks may also contact customers, take orders, and inform clients of changes to their accounts. Brokerage clerks work in the operations departments of securities firms, on trading floors, and in branch offices. Technology has had a major impact on these positions over the last several years. A significant and growing number of brokerage clerks use custom-designed software programs to process transactions more quickly. Only a few customized accounts are still handled manually.

A *broker's assistant*, also called a *sales assistant*, is the most common type of brokerage clerk. These clerks typically assist a small number of brokers, for whom they take client calls, write up order tickets, process the paperwork for opening and closing accounts, record a client's purchases and sales, and inform clients of changes to their accounts. All broker's assistants must be knowledgeable about investment products so that they can communicate clearly with clients. Those who are licensed by the Financial Industry Regulatory Authority (FINRA) can make recommendations to clients at the instruction of the broker.

Brokerage clerks in the operations areas of securities firms perform many duties to help the sale and purchase of stocks, bonds, commodities, and other kinds of investments. They also produce the necessary records of all transactions that occur in their area of the business. *Purchase-and-sale clerks* match orders to buy with orders to sell. They balance and verify trades of stock by comparing the records of the selling firm with those of the buying firm. *Dividend clerks* ensure timely payments of stock or cash dividends to clients of a particular brokerage firm. *Transfer clerks* execute customer requests for changes to security registration and examine stock certificates to make sure that they adhere to banking regulations.

**Projections data from the National Employment Matrix**

| Occupational Title | SOC Code | Employment, 2006 | Projected employment, 2016 | Change, 2006-16 | |
|---|---|---|---|---|---|
| | | | | Number | Percent |
| Brokerage clerks ........................................................................ | 43-4011 | 73,000 | 88,000 | 15,000 | 20 |

NOTE: Data in this table are rounded.

*Receive-and-deliver clerks* handle the receipt and delivery of securities among firms and institutions. *Margin clerks* record and monitor activity in customers' accounts to ensure that clients make payments and stay within legal boundaries concerning their purchases of stock.

*Work environment.* Brokerage clerks work in offices and on trading floors, areas that are clean and well lit but which may be noisy at times. The workload is generally manageable but can become very heavy when the market fluctuates rapidly. Brokerage clerks generally work a standard 40-hour week, but they may work overtime during particularly busy periods.

## Training, Other Qualifications, and Advancement

Most brokerage clerks learn their jobs through a few months of on-the-job training and experience. Once they have worked in the firm for a few years, many clerks advance to sales representative or broker positions.

*Education and training.* Some brokerage clerk positions require only a high school diploma, but graduates from two- and four-year college degree programs are increasingly preferred. Positions dealing with the public, such as broker's or sales assistant, and those dealing with more complicated financial records are especially likely to require a college degree.

Most new employees are trained on the job, working under the close supervision of more experienced employees. Some firms offer formal training that may include courses in telephone etiquette, computer use, and customer service skills. They may also offer training programs to help clerks study for the broker licensing exams.

*Licensure.* Licenses are not strictly required for most brokerage clerk positions, but a Series seven brokerage license can make a clerk more valuable to the broker. This license gives the holder the ability to act as a registered representative of the firm. A registered representative has the right to answer more of a client's questions and to pass along securities recommendations from the broker. In order to receive this license, a clerk must pass the General Securities Registered Representative Examination (Series seven exam), administered by FINRA, and be an employee of a registered firm for at least four months.

*Other qualifications.* Brokerage clerk jobs require good organizational and communication skills, as well as attention to detail. Computer skills are extremely important, as most of the work is done by computer. An aptitude for working with numbers is also very helpful, as is a basic knowledge of accounting.

*Advancement.* Clerks may be promoted to sales representative positions or other professional positions within the securities industry.

Employment as a brokerage clerk may also be a stepping-stone into a position as a broker.

## Employment

Brokerage clerks held about 73,000 jobs in 2006. More than 9 out of 10 worked for securities and commodities, banking, and other financial industries.

## Job Outlook

The job outlook for prospective brokerage clerks is good. As the securities industry grows, the number of clerks will increase. Opportunities will be abundant relative to other securities industry occupations, due to advancement of other clerks and job growth.

*Employment change.* Employment of brokerage clerks is expected to grow by 20 percent during the 2006–2016 decade, which is faster than the average for all occupations. With more people investing in securities, brokerage clerks will be required to process larger volumes of transactions. Moreover, regulatory changes have resulted in more legal documentation and recordkeeping requirements. Demand will be tempered, however, by continually improving technologies that allow increased automation of many tasks. Further, clerks are often seen as reducing profits, since they do not bring in customers, making them particularly prone to layoffs. Because of intense competition, especially among discount brokerages, companies must continually focus on cutting costs, meaning that many responsibilities formerly handled by clerks are now handled by the brokers themselves.

*Job prospects.* Because brokerage clerks are often entry-level workers, many opportunities will result from the advancement of other clerks. Prospects will be good for qualified workers. New entrants who have strong sales skills and an aptitude for understanding numbers will have the best opportunities. While not required, a 4-year degree can also be very helpful.

## Earnings

Median annual earnings of brokerage clerks were $36,390 in May 2006. The middle 50 percent earned between $29,480 and $46,030. The lowest 10 percent earned less than $24,590 and the highest 10 percent earned more than $57,600.

## Related Occupations

Brokerage clerks compute and record data. Other workers who perform calculations and record data include bill and account collectors; billing and posting clerks and machine operators; bookkeeping, accounting, and auditing clerks; and tellers.

## Sources of Additional Information

For more information on employment in the securities industry, contact

▸ Securities Industry and Financial Markets Association, 120 Broadway, 35th Floor, New York, NY 10271. Internet: http://www.sifma.org

For information on licensing, contact

▸ Financial Industry Regulatory Authority (FINRA), 1735 K St. NW, Washington, DC 20006. Internet: http://www.finra.org

# Building Cleaning Workers

(O*NET 37-1011.00, 37-2011.00, 37-2012.00, and 37-2019.99 )

## Significant Points

■ This very large occupation requires few skills to enter and each year has one of the largest numbers of job openings of any occupation.

■ Most job openings result from the need to replace the many workers who leave these jobs because they provide low pay and few benefits, limited opportunities for training or advancement, and often only part-time or temporary work.

■ Most new jobs will occur in businesses providing janitorial and cleaning services on a contract basis.

## Nature of the Work

Building cleaning workers—including janitors, maids, housekeeping cleaners, window washers, and rug shampooers—keep office buildings, hospitals, stores, apartment houses, hotels, and residences clean, sanitary, and in good condition. Some do only cleaning, while others have a wide range of duties.

*Janitors and cleaners* perform a variety of heavy cleaning duties, such as cleaning floors, shampooing rugs, washing walls and glass, and removing rubbish. They may fix leaky faucets, empty trash cans, do painting and carpentry, replenish bathroom supplies, mow lawns, and see that heating and air-conditioning equipment works properly. On a typical day, janitors may wet- or dry-mop floors, clean bathrooms, vacuum carpets, dust furniture, make minor repairs, and exterminate insects and rodents. They may also clean snow or debris from sidewalks in front of buildings and notify management of the need for major repairs. While janitors typically perform most of the duties mentioned, cleaners tend to work for companies that specialize in one type of cleaning activity, such as washing windows.

*Maids and housekeeping cleaners* perform any combination of light cleaning duties to keep private households or commercial establishments, such as hotels, restaurants, hospitals, and nursing homes, clean and orderly. In hotels, aside from cleaning and maintaining the premises, maids and housekeeping cleaners may deliver ironing boards, cribs, and rollaway beds to guests' rooms. In hospitals, they also may wash bed frames, make beds, and disinfect and sanitize equipment and supplies with germicides. Janitors, maids, and cleaners use many kinds of equipment, tools, and cleaning materials. For one job they may need standard cleaning implements; another may require an electric floor polishing machine and a special cleaning solution. Improved building materials, chemical cleaners, and power equipment have made many tasks easier and less time consuming, but cleaning workers must learn the proper use of equipment and cleaners to avoid harming floors, fixtures, building occupants, and themselves.

*Cleaning supervisors* coordinate, schedule, and supervise the activities of janitors and cleaners. They assign tasks and inspect building areas to see that work has been done properly; they also issue supplies and equipment and inventory stocks to ensure that supplies on hand are adequate. They may be expected to screen and hire job applicants; train new and experienced employees; and recommend promotions, transfers, or dismissals. Supervisors may prepare reports concerning the occupancy of rooms, hours worked, and department expenses. Some also perform cleaning duties.

*Cleaners and servants in private households* dust and polish furniture; sweep, mop, and wax floors; vacuum; and clean ovens, refrigerators, and bathrooms. They also may wash dishes, polish silver, and change and make beds. Some wash, fold, and iron clothes; a few wash windows. General houseworkers also may take clothes and laundry to the cleaners, buy groceries, and perform many other errands.

Building cleaning workers in large office and residential buildings, and more recently in large hotels, often work in teams consisting of workers who specialize in vacuuming, picking up trash, and cleaning restrooms, among other things. Supervisors conduct inspections to ensure that the building is cleaned properly and the team is functioning efficiently. In hotels, one member of the team is responsible for reporting electronically to the supervisor when rooms are cleaned.

*Work environment.* Because most office buildings are cleaned while they are empty, many cleaning workers work evening hours. Some, however, such as school and hospital custodians, work in the daytime. When there is a need for 24-hour maintenance, janitors may be assigned to shifts. Most full-time building cleaners work about 40 hours a week. Part-time cleaners usually work in the evenings and on weekends.

Most building cleaning workers work indoors, but some work outdoors part of the time, sweeping walkways, mowing lawns, or shoveling snow. Working with machines can be noisy, and some tasks, such as cleaning bathrooms and trash rooms, can be dirty and unpleasant. Janitors may suffer cuts, bruises, and burns from machines, hand tools, and chemicals. They spend most of their time on their feet, sometimes lifting or pushing heavy furniture or equipment. Many tasks, such as dusting or sweeping, require constant bending, stooping, and stretching. Lifting the increasingly heavier mattresses at nicer hotels in order to change the linens can cause back injuries and sprains.

## Training, Other Qualifications, and Advancement

Most building cleaning workers, except supervisors, have a high school degree or less and mainly learn their skills on the job or in informal training sessions sponsored by their employers. Supervisors, though, generally have at least a high school diploma and often some college.

**Projections data from the National Employment Matrix**

| Occupational Title | SOC Code | Employment, 2006 | Projected employment, 2016 | Change, 2006-16 | |
|---|---|---|---|---|---|
| | | | | Number | Percent |
| Building cleaning workers ................................................................. | — | 4,154,000 | 4,723,000 | 569,000 | 14 |
| First-line supervisors/managers of housekeeping and janitorial workers................................................................. | 37-1011 | 282,000 | 318,000 | 36,000 | 13 |
| Building cleaning workers ....................................................... | 37-2010 | 3,872,000 | 4,405,000 | 533,000 | 14 |
| Janitors and cleaners, except maids and housekeeping cleaners ................................................................. | 37-2011 | 2,387,000 | 2,732,000 | 345,000 | 14 |
| Maids and housekeeping cleaners..................................... | 37-2012 | 1,470,000 | 1,656,000 | 186,000 | 13 |
| Building cleaning workers, all other....................................... | 37-2019 | 16,000 | 18,000 | 2,400 | 15 |

NOTE: Data in this table are rounded.

*Education and training.* No special education is required for most entry-level janitorial or cleaning jobs, but workers should be able to perform simple arithmetic and follow instructions. High school shop courses are helpful for jobs involving repair work. Most building cleaners learn their skills on the job. Beginners usually work with an experienced cleaner, doing routine cleaning. As they gain more experience, they are assigned more complicated tasks. In some cities, programs run by unions, government agencies, or employers teach janitorial skills. Students learn how to clean buildings thoroughly and efficiently; how to select and safely use various cleansing agents; and how to operate and maintain machines, such as wet and dry vacuums, buffers, and polishers. Students learn to plan their work, to follow safety and health regulations, to interact positively with people in the buildings they clean, and to work without supervision. Instruction in minor electrical, plumbing, and other repairs also may be given.

Supervisors of building cleaning workers usually need at least a high school diploma, but many have some college or more, especially those who work at places where clean rooms and well-functioning buildings are a necessity, such as in hospitals and hotels.

*Other qualifications.* Those who come in contact with the public should have good communication skills. Employers usually look for dependable, hard-working individuals who are in good health, follow directions well, and get along with other people.

*Certification and advancement.* A small number of cleaning supervisors and managers are members of the International Executive Housekeepers Association, which offers two kinds of certification programs for cleaning supervisors and managers: Certified Executive Housekeeper (CEH) and Registered Executive Housekeeper (REH). The CEH designation is offered to those with a high school education, while the REH designation is offered to those who have a four-year college degree. Both designations are earned by attending courses and passing exams and both must be renewed every three years to ensure that workers keep abreast of new cleaning methods. Those with the REH designation usually oversee the cleaning services of hotels, hospitals, casinos, and other large institutions that rely on well-trained experts for their cleaning needs.

Advancement opportunities for workers usually are limited in organizations where they are the only maintenance worker. Where there is a large maintenance staff, however, cleaning workers can be promoted to supervisor or to area supervisor or manager. In many establishments, they are required to take some in-service training to improve their housekeeping techniques and procedures and to

enhance their supervisory skills. A high school diploma improves the chances for advancement. Some janitors set up their own maintenance or cleaning businesses.

## Employment

Building cleaning workers held about 4.2 million jobs in 2006. More than 7 percent were self-employed.

Janitors and cleaners worked in nearly every type of establishment and held about 2.4 million jobs. They accounted for more than 57 percent of all building cleaning workers. More than 31 percent worked for firms supplying building maintenance services on a contract basis, about 20 percent were employed in public or private educational services, and 2 percent worked in hotels or motels. Other employers included hospitals; restaurants; religious institutions; manufacturing firms; government agencies; and operators of apartment buildings, office buildings, and other types of real estate.

First-line supervisors of housekeeping and janitorial workers held more than 282,000 jobs. Approximately 20 percent worked in firms supplying building maintenance services on a contract basis, while approximately 11 percent were employed in hotels or motels. About 4 percent worked for state and local governments, primarily at schools and colleges. Others worked for hospitals, nursing homes and other residential care facilities.

Maids and housekeepers held about 1.5 million jobs. Private households employed the most maids and housekeepers—almost 29 percent—while hotels, motels, and other traveler accommodations employed about the same percentage, almost 29 percent. Hospitals, nursing homes, and other residential care facilities employed large numbers, also. Although cleaning jobs can be found in all cities and towns, most are located in highly populated areas where there are many office buildings, schools, apartment houses, nursing homes, and hospitals.

## Job Outlook

Overall employment of building cleaning workers is expected to grow faster than average for all occupations through 2016, as more office complexes, apartment houses, schools, factories, hospitals, and other buildings requiring cleaning are built to accommodate a growing population and economy.

*Employment change.* The number of building cleaning workers is expected to grow 14 percent between 2006 and 2016, which is faster than the average for all occupations. This occupation will have, in fact, one of the largest numbers of new jobs arise, about 570,000 over the 2006–2016 period.

Much of the growth in these occupations will come from cleaning residential properties. As families become more pressed for time, they increasingly hire cleaning and handyman services to perform a variety of tasks in their homes. Also, as the population ages, older people will need to hire cleaners to help maintain their houses. In addition, housekeeping cleaners will be needed to clean the growing number of residential care facilities for the elderly. These facilities, including assisted-living residences, generally provide housekeeping services as part of the rent. Although there have been some improvements in productivity in the way buildings are cleaned and maintained—using teams of cleaners, for example, and better cleaning supplies—cleaning still is very much a labor-intensive job.

As many firms reduce costs by contracting out the cleaning and maintenance of buildings, businesses providing janitorial and cleaning services on a contract basis are expected to have the greatest number of new jobs in this field.

*Job prospects.* In addition to job openings arising due to growth, numerous openings should result from the need to replace those who leave this very large occupation each year. Limited promotion potential, low pay, and the fact that many jobs are part-time and temporary, induce many to leave the occupation, thereby contributing to the number of job openings and the need to replace these workers.

Building cleaners usually find work by answering newspaper advertisements, applying directly to organizations where they would like to work, contacting local labor unions, or contacting state employment service offices.

## Earnings

Median annual earnings of janitors and cleaners, except maids and housekeeping cleaners, were $19,930 in May 2006. The middle 50 percent earned between $16,220 and $25,640. The lowest 10 percent earned less than $14,010 and the highest 10 percent earned more than $33,060. Median annual earnings in 2006 in the industries employing the largest numbers of janitors and cleaners, except maids and housekeeping cleaners, were as follows:

| | |
|---|---|
| Elementary and secondary schools | $24,010 |
| Local government | 23,930 |
| Colleges, universities, and professional schools | 23,170 |
| General medical and surgical hospitals | 21,670 |
| Services to buildings and dwellings | 17,870 |

Median annual earnings of maids and housekeepers were $17,580 in May 2006. The middle 50 percent earned between $15,060 and $21,440. The lowest 10 percent earned less than $13,140, and the highest 10 percent earned more than $26,390. Median annual earnings in 2006 in the industries employing the largest numbers of maids and housekeepers were as follows:

| | |
|---|---|
| General medical and surgical hospitals | $20,080 |
| Community care facilities for the elderly | 17,900 |
| Nursing care facilities | 17,690 |
| Services to buildings and dwellings | 17,540 |
| Traveler accommodation | 16,790 |

Median annual earnings of first-line supervisors and managers of housekeeping and janitorial workers were $31,290 in May 2006. The middle 50 percent earned between $24,230 and $40,670. The lowest 10 percent earned less than $19,620, and the highest 10 percent earned more than $51,490. Median annual earnings in May 2006 in the industries employing the largest numbers of first-line supervisors and managers of housekeeping and janitorial workers were as follows:

| | |
|---|---|
| Local government | $38,170 |
| Elementary and secondary schools | 35,660 |
| Nursing care facilities | 30,570 |
| Services to buildings and dwellings | 29,730 |
| Traveler accommodation | 26,730 |

## Related Occupations

Workers who specialize in one of the many job functions of janitors and cleaners include pest control workers; general maintenance and repair workers; and grounds maintenance workers.

## Sources of Additional Information

Information about janitorial jobs may be obtained from state employment service offices.

For information on certification in executive housekeeping, contact

▶ International Executive Housekeepers Association, Inc., 1001 Eastwind Dr., Suite 301, Westerville, OH 43081-3361. Internet: http://www.ieha.org

## Bus Drivers

(O*NET 53-3021.00 and 53-3022.00)

### Significant Points

■ Opportunities should be good, particularly for school bus drivers; applicants for higher paying public transit bus driver positions may encounter competition.

■ State and federal governments establish bus driver qualifications and standards, which include a commercial driver's license.

■ Work schedules vary considerably among various types of bus drivers.

■ Bus drivers must possess strong customer service skills, including communication skills and the ability to manage large groups of people with varying needs.

### Nature of the Work

Bus drivers provide transportation for millions of people, from commuters to school children to vacationers. There are two major kinds of bus drivers. *Transit and intercity bus drivers* transport people within or across states, along routes run within a metropolitan area or county, or on chartered excursions and tours. *School bus drivers* take children to and from schools and related events.

Bus drivers pick up and drop off passengers at bus stops, stations, or—in the case of students—at regularly scheduled neighborhood locations, all according to strict time schedules. Drivers must operate vehicles safely, sometimes in heavy traffic. They also cannot let light traffic put them ahead of schedule so that they miss passengers. Bus drivers drive a range of vehicles from 15-passenger buses to 60-foot articulated buses that can carry more than 100 passengers.

Local transit and intercity bus drivers stock up on tickets or transfers and prepare trip reports after reporting to their assigned terminal or garage. In some transportation firms, maintenance departments are responsible for keeping vehicles in good condition; in others, drivers check their vehicle's tires, brakes, windshield wipers, lights, oil, fuel, and water supply before beginning their routes. Drivers usually verify that the bus has safety equipment, such as fire extinguishers, first aid kits, and emergency reflectors.

During their shift, local transit and intercity bus drivers collect fares; answer questions about schedules, routes, and transfer points; and sometimes announce stops. Intercity bus drivers may make only a single one-way trip to a distant city or a round trip each day. They may stop at towns just a few miles apart or only at large cities hundreds of miles apart. Local transit bus drivers may make several trips each day over the same city and suburban streets, stopping as frequently as every few blocks.

Local transit bus drivers submit daily trip reports with a record of trips, significant schedule delays, and mechanical problems. Intercity drivers who drive across state or national boundaries must comply with U.S. Department of Transportation regulations. These include completing vehicle inspection reports and recording distances traveled and the times they spend driving, performing other duties, and off duty.

Some intercity drivers operate motor coaches which transport passengers on chartered trips and sightseeing tours. Drivers routinely interact with customers and tour guides to make the trip as comfortable and informative as possible. They are directly responsible for keeping to strict schedules, adhering to the guidelines of the tour's itinerary, and ensuring the overall success of the trip. These drivers act as customer service representatives, tour guides, program directors, and safety guides. Trips frequently last more than a day. The driver may be away for more than a week if assigned to an extended tour.

*School bus drivers* usually drive the same routes each day, stopping to pick up pupils in the morning and returning them to their homes in the afternoon. Some school bus drivers also transport students and teachers on field trips or to sporting events. In addition to driving, some school bus drivers work part time in the school system as janitors, mechanics, or classroom assistants when not driving buses.

Bus drivers must be alert to prevent accidents, especially in heavy traffic or in bad weather, and to avoid sudden stops or swerves that jar passengers. School bus drivers must exercise particular caution when children are getting on or off the bus. They must maintain order on their bus and enforce school safety standards by allowing only students to board. In addition, they must know and enforce the school system's rules regarding student conduct. As the number of students with physical or behavioral disabilities increases, school bus drivers must learn how to accommodate their special needs.

Some school bus drivers can take their bus home or park it in a more convenient area rather than reporting to an assigned terminal or garage. School bus drivers do not collect fares. Instead, they prepare weekly reports on the number of students, trips or "runs," work hours, miles, and fuel consumption. Their supervisors set time schedules and routes for the day or week.

*Work environment.* Driving a bus through heavy traffic while dealing with passengers is more stressful and fatiguing than physically strenuous. Many drivers enjoy the opportunity to work without direct supervision, with full responsibility for their bus and passengers. To improve working conditions and retain drivers, many bus lines provide ergonomically designed seats and controls for drivers. Many bus companies use Global Positioning Systems to help dispatchers manage their bus fleets and help drivers navigate.

Work schedules vary considerably among various types of bus drivers. Intercity bus drivers may work nights, weekends, and holidays and often spend nights away from home, during which they stay in hotels at company expense. Senior drivers with regular routes have regular weekly work schedules, but others do not have regular schedules and must be prepared to report for work on short notice. They report for work only when called for a charter assignment or to drive extra buses on a regular route. Intercity bus travel and charter work tend to be seasonal. From May through August, drivers might work the maximum number of hours per week that regulations allow. During winter, junior drivers might work infrequently, except for busy holiday travel periods, and may be furloughed at times.

School bus drivers work only when schools are in session. Many work 20 hours a week or less, driving one or two routes in the morning and afternoon. Drivers taking field or athletic trips, or who also have midday kindergarten routes, may work more hours a week.

Regular local transit bus drivers usually have a five-day work week; Saturdays and Sundays are considered regular workdays. Some drivers work evenings and after midnight. To accommodate commuters, many work "split shifts"—for example, 6 a.m. to 10 a.m. and 3 p.m. to 7 p.m., with time off in between.

Intercity bus drivers operating tour and charter buses may work any day and all hours of the day, including weekends and holidays. Their hours are dictated by the destinations, schedules, and itineraries of chartered tours. Like all commercial drivers, their weekly hours must be consistent with the Department of Transportation's rules and regulations concerning hours of service. For example, drivers may drive for 10 hours and work for up to 15 hours—including driving and non-driving duties—before having 8 hours off duty. Drivers may only drive for 60 hours in 7 days or 70 hours in 8 days. They are required to document their time in a logbook.

## Training, Other Qualifications, and Advancement

State and federal governments establish bus driver qualifications and standards, which include a commercial driver's license (CDL) with the proper endorsements. Many employers provide several weeks of training and help new employees obtain their CDL. Other employers prefer those with truck or other driving experience.

*Education and training.* Many employers prefer high school graduates and require a written test of ability to follow complex bus schedules. Some intercity and public transit bus companies require several years of experience driving a bus or truck. Most intercity bus companies and local transit systems give driver trainees two to eight weeks of classroom and behind-the-wheel instruction. In the classroom, trainees learn Department of Transportation and company work rules, safety regulations, state and municipal driving regulations, and safe driving practices. They also learn to read schedules, determine fares, keep records, and deal courteously with passengers.

School bus drivers receive between one and four weeks of driving instruction and classroom training on state and local laws, regulations, and policies; safe driving practices; driver-pupil relations; first aid; emergency evacuation procedures; and the special needs of students who are disabled or emotionally troubled. School bus drivers also must be aware of the school system's rules for discipline and conduct for bus drivers and the students they transport. Many people who become school bus drivers have never driven any vehicle larger than an automobile.

During training, all bus drivers practice driving on set courses. They practice turns and zigzag maneuvers, backing up, and driving in narrow lanes. Then, they drive in light traffic and, eventually, on congested highways and city streets. They also make trial runs without passengers to improve their driving skills and learn the routes. Local transit trainees memorize and drive each of the runs operating out of their assigned garage. New drivers make regularly scheduled trips with passengers, accompanied by an experienced driver who gives helpful tips, answers questions, and evaluates the new driver's performance. Most bus drivers get brief supplemental training periodically to stay informed of safety issues and regulatory changes.

*Licensure.* Bus driver qualifications and standards are established by state and federal regulations. All drivers must comply with federal regulations and with any state regulations that exceed federal requirements. Federal regulations require drivers who operate commercial motor vehicles in excess of 26,000 pounds gross vehicle weight rating or designed to carry 16 or more people, including the driver, to hold a commercial driver's license with the appropriate endorsements from the state in which they live. As with all commercial drivers, bus drivers who drive across state or national boundaries, as motor coach drivers frequently do, must comply with U.S. Department of Transportation regulations, state regulations, and the regulations of other countries.

To qualify for a commercial driver's license, applicants must pass a knowledge test on rules and regulations and then demonstrate in a skills test that they can operate a bus safely. A national database records all driving violations incurred by people who hold commercial licenses, and a state may not issue a license to a person who has already had a license suspended or revoked in another state. To be issued a commercial license, a driver must surrender all other driver's licenses. All bus drivers must also have a passenger endorsement for their license, which requires passing a knowledge test and demonstrating the necessary skills in a vehicle of the same type as the one they would be driving on the job. Information on how to apply for a commercial driver's license and each type of endorsement can be obtained from state motor vehicle administrations.

Although many states allow those who are 18 years of age and older to drive buses within state borders, the U.S. Department of Transportation establishes minimum qualifications for bus drivers engaged in interstate commerce. Federal Motor Carrier Safety Regulations require drivers to be at least 21 years old and to pass a physical examination once every two years. The main physical requirements include good hearing, at least 20/40 vision with or without glasses or corrective lenses, and a 70-degree field of vision in each eye. Drivers cannot be colorblind. They must be able to hear a forced whisper in one ear at not less than 5 feet, with or without a hearing aide. Drivers must have normal blood pressure and normal use of their arms and legs. They may not use any controlled substances, unless prescribed by a licensed physician. People with epilepsy or with diabetes controlled by insulin are not permitted to be interstate bus drivers. Federal regulations also require employers to test their drivers for alcohol and drug use as a condition of employment and require periodic random tests of the drivers while they are on duty. In addition, a driver must not have been convicted of a felony involving the use of a motor vehicle or a crime involving drugs, driving under the influence of drugs or alcohol, refusing to submit to an alcohol test required by a state or its implied consent laws or regulations, leaving the scene of a crime, or causing a fatality through negligent operation of a commercial vehicle.

All drivers also must be able to read and speak English well enough to read road signs, prepare reports, and communicate with law enforcement officers and the public. In addition, drivers must take a written examination on the Motor Carrier Safety Regulations of the U.S. Department of Transportation.

School bus drivers are required to obtain a commercial driver's license with a school bus endorsement from the state in which they live. To receive this endorsement, they must pass a written test and demonstrate necessary skills in a bus of the same type that they would be driving on their route. Both of these tests are specific to school buses and are in addition to the testing required to receive a commercial license and the passenger endorsement.

*Other qualifications.* Many intercity and public transit bus companies prefer applicants who are at least 24 years old. Because bus drivers deal with passengers, they must be courteous. They need an even temperament and emotional stability because driving in heavy, fast-moving, or stop-and-go traffic and dealing with passengers can be stressful. Drivers must have strong customer service skills, including communication skills and the ability to coordinate and manage large groups of people. In some states, school bus drivers must pass a background investigation to uncover any criminal record or history of mental problems.

*Advancement.* New intercity and local transit drivers usually are placed on an "extra" list to drive chartered runs, extra buses on regular runs, and special runs, such as those during morning and evening rush hours and to sports events. New drivers also substitute for regular drivers who are ill or on vacation. New drivers remain on the extra list and may work only part time, perhaps for several years, until they have enough seniority to get a regular run.

Senior drivers may bid for the runs that they prefer, such as those with more work hours, lighter traffic, weekends off, or—in the case of intercity bus drivers—higher earnings or fewer workdays per week.

**Projections data from the National Employment Matrix**

| Occupational Title | SOC Code | Employment, 2006 | Projected employment, 2016 | Change, 2006-16 | |
|---|---|---|---|---|---|
| | | | | Number | Percent |
| Bus drivers .................................................................. | 53-3020 | 653,000 | 721,000 | 67,000 | 10 |
| Bus drivers, transit and intercity ................................. | 53-3021 | 198,000 | 223,000 | 25,000 | 13 |
| Bus drivers, school ..................................................... | 53-3022 | 455,000 | 497,000 | 42,000 | 9 |

NOTE: Data in this table are rounded.

Opportunities for promotion are generally limited. However, experienced drivers may become supervisors or dispatchers—assigning buses to drivers, checking whether drivers are on schedule, rerouting buses to avoid blocked streets or other problems, and dispatching extra vehicles and service crews to scenes of accidents and breakdowns. In transit agencies with rail systems, drivers may become train operators or station attendants. Some bus drivers become either instructors of new bus drivers or master-instructors, who train new instructors. Few drivers become managers. Promotion in publicly owned bus systems is often determined by competitive civil service examination. Some motor coach drivers purchase their own equipment and open their own business.

## Employment

Bus drivers held about 653,000 jobs in 2006. About 34 percent worked part time. Around 70 percent of all bus drivers were school bus drivers working primarily for school systems or for companies providing school bus services under contract. Most of the remainder worked for private and local government transit systems; some also worked for intercity and charter bus lines.

## Job Outlook

Average job growth and good employment opportunities are expected for bus drivers. Those seeking higher paying public transit bus driver positions may encounter competition. Individuals who have good driving records and who are willing to work a part-time or irregular schedule will probably have the best job prospects.

*Employment change.* Overall employment of bus drivers is expected to grow 10 percent between 2006 and 2016, about as fast as the average for all occupations. New drivers will be needed primarily to meet the transportation needs of the growing general population and school-aged population.

Employment growth for local transit and intercity bus drivers is projected to be 13 percent over the 2006–2016 decade, about as fast as average for all occupations, primarily because of the increasing popularity of mass transit due to congestion and rising fuel prices and the demand for transit services in expanding metropolitan areas. Competition from other modes of transportation—airplane, train, or automobile—will temper job growth among intercity bus drivers. Most growth in intercity bus transportation will occur in group charters to locations not served by other modes of transportation. Like automobiles, buses have a far greater number of possible destinations than airplanes or trains. Since they offer greater cost savings and convenience than automobiles do, buses usually are the most economical option for tour groups traveling to out-of-the-way destinations.

The number of school bus drivers is expected to increase 9 percent over the next 10 years, which is also about as fast as the average for all occupations. This growth is somewhat slower than in the past. School enrollments are projected to increase in 37 states, decrease in 12 states and stay constant in 1 state. However, the net effect will still be a slowdown in the rate of school enrollment and, therefore, in employment growth of school bus drivers. This, as well as the part-time nature of the occupation, will result in most openings for school bus drivers being to replace those who leave the occupation.

*Job prospects.* People seeking jobs as bus drivers likely will have good opportunities. Employment growth will create jobs, but most job openings are expected because of the need to replace workers who take jobs in other occupations or who retire or leave the occupation for other reasons.

Individuals who have good driving records and who are willing to work a part-time or irregular schedule probably will have the best job prospects. School bus driving jobs, particularly in rapidly growing suburban areas, should be easiest to acquire because most are part-time positions with high turnover and less training required than for other bus-driving jobs. Those seeking higher paying public transit bus driver positions may encounter competition. Opportunities for intercity driving positions should be good, although employment prospects for motor coach drivers will depend on tourism, which fluctuates with the economy.

Full-time bus drivers rarely are laid off during recessions. In local transit and intercity bus systems, if the number of passengers decreases, employers might reduce the hours of part-time bus drivers or consolidate routes since fewer buses would be required. Seasonal layoffs are common. Many intercity bus drivers with little seniority, for example, are furloughed during the winter when regularly scheduled and charter business declines. School bus drivers seldom work during the summer or school holidays.

## Earnings

Median hourly wage-and-salary earnings of transit and intercity bus drivers were $15.43 in May 2006. The middle 50 percent earned between $11.56 and $19.86 per hour. The lowest 10 percent earned less than $9.26, and the highest 10 percent earned more than $24.08 per hour. Median hourly earnings in the industries employing the largest numbers of transit and intercity bus drivers were

Interurban and rural bus transportation ................$17.16

Urban transit systems .........................................14.07

School and employee bus transportation.................12.35

Other transit and ground passenger transportation....11.51

Charter bus industry ...........................................11.50

Median hourly wage-and-salary earnings of school bus drivers were $11.93 in May 2006. The middle 50 percent earned between $8.99 and $14.82 per hour. The lowest 10 percent earned less than $6.58, and the highest 10 percent earned more than $17.61 per hour. Median hourly earnings in the industries employing the largest numbers of school bus drivers were

School and employee bus transportation................$12.55
Elementary and secondary schools ...........................11.59
Other transit and ground passenger transportation....11.11
Child day care services.............................................9.50
Individual and family services..................................9.17

The benefits bus drivers receive from their employers vary greatly. Most intercity and local transit bus drivers receive paid health and life insurance, sick leave, vacation leave, and free bus rides on any of the regular routes of their line or system. School bus drivers receive sick leave, and many are covered by health and life insurance and pension plans. Because they generally do not work when school is not in session, they do not get vacation leave.

About 41 percent of bus drivers were members of or were covered by union contracts in 2006. Many intercity and local transit bus drivers are members of the Amalgamated Transit Union. Some drivers belong to the United Transportation Union or to the International Brotherhood of Teamsters.

## Related Occupations

Other workers who drive vehicles on highways and city streets include taxi drivers and chauffeurs, and truck drivers and driver/sales workers. Some local transit bus drivers enter rail transportation occupations by becoming subway or light rail operators.

## Sources of Additional Information

For information on employment opportunities, contact local transit systems, intercity bus lines, school systems, or the local offices of the state employment service.

General information on school bus driving is available from

▸ National Association of State Directors of Pupil Transportation Services, P.O. Box 5446, Steamboat Springs, CO 80477. Internet: http://www.nasdpts.org

▸ National School Transportation Association, 113 South West St., 4th Floor, Alexandria, VA 22314. Internet: http://www.yellowbuses.org

General information on motor coach driving is available from

▸ United Motorcoach Association, 113 South West St., 4th Floor, Alexandria, VA 22314. Internet: http://www.uma.org

## Carpenters

(O*NET 47-2031.00, 47-2031.01, and 47-2031.02)

## Significant Points

■ About 32 percent of all carpenters—the largest construction trade—are self-employed.

■ Job opportunities should be best for those with the most training and skills.

■ Between 3 and 4 years of both on-the-job training and classroom instruction usually is needed to become a skilled carpenter.

## Nature of the Work

Carpenters are involved in many different kinds of construction, from the building of highways and bridges to the installation of kitchen cabinets. Carpenters construct, erect, install, and repair structures and fixtures made from wood and other materials.

Each carpentry task is somewhat different, but most involve the same basic steps. Working from blueprints or instructions from supervisors, carpenters first do the layout—measuring, marking, and arranging materials—in accordance with local building codes. They cut and shape wood, plastic, fiberglass, or drywall using hand and power tools, such as chisels, planes, saws, drills, and sanders. They then join the materials with nails, screws, staples, or adhesives. In the last step, carpenters do a final check of the accuracy of their work with levels, rules, plumb bobs, framing squares, and surveying equipment, and make any necessary adjustments.

When working with prefabricated components, such as stairs or wall panels, the carpenter's task is somewhat simpler because it does not require as much layout work or the cutting and assembly of as many pieces. Prefabricated components are designed for easy and fast installation and generally can be installed in a single operation.

Some carpenters do many different carpentry tasks, while others specialize in one or two. Carpenters who remodel homes and other structures, for example, need a broad range of carpentry skills. As part of a single job, for example, they might frame walls and partitions, put in doors and windows, build stairs, install cabinets and molding, and complete many other tasks. Because these carpenters are so well-trained, they often can switch from residential building to commercial construction or remodeling work, depending on which offers the best work opportunities.

Carpenters who work for large construction contractors or specialty contractors may perform only a few regular tasks, such as constructing wooden forms for pouring concrete, or erecting scaffolding. Some carpenters build tunnel bracing, or brattices, in underground passageways and mines to control the circulation of air through the passageways and to worksites. Others build concrete forms for tunnel, bridge, or sewer construction projects.

**Projections data from the National Employment Matrix**

| Occupational Title | SOC Code | Employment, 2006 | Projected employment, 2016 | Change, 2006-16 | |
|---|---|---|---|---|---|
| | | | | Number | Percent |
| Carpenters ................................................................. | 47-2031 | 1,462,000 | 1,612,000 | 150,000 | 10 |

NOTE: Data in this table are rounded.

Carpenters employed outside the construction industry perform a variety of installation and maintenance work. They may replace panes of glass, ceiling tiles, and doors, as well as repair desks, cabinets, and other furniture. Depending on the employer, carpenters install partitions, doors, and windows; change locks; and repair broken furniture. In manufacturing firms, carpenters may assist in moving or installing machinery.

*Work environment.* As is true of other building trades, carpentry work is sometimes strenuous. Prolonged standing, climbing, bending, and kneeling often are necessary. Carpenters risk injury working with sharp or rough materials, using sharp tools and power equipment, and working in situations where they might slip or fall. Although many carpenters work indoors, those that work outdoors are subject to variable weather conditions.

Most carpenters work a standard 40 hour week. Hours may be longer during busy periods.

## Training, Other Qualifications, and Advancement

Carpenters learn their trade through formal and informal training programs. Between three and four years of both on-the-job training and classroom instruction usually is needed to become a skilled carpenter. There are a number of ways to train, but a more formal training program often improves job opportunities.

*Education and training.* Learning to be a carpenter can start in high school. Classes in English, algebra, geometry, physics, mechanical drawing, blueprint reading, and general shop will prepare students for the further training they will need.

After high school, there are a number of different ways to obtain the necessary training. Some people get a job as a carpenter's helper, assisting more experienced workers. At the same time, the helper might attend a trade or vocational school, or community college to receive further trade-related training and eventually become a carpenter.

Some employers offer employees formal apprenticeships. These programs combine on-the-job training with related classroom instruction. Apprentices usually must be at least 18 years old and meet local requirements. Apprenticeship programs usually last three to four years, but length varies with the apprentice's skill.

On the job, apprentices learn elementary structural design and become familiar with common carpentry jobs, such as layout, form building, rough framing, and outside and inside finishing. They also learn to use the tools, machines, equipment, and materials of the trade. In the classroom, apprentices learn safety, first aid, blueprint reading, freehand sketching, basic mathematics, and various carpentry techniques. Both in the classroom and on the job, they learn the relationship between carpentry and the other building trades.

The number of apprenticeship programs is limited, however, so only a small proportion of carpenters learn their trade through these programs. Most apprenticeships are offered by commercial and industrial building contractors with union membership.

Some people who are interested in carpentry careers choose to get their classroom training before seeking a job. There are a number of public and private vocational-technical schools and training academies affiliated with unions and contractors that offer training to become a carpenter. Employers often look favorably upon these students and usually start them at a higher level than those without the training.

*Other qualifications.* Carpenters need manual dexterity, eye-hand coordination, physical fitness, and a good sense of balance. The ability to solve arithmetic problems quickly and accurately also is required. In addition, military service or a good work history is viewed favorably by employers.

*Certification and advancement.* Carpenters who complete formal apprenticeship programs receive certification as journeypersons. Some carpenters earn other certifications in scaffold building, high torque bolting, or pump work. These certifications prove that carpenters are able to perform these tasks, which can lead to additional responsibilities.

Carpenters usually have more opportunities than most other construction workers to become general construction supervisors because carpenters are exposed to the entire construction process. For those who would like to advance, it is increasingly important to be able to communicate in both English and Spanish in order to relay instructions and safety precautions to workers; Spanish-speaking workers make up a large part of the construction workforce in many areas. Carpenters may advance to carpentry supervisor or general construction supervisor positions. Others may become independent contractors. Supervisors and contractors need good communication skills to deal with clients and subcontractors. They should be able to identify and estimate the quantity of materials needed to complete a job and accurately estimate how long a job will take to complete and what it will cost.

## Employment

Carpenters are employed throughout the country in almost every community and make up the largest building trades occupation. They held about 1.5 million jobs in 2006.

About 32 percent worked in construction of buildings and about 23 percent worked for specialty trade contractors. Most of the rest of the wage and salary workers worked for manufacturing firms, government agencies, retail establishments, and a wide variety of other industries. About 32 percent of all carpenters were self-employed. Some carpenters change employers each time they finish a construction job. Others alternate between working for a contractor and working as contractors themselves on small jobs, depending on where the work is available.

## Job Outlook

Average job growth, coupled with replacement needs, create a large number of openings each year. Job opportunities should be best for those with the most training and skills.

*Employment change.* Employment of carpenters is expected to increase by 10 percent during the 2006–2016 decade, about as fast as the average for all occupations. The need for carpenters should grow as construction activity increases in response to demand for new housing and office and retail space, and for modernizing and expanding schools and industrial plants. A strong home remodeling market also will create demand for carpenters. Moreover, construction of roads and bridges as well as restaurants, hotels, and other businesses will increase the demand for carpenters in the coming decade.

Some of the demand for carpenters, however, will be offset by expected productivity gains resulting from the increasing use of prefabricated components and improved fasteners and tools. Prefabricated wall panels, roof assemblies, and stairs, as well as prehung doors and windows can be installed very quickly. Instead of having to be built on the worksite, prefabricated walls, partitions, and stairs can be lifted into place in one operation; beams and, in some cases, entire roof assemblies, are lifted into place using a crane. As prefabricated components become more standardized, builders will use them more often. In addition, improved adhesives are reducing the time needed to join materials, and lightweight, cordless, and pneumatic tools—such as nailers and drills—will all continue to make carpenters more productive. New and improved tools, equipment, techniques, and materials also have made carpenters more versatile, allowing them to perform more carpentry tasks.

*Job prospects.* Job opportunities should be best for those with the most training and skills. Job growth and replacement needs for those who leave the occupation create a large number of openings each year. Many people with limited skills take jobs as carpenters but eventually leave the occupation because they dislike the work or cannot find steady employment.

Carpenters with all-around skills will have better opportunities for steady work than carpenters who can perform only a few relatively simple, routine tasks. Carpenters can experience periods of unemployment because of the short-term nature of many construction projects, winter slowdowns in construction activity in northern areas, and the cyclical nature of the construction industry.

Employment of carpenters, like that of many other construction workers, is sensitive to the fluctuations of the economy. Workers in these trades may experience periods of unemployment when the overall level of construction falls. On the other hand, shortages of these workers may occur in some areas during peak periods of building activity.

Job opportunities for carpenters also vary by geographic area. Construction activity parallels the movement of people and businesses and reflects differences in local economic conditions. The areas with the largest population increases will also provide the best opportunities for jobs as carpenters and for apprenticeships for people seeking to become carpenters.

## Earnings

In May 2006, median hourly earnings of wage and salary carpenters were $17.57. The middle 50 percent earned between $13.55 and $23.85. The lowest 10 percent earned less than $10.87, and the highest 10 percent earned more than $30.45. Median hourly earnings in the industries employing the largest numbers of carpenters were as follows:

| | |
|---|---|
| Residential building construction | $17.39 |
| Foundation, structure, and building exterior contractors | 17.03 |
| Nonresidential building construction | 15.12 |
| Building finishing contractors | 13.76 |
| Employment services | 10.88 |

Earnings can be reduced on occasion, because carpenters lose work time in bad weather and during recessions when jobs are unavailable. Earnings may be increased by overtime during busy periods.

Some carpenters are members of the United Brotherhood of Carpenters and Joiners of America.

## Related Occupations

Carpenters are skilled construction workers. Other skilled construction occupations include brickmasons, blockmasons, and stonemasons; cement masons, concrete finishers, segmental pavers, and terrazzo workers; drywall installers, ceiling tile installers, and tapers; electricians; pipelayers, plumbers, pipefitters, and steamfitters; and plasterers and stucco masons.

## Sources of Additional Information

For information about carpentry apprenticeships or other work opportunities in this trade, contact local carpentry contractors, locals of the union mentioned above, local joint union-contractor apprenticeship committees, or the nearest office of the state employment service or apprenticeship agency. You can also find information on the registered apprenticeship system with links to state apprenticeship programs on the U.S. Department of Labor's Web site: http://www.doleta.gov/atels_bat. Apprenticeship information is also available from the U.S. Department of Labor's toll free helpline: 1 (877) 872-5627.

For information on training opportunities and carpentry in general, contact

- ▶ Associated Builders and Contractors, 4250 North Fairfax Dr., 9th Floor, Arlington, VA 22203. Internet: http://www.trytools.org
- ▶ Associated General Contractors of America, Inc., 2300 Wilson Blvd., Suite 400, Arlington, VA 22201. Internet: http://www.agc.org
- ▶ National Center for Construction Education and Research, 3600 NW 43rd St., Bldg. G, Gainesville, FL 32606. Internet: http://www.nccer.org
- ▶ National Association of Home Builders, Home Builders Institute, 1201 15th St. NW, Washington, DC 20005. Internet: http://www.hbi.org
- ▶ United Brotherhood of Carpenters and Joiners of America, Carpenters Training Fund, 6801 Placid St., Las Vegas, NV 89119. Internet: http://www.carpenters.org

For general information on apprenticeships and how to get them, see the *Occupational Outlook Quarterly* article "Apprenticeships: Career training, credentials—and a paycheck in your pocket," online at http://www.bls.gov/opub/ooq/2002/summer/art01.pdf and in print at many libraries and career centers.

## Chefs, Cooks, and Food Preparation Workers

(O*NET 35-1011.00, 35-2011.00, 35-2012.00, 35-2013.00, 35-2014.00, 35-2015.00, 35-2019.99, and 35-2021.00)

## Significant Points

- Many cooks and food preparation workers are young—37 percent are below the age of 24.
- One-third of these workers are employed part time.
- Job openings are expected to be plentiful because many of these workers will leave the occupation for full-time employment or better wages.

## Nature of the Work

Chefs, cooks, and food preparation workers prepare, season, and cook a wide range of foods—from soups, snacks, and salads to entrees, side dishes, and desserts. They work in a variety of restaurants and other food services establishments. Chefs and cooks create recipes and prepare meals, while food preparation workers peel and cut vegetables, trim meat, prepare poultry, and perform other duties, such as keeping work areas clean and monitoring temperatures of ovens and stovetops.

Specifically, *chefs* and *cooks* measure, mix, and cook ingredients according to recipes, using a variety of equipment, including pots, pans, cutlery, ovens, broilers, grills, slicers, grinders, and blenders. Chefs and head cooks also are responsible for directing the work of other kitchen workers, estimating food requirements, and ordering food supplies.

*Food preparation workers* perform routine, repetitive tasks under the direction of chefs and cooks. These workers ready the ingredients for complex dishes by slicing and dicing vegetables, and composing salads and cold items. They weigh and measure ingredients, go after pots and pans, and stir and strain soups and sauces. Food preparation workers may cut and grind meats, poultry, and seafood in preparation for cooking. They also clean work areas, equipment, utensils, dishes, and silverware.

Larger restaurants and food services establishments tend to have varied menus and larger kitchen staffs. Staffs often include several chefs and cooks, sometimes called assistant or line cooks. Each chef or cook works an assigned station that is equipped with the types of stoves, grills, pans, and ingredients needed for the foods prepared at that station. Job titles often reflect the principal ingredient prepared or the type of cooking performed—vegetable cook, fry cook, or grill cook, for example. These cooks also may direct or work with other food preparation workers.

*Executive chefs* and *head cooks* coordinate the work of the kitchen staff and direct the preparation of meals. They determine serving sizes, plan menus, order food supplies, and oversee kitchen operations to ensure uniform quality and presentation of meals. An executive chef, for example, is in charge of all food service operations and also may supervise the many kitchens of a hotel, restaurant group, or corporate dining operation. A *chef de cuisine* reports to an executive chef and is responsible for the daily operations of a single kitchen. A *sous chef*, or sub chef, is the second-in-command and runs the kitchen in the absence of the chef. Many chefs earn fame both for themselves and for their kitchens because of the quality and distinctive nature of the food they serve.

Responsibilities depend on where cooks work. *Institution and cafeteria cooks*, for example, work in the kitchens of schools, cafeterias, businesses, hospitals, and other institutions. For each meal, they prepare a large quantity of a limited number of entrees, vegetables, and desserts according to preset menus. Meals generally are prepared in advance so diners seldom get the opportunity to special order a meal. *Restaurant cooks* usually prepare a wider selection of dishes, cooking most orders individually. *Short-order cooks* prepare foods in restaurants and coffee shops that emphasize fast service and quick food preparation. They grill and garnish hamburgers, prepare sandwiches, fry eggs, and cook French fries, often working on several orders at the same time. *Fast-food cooks* prepare a limited selection of menu items in fast-food restaurants. They cook and package batches of food, such as hamburgers and fried chicken, to be kept warm until served.

The number and types of workers employed in kitchens also depends on the type of establishment. Small, full-service restaurants offering casual dining often feature a limited number of easy-to-prepare items supplemented by short-order specialties and ready-made desserts. Typically, one cook prepares all the food with the help of a short-order cook and one or two other kitchen workers.

Grocery and specialty food stores employ chefs, cooks, and food preparation workers to develop recipes and prepare meals for customers to carry out. Typically, entrees, side dishes, salads, or other items are prepared in large quantities and stored at an appropriate temperature. Counter assistants portion and package items according to customer orders for serving at home.

Some cooks, called research chefs, combine culinary skills with knowledge of food science to develop recipes for chain restaurants and food processors and manufacturers. They test new formulas and flavors for prepared foods and determine the most efficient and safest way to prepare new foods.

Some cooks work for individuals rather than for restaurants, cafeterias, or food manufacturers. These *private household cooks* plan and prepare meals in private homes according to the client's tastes or dietary needs. They order groceries and supplies, clean the kitchen, and wash dishes and utensils. They also may serve meals. Private chefs are employed directly by a single individual or family or sometimes by corporations or institutions, such as universities and embassies, to perform cooking and entertaining tasks. These chefs usually live in and may travel with their employer. Because of the sensitive nature of their employment, they are usually required to sign confidentiality agreements. As part of the job, private chefs often perform additional services, such as paying bills, coordinating schedules, and planning events.

Another type of private household cooks, called personal chefs, usually prepare a week's worth of meals in the client's home for the client to heat and serve according to directions throughout the week. Personal chefs are self-employed or employed by a company that provides this service.

*Work environment.* Many restaurant and institutional kitchens have modern equipment, convenient work areas, and air conditioning, but kitchens in older and smaller eating places are often not as well designed. Kitchen staffs invariably work in small quarters against hot stoves and ovens. They are under constant pressure to prepare meals quickly, while ensuring quality is maintained and safety and sanitation guidelines are observed. Because the pace can be hectic during peak dining times, workers must be able to communicate clearly so that food orders are completed correctly.

Working conditions vary with the type and quantity of food prepared and the local laws governing food service operations. Workers usually must stand for hours at a time, lifting heavy pots and kettles, and working near hot ovens and grills. Job hazards include slips and falls, cuts, and burns, but injuries are seldom serious.

Work hours in restaurants may include early mornings, late evenings, holidays, and weekends. Work schedules of chefs, cooks and other kitchen workers in factory and school cafeterias may be more regular. In 2006, about 29 percent of cooks and 44 percent of food preparation workers had part-time schedules, compared to 15 percent of workers throughout the economy. Work schedules in fine-dining restaurants, however, tend to be longer because of the time required to prepare ingredients in advance. Many executive chefs regularly work 12-hour days because they oversee the delivery of foodstuffs early in the day, plan the menu, and prepare those menu items that take the most skill.

The wide range in dining hours and the need for fully-staffed kitchens during all open hours creates work opportunities for students, youth, and other individuals seeking supplemental income, flexible work hours, or variable schedules. Eighteen percent of cooks and food preparation workers were 16 to 19 years old in 2006; nineteen percent were age 20 to 24. Ten percent had variable schedules. Kitchen workers employed by schools may work during the school year only, usually for 9 or 10 months. Similarly, resort establishments usually only offer seasonal employment.

## Training, Other Qualifications, and Advancement

On-the-job training is most common for fast-food cooks, short-order cooks, and food preparation workers. Chefs and others with more advanced cooking duties often attend cooking school. Vocational training programs are available to many high school students, but advanced positions usually require training after high school. Experience, an ability to develop and enhance cooking skills, and a strong desire to cook are the most common requirements for advancement.

*Education and training.* A high school diploma is not required for beginning jobs, but it is recommended for those planning a career as a cook or chef. Most fast-food or short-order cooks and food preparation workers require little education or training to start because most skills are learned on the job. Training generally starts with basic sanitation and workplace safety and continues with instruction on food handling, preparation, and cooking procedures. Training in food handling, sanitation, and health and safety procedures are mandatory in most jurisdictions for all workers. Those who become proficient and who show an interest in learning complicated cooking techniques may advance to more demanding cooking positions or into supervisory positions.

Some high school or vocational school programs offer courses in basic food safety and handling procedures, cooking, and general business and computer classes that can be helpful for those who might someday want to be a chef or to open their own restaurant. Many school districts, in cooperation with state departments of education, provide on-the-job training and summer workshops for cafeteria kitchen workers who aspire to become cooks. Food service management companies or hotel and restaurant chains, also offer paid internships and summer jobs to those starting out in the field. Internships provide valuable experience and can lead to placement in more formal chef training programs.

When hiring chefs and others in advanced cooking positions, however, employers usually prefer applicants who have training after high school. These training programs range from a few months to two years or more. Vocational or trade-school programs typically offer basic training in food handling and sanitation procedures, nutrition, slicing and dicing methods for various kinds of meats and vegetables, and basic cooking methods, such as baking, broiling, and grilling. Longer programs leading to a certificate or a two- or four-year degree train chefs for fine-dining or upscale restaurants. They offer a wider array of training specialties, such as advanced cooking techniques; cooking for banquets, buffets, or parties; and cuisines and cooking styles from around the world.

A growing number of chefs participate in these longer training programs through independent cooking schools, professional culinary institutes, two- or four-year college degree programs in hospitality or culinary arts, or in the armed forces. Some large hotels and restaurants also operate their own training and job-placement programs for chefs and cooks. Executive chefs and head cooks who work in fine-dining restaurants require many years of training and experience and an intense desire to cook.

Although curricula may vary, students in culinary training programs spend most of their time in kitchens learning to prepare meals by practicing cooking skills. They learn good knife techniques and proper use and care of kitchen equipment. Training programs also include courses in nutrition, menu planning, portion control, purchasing and inventory methods, proper food storage procedures, and use of leftover food to minimize waste. Students also learn sanitation and public health rules for handling food. Training in food service management, computer accounting and inventory software, and banquet service are featured in some training programs. Most formal training programs also require students to get experience in a commercial kitchen through an internship, apprenticeship, or out-placement program.

Many chefs are trained on the job, receiving real work experience and training from chef-mentors in the restaurants where they work. Professional culinary institutes, industry associations, and trade unions sponsor formal apprenticeship programs in coordination with the U.S. Department of Labor.

The American Culinary Federation accredits more than 200 formal academic training programs and sponsors apprenticeship programs around the country. Typical apprenticeships last two years and combine classroom training and work experience. Accreditation is an indication that a culinary program meets recognized standards regarding course content, facilities, and quality of instruction.

*Other qualifications.* Chefs, cooks, and food preparation workers must be efficient, quick, and work well as part of a team. Manual dexterity is helpful for cutting, chopping, and plating. These workers also need creativity and a keen sense of taste and smell. Personal cleanliness is essential because most states require health certificates indicating that workers are free from communicable diseases. Knowledge of a foreign language can be an asset because it may improve communication with other restaurant staff, vendors, and the restaurant's clientele.

*Certification and advancement.* The American Culinary Federation certifies pastry professionals, personal chefs, and culinary educators in addition to various levels of chefs. Certification standards are based primarily on experience and formal training. Although certification is not required, it can help to prove accomplishment and lead to advancement and higher-paying positions.

Advancement opportunities for chefs, cooks, and food preparation workers depend on their training, work experience, and ability to perform more responsible and sophisticated tasks. Many food preparation workers, for example, may move into assistant or line cook positions. Chefs and cooks who demonstrate an eagerness to learn new cooking skills and to accept greater responsibility may also move up and be asked to train or supervise lesser skilled kitchen staff. Others may move to larger or more prestigious kitchens and restaurants.

Some chefs and cooks go into business as caterers or personal chefs or open their own restaurant. Others become instructors in culinary training programs. A number of cooks and chefs advance to executive chef positions or food service management positions, particularly in hotels, clubs, or larger, more elegant restaurants.

## Employment

Chefs, cooks, and food preparation workers held 3.1 million jobs in 2006. The distribution of jobs among the various types of chefs, cooks, and food preparation workers was as follows:

| | |
|---|---|
| Food preparation workers | 902,000 |
| Cooks, restaurant | 850,000 |
| Cooks, fast food | 629,000 |
| Cooks, institution and cafeteria | 401,000 |
| Cooks, short order | 195,000 |
| Chefs and head cooks | 115,000 |
| Cooks, private household | 4,900 |
| Cooks, all other | 16,000 |

Two-thirds of all chefs, cooks, and food preparation workers were employed in restaurants and other food services and drinking places. About 15 percent worked in institutions such as schools, universities, hospitals, and nursing care facilities. Grocery stores, hotels, and gasoline stations with convenience stores employed most of the remainder.

## Job Outlook

Job opportunities for chefs, cooks, and food preparation workers are expected to be plentiful because of the continued growth and expansion of food services outlets, resulting in average employment growth, and because of the large numbers of workers who leave these occupations and need to be replaced. However, those seeking the highest-paying positions will face keen competition.

*Employment change.* Employment of chefs, cooks, and food preparation workers is expected to increase by 11 percent over the 2006–2016 decade, which is about as fast as the average for all occupations. This occupation will have among the largest numbers of new jobs arise, about 351,000 over the period. Growth will be spurred by increases in population, household income, and demand for convenience that will lead to more people dining out and taking vacations that include hotel stays and restaurant visits. In addition, employment of chefs, cooks, and food preparation workers who prepare meals-to-go, such as those who work in the prepared foods sections of grocery or specialty food stores, should grow faster than average as these stores compete with restaurants for people's food dollars. Also, there is a growing consumer desire for convenient, healthier, made-from-scratch meals.

Projected employment growth varies by detailed occupation. The number of higher-skilled chefs and cooks working in full-service restaurants—those that offer table service and more varied menus— is expected to increase about as fast as the average for all occupations. Much of this increase will come from job growth in more casual dining settings, rather than in up-scale full-service restaurants. Dining trends suggest that an increasing number of meals are eaten away from home, which creates growth in family dining restaurants, but greater limits on expense-account meals is expected to generate slower growth for up-scale restaurants.

Employment of food preparation workers is expected to grow faster than the average for all occupations, reflecting diners' desires for convenience as they shop for carryout meals in a greater variety of places, including full-service restaurants, limited-service eating places, and grocery stores.

Employment of fast-food cooks is expected to grow about as fast as the average for all occupations. Duties of cooks in fast-food restaurants are limited; most workers are likely to be combined food preparation and serving workers, rather than fast-food cooks. Employment of short-order cooks is expected to increase more slowly than average.

Employment of institution and cafeteria chefs and cooks will show growth about as fast as the average. Their employment will not keep pace with the rapid growth in the educational and health services industries—where their employment is concentrated. Offices, schools, and hospitals increasingly contract out their food services in an effort to make "institutional food" more attractive to office workers, students, staff, visitors, and patients. Much of the growth of these workers will be in contract food service establishments that provide catering services or food management and staff for employee dining rooms, sports complexes, convention centers, and educational or health care facilities.

Employment of private household cooks is projected to grow by 9 percent, about as fast as the average. While the employment of personal chefs is expected to increase—reflecting the growing popular-

**Projections data from the National Employment Matrix**

| Occupational Title | SOC Code | Employment, 2006 | Projected employment, 2016 | Change, 2006-16 | |
|---|---|---|---|---|---|
| | | | | Number | Percent |
| Chefs, cooks, and food preparation workers..................................... | — | 3,113,000 | 3,464,000 | 351,000 | 11 |
| Chefs and head cooks......................................................... | 35-1011 | 115,000 | 124,000 | 8,700 | 8 |
| Cooks and food preparation workers ............................................ | 35-2000 | 2,998,000 | 3,340,000 | 342,000 | 11 |
| Cooks ...................................................... | 35-2010 | 2,097,000 | 2,301,000 | 204,000 | 10 |
| Cooks, fast food ........................................ | 35-2011 | 629,000 | 681,000 | 52,000 | 8 |
| Cooks, institution and cafeteria................... | 35-2012 | 401,000 | 445,000 | 43,000 | 11 |
| Cooks, private household................................ | 35-2013 | 4,900 | 5,400 | 400 | 9 |
| Cooks, restaurant.......................................... | 35-2014 | 850,000 | 948,000 | 98,000 | 12 |
| Cooks, short order........................................ | 35-2015 | 195,000 | 205,000 | 9,500 | 5 |
| Cooks, all other ........................................... | 35-2019 | 16,000 | 16,000 | 500 | 3 |
| Food preparation workers ....................................................... | 35-2021 | 902,000 | 1,040,000 | 138,000 | 15 |

NOTE: Data in this table are rounded.

ity and convenience of eating restaurant-quality meals at home—the number of private chefs will not grow as fast, reflecting slower growth in private household service employment.

*Job prospects.* Job openings for chefs, cooks, and food preparation workers are expected to be plentiful through 2016; however, competition should be keen for jobs in the top kitchens of higher end restaurants. Although job growth will create many new positions, the overwhelming majority of job openings will stem from the need to replace workers who leave this large occupational group. Many chef, cook, and food preparation worker jobs are attractive to people seeking first-time or short-term employment, additional income, or a flexible schedule. Employers typically hire a large number of part-time workers, but many of these workers soon transfer to other occupations or stop working, creating numerous openings for those entering the field. At higher end restaurants, the fast pace, long hours, and high energy levels required to succeed also cause some top chefs and cooks to leave for other jobs, creating job openings.

# Earnings

Earnings of chefs, cooks, and food preparation workers vary greatly by region and the type of employer. Earnings usually are highest in elegant restaurants and hotels, where many executive chefs are employed, and in major metropolitan and resort areas.

Median annual wage-and-salary earnings of chefs and head cooks were $34,370 in May 2006. The middle 50 percent earned between $25,910 and $46,040. The lowest 10 percent earned less than $20,160, and the highest 10 percent earned more than $60,730. Median annual earnings in the industries employing the largest number of chefs and head cooks were

| | |
|---|---|
| Other amusement and recreation industries ..........$46,460 | |
| Traveler accommodation ........................................40,020 | |
| Special food services ...........................................36,450 | |
| Full-service restaurants.........................................32,360 | |
| Limited-service eating places ...............................27,560 | |

Median annual wage-and-salary earnings of cooks, private household were $22,870 in May 2006. The middle 50 percent earned between $17,960 and $31,050. The lowest 10 percent earned less than $14,690, and the highest 10 percent earned more than $55,040.

Median annual wage-and-and salary earnings of institution and cafeteria cooks were $20,410 in May 2006. The middle 50 percent earned between $16,280 and $25,280. The lowest 10 percent earned less than $13,450, and the highest 10 percent earned more than $30,770. Median annual earnings in the industries employing the largest numbers of institution and cafeteria cooks were

| | |
|---|---|
| General medical and surgical hospitals ................$22,980 | |
| Special food services ...........................................21,650 | |
| Community care facilities for the elderly................20,910 | |
| Nursing care facilities ..........................................20,470 | |
| Elementary and secondary schools ........................18,770 | |

Median annual wage-and-salary earnings of restaurant cooks were $20,340 in May 2006. The middle 50 percent earned between $16,860 and $24,260. The lowest 10 percent earned less than $14,370, and the highest 10 percent earned more than $28,850. Median annual earnings in the industries employing the largest numbers of restaurant cooks were

| | |
|---|---|
| Traveler accommodations ...................................$23,400 | |
| Full-service restaurants.........................................20,100 | |
| Limited-service eating places ...............................18,200 | |

Median annual wage-and-salary earnings of short-order cooks were $17,880 in May 2006. The middle 50 percent earned between $14,960 and $21,820. The lowest 10 percent earned less than $12,930, and the highest 10 percent earned more than $26,110. Median annual earnings in full-service restaurants were $18,340.

Median annual wage-and-salary earnings of food preparation workers were $17,410 in May 2006. The middle 50 percent earned between $14,920 and $21,230. The lowest 10 percent earned less than $13,190, and the highest 10 percent earned more than $25,940. Median annual earnings in the industries employing the largest number of food preparation workers were

| | |
|---|---|
| Grocery stores ..................................................$18,920 | |
| Full-service restaurants.........................................17,390 | |
| Limited-service eating places ...............................15,550 | |

Median annual wage-and-salary earnings of fast-food cooks were $15,410 in May 2006. The middle 50 percent earned between $13,730 and $17,700. The lowest 10 percent earned less than

$12,170, and the highest 10 percent earned more than $20,770. Median annual earnings were $15,360 in full-service restaurants and $15,350 in limited-service eating places.

Some employers provide employees with uniforms and free meals, but federal law permits employers to deduct from their employees' wages the cost or fair value of any meals or lodging provided, and some employers do so. Chefs, cooks, and food preparation workers who work full time often receive typical benefits, but part-time and hourly workers usually do not.

In some large hotels and restaurants, kitchen workers belong to unions. The principal unions are the Hotel Employees and Restaurant Employees International Union and the Service Employees International Union.

## Related Occupations

People who perform tasks similar to those of chefs, cooks, and food preparation workers include those in food processing occupations, such as butchers and meat cutters, and bakers. Others who work closely with these workers include food service managers and food and beverage serving and related workers.

## Sources of Additional Information

Information about job opportunities may be obtained from local employers and local offices of the state employment service.

Career information about chefs, cooks, and other kitchen workers, including a directory of two- and four-year colleges that offer courses or training programs is available from

▸ National Restaurant Association, 1200 17th St. NW, Washington, DC 20036. Internet: http://www.restaurant.org

Information on the American Culinary Federation's apprenticeship and certification programs for cooks and a list of accredited culinary programs is available from

▸ American Culinary Federation, 180 Center Place Way, St. Augustine, FL 32095. Internet: http://www.acfchefs.org

For information about becoming a personal or private chef, contact

▸ American Personal & Private Chef Association, 4572 Delaware St., San Diego, CA 92116. Internet: http://www.personalchef.com

For information about culinary apprenticeship programs registered with the U.S. Department of Labor, contact the local office of your state employment service agency, check the department's apprenticeship web site: http://www.doleta.gov/atels_bat, or call the toll free helpline: (877) 872-5627.

## Child Care Workers

(O*NET 39-9011.00 and 39-9011.01)

### Significant Points

- About 35 percent of child care workers are self-employed, most of whom provided child care in their homes.

- Training requirements range from a high school diploma to a college degree, although a high school diploma and a little experience are adequate for many jobs.

- Many workers leave these jobs every year, creating good job opportunities.

### Nature of the Work

Child care workers nurture and care for children who have not yet entered formal schooling. They also supervise older children before and after school. These workers play an important role in children's development by caring for them when parents are at work or away for other reasons. In addition to attending to children's basic needs, child care workers organize activities and implement curricula that stimulate children's physical, emotional, intellectual, and social growth. They help children explore individual interests, develop talents and independence, build self-esteem, and learn how to get along with others.

Child care workers generally are classified into three different groups based on where they work: private household workers, who care for children at the children's home; family child care providers, who care for children in the provider's own home; and child care workers who work at separate child care centers.

Private household workers who are employed on an hourly basis usually are called *babysitters*. These child care workers bathe, dress, and feed children; supervise their play; wash their clothes; and clean their rooms. Babysitters also may put children to bed and wake them, read to them, involve them in educational games, take them for doctors' visits, and discipline them. Those who are in charge of infants, sometimes called *infant nurses*, also prepare bottles and change diapers. *Nannies* for a single family. They generally take care of children from birth to age 12, tending to the child's early education, nutrition, health, and other needs. They also may perform the duties of a housekeeper, including cleaning and laundry.

Family child care providers often work alone with a small group of children, though some work in larger settings with multiple adults. Child care centers generally have more than one adult per group of children; in groups of older children, a child care worker may assist a more experienced preschool teacher.

Most child care workers perform a combination of basic care and teaching duties, but the majority of their time is spent on care giving activities. Workers whose primary responsibility is teaching are classified as preschool teachers. However, many basic care activities also are opportunities for children to learn. For example, a worker who shows a child how to tie a shoelace teaches the child while also providing for that child's basic needs.

Child care workers spend most of their day working with children. However, they do maintain contact with parents or guardians through informal meetings or scheduled conferences to discuss each child's progress and needs. Many child care workers keep records of each child's progress and suggest ways in which parents can stimulate their child's learning and development at home. Some child care centers and before- and after-school programs actively recruit parent volunteers to work with the children and participate in administrative decisions and program planning.

Young children learn mainly through play. Child care workers recognize this and capitalize on children's play to further language development (storytelling and acting games), improve social skills (working together to build a neighborhood in a sandbox), and introduce scientific and mathematical concepts (balancing and counting blocks when building a bridge or mixing colors when painting). Often a less structured approach is used to teach young children, including small-group lessons; one-on-one instruction; and creative activities such as art, dance, and music. Child care workers play a vital role in preparing children to build the skills they will need in school.

Child care workers in child care centers or family child care homes greet young children as they arrive, help them with their jackets, and select an activity of interest. When caring for infants, they feed and change them. To ensure a well-balanced program, child care workers prepare daily and long-term schedules of activities. Each day's activities balance individual and group play, as well as quiet and active time. Children are given some freedom to participate in activities in which they are interested. As children age, child care workers may provide more guided learning opportunities, particularly in the areas of math and reading.

Concern over school-aged children being home alone before and after school has spurred many parents to seek alternative ways for their children to constructively spend their time. The purpose of before- and after-school programs is to watch over school-aged children during the gap between school hours and the end of their parents' daily work hours. These programs also may operate during the summer and on weekends. Workers in before- and after-school programs may help students with their homework or engage them in other extracurricular activities. These activities may include field trips, sports, or learning about computers, painting, photography, or other fun subjects. Some child care workers are responsible for taking children to school in the morning and picking them up from school in the afternoon. Before- and after-school programs may be operated by public school systems, local community centers, or other private organizations.

Helping to keep children healthy is another important part of the job. Child care workers serve nutritious meals and snacks and teach good eating habits and personal hygiene. They ensure that children have proper rest periods. They identify children who may not feel well and, in some cases, may help parents locate programs that will provide basic health services. Child care workers also watch for children who show signs of emotional or developmental problems and discuss these matters with their supervisor and the child's parents. Early identification of children with special needs—such as those with behavioral, emotional, physical, or learning disabilities—is important to improve their future learning ability. Special education

teachers often work with preschool children to provide the individual attention they need.

*Work environment.* Helping children grow, learn, and gain new skills can be very rewarding. The work is sometimes routine but new activities and challenges mark each day. Child care can be physically and emotionally taxing, as workers constantly stand, walk, bend, stoop, and lift to attend to each child's interests and problems.

States regulate child care facilities, the number of children per child care worker, staff qualifications, and the health and safety of the children. State regulations in all of these areas vary. To ensure that children in child care centers receive proper supervision, state or local regulations may require a certain ratio of workers to children. The ratio varies with the age of the children. Child development experts generally recommend that a single caregiver be responsible for no more than 3 or 4 infants (less than 1 year old) and toddler's (1 to 2 years old) or 6 or 7 preschool-aged children (between 2 and 5 years old). In before- and after-school programs, workers may be responsible for many school-aged children at a time.

Family child care providers work out of their own homes. While this arrangement provides convenience, it also requires that their homes be accommodating to young children. Private household workers usually work in the homes or apartments of their employers. Most live in their own homes and travel to work, though some live in the home of their employer and generally are provided with their own room and bath. They often come to feel like part of their employer's family.

The work hours of child care workers vary widely. Child care centers usually are open year round, with long hours so that parents can drop off and pick up their children before and after work. Some centers employ full-time and part-time staff with staggered shifts to cover the entire day. Some workers are unable to take regular breaks during the day due to limited staffing. Public and many private preschool programs operate during the typical 9- or 10-month school year, employing both full-time and part-time workers. Family child care providers have flexible hours and daily routines, but they may work long or unusual hours to fit parents' work schedules. Live-in nannies usually work longer hours than do those who have their own homes. However, although nannies may work evenings or weekends, they usually get other time off.

# Training, Other Qualifications, and Advancement

Licensure and training requirements vary greatly by state, but many jobs require little more than a high school diploma.

*Education and training.* The training and qualifications required of child care workers vary widely. Each state has its own licensing requirements that regulate caregiver training. These requirements range from a high school diploma, a national Child Development Associate (CDA) credential to community college courses or a college degree in child development or early childhood education. State requirements are generally higher for workers at child care centers than for family child care providers. Child care workers in private settings who care for only a few children often are not regulated by states at all. Child care workers generally can obtain some form of employment with a high school diploma and little or no experience,

Projections data from the National Employment Matrix

| Occupational Title | SOC Code | Employment, 2006 | Projected employment, 2016 | Change, 2006-16 | |
|---|---|---|---|---|---|
| | | | | Number | Percent |
| Child care workers ............................................................. | 39-9011 | 1,388,000 | 1,636,000 | 248,000 | 18 |

NOTE: Data in this table are rounded.

but certain private firms and publicly funded programs have more demanding training and education requirements. Some employers may prefer workers who have taken secondary or postsecondary courses in child development and early childhood education or who have work experience in a child care setting. Other employers require their own specialized training. An increasing number of employers require an associate degree in early childhood education.

*Licensure.* Many states require child care centers, including those in private homes, to be licensed if they care for more than a few children. In order to obtain their license, child care centers may require child care workers to pass a background check and get immunizations. Furthermore, child care workers may need to be trained in first aid and CPR and receive continuous training on topics of health and safety.

*Other qualifications.* Child care workers must anticipate and prevent problems, deal with disruptive children, provide fair but firm discipline, and be enthusiastic and constantly alert. They must communicate effectively with the children and their parents, as well as with teachers and other child care workers. Workers should be mature, patient, understanding, and articulate and have energy and physical stamina. Skills in music, art, drama, and storytelling also are important. Self-employed child care workers must have business sense and management abilities.

*Certification and advancement.* Some employers prefer to hire child care workers who have earned a nationally recognized Child Development Associate (CDA) credential or the Certified Childcare Professional (CCP) designation from the Council for Professional Recognition and the National Child Care Association, respectively. Requirements include child care experience and coursework, such as college courses or employer-provided seminars.

Opportunities for advancement are limited. However, as child care workers gain experience, some may advance to supervisory or administrative positions in large child care centers or preschools. Often, these positions require additional training, such as a bachelor's or master's degree. Other workers move on to work in resource and referral agencies, consulting with parents on available child services. A few workers become involved in policy or advocacy work related to child care and early childhood education. With a bachelor's degree, workers may become preschool teachers or become certified to teach in public or private schools. Some workers set up their own child care businesses.

## Employment

Child care workers held about 1.4 million jobs in 2006. Many worked part time. About 35 percent of child care workers were self-employed; most of these were family child care providers.

Child day care services employed about 18 percent of all child care workers and about 20 percent work for private households. The remainder worked primarily in educational services; nursing and residential care facilities; religious organizations; amusement and recreation industries; civic and social organizations; individual and family services; and local government, excluding education and hospitals. Some child care programs are for-profit centers, which may be affiliated with a local or national company. Religious institutions, community agencies, school systems, and state and local governments operate nonprofit programs. A very small percentage of private industry establishments operate onsite child care centers for the children of their employees.

## Job Outlook

Child care workers are expected to experience job growth that is faster than the average for all occupations. Job prospects will be excellent because of the many workers who leave and need to be replaced.

*Employment change.* Employment of child care workers is projected to increase by 18 percent between 2006 and 2016, which is faster than the average for all occupations. Child care workers will have a very large number of new jobs arise, almost 248,000 over the projections decade. The proportion of children being cared for exclusively by parents or other relatives is likely to continue to decline, spurring demand for additional child care workers. Concern about the safety and supervision of school-aged children during nonschool hours also should increase demand for before- and after-school programs and the child care workers who staff them.

The growth in demand for child care workers will be moderated, however, by an increasing emphasis on early childhood education programs, which hire mostly preschool workers instead of child care workers. While only a few states currently provide targeted or universal preschool programs, many more are considering or starting such programs. A rise in enrollment in private preschools is likely as the value of formal education before kindergarten becomes more widely accepted. Since the majority of workers in these programs are classified as preschool teachers, this growth in preschool enrollment will mean less growth among child care workers.

*Job prospects.* High replacement needs should create good job opportunities for child care workers. Qualified persons who are interested in this work should have little trouble finding and keeping a job. Many child care workers must be replaced each year as they leave the occupation to fulfill family responsibilities, to study, or for other reasons. Others leave because they are interested in pursuing other occupations or because of low wages.

## Earnings

Pay depends on the educational attainment of the worker and the type of establishment. Although the pay generally is very low, more education usually means higher earnings. Median annual earnings of wage-and-salary child care workers were $17,630 in May 2006. The middle 50 percent earned between $14,790 and $21,930. The lowest 10 percent earned less than $12,910, and the highest 10 percent earned more than $27,050. Median annual earnings in the industries employing the largest numbers of child care workers in 2006 were as follows:

| | |
|---|---|
| Other residential care facilities | $20,770 |
| Elementary and secondary schools | 20,220 |
| Civic and social organizations | 16,460 |
| Child day care services | 16,320 |
| Other amusement and recreation industries | 16,300 |

Earnings of self-employed child care workers vary depending on the number of hours worked, the number and ages of the children, and the location.

Benefits vary but are minimal for most child care workers. Many employers offer free or discounted child care to employees. Some offer a full benefits package, including health insurance and paid vacations, but others offer no benefits at all. Some employers offer seminars and workshops to help workers learn new skills. A few are willing to cover the cost of courses taken at community colleges or technical schools. Live-in nannies receive free room and board.

## Related Occupations

Child care work requires patience; creativity; an ability to nurture, motivate, teach, and influence children; and leadership, organizational, and administrative skills. Others who work with children and need these qualities and skills include teacher assistants; teachers—preschool, kindergarten, elementary, middle, and secondary; and teachers—special education.

## Sources of Additional Information

For an electronic question-and-answer service on child care, information on becoming a child care provider, and other resources, contact

▸ National Child Care Information Center, 243 Church St. NW, 2nd floor, Vienna, VA 22180. Internet: http://www.nccic.org

For eligibility requirements and a description of the Child Development Associate credential, contact

▸ Council for Professional Recognition, 2460 16th St. NW, Washington, DC 20009-3575. Internet: http://www.cdacouncil.org

For eligibility requirements and a description of the Certified Childcare Professional designation, contact

▸ National Child Care Association, 2025 M St. NW, Suite 800, Washington, DC 20036. Internet: http://www.nccanet.org

For information about a career as a nanny, contact

▸ International Nanny Association, 191 Clarksville Rd., Princeton Junction, NJ 08550-3111. Telephone (toll free): 888-878-1477. Internet: http://www.nanny.org

State departments of human services or social services can supply state regulations and training requirements for child care workers.

# Computer and Information Systems Managers

(O*NET 11-3021.00)

## Significant Points

■ Employment of computer and information systems managers is expected to grow faster than the average for all occupations through the year 2016.

■ Many managers possess advanced technical knowledge gained from working in a computer occupation.

■ Job opportunities will be best for applicants with a strong understanding of business and good communication skills.

## Nature of the Work

In the modern workplace, it is imperative that technology works both effectively and reliably. Computer and information systems managers play a vital role in the implementation of technology within their organizations. They do everything from helping to construct a business plan to overseeing network security to directing Internet operations.

Computer and information systems managers plan, coordinate, and direct research and facilitate the computer-related activities of firms. They help determine both technical and business goals in consultation with top management and make detailed plans for the accomplishment of these goals. This requires a strong understanding of both technology and business practices.

Computer and information systems managers direct the work of systems analysts, computer programmers, support specialists, and other computer-related workers. They plan and coordinate activities such as installation and upgrading of hardware and software, programming and systems design, development of computer networks, and implementation of Internet and intranet sites. They are increasingly involved with the upkeep, maintenance, and security of networks. They analyze the computer and information needs of their organizations from an operational and strategic perspective and determine immediate and long-range personnel and equipment requirements. They assign and review the work of their subordinates and stay abreast of the latest technology to ensure the organization does not lag behind competitors.

The duties of computer and information systems managers vary greatly. *Chief technology officers (CTOs)*, for example, evaluate the newest and most innovative technologies and determine how these can help their organizations. The chief technology officer often reports to the organization's chief information officer, manages and plans technical standards, and tends to the daily information technology issues of the firm. Because of the rapid pace of technological change, chief technology officers must constantly be on the lookout for developments that could benefit their organizations. Once a useful tool has been identified, the CTO must determine an implementation strategy and sell that strategy to management.

*Management information systems (MIS) directors* or *information technology (IT) directors* manage computing resources for their organizations. They often work under the chief information officer and plan and direct the work of subordinate information technology employees. These managers ensure the availability, continuity, and security of data and information technology services in their organizations. In this capacity, they oversee a variety of user services, such as an organization's help desk, which employees can call with questions or problems. MIS directors also may make hardware and software upgrade recommendations based on their experience with an organization's technology.

*Project managers* develop requirements, budgets, and schedules for their firms' information technology projects. They coordinate such projects from development through implementation, working with internal and external clients, vendors, consultants, and computer specialists. These managers are increasingly involved in projects that upgrade the information security of an organization.

*Work environment.* Computer and information systems managers spend most of their time in offices. Most work at least 40 hours a week, and some may have to work evenings and weekends to meet deadlines or solve unexpected problems. Some computer and information systems managers may experience considerable pressure in meeting technical goals with short deadlines or tight budgets. As networks continue to expand and more work is done remotely, computer and information systems managers have to communicate with and oversee off-site employees using modems, laptops, e-mail, and the Internet.

Like other workers who spend most of their time using computers, computer and information systems managers are susceptible to eyestrain, back discomfort, and hand and wrist problems such as carpal tunnel syndrome.

## Training, Other Qualifications, and Advancement

Computer and information systems managers are generally experienced workers who have both technical expertise and an understanding of business and management principles. A strong educational background and experience in a variety of technical fields are needed.

*Education and training.* A bachelor's degree usually is required for management positions, although employers often prefer a graduate degree, especially an MBA with technology as a core component. This degree differs from a traditional MBA in that there is a heavy emphasis on information technology in addition to the standard business curriculum. This preparation is becoming important because more computer and information systems managers are making important technology decisions as well as business decisions for their organizations.

Some universities offer degrees in management information systems. These degrees blend technical subjects with business, accounting, and communications courses. A few computer and information systems managers attain their positions with only an associate or trade school degree, but they must have sufficient experience and must have acquired additional skills on the job. To aid their professional advancement, many managers with an associate degree eventually earn a bachelor's or master's degree while working.

*Certification and other qualifications.* Computer and information systems managers need a broad range of skills. Employers look for managers who have experience with the specific software or technology used on the job, as well as a background in either consulting or business management. The expansion of electronic commerce has elevated the importance of business insight, and consequently, many computer and information systems managers are called on to make important business decisions. Managers need a keen understanding of people, management processes, and customers' needs.

Advanced technical knowledge is essential for computer and information systems managers, who must understand and guide the work of their subordinates yet also explain the work in nontechnical terms to senior managers and potential customers. Therefore, many computer and information systems managers have worked as a systems analyst, for example, or as a computer support specialist, programmer, or other information technology professional.

Although certification is not necessarily required for most computer and information systems manager positions, there is a wide variety of certifications available that may be helpful in getting a job. These certifications are often product-specific, and they are generally administered by software or hardware companies rather than independent organizations.

As computer systems become more closely connected with day-to-day operations of businesses, computer and information systems managers are also expected to be aware of business practices. They must possess strong interpersonal, communication, and leadership skills because they are required to interact not only with staff members, but also with other people inside and outside their organizations. They must possess team skills to work on group projects and other collaborative efforts. They also must have an understanding of how a business functions, how it earns revenue, and how technology relates to the core competencies of the business. As a result, many firms now prefer to give these positions to people who have spent time outside purely technical fields.

*Advancement.* Computer and information systems managers may advance to progressively higher leadership positions in the information technology department. A project manager might, for instance, move up to the chief technology officer position and then to chief information officer. On occasion, some may become managers in non-technical areas such as marketing, human resources, or sales because in high technology firms an understanding of technical issues is helpful in those areas.

## Employment

Computer and information systems managers held about 264,000 jobs in 2006. About 1 in 4 computer managers worked in service-providing industries, mainly in computer systems design and related services. This industry provides services related to the commercial use of computers on a contract basis, including custom computer programming services; computer systems integration design services; computer facilities management services, including computer systems or data-processing facilities support services; and other computer-related services, such as disaster recovery services and software installation. Other large employers include insurance and financial firms, government agencies, and manufacturers.

**Projections data from the National Employment Matrix**

| Occupational Title | SOC Code | Employment, 2006 | Projected employment, 2016 | Change, 2006-16 | |
|---|---|---|---|---|---|
| | | | | Number | Percent |
| Computer and information systems managers ................................. | 11-3021 | 264,000 | 307,000 | 43,000 | 16 |

NOTE: Data in this table are rounded.

## Job Outlook

The increasing use of technology in the workplace is projected to lead to faster-than-average growth in this occupation. Because of employment increases and the high demand for technical workers, prospects should be excellent for qualified job candidates.

*Employment change.* Employment of computer and information systems managers is expected to grow 16 percent over the 2006–2016 decade, which is faster than the average for all occupations. New applications of technology in the workplace will continue to drive demand for workers, fueling the need for more managers.

Despite the downturn in the technology sector in the early part of the decade, the outlook for computer and information systems managers remains strong. To remain competitive, firms will continue to install sophisticated computer networks and set up more complex intranets and Web sites. Keeping a computer network running smoothly is essential to almost every organization.

Because so much business is carried out over computer networks, security will continue to be an important issue for businesses and other organizations. Although software developers continue to improve their products to remove vulnerabilities, attackers are becoming ever more complex in their methods. Organizations need to understand how their systems are vulnerable and how to protect their infrastructure and Internet sites from hackers, viruses, and other attacks. The emergence of security as a key concern for businesses should lead to strong growth for computer managers. Firms will increasingly hire security experts to fill key leadership roles in their information technology departments because the integrity of their computing environments is of utmost importance. As a result, there will be a high demand for managers proficient in computer security issues.

With the explosive growth of electronic commerce and the capacity of the Internet to create new relationships with customers, the role of computer and information systems managers will continue to evolve. Workers who have experience in Web applications and Internet technologies will become increasingly vital to their companies.

Opportunities for those who wish to become computer and information systems managers should be closely related to the growth of the occupations they supervise and the industries in which they are found.

*Job prospects.* Prospects for qualified computer and information systems managers should be excellent. Fast-paced occupational growth and the limited supply of technical workers will lead to a wealth of opportunities for qualified individuals. While technical workers remain relatively scarce in the United States, the demand for them continues to rise. This situation was exacerbated by the economic downturn in the early 2000s, when many technical professionals lost their jobs. Since then, many workers have chosen to avoid this work since it is perceived to have poor prospects.

Workers with specialized technical knowledge and strong communications skills will have the best prospects. People with management skills and an understanding of business practices and principles will have excellent opportunities, as companies are increasingly looking to technology to drive their revenue.

## Earnings

Earnings for computer and information systems managers vary by specialty and level of responsibility. Median annual earnings of these managers in May 2006 were $101,580. The middle 50 percent earned between $79,240 and $129,250. Median annual earnings in the industries employing the largest numbers of computer and information systems managers in May 2006 were as follows:

| | |
|---|---|
| Computer systems design and related services | ....$109,130 |
| Management of companies and enterprises | ..........105,980 |
| Data processing, hosting, and related services | ......105,200 |
| Insurance carriers | .............................................102,180 |
| Colleges, universities, and professional schools | ......83,280 |

The Robert Half Technology 2007 Salary Guide lists the following annual salary ranges for various computer and information systems manager positions: Chief Technology Officer (CTO), $101,000–$157,750; Chief Security Officer, $97,500–$141,000; Vice President of Information Technology, $107,500–$157,750; Information Technology Manager, Technical Services Manager, $62,500–$88,250.

In addition, computer and information systems managers, especially those at higher levels, often receive employment-related benefits, such as expense accounts, stock option plans, and bonuses.

## Related Occupations

The work of computer and information systems managers is closely related to that of computer programmers, computer software engineers, computer systems analysts, computer scientists and database administrators, and computer support specialists and systems administrators. Computer and information systems managers also have some high-level responsibilities similar to those of top executives.

## Sources of Additional Information

For information about a career as a computer and information systems manager, contact

▸ Association of Information Technology Professionals, 401 North Michigan Ave., Suite 2400, Chicago, IL 60611. Internet: http://www.aitp.org

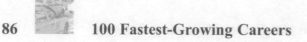

# Computer Scientists and Database Administrators

(O*NET 15-1011.00, 15-1061.00, 15-1081.00, 15-1099.04, 15-1099.05, and 15-1099.99)

## Significant Points

- Education requirements range from an associate degree to a doctoral degree.

- Employment is expected to increase much faster than the average as organizations continue to expand their use of technology.

- Workers must be able to learn new technologies quickly for these constantly evolving occupations.

## Nature of the Work

The rapid and widespread use of computers and information technology has generated a need for highly trained workers proficient in various job functions. These computer specialists include computer scientists, database administrators, and network systems and data communication analysts. Job tasks and occupational titles used to describe these workers evolve rapidly and continually, reflecting new areas of specialization or changes in technology, as well as the preferences and practices of employers.

*Computer scientists* work as theorists, researchers, or inventors. Their jobs are distinguished by the higher level of theoretical expertise and innovation they apply to complex problems and the creation or application of new technology. The areas of computer science research range from complex theory to hardware design to programming-language design. Some researchers work on multidisciplinary projects, such as developing and advancing uses of virtual reality, extending human-computer interaction, or designing robots. They may work on design teams with electrical engineers and other specialists.

Computer science researchers employed by academic institutions have job functions that are similar in many ways to those employed by other organizations. In general, researchers in academic settings have more flexibility to focus on pure theory, while those working in other organizations usually focus on projects that have the possibility of producing patents and profits. However, some researchers in non-academic settings have considerable latitude in determining the direction of their research.

With the Internet and electronic business generating large volumes of data, there is a growing need to be able to store, manage, and extract data effectively. *Database administrators* work with database management systems software and determine ways to organize and store data. They identify user needs and set up new computer databases. In many cases, database administrators must integrate data from outdated systems into a new system. They also test and coordinate modifications to the system when needed, and troubleshoot problems when they occur. An organization's database administrator ensures the performance of the system, understands the platform on which the database runs, and adds new users to the system. Because many databases are connected to the Internet, database administrators also must plan and coordinate security measures with network administrators. With the growing volume of sensitive data and the increasing interconnectedness of computer networks, data integrity, backup systems, and database security have become increasingly important aspects of the job of database administrators.

*Network systems and data communications analysts*, also referred to as *network architects*, design, test, and evaluate systems such as local area networks (LANs), wide area networks (WANs), the Internet, intranets, and other data communications systems. Systems are configured in many ways and can range from a connection between two offices in the same building to globally distributed networks, voice mail, and e-mail systems of a multinational organization. Network systems and data communications analysts perform network modeling, analysis, and planning, often requiring both hardware and software solutions. For example, a network may involve the installation of several pieces of hardware, such as routers and hubs, wireless adaptors, and cables, while also requiring the installation and configuration of software, such as network drivers. Analysts also may research related products and make necessary hardware and software recommendations.

*Telecommunications specialists* focus on the interaction between computer and communications equipment. These workers design voice and data communication systems, supervise the installation of the systems, and provide maintenance and other services to clients after the systems are installed.

The growth of the Internet and the expansion of the World Wide Web (the graphical portion of the Internet) have generated a variety of occupations related to the design, development, and maintenance of Web sites and their servers. For example, *webmasters* are responsible for all technical aspects of a Web site, including performance issues such as speed of access, and for approving the content of the site. *Internet developers* or *Web developers*, also called *Web designers*, are responsible for day-to-day site creation and design.

*Work environment.* Computer scientists and database administrators normally work in offices or laboratories in comfortable surroundings. They typically work about 40 hours a week, the same as many other professional or office workers. However, evening or weekend work may be necessary to meet deadlines or to solve specific problems. Telecommuting is increasingly common for many computer professionals as networks expand, allowing more work to be done from remote locations through modems, laptops, electronic mail, and the Internet. However, some work still must be done in the office for security or other reasons.

Like other workers who spend long periods in front of a computer terminal typing on a keyboard, computer scientists and database administrators are susceptible to eyestrain, back discomfort, and hand and wrist problems such as carpal tunnel syndrome or cumulative trauma disorder.

## Training, Other Qualifications, and Advancement

Rapidly changing technology requires an increasing level of skill and education on the part of workers in these occupations. Employers look for professionals with an ever-broader background and range of skills, including technical knowledge and also communication and other interpersonal skills.

*Education and training.* While there is no universally accepted way to prepare for a job as a network systems analyst, computer scientist, or database administrator, most employers place a premium on some formal college education. A bachelor's degree is a prerequisite for many jobs; however, some jobs may require only a two-year degree. Relevant work experience also is very important. For more technically complex jobs, persons with graduate degrees are preferred. Most computer scientist positions require a Ph.D. degree, as their main job function is research. Computer scientists having only a bachelor's or master's degree are generally limited in their ability to advance.

For database administrator and network systems and data communication analyst positions, most employers seek applicants who have bachelor's degrees in computer science, information science, or management information systems (MIS). MIS programs usually are part of the business school or college and differ considerably from computer science programs, emphasizing business and management-oriented coursework and business computing courses. Employers increasingly prefer applicants with a master's degree in business administration (MBA) with a concentration in information systems, as more firms move their business to the Internet. For some network systems and data communication analysts, such as webmasters, an associate degree or certificate is sufficient, although more advanced positions might require a computer-related bachelor's degree.

Most community colleges and many independent technical institutes and proprietary schools offer an associate's degree in computer science or a related information technology field. Many of these programs may be geared more toward meeting the needs of local businesses and are more occupation specific than are four-year degree programs. Some jobs may be better suited to the level of training that such programs offer. Employers usually look for people who have broad knowledge and experience related to computer systems and technologies, strong problem-solving and analytical skills, and good interpersonal skills. Courses in computer science or systems design offer good preparation for a job in these computer occupations. For jobs in a business environment, employers usually want systems analysts to have business management or closely related skills, while a background in the physical sciences, applied mathematics, or engineering is preferred for work in scientifically oriented organizations. Art or graphic design skills may be desirable for webmasters or Web developers.

Despite employers' preference for those with technical degrees, individuals with post-secondary degrees in a variety of other subjects may find employment in these occupations. Given the rapid pace of technological change, a degree generally has more value as a demonstration of an individual's ability to learn, rather than as a certification of a certain skill set. Generally speaking, coursework in computer science and an undergraduate degree are sufficient qualifications, especially if the applicant has a reasonable amount of experience.

*Certification and other qualifications.* Computer scientists and database administrators must be able to think logically and have good communication skills. Because they often deal with a number of tasks simultaneously, the ability to concentrate and pay close attention to detail also is important. Although computer specialists sometimes work independently, they frequently work in teams on large projects. As a result, they must be able to communicate effectively with computer personnel, such as programmers and managers, as well as with users or other staff who may have no technical computer background.

Jobseekers can enhance their employment opportunities by earning certifications, most of which are offered through private companies, with many related to specific products. Many employers regard these certifications as the industry standard. For example, one method of acquiring enough knowledge to get a job as a database administrator is to become certified in database management with a certain software package. Voluntary certification also is available through various organizations associated with computer specialists. Professional certification may afford a jobseeker a competitive advantage.

Because technology is so closely connected to the functioning of businesses, many workers in these occupations come from elsewhere in the business or industry to become computer specialists. This background can be very useful, in that it helps them to better understand how their networking and database tools are being used within the organization.

*Advancement.* Computer scientists may advance into managerial or project leadership positions. Many having advanced degrees choose to leave private industry for academic positions. Database administrators may advance into managerial positions, such as chief technology officer, on the basis of their experience managing data and enforcing security. Computer specialists with work experience and considerable expertise in a particular subject or a certain application may find lucrative opportunities as independent consultants or may choose to start their own computer consulting firms.

Technological advances come so rapidly in the computer field that continuous study is necessary to keep one's skills up to date. Employers, hardware and software vendors, colleges and universities, and private training institutions offer continuing education. Additional training may come from professional development seminars offered by professional computing societies.

# Employment

Computer scientists and database administrators held about 542,000 jobs in May 2006, including about 58,000 who were self-employed. Employment was distributed among the detailed occupations as follows:

| | |
|---|---|
| Network systems and data communication analysts | 262,000 |
| Computer specialists, all other | 136,000 |
| Database administrators | 119,000 |
| Computer and information scientists, research | 25,000 |

Although they are increasingly employed in every sector of the economy, the greatest concentration of these workers is in the computer systems design and related services industry. Firms in this industry provide services related to the commercial use of computers on a contract basis, including custom computer programming services; computer systems integration design services; computer

**Projections data from the National Employment Matrix**

| Occupational Title | SOC Code | Employment, 2006 | Projected employment, 2016 | Change, 2006-2016 | |
|---|---|---|---|---|---|
| | | | | Number | Percent |
| Computer scientists and database administrators ............................. | — | 542,000 | 742,000 | 200,000 | 37 |
| Computer and information scientists, research ........................... | 15-1011 | 25,000 | 31,000 | 5,400 | 22 |
| Database administrators ................................................................. | 15-1061 | 119,000 | 154,000 | 34,000 | 29 |
| Network systems and data communications analysts ................... | 15-1081 | 262,000 | 402,000 | 140,000 | 53 |
| Computer specialists, all other ...................................................... | 15-1099 | 136,000 | 157,000 | 21,000 | 15 |

NOTE: Data in this table are rounded.

facilities management services, including computer systems or data processing facilities support services for clients; and other computer-related services, such as disaster recovery services and software installation. Many computer scientists and database administrators are employed by Internet service providers; Web search portals; and data processing, hosting, and related services firms. Others work for government, manufacturers of computer and electronic products, insurance companies, financial institutions, and universities.

A growing number of computer specialists, such as network and data communications analysts, are employed on a temporary or contract basis; many of these individuals are self-employed, working independently as contractors or consultants. For example, a company installing a new computer system may need the services of several network systems and data communication analysts just to get the system running. Because not all of the analysts would be needed once the system is functioning, the company might contract for such employees with a temporary help agency or consulting firm, or with the network systems analysts themselves. Such jobs may last from several months to 2 years or more. This growing practice enables companies to bring in people with the exact skills they need to complete a particular project, rather than having to spend time or money training or retraining existing workers. Often, experienced consultants then train a company's in-house staff as a project develops.

## Job Outlook

Computer scientists and database administrators are projected to be one of the fastest growing occupations over the next decade. Strong employment growth combined with a limited supply of qualified workers will result in excellent employment prospects for this occupation and a high demand for their skills.

*Employment change.* The computer scientists and database administrators occupation is expected to grow 37 percent from 2006 to 2016, much faster than average for all occupations. Employment of these computer specialists is expected to grow as organizations continue to adopt and integrate increasingly sophisticated technologies. Job increases will be driven by very rapid growth in computer systems design and related services, which is projected to be one of the fastest growing industries in the U.S. economy.

The demand for networking to facilitate the sharing of information, the expansion of client-server environments, and the need for computer specialists to use their knowledge and skills in a problem-solving capacity will be major factors in the rising demand for computer scientists and database administrators. Firms will continue to seek out computer specialists who are able to implement the latest technologies and are able to apply them to meet the needs of businesses as they struggle to maintain a competitive advantage.

As computers continue to become more central to business functions, more sophisticated and complex technology is being implemented across all organizations, fueling demand for computer scientists and database administrators. There is growing demand for network systems and data communication analysts to help firms maximize their efficiency with available technology. Expansion of electronic commerce—doing business on the Internet—and the continuing need to build and maintain databases that store critical information on customers, inventory, and projects are fueling demand for database administrators familiar with the latest technology. Because of the increasing reliance on the Internet among businesses, information security is an increasing concern.

The development of new technologies leads to demand for various kinds of workers. The expanding integration of Internet technologies into businesses, for example, has resulted in a growing need for specialists who can develop and support Internet and intranet applications. The growth of electronic commerce means that more establishments use the Internet to conduct their business online. It also means more security specialists are needed to protect their systems. The spread of such new technologies translates into a need for information technology professionals who can help organizations use technology to communicate with employees, clients, and consumers. Explosive growth in these areas also is expected to fuel demand for specialists who are knowledgeable about network, data, and communications security.

*Job prospects.* Computer scientists and database administrators should continue to enjoy excellent job prospects. As technology becomes more sophisticated and complex, however, these positions will demand a higher level of skill and expertise from their employees. Individuals with an advanced degree in computer science or computer engineering or with an MBA with a concentration in information systems should enjoy favorable employment prospects. College graduates with a bachelor's degree in computer science, computer engineering, information science, or MIS also should enjoy favorable prospects, particularly if they have supplemented their formal education with practical experience. Because employers continue to seek computer specialists who can combine strong technical skills with good business skills, individuals with a combination of experience inside and outside the IT arena will have the best job prospects.

In addition to growth, many job openings will arise from the need to replace workers who move into managerial positions or other occupations or who leave the labor force.

## Earnings

Median annual earnings of computer and information scientists, research, were $93,950 in May 2006. The middle 50 percent earned between $71,930 and $118,100. The lowest 10 percent earned less than $53,590, and the highest 10 percent earned more than $144,880. Median annual earnings of computer and information scientists employed in computer systems design and related services in May 2006 were $95,340.

Median annual earnings of database administrators were $64,670 in May 2006. The middle 50 percent earned between $48,560 and $84,830. The lowest 10 percent earned less than $37,350, and the highest 10 percent earned more than $103,010. In May 2006, median annual earnings of database administrators employed in computer systems design and related services were $72,510, and for those in management of companies and enterprises, earnings were $67,680.

Median annual earnings of network systems and data communication analysts were $64,600 in May 2006. The middle 50 percent earned between $49,510 and $82,630. The lowest 10 percent earned less than $38,410, and the highest 10 percent earned more than $101,740. Median annual earnings in the industries employing the largest numbers of network systems and data communications analysts in May 2006 are shown below:

| | |
|---|---|
| Wired telecommunications carriers | $72,480 |
| Management of companies and enterprises | 68,490 |
| Management, scientific, and technical consulting services | 67,830 |
| Computer systems design and related services | 67,080 |
| State government | 52,020 |

Median annual earnings of all other computer specialists were $68,570 in May 2006. Median annual earnings of all other computer specialists employed in computer systems design and related services were $67,370, and, for those in management of companies and enterprises, earnings were $63,610 in May 2006.

Robert Half International, a firm providing specialized staffing services, noted the following salary ranges for computer-related occupations in their 2007 Salary Guide:

| | |
|---|---|
| Database manager | $84,750 - $116,000 |
| Network architect | 78,000 - 112,250 |
| Database developer | 73,500 - 103,000 |
| Senior web developer | 71,000 - 102,000 |
| Database administrator | 70,250 - 102,000 |
| Network manager | 68,750 - 93,000 |
| Web developer | 54,750 - 81,500 |
| LAN/WAN administrator | 51,000 - 71,500 |
| Web administrator | 49,750 - 74,750 |
| Web designer | 47,000 - 71,500 |
| Telecommunications specialist | 47,500 - 69,500 |

## Related Occupations

Others who work with large amounts of data are computer programmers, computer software engineers, computer and information systems managers, engineers, mathematicians, statisticians, and actuaries.

## Sources of Additional Information

Further information about computer careers is available from

▸ Association for Computing Machinery (ACM), 1515 Broadway, New York, NY 10036. Internet: http://www.acm.org

▸ Institute of Electrical and Electronics Engineers Computer Society, Headquarters Office, 1730 Massachusetts Ave. NW, Washington, DC 20036-1992. Internet: http://www.computer.org

▸ Software & Information Industry Association, 1090 Vermont Ave. NW, 6th floor, Washington, DC 20005. Internet: http://www.siia.net

# Computer Software Engineers

(O*NET 15-1031.00 and 15-1032.00)

## Significant Points

■ Computer software engineers are one of the occupations projected to grow the fastest and add the most new jobs over the 2006–2016 decade.

■ Excellent job prospects are expected for applicants with at least bachelor's degree in computer engineering or computer science and with practical work experience.

■ Computer software engineers must continually strive to acquire new skills in conjunction with the rapid changes that occur in computer technology.

## Nature of the Work

Computer software engineers apply the principles of computer science and mathematical analysis to the design, development, testing, and evaluation of the software and systems that make computers work. The tasks performed by these workers evolve quickly, reflecting new areas of specialization or changes in technology, as well as the preferences and practices of employers.

Software engineers can be involved in the design and development of many types of software, including computer games, word processing and business applications, operating systems and network distribution, and compilers, which convert programs to machine language for execution on a computer.

Computer software engineers begin by analyzing users' needs, and then design, test, and develop software to meet those needs. During this process they create the detailed sets of instructions, called algorithms, that tell the computer what to do. They also may be responsible for converting these instructions into a computer language, a process called programming or coding, but this usually is the responsibility of *computer programmers*. Computer software engineers must be experts in operating systems and middleware to ensure that the underlying systems will work properly.

*Computer applications software engineers* analyze users' needs and design, construct, and maintain general computer applications software or specialized utility programs. These workers use different programming languages, depending on the purpose of the program. The programming languages most often used are C, C++, and Java, with Fortran and COBOL used less commonly. Some software engineers develop both packaged systems and systems software or create customized applications.

*Computer systems software engineers* coordinate the construction, maintenance, and expansion of an organization's computer systems. Working with the organization, they coordinate each department's computer needs—ordering, inventory, billing, and payroll record-keeping, for example—and make suggestions about its technical direction. They also might set up the organization's intranets—networks that link computers within the organization and ease communication among various departments.

Systems software engineers also work for companies that configure, implement, and install the computer systems of other organizations. These workers may be members of the marketing or sales staff, serving as the primary technical resource for sales workers. They also may help with sales and provide customers with technical support. Since the selling of complex computer systems often requires substantial customization to meet the needs of the purchaser, software engineers help to identify and explain needed changes. In addition, systems software engineers are responsible for ensuring security across the systems they are configuring.

Computer software engineers often work as part of a team that designs new hardware, software, and systems. A core team may comprise engineering, marketing, manufacturing, and design people, who work together to release a product.

*Work environment.* Computer software engineers normally work in clean, comfortable offices or in laboratories in which computer equipment is located. Software engineers who work for software vendors and consulting firms frequently travel overnight to meet with customers. Telecommuting is also becoming more common, allowing workers to do their jobs from remote locations.

Most software engineers work at least 40 hours a week, but about 17 percent work more than 50 hours a week. Software engineers also may have to work evenings or weekends to meet deadlines or solve unexpected technical problems.

Like other workers who spend long hours typing at a computer, software engineers are susceptible to eyestrain, back discomfort, and hand and wrist problems such as carpal tunnel syndrome.

# Training, Other Qualifications, and Advancement

Most employers prefer applicants who have at least a bachelor's degree and experience with a variety of computer systems and technologies. In order to remain competitive, computer software engineers must continually strive to acquire the latest technical skills. Advancement opportunities are good for those with relevant experience.

*Education and training.* Most employers prefer applicants who have at least a bachelor's degree and broad knowledge of, and experience with, a variety of computer systems and technologies. The usual college major for applications software engineers is computer science or software engineering. Systems software engineers often study computer science or computer information systems. Graduate degrees are preferred for some of the more complex jobs. In 2006, about 80 percent of workers had a bachelor's degree or higher.

Academic programs in software engineering may offer the program as a degree option or in conjunction with computer science degrees. Because of increasing emphasis on computer security, software engineers with advanced degrees in areas such as mathematics and systems design will be sought after by software developers, government agencies, and consulting firms.

Students seeking software engineering jobs enhance their employment opportunities by participating in internships or co-ops. These experiences provide students with broad knowledge and experience, making them more attractive to employers. Inexperienced college graduates may be hired by large computer and consulting firms that train new employees in intensive, company-based programs.

*Certification and other qualifications.* Systems software vendors offer certification and training programs, but most training authorities say that program certification alone is not sufficient for the majority of software engineering jobs.

People interested in jobs as computer software engineers must have strong problem-solving and analytical skills. They also must be able to communicate effectively with team members, other staff, and the customers they meet. Because they often deal with a number of tasks simultaneously, they must be able to concentrate and pay close attention to detail.

As technology advances, employers will need workers with the latest skills. Computer software engineers must continually strive to acquire new skills if they wish to remain in this dynamic field. To help keep up with changing technology, workers may take continuing education and professional development seminars offered by employers, software vendors, colleges and universities, private training institutions, and professional computing societies. Computer software engineers also need skills related to the industry in which they work. Engineers working for a bank, for example, should have some expertise in finance so that they understand banks' computer needs.

*Advancement.* As with most occupations, advancement opportunities for computer software engineers increase with experience. Entry-level computer software engineers are likely to test designs. As they become more experienced, engineers may begin helping to design and develop software. Eventually, they may advance to become a project manager, manager of information systems, or chief information officer, especially if they have business skills and training. Some computer software engineers with several years of experience or expertise find lucrative opportunities working as systems designers or independent consultants.

**Projections data from the National Employment Matrix**

| Occupational Title | SOC Code | Employment, 2006 | Projected employment, 2016 | Change, 2006-2016 | |
|---|---|---|---|---|---|
| | | | | Number | Percent |
| Computer software engineers ............................................................ | 15-1030 | 857,000 | 1,181,000 | 324,000 | 38 |
| Computer software engineers, applications ................................... | 15-1031 | 507,000 | 733,000 | 226,000 | 45 |
| Computer software engineers, systems software ......................... | 15-1032 | 350,000 | 449,000 | 99,000 | 28 |

NOTE: Data in this table are rounded.

## Employment

Computer software engineers held about 857,000 jobs in 2006. Approximately 507,000 were computer applications software engineers, and about 350,000 were computer systems software engineers. Although they are employed in most industries, the largest concentration of computer software engineers—more than 29 percent—is in computer systems design and related services. Many computer software engineers also work for establishments in other industries, such as software publishers, government agencies, manufacturers of computers and related electronic equipment, financial institutions, insurance providers, and management of companies and enterprises.

An increasing number of computer software engineers work as independent consultants on a temporary or contract basis, many of whom are self-employed. About 17,000 computer software engineers were self-employed in 2006.

## Job Outlook

Job prospects should be excellent, as computer software engineers are expected to be among the fastest-growing occupations through the year 2016.

*Employment change.* Employment of computer software engineers is projected to increase by 38 percent over the 2006 to 2016 period, which is much faster than the average for all occupations. This occupation will generate about 324,000 new jobs, over the projections decade, one of the largest employment increases of any occupation.

Employment growth will result as businesses and other organizations adopt and integrate new technologies and seek to maximize the efficiency of their computer systems. Competition among businesses will continue to create incentive for sophisticated technological innovations, and organizations will need more computer software engineers to implement these changes.

Demand for computer software engineers will also increase as computer networking continues to grow. For example, expanding Internet technologies have spurred demand for computer software engineers who can develop Internet, intranet, and World Wide Web applications. Likewise, electronic data-processing systems in business, telecommunications, government, and other settings continue to become more sophisticated and complex. Implementing, safeguarding, and updating computer systems and resolving problems will fuel the demand for growing numbers of systems software engineers.

New growth areas will also continue to arise from rapidly evolving technologies. The increasing uses of the Internet, the proliferation of Web sites, and mobile technology such as wireless Internet have created a demand for a wide variety of new products. As individuals and businesses rely more on hand-held computers and wireless networks, it will be necessary to integrate current computer systems with this new, more mobile technology.

In addition, information security concerns have given rise to new software needs. Concerns over "cyber security" should result in businesses and government continuing to invest heavily in software that protects their networks and vital electronic infrastructure from attack. The expansion of this technology in the next 10 years will lead to an increased need for computer engineers to design and develop the software and systems to run these new applications and integrate them into older systems.

As with other information technology jobs, outsourcing of software development to other countries may temper somewhat employment growth of computer software engineers. Firms may look to cut costs by shifting operations to foreign countries with lower prevailing wages and highly educated workers. Jobs in software engineering are less prone to being offshored than are jobs in other computer specialties, however, because software engineering requires innovation and intense research and development.

*Job prospects.* As a result of rapid employment growth over the 2006 to 2016 decade, job prospects for computer software engineers should be excellent. Those with practical experience and at least a bachelor's degree in computer engineering or computer science should have the best opportunities. Employers will continue to seek computer professionals with strong programming, systems analysis, interpersonal, and business skills. In addition to jobs created through employment growth, many job openings will result from the need to replace workers who move into managerial positions, transfer to other occupations, or leave the labor force. Consulting opportunities for computer software engineers also should continue to grow as businesses seek help to manage, upgrade, and customize their increasingly complicated computer systems.

## Earnings

In May 2006, median annual earnings of wage-and-salary computer applications software engineers were $79,780. The middle 50 percent earned between $62,830 and $98,470. The lowest 10 percent earned less than $49,350, and the highest 10 percent earned more than $119,770. Median annual earnings in the industries employing the largest numbers of computer applications software engineers in May 2006 were as follows:

Software publishers ............................................$84,560

Computer systems design and related services ........78,850

Management, scientific, and technical
    consulting services ............................................78,850

Management of companies and enterprises ............78,580

Insurance carriers ............................................74,230

In May 2006, median annual earnings of wage-and-salary computer systems software engineers were $85,370. The middle 50 percent earned between $67,620 and $105,330. The lowest 10 percent earned less than $53,580, and the highest 10 percent earned more than $125,750. Median annual earnings in the industries employing the largest numbers of computer systems software engineers in May 2006 are as follows:

| | |
|---|---|
| Research and development in the physical, engineering, and life sciences | $97,220 |
| Scientific research and development services | 97,180 |
| Computer and peripheral equipment manufacturing | 93,240 |
| Software publishers | 87,450 |
| Computer systems design and related services | 84,660 |
| Data processing, hosting, and related services | 78,270 |

According to the National Association of Colleges and Employers, starting salary offers for graduates with a bachelor's degree in computer engineering averaged $56,201 in 2007. Starting salary offers for graduates with a bachelor's degree in computer science averaged $53,396.

According to Robert Half Technology, starting salaries for software engineers in software development ranged from $66,500 to $99,750 in 2007. For network engineers, starting salaries ranged from $65,750 to $90,250.

## Related Occupations

Other workers who use mathematics and logic extensively include computer systems analysts, computer scientists and database administrators, computer programmers, computer hardware engineers, computer support specialists and systems administrators, engineers, commercial and industrial designers, statisticians, mathematicians, and actuaries.

## Sources of Additional Information

Additional information on a career in computer software engineering is available from the following organizations:

▸ Association for Computing Machinery (ACM), 2 Penn Plaza, Suite 701, NY 10121-0701. Internet: http://www.acm.org

▸ Institute of Electronics and Electrical Engineers Computer Society, Headquarters Office, 1730 Massachusetts Ave. NW, Washington, DC 20036-1992. Internet: http://www.computer.org

▸ National Workforce Center for Emerging Technologies, 3000 Landerholm Circle SE, Bellevue, WA 98007. Internet: http://www.nwcet.org

▸ University of Washington Computer Science and Engineering Department, AC101 Paul G. Allen Center, Box 352350, 185 Stevens Way, Seattle, WA 98195-2350. Internet: http://www.cs.washington.edu/WhyCSE

# Computer Support Specialists and Systems Administrators

(O*NET 15-1041.00, 15-1071.00, and 15-1071.01)

## Significant Points

■ Growth in computer support specialist jobs will be about as fast as the average, while growth in network and computer system administrator jobs will be much faster than average.

■ There are many paths of entry to these occupations.

■ Job prospects should be best for college graduates with relevant skills and experience; certifications and practical experience are essential for people without degrees.

## Nature of the Work

In the last decade, computers have become an integral part of everyday life at home, work, school, and nearly everywhere else. Of course, almost every computer user encounters a problem occasionally, whether it is the annoyance of a forgotten password or the disaster of a crashing hard drive. The explosive use of computers has created demand for specialists who provide advice to users, as well as for the day-to-day administration, maintenance, and support of computer systems and networks.

*Computer support specialists* provide technical assistance, support, and advice to customers and other users. This occupational group includes *technical support specialists* and *help-desk technicians*. These troubleshooters interpret problems and provide technical support for hardware, software, and systems. They answer telephone calls, analyze problems by using automated diagnostic programs, and resolve recurring difficulties. Support specialists work either within a company that uses computer systems or directly for a computer hardware or software vendor. Increasingly, these specialists work for help-desk or support services firms, for which they provide computer support to clients on a contract basis.

Technical support specialists respond to inquiries from their organizations' computer users and may run automatic diagnostics programs to resolve problems. They also install, modify, clean, and repair computer hardware and software. In addition, they may write training manuals and train computer users in how to use new computer hardware and software. These workers also oversee the daily performance of their company's computer systems and evaluate how useful software programs are.

Help-desk technicians respond to telephone calls and e-mail messages from customers looking for help with computer problems. In responding to these inquiries, help-desk technicians must listen carefully to the customer, ask questions to diagnose the nature of the problem, and then patiently walk the customer through the problem-solving steps.

Help-desk technicians deal directly with customer issues and companies value them as a source of feedback on their products. They are consulted for information about what gives customers the most trouble, as well as other customer concerns. Most computer support specialists start out at the help desk.

*Network* and *computer systems administrators* design, install, and support an organization's computer systems. They are responsible for local-area networks (LAN), wide-area networks (WAN), network segments, and Internet and intranet systems. They work in a variety of environments, including professional offices, small businesses, government organizations, and large corporations. They maintain network hardware and software, analyze problems, and monitor networks to ensure their availability to system users. These workers gather data to identify customer needs and then use the information to identify, interpret, and evaluate system and network requirements. Administrators also may plan, coordinate, and implement network security measures.

Systems administrators are responsible for maintaining network efficiency. They ensure that the design of an organization's computer system allows all of the components, including computers, the network, and software, to work properly together. Furthermore, they monitor and adjust the performance of existing networks and continually survey the current computer site to determine future network needs. Administrators also troubleshoot problems reported by users and by automated network monitoring systems and make recommendations for future system upgrades.

In some organizations, *computer security specialists* may plan, coordinate, and implement the organization's information security. These workers educate users about computer security, install security software, monitor networks for security breaches, respond to cyber attacks, and, in some cases, gather data and evidence to be used in prosecuting cyber crime. The responsibilities of computer security specialists have increased in recent years as cyber attacks have become more common. This and other growing specialty occupations reflect an increasing emphasis on client-server applications, the expansion of Internet and intranet applications, and the demand for more end-user support.

*Work environment.* Computer support specialists and systems administrators normally work in well-lighted, comfortable offices or computer laboratories. They usually work about 40 hours a week, but if their employer requires computer support over extended hours, they may be "on call" for rotating evening or weekend work. Overtime may be necessary when unexpected technical problems arise. Like other workers who type on a keyboard for long periods, computer support specialists and systems administrators are susceptible to eyestrain, back discomfort, and hand and wrist problems such as carpal tunnel syndrome.

Computer support specialists and systems administrators constantly interact with customers and fellow employees as they answer questions and give advice. Those who work as consultants are away from their offices much of the time, sometimes spending months working in a client's office.

As computer networks expand, more computer support specialists and systems administrators may be able to provide technical support from remote locations. This capability would reduce or eliminate travel to the customer's workplace. Systems administrators also can administer and configure networks and servers remotely, although this practice is not as common as it is among computer support specialists.

## Training, Other Qualifications, and Advancement

A college degree is required for some computer support specialist positions, but certification and relevant experience may be sufficient for others. A bachelor's degree is required for many network and computer systems administrator positions. For both occupations, strong analytical and communication skills are essential.

*Education and training.* Due to the wide range of skills required, there are many paths of entry to a job as a computer support specialist or systems administrator. Training requirements for computer support specialist positions vary, but many employers prefer to hire applicants with some formal college education. A bachelor's degree in computer science or information systems is a prerequisite for some jobs; other jobs, however, may require only a computer-related associate degree. And for some jobs, relevant computer experience and certifications may substitute for formal education. For systems administrator jobs, many employers seek applicants with bachelor's degrees, although not necessarily in a computer-related field.

A number of companies are becoming more flexible about requiring a college degree for support positions. In the absence of a degree, however, certification and practical experience are essential. Certification training programs, offered by a variety of vendors and product makers, may help some people to qualify for entry-level positions.

*Other qualifications.* People interested in becoming a computer support specialist or systems administrator must have strong problem-solving, analytical, and communication skills because troubleshooting and helping others are vital parts of the job. The constant interaction with other computer personnel, customers, and employees requires computer support specialists and systems administrators to communicate effectively on paper, via e-mail, over the phone, or in person. Strong writing skills are useful in preparing manuals for employees and customers.

*Advancement.* Beginning computer support specialists usually work for organizations that deal directly with customers or in-house users. Support specialists may advance into positions in which they use what they have learned from customers to improve the design and efficiency of future products. Job promotions usually depend more on performance than on formal education. Eventually, some computer support specialists become software engineers, designing products rather than assisting users. Computer support specialists in hardware and software companies often enjoy great upward mobility; advancement sometimes comes within months of becoming employed.

Entry-level network and computer systems administrators are involved in routine maintenance and monitoring of computer systems, typically working behind the scenes in an organization. After gaining experience and expertise, they often are able to advance to more senior-level positions. For example, senior network and computer systems administrators may make presentations to executives and managers on the security of the company computer network. They also may translate the needs of an organization into a set of technical requirements based on the available technology. As with support specialists, administrators may become software engineers involved in system and network design.

**Projections data from the National Employment Matrix**

| Occupational Title | SOC Code | Employment, 2006 | Projected employment, 2016 | Change, 2006-2016 | |
|---|---|---|---|---|---|
| | | | | Number | Percent |
| Computer support specialists and systems administrators................ | — | 862,000 | 1,016,000 | 155,000 | 18 |
| Computer support specialists ....................................................... | 15-1041 | 552,000 | 624,000 | 71,000 | 13 |
| Network and computer systems administrators ........................... | 15-1071 | 309,000 | 393,000 | 83,000 | 27 |

NOTE: Data in this table are rounded.

As technology continues to improve, computer support specialists and systems administrators must strive to acquire new skills. Many continuing education programs are provided by employers, hardware and software vendors, colleges and universities, and private training institutions. Professional development seminars offered by computing services firms also can enhance skills and advancement opportunities.

## Employment

Computer support specialists and systems administrators held about 862,000 jobs in 2006. Of these, approximately 552,000 were computer support specialists and about 309,000 were network and computer systems administrators. Although they worked in a wide range of industries, about 23 percent of all computer support specialists and systems administrators were employed in professional, scientific, and technical services industries, principally computer systems design and related services. Substantial numbers of these workers were also employed in administrative and support services companies, financial institutions, insurance companies, government agencies, educational institutions, software publishers, telecommunications organizations, health care organizations, and management of companies and enterprises.

Employers of computer support specialists and systems administrators range from startup companies to established industry leaders. As computer networks become an integral part of business, industries not typically associated with computers—such as construction—increasingly need computer support workers.

## Job Outlook

Employment of computer support specialists and systems administrators is expected to increase faster than the average. Job prospects should be best for those with a college degree and relevant experience.

*Employment change.* Employment of computer support specialists and systems administrators is expected to increase by 18 percent from 2006 to 2016, which is much faster than the average for all occupations. In addition, this occupation is expected to add 155,000 jobs over the projection decade.

Employment of computer support specialists is expected to increase by 13 percent from 2006 to 2016, which is about as fast as the average for all occupations. Demand for these workers will result as organizations and individuals continue to adopt increasingly sophisticated technology. Job growth will continue to be driven by the ongoing expansion of the computer system design and related services industry, which is projected to remain one of the fastest-growing industries in the U.S. economy. Growth will not be as explosive as during the previous decade, however, because the information

technology industry is maturing and because some of these jobs are expected to be outsourced offshore where prevailing wages are lower. Physical location is not as important for computer support specialists as it is for other occupations because these workers can provide assistance remotely and support services are provided around the clock across time zones.

Job growth among computer support specialists reflects the rapid evolution of technology. As computers and software become more complex, support specialists will be needed to provide technical assistance to customers and other users. The adoption of new mobile technologies, such as the wireless Internet, will continue to create a need for these workers to familiarize and educate computer users. Consulting jobs for computer support specialists also should continue to increase as businesses seek help managing, upgrading, and customizing ever more complex computer systems.

Employment of network and computer systems administrators is expected to increase by 27 percent from 2006 to 2016, which is much faster than the average for all occupations. Computer networks have become an integral part of business, and demand for these workers will increase as firms continue to invest in new technologies. The wide use of electronic commerce and the increasing adoption of mobile technologies mean that more establishments will use the Internet to conduct business online. This growth translates into a need for systems administrators who can help organizations use technology to communicate with employees, clients, and consumers.

Demand for computer security specialists will grow as businesses and government continue to invest heavily in "cyber security," protecting vital computer networks and electronic infrastructures from attack. The information security field is expected to generate many new system administrator jobs over the next decade as firms across all industries place a high priority on safeguarding their data and systems.

Employment of network and computer systems administrators, however, may be tempered somewhat by offshore outsourcing, as firms transfer work to countries with lower-prevailing wages and highly skilled work forces. Systems administrators may increasingly be able to manage computer systems from remote locations as technology advances.

*Job prospects.* Job prospects should be best for college graduates who possess the latest technological skills, particularly graduates who have supplemented their formal education with relevant work experience. Employers will continue to seek computer specialists who possess strong fundamental computer skills combined with good interpersonal and communication skills. Due to the demand for computer support specialists and systems administrators over the next decade, those who have strong computer skills but do not have a college degree should continue to qualify for some entry-level positions.

## Earnings

Median annual earnings of wage-and-salary computer support specialists were $41,470 in May 2006. The middle 50 percent earned between $32,110 and $53,640. The lowest 10 percent earned less than $25,290, and the highest 10 percent earned more than $68,540. Median annual earnings in the industries employing the largest numbers of computer support specialists in May 2006 were as follows:

Software publishers ............................................$46,270

Management of companies and enterprises ............42,770

Computer systems design and related services ........42,510

Colleges, universities, and professional schools ......40,130

Elementary and secondary schools ........................37,880

Median annual earnings of wage-and-salary network and computer systems administrators were $62,130 in May 2006. The middle 50 percent earned between $48,520 and $79,160. The lowest 10 percent earned less than $38,610, and the highest 10 percent earned more than $97,080. Median annual earnings in the industries employing the largest numbers of network and computer systems administrators in May 2006 were as follows:

Wired telecommunications carriers ......................$70,790

Computer systems design and related services ........66,680

Management of companies and enterprises ............66,020

Colleges, universities, and professional schools ......54,590

Elementary and secondary schools ........................53,750

According to Robert Half Technology, starting salaries in 2007 ranged from $27,500 to $37,000 for help-desk workers. Starting salaries for desktop support analysts ranged from $46,500 to $65,250. For systems administrators, starting salaries ranged from $50,000 to $75,750.

## Related Occupations

Other computer specialists include computer programmers, computer software engineers, computer systems analysts, and computer scientists and database administrators. Other workers who respond to customer inquiries are customer service representatives.

## Sources of Additional Information

For additional information about a career as a computer support specialist, contact

▸ Association of Support Professionals, 122 Barnard Ave., Watertown, MA 02472.

For additional information about a career as a systems administrator, contact

▸ The League of Professional System Administrators, 15000 Commerce Parkway, Suite C, Mount Laurel, NJ 08054. Internet: http://lopsa.org/

▸ National Workforce Center for Emerging Technologies, 3000 Landerholm Circle SE, Bellevue, WA 98007. Internet: http://www.nwcet.org

# Computer Systems Analysts

(O*NET 15-1051.00, 15-1099.01, 15-1099.02, and 15-1099.03)

## Significant Points

■ Employers generally prefer applicants who have at least a bachelor's degree in computer science, information science, or management information systems (MIS).

■ Employment is expected to increase much faster than the average and more new jobs are expected to arise than in all but a few other occupations.

■ Very good job prospects are expected as organizations continue to adopt increasingly sophisticated technologies.

## Nature of the Work

All organizations rely on computer and information technology to conduct business and operate efficiently. Computer systems analysts help organizations to use technology effectively and to incorporate rapidly changing technologies into their existing systems. The work of computer systems analysts evolves rapidly, reflecting new areas of specialization and changes in technology.

Computer systems analysts solve computer problems and use computer technology to meet the needs of an organization. They may design and develop new computer systems by choosing and configuring hardware and software. They may also devise ways to apply existing systems' resources to additional tasks. Most systems analysts work with specific types of computer systems—for example, business, accounting, or financial systems or scientific and engineering systems—that vary with the kind of organization. Analysts who specialize in helping an organization select the proper system software and infrastructure are often called *system architects*. Analysts who specialize in developing and fine-tuning systems often are known as *systems designers*.

To begin an assignment, systems analysts consult managers and users to define the goals of the system. Analysts then design a system to meet those goals. They specify the inputs that the system will access, decide how the inputs will be processed, and format the output to meet users' needs. Analysts use techniques such as structured analysis, data modeling, information engineering, mathematical model building, sampling, and cost accounting to make sure their plans are efficient and complete. They also may prepare cost-benefit and return-on-investment analyses to help management decide whether implementing the proposed technology would be financially feasible.

When a system is approved, systems analysts determine what computer hardware and software will be needed to set it up. They coordinate tests and observe the initial use of the system to ensure that it performs as planned. They prepare specifications, flow charts, and process diagrams for computer programmers to follow; then they work with programmers to "debug," or eliminate errors, from the system. Systems analysts who do more in-depth testing may be called *software quality assurance analysts*. In addition to running tests, these workers diagnose problems, recommend solutions, and determine whether program requirements have been met.

**Projections data from the National Employment Matrix**

| Occupational Title | SOC Code | Employment, 2006 | Projected employment, 2016 | Change, 2006-2016 | |
|---|---|---|---|---|---|
| | | | | Number | Percent |
| Computer systems analysts ............................................................. | 15-1051 | 504,000 | 650,000 | 146,000 | 29 |

NOTE: Data in this table are rounded.

In some organizations, *programmer-analysts* design and update the software that runs a computer. They also create custom applications tailored to their organization's tasks. Because they are responsible for both programming and systems analysis, these workers must be proficient in both areas. As this dual proficiency becomes more common, analysts are increasingly working with databases, object-oriented programming languages, client–server applications, and multimedia and Internet technology.

One challenge created by expanding computer use is the need for different computer systems to communicate with each other. Systems analysts work to make the computer systems within an organization, or across organizations, compatible so that information can be shared. Many systems analysts are involved with these "networking" tasks, connecting all the computers internally, in an individual office, department, or establishment, or externally, as when setting up e-commerce networks to facilitate business among companies.

*Work environment.* Computer systems analysts work in offices or laboratories in comfortable surroundings. They usually work about 40 hours a week—about the same as many other professional or office workers. Evening or weekend work may be necessary, however, to meet deadlines or solve specific problems. Many analysts telecommute, using computers to work from remote locations.

Like other workers who spend long periods typing on a computer, computer systems analysts are susceptible to eyestrain, back discomfort, and hand and wrist problems such as carpal tunnel syndrome or cumulative trauma disorder.

# Training, Other Qualifications, and Advancement

Training requirements for computer systems analysts vary depending on the job, but many employers prefer applicants who have a bachelor's degree. Relevant work experience also is very important. Advancement opportunities are good for those with the necessary skills and experience.

*Education and training.* When hiring computer systems analysts, employers usually prefer applicants who have at least a bachelor's degree. For more technically complex jobs, people with graduate degrees are preferred.

The level and type of education that employers require reflects changes in technology. Employers often scramble to find workers capable of implementing the newest technologies. Workers with formal education or experience in information security, for example, are currently in demand because of the growing use of computer networks, which must be protected from threats.

For jobs in a technical or scientific environment, employers often seek applicants who have at least a bachelor's degree in a technical field, such as computer science, information science, applied math-

ematics, engineering, or the physical sciences. For jobs in a business environment, employers often seek applicants with at least a bachelor's degree in a business-related field such as management information systems (MIS). Increasingly, employers are seeking individuals who have a master's degree in business administration (MBA) with a concentration in information systems.

Despite the preference for technical degrees, however, people who have degrees in other majors may find employment as systems analysts if they also have technical skills. Courses in computer science or related subjects combined with practical experience can qualify people for some jobs in the occupation.

Employers generally look for people with expertise relevant to the job. For example, systems analysts who wish to work for a bank should have some expertise in finance, and systems analysts who wish to work for a hospital should have some knowledge of health management.

Technological advances come so rapidly in the computer field that continuous study is necessary to remain competitive. Employers, hardware and software vendors, colleges and universities, and private training institutions offer continuing education to help workers attain the latest skills. Additional training may come from professional development seminars offered by professional computing societies.

*Other qualifications.* Employers usually look for people who have broad knowledge and experience related to computer systems and technologies, strong problem-solving and analytical skills, and the ability to think logically. In addition, because they often deal with a number of tasks simultaneously, the ability to concentrate and pay close attention to detail is important. Although these workers sometimes work independently, they frequently work in teams on large projects. Therefore, they must have good interpersonal skills and be able to communicate effectively with computer personnel, users, and other staff who may have no technical background.

*Advancement.* With experience, systems analysts may be promoted to senior or lead systems analyst. Those who possess leadership ability and good business skills also can become computer and information systems managers or can advance into other management positions such as manager of information systems or chief information officer. Those with work experience and considerable expertise in a particular subject or application may find lucrative opportunities as independent consultants, or may choose to start their own computer consulting firms.

# Employment

Computer systems analysts held about 504,000 jobs in 2006. Although they are increasingly employed in every sector of the economy, the greatest concentration of these workers is in the computer systems design and related services industry. Computer systems analysts are also employed by governments; insurance companies; financial institutions; hospitals; management, scientific, and technical consulting services firms; data processing services firms; professional and commercial equipment wholesalers; universities; and management of companies and enterprises.

A growing number of systems analysts are employed on a temporary or contract basis; many of these individuals are self-employed, working independently as contractors or consultants. About 29,000 computer systems analysts were self-employed in 2006.

## Job Outlook

Employment is expected to grow much faster than the average for all occupations. As a result of this rapid growth, job prospects should be very good.

*Employment change.* Employment of computer systems analysts is expected to grow by 29 percent from 2006 to 2016, which is much faster than the average for all occupations. In addition, the 146,000 new jobs that are expected to arise over the projections decade will be substantial. Demand for these workers will increase as organizations continue to adopt and integrate increasingly sophisticated technologies. Job growth will not be as rapid as during the preceding decade, however, as the information technology sector matures and as routine work is increasingly outsourced offshore to foreign countries with lower prevailing wages.

The growth of electronic commerce and the integration of Internet technologies into business have resulted in a growing need for specialists who can develop and support Internet and intranet applications. Moreover, falling prices of computer hardware and software should continue to induce more businesses to expand their computerized operations and incorporate new technologies.

The demand for computer networking within organizations will also drive demand for computer systems analysts. The introduction of the wireless Internet, known as WiFi, and of personal mobile computers has created a need for new systems that can integrate these technologies into existing networks. Explosive growth in these areas is expected to fuel demand for analysts who are knowledgeable about systems integration and network, data, and communications security.

As more sophisticated and complex technology is implemented across all organizations, demand for systems analysts will remain strong. These workers will be called upon to solve problems and to integrate new technologies with existing ones. Also, the increasing importance being placed on "cybersecurity"—the protection of electronic information—will result in a need for workers skilled in information security.

As with other information technology jobs, employment growth may be tempered somewhat as some computer systems analyst jobs are outsourced offshore. Firms may look to cut costs by shifting operations to foreign countries with lower prevailing wages and highly educated workers who have strong technical skills.

*Job prospects.* Job prospects should be very good. Job openings will occur as a result of strong job growth and from the need to replace workers who move into managerial positions or other occupations, or who leave the labor force. As technology becomes more sophisticated and complex, employers demand a higher level of skill and

expertise from their employees. Individuals with an advanced degree in computer science or computer engineering or with an MBA with a concentration in information systems should have the best prospects. College graduates with a bachelor's degree in computer science, computer engineering, information science, or management information systems also should enjoy very good prospects, particularly if they have supplemented their formal education with practical experience. Because employers continue to seek computer specialists who can combine strong technical skills with good interpersonal and business skills, graduates with non-computer-science degrees who have had courses in computer programming, systems analysis, and other information technology subjects also should continue to find jobs in computer fields.

## Earnings

Median annual earnings of wage-and-salary computer systems analysts were $69,760 in May 2006. The middle 50 percent earned between $54,320 and $87,600 a year. The lowest 10 percent earned less than $42,780, and the highest 10 percent earned more than $106,820. Median annual earnings in the industries employing the largest numbers of computer systems analysts in May 2006 were

| | |
|---|---|
| Professional and commercial equipment and supplies merchant wholesalers | $81,080 |
| Computer systems design and related services | 71,680 |
| Management of companies and enterprises | 71,090 |
| Insurance carriers | 69,990 |
| State government | 61,340 |

According to the National Association of Colleges and Employers, starting offers for graduates with a bachelor's degree in computer science averaged $53,396. Starting offers for graduates with a bachelor's degree in information sciences and systems averaged $50,852. For those with a degree in management information systems/business data processing, starting offers averaged $47,648.

According to Robert Half Technology, starting salaries for systems analysts ranged from $64,000 to $87,000 in 2007. Starting salaries for business systems analysts ranged from $61,250 to $86,500. Starting salaries for developer/programmer analysts ranged from $55,250 to $90,250.

## Related Occupations

Other workers who use computers extensively and who use logic and creativity to solve business and technical problems include computer programmers, computer software engineers, computer and information systems managers, engineers, mathematicians, statisticians, operations research analysts, management analysts, and actuaries.

## Sources of Additional Information

Further information about computer careers is available from

▸ Association for Computing Machinery (ACM), 2 Penn Plaza, Suite 701, New York, NY 10121-0701. Internet: http://www.acm.org

▸ Institute of Electrical and Electronics Engineers Computer Society, Headquarters Office, 1730 Massachusetts Ave. NW, Washington, DC 20036-1992. Internet: http://www.computer.org

▸ National Workforce Center for Emerging Technologies, 3000 Landerholm Circle SE, Bellevue, WA 98007. Internet: http://www.nwcet.org

▸ University of Washington Computer Science and Engineering Department, AC101 Paul G. Allen Center, Box 352350, 185 Stevens Way, Seattle, WA 98195-2350. Internet: http://www.cs.washington.edu/WhyCSE

# Construction and Building Inspectors

(O*NET 47-4011.00)

## Significant Points

■ About 41 percent of inspectors work for local governments, primarily municipal or county building departments.

■ Many home inspectors are self-employed.

■ Opportunities should be best for experienced construction supervisors and craftworkers who have some college education, engineering or architectural training, or certification as construction inspectors or plan examiners.

## Nature of the Work

Construction and building inspectors examine buildings, highways and streets, sewer and water systems, dams, bridges, and other structures. They ensure that their construction, alteration, or repair complies with building codes and ordinances, zoning regulations, and contract specifications. Building codes and standards are the primary means by which building construction is regulated in the United States for the health and safety of the general public. National model building and construction codes are published by the International Code Council (ICC), although many localities have additional ordinances and codes that modify or add to the national model codes. To monitor compliance with regulations, inspectors make an initial inspection during the first phase of construction and follow up with further inspections throughout the construction project. However, no inspection is ever exactly the same. In areas where certain types of severe weather or natural disasters—such as earthquakes or hurricanes—are more common, inspectors monitor compliance with additional safety regulations designed to protect structures and occupants during those events.

There are many types of inspectors. *Building inspectors* inspect the structural quality and general safety of buildings. Some specialize in for example, structural steel or reinforced-concrete structures. Before construction begins, *plan examiners* determine whether the plans for the building or other structure comply with building codes and whether they are suited to the engineering and environmental demands of the building site. To inspect the condition of the soil and the positioning and depth of the footings, inspectors visit the worksite before the foundation is poured. Later, they return to the site to inspect the foundation after it has been completed. The size and type of structure, as well as the rate at which it proceeds toward completion, determine the number of other site visits they must make. Upon completion of the project, they make a final, comprehensive inspection.

In addition to structural characteristics, a primary concern of building inspectors is fire safety. They inspect structures' fire sprinklers, alarms, smoke control systems, and fire exits. Inspectors assess the type of construction, contents of the building, adequacy of fire protection equipment, and risks posed by adjoining buildings.

*Electrical inspectors* examine the installation of electrical systems and equipment to ensure that they function properly and comply with electrical codes and standards. They visit worksites to inspect new and existing sound and security systems, wiring, lighting, motors, and generating equipment. They also inspect the installation of the electrical wiring for heating and air-conditioning systems, appliances, and other components.

*Elevator inspectors* examine lifting and conveying devices such as elevators, escalators, moving sidewalks, lifts and hoists, inclined railways, ski lifts, and amusement rides.

*Home inspectors* conduct inspections of newly built or previously owned homes, condominiums, town homes, manufactured homes, apartments, and at times commercial buildings. Home inspection has become a standard practice in the home-purchasing process. Home inspectors are most often hired by prospective home buyers to inspect and report on the condition of a home's systems, components, and structure. Although they look for and report violations of building codes, they do not have the power to enforce compliance with the codes. Typically, they are hired either immediately prior to a purchase offer on a home or as a contingency to a sales contract. In addition to examining structural quality, home inspectors inspect all home systems and features, including roofing as well as the exterior, attached garage or carport, foundation, interior, plumbing, and electrical, heating, and cooling systems. Some home inspections are done for homeowners who want an evaluation of their home's condition, for example, prior to putting the home on the market or as a way to diagnose problems.

*Mechanical inspectors* inspect the installation of the mechanical components of commercial kitchen appliances, heating and air-conditioning equipment, gasoline and butane tanks, gas and oil piping, and gas-fired and oil-fired appliances. Some specialize in boilers or ventilating equipment as well.

*Plumbing inspectors* examine plumbing systems, including private disposal systems, water supply and distribution systems, plumbing fixtures and traps, and drain, waste, and vent lines.

*Public works inspectors* ensure that federal, state, and local government construction of water and sewer systems, highways, streets, bridges, and dams conforms to detailed contract specifications. They inspect excavation and fill operations, the placement of forms for concrete, concrete mixing and pouring, asphalt paving, and grading operations. They record the work and materials used so that contract payments can be calculated. Public works inspectors may specialize in highways, structural steel, reinforced concrete, or ditches. Others specialize in dredging operations required for bridges and dams or for harbors.

The owner of a building or structure under construction employs *specification inspectors* to ensure that work is done according to

**Projections data from the National Employment Matrix**

| Occupational Title | SOC Code | Employment, 2006 | Projected employment, 2016 | Change, 2006-16 | |
| --- | --- | --- | --- | --- | --- |
| | | | | Number | Percent |
| Construction and building inspectors................................................ | 47-4011 | 110,000 | 130,000 | 20,000 | 18 |

NOTE: Data in this table are rounded.

design specifications. Specification inspectors represent the owner's interests, not those of the general public. Insurance companies and financial institutions also may use their services.

Details concerning construction projects, building and occupancy permits, and other documentation generally are stored on computers so that they can easily be retrieved and updated. For example, inspectors may use laptop computers to record their findings while inspecting a site. Most inspectors use computers to help them monitor the status of construction inspection activities and keep track of permits issued, and some can access all construction and building codes from their computers on the jobsite, decreasing the need for paper binders. However, many inspectors continue to use a paper checklist to detail their findings.

Although inspections are primarily visual, inspectors may use tape measures, survey instruments, metering devices, and equipment such as concrete strength measurers. They keep a log of their work, take photographs, and file reports. Many inspectors also use laptops or other portable electronic devices onsite to facilitate the accuracy of their written reports, as well as e-mail and fax machines to send out the results. If necessary, they act on their findings. For example, government and construction inspectors notify the construction contractor, superintendent, or supervisor when they discover a violation of a code or ordinance or something that does not comply with the contract specifications or approved plans. If the problem is not corrected within a reasonable or otherwise specified period, government inspectors have authority to issue a "stop-work" order.

Many inspectors also investigate construction or alterations being done without proper permits. Inspectors who are employees of municipalities enforce laws pertaining to the proper design, construction, and use of buildings. They direct violators of permit laws to obtain permits and to submit to inspection.

*Work environment.* Construction and building inspectors usually work alone. However, several may be assigned to large, complex projects, particularly because inspectors tend to specialize in different areas of construction. Although they spend considerable time inspecting construction worksites, inspectors also spend time in a field office reviewing blueprints, answering letters or telephone calls, writing reports, and scheduling inspections.

Many construction sites are dirty and may be cluttered with tools, materials, or debris. Inspectors may have to climb ladders or many flights of stairs or crawl around in tight spaces. Although their work generally is not considered hazardous, inspectors, like other construction workers, wear hardhats and adhere to other safety requirements while at a construction site.

Inspectors normally work regular hours. However, they may work additional hours during periods when a lot of construction is taking place. Also, if an accident occurs at a construction site, inspectors must respond immediately and may work additional hours to complete their report. Non-government inspectors—especially those

who are self-employed—may have a varied work schedule, at times working evenings and weekends.

## Training, Other Qualifications, and Advancement

Although requirements vary considerably, construction and building inspectors should have a thorough knowledge of construction materials and practices. In some states, construction and building inspectors are required to obtain a special license or certification, so it is important to check with the appropriate state agency.

*Education and training.* Most employers require at least a high school diploma or the equivalent, even for workers with considerable experience. More often, employers look for persons who have studied engineering or architecture or who have a degree from a community or junior college with courses in building inspection, home inspection, construction technology, drafting, and mathematics. Many community colleges offer certificate or associate degree programs in building inspection technology. Courses in blueprint reading, algebra, geometry, and English also are useful. A growing number of construction and building inspectors are entering the occupation with a college degree, which often can substitute for previous experience. The distribution of all construction and building inspectors by their highest level of educational attainment in 2006 was:

| | Percent |
| --- | --- |
| High school graduate or less | 31 |
| Some college, no degree | 28 |
| Associate's degree | 12 |
| Bachelor's degree | 26 |
| Graduate degree | 2 |

The level of training requirements varies by type of inspector and state. In general, construction and building inspectors receive much of their training on the job, although they must learn building codes and standards on their own. Working with an experienced inspector, they learn about inspection techniques; codes, ordinances, and regulations; contract specifications; and recordkeeping and reporting duties. Supervised onsite inspections also may be a part of the training. Other requirements can include various courses and assigned reading. Some courses and instructional material are available online as well as through formal venues.

*Licensure and certification.* Many states and local jurisdictions require some type of license or certification for employment as a construction and building inspector. Requirements may vary by state or local municipality. Typical requirements for licensure or certification include previous experience, a minimum educational attainment level, such as a high school diploma, and possibly the passing of a state-approved examination. Some states have individual licensing programs for inspectors, while others may require certification by such associations as the International Code Council, International Association of Plumbing and Mechanical Officials, and National Fire Protection Association.

Similarly, some states require home inspectors to obtain a state issued license or certification. Currently, 33 states have regulations affecting home inspectors. Requirements for a license or certification vary by state, but may include obtaining a minimum level of education, having a set amount of experience with inspections, purchasing liability insurance of a certain amount, and the passing of an examination. Renewal is usually every few years and annual continuing education is almost always required.

*Other qualifications.* Because inspectors must possess the right mix of technical knowledge, experience, and education, employers prefer applicants who have both formal training and experience. For example, many inspectors previously worked as carpenters, electricians, or plumbers. Home inspectors combine knowledge of multiple specialties, so many of them come into the occupation having a combination of certifications and previous experience in various construction trades.

Construction and building inspectors must be in good physical condition in order to walk and climb about construction and building sites. They also must have a driver's license so that they can get to scheduled appointments.

*Advancement.* Being a member of a nationally recognized inspection association enhances employment opportunities and may be required by some employers. Even if it is not required, certification can enhance an inspector's opportunities for employment and advancement to more responsible positions. To become certified, inspectors with substantial experience and education must pass examinations on topics including code requirements, construction techniques and materials, standards of practice, and codes of ethics. The International Code Council offers multiple voluntary certifications, as do many other professional associations. Many categories of certification are awarded for inspectors and plan examiners in a variety of specialties, including the Certified Building Official (CBO) certification, for code compliance, and the Residential Building Inspector (RBI) certification, for home inspectors. In a few cases, there are no education or experience prerequisites, and certification consists of passing an examination in a designated field either at a regional location or online. In addition, federal, state, and many local governments may require inspectors to pass a civil service exam.

Because they advise builders and the general public on building codes, construction practices, and technical developments, construction and building inspectors must keep abreast of changes in these areas. Continuing education is required by many states and certifying organizations. Numerous employers provide formal training to broaden inspectors' knowledge of construction materials, practices, and techniques. Inspectors who work for small agencies or firms that do not conduct their own training programs can expand their knowledge and upgrade their skills by attending state-sponsored training programs, by taking college or correspondence courses, or by attending seminars and conferences sponsored by various related organizations, including professional organizations. An engineering

or architectural degree often is required for advancement to supervisory positions.

## Employment

Construction and building inspectors held about 110,000 jobs in 2006. Local governments—primarily municipal or county building departments—employed 41 percent. Employment of local government inspectors is concentrated in cities and in suburban areas undergoing rapid growth. Local governments in larger jurisdictions may employ large inspection staffs, including many plan examiners or inspectors who specialize in structural steel, reinforced concrete, and boiler, electrical, and elevator inspection. In smaller jurisdictions, only one or a few inspectors who specialize in multiple areas may be on staff.

Another 26 percent of construction and building inspectors worked for architectural and engineering services firms, conducting inspections for a fee or on a contract basis. Many of these were home inspectors working on behalf of potential real estate purchasers. Most of the remaining inspectors were employed in other service-providing industries or by state governments. About 1 in 10 construction and building inspectors was self-employed. Since many home inspectors are self-employed, it is likely that most self-employed construction and building inspectors were home inspectors.

## Job Outlook

Job opportunities in construction and building inspection should be best for highly experienced supervisors and construction craft workers who have some college education, engineering or architectural training, or certification as inspectors or plan examiners. Inspectors should experience faster than average employment growth.

*Employment change.* Employment of construction and building inspectors is expected to grow by 18 percent over the 2006–2016 decade, which is faster than the average for all occupations. Concern for public safety and a desire for improvement in the quality of construction should continue to stimulate demand for construction and building inspectors in government as well as in firms specializing in architectural, engineering, and related services. As the result of new technology such as building information modeling (BIM), the availability of a richer set of buildings data in a more timely and transparent manner will make it easier to conduct plan reviews. This will lead to more time and resources spent on inspections. In addition, the growing focus on natural and manmade disasters is increasing the level of interest in and need for qualified inspectors. Issues such as green and sustainable design are new areas of focus that will also drive the demand for construction and building inspectors.

The routine practice of obtaining home inspections is a relatively recent development, causing employment of home inspectors to increase rapidly. Although employment of home inspectors is expected to continue to increase, the attention given to this specialty, combined with the desire of some construction workers to move into less strenuous and potentially higher paying work, may result in reduced growth of home inspectors in some areas. In addition, increasing state regulations are starting to limit entry into the specialty only to those who have a given level of previous experience and are certified.

***Job prospects.*** Inspectors are involved in all phases of construction, including maintenance and repair work, and are therefore less likely to lose their jobs when new construction slows during recessions. Those who are self-employed, such as home inspectors, are more likely to be affected by economic downturns or fluctuations in the real estate market. However, those with a thorough knowledge of construction practices and skills in areas such as reading and evaluating blueprints and plans will be better off. Inspectors with previous related experience in construction, a postsecondary degree, and engineering or architectural training will have the best prospects. In addition to openings stemming from the expected employment growth, some job openings will arise from the need to replace inspectors who transfer to other occupations or leave the labor force.

## Earnings

Median annual earnings of wage and salary construction and building inspectors were $46,570 in May 2006. The middle 50 percent earned between $36,610 and $58,780. The lowest 10 percent earned less than $29,210, and the highest 10 percent earned more than $72,590. Median annual earnings in the industries employing the largest numbers of construction and building inspectors were

| | |
|---|---|
| Architectural, engineering, and related services | $46,850 |
| Local government | 46,040 |
| State government | 43,680 |

Building inspectors, including plan examiners, generally earn the highest salaries. Salaries in large metropolitan areas are substantially higher than those in small jurisdictions.

Benefits vary by place of employment. Those working for the government and private companies typically receive standard benefits, including health and medical insurance, a retirement plan, and paid annual leave. Those who are self-employed may have to provide their own benefits.

More than a quarter of all construction and building inspectors belonged to a union in 2006.

## Related Occupations

Because construction and building inspectors are familiar with construction principles, the most closely related occupations are construction occupations, especially carpenters, plumbers, and electricians. Construction and building inspectors also combine knowledge of construction principles and law with an ability to coordinate data, diagnose problems, and communicate with people. Workers in other occupations using a similar combination of skills include architects, except landscape and naval; appraisers and assessors of real estate; construction managers; civil engineers; cost estimators; engineering technicians; and surveyors, cartographers, photogrammetrists, and surveying technicians.

## Sources of Additional Information

Information about building codes, certification, and a career as a construction or building inspector is available from

▶ International Code Council, 500 New Jersey Avenue NW, 6th Floor, Washington, DC 20001-2070. Internet: http://www.iccsafe.org

▶ National Fire Protection Association, 1 Batterymarch Park, Quincy, Massachusetts, 02169-7471. Internet: http://www.nfpa.org

For more information about construction inspectors, contact

▶ Association of Construction Inspectors, 1224 North Nokomis NE, Alexandria, MN 56308.

For more information about electrical inspectors, contact

▶ International Association of Electrical Inspectors, 901 Waterfall Way, Suite 602, Richardson, TX 75080-7702. Internet: http://www.iaei.org

For more information about elevator inspectors, contact

▶ National Association of Elevator Safety Authorities International, 6957 Littlerock Rd SW, Ste A, Tumwater, WA 98512. Internet: http://www.naesai.org

For more information about education and training for mechanical and plumbing inspectors, contact

▶ International Association for Plumbing and Mechanical Officials, 5001 E. Philadelphia St., Ontario, CA 91761. Internet: http://www.iapmo.org/iapmo

For information about becoming a home inspector, contact any of the following organizations:

▶ American Society of Home Inspectors, 932 Lee St., Suite 101, Des Plaines, IL 60016. Internet: http://www.ashi.org

▶ National Association of Home Inspectors, 4248 Park Glen Rd., Minneapolis, MN 55416. Internet: http://www.nahi.org

For information about a career as a state or local government construction or building inspector, contact your state or local employment service.

## Construction Laborers

(O*NET 47-2061.00)

## Significant Points

■ Many construction laborer jobs require a variety of basic skills, but others require specialized training and experience.

■ Most construction laborers learn on the job, but formal apprenticeship programs provide the most thorough preparation.

■ Job opportunities vary by locality, but in many areas there will be competition, especially for jobs requiring limited skills.

■ Laborers who have specialized skills or who can relocate near new construction projects should have the best opportunities.

## Nature of the Work

Construction laborers can be found on almost all construction sites performing a wide range of tasks from the very easy to the potentially hazardous. They can be found at building, highway, and heavy construction sites; residential and commercial sites; tunnel and shaft excavations; and demolition sites. Many of the jobs they perform require physical strength, training, and experience. Other jobs require little skill and can be learned in a short amount of time. While most construction laborers specialize in a type of construction, such as highway or tunnel construction, some are generalists who perform many different tasks during all stages of construction. Construction laborers, who work in underground construction, such as in tunnels, or in demolition are more likely to specialize in only those areas.

Construction laborers clean and prepare construction sites. They remove trees and debris, tend pumps, compressors and generators, and build forms for pouring concrete. They erect and disassemble scaffolding and other temporary structures. They load, unload, identify, and distribute building materials to the appropriate location according to project plans and specifications. Laborers also tend machines; for example, they may mix concrete using a portable mixer or tend a machine that pumps concrete, grout, cement, sand, plaster, or stucco through a spray gun for application to ceilings and walls. They often help other craftworkers, including carpenters, plasterers, operating engineers, and masons.

Construction laborers are responsible for oversight of the installation and maintenance of traffic control devices and patterns. At highway construction sites, this work may include clearing and preparing highway work zones and rights of way; installing traffic barricades, cones, and markers; and controlling traffic passing near, in, and around work zones. They also dig trenches, install sewer, water, and storm drain pipes, and place concrete and asphalt on roads. Other highly specialized tasks include operating laser guidance equipment to place pipes; operating air, electric, and pneumatic drills; and transporting and setting explosives for tunnel, shaft, and road construction.

Some construction laborers help with the removal of hazardous materials, such as asbestos, lead, or chemicals.

Construction laborers operate a variety of equipment including pavement breakers; jackhammers; earth tampers; concrete, mortar, and plaster mixers; electric and hydraulic boring machines; torches; small mechanical hoists; laser beam equipment; and surveying and measuring equipment. They may use computers and other high-tech input devices to control robotic pipe cutters and cleaners. To perform their jobs effectively, construction laborers must be familiar with the duties of other craftworkers and with the materials, tools, and machinery they use.

Construction laborers often work as part of a team with other skilled craftworkers, jointly carrying out assigned construction tasks. At other times, construction laborers may work alone, reading and interpreting instructions, plans, and specifications with little or no supervision.

*Work environment.* Most laborers do physically demanding work. They may lift and carry heavy objects, and stoop, kneel, crouch, or crawl in awkward positions. Some work at great heights, or outdoors in all weather conditions. Some jobs expose workers to harmful materials or chemicals, fumes, odors, loud noise, or dangerous machinery. Some laborers may be exposed to lead-based paint, asbestos, or other hazardous substances during their work especially when working in confined spaces. To avoid injury, workers in these jobs wear safety clothing, such as gloves, hardhats, protective chemical suits, and devices to protect their eyes, respiratory system, or hearing. While working in underground construction, construction laborers must be especially alert to safely follow procedures and must deal with a variety of hazards.

Construction laborers generally work 8-hour shifts, although longer shifts are common. Overnight work may be required when working on highways. In some parts of the country, construction laborers may work only during certain seasons. They may also experience weather-related work stoppages at any time of the year.

## Training, Other Qualifications, and Advancement

Many construction laborer jobs require a variety of basic skills, but others require specialized training and experience. Most construction laborers learn on the job, but formal apprenticeship programs provide the most thorough preparation.

*Education and training.* While some construction laborer jobs have no specific educational qualifications or entry-level training, apprenticeships for laborers require a high school diploma or equivalent. High school classes in English, mathematics, physics, mechanical drawing, blueprint reading, welding, and general shop can be helpful.

Most workers start by getting a job with a contractor who provides on-the-job training. Increasingly, construction laborers find work through temporary help agencies that send laborers to construction sites for short-term work. Entry-level workers generally help more experienced workers. They perform routine tasks, such as cleaning and preparing the worksite and unloading materials. When the opportunity arises, they learn from experienced construction trades workers how to do more difficult tasks, such as operating tools and equipment. Construction laborers may also choose or be required to attend a trade or vocational school or community college to receive further trade-related training.

Some laborers receive more formal training. A number of employers, particularly large nonresidential construction contractors with union membership, offer employees formal apprenticeships, which provide the best preparation. These programs include between two and four years of classroom and on-the-job training. In the first 200 hours, workers learn basic construction skills such as blueprint reading, the correct use of tools and equipment, and safety and health procedures. The remainder of the curriculum consists of specialized skills training in three of the largest segments of the construction industry: building construction, heavy and highway construction, and environmental remediation, such as lead or asbestos abatement, and mold or hazardous waste remediation.

Workers who use dangerous equipment or handle toxic chemicals usually receive specialized safety training. Laborers who remove hazardous materials are required to take union or employer-sponsored Occupational Safety and Health Administration safety training.

Apprenticeship applicants usually must be at least 18 years old and meet local requirements. Because the number of apprenticeship programs is limited, however, only a small proportion of laborers learn their trade in this way.

*Other qualifications.* Laborers need manual dexterity, eye-hand coordination, good physical fitness, a good sense of balance, and an ability to work as a member of a team. The ability to solve arithmetic problems quickly and accurately may be required. In addition, military service or a good work history is viewed favorably by contractors.

**Projections data from the National Employment Matrix**

| Occupational Title | SOC Code | Employment, 2006 | Projected employment, 2016 | Change, 2006-16 | |
|---|---|---|---|---|---|
| | | | | Number | Percent |
| Construction laborers ................................................................ | 47-2061 | 1,232,000 | 1,366,000 | 134,000 | 11 |

NOTE: Data in this table are rounded.

*Certification and advancement.* Laborers may earn certifications in welding, scaffold erecting, and concrete finishing. These certifications help workers prove that they have the knowledge to perform more complex tasks.

Through training and experience, laborers can move into other construction occupations. Laborers may also advance to become construction supervisors or general contractors. For those who would like to advance, it is increasingly important to be able to communicate in both English and Spanish in order to relay instructions and safety precautions to workers with limited understanding of English; Spanish-speaking workers make up a large part of the construction workforce in many areas. Supervisors and contractors need good communication skills to deal with clients and subcontractors.

In addition, supervisors and contractors should be able to identify and estimate the quantity of materials needed to complete a job, and accurately estimate how long a job will take to complete and what it will cost. Computer skills also are important for advancement as construction becomes increasingly mechanized and computerized.

## Employment

Construction laborers held about 1.2 million jobs in 2006. They worked throughout the country but, like the general population, were concentrated in metropolitan areas. About 67 percent of construction laborers work in the construction industry, including 30 percent who work for specialty trade contractors. About 17 percent were self-employed in 2006.

## Job Outlook

Employment is expected to grow about as fast as the average. In many areas, there will be competition for jobs, especially for those requiring limited skills. Laborers who have specialized skills or who can relocate near new construction projects should have the best opportunities.

*Employment change.* Employment of construction laborers is expected to grow by 11 percent between 2006 and 2016, about as fast as the average for all occupations. The construction industry in general is expected to grow more slowly than it has in recent years. Due to the large variety of tasks that laborers perform, demand for laborers will mirror the level of overall construction activity.

Construction laborer jobs will be adversely affected by automation as some jobs are replaced by new machinery and equipment that improves productivity and quality. Also, laborers will be increasingly employed by staffing agencies that will contract out laborers to employers on a temporary basis, and in many areas employers will continue to rely on day laborers instead of full-time laborers on staff.

*Job prospects.* In many geographic areas there will be competition, especially for jobs requiring limited skills, due to a plentiful supply of workers who are willing to work as day laborers. In other areas, however, opportunities will be better. Overall opportunities will be best for those with experience and specialized skills and for those who can relocate to areas with new construction projects. Opportunities will also be better for laborers specializing in road construction.

Employment of construction laborers, like that of many other construction workers, is sensitive to the fluctuations of the economy. Workers in these trades may experience periods of unemployment when the overall level of construction falls. On the other hand, shortages of these workers may occur in some areas during peak periods of building activity.

## Earnings

Median hourly earnings of wage and salary construction laborers in May 2006 were $12.66. The middle 50 percent earned between $9.95 and $17.31. The lowest 10 percent earned less than $8.16, and the highest 10 percent earned more than $24.19. Median hourly earnings in the industries employing the largest number of construction laborers were as follows:

| | |
|---|---|
| Nonresidential building construction | $13.62 |
| Other specialty trade contractors | 12.93 |
| Residential building construction | 12.82 |
| Foundation, structure, and building exterior contractors | 12.41 |
| Employment services | 9.90 |

Earnings for construction laborers can be reduced by poor weather or by downturns in construction activity, which sometimes result in layoffs. Apprentices or helpers usually start out earning about 60 percent of the wage rate paid to experienced workers. Pay increases as apprentices gain experience and learn new skills. Some laborers belong to the Laborers' International Union of North America.

## Related Occupations

The work of construction laborers is closely related to other construction occupations. Other workers who perform similar physical work include persons in material moving occupations; forest, conservation, and logging workers; and grounds maintenance workers.

## Sources of Additional Information

For information about jobs as a construction laborer, contact local building or construction contractors, local joint labor-management apprenticeship committees, apprenticeship agencies, or the local office of your State Employment Service. You can also find information on the registered apprenticeships together with links to state apprenticeship programs on the U.S. Department of Labor's Web site: http://www.doleta.gov/atels_bat. Apprenticeship information is also available from the U.S. Department of Labor's toll-free helpline: (877) 872-5627. For general information on apprenticeships and how to get them, see the *Occupational Outlook Quarterly* article "Apprenticeships: Career training, credentials—and a paycheck in your pocket," online at http://www.bls.gov/opub/ooq/2002/summer/art01.pdf and in print at many libraries and career centers.

For information on education programs for laborers, contact

- Laborers-AGC Education and Training Fund, 37 Deerfield Rd., P.O. Box 37, Pomfret Center, CT 06259. Internet: http://www.laborerslearn.org

- National Center for Construction Education and Research, P.O. Box 141104, Gainesville, FL 32614-1104. Internet: http://www.nccer.org

# Construction Managers

(O*NET 11-9021.00)

## Significant Points

- Construction managers must be available—often 24 hours a day—to deal with delays, bad weather, or emergencies at the jobsite.

- Employers prefer jobseekers who combine construction industry work experience with a bachelor's degree in construction science, construction management, or civil engineering.

- Although certification is not required, there is a growing movement toward certification of construction managers.

- Excellent job opportunities are expected.

## Nature of the Work

Construction managers plan, direct, and coordinate a wide variety of construction projects, including the building of all types of residential, commercial, and industrial structures, roads, bridges, wastewater treatment plants, and schools and hospitals. Construction managers may oversee an entire project or just part of one. They schedule and coordinate all design and construction processes, including the selection, hiring, and oversight of specialty trade contractors, but they usually do not do any actual construction of the structure.

Construction managers are salaried or self-employed managers who oversee construction supervisors and workers. They are often called project managers, constructors, construction superintendents, project engineers, program managers, construction supervisors, or general contractors. Construction managers may be owners or salaried employees of a construction management or contracting firm, or they may work under contract or as a salaried employee of the property owner, developer, or contracting firm overseeing the construction project.

These managers coordinate and supervise the construction process from the conceptual development stage through final construction, making sure that the project gets done on time and within budget. They often work with owners, engineers, architects, and others who are involved in the construction process. Given the designs for buildings, roads, bridges, or other projects, construction managers oversee the planning, scheduling, and implementation of those designs.

Large construction projects, such as an office building or industrial complex, are often too complicated for one person to manage. These projects are divided into many segments: site preparation, including land clearing and earth moving; sewage systems; landscaping and road construction; building construction, including excavation and laying of foundations and erection of the structural framework, floors, walls, and roofs; and building systems, including fire protection, electrical, plumbing, air conditioning, and heating. Construction managers may be in charge of one or more of these activities.

Construction managers determine the best way to get materials to the building site and the most cost-effective plan and schedule for completing the project. They divide all required construction site activities into logical steps, budgeting the time required to meet established deadlines. This may require sophisticated estimating and scheduling techniques and use of computers with specialized software.

They also oversee the selection of general contractors and trade contractors to complete specific pieces of the project—which could include everything from structural metalworking and plumbing to painting and carpet installation. Construction managers determine the labor requirements and, in some cases, supervise or monitor the hiring and dismissal of workers. They oversee the performance of all trade contractors and are responsible for ensuring that all work is completed on schedule.

Construction managers direct and monitor the progress of construction activities, sometimes through construction supervisors or other construction managers. They oversee the delivery and use of materials, tools, and equipment; worker productivity and safety; and the quality of construction. They are responsible for obtaining all necessary permits and licenses and, depending upon the contractual arrangements, direct or monitor compliance with building and safety codes, other regulations, and requirements set by the project's insurers.

***Work environment.*** Working out of a main office or out of a field office at the construction site, construction managers monitor the overall construction project. Decisions regarding daily construction activities generally are made at the jobsite. Managers may travel extensively when the construction site is not close to their main office or when they are responsible for activities at two or more sites. Management of overseas construction projects usually entails temporary residence in another country.

Often "on call" 24 hours a day, construction managers deal with delays, the effects of bad weather, or emergencies at the site. Most work more than a standard 40-hour week because construction may proceed around the clock. They may need to work this type of schedule for days or weeks to meet special project deadlines, especially if there are delays.

Although the work usually is not considered inherently dangerous, construction managers must be careful while performing onsite services.

# Training, Other Qualifications, and Advancement

Employers increasingly prefer to hire construction managers with a bachelor's degree in construction science, construction management, building science, or civil engineering, although it is also possible for experienced construction workers to move up to become construction managers. In addition to having education and experience, construction managers must understand contracts, plans, specifications, and regulations.

*Education and training.* For construction manager jobs, employers increasingly prefer to hire individuals who have a bachelor's degree in construction science, construction management, building science, or civil engineering plus work experience. Practical construction experience is very important, whether gained through an internship, a cooperative education program, a job in the construction trades, or another job in the industry. Traditionally, people advanced to construction management positions after having substantial experience as construction craftworkers—carpenters, masons, plumbers, or electricians, for example—or after having worked as construction supervisors or as owners of independent specialty contracting firms. However, as construction processes become increasingly complex, employers are placing more importance on specialized education after high school.

About 105 colleges and universities offer bachelor's degree programs in construction science, building science, and construction engineering. These programs include courses in project control and development, site planning, design, construction methods, construction materials, value analysis, cost estimating, scheduling, contract administration, accounting, business and financial management, safety, building codes and standards, inspection procedures, engineering and architectural sciences, mathematics, statistics, and information technology. Graduates from four-year degree programs usually are hired as assistants to project managers, field engineers, schedulers, or cost estimators. An increasing number of graduates in related fields—engineering or architecture, for example—also enter construction management, often after acquiring substantial experience on construction projects.

About 60 colleges and universities offer a master's degree program in construction management or construction science. Master's degree recipients, especially those with work experience in construction, typically become construction managers in very large construction or construction management companies. Often, individuals who hold a bachelor's degree in an unrelated field seek a master's degree in construction management or construction science to work in the construction industry. Some construction managers obtain a master's degree in business administration or finance to further their career prospects. Doctoral degree recipients usually become college professors or conduct research.

A number of two-year colleges throughout the country offer construction management or construction technology programs. Many individuals also attend training and educational programs sponsored by industry associations, often in collaboration with postsecondary institutions.

*Other qualifications.* Construction managers should be flexible and work effectively in a fast-paced environment. They should be decisive and work well under pressure, particularly when faced with unexpected occurrences or delays. The ability to coordinate several major activities at once, while analyzing and resolving specific problems, is essential, as is an understanding of engineering, architectural, and other construction drawings. Familiarity with computers and software programs for job costing, online collaboration, scheduling, and estimating also is important.

Good oral and written communication skills also are important, as are leadership skills. Managers must be able to establish a good working relationship with many different people, including owners, other managers, designers, supervisors, and craftworkers. The ability to converse fluently in Spanish is increasingly an asset because Spanish is the first language of many workers in the construction industry.

*Certification and advancement.* There is a growing movement toward certification of construction managers. Although certification is not required to work in the construction industry, it can be valuable because it provides evidence of competence and experience. Both the American Institute of Constructors and the Construction Management Association of America have established voluntary certification programs for construction managers. Requirements combine written examinations with verification of education and professional experience. The American Institute of Constructors awards the Associate Constructor (AC) and Certified Professional Constructor (CPC) designations to candidates who meet its requirements and pass the appropriate construction examinations. The Construction Management Association of America awards the Certified Construction Manager (CCM) designation to workers who have the required experience and who pass a technical examination. Applicants for this designation also must complete a self-study course that covers the professional role of a construction manager, legal issues, allocation of risk, and other topics related to construction management.

Advancement opportunities for construction managers vary depending upon an individual's performance and the size and type of company for which they work. Within large firms, managers may eventually become top-level managers or executives. Highly experienced individuals may become independent consultants; some serve as expert witnesses in court or as arbitrators in disputes. Those with the required capital may establish their own construction management services, specialty contracting, or general contracting firm.

# Employment

Construction managers held 487,000 jobs in 2006. About 57 percent were self-employed, many as owners of general or specialty trade construction firms. Most salaried construction managers were employed in the construction industry, 13 percent by specialty trade contractor businesses—for example, plumbing, heating, air-conditioning, and electrical contractors—9 percent in residential building construction; and 9 percent in nonresidential building construction. Others were employed by architectural, engineering, and related services firms and by local governments.

**Projections data from the National Employment Matrix**

| Occupational Title | SOC Code | Employment, 2006 | Projected employment, 2016 | Change, 2006-16 | |
|---|---|---|---|---|---|
| | | | | Number | Percent |
| Construction managers............................................................. | 11-9021 | 487,000 | 564,000 | 77,000 | 16 |

NOTE: Data in this table are rounded.

# Job Outlook

Faster-than-average employment growth is expected. Additionally, excellent job opportunities will exist as the number of job openings exceeds the number of qualified applicants.

Employment change. Employment of construction managers is projected to increase by 16 percent during the 2006–2016 decade, faster than the average for all occupations. More construction managers will be needed as the level of construction activity continues to grow. Population and business growth will result in more construction of residential homes, office buildings, shopping malls, hospitals, schools, restaurants, and other structures that require construction managers.

The increasing complexity of construction projects will also boost demand for specialized management-level personnel within the construction industry. Sophisticated technology and the proliferation of laws setting standards for buildings and construction materials, worker safety, energy efficiency, environmental protection, and the potential for adverse litigation have further complicated the construction process. Advances in building materials and construction methods; the need to replace portions of the nation's infrastructure; and the growing number of multipurpose buildings and energy-efficient structures will further add to the demand for more construction managers.

Job prospects. Excellent employment opportunities for construction managers are expected through 2016 because the number of job openings will exceed the number of qualified individuals seeking to enter the occupation. This situation is expected to continue even as college construction management programs expand to meet the current high demand for graduates. The construction industry often does not attract sufficient numbers of qualified job seekers because working conditions are considered poor.

In addition to job openings arising from employment growth, many additional openings should result annually from the need to replace workers who transfer to other occupations or leave the labor force for other reasons. A substantial number of seasoned managers are also expected to retire over the next decade, likely resulting in a large number of openings.

Prospects for individuals seeking construction manager jobs in construction management, architectural and engineering services, and construction contracting firms should be best for people who have a bachelor's or higher degree in construction science, construction management, or civil engineering plus practical experience working in construction. Employers will increasingly prefer applicants with college degrees, internships, and a strong background in building technology. Construction managers will also have many opportunities to start their own firms.

Employment of construction managers, like that of many other construction workers, is sensitive to the fluctuations of the economy.

Workers in these trades may experience periods of unemployment when the overall level of construction falls. On the other hand, shortages of these workers may occur in some areas during peak periods of building activity.

# Earnings

Earnings of salaried construction managers and self-employed independent construction contractors vary depending upon the size and nature of the construction project, its geographic location, and economic conditions. In addition to typical benefits, many salaried construction managers receive bonuses and use of company motor vehicles.

Median annual earnings of wage and salary construction managers in May 2006 were $73,700. The middle 50 percent earned between $56,090 and $98,350. The lowest-paid 10 percent earned less than $43,210, and the highest-paid 10 percent earned more than $135,780. Median annual earnings in the industries employing the largest numbers of construction managers were as follows:

| | |
|---|---|
| Building equipment contractors | $75,200 |
| Electrical contractors | 74,380 |
| Nonresidential building construction | 74,080 |
| Foundation, structure, and building exterior contractors | 71,640 |
| Residential building construction | 69,400 |

The earnings of self-employed workers are not included in these numbers.

According to a July 2007 salary survey by the National Association of Colleges and Employers, people with a bachelor's degree in construction science/management received job offers averaging $46,930 a year.

# Related Occupations

Construction managers participate in the conceptual development of a construction project and oversee its organization, scheduling, and implementation. Other workers who perform similar functions include architects, except landscape and naval; civil engineers; cost estimators; landscape architects; and engineering and natural sciences managers.

# Sources of Additional Information

For information about constructor certification, contact

▸ American Institute of Constructors, 717 Princess St., Alexandria, VA 22314. Internet: http://www.aicnet.org

For information about construction management and construction manager certification, contact

▶ Construction Management Association of America, 7918 Jones Branch Dr., Suite 540, McLean, VA 22102. Internet: http://www.cmaanet.org

Information on accredited construction science and management educational programs and accreditation requirements is available from

▶ American Council for Construction Education, 1717 North Loop 1604 E, Suite 320, San Antonio, TX 78232. Internet: http://www.acce-hq.org

▶ National Center for Construction Education and Research, P.O. Box 141104, Gainesville, FL 32614. Internet: http://www.nccer.org

# Correctional Officers

(O*NET 33-1011.00, 33-3011.00, and 33-3012.00)

## Significant Points

■ The work can be stressful and hazardous.

■ Most correctional officers are employed in state and local government prisons and jails.

■ Job opportunities are expected to be excellent.

## Nature of the Work

Correctional officers, also known as *detention officers*, are responsible for overseeing individuals who have been arrested and are awaiting trial or who have been convicted of a crime and sentenced to serve time in a jail, reformatory, or penitentiary.

The jail population changes constantly as some are released, some are convicted and transferred to prison, and new offenders are arrested and enter the system. Correctional officers in local jails admit and process about 12 million people a year, with about 700,000 offenders in jail at any given time. Correctional officers in state and federal prisons watch over the approximately 1.5 million offenders who are incarcerated there at any given time.

Correctional officers maintain security and inmate accountability to prevent disturbances, assaults, and escapes. Officers have no law enforcement responsibilities outside the institution where they work.

Regardless of the setting, correctional officers maintain order within the institution and enforce rules and regulations. To help ensure that inmates are orderly and obey rules, correctional officers monitor the activities and supervise the work assignments of inmates. Sometimes, officers must search inmates and their living quarters for contraband like weapons or drugs, settle disputes between inmates, and enforce discipline. Correctional officers periodically inspect the facilities, checking cells and other areas of the institution for unsanitary conditions, contraband, fire hazards, and any evidence of infractions of rules. In addition, they routinely inspect locks, window bars, grilles, doors, and gates for signs of tampering. Finally, officers inspect mail and visitors for prohibited items.

Correctional officers report orally and in writing on inmate conduct and on the quality and quantity of work done by inmates. Officers also report security breaches, disturbances, violations of rules, and any unusual occurrences. They usually keep a daily log or record of their activities. Correctional officers cannot show favoritism and must report any inmate who violates the rules. If a crime is committed within their institution or an inmate escapes, they help the responsible law enforcement authorities investigate or search for the escapee. In jail and prison facilities with direct supervision of cellblocks, officers work unarmed. They are equipped with communications devices so that they can summon help if necessary. These officers often work in a cellblock alone, or with another officer, among the 50 to 100 inmates who reside there. The officers enforce regulations primarily through their interpersonal communication skills and through the use of progressive sanctions, such as the removal of some privileges.

In the highest security facilities, where the most dangerous inmates are housed, correctional officers often monitor the activities of prisoners from a centralized control center with closed-circuit television cameras and a computer tracking system. In such an environment, the inmates may not see anyone but officers for days or weeks at a time and may leave their cells only for showers, solitary exercise time, or visitors. Depending on the offenders' security classification within the institution, correctional officers may have to restrain inmates in handcuffs and leg irons to safely escort them to and from cells and other areas and to see authorized visitors. Officers also escort prisoners between the institution and courtrooms, medical facilities, and other destinations outside the institution.

Bailiffs, also known as *marshals* or *court officers*, are law enforcement officers who maintain safety and order in courtrooms. Their duties, which vary by location, include enforcing courtroom rules, assisting judges, guarding juries from outside contact, delivering court documents, and providing general security for courthouses.

*Work environment.* Working in a correctional institution can be stressful and hazardous. Every year, correctional officers are injured in confrontations with inmates. Correctional officers may work indoors or outdoors. Some correctional institutions are well lighted, temperature controlled, and ventilated, but others are old, overcrowded, hot, and noisy. Although both jails and prisons can be dangerous places to work, prison populations are more stable than jail populations, and correctional officers in prisons know the security and custodial requirements of the prisoners with whom they are dealing.

Correctional officers usually work an 8-hour day, 5 days a week, on rotating shifts. Because prison and jail security must be provided around the clock, officers work all hours of the day and night, weekends, and holidays. In addition, officers may be required to work paid overtime.

## Training, Other Qualifications, and Advancement

Correctional officers learn most of what they need to know for their work through on-the-job training. Qualifications vary by agency, but all agencies require a high school diploma or equivalent, and some also require some college education or full-time work experience.

*Education and training.* A high school diploma or graduation equivalency degree is required by all employers. The Federal Bureau of Prisons requires entry-level correctional officers to have at least a bachelor's degree; three years of full-time experience in a field providing counseling, assistance, or supervision to individuals;

**Projections data from the National Employment Matrix**

| Occupational Title | SOC Code | Employment, 2006 | Projected employment, 2016 | Change, 2006-16 | |
|---|---|---|---|---|---|
| | | | | Number | Percent |
| Correctional officers................................................................. | — | 500,000 | 582,000 | 82,000 | 16 |
| First-line supervisors/managers of correctional officers.............. | 33-1011 | 40,000 | 45,000 | 5,000 | 13 |
| Bailiffs, correctional officers, and jailers .................................... | 33-3010 | 460,000 | 537,000 | 77,000 | 17 |
| Bailiffs............................................................................... | 33-3011 | 19,000 | 21,000 | 2,100 | 11 |
| Correctional officers and jailers .............................................. | 33-3012 | 442,000 | 516,000 | 75,000 | 17 |

NOTE: Data in this table are rounded.

or a combination of the two. Some state and local corrections agencies require some college credits, but law enforcement or military experience may be substituted to fulfill this requirement.

Federal, state, and some local departments of corrections provide training for correctional officers based on guidelines established by the American Correctional Association and the American Jail Association. Some states have regional training academies that are available to local agencies. At the conclusion of formal instruction, all state and local correctional agencies provide on-the-job training, including training on legal restrictions and interpersonal relations. Many systems require firearms proficiency and self-defense skills. Officer trainees typically receive several weeks or months of training in an actual job setting under the supervision of an experienced officer. However, on-the-job training varies widely from agency to agency.

Academy trainees generally receive instruction in a number of subjects, including institutional policies, regulations, and operations, as well as custody and security procedures. New federal correctional officers must undergo 200 hours of formal training within the first year of employment. They also must complete 120 hours of specialized training at the U.S. Federal Bureau of Prisons residential training center at Glynco, GA, within 60 days of their appointment. Experienced officers receive annual in-service training to keep abreast of new developments and procedures.

Some correctional officers are members of prison tactical response teams, which are trained to respond to disturbances, riots, hostage situations, forced cell moves, and other potentially dangerous confrontations. Team members practice disarming prisoners wielding weapons, protecting themselves and inmates against the effects of chemical agents, and other tactics.

*Other qualifications.* All institutions require correctional officers to be at least 18 to 21 years of age, be a U.S. citizen or permanent resident, and have no felony convictions. Some require previous experience in law enforcement or the military, but college credits can be substituted to fulfill this requirement. Others require demonstration of job stability, usually by accumulating two years of work experience, which need not be related to corrections or law enforcement.

Correctional officers must be in good health. Candidates for employment generally are required to meet formal standards of physical fitness, eyesight, and hearing. In addition, many jurisdictions use standard tests to determine applicant suitability to work in a correctional environment. Good judgment and the ability to think and act quickly are indispensable. Applicants are typically screened for drug abuse, subject to background checks, and required to pass a written examination.

*Advancement.* Qualified officers may advance to the position of correctional sergeant. Correctional sergeants supervise correctional officers and usually are responsible for maintaining security and directing the activities of other officers during an assigned shift or in an assigned area. Ambitious and qualified correctional officers can be promoted to supervisory or administrative positions all the way up to warden. Promotion prospects may be enhanced by attending college. Officers sometimes transfer to related jobs, such as probation officer, parole officer, and correctional treatment specialist.

## Employment

Correctional officers held about 500,000 jobs in 2006. About 3 of every 5 jobs were in state correctional institutions such as prisons, prison camps, and youth correctional facilities. About 18,000 jobs for correctional officers were in federal correctional institutions, and about 16,000 jobs were in privately owned and managed prisons.

Most of the remaining jobs were in city and county jails or in other institutions run by local governments. Some 300 of these jails, all of them in urban areas, are large, housing over 1,000 inmates. Most correctional officers employed in jails, however, work in institutions located in rural areas with smaller inmate populations.

Other correctional officers oversee individuals being held by the U.S. Immigration and Naturalization Service pending release or deportation or work for correctional institutions that are run by private, for-profit organizations.

## Job Outlook

Employment growth is expected to be faster than the average for all occupations, and job opportunities are expected to be excellent.

*Employment change.* Employment of correctional officers is expected to grow 16 percent between 2006 and 2016, faster than the average for all occupations. Increasing demand for correctional officers will stem from population growth and rising rates of incarceration. Mandatory sentencing guidelines calling for longer sentences and reduced parole for inmates are a primary reason for historically increasing incarceration rates. Some states are reconsidering mandatory sentencing guidelines because of budgetary constraints, court decisions, and doubts about their effectiveness. Additionally, the Supreme Court recently ruled to make federal sentencing guidelines voluntary, rather than mandatory, for judges. It is unclear how many states will change their sentencing policies and how long it will be before any changes affect the prison population. Nevertheless, these developments could moderate future increases in the prison population and cause employment of correctional officers to grow more slowly than they have in the past.

Some employment opportunities also will arise in the private sector, as public authorities contract with private companies to provide and staff corrections facilities. Both state and federal corrections agencies are increasingly using private prisons.

*Job prospects.* Job opportunities for correctional officers are expected to be excellent. The need to replace correctional officers who transfer to other occupations, retire, or leave the labor force, coupled with rising employment demand, will generate thousands of job openings each year. In the past, some local and state corrections agencies have experienced difficulty in attracting and keeping qualified applicants, largely because of low salaries, shift work, and the concentration of jobs in rural locations. This situation is expected to continue.

Layoffs of correctional officers are rare because of increasing offender populations.

## Earnings

Median annual earnings of correctional officers and jailers were $35,760 in May 2006. The middle 50 percent earned between $28,320 and $46,500. The lowest 10 percent earned less than $23,600, and the highest 10 percent earned more than $58,580. Median annual earnings in the public sector were $47,750 in the federal government, $36,140 in state government, and $34,820 in local government. In the facilities support services industry, where the relatively small number of officers employed by privately operated prisons is classified, median annual earnings were $25,050.

Median annual earnings of first-line supervisors/managers of correctional officers were $52,580 in May 2006. The middle 50 percent earned between $38,920 and $67,820. The lowest 10 percent earned less than $33,270, and the highest 10 percent earned more than $81,230. Median annual earnings were $51,500 in state government and $52,940 in local government.

Median annual earnings of bailiffs were $34,210 in May 2006. The middle 50 percent earned between $25,130 and $48,010. The lowest 10 percent earned less than $18,390, and the highest 10 percent earned more than $58,270. Median annual earnings were $30,510 in local government.

According to the Federal Bureau of Prisons, the starting salary for federal correctional officers was $28,862 a year in 2007. Starting federal salaries were slightly higher in areas where prevailing local pay levels were higher.

In addition to typical benefits, correctional officers employed in the public sector usually are provided with uniforms or a clothing allowance to purchase their own uniforms. Civil service systems or merit boards cover officers employed by the federal government and most state governments. Their retirement coverage entitles correctional officers to retire at age 50 after 20 years of service or at any age with 25 years of service.

## Related Occupations

A number of options are available to those interested in careers in protective services and security. Security guards and gaming surveillance officers protect people and property against theft, vandalism, illegal entry, and fire. Police and detectives maintain law and order, prevent crime, and arrest offenders. Probation officers and correctional treatment specialists monitor and counsel offenders and evaluate their progress in becoming productive members of society.

## Sources of Additional Information

Further information about correctional officers is available from

▸ American Correctional Association, 206 N. Washington St., Suite 200, Alexandria, VA 22314. Internet: http://www.aca.org

▸ American Jail Association, 1135 Professional Ct., Hagerstown, MD 21740. Internet: http://www.corrections.com/aja

▸ Information on entrance requirements, training, and career opportunities for correctional officers at the federal level may be obtained from the Federal Bureau of Prisons. Internet: http://www.bop.gov

Information on obtaining a position as a correctional officer with the federal government is available from the Office of Personnel Management through USAJOBS, the federal government's official employment information system. This resource for locating and applying for job opportunities can be accessed through the Internet at http://www.usajobs.opm.gov or through an interactive voice response telephone system at (703) 724-1850 or TDD (978) 461-8404. These numbers are not toll free, and charges may result.

## Cost Estimators

(O*NET 13-1051.00)

## Significant Points

■ About 62 percent of cost estimators work in the construction industry, and another 15 percent are employed in manufacturing industries.

■ Voluntary certification can be valuable to cost estimators; some individual employers may require professional certification for employment.

■ Very good employment opportunities are expected.

■ In construction and manufacturing, job prospects should be best for those with industry work experience and a bachelor's degree in a related field.

## Nature of the Work

Accurately forecasting the scope, cost, and duration of future projects is vital to the survival of any business. Cost estimators develop the cost information that business owners or managers need to make a bid for a contract or to decide on the profitability of a proposed new product or project. They also determine which endeavors are making a profit.

Regardless of the industry in which they work, estimators compile and analyze data on all of the factors that can influence costs, such as materials; labor; location; duration of the project; and special machinery requirements, including computer hardware and software. Job duties vary widely depending on the type and size of the project.

The methods for estimating costs can differ greatly by industry. On a construction project, for example, the estimating process begins with the decision to submit a bid. After reviewing various preliminary drawings and specifications, the estimator visits the site of the proposed project. The estimator needs to gather information on access to the site; the availability of electricity, water, and other services; and surface topography and drainage. The estimator usually records this information in a signed report that is included in the final project estimate.

After the site visit, the estimator determines the quantity of materials and labor the firm will need to furnish. This process, called the quantity survey or "takeoff," involves completing standard estimating forms, filling in dimensions, numbers of units, and other information. A cost estimator working for a general contractor, for example, estimates the costs of all of the items that the contractor must provide. Although subcontractors estimate their costs as part of their own bidding process, the general contractor's cost estimator often analyzes bids made by subcontractors. Also during the takeoff process, the estimator must make decisions concerning equipment needs, the sequence of operations, the size of the crew required, and physical constraints at the site. Allowances for wasted materials, inclement weather, shipping delays, and other factors that may increase costs also must be incorporated in the estimate.

After completing the quantity surveys, the estimator prepares a cost summary for the entire project, including the costs of labor, equipment, materials, subcontracts, overhead, taxes, insurance, markup, and any other costs that may affect the project. The chief estimator then prepares the bid proposal for submission to the owner.

Construction cost estimators also may be employed by the project's architect or owner to estimate costs or to track actual costs relative to bid specifications as the project develops. Estimators often specialize in large construction companies employing more than one estimator. For example, one may estimate only electrical work and another may concentrate on excavation, concrete, and forms.

In manufacturing and other firms, cost estimators usually are assigned to the engineering, cost, or pricing department. The estimator's goal is to accurately estimate the costs associated with making products. The job may begin when management requests an estimate of the costs associated with a major redesign of an existing product or the development of a new product or production process. When estimating the cost of developing a new product, for example, the estimator works with engineers, first reviewing blueprints or conceptual drawings to determine the machining operations, tools, gauges, and materials that would be required. The estimator then prepares a parts list and determines whether it is more efficient to produce or to purchase the parts. To do this, the estimator asks for price information from potential suppliers. The next step is to determine the cost of manufacturing each component of the product. Some high-technology products require a considerable amount of computer programming during the design phase. The cost of software development is one of the fastest-growing and most difficult activities to estimate. As a result, some cost estimators now specialize in estimating only computer software development and related costs.

The cost estimator then prepares time-phase charts and learning curves. Time-phase charts indicate the time required for tool design

and fabrication, tool "debugging"—finding and correcting all problems—manufacturing of parts, assembly, and testing. Learning curves graphically represent the rate at which the performance of workers producing parts for the new product improves with practice. These curves are commonly called "cost reduction" curves because many problems—such as engineering changes, rework, shortages of parts, and lack of operator skills—diminish as the number of units produced increases, resulting in lower unit costs.

Using all of this information, the estimator then calculates the standard labor hours necessary to produce a specified number of units. Standard labor hours are then converted to dollar values, to which are added factors for waste, overhead, and profit to yield the unit cost in dollars. The estimator then compares the cost of purchasing parts with the firm's estimated cost of manufacturing them to determine which is cheaper.

Computers play an integral role in cost estimation because estimating often involves complex mathematical calculations and requires advanced mathematical techniques. For example, to undertake a parametric analysis (a process used to estimate costs per unit based on square footage or other specific requirements of a project), cost estimators use a computer database containing information on the costs and conditions of many other similar projects. Although computers cannot be used for the entire estimating process, they can relieve estimators of much of the drudgery associated with routine, repetitive, and time-consuming calculations. New and improved cost estimating software has led to more efficient computations, leaving estimators greater time to visit and analyze projects.

Operations research, production control, cost, and price analysts who work for government agencies may do significant amounts of cost estimating in the course of their regular duties. In addition, the duties of construction managers may include estimating costs.

***Work environment.*** Although estimators spend most of their time in a comfortable office, construction estimators also visit worksites that can be dusty, dirty, and occasionally hazardous. Likewise, estimators in manufacturing spend time on the factory floor, where it also can be noisy and dirty. In some industries, frequent travel between a firm's headquarters and its subsidiaries or subcontractors may be required.

Estimators normally work a 40-hour week, but overtime is common. Cost estimators often work under pressure and stress, especially when facing bid deadlines. Inaccurate estimating can cause a firm to lose a bid or to lose money on a job that was not accurately estimated.

## Training, Other Qualifications, and Advancement

Job entry requirements for cost estimators vary by industry. In the construction industry, employers increasingly prefer to hire cost estimators with a bachelor's degree in construction science, construction management, or building science, although it is also possible for experienced construction workers to become cost estimators. Employers in manufacturing usually prefer someone with a bachelor's degree in mathematics, statistics, or engineering.

**Projections data from the National Employment Matrix**

| Occupational Title | SOC Code | Employment, 2006 | Projected employment, 2016 | Change, 2006-16 | |
| --- | --- | --- | --- | --- | --- |
| | | | | Number | Percent |
| Cost estimators................................................................ | 13-1051 | 221,000 | 262,000 | 41,000 | 19 |

NOTE: Data in this table are rounded.

***Education and training.*** In the construction industry, employers increasingly prefer individuals with a degree in building science, construction management, or construction science, all of which usually include several courses in cost estimating. Most construction estimators also have considerable construction experience, gained through work in the industry, internships, or cooperative education programs. Applicants with a thorough knowledge of construction materials, costs, and procedures in areas ranging from heavy construction to electrical work, plumbing systems, or masonry work have a competitive edge.

In manufacturing industries, employers prefer to hire individuals with a degree in engineering, physical science, operations research, mathematics, or statistics or in accounting, finance, business, economics, or a related subject. In most industries, experience in quantitative techniques is important.

Many colleges and universities include cost estimating as part of bachelor's and associate degree curriculums in civil engineering, industrial engineering, and construction management or construction engineering technology. In addition, cost estimating is often part of master's degree programs in construction science or construction management. Organizations representing cost estimators, such as the Association for the Advancement of Cost Engineering (AACE International) and the Society of Cost Estimating and Analysis (SCEA), also sponsor educational and professional development programs. These programs help students, estimators-in-training, and experienced estimators learn about changes affecting the profession. Specialized courses and programs in cost estimating techniques and procedures also are offered by many technical schools, community colleges, and universities.

Estimators also receive much training on the job because every company has its own way of handling estimates. Working with an experienced estimator, newcomers become familiar with each step in the process. Those with no experience reading construction specifications or blueprints first learn that aspect of the work. Then they may accompany an experienced estimator to the construction site or shop floor, where they observe the work being done, take measurements, or perform other routine tasks. As they become more knowledgeable, estimators learn how to tabulate quantities and dimensions from drawings and how to select the appropriate prices for materials.

***Other qualifications.*** Cost estimators should have an aptitude for mathematics; be able to quickly analyze, compare, and interpret detailed but sometimes poorly defined information; and be able to make sound and accurate judgments based on this information. The ability to focus on details while analyzing and overcoming larger obstacles is essential. Assertiveness and self-confidence in presenting and supporting conclusions are also important, as are strong communications and interpersonal skills, because estimators may work as part of a team alongside managers, owners, engineers, and design professionals. Cost estimators also need knowledge of computers, including word-processing and spreadsheet packages. In some instances, familiarity with special estimation software or programming skills also may be required.

***Certification and advancement.*** Voluntary certification can be valuable to cost estimators because it provides professional recognition of the estimator's competence and experience. In some instances, individual employers may even require professional certification for employment. Both AACE International and SCEA administer certification programs. To become certified, estimators usually must have between two and eight years of estimating experience and must pass an examination. In addition, certification requirements may include the publication of at least one article or paper in the field.

For most estimators, advancement takes the form of higher pay and prestige. Some move into management positions, such as project manager for a construction firm or manager of the industrial engineering department for a manufacturer. Others may go into business for themselves as consultants, providing estimating services for a fee to government or to construction or manufacturing firms.

## Employment

Cost estimators held about 221,000 jobs in 2006. About 62 percent of estimators were in the construction industry, and another 15 percent were employed in manufacturing. The remainder worked in a wide range of other industries.

Cost estimators work throughout the country, usually in or near major industrial, commercial, and government centers and in cities and suburban areas undergoing rapid change or development.

## Job Outlook

Employment of cost estimators is expected to grow faster than average. Very good employment opportunities are expected.

***Employment change.*** Employment is expected to grow by 19 percent between 2006 and 2016, which is faster than the average for all occupations. Employment growth in the construction industry, in which most cost estimators are employed, will account for the majority of new jobs in this occupation. Construction and repair of highways, streets, bridges, subway systems, airports, water and sewage systems, and electric power plants and transmission lines will stimulate demand for many more cost estimators. Similarly, increasing population and business growth will result in more construction of residential homes, office buildings, shopping malls, hospitals, schools, restaurants, and other structures that require cost estimators. As the population ages, the demand for nursing and extended-care facilities will also increase. The growing complexity of construction projects will also boost demand for cost estimators as a larger number of workers specialize in a particular area of construction.

*Job prospects.* Because there are no formal bachelor's degree programs in cost estimating, some employers have difficulty recruiting qualified cost estimators, resulting in very good employment opportunities. Job prospects in construction should be best for those who have a degree in construction science, construction management, or building science plus practical experience in the various phases of construction or in a specialty craft area. For cost estimating jobs in manufacturing, those with degrees in mathematics, statistics, engineering, accounting, business administration, or economics should have the best job prospects.

In addition to job openings arising from employment growth, many additional openings should result annually from the need to replace workers who transfer to other occupations due to the sometimes stressful nature of the work or who retire or leave the occupation for other reasons.

Employment of cost estimators, like that of many other construction workers, is sensitive to the fluctuations of the economy. Workers in these trades may experience periods of unemployment when the overall level of construction falls. On the other hand, shortages of these workers may occur in some areas during peak periods of building activity.

## Earnings

Salaries of cost estimators vary widely by experience, education, size of firm, and industry. Median annual earnings of wage and salary cost estimators in May 2006 were $52,940. The middle 50 percent earned between $40,320 and $69,460. The lowest 10 percent earned less than $31,600, and the highest 10 percent earned more than $88,310. Median annual earnings in the industries employing the largest numbers of cost estimators were

| | |
|---|---|
| Nonresidential building construction | $60,870 |
| Building equipment contractors | 56,170 |
| Foundation, structure, and building exterior contractors | 52,520 |
| Residential building construction | 52,460 |
| Building finishing contractors | 51,610 |

According to a July 2007 salary survey by the National Association of Colleges and Employers, those with bachelor's degrees in construction science/management received job offers averaging $46,930 a year.

## Related Occupations

Other workers who quantitatively analyze information include accountants and auditors; budget analysts; claims adjusters, appraisers, examiners, and investigators; economists; financial analysts and personal financial advisors; insurance underwriters; loan officers; market and survey researchers; and operations research analysts. In addition, the duties of industrial production managers and construction managers also may involve analyzing costs.

## Sources of Additional Information

Information about career opportunities, certification, educational programs, and cost-estimating techniques may be obtained from the following organizations:

▸ Association for the Advancement of Cost Engineering (AACE International), 209 Prairie Ave., Suite 100, Morgantown, WV 26501. Internet: http://www.aacei.org

▸ Society of Cost Estimating and Analysis, 527 Maple Ave. East, Suite 301, Vienna, VA 22180. Internet: http://www.sceaonline.net

## Counselors

(O*NET 21-1011.00, 21-1012.00, 21-1013.00, 21-1014.00, 21-1015.00, and 21-1019.99)

## Significant Points

■ A master's degree generally is required to become a licensed counselor.

■ Job opportunities for counselors should be very good because job openings are expected to exceed the number of graduates from counseling programs.

■ The health care and social assistance industry employs about 47 percent of counselors, and state and local government employ about 11 percent.

## Nature of the Work

Counselors assist people with personal, family, educational, mental health, and career problems. Their duties vary greatly depending on their occupational specialty, which is determined by the setting in which they work and the population they serve.

*Educational, vocational, and school counselors* provide individuals and groups with career and educational counseling. School counselors assist students of all levels, from elementary school to postsecondary education. They advocate for students and work with other individuals and organizations to promote the academic, career, personal, and social development of children and youth. School counselors help students evaluate their abilities, interests, talents, and personalities to develop realistic academic and career goals. Counselors use interviews, counseling sessions, interest and aptitude assessment tests, and other methods to evaluate and advise students. They also operate career information centers and career education programs. Often, counselors work with students who have academic and social development problems or other special needs.

*Elementary school counselors* observe children during classroom and play activities and confer with their teachers and parents to evaluate the children's strengths, problems, or special needs. In conjunction with teachers and administrators, they make sure that the curriculum addresses both the academic and the developmental needs of students. Elementary school counselors do less vocational and academic counseling than high school counselors.

*High school counselors* advise students regarding college majors, admission requirements, entrance exams, financial aid, trade or technical schools, and apprenticeship programs. They help students develop job search skills, such as resume writing and interviewing techniques. College career planning and placement counselors assist alumni or students with career development and job-hunting techniques.

School counselors at all levels help students to understand and deal with social, behavioral, and personal problems. These counselors emphasize preventive and developmental counseling to provide students with the life skills needed to deal with problems before they worsen and to enhance students' personal, social, and academic growth. Counselors provide special services, including alcohol and drug prevention programs and conflict resolution classes. They also try to identify cases of domestic abuse and other family problems that can affect a student's development.

Counselors interact with students individually, in small groups, or as an entire class. They consult and collaborate with parents, teachers, school administrators, school psychologists, medical professionals, and social workers to develop and implement strategies to help students succeed.

*Vocational counselors*, also called *employment* or *career counselors*, provide mainly career counseling outside the school setting. Their chief focus is helping individuals with career decisions. Vocational counselors explore and evaluate the client's education, training, work history, interests, skills, and personality traits. They may arrange for aptitude and achievement tests to help the client make career decisions. They also work with individuals to develop their job-search skills and assist clients in locating and applying for jobs. In addition, career counselors provide support to people experiencing job loss, job stress, or other career transition issues.

*Rehabilitation counselors* help people deal with the personal, social, and vocational effects of disabilities. They counsel people with disabilities resulting from birth defects, illness or disease, accidents, or other causes. They evaluate the strengths and limitations of individuals, provide personal and vocational counseling, and arrange for medical care, vocational training, and job placement. Rehabilitation counselors interview both individuals with disabilities and their families, evaluate school and medical reports, and confer with physicians, psychologists, occupational therapists, and employers to determine the capabilities and skills of the individual. They develop rehabilitation programs by conferring with clients; these programs often include training to help clients develop job skills. Rehabilitation counselors also work toward increasing the client's capacity to live independently.

*Mental health counselors* work with individuals, families, and groups to address and treat mental and emotional disorders and to promote mental health. They are trained in a variety of therapeutic techniques used to address issues, including depression, addiction and substance abuse, suicidal impulses, stress, problems with self-esteem, and grief. They also help with job and career concerns, educational decisions, issues related to mental and emotional health, and family, parenting, marital, or other relationship problems. Mental health counselors often work closely with other mental health specialists, such as psychiatrists, psychologists, clinical social workers, psychiatric nurses, and school counselors.

*Substance abuse and behavioral disorder counselors* help people who have problems with alcohol, drugs, gambling, and eating disorders. They counsel individuals who are addicted to drugs, helping them to identify behaviors and problems related to their addiction.

Counseling can be done on an individual basis, but is frequently done in a group setting. These counselors will often also work with family members who are affected by the addictions of their loved ones. Counselors also conduct programs aimed at preventing addictions.

*Marriage and family therapists* apply family systems theory, principals and techniques to individuals, families, and couples to resolve emotional conflicts. In doing so, they modify people's perceptions and behaviors, enhance communication and understanding among family members, and help to prevent family and individual crises. Marriage and family therapists also may engage in psychotherapy of a non-medical nature, make appropriate referrals to psychiatric resources, perform research, and teach courses about human development and interpersonal relationships.

Other counseling specialties include gerontological, multicultural, and genetic counseling. A gerontological counselor provides services to elderly people and their families as they face changing lifestyles. Genetic counselors provide information and support to families who have members with birth defects or genetic disorders and to families who may be at risk for a variety of inherited conditions. These counselors identify families at risk, interpret information about the disorder, analyze inheritance patterns and risks of recurrence, and review available options with the family.

**Work environment.** Work environment can vary greatly depending on occupational specialty. School counselors work predominantly in schools, where they usually have an office but also may work in classrooms. Other counselors may work in a private practice, community health organization, or hospital. Many counselors work in an office where they see clients throughout the day. Because privacy is essential for confidential and frank discussions with clients, counselors usually have private offices.

The work schedules of counselors depend on occupational specialty and work setting. Some school counselors work the traditional 9- to 10-month school year with a 2- to 3-month vacation, but increasing numbers, are employed on 11-month or full-year contracts, particularly those working in middle and high schools. They usually work the same hours as teachers, but they may travel more frequently to attend conferences and conventions. College career planning and placement counselors work long and irregular hours during student recruiting periods.

Rehabilitation counselors usually work a standard 40-hour week. Self-employed counselors and those working in mental health and community agencies, such as substance abuse and behavioral disorder counselors, frequently work evenings to counsel clients who work during the day. Both mental health counselors and marriage and family therapists also often work flexible hours to accommodate families in crisis or working couples who must have evening or weekend appointments.

## Training, Other Qualifications, and Advancement

Education and training requirements for counselors are often very detailed and vary by state and specialty. Prospective counselors should check with state and local governments, employers, and national voluntary certification organizations to determine which requirements apply.

**Projections data from the National Employment Matrix**

| Occupational Title | SOC Code | Employment, 2006 | Projected employment, 2016 | Change, 2006-2016 | |
|---|---|---|---|---|---|
| | | | | Number | Percent |
| Counselors................................................................ | 21-1010 | 635,000 | 771,000 | 136,000 | 21 |
| Substance abuse and behavioral disorder counselors................... | 21-1011 | 83,000 | 112,000 | 29,000 | 34 |
| Educational, vocational, and school counselors.......................... | 21-1012 | 260,000 | 292,000 | 33,000 | 13 |
| Marriage and family therapists ....................................... | 21-1013 | 25,000 | 32,000 | 7,400 | 30 |
| Mental health counselors ............................................. | 21-1014 | 100,000 | 130,000 | 30,000 | 30 |
| Rehabilitation counselors............................................. | 21-1015 | 141,000 | 173,000 | 32,000 | 23 |
| Counselors, all other .................................................. | 21-1019 | 27,000 | 32,000 | 4,500 | 17 |

NOTE: Data in this table are rounded.

*Education and training.* Education requirements vary based on occupational specialty and state licensure and certification requirements. A master's degree is usually required to be licensed as a counselor. Some states require counselors in public employment to have a master's degree; others accept a bachelor's degree with appropriate counseling courses. Counselor education programs in colleges and universities are often found in departments of education or psychology. Fields of study include college student affairs, elementary or secondary school counseling, education, gerontological counseling, marriage and family therapy, substance abuse counseling, rehabilitation counseling, agency or community counseling, clinical mental health counseling, career counseling, and related fields. Courses are often grouped into eight core areas: human growth and development, social and cultural diversity, relationships, group work, career development, assessment, research and program evaluation, and professional identity. In an accredited master's degree program, 48 to 60 semester hours of graduate study, including a period of supervised clinical experience in counseling, are required.

Some employers provide training for newly hired counselors. Others may offer time off or tuition assistance to complete a graduate degree. Often counselors must participate in graduate studies, workshops, and personal studies to maintain their certificates and licenses.

*Licensure.* Licensure requirements differ greatly by state, occupational specialty, and work setting. Many states require school counselors to hold a state school counseling certification and to have completed at least some graduate course work; most require the completion of a master's degree. Some states require school counselors to be licensed, which generally requires continuing education credits. Some states require public school counselors to have both counseling and teaching certificates and to have had some teaching experience.

For counselors based outside of schools, 49 states and the District of Columbia have some form of counselor licensure that governs the practice of counseling. Requirements typically include the completion of a master's degree in counseling, the accumulation of two years or 3,000 hours of supervised clinical experience beyond the master's degree level, the passage of a state-recognized exam, adherence to ethical codes and standards, and the completion of annual continuing education requirements. However, counselors working in certain settings or in a particular specialty may face different licensure requirements. For example, a career counselor working in private practice may need a license, but a counselor working for a college career center may not. In addition, substance abuse and behavior disorder counselors are generally governed by a different state agency or board than other counselors. The criteria for their licensure vary greatly and in some cases, these counselors may only need a high school diploma and certification. Those interested in entering the field must research state and specialty requirements to determine what qualifications they must have.

*Other qualifications.* People interested in counseling should have a strong desire to help others and should be able to inspire respect, trust, and confidence. They should be able to work independently or as part of a team. Counselors must follow the code of ethics associated with their respective certifications and licenses.

Counselors must possess high physical and emotional energy to handle the array of problems that they address. Dealing daily with these problems can cause stress.

*Certification and advancement.* Some counselors elect to be certified by the National Board for Certified Counselors, Inc., which grants a general practice credential of National Certified Counselor. To be certified, a counselor must hold a master's degree with a concentration in counseling from a regionally accredited college or university; have at least two years of supervised field experience in a counseling setting (graduates from counselor education programs accredited by the Council for Accreditation of Counseling and Related Educational Programs are exempted); provide two professional endorsements, one of which must be from a recent supervisor; and must have a passing score on the board's examination. This national certification is voluntary and is distinct from state licensing. However, in some states, those who pass the national exam are exempted from taking a state certification exam. The board also offers specialty certifications in school, clinical mental health, and addiction counseling. These specialty certifications require passage of a supplemental exam. To maintain their certifications, counselors retake and pass the exam or complete 100 credit hours of acceptable continuing education every five years.

The Commission on Rehabilitation Counselor Certification offers voluntary national certification for rehabilitation counselors. Many state and local governments and other employers require rehabilitation counselors to have this certification. To become certified, rehabilitation counselors usually must graduate from an accredited educational program, complete an internship, and pass a written examination. Certification requirements vary, however, according to an applicant's educational history. Employment experience, for example, is required for those with a counseling degree in a specialty other than rehabilitation. To maintain their certification, counselors must successfully retake the certification exam or complete

100 credit hours of acceptable continuing education every five years.

Other counseling organizations also offer certification in particular counseling specialties. Usually, becoming certified is voluntary, but having certification may enhance job prospects.

Prospects for advancement vary by counseling field. School counselors can become directors or supervisors of counseling, guidance, or pupil personnel services; or, usually with further graduate education, become counselor educators, counseling psychologists, or school administrators. Some counselors choose to work for a state's department of education.

Some marriage and family therapists, especially those with doctorates in family therapy, become supervisors, teachers, researchers, or advanced clinicians in the discipline. Counselors may also become supervisors or administrators in their agencies. Some counselors move into research, consulting, or college teaching or go into private or group practice. Some may choose to pursue a doctoral degree to improve their chances for advancement.

## Employment

Counselors held about 635,000 jobs in 2006. Employment was distributed among the counseling specialties as follows:

Educational, vocational, and school counselors ....260,000

Rehabilitation counselors ....................................141,000

Mental health counselors ....................................100,000

Substance abuse and behavioral disorder
    counselors ...................................................83,000

Marriage and family therapists.............................25,000

Counselors, all other ...........................................27,000

Educational, vocational, and school counselors work primarily in elementary and secondary schools and colleges and universities. Other types of counselors work in a wide variety of public and private establishments, including healthcare facilities; job training, career development, and vocational rehabilitation centers; social agencies; correctional institutions; and residential care facilities, such as halfway houses for criminal offenders and group homes for children, the elderly, and the disabled. Some substance abuse and behavioral disorder counselors work in therapeutic communities where people with addictions live while undergoing treatment. Counselors also work in organizations engaged in community improvement and social change, drug and alcohol rehabilitation programs, and state and local government agencies.

A growing number of counselors are self-employed and work in group practices or private practice, due in part to new laws allowing counselors to be paid for their services by insurance companies and to the growing recognition that counselors are well-trained, effective professionals.

## Job Outlook

Employment for counselors is expected to grow much faster than the average for all occupations through 2016. However, job growth will vary by location and occupational specialty. Job prospects should be good due to growth and the need to replace people leaving the field.

*Employment change.* Overall employment of counselors is expected to increase by 21 percent between 2006 and 2016, which is much faster than the average for all occupations. However, growth is expected to vary by specialty.

Employment of substance abuse and behavioral disorder counselors is expected to grow 34 percent, which is much faster than the average for all occupations. As society becomes more knowledgeable about addiction, it is increasingly common for people to seek treatment. Furthermore, drug offenders are increasingly being sent to treatment programs rather than jail.

Employment for educational, vocational and school counselors is expected to grow 13 percent, which is about as fast as the average for all occupations. Demand for vocational or career counselors should grow as multiple job and career changes become common and as workers become increasingly aware of counseling services. In addition, state and local governments will employ growing numbers of counselors to assist beneficiaries of welfare programs who exhaust their eligibility and must find jobs. Other opportunities for employment of counselors will arise in private job-training centers that provide training and other services to laid-off workers and others seeking to acquire new skills or careers. Demand for school counselors may increase due in large part to increases in student enrollments at postsecondary schools and colleges and as more states require elementary schools to employ counselors. Expansion of the responsibilities of school counselors should also lead to increases in their employment. For example, counselors are becoming more involved in crisis and preventive counseling, helping students deal with issues ranging from drug and alcohol abuse to death and suicide. Although schools and governments realize the value of counselors in helping their students to achieve academic success, budget constraints at every school level will dampen job growth of school counselors. Federal grants and subsidies may help to offset tight budgets and allow the reduction in student-to-counselor ratios to continue.

Employment of mental health counselors is expected to grow by 30 percent, which is much faster than the average for all occupations. Mental health counselors will be needed to staff statewide networks that are being established to improve services for children and adolescents with serious emotional disturbances and for their families. Under managed care systems, insurance companies are increasingly providing for reimbursement of counselors as a less costly alternative to psychiatrists and psychologists.

Jobs for rehabilitation counselors are expected to grow by 23 percent, which is much faster than the average for all occupations. The number of people who will need rehabilitation counseling is expected to grow as advances in medical technology allow more people to survive injury or illness and live independently again. In addition, legislation requiring equal employment rights for people with disabilities will spur demand for counselors, who not only help these people make a transition to the workforce but also help companies to comply with the law.

Marriage and family therapists will experience growth of 30 percent, which is much faster than the average for all occupations. This is due in part to an increased recognition of the field. It is more common for people to seek help for their marital and family problems than it was in the past.

*Job prospects.* Job prospects vary greatly based on the occupational specialty. Prospects for rehabilitation counselors are excellent because many people are leaving the field or retiring. Furthermore, opportunities are very good in substance abuse and behavioral disorder counseling because relatively low wages and long hours make recruiting new entrants difficult. For school counselors, job prospects should be good because many people are leaving the occupation to retire; however, opportunities may be more favorable in rural and urban areas, rather than the suburbs, because it is often difficult to recruit people to these areas.

## Earnings

Median annual earnings of wage and salary educational, vocational, and school counselors in May 2006 were $47,530. The middle 50 percent earned between $36,120 and $60,990. The lowest 10 percent earned less than $27,240, and the highest 10 percent earned more than $75,920. School counselors can earn additional income working summers in the school system or in other jobs. Median annual earnings in the industries employing the largest numbers of educational, vocational, and school counselors were as follows:

| | |
|---|---|
| Elementary and secondary schools | $53,750 |
| Junior colleges | 48,240 |
| Colleges, universities, and professional schools | 41,780 |
| Individual and family services | 32,370 |
| Vocational rehabilitation services | 31,340 |

Median annual earnings of wage and salary substance abuse and behavioral disorder counselors in May 2006 were $34,040. The middle 50 percent earned between $27,330 and $42,650. The lowest 10 percent earned less than $22,600, and the highest 10 percent earned more than $52,340.

Median annual earnings of wage and salary mental health counselors in May 2006 were $34,380. The middle 50 percent earned between $26,780 and $45,610. The lowest 10 percent earned less than $21,890, and the highest 10 percent earned more than $59,700.

Median annual earnings of wage and salary rehabilitation counselors in May 2006 were $29,200. The middle 50 percent earned between $22,980 and $39,000. The lowest 10 percent earned less than $19,260, and the highest 10 percent earned more than $53,170.

For substance abuse, mental health, and rehabilitation counselors, government employers generally pay the highest wages, followed by hospitals and social service agencies. Residential care facilities often pay the lowest wages.

Median annual earnings of wage and salary marriage and family therapists in May 2006 were $43,210. The middle 50 percent earned between $32,950 and $54,150. The lowest 10 percent earned less than $25,280, and the highest 10 percent earned more than $69,050. Median annual earnings were $36,020 in individual and family social services, the industry employing the largest number of marriage and family therapists.

Self-employed counselors who have well-established practices, as well as counselors employed in group practices, usually have the highest earnings.

## Related Occupations

Counselors help people evaluate their interests, abilities, and disabilities and deal with personal, social, academic, and career problems. Others who help people in similar ways include teachers, social and human service assistants, social workers, psychologists, physicians and surgeons, registered nurses, occupational therapists, and human resources, training, and labor relations managers and specialists.

## Sources of Additional Information

For general information about counseling, as well as information on specialties such as college, mental health, rehabilitation, multicultural, career, marriage and family, and gerontological counseling, contact

▸ American Counseling Association, 5999 Stevenson Ave., Alexandria, VA 22304. Internet: http://www.counseling.org

For information on school counselors, contact

▸ American School Counselors Association, 1101 King St., Suite 625, Alexandria, VA 22314. Internet: http://www.schoolcounselor.org

For information on mental health counselors, contact

▸ American Mental Health Counselors Association, 801 N. Fairfax Street, Suite 304, Alexandria, VA 22314. Internet: http://www.amhca.org

For information on marriage and family therapists, contact

▸ American Association for Marriage and Family Therapy, 112 South Alfred Street, Alexandria, VA 22314 Internet: http://www.aamft.org

For information on accredited counseling and related training programs, contact

▸ Council for Accreditation of Counseling and Related Educational Programs, American Counseling Association, 5999 Stevenson Ave., 4th floor, Alexandria, VA 22304. Internet: http://www.cacrep.org

For information on national certification requirements for counselors, contact

▸ National Board for Certified Counselors, Inc., 3 Terrace Way, Suite D, Greensboro, NC 27403. Internet: http://www.nbcc.org

State departments of education can supply information on colleges and universities offering guidance and counseling training that meets state certification and licensure requirements.

State employment service offices have information about job opportunities and entrance requirements for counselors.

## Counter and Rental Clerks

(O*NET 41-2021.00)

## Significant Points

■ Jobs usually require little or no experience or formal education.

■ Employment is projected to grow much faster than average as businesses strive to improve customer service.

■ Many full-time and part-time job opportunities should be available, primarily because of the need to replace workers who leave this occupation.

## Nature of the Work

Counter and rental clerks take orders for rentals and services. Many rent cars or home improvement equipment, for example. Regardless of where they work, counter and rental clerks must be knowledgeable about the company's goods and services, policies, and procedures. Depending on the type of establishment, counter and rental clerks use their knowledge to give advice on a wide variety of products and services, ranging from hydraulic tools to shoe repair. For example, in the car rental industry, these workers tell customers about the features of different types of automobiles and about daily and weekly rental costs. They also ensure that customers meet age and other requirements for renting cars, and they indicate when and in what condition the cars must be returned. Those in the equipment rental industry have similar duties but also must know how to operate and care for the machinery rented. In drycleaning establishments, counter clerks inform customers when items will be ready and about the effects, if any, of the chemicals used on certain garments. In video rental stores, counter clerks advise customers about the use of video and game players and the length of the rental period. They scan returned movies and games, restock shelves, handle money, and log daily reports.

When taking orders, counter and rental clerks use various types of equipment. In some establishments, they write out tickets and order forms, although most use computers or barcode scanners. Most of these computer systems are user friendly, require very little data entry, and are customized for each firm. Scanners read the product code and display a description of the item on a computer screen. However, clerks must ensure that the information on the screen matches the product.

*Work environment.* Firms employing counter and rental clerks usually operate nights and weekends for the convenience of their customers. As a result, many employers offer flexible schedules. Some counter and rental clerks work 40-hour weeks, but many are on part-time schedules—usually during rush periods, such as weekends, evenings, and holidays.

Working conditions usually are pleasant; most stores and service establishments are clean, well lighted, and temperature controlled. However, clerks are on their feet much of the time and may be confined behind a small counter area. Some may need to move, lift, or carry heavy machinery or other equipment. The job requires constant interaction with the public and can be stressful, especially during busy periods.

## Training, Other Qualifications, and Advancement

Most counter and rental clerk jobs are entry-level positions that require little or no experience and minimal formal education.

*Education and training.* Many employers prefer workers with at least a high school diploma. In most companies, counter and rental clerks are trained on the job, sometimes through the use of videos, brochures, and pamphlets.

Clerks usually learn the firm's policies and procedures and how to operate a firm's equipment from more experienced workers. However, some employers have formal classroom training programs lasting between a few hours and a few weeks. Topics covered in this training include the nature of the industry, the company and its policies and procedures, operation of equipment, sales techniques, and customer service. Counter and rental clerks also must become familiar with the different products and services rented or provided by their company to give customers the best possible service.

*Other qualifications.* Counter and rental clerks should enjoy working with people and should be tactful and polite, even with difficult customers. They also should be able to handle several tasks at once, while continuing to provide friendly service. In addition, good oral and written communication skills are essential.

*Advancement.* Advancement opportunities depend on the size and type of company. Many establishments that employ counter or rental clerks tend to be small businesses, making advancement difficult. In larger establishments, however, jobs such as counter and rental clerks offer good opportunities for workers to learn about their company's products and business practices. That can lead to more responsible positions. Some counter and rental clerks are promoted to event planner, assistant manager, or salesperson. Some pursue related positions. A clerk that fixes rented equipment might become a mechanic, for example.

In certain industries, such as equipment repair, counter and rental jobs may be an additional or alternative source of income for workers with multiple jobs or for those who are semiretired. For example, retired mechanics could prove invaluable at tool rental centers because of their knowledge of, and familiarity with, tools.

## Employment

Counter and rental clerks held about 477,000 jobs in 2006. About 22 percent of clerks worked in consumer goods rental, which includes video rental stores. Other large employers included drycleaning and laundry services; automotive equipment rental and leasing services; automobile dealers; amusement, gambling, and recreation industries; and grocery stores.

Counter and rental clerks are employed throughout the country but are concentrated in metropolitan areas, where personal services and renting and leasing services are in greater demand.

## Job Outlook

Much faster than average employment growth coupled with the need to replace workers who leave this occupation should result in many full-time and part-time job opportunities.

*Employment change.* Employment of counter and rental clerks is expected to increase by 23 percent during the 2006–2016 decade, much faster than the average for all occupations. Because all types of businesses strive to improve customer service by hiring more clerks, fast employment growth is expected in most industries; growth in amusement and recreation industries is expected to be especially fast.

*Job prospects.* Many full-time and part-time job opportunities should be available, primarily because of the need to replace experienced workers who transfer to other occupations or leave the labor force.

**Projections data from the National Employment Matrix**

| Occupational Title | SOC Code | Employment, 2006 | Projected employment, 2016 | Change, 2006-16 | |
|---|---|---|---|---|---|
| | | | | Number | Percent |
| Counter and rental clerks ............................................................ | 41-2021 | 477,000 | 586,000 | 109,000 | 23 |

NOTE: Data in this table are rounded.

## Earnings

Counter and rental clerks typically start at the minimum wage, which, in establishments covered by federal law, was $5.85 an hour in 2007. In some states, the law sets the minimum wage higher, and establishments must pay at least that amount. Wages also tend to be higher in areas where there is intense competition for workers. In addition to wages, some counter and rental clerks receive commissions based on the number of contracts they complete or services they sell.

Median hourly earnings of counter and rental clerks in May 2006 were $9.41. The middle 50 percent earned between $7.58 and $13.05 an hour. The lowest 10 percent earned less than $6.56 an hour, and the highest 10 percent earned more than $18.17 an hour. Median hourly earnings in the industries employing the largest number of counter and rental clerks in May 2006 were

| | |
|---|---|
| Automobile dealers ..............................................$19.15 |
| Automotive equipment rental and leasing ................10.79 |
| Lessors of real estate...........................................10.31 |
| Consumer goods rental .........................................8.07 |
| Drycleaning and laundry services............................7.95 |

Full-time workers typically receive health and life insurance, paid vacation, and sick leave. Benefits for counter and rental clerks who work part time or work for independent stores tend to be significantly less than for those who work full time. Many companies offer discounts to full-time and part-time employees on the goods or services they provide.

## Related Occupations

Counter and rental clerks take orders and receive payment for services rendered. Other workers with similar duties include tellers, cashiers, food and beverage serving and related workers, gaming cage workers, Postal Service workers, and retail salespersons.

## Sources of Additional Information

For general information on employment in the equipment rental industry, contact

▸ American Rental Association, 1900 19th St., Moline, IL 61265. Internet: http://www.ararental.org

For more information about the work of counter clerks in drycleaning and laundry establishments, contact

▸ International Fabricare Institute, 14700 Sweitzer Ln., Laurel, MD 20707. Internet: http://www.ifi.org

# Customer Service Representatives

(O*NET 43-4051.00, 43-4051.01, and 43-4051.02)

## Significant Points

■ Job prospects are expected to be excellent.

■ Most jobs require only a high school diploma but educational requirements are rising.

■ Strong verbal communication and listening skills are important.

## Nature of the Work

Customer service representatives are employed by many different types of companies to serve as a direct point of contact for customers. They are responsible for ensuring that their company's customers receive an adequate level of service or help with their questions and concerns. These customers may be individual consumers or other companies, and their service needs can vary considerably.

All customer service representatives interact with customers to provide information in response to inquiries about products or services and to handle and resolve complaints. They communicate with customers through a variety of means—by telephone; by e-mail, fax, or regular mail; or in person. Some customer service representatives handle general questions and complaints, whereas others specialize in a particular area.

Many customer inquiries involve routine questions and requests. For example, customer service representatives may be asked to provide a customer with their credit card balance, or to check on the status of an order. However, other questions are more involved, and may require additional research or further explanation on the part of the customer service representative. In handling customers' complaints, they must attempt to resolve the problem according to guidelines established by the company. These procedures may involve asking questions to determine the validity of a complaint; offering possible solutions; or providing customers with refunds, exchanges, or other offers, like discounts or coupons. In some cases, customer service representatives are required to follow up with an individual customer until a question is answered or an issue is resolved.

Some customer service representatives help people decide what types of products or services would best suit their needs. They may even aid customers in completing purchases or transactions. Although the primary function of customer service representatives is not sales, some may spend time encouraging customers to purchase additional products or services. Customer service representatives also may make changes or updates to a customer's profile or account information. They may keep records of transactions and update and maintain databases of information.

Most customer service representatives use computers and telephones extensively in their work. Customer service representatives frequently enter information into a computer as they are speaking to customers. Often, companies have large amounts of data, such as account information, that is pulled up on a computer screen while the representative is talking to a customer so he or she can answer specific questions. Customer service representatives also usually have answers to the most common customer questions, or guidelines for dealing with complaints. In the event that they encounter a question or situation to which they do not know how to respond, workers consult with a supervisor to determine the best course of action. They generally use multiline telephone systems, which may route calls directly to the most appropriate representative. However, at times, they must transfer calls to someone who may be better able to respond to the customer's needs.

In some organizations, customer service representatives spend their entire day on the telephone. In others, they may spend part of their day answering e-mails and the remainder of the day taking calls. For some, most of their contact with the customer is face to face. Customer service representatives need to remain aware of the amount of time spent with each customer so that they can fairly distribute their time among the people who require their assistance. This is particularly important for those whose primary activities are answering telephone calls and whose conversations are required to be kept within a set time limit. For those working in call centers, there is usually very little time between telephone calls. When working in call centers, customer service representatives are likely to be under close supervision. Telephone calls may be taped and reviewed by supervisors to ensure that company policies and procedures are being followed.

Job responsibilities also can differ, depending on the industry in which a customer service representative is employed. For example, those working in the branch office of a bank may assume the responsibilities of other workers, such as teller or new account clerk, as needed. In insurance agencies, a customer service representative interacts with agents, insurance companies, and policyholders. These workers handle much of the paperwork related to insurance policies, such as policy applications and changes and renewals to existing policies. They answer questions regarding policy coverage, help with reporting claims, and do anything else that may need to be done. Although they must have similar credentials and knowledge of insurance products as insurance agents, the duties of a customer service representative differ from those of an agent as they are not responsible for seeking potential customers. Customer service representatives employed by utilities and communications companies assist individuals interested in opening accounts for various utilities such as electricity and gas, or for communication services such as cable television and telephone. They explain various options and receive orders for services to be installed, turned on, turned off, or changed. They also may look into and resolve complaints about billing and other service.

***Work environment.*** Although customer service representatives work in a variety of settings, most work in areas that are clean and well lit. Many work in call or customer contact centers where workers generally have their own workstation or cubicle space equipped with a telephone, headset, and computer. Because many call centers are open extended hours, beyond the traditional work day, or are staffed around the clock, these positions may require workers to take on early morning, evening, or late night shifts. Weekend or holiday work also may be necessary. As a result, the occupation is well suited to flexible work schedules. About 17 percent of customer service representatives work part time. The occupation also offers the opportunity for seasonal work in certain industries, often through temporary help agencies.

Call centers may be crowded and noisy, and work may be repetitious and stressful, with little time between calls. Workers usually must attempt to minimize the length of each call, while still providing excellent service. To ensure that these procedures are followed, conversations may be monitored by supervisors, which be stressful. Also, long periods spent sitting, typing, or looking at a computer screen may cause eye and muscle strain, backaches, headaches, and repetitive motion injuries.

Customer service representatives working outside of a call center environment may interact with customers through several different means. For example, workers employed by an insurance agency or in a grocery store may have customers approach them in person or contact them by telephone, computer, mail, or fax. Many of these customer service representatives work a standard 40-hour week; however, their hours generally depend on their employer's hours of operation. Work environments outside of a call center also vary accordingly. Most customer service representatives work either in an office or at a service or help desk.

Customer service representatives may have to deal with difficult or irate customers, which can be challenging. However, the ability to resolve customers' problems has the potential to be very rewarding.

## Training, Other Qualifications, and Advancement

Most jobs require at least a high school diploma. However, employers are increasingly seeking candidates with some college education. Most employers provide training to workers before they begin serving customers.

***Education and training.*** Most customer service representative jobs require only a high school diploma. However, because employers are demanding a higher skilled workforce, many customer service jobs now require an associate or bachelor's degree. High school and college level courses in computers, English, or business are helpful in preparing for a job in customer service.

Training requirements vary by industry. Almost all customer service representatives are provided with some training prior to beginning work. This training generally includes customer service and phone skills; information on products and services; information about common customer problems; the use of the telephone and computer systems; and company policies and regulations. Length of training varies, but usually lasts at least several weeks. Because of a constant need to update skills and knowledge, most customer service representatives continue to receive training throughout their career. This is particularly true of workers in industries such as banking, in which regulations and products are continually changing.

*Other qualifications.* Because customer service representatives constantly interact with the public, good communication and problem-solving skills are a must. Verbal communication and listening skills are especially important. For workers who communicate through e-mail, good typing, spelling, and writing skills are necessary. Basic to intermediate computer knowledge and good interpersonal skills also are important qualities for people who wish to be successful in the field.

Customer service representatives play a critical role in providing an interface between customers and companies. As a result, employers seek out people who are friendly and possess a professional manner. The ability to deal patiently with problems and complaints and to remain courteous when faced with difficult or angry people is very important. Also, a customer service representative needs to be able to work independently within specified time constraints. Workers should have a clear and pleasant speaking voice and be fluent in English. However, the ability to speak a foreign language is becoming increasingly necessary.

Although some positions may require previous industry, office, or customer service experience, many customer service jobs are entry level. However, within insurance agencies and brokerages, these jobs usually are not entry-level positions. Workers must have previous experience in insurance and often are required by state regulations to be licensed like insurance sales agents. A variety of designations are available to demonstrate that a candidate has sufficient knowledge and skill, and continuing education courses and training often are offered through the employer.

*Advancement.* Customer service jobs are often good introductory positions into a company or an industry. In some cases, experienced workers can move up within the company into supervisory or managerial positions or they may move into areas such as product development, in which they can use their knowledge to improve products and services. As they gain more knowledge of industry products and services, customer service representatives in insurance may advance to other, higher level positions, such as insurance sales agent.

## Employment

Customer service representatives held about 2.2 million jobs in 2006. Although they were found in a variety of industries, about 23 percent of customer service representatives worked in finance and insurance. The largest numbers were employed by insurance carriers, insurance agencies and brokerages, and banks and credit unions.

About 14 percent of customer service representatives were employed in administrative and support services. These workers were concentrated in the business support services industry (which includes telephone call centers) and employment services (which includes temporary help services and employment placement agencies). Another 11 percent of customer service representatives were employed in retail trade establishments such as general merchandise stores and food and beverage stores. Other industries that employ significant numbers of customer service representatives include information, particularly the telecommunications industry; manufacturing, such as printing and related support activities; and wholesale trade.

## Job Outlook

Customer service representatives are expected to experience growth that is much faster than the average for all occupations through the projection period. Furthermore, job prospects should excellent as workers who leave the occupation will need to be replaced.

*Employment Change.* Employment of customer service representatives is expected to increase 25 percent from 2006 to 2016, which is much faster than the average for all occupations. This occupation will have one of the largest numbers of new jobs arise, about 545,000 over the 2006–2016 projection period. Beyond growth stemming from expansion of the industries in which customer service representatives are employed, a need for additional customer service representatives is likely to result from heightened reliance on these workers. Customer service is very important to the success of any organization that deals with customers, and strong customer service can build sales, visibility, and loyalty as companies try to distinguish themselves from competitors. In many industries, gaining a competitive edge and retaining customers will be increasingly important over the next decade. This is particularly true in industries such as financial services, communications, and utilities, which already employ numerous customer service representatives. As the trend towards consolidation in industries continues, centralized call centers will provide an effective method for delivering a high level of customer service. As a result, employment of customer service representatives may grow at a faster rate in call centers than in other areas. However, this growth may be tempered by a variety of factors such as technological improvements that make it increasingly feasible and cost-effective for call centers to be built or relocated outside of the United States.

Technology is affecting the occupation in many ways. The Internet and automated teller machines have provided customers with means of obtaining information and conducting transactions that do not entail interacting with another person. Technology also allows for greater streamlining of processes, while at the same time increasing the productivity of workers. The use of computer software to filter e-mails, generating automatic responses or directing messages to the appropriate representative, and the use of similar systems to answer or route telephone inquiries are likely to become more prevalent in the future. Also, with rapidly improving telecommunications, some organizations have begun to position their call centers overseas.

Despite such developments, the need for customer service representatives is expected to remain strong. In many ways, technology has heightened consumers' expectations for information and services, and the availability of information online seems to have generated more need for customer service representatives, particularly to respond to e-mail. Also, technology cannot replace human skills. As more sophisticated technologies are able to resolve many customers' questions and concerns, the nature of the inquiries handled by customer service representatives is likely to become increasingly complex.

Furthermore, the job responsibilities of customer service representatives are expanding. As companies downsize or take other measures to increase profitability, workers are being trained to perform additional duties such as opening bank accounts or cross-selling products. As a result, employers increasingly may prefer customer

**Projections data from the National Employment Matrix**

| Occupational Title | SOC Code | Employment, 2006 | Projected employment, 2016 | Change, 2006-16 | |
|---|---|---|---|---|---|
| | | | | Number | Percent |
| Customer service representatives.................................................... | 43-4051 | 2,202,000 | 2,747,000 | 545,000 | 25 |

NOTE: Data in this table are rounded.

service representatives who have education beyond high school, such as some college or even a college degree.

While jobs in some industries—such as retail trade—may be affected by economic downturns, the customer service occupation generally is resistant to major fluctuations in employment.

*Job prospects.* Prospects for obtaining a job in this field are expected to be excellent, with more job openings than jobseekers. Bilingual jobseekers, in particular, may enjoy favorable job prospects. In addition, numerous job openings will result from the need to replace experienced customer service representatives who transfer to other occupations or leave the labor force. Replacement needs are expected to be significant in this large occupation because many young people work as customer service representatives before switching to other jobs.

This occupation is well suited to flexible work schedules, and many opportunities for part-time work will continue to be available, particularly as organizations attempt to cut labor costs by hiring more temporary workers.

## Earnings

In May 2006, median hourly earnings for wage and salary customer service representatives were $13.62. The middle 50 percent earned between $10.73 and $17.40. The lowest 10 percent earned less than $8.71 and the highest 10 percent earned more than $22.11.

Earnings for customer service representatives vary according to level of skill required, experience, training, location, and size of firm. Median hourly earnings in the industries employing the largest numbers of these workers in May 2006 were

| | |
|---|---|
| Insurance carriers .............................................$15.00 | |
| Agencies, brokerages, and other insurance-related activities.................................................14.51 | |
| Depository Credit Intermediation ............................13.68 | |
| Employment services .............................................11.74 | |
| Telephone call centers .........................................10.29 | |

In addition to receiving an hourly wage, full-time customer service representatives who work evenings, nights, weekends, or holidays may receive shift differential pay. Also, because call centers are often open during extended hours, or even 24 hours a day, some customer service representatives have the benefit of being able to work a schedule that does not conform to the traditional work week. Other benefits can include life and health insurance, pensions, bonuses, employer-provided training, and discounts on the products and services the company offers.

## Related Occupations

Customer service representatives interact with customers to provide information in response to inquiries about products and services and

to handle and resolve complaints. Other occupations in which workers have similar dealings with customers and the public are information and record clerks; financial clerks such as tellers and new account clerks; insurance sales agents; securities, commodities, and financial services sales agents; retail salespersons; computer support specialists; and gaming services workers.

## Sources of Additional Information

State employment service offices can provide information about employment opportunities for customer service representatives.

## Demonstrators, Product Promoters, and Models

(O*NET 41-9011.00 and 41-9012.00)

## Significant Points

- Job openings should be plentiful for demonstrators and product promoters, but keen competition is expected for modeling jobs.
- Most jobs are part time or have variable work schedules, and many jobs require frequent travel.
- Formal training is limited and education beyond high school usually is not required.

## Nature of the Work

Demonstrators, product promoters, and models create public interest in buying products such as clothing, cosmetics, food, and housewares. The information they provide helps consumers make choices among the wide variety of products and services they can buy.

Demonstrators and product promoters encourage people and stores to buy a product by demonstrating it to prospective customers and answering their questions. They may sell the demonstrated merchandise or gather names of prospects to contact later or pass on to sales staff. *Demonstrators* promote sales of a product to consumers, while *product promoters* encourage sales to retail stores and help them market products effectively.

Demonstrators and product promoters generate sales of both sophisticated and simple products, ranging from computer software to mops. They attract an audience by offering samples, administering contests, distributing prizes and coupons, and using direct-mail advertising. They must greet and catch the attention of possible customers and quickly identify those who are interested and able to buy. They inform and educate customers about the features of products and demonstrate their use with apparent ease to inspire confidence in the product and its manufacturer. They also distribute information, such as brochures and order forms. Some demonstrations are intended to generate immediate sales through impulse buying, whereas others increase the likelihood of future sales by increasing brand awareness.

Demonstrations and product promotions are conducted in retail and grocery stores, shopping malls, trade shows, and outdoor fairs. Locations are selected based on the nature of the product and the type of audience. Demonstrations at large events may require teams of demonstrators to efficiently handle large crowds. Some demonstrators promote products on videotape or on television programs, such as "infomercials" or home shopping programs.

Demonstrators and product promoters may prepare the content of a presentation and alter it to target a specific audience or to keep it current. They may participate in the design of an exhibit or customize it for particular audiences. Results obtained by demonstrators and product promoters are analyzed, and presentations are adjusted to make them more effective. Demonstrators and product promoters also may be involved in transporting, assembling, and disassembling materials used in demonstrations.

A demonstrator's presentation may include visuals, models, case studies, testimonials, test results, and surveys. The equipment used for a demonstration varies with the product being demonstrated. A food product demonstration might require the use of cooking utensils, while a software demonstration could require the use of a multimedia computer. Demonstrators must be familiar with the product to be able to relate detailed information to customers and to answer any questions that arise before, during, or after a demonstration. Therefore, they may research the product presented, the products of competitors, and the interests and concerns of the target audience before conducting a demonstration. Demonstrations of complex products often need practice.

*Models* pose for photos, paintings, or sculptures. They display clothing, such as dresses, coats, underclothing, swimwear, and suits, for a variety of audiences and in various types of media. They model accessories, such as handbags, shoes, and jewelry, and promote beauty products, including fragrances and cosmetics. The most successful models, called supermodels, hold celebrity status and often use their image to sell books, calendars, fitness videos, and other products. In addition to modeling, they may appear in movies and television shows.

Models appear in printed publications, live modeling events, and television to advertise and promote products and services. Most modeling jobs are for printed publications, and models usually do a combination of editorial, commercial, and catalog work. Editorial print modeling uses still photographs of models for fashion magazine covers and to accompany feature articles. Commercial print modeling includes work for advertisements in magazines, newspapers, and billboards. Catalog models appear in department store and mail order catalogs.

During a photo shoot, a model poses to demonstrate the features of clothing and products. Models make small changes in posture and facial expression to capture the look desired by the client. As they shoot film, photographers instruct models to pose in certain positions and to interact with their physical surroundings. Models work closely with photographers, hair and clothing stylists, makeup artists, and clients to produce the desired look and to finish the photo shoot on schedule. Stylists and makeup artists prepare the model for the photo shoot, provide touchups, and change the look of models throughout the day. If stylists are not provided, models must apply their own makeup and bring their own clothing. Because the client spends time and money planning for and preparing an advertising campaign, the client usually is present to ensure that the work is satisfactory.

Editorial printwork generally pays less than other types of modeling but provides exposure for a model and can lead to commercial modeling opportunities. Often, beginning fashion models work in foreign countries where fashion magazines are more plentiful.

Live modeling is done in a variety of locations. Live models stand, turn, and walk to demonstrate clothing to a variety of audiences. At fashion shows and in showrooms, garment buyers are the primary audience. Runway models display clothes that either are intended for direct sale to consumers or are the artistic expressions of the designer. High fashion, or haute couture, runway models walk a runway before an audience of photographers, journalists, designers, and garment buyers. Live modeling also is done in apparel marts, department stores, and fitting rooms of clothing designers. In retail establishments, models display clothing directly for shoppers and may be required to describe the features and price of the clothing. Other models pose for sketch artists, painters, and sculptors.

Models may compete with actors and actresses for work in television and may even receive speaking parts. Television work includes commercials, cable television programs, and even game shows. However, competition for television work is intense because of the potential for high earnings and extensive exposure.

Because advertisers need to target very specific segments of the population, models may specialize in a certain area. Petite and plus-size fashions are modeled by women whose dress size is smaller or larger than that worn by the typical model. Models who are disabled may be used to model fashions or products for disabled consumers. "Parts" models have a body part, such as a hand or foot, which is particularly well-suited to model products such as fingernail polish or shoes.

Almost all models work through agents. Agents provide a link between models and clients. Clients pay models, while the agency receives a portion of the model's earnings for its services. Agents scout for new faces, advise and train new models, and promote them to clients. A typical modeling job lasts only 1 day, so modeling agencies differ from other employment agencies in that they maintain an ongoing relationship with the model. Agents find and nurture relationships with clients, arrange auditions called "go-sees," and book shoots if a model is hired. They also provide bookkeeping and billing services to models and may offer them financial planning services. Relatively short careers and variable incomes make financial planning an important issue for many models.

With the help of agents, models spend a considerable amount of time promoting and developing themselves. Models assemble and maintain portfolios, print composite cards, and travel to go-sees. A portfolio is a collection of a model's previous work that is carried to all go-sees and bookings. A composite card contains the best photographs from a model's portfolio, along with his or her measurements. Increasingly, composite cards are being sent electronically to clients and printed portfolios are being replaced with digital portfolios.

Models must gather information before a job. From an agent, they learn the pay, date, time, and length of the shoot. Also, models need to ask if hair, makeup, and clothing stylists will be provided. It is helpful to know what product is being promoted and what image they should project. Some models research the client and the product being modeled to prepare for a shoot. Models use a document called a voucher to record the rate of pay and the actual duration of the job. The voucher is used for billing purposes after both the client and model sign it. Once a job is completed, models must check in with their agency and plan for the next appointment.

*Work environment.* More than half of all demonstrators, product promoters, and models work part time and about 1 in 4 have variable work schedules. Many positions last 6 months or less.

Demonstrators and product promoters may work long hours while standing or walking, with little opportunity to rest. Some of them travel frequently, and night and weekend work often is required. The atmosphere of a crowded trade show or state fair is often hectic, and demonstrators and product promoters may feel pressure to influence the greatest number of consumers possible in a very limited amount of time. However, many enjoy the opportunity to interact with a variety of people.

Models work under a variety of conditions, which can often be both difficult and glamorous. The coming season's fashions may be modeled in a comfortable, climate-controlled studio or in a cold, damp outdoor location. Schedules can be demanding, and models must keep in constant touch with an agent so that they do not miss an opportunity for work. Being away from friends and family, and needing to focus on the photographer's instructions despite constant interruption for touchups, clothing, and set changes can be stressful. Yet, successful models interact with a variety of people and enjoy frequent travel. They may meet potential clients at several go-sees in one day and often travel to work in distant cities, foreign countries, and exotic locations.

## Training, Other Qualifications, and Advancement

Postsecondary education, while helpful, usually is not required for demonstrators, product promoters, and models.

*Education and training.* Demonstrators and product promoters usually receive on-the-job training. Training is primarily product oriented because a demonstrator must be familiar with the product to demonstrate it properly. The length of training varies with the complexity of the product. Experience with the product or familiarity with similar products may be required for demonstration of complex products, such as computers. During the training process, demonstrators may be introduced to the manufacturer's corporate philosophy and preferred methods for dealing with customers.

Some aspiring models opt to attend modeling schools. Modeling schools provide training in posing, walking, makeup application, and other basic tasks, but attending such schools does not necessarily lead to job opportunities. In fact, many agents prefer beginning models with little or no previous experience and discourage models from attending modeling schools and purchasing professional photographs. Agents continually scout for new faces, and many of the top models are discovered in this way. Most agencies review snap-

shots or have "open calls", during which models are seen in person; this service usually is provided free of charge. Some agencies sponsor modeling contests and searches. Very few people who send in snapshots or attend open calls are offered contracts.

Agencies advise models on how to dress, wear makeup, and conduct themselves properly during go-sees and bookings. Because models' advancement depends on their previous work, development of a good portfolio is key to getting assignments. The higher the quality and currency of the photos in the portfolio, the more likely it is that the model will find work.

*Other qualifications.* Employers look for demonstrators and product promoters with good communication skills and a pleasant appearance and personality. Demonstrators and product promoters must be comfortable with public speaking. They should be able to entertain an audience and use humor, spontaneity, and personal interest in the product as promotional tools. Foreign language skills are helpful.

Models should be photogenic and have a basic knowledge of hair styling, makeup, and clothing. Some local governments require models under the age of 18 to hold a work permit. An attractive physical appearance is necessary to become a successful model. A model should have flawless skin, healthy hair, and attractive facial features. Specific requirements depend on the client, but most models must be within certain ranges for height, weight, and clothing size in order to meet the practical needs of fashion designers, photographers, and advertisers. Requirements may change slightly from time to time as our society's perceptions of physical beauty change. However, most fashion designers feel that their clothing looks best on tall, thin models. Although physical requirements may be relaxed for some types of modeling jobs, opportunities are limited for those who do not meet these basic requirements.

A model's career depends on preservation of his or her physical characteristics, so models must control their diet, exercise regularly, and get enough sleep in order to stay healthy. Haircuts, pedicures, and manicures are necessary work-related expenses for models.

In addition to being attractive, models must be photogenic. The ability to relate to the camera in order to capture the desired look on film is essential and agents test prospective models using snapshots or professional photographs. For photographic and runway work, models must be able to move gracefully and confidently. Training in acting, voice, and dance is useful and allows a model to be considered for television work. Foreign language skills are useful because successful models travel frequently to foreign countries.

Models must interact with a large number of people and personality plays an important role in success. They must be professional, polite, and prompt as every contact could lead to future employment. Organizational skills are necessary to manage personal lives, financial matters, and work and travel schedules. Competition for jobs is keen and clients' needs are very specific so patience and persistence are essential.

*Advancement.* Demonstrators and product promoters who perform well and show leadership abilities may advance to other marketing and sales occupations or open their own business.

Models advance by working more regularly and being selected for assignments that have higher pay. They may begin to appear in magazine, print campaigns, commercials, or runway shows with a higher

**Projections data from the National Employment Matrix**

| Occupational Title | SOC Code | Employment, 2006 | Projected employment, 2016 | Change, 2006-16 | |
|---|---|---|---|---|---|
| | | | | Number | Percent |
| Models, demonstrators, and product promoters............................... | 41-9010 | 107,000 | 126,000 | 19,000 | 18 |
| Demonstrators and product promoters......................................... | 41-9011 | 105,000 | 124,000 | 19,000 | 18 |
| Models.......................................................................... | 41-9012 | 2,000 | 2,200 | 200 | 10 |

NOTE: Data in this table are rounded.

profile. They may begin to work with clients who will provide them with more national exposure. A model's selection of an agency is an important factor for advancement in the occupation. The better the reputation and skill of the agency, the more assignments a model is likely to get. Prospective clients prefer to work with agents, making it very difficult for a model to pursue a freelance career. Modeling careers are relatively short and most models eventually transfer to other occupations.

## Employment

Demonstrators, product promoters, and models held about 107,000 jobs in 2006. Of these, models held only about 2,000 jobs in 2006. About 22 percent of all salaried jobs for demonstrators, product promoters, and models were in retail trade, especially general merchandise stores, and 14 percent were in administrative and support services—which includes employment services. Other jobs were found in advertising and related services.

## Job Outlook

Employment of demonstrators, product promoters, and models is expected to grow faster than the average for all occupations through 2016. Job openings for demonstrators and product promoters should be plentiful over the next decade but models should face keen competition for the small number of openings.

*Employment change.* Demonstrators and product promoters are expected to experience 18 percent growth between 2006 and 2016, which is faster than the average for all occupations. Job growth should be driven by increases in the number and size of trade shows and greater use of these workers in department stores and various retail shops for in-store promotions. Product demonstration is considered a very effective marketing tool. New jobs should arise as firms devote a greater percentage of marketing budgets to product demonstration. However, it is also an expensive method of marketing, which will somewhat limit growth.

Employment of models is expected to grow by 10 percent between 2006 and 2016, which is as fast as the average for all occupations. Growth in the employment of models will be driven by their continued use in advertising products. Advertisers will continue to use models in fashion shows, catalogs, and print campaigns as a method to increase awareness of their product.

*Job prospects.* Job openings should be plentiful for demonstrators and product promoters. Employers may have difficulty finding qualified demonstrators who are willing to fill part-time, short-term positions. On the other hand, modeling is considered a glamorous occupation, with limited formal entry requirements. Consequently,

those who wish to pursue a modeling career can expect keen competition for jobs. The modeling profession typically attracts many more jobseekers than there are job openings available. Only models who closely meet the unique requirements of the occupation will achieve regular employment. The increasing diversification of the general population should boost demand for models more representative of diverse racial and ethnic groups. Work for male models also should increase as society becomes more receptive to the marketing of men's fashions. Because fashions change frequently, demand for a model's look may fluctuate. Most models experience periods of unemployment.

Employment of demonstrators, product promoters, and models is affected by downturns in the business cycle. Many firms tend to reduce advertising budgets during recessions

## Earnings

Demonstrators and product promoters had median hourly earnings of $10.65 in May 2006. The middle 50 percent earned between $8.77 and $13.91. The lowest 10 percent earned less than $7.70, and the highest 10 percent earned more than $19.27. Employers of demonstrators, product promoters, and models generally pay for job-related travel expenses.

Median hourly earnings of models were $11.22 in May 2006. The middle 50 percent earned between $9.52 and $14.42. The lowest 10 percent earned less than $7.67, and the highest 10 percent earned more than $18.68. Earnings vary for different types of modeling, and depend on the experience and reputation of the model. Female models typically earn more than male models for similar work. Hourly earnings can be relatively high, particularly for supermodels and others in high demand, but models may not have work every day, and jobs may last only a few hours. Models occasionally receive clothing or clothing discounts instead of, or in addition to, regular earnings. Almost all models work with agents, and pay 15 to 20 percent of their earnings in return for an agent's services. Models who do not find immediate work may receive payments, called advances, from agents to cover promotional and living expenses. Models must provide their own health and retirement benefits.

## Related Occupations

Demonstrators, product promoters, and models create public interest in buying clothing, products, and services. Others who create interest in a product or service include actors, producers, and directors; insurance sales agents; real estate brokers; retail salespersons; sales representatives, wholesale and manufacturing; and reservation and transportation ticket agents and travel clerks.

## Sources of Additional Information

For information about modeling schools and agencies in your area, contact a local consumer affairs organization such as the Better Business Bureau.

## Dental Assistants

(O*NET 31-9091.00)

## Significant Points

- Job prospects should be excellent.

- Dentists are expected to hire more assistants to perform routine tasks so that they may devote their own time to more complex procedures.

- Many assistants learn their skills on the job, although an increasing number are trained in dental-assisting programs; most programs take 1 year or less to complete.

## Nature of the Work

Dental assistants work closely with, and under the supervision of, dentists. Assistants perform a variety of patient care, office, and laboratory duties.

Dental assistants should not be confused with dental hygienists, who are licensed to perform different clinical tasks.

Dental assistants sterilize and disinfect instruments and equipment, prepare and lay out the instruments and materials required to treat each patient, and obtain patients' dental records. Assistants make patients as comfortable as possible in the dental chair and prepare them for treatment. During dental procedures, assistants work alongside the dentist to provide assistance. They hand instruments and materials to dentists and keep patients' mouths dry and clear by using suction or other devices. They also instruct patients on post-operative and general oral health care.

Dental assistants may prepare materials for impressions and restorations, take dental x rays, and process x-ray film as directed by a dentist. They also may remove sutures, apply topical anesthetics to gums or cavity-preventive agents to teeth, remove excess cement used in the filling process, and place rubber dams on the teeth to isolate them for individual treatment. Some states are expanding dental assistants' duties to include tasks such as coronal polishing and restorative dentistry functions for those assistants that meet specific training and experience requirements.

Dental assistants with laboratory duties make casts of the teeth and mouth from impressions, clean and polish removable appliances, and make temporary crowns. Those with office duties schedule and confirm appointments, receive patients, keep treatment records, send bills, receive payments, and order dental supplies and materials.

*Work environment.* Dental assistants work in a well-lighted, clean environment. Their work area usually is near the dental chair so that they can arrange instruments, materials, and medication and hand them to the dentist when needed. Dental assistants must wear gloves, masks, eyewear, and protective clothing to protect them-selves and their patients from infectious diseases. Assistants also follow safety procedures to minimize the risks associated with the use of x-ray machines.

About half of dental assistants have a 35- to 40-hour work week. Most of the rest work part-time or have variable schedules. Depending on the hours of the dental office where they work, assistants may have to work on Saturdays or evenings. Some dental assistants hold multiple jobs by working at dental offices that are open on different days or scheduling their work at a second office around the hours they work at their primary office.

## Training, Other Qualifications, and Advancement

Many assistants learn their skills on the job, although an increasing number are trained in dental-assisting programs offered by community and junior colleges, trade schools, technical institutes, or the Armed Forces.

*Education and training.* High school students interested in a career as a dental assistant should take courses in biology, chemistry, health, and office practices. For those wishing to pursue further education, the Commission on Dental Accreditation within the American Dental Association (ADA) approved 269 dental-assisting training programs in 2006. Programs include classroom, laboratory, and preclinical instruction in dental-assisting skills and related theory. In addition, students gain practical experience in dental schools, clinics, or dental offices. Most programs take one year or less to complete and lead to a certificate or diploma. Two-year programs offered in community and junior colleges lead to an associate degree. All programs require a high school diploma or its equivalent, and some require science or computer-related courses for admission. A number of private vocational schools offer four- to six-month courses in dental assisting, but the Commission on Dental Accreditation does not accredit these programs.

A large number of dental assistants learn through on-the-job training. In these situations, the employing dentist or other dental assistants in the dental office teach the new assistant dental terminology, the names of the instruments, how to perform daily duties, how to interact with patients, and other things necessary to help keep the dental office running smoothly. While some things can be picked up easily, it may be a few months before new dental assistants are completely knowledgeable about their duties and comfortable doing all of their tasks without assistance.

A period of on-the-job training is often required even for those that have completed a dental-assisting program or have some previous experience. Different dentists may have their own styles of doing things that need to be learned before an assistant can be comfortable working with them. Office-specific information, such as where files are kept, will need to be learned at each new job. Also, as dental technology changes, dental assistants need to stay familiar with the tools and procedures that they will be using or helping dentists to use. On-the-job training is often sufficient to keep assistants up-to-date on these matters.

*Licensure.* Most states regulate the duties that dental assistants are allowed to perform. Some states require licensure or registration, which may include passing a written or practical examination. There

**Projections data from the National Employment Matrix**

| Occupational Title | SOC Code | Employment, 2006 | Projected employment, 2016 | Change, 2006-16 | |
|---|---|---|---|---|---|
| | | | | Number | Percent |
| Dental assistants................................................................. | 31-9091 | 280,000 | 362,000 | 82,000 | 29 |

NOTE: Data in this table are rounded.

are a variety of schools offering courses—approximately 10 to 12 months in length—that meet their state's requirements. Other states require dental assistants to complete state-approved education courses of four to 12 hours in length. Some states offer registration of other dental assisting credentials with little or no education required. Some states require continuing education to maintain licensure or registration. A few states allow dental assistants to perform any function delegated to them by the dentist.

Individual states have adopted different standards for dental assistants who perform certain advanced duties. In some states, for example, dental assistants who perform radiological procedures must complete additional training. Completion of the Radiation Health and Safety examination offered by Dental Assisting National Board (DANB) meets the standards in more than 30 states. Some states require completion of a state-approved course in radiology as well.

*Certification and other qualifications.* Certification is available through the Dental Assisting National Board (DANB) and is recognized or required in more than 30 states. Certification is an acknowledgment of an assistant's qualifications and professional competence and may be an asset when one is seeking employment. Candidates may qualify to take the DANB certification examination by graduating from an ADA-accredited dental assisting education program or by having two years of full-time, or four years of part-time, experience as a dental assistant. In addition, applicants must have current certification in cardiopulmonary resuscitation. For annual recertification, individuals must earn continuing education credits. Other organizations offer registration, most often at the state level.

Dental assistants must be a second pair of hands for a dentist; therefore, dentists look for people who are reliable, work well with others, and have good manual dexterity.

*Advancement.* Without further education, advancement opportunities are limited. Some dental assistants become office managers, dental-assisting instructors, dental product sales representatives, or insurance claims processors for dental insurance companies. Others go back to school to become dental hygienists. For many, this entry-level occupation provides basic training and experience and serves as a steppingstone to more highly skilled and higher paying jobs.

## Employment

Dental assistants held about 280,000 jobs in 2006. Almost all jobs for dental assistants were in offices of dentists. A small number of jobs were in the federal, state, and local governments or in offices of physicians. About 35 percent of dental assistants worked part time, sometimes in more than one dental office.

## Job Outlook

Employment is expected to increase much faster than average; job prospects are expected to be excellent.

*Employment change.* Employment is expected to grow 29 percent from 2006 to 2016, which is much faster than the average for all occupations. In fact, dental assistants are expected to be among the fastest growing occupations over the 2006–2016 projection period.

Population growth, greater retention of natural teeth by middle-aged and older people, and an increased focus on preventative dental care for younger generations will fuel demand for dental services. Older dentists, who have been less likely to employ assistants or have employed fewer, are leaving the occupation and will be replaced by recent graduates, who are more likely to use one or more assistants. In addition, as dentists' workloads increase, they are expected to hire more assistants to perform routine tasks, so that they may devote their own time to more complex procedures.

*Job prospects.* Job prospects for dental assistants should be excellent. In addition to job openings due to employment growth, numerous job openings will arise out of the need to replace assistants who transfer to other occupations, retire, or leave for other reasons. Many opportunities for entry-level positions offer on-the-job training, but some dentists prefer to hire experienced assistants or those who have completed a dental-assisting program.

## Earnings

Median hourly earnings of dental assistants were $14.53 in May 2006. The middle 50 percent earned between $11.94 and $17.44 an hour. The lowest 10 percent earned less than $9.87, and the highest 10 percent earned more than $20.69 an hour.

Benefits vary substantially by practice setting and may be contingent upon full-time employment. According to the American Dental Association, 87 percent of dentists offer reimbursement for continuing education courses taken by their assistants.

## Related Occupations

Other workers supporting health practitioners include dental hygienists, medical assistants, surgical technologists, pharmacy aides, pharmacy technicians, occupational therapist assistants and aides, and physical therapist assistants and aides.

## Sources of Additional Information

Information about career opportunities and accredited dental assistant programs is available from

▸ Commission on Dental Accreditation, American Dental Association, 211 East Chicago Ave., Suite 1814, Chicago, IL 60611. Internet: http://www.ada.org

For information on becoming a Certified Dental Assistant and a list of state boards of dentistry, contact

▸ Dental Assisting National Board, Inc., 676 North Saint Clair St., Suite 1880, Chicago, IL 60611. Internet: http://www.danb.org

For more information on a career as a dental assistant and general information about continuing education, contact

▸ American Dental Assistants Association, 35 East Wacker Dr., Suite 1730, Chicago, IL 60601. Internet: http://www.dentalassistant.org

For more information about continuing education courses, contact

▸ National Association of Dental Assistants, 900 South Washington St., Suite G-13, Falls Church, VA 22046.

# Dental Hygienists

(O*NET 29-2021.00)

## Significant Points

- A degree from an accredited dental hygiene school and a state license are required for this job.

- Dental hygienists rank among the fastest growing occupations.

- Job prospects are expected to remain excellent.

- More than half work part time, and flexible scheduling is a distinctive feature of this job.

## Nature of the Work

Dental hygienists remove soft and hard deposits from teeth, teach patients how to practice good oral hygiene, and provide other preventive dental care. They examine patients' teeth and gums, recording the presence of diseases or abnormalities.

Dental hygienists use an assortment of different tools to complete their tasks. Hand and rotary instruments and ultrasonic devices are used to clean and polish teeth, including removing calculus, stains, and plaque. Hygienists use x-ray machines to take dental pictures, and sometimes develop the film. They may use models of teeth to explain oral hygiene, perform root planning as a periodontal therapy, or apply cavity-preventative agents such as fluorides and pit and fissure sealants. In some states, hygienists are allowed to administer anesthetics, while in others they administer local anesthetics using syringes. Some states also allow hygienists to place and carve filling materials, temporary fillings, and periodontal dressings; remove sutures; and smooth and polish metal restorations.

Dental hygienists also help patients develop and maintain good oral health. For example, they may explain the relationship between diet and oral health or inform patients how to select toothbrushes and show them how to brush and floss their teeth.

Hygienists sometimes make a diagnosis and other times may prepare clinical and laboratory diagnostic tests for the dentist to interpret. Hygienists sometimes work chair side with the dentist during treatment.

*Work environment.* Dental hygienists work in clean, well-lighted offices. Important health safeguards include strict adherence to proper radiological procedures and the use of appropriate protective devices when administering anesthetic gas. Dental hygienists also wear safety glasses, surgical masks, and gloves to protect themselves and patients from infectious diseases.

Flexible scheduling is a distinctive feature of this job. Full-time, part-time, evening, and weekend schedules are widely available. Dentists frequently hire hygienists to work only 2 or 3 days a week, so hygienists may hold jobs in more than one dental office. More than half of all dental hygienists worked part time—less than 35 hours a week.

## Training, Other Qualifications, and Advancement

Prospective dental hygienists must become licensed in the state in which they wish to practice. A degree from an accredited dental hygiene school is usually required along with licensure examinations.

*Education and training.* A high school diploma and college entrance test scores are usually required for admission to a dental hygiene program. High school students interested in becoming a dental hygienist should take courses in biology, chemistry, and mathematics. Also, some dental hygiene programs require applicants to have completed at least one year of college. Specific entrance requirements vary from one school to another.

In 2006, there were 286 dental hygiene programs accredited by the Commission on Dental Accreditation. Most dental hygiene programs grant an associate degree, although some also offer a certificate, a bachelor's degree, or a master's degree. A minimum of an associate degree or certificate in dental hygiene is generally required for practice in a private dental office. A bachelor's or master's degree usually is required for research, teaching, or clinical practice in public or school health programs.

Schools offer laboratory, clinical, and classroom instruction in subjects such as anatomy, physiology, chemistry, microbiology, pharmacology, nutrition, radiography, histology (the study of tissue structure), periodontology (the study of gum diseases), pathology, dental materials, clinical dental hygiene, and social and behavioral sciences.

*Licensure.* Dental hygienists must be licensed by the state in which they practice. Nearly all states require candidates to graduate from an accredited dental hygiene school and pass both a written and clinical examination. The American Dental Association's Joint Commission on National Dental Examinations administers the written examination, which is accepted by all states and the District of Columbia. State or regional testing agencies administer the clinical examination. In addition, most states require an examination on the legal aspects of dental hygiene practice. Alabama is the only state that allows candidates to take its examinations if they have been trained through a state-regulated on-the-job program in a dentist's office.

*Other qualifications.* Dental hygienists should work well with others because they work closely with dentists and dental assistants as well as dealing directly with patients. Hygienists also need good manual dexterity, because they use dental instruments within a patient's mouth, with little room for error.

**Projections data from the National Employment Matrix**

| Occupational Title | SOC Code | Employment, 2006 | Projected employment, 2016 | Change, 2006-2016 | |
|---|---|---|---|---|---|
| | | | | Number | Percent |
| Dental hygienists.................................................................... | 29-2021 | 167,000 | 217,000 | 50,000 | 30 |

NOTE: Data in this table are rounded.

## Employment

Dental hygienists held about 167,000 jobs in 2006. Because multiple job holding is common in this field, the number of jobs exceeds the number of hygienists. Almost all jobs for dental hygienists were in offices of dentists. A very small number worked for employment services, offices of physicians, or other industries.

## Job Outlook

Dental hygienists rank among the fastest growing occupations, and job prospects are expected to remain excellent.

*Employment change.* Employment of dental hygienists is expected to grow 30 percent through 2016, much faster than the average for all occupations. This projected growth ranks dental hygienists among the fastest growing occupations, in response to increasing demand for dental care and the greater use of hygienists.

The demand for dental services will grow because of population growth, older people increasingly retaining more teeth, and a growing focus on preventative dental care. To meet this demand, facilities that provide dental care, particularly dentists' offices, will increasingly employ dental hygienists, and more hygienists per office, to perform services that have been performed by dentists in the past.

*Job prospects.* Job prospects are expected to remain excellent. Older dentists, who have been less likely to employ dental hygienists, are leaving the occupation and will be replaced by recent graduates, who are more likely to employ one or more hygienists. In addition, as dentists' workloads increase, they are expected to hire more hygienists to perform preventive dental care, such as cleaning, so that they may devote their own time to more complex procedures.

## Earnings

Median hourly earnings of dental hygienists were $30.19 in May 2006. The middle 50 percent earned between $24.63 and $35.67 an hour. The lowest 10 percent earned less than $19.45, and the highest 10 percent earned more than $41.60 an hour.

Earnings vary by geographic location, employment setting, and years of experience. Dental hygienists may be paid on an hourly, daily, salary, or commission basis.

Benefits vary substantially by practice setting and may be contingent upon full-time employment. According to the American Dental Association, 86 percent of hygienists receive hospital and medical benefits.

## Related Occupations

Other workers supporting health practitioners in an office setting include dental assistants, medical assistants, occupational therapist assistants and aides, physical therapist assistants and aides, physician assistants, and registered nurses. Dental hygienists sometimes work with radiation technology, as do radiation therapists.

## Sources of Additional Information

For information on a career in dental hygiene, including educational requirements, contact

▸ Division of Education, American Dental Hygienists Association, 444 N. Michigan Ave., Suite 3400, Chicago, IL 60611. Internet: http://www.adha.org

For information about accredited programs and educational requirements, contact

▸ Commission on Dental Accreditation, American Dental Association, 211 E. Chicago Ave., Suite 1814, Chicago, IL 60611. Internet: http://www.ada.org

The State Board of Dental Examiners in each state can supply information on licensing requirements.

# Education Administrators

(O*NET 11-9031.00, 11-9032.00, 11-9033.00, and 11-9039.99)

## Significant Points

■ Many jobs require a master's or doctoral degree and experience in a related occupation, such as teaching or admissions counseling.

■ Strong interpersonal and communication skills are essential because much of an administrator's job involves working and collaborating with others.

■ Excellent opportunities are expected since a large proportion of education administrators is expected to retire over the next 10 years.

## Nature of the Work

Successful operation of an educational institution requires competent administrators. Education administrators provide instructional leadership and manage the day-to-day activities in schools, preschools, day care centers, and colleges and universities. They also direct the educational programs of businesses, correctional institutions, museums, and job training and community service organizations.

Education administrators set educational standards and goals and establish the policies and procedures to achieve them. They also supervise managers, support staff, teachers, counselors, librarians, coaches, and other employees. They develop academic programs, monitor students' educational progress, train and motivate teachers and other staff, manage career counseling and other student services, administer recordkeeping, prepare budgets, and perform many other duties. They also handle relations with parents, prospective and current students, employers, and the community. In an organization such as a small day care center, one administrator may handle all these functions. In universities or large school systems, responsibilities are divided among many administrators, each with a specific function.

Educational administrators who manage elementary, middle, and secondary schools are called *principals*. They set the academic tone and actively work with teachers to develop and maintain high curriculum standards, develop mission statements, and set performance goals and objectives. Principals confer with staff to advise, explain, or answer procedural questions. They hire, evaluate, and help improve the skills of teachers and other staff. They visit classrooms, observe teaching methods, review instructional objectives, and examine learning materials. Principals must use clear, objective guidelines for teacher appraisals because pay often is based on performance ratings.

Principals also meet and interact with other administrators, students, parents, and representatives of community organizations. Decision-making authority has increasingly shifted from school district central offices to individual schools. School principals have greater flexibility in setting school policies and goals, but when making administrative decisions they must pay attention to the concerns of parents, teachers, and other members of the community.

Preparing budgets and reports on various subjects, including finances and attendance, and overseeing the requisition and allocation of supplies also is an important responsibility of principals. As school budgets become tighter, many principals have become more involved in public relations and fundraising to secure financial support for their schools from local businesses and the community.

Principals must take an active role to ensure that students meet national, state, and local academic standards. Many principals develop partnerships with local businesses and school-to-work transition programs for students. Increasingly, principals must be sensitive to the needs of the rising number of non-English-speaking students and a culturally diverse student body. In some areas, growing enrollments also are a cause for concern because they lead to overcrowding at many schools. When addressing problems of inadequate resources, administrators serve as advocates for the building of new schools or the repair of existing ones. During summer months, principals are responsible for planning for the upcoming year, overseeing summer school, participating in workshops for teachers and administrators, supervising building repairs and improvements, and working to make sure the school has adequate staff for the school year.

Schools continue to be involved with students' emotional welfare as well as their academic achievement. As a result, principals face responsibilities outside the academic realm. For example, many schools have growing numbers of students from dual-income and single-parent families or students who are themselves teenage parents. To support these students and their families, some schools have established before- and after-school child-care programs or family resource centers, which also may offer parenting classes and social service referrals. With the help of community organizations, some principals have established programs to combat increases in crime, drug and alcohol abuse, and sexually transmitted diseases among students.

*Assistant principals* aid the principal in the overall administration of the school. Some assistant principals hold this position for several years, during which time they prepare for advancement to principal; others are assistant principals throughout their careers. They are primarily responsible for scheduling student classes; ordering textbooks and supplies; and coordinating transportation, custodial, cafeteria, and other support services. They usually handle student discipline and attendance problems, social and recreational programs, and health and safety matters. They also may counsel students on personal, educational, or vocational matters. With the advent of site-based management, assistant principals are playing a greater role in ensuring the academic success of students by helping to develop new curriculums, evaluating teachers, and dealing with school-community relations—responsibilities previously assumed solely by the principal. The number of assistant principals that a school employs may vary, depending on the number of students.

*Administrators* in school district central offices oversee public schools under their jurisdiction. This group includes those who direct subject-area programs such as English, music, vocational education, special education, and mathematics. They supervise instructional coordinators and curriculum specialists and work with them to evaluate and improve curriculums and teaching techniques. Administrators also may oversee career counseling programs and testing that measures students' abilities and helps to place them in appropriate classes. Others may also direct programs such as school psychology, athletics, curriculum and instruction, and professional development. With site-based management, administrators have transferred primary responsibility for many of these programs to the principals, assistant principals, teachers, instructional coordinators, and other staff in the schools.

In preschools and child care centers, which are usually much smaller than other educational institutions, the director or supervisor of the school or center often serves as the sole administrator. Their job is similar to that of other school administrators in that they oversee daily activities and operation of the schools, hire and develop staff, and make sure that the school meets required regulations and educational standards.

In colleges and universities, *provosts*, also known as *chief academic officers*, assist presidents, make faculty appointments and tenure decisions, develop budgets, and establish academic policies and programs. With the assistance of *academic deans* and *deans of faculty*, they also direct and coordinate the activities of deans of individual colleges and chairpersons of academic departments. Fundraising is the chief responsibility of the *director of development* and also is becoming an essential part of the job for all administrators.

*College or university department heads* or *chairpersons* are in charge of departments that specialize in particular fields of study, such as English, biological science, or mathematics. In addition to teaching, they coordinate schedules of classes and teaching assignments; propose budgets; recruit, interview, and hire applicants for teaching positions; evaluate faculty members; encourage faculty development; serve on committees; and perform other administrative duties. In overseeing their departments, chairpersons must consider and balance the concerns of faculty, administrators, and students.

Higher education administrators also direct and coordinate the provision of student services. *Vice presidents of student affairs or student life, deans of students*, and *directors of student services* may direct and coordinate admissions, foreign student services, health and counseling services, career services, financial aid, and housing and residential life, as well as social, recreational, and related programs. In small colleges, they may counsel students. In larger colleges and universities, separate administrators may handle each of these services. *Registrars* are custodians of students' records. They register students, record grades, prepare student transcripts, evaluate academic records, assess and collect tuition and fees, plan and implement commencement, oversee the preparation of college catalogs and schedules of classes, and analyze enrollment and demographic statistics. *Directors of admissions* manage the process of recruiting, evaluating, and admitting students and work closely with *financial aid directors*, who oversee scholarship, fellowship, and loan programs. Registrars and admissions officers at most institutions need computer skills because they use electronic student information systems. For example, for those whose institutions present college catalogs, schedules, and other information on the Internet, knowledge of online resources, imaging, and other computer skills is important. *Athletic directors* plan and direct intramural and intercollegiate athletic activities, seeing to publicity for athletic events, preparation of budgets, and supervision of coaches. Other increasingly important administrators direct public relations, distance learning, and technology.

*Work environment.* Education administrators hold leadership positions with significant responsibility. Most find working with students extremely rewarding, but as the responsibilities of administrators have increased in recent years, so has the stress. Coordinating and interacting with faculty, parents, students, community members, business leaders, and state and local policymakers can be fast-paced and stimulating, but also stressful and demanding. Principals and assistant principals, whose varied duties include discipline, may find working with difficult students to be challenging. They are also increasingly being held accountable for ensuring that their schools meet recently imposed state and federal guidelines for student performance and teacher qualifications.

About 1 in 3 education administrators work more than 40 hours a week and often supervise school activities at night and on weekends. Most administrators work year round, although some work only during the academic year.

## Training, Other Qualifications, and Advancement

Most education administrators begin their careers as teachers and prepare for advancement into education administration by completing a master's or doctoral degree. Because of the diversity of duties and levels of responsibility, educational backgrounds and experience vary considerably among these workers.

*Education and training.* Principals, assistant principals, central office administrators, academic deans, and preschool directors usually have held teaching positions before moving into administration. Some teachers move directly into principal positions; others first become assistant principals or gain experience in other administrative jobs at either the school or district level in positions such as

department head, curriculum specialist, or subject matter advisor. In some cases, administrators move up from related staff jobs such as recruiter, school counselor, librarian, residence hall director, or financial aid or admissions counselor.

In most public schools, principals, assistant principals, and school district administrators need a master's degree in education administration or educational leadership. Some principals and central office administrators have a doctorate or specialized degree in education administration. In private schools, some principals and assistant principals hold only a bachelor's degree, but the majority have a master's or doctoral degree.

Educational requirements for administrators of preschools and child care centers vary depending on the setting of the program and the state of employment. Administrators who oversee preschool programs in public schools are often required to have at least a bachelor's degree. Child care directors who supervise private programs are usually not required to have a degree; however, most states require a preschool education credential, which often includes some postsecondary coursework.

College and university academic deans and chairpersons usually advance from professorships in their departments, for which they need a master's or doctoral degree; further education is not typically necessary. Admissions, student affairs, and financial aid directors and registrars sometimes start in related staff jobs with bachelor's degrees—any field usually is acceptable—and obtain advanced degrees in college student affairs, counseling, or higher education administration. A Ph.D. or Ed.D. usually is necessary for top student affairs positions. Computer literacy and a background in accounting or statistics may be assets in admissions, records, and financial work.

Advanced degrees in higher education administration, educational leadership, and college student affairs are offered in many colleges and universities. Education administration degree programs include courses in school leadership, school law, school finance and budgeting, curriculum development and evaluation, research design and data analysis, community relations, politics in education, and counseling. The National Council for Accreditation of Teacher Education (NCATE) and the Educational Leadership Constituent Council (ELCC) accredit programs designed for elementary and secondary school administrators. Although completion of an accredited program is not required, it may assist in fulfilling licensure requirements.

*Licensure and certification.* Most states require principals to be licensed as school administrators. License requirements vary by state, but nearly all states require either a master's degree or some other graduate-level training. Some states also require candidates for licensure to pass a test. On-the-job training, often with a mentor, is increasingly required or recommended for new school leaders. Some states require administrators to take continuing education courses to keep their license, thus ensuring that administrators have the most up-to-date skills. The number and types of courses required to maintain licensure vary by state. Principals in private schools are not subject to state licensure requirements.

Nearly all states require child care and preschool center directors to be licensed. Licensing usually requires a number of years of experience or hours of coursework or both. Sometimes it requires a college

**Projections data from the National Employment Matrix**

| Occupational Title | SOC Code | Employment, 2006 | Projected employment, 2016 | Change, 2006-16 | |
|---|---|---|---|---|---|
| | | | | Number | Percent |
| Education administrators ................................................... | 11-9030 | 443,000 | 496,000 | 53,000 | 12 |
|    Education administrators, preschool and child care center/ program ..................................................................... | 11-9031 | 56,000 | 69,000 | 13,000 | 24 |
|    Education administrators, elementary and secondary school ....... | 11-9032 | 226,000 | 243,000 | 17,000 | 8 |
|    Education administrators, postsecondary..................................... | 11-9033 | 131,000 | 150,000 | 19,000 | 14 |
|    Education administrators, all other .......................................... | 11-9039 | 30,000 | 33,000 | 3,700 | 13 |

NOTE: Data in this table are rounded.

degree. Often, directors are also required to earn a general preschool education credential, such as the Child Development Associate credential (CDA), sponsored by the Council for Professional Recognition, or some other credential designed specifically for directors.

One credential specifically for directors is the National Administration Credential, offered by the National Child Care Association. The credential requires experience and training in child care center management.

There are usually no licensing requirements for administrators at postsecondary institutions.

*Other qualifications.* To be considered for education administrator positions, workers must first prove themselves in their current jobs. In evaluating candidates, supervisors look for leadership, determination, confidence, innovativeness, and motivation. The ability to make sound decisions and to organize and coordinate work efficiently is essential. Because much of an administrator's job involves interacting with others—such as students, parents, teachers, and the community—a person in such a position must have strong interpersonal skills and be an effective communicator and motivator. Knowledge of leadership principles and practices, gained through work experience and formal education, is important. A familiarity with computer technology is a necessity for principals, who are required to gather information and coordinate technical resources for their students, teachers, and classrooms.

*Advancement.* Education administrators advance through promotion to higher-level administrative positions or by transferring to comparable positions at larger schools or systems. They also may become superintendents of school systems or presidents of educational institutions.

## Employment

Education administrators held about 443,000 jobs in 2006. Of these, 56,000 were preschool or child care administrators, 226,000 were elementary or secondary school administrators, and 131,000 were postsecondary administrators. The great majority—over 80 percent—worked in public or private educational institutions. Most of the remainder worked in child daycare centers, religious organizations, job training centers, and businesses and other organizations that provided training for their employees.

## Job Outlook

Employment of education administrators is projected to grow about as fast as average as education and training take on greater importance in everyone's lives. Job opportunities for many of these posi-

tions should be excellent because a large proportion of education administrators are expected to retire over the next 10 years.

*Employment change.* Employment of education administrators is expected to grow by 12 percent between 2006 and 2016, about as fast as the average for all occupations, primarily due to growth in enrollments of school-age children. Enrollment of students in elementary and secondary schools is expected to grow slowly over the next decade, which will limit the growth of principals and other administrators in these schools. However, the number of administrative positions will continue to increase as more administrative responsibilities are placed on individual schools, particularly related to monitoring student achievement. Preschool and child care center administrators are expected to experience substantial growth due to increasing enrollments in formal child care programs as fewer young children are cared for in private homes. Additionally, as more states implement or expand public preschool programs, more preschool directors will be needed.

The number of students at the postsecondary level is projected to grow more rapidly than other student populations, creating significant demand for administrators at that level. A significant portion of the growth will occur in the private and for-profit segments of higher education. Many of these schools cater to working adults who might not ordinarily participate in postsecondary education. These schools allow students to earn a degree, receive job-specific training, or update their skills in a convenient manner, such as through part-time programs or distance learning. As the number of these schools continues to grow, more administrators will be needed to oversee them.

*Job prospects.* Principals and assistant principals should have very favorable job prospects. A sharp increase in responsibilities in recent years has made the job more stressful and has discouraged some teachers from taking positions in administration. Principals are now being held more accountable for the performance of students and teachers, while at the same time they are required to adhere to a growing number of government regulations. In addition, overcrowded classrooms, safety issues, budgetary concerns, and teacher shortages in some areas are creating additional stress for administrators. Many teachers feel that the increase in pay for becoming an administrator is not high enough to compensate for the greater responsibilities.

Opportunities may vary by region of the country. Enrollments are expected to increase the fastest in the West and South, where the population is growing faster, and to decline or remain stable in the Northeast and the Midwest. School administrators also are in greater demand in rural and urban areas, where pay is generally lower than in the suburbs.

Although competition among faculty for prestigious positions as academic deans and department heads is likely to remain keen, fewer applicants are expected for nonacademic administrative jobs, such as director of admissions or student affairs. Furthermore, many people are discouraged from seeking administrator jobs by the requirement that they have a master's or doctoral degree in education administration—as well as by the opportunity to earn higher salaries in other occupations.

## Earnings

In May 2006, elementary and secondary school administrators had median annual earnings of $77,740; postsecondary school administrators had median annual earnings of $73,990, while administrators in preschool and child care centers earned a median of $37,740 per year. Salaries of education administrators depend on several factors, including the location and enrollment level in the school or school district.

According to a survey of public schools, conducted by the Educational Research Service, average salaries for principals and assistant principals in the 2006-07 school year were as follows:

Principals:

|  |  |
|---|---|
| Senior high school | $92,965 |
| Jr. high/middle school | 87,866 |
| Elementary school | 82,414 |

Assistant principals:

|  |  |
|---|---|
| Senior high school | $75,121 |
| Jr. high/middle school | 73,020 |
| Elementary school | 67,735 |

According to the College and University Professional Association for Human Resources, median annual salaries for selected administrators in higher education in 2006-07 were as follows:

| | |
|---|---|
| Chief academic officer | $140,595 |

Academic deans:

|  |  |
|---|---|
| Business | $135,080 |
| Arts and sciences | 121,942 |
| Graduate programs | 120,120 |
| Education | 117,450 |
| Nursing | 112,497 |
| Health-related professions | 110,346 |
| Continuing education | 99,595 |
| Occupational studies/vocational education | 83,108 |

Other administrators:

|  |  |
|---|---|
| Chief development officer | $125,000 |
| Dean of students | 80,012 |
| Director, student financial aid | 68,000 |
| Registrar | 66,008 |
| Director, student activities | 50,000 |

Benefits for education administrators are generally very good. Many get 4 or 5 weeks of vacation every year and have generous health and pension packages. Many colleges and universities offer free tuition to employees and their families.

## Related Occupations

Education administrators apply organizational and leadership skills to provide services to individuals. Workers in related occupations include administrative services managers; office and administrative support worker supervisors and managers; and human resources, training, and labor relations managers and specialists. Education administrators also work with students and have backgrounds similar to those of counselors; librarians; instructional coordinators; teachers—preschool, kindergarten, elementary, middle, and secondary; and teachers—postsecondary.

## Sources of Additional Information

For information on principals, contact

▸ The National Association of Elementary School Principals, 1615 Duke St., Alexandria, VA 22314-3483. Internet: http://www.naesp.org

▸ The National Association of Secondary School Principals, 1904 Association Drive, Reston, VA 20191-1537. Internet: http://www.nassp.org

For a list of nationally recognized programs in elementary and secondary educational administration, contact

▸ The Educational Leadership Constituent Council, 1904 Association Drive, Reston, VA 20191. Internet: http://www.npbea.org/ELCC/index.html

For information on collegiate registrars and admissions officers, contact

▸ American Association of Collegiate Registrars and Admissions Officers, One Dupont Circle NW, Suite 520, Washington, DC 20036-1171. Internet: http://www.aacrao.org

For information on professional development and graduate programs for college student affairs administrators, contact

▸ NASPA, Student Affairs Administrators in Higher Education, 1875 Connecticut Ave. NW, Suite 418, Washington, DC 20009. Internet: http://www.naspa.org

For information on the National Administrator Credential for child care directors, contact

▸ National Child Care Association, 2025 M St. NW, Suite 800, Washington, DC 20036. Internet: http://www.nccanet.org

For information on the Child Development Associate Credential, contact

▸ Council for Professional Recognition, 2460 16th St. NW, Washington, DC 20009. Internet: http://www.cdacouncil.org

## Emergency Medical Technicians and Paramedics

(O*NET 29-2041.00)

## Significant Points

- Employment is projected to grow faster than the average as paid positions replace unpaid volunteers.

- Emergency medical technicians and paramedics need formal training and certification, but requirements vary by state.

- Emergency services function 24 hours a day so emergency medical technicians and paramedics have irregular working hours.

- Opportunities will be best for those who have earned advanced certifications.

## Nature of the Work

People's lives often depend on the quick reaction and competent care of emergency medical technicians (EMTs) and paramedics. Incidents as varied as automobile accidents, heart attacks, slips and falls, childbirth, and gunshot wounds all require immediate medical attention. EMTs and paramedics provide this vital service as they care for and transport the sick or injured to a medical facility.

In an emergency, EMTs and paramedics are typically dispatched by a 911 operator to the scene, where they often work with police and fire fighters. Once they arrive, EMTs and paramedics assess the nature of the patient's condition while trying to determine whether the patient has any pre-existing medical conditions. Following medical protocols and guidelines, they provide appropriate emergency care and, when necessary, transport the patient. Some paramedics are trained to treat patients with minor injuries on the scene of an accident or they may treat them at their home without transporting them to a medical facility. Emergency treatment is carried out under the medical direction of physicians.

EMTs and paramedics may use special equipment, such as backboards, to immobilize patients before placing them on stretchers and securing them in the ambulance for transport to a medical facility. These workers generally work in teams. During the transport of a patient, one EMT or paramedic drives while the other monitors the patient's vital signs and gives additional care as needed. Some paramedics work as part of a helicopter's flight crew to transport critically ill or injured patients to hospital trauma centers.

At the medical facility, EMTs and paramedics help transfer patients to the emergency department, report their observations and actions to emergency department staff, and may provide additional emergency treatment. After each run, EMTs and paramedics replace used supplies and check equipment. If a transported patient had a contagious disease, EMTs and paramedics decontaminate the interior of the ambulance and report cases to the proper authorities.

EMTs and paramedics also provide transportation for patients from one medical facility to another, particularly if they work for private ambulance services. Patients often need to be transferred to a hospital that specializes in their injury or illness or to a nursing home.

Beyond these general duties, the specific responsibilities of EMTs and paramedics depend on their level of qualification and training. The National Registry of Emergency Medical Technicians (NREMT) certifies emergency medical service providers at five levels: First Responder; EMT-Basic; EMT-Intermediate, which has two levels called 1985 and 1999; and Paramedic. Some states, however, have their own certification programs and use distinct names and titles.

The EMT-Basic represents the first component of the emergency medical technician system. An EMT trained at this level is prepared to care for patients at the scene of an accident and while transporting patients by ambulance to the hospital under medical direction. The EMT-Basic has the emergency skills to assess a patient's condition and manage respiratory, cardiac, and trauma emergencies.

The EMT-Intermediate has more advanced training. However, the specific tasks that those certified at this level are allowed to perform varies greatly from state to state.

EMT-Paramedics provide the most extensive pre-hospital care. In addition to carrying out the procedures of the other levels, paramedics may administer drugs orally and intravenously, interpret electrocardiograms (EKGs), perform endotracheal intubations, and use monitors and other complex equipment. However, like EMT-Intermediate, what paramedics are permitted to do varies by state.

*Work environment.* EMTs and paramedics work both indoors and out, in all types of weather. They are required to do considerable kneeling, bending, and heavy lifting. These workers risk noise-induced hearing loss from sirens and back injuries from lifting patients. In addition, EMTs and paramedics may be exposed to diseases such as hepatitis-B and AIDS, as well as violence from mentally unstable patients. The work is not only physically strenuous but can be stressful, sometimes involving life-or-death situations and suffering patients. Nonetheless, many people find the work exciting and challenging and enjoy the opportunity to help others.

EMTs and paramedics employed by fire departments work about 50 hours a week. Those employed by hospitals frequently work between 45 and 60 hours a week, and those in private ambulance services, between 45 and 50 hours. Some of these workers, especially those in police and fire departments, are on call for extended periods. Because emergency services function 24 hours a day, EMTs and paramedics have irregular working hours.

## Training, Other Qualifications, and Advancement

Generally, a high school diploma is required to enter a training program to become an EMT or paramedic. Workers must complete a formal training and certification process.

*Education and training.* A high school diploma is usually required to enter a formal emergency medical technician training program. Training is offered at progressive levels: EMT-Basic, EMT-Intermediate, and EMT-Paramedic.

At the EMT-Basic level, coursework emphasizes emergency skills, such as managing respiratory, trauma, and cardiac emergencies, and patient assessment. Formal courses are often combined with time in an emergency room or ambulance. The program provides instruction and practice in dealing with bleeding, fractures, airway obstruction,

**Projections data from the National Employment Matrix**

| Occupational Title | SOC Code | Employment, 2006 | Projected employment, 2016 | Change, 2006-2016 | |
|---|---|---|---|---|---|
| | | | | Number | Percent |
| Emergency medical technicians and paramedics............................. | 29-2041 | 201,000 | 240,000 | 39,000 | 19 |

NOTE: Data in this table are rounded.

cardiac arrest, and emergency childbirth. Students learn how to use and maintain common emergency equipment, such as backboards, suction devices, splints, oxygen delivery systems, and stretchers. Graduates of approved EMT-Basic training programs must pass a written and practical examination administered by the state certifying agency or the NREMT.

At the EMT-Intermediate level, training requirements vary by state. The nationally defined levels (EMT-Intermediate 1985 and EMT-Intermediate 1999) typically require 30 to 350 hours of training based on scope of practice. Students learn advanced skills such the use of advanced airway devices, intravenous fluids, and some medications.

The most advanced level of training for this occupation is EMT-Paramedic. At this level, the caregiver receives training in anatomy and physiology as well as advanced medical skills. Most commonly, the training is conducted in community colleges and technical schools over one to two years and may result in an associate's degree. Such education prepares the graduate to take the NREMT examination and become certified as a Paramedic. Extensive related coursework and clinical and field experience is required. Refresher courses and continuing education are available for EMTs and paramedics at all levels.

*Licensure.* All 50 states require certification for each of the EMT levels. In most states and the District of Columbia registration with the NREMT is required at some or all levels of certification. Other states administer their own certification examination or provide the option of taking either the NREMT or state examination. To maintain certification, EMTs and paramedics must recertify, usually every two years. Generally, they must be working as an EMT or paramedic and meet a continuing education requirement.

*Other qualifications.* EMTs and paramedics should be emotionally stable, have good dexterity, agility, and physical coordination, and be able to lift and carry heavy loads. They also need good eyesight (corrective lenses may be used) with accurate color vision.

*Advancement.* Paramedics can become supervisors, operations managers, administrative directors, or executive directors of emergency services. Some EMTs and paramedics become instructors, dispatchers, or physician assistants; others move into sales or marketing of emergency medical equipment. A number of people become EMTs and paramedics to test their interest in health care before training as registered nurses, physicians, or other health workers.

## Employment

EMTs and paramedics held about 201,000 jobs in 2006. Most career EMTs and paramedics work in metropolitan areas. Volunteer EMTs and paramedics are more common in small cities, towns, and rural areas. These individuals volunteer for fire departments, emergency

medical services, or hospitals and may respond to only a few calls per month. About 30 percent of EMTs or paramedics belong to a union.

Paid EMTs and paramedics were employed in a number of industries. About 4 out of 10 worked as employees of private ambulance services. About 3 out of 10 worked in local government for fire departments, public ambulance services, and emergency medical services. Another 2 out of 10 worked full time in hospitals within the medical facility or responded to calls in ambulances or helicopters to transport critically ill or injured patients. The remainder worked in various industries providing emergency services.

## Job Outlook

Employment for EMTs and paramedics is expected to grow faster than the average for all occupations through 2016. Job prospects should be good, particularly in cities and private ambulance services.

*Employment change.* Employment of emergency medical technicians and paramedics is expected to grow by 19 percent between 2006 and 2016, which is faster than the average for all occupations. Full-time paid EMTs and paramedics will be needed to replace unpaid volunteers. It is becoming increasing difficult for emergency medical services to recruit and retain unpaid volunteers because of the amount of training and the large time commitment these positions require. As a result, more paid EMTs and paramedics are needed. Furthermore, as a large segment of the population—aging members of the baby boom generation—becomes more likely to have medical emergencies, demand will increase for EMTs and paramedics. There also will still be demand for part-time, volunteer EMTs and paramedics in rural areas and smaller metropolitan areas.

*Job prospects.* Job prospects should be favorable. Many job openings will arise from growth and from the need to replace workers who leave the occupation because of the limited potential for advancement, as well as the modest pay and benefits in private-sector jobs.

Job opportunities should be best in private ambulance services. Competition will be greater for jobs in local government, including fire, police, and independent third-service rescue squad departments which tend to have better salaries and benefits. EMTs and paramedics who have advanced education and certifications, such as Paramedic level certification, should enjoy the most favorable job prospects as clients and patients demand higher levels of care before arriving at the hospital.

## Earnings

Earnings of EMTs and paramedics depend on the employment setting and geographic location of their jobs, as well as their training and experience. Median annual earnings of EMTs and paramedics were $27,070 in May 2006. The middle 50 percent earned between $21,290 and $35,210. The lowest 10 percent earned less than $17,300, and the highest 10 percent earned more than $45,280. Median annual earnings in the industries employing the largest numbers of EMTs and paramedics in May 2006 were $23,250 in general medical and surgical hospitals and $20,350 in ambulance services.

Those in emergency medical services who are part of fire or police departments typically receive the same benefits as firefighters or police officers. For example, many are covered by pension plans that provide retirement at half pay after 20 or 25 years of service or if the worker is disabled in the line of duty.

## Related Occupations

Other workers in occupations that require quick and level-headed reactions to life-or-death situations are air traffic controllers, firefighting occupations, physician assistants, police and detectives, and registered nurses.

## Sources of Additional Information

General information about emergency medical technicians and paramedics is available from

▸ National Association of Emergency Medical Technicians, P.O. Box 1400, Clinton, MS 39060-1400. Internet: http://www.naemt.org

▸ National Highway Traffic Safety Administration, EMS Division, 400 7th St. SW, NTS-14, Washington, DC 20590. Internet: http://www.nhtsa.dot.gov/portal/site/nhtsa/menuItem.2d0771e91315babbbf30811060008a0c/

▸ National Registry of Emergency Medical Technicians, Rocco V. Morando Bldg., 6610 Busch Blvd., P.O. Box 29233, Columbus, OH 43229. Internet: http://www.nremt.org

# Engineers

(O*NET 17-2011.00, 17-2021.00, 17-2031.00, 17-2041.00, 17-2051.00, 17-2061.00, 17-2071.00, 17-2072.00, 17-2081.00, 17-2111.00, 17-2111.01, 17-2111.02, 17-2111.03, 17-2112.00, 17-2121.00, 17-2121.01, 17-2121.02, 17-2131.00, 17-2141.00, 17-2151.00, 17-2161.00, 17-2171.00, and 17-2199.99)

## Significant Points

■ Overall job opportunities in engineering are expected to be good, but will vary by specialty.

■ A bachelor's degree in engineering is required for most entry-level jobs.

■ Starting salaries are among the highest of all college graduates.

■ Continuing education is critical for engineers as technology evolves.

## Nature of the Work

Engineers apply the principles of science and mathematics to develop economical solutions to technical problems. Their work is the link between scientific discoveries and the commercial applications that meet societal and consumer needs.

Many engineers develop new products. During this process, they consider several factors. For example, in developing an industrial robot, engineers precisely specify the functional requirements; design and test the robot's components; integrate the components to produce the final design; and evaluate the design's overall effectiveness, cost, reliability, and safety. This process applies to the development of many different products, such as chemicals, computers, power plants, helicopters, and toys.

In addition to design and development, many engineers work in testing, production, or maintenance. These engineers supervise production in factories, determine the causes of component failure, and test manufactured products to maintain quality. They also estimate the time and cost to complete projects. Supervisory engineers are responsible for major components or entire projects.

Engineers use computers extensively to produce and analyze designs; to simulate and test how a machine, structure, or system operates; to generate specifications for parts; and to monitor product quality and control process efficiency. Nanotechnology, which involves the creation of high-performance materials and components by integrating atoms and molecules, also is introducing entirely new principles to the design process.

Most engineers specialize. Following are details on the 17 engineering specialties covered in the federal government's Standard Occupational Classification (SOC) system. Numerous other specialties are recognized by professional societies, and each of the major branches of engineering has numerous subdivisions. Civil engineering, for example, includes structural and transportation engineering, and materials engineering includes ceramic, metallurgical, and polymer engineering. Engineers also may specialize in one industry, such as motor vehicles, or in one type of technology, such as turbines or semiconductor materials.

**Aerospace engineers** design, develop, and test aircraft, spacecraft, and missiles and supervise the manufacture of these products. Those who work with aircraft are called *aeronautical engineers,* and those working specifically with spacecraft are *astronautical engineers.* Aerospace engineers develop new technologies for use in aviation, defense systems, and space exploration, often specializing in areas such as structural design, guidance, navigation and control, instrumentation and communication, or production methods. They also may specialize in a particular type of aerospace product, such as commercial aircraft, military fighter jets, helicopters, spacecraft, or missiles and rockets, and may become experts in aerodynamics, thermodynamics, celestial mechanics, propulsion, acoustics, or guidance and control systems.

**Agricultural engineers** apply knowledge of engineering technology and science to agriculture and the efficient use of biological resources. Because of this, they are also referred to as *biological and agricultural engineers.* They design agricultural machinery, equipment, sensors, processes, and structures, such as those used for crop storage. Some engineers specialize in areas such as power systems and machinery design; structures and environment engineering; and food and bioprocess engineering. They develop ways to conserve soil and water and to improve the processing of agricultural products. Agricultural engineers often work in research and development, production, sales, or management.

**Biomedical engineers** develop devices and procedures that solve medical and health-related problems by combining their knowledge of biology and medicine with engineering principles and practices. Many do research, along with life scientists, chemists, and medical scientists, to develop and evaluate systems and products such as artificial organs, prostheses (artificial devices that replace missing body parts), instrumentation, medical information systems, and health management and care delivery systems. Biomedical engineers may also design devices used in various medical procedures, imaging systems such as magnetic resonance imaging (MRI), and devices for automating insulin injections or controlling body functions. Most engineers in this specialty need a sound background in another engineering specialty, such as mechanical or electronics engineering, in addition to specialized biomedical training. Some specialties within biomedical engineering include biomaterials, biomechanics, medical imaging, rehabilitation engineering, and orthopedic engineering.

**Chemical engineers** apply the principles of chemistry to solve problems involving the production or use of chemicals and biochemicals. They design equipment and processes for large-scale chemical manufacturing, plan and test methods of manufacturing products and treating byproducts, and supervise production. Chemical engineers also work in a variety of manufacturing industries other than chemical manufacturing, such as those producing energy, electronics, food, clothing, and paper. They also work in health care, biotechnology, and business services. Chemical engineers apply principles of physics, mathematics, and mechanical and electrical engineering, as well as chemistry. Some may specialize in a particular chemical process, such as oxidation or polymerization. Others specialize in a particular field, such as nanomaterials, or in the development of specific products. They must be aware of all aspects of chemicals manufacturing and how the manufacturing process affects the environment and the safety of workers and consumers.

**Civil engineers** design and supervise the construction of roads, buildings, airports, tunnels, dams, bridges, and water supply and sewage systems. They must consider many factors in the design process, from the construction costs and expected lifetime of a project to government regulations and potential environmental hazards such as earthquakes and hurricanes. Civil engineering, considered one of the oldest engineering disciplines, encompasses many specialties. The major ones are structural, water resources, construction, environmental, transportation, and geotechnical engineering. Many civil engineers hold supervisory or administrative positions, from supervisor of a construction site to city engineer. Others may work in design, construction, research, and teaching.

**Computer hardware engineers** research, design, develop, test, and oversee the manufacture and installation of computer hardware. Hardware includes computer chips, circuit boards, computer systems, and related equipment such as keyboards, modems, and printers. The work of computer hardware engineers is very similar to that of electronics engineers in that they may design and test circuits and other electronic components, but computer hardware engineers do that work only as it relates to computers and computer-related equipment. The rapid advances in computer technology are largely a result of the research, development, and design efforts of these engineers.

**Electrical engineers** design, develop, test, and supervise the manufacture of electrical equipment. Some of this equipment includes electric motors; machinery controls, lighting, and wiring in buildings; automobiles; aircraft; radar and navigation systems; and power generation, control, and transmission devices used by electric utilities. Although the terms electrical and electronics engineering often are used interchangeably in academia and industry, electrical engineers have traditionally focused on the generation and supply of power, whereas electronics engineers have worked on applications of electricity to control systems or signal processing. Electrical engineers specialize in areas such as power systems engineering or electrical equipment manufacturing.

**Electronics engineers, except computer** are responsible for a wide range of technologies, from portable music players to the global positioning system (GPS), which can continuously provide the location, for example, of a vehicle. Electronics engineers design, develop, test, and supervise the manufacture of electronic equipment such as broadcast and communications systems. Many electronics engineers also work in areas closely related to computers. However, engineers whose work is related exclusively to computer hardware are considered computer hardware engineers. Electronics engineers specialize in areas such as communications, signal processing, and control systems or have a specialty within one of these areas—control systems or aviation electronics, for example.

**Environmental engineers** develop solutions to environmental problems using the principles of biology and chemistry. They are involved in water and air pollution control, recycling, waste disposal, and public health issues. Environmental engineers conduct hazardous-waste management studies in which they evaluate the significance of the hazard, advise on treatment and containment, and develop regulations to prevent mishaps. They design municipal water supply and industrial wastewater treatment systems. They conduct research on the environmental impact of proposed construction projects, analyze scientific data, and perform quality-control checks. Environmental engineers are concerned with local and worldwide environmental issues. They study and attempt to minimize the effects of acid rain, global warming, automobile emissions, and ozone depletion. They may also be involved in the protection of wildlife. Many environmental engineers work as consultants, helping their clients to comply with regulations, to prevent environmental damage, and to clean up hazardous sites.

**Health and safety engineers, except mining safety engineers and inspectors** prevent harm to people and property by applying knowledge of systems engineering and mechanical, chemical, and human performance principles. Using this specialized knowledge, they identify and measure potential hazards, such as the risk of fires or the dangers involved in handling of toxic chemicals. They recommend appropriate loss prevention measures according to the probability of harm and potential damage. Health and safety engineers develop procedures and designs to reduce the risk of illness, injury, or damage. Some work in manufacturing industries to ensure the designs of new products do not create unnecessary hazards. They must be able to anticipate, recognize, and evaluate hazardous conditions, as well as develop hazard control methods.

**Industrial engineers** determine the most effective ways to use the basic factors of production—people, machines, materials, information, and energy—to make a product or provide a service. They are primarily concerned with increasing productivity through the management of people, methods of business organization, and technology. To maximize efficiency, industrial engineers carefully study the product requirements and design manufacturing and information systems to meet those requirements with the help of mathematical methods and models. They develop management control systems to aid in financial planning and cost analysis, and design production planning and control systems to coordinate activities and ensure product quality. They also design or improve systems for the physical distribution of goods and services and determine the most efficient plant locations. Industrial engineers develop wage and salary administration systems and job evaluation programs. Many industrial engineers move into management positions because the work is closely related to the work of managers.

**Marine engineers and naval architects** are involved in the design, construction, and maintenance of ships, boats, and related equipment. They design and supervise the construction of everything from aircraft carriers to submarines, and from sailboats to tankers. Naval architects work on the basic design of ships, including hull form and stability. Marine engineers work on the propulsion, steering, and other systems of ships. Marine engineers and naval architects apply knowledge from a range of fields to the entire design and production process of all water vehicles. Other workers who operate or supervise the operation of marine machinery on ships and other vessels sometimes may be called marine engineers or, more frequently, ship engineers, but they do different work.

**Materials engineers** are involved in the development, processing, and testing of the materials used to create a range of products, from computer chips and aircraft wings to golf clubs and snow skis. They work with metals, ceramics, plastics, semiconductors, and composites to create new materials that meet certain mechanical, electrical, and chemical requirements. They also are involved in selecting materials for new applications. Materials engineers have developed the ability to create and then study materials at an atomic level, using advanced processes to replicate the characteristics of materials and their components with computers. Most materials engineers specialize in a particular material. For example, metallurgical engineers specialize in metals such as steel, and ceramic engineers develop ceramic materials and the processes for making them into useful products such as glassware or fiber optic communication lines.

**Mechanical engineers** research, design, develop, manufacture, and test tools, engines, machines, and other mechanical devices. Mechanical engineering is one of the broadest engineering disciplines. Engineers in this discipline work on power-producing machines such as electric generators, internal combustion engines, and steam and gas turbines. They also work on power-using machines such as refrigeration and air-conditioning equipment, machine tools, material handling systems, elevators and escalators, industrial production equipment, and robots used in manufacturing. Mechanical engineers also design tools that other engineers need for their work. In addition, mechanical engineers work in manufacturing or agriculture production, maintenance, or technical sales; many become administrators or managers.

**Mining and geological engineers, including mining safety engineers** find, extract, and prepare coal, metals, and minerals for use by manufacturing industries and utilities. They design open-pit and underground mines, supervise the construction of mine shafts and tunnels in underground operations, and devise methods for transporting minerals to processing plants. Mining engineers are responsible for the safe, economical, and environmentally sound operation of mines. Some mining engineers work with geologists and metallurgical engineers to locate and appraise new ore deposits. Others develop new mining equipment or direct mineral-processing operations that separate minerals from the dirt, rock, and other materials with which they are mixed. Mining engineers frequently specialize in the mining of one mineral or metal, such as coal or gold. With increased emphasis on protecting the environment, many mining engineers work to solve problems related to land reclamation and water and air pollution. Mining safety engineers use their knowledge of mine design and practices to ensure the safety of workers and to comply with state and federal safety regulations. They inspect walls and roof surfaces, monitor air quality, and examine mining equipment for compliance with safety practices.

**Nuclear engineers** research and develop the processes, instruments, and systems used to derive benefits from nuclear energy and radiation. They design, develop, monitor, and operate nuclear plants to generate power. They may work on the nuclear fuel cycle—the production, handling, and use of nuclear fuel and the safe disposal of waste produced by the generation of nuclear energy—or on the development of fusion energy. Some specialize in the development of nuclear power sources for naval vessels or spacecraft; others find industrial and medical uses for radioactive materials, as in equipment used to diagnose and treat medical problems.

**Petroleum engineers** search the world for reservoirs containing oil or natural gas. Once these resources are discovered, petroleum engineers work with geologists and other specialists to understand the geologic formation and properties of the rock containing the reservoir, determine the drilling methods to be used, and monitor drilling and production operations. They design equipment and processes to achieve the maximum profitable recovery of oil and gas. Because only a small proportion of oil and gas in a reservoir flows out under natural forces, petroleum engineers develop and use various enhanced recovery methods. These include injecting water, chemicals, gases, or steam into an oil reservoir to force out more of the oil and doing computer-controlled drilling or fracturing to connect a larger area of a reservoir to a single well. Because even the best techniques in use today recover only a portion of the oil and gas in a reservoir, petroleum engineers research and develop technology and methods to increase recovery and lower the cost of drilling and production operations.

*Work environment.* Most engineers work in office buildings, laboratories, or industrial plants. Others may spend time outdoors at construction sites and oil and gas exploration and production sites, where they monitor or direct operations or solve onsite problems. Some engineers travel extensively to plants or worksites here and abroad.

Many engineers work a standard 40-hour week. At times, deadlines or design standards may bring extra pressure to a job, requiring engineers to work longer hours.

# Training, Other Qualifications, and Advancement

Engineers typically enter the occupation with a bachelor's degree in an engineering specialty, but some basic research positions may require a graduate degree. Engineers offering their services directly to the public must be licensed. Continuing education to keep current with rapidly changing technology is important for engineers.

*Education and training.* A bachelor's degree in engineering is required for almost all entry-level engineering jobs. College graduates with a degree in a natural science or mathematics occasionally may qualify for some engineering jobs, especially in specialties in high demand. Most engineering degrees are granted in electrical, electronics, mechanical, or civil engineering. However, engineers trained in one branch may work in related branches. For example, many aerospace engineers have training in mechanical engineering. This flexibility allows employers to meet staffing needs in new technologies and specialties in which engineers may be in short supply. It also allows engineers to shift to fields with better employment prospects or to those that more closely match their interests.

Most engineering programs involve a concentration of study in an engineering specialty, along with courses in both mathematics and the physical and life sciences. Many programs also include courses in general engineering. A design course, sometimes accompanied by a computer or laboratory class or both, is part of the curriculum of most programs. General courses not directly related to engineering, such as those in the social sciences or humanities, are also often required.

In addition to the standard engineering degree, many colleges offer two-year or four-year degree programs in engineering technology. These programs, which usually include various hands-on laboratory classes that focus on current issues in the application of engineering principles, prepare students for practical design and production work, rather than for jobs that require more theoretical and scientific knowledge. Graduates of four-year technology programs may get jobs similar to those obtained by graduates with a bachelor's degree in engineering. Engineering technology graduates, however, are not qualified to register as professional engineers under the same terms as graduates with degrees in engineering. Some employers regard technology program graduates as having skills between those of a technician and an engineer.

Graduate training is essential for engineering faculty positions and many research and development programs, but is not required for the majority of entry-level engineering jobs. Many experienced engineers obtain graduate degrees in engineering or business administration to learn new technology and broaden their education. Many high-level executives in government and industry began their careers as engineers.

About 1,830 programs at colleges and universities offer bachelor's degrees in engineering that are accredited by the Accreditation Board for Engineering and Technology (ABET), Inc., and there are another 710 accredited programs in engineering technology. ABET accreditation is based on a program's faculty, curriculum, and facilities; the achievement of a program's students; program improvements; and institutional commitment to specific principles of quality and ethics. Although most institutions offer programs in the major branches of engineering, only a few offer programs in the smaller specialties. Also, programs of the same title may vary in content. For example, some programs emphasize industrial practices, preparing students for a job in industry, whereas others are more theoretical and are designed to prepare students for graduate work. Therefore, students should investigate curriculums and check accreditations carefully before selecting a college.

Admissions requirements for undergraduate engineering schools include a solid background in mathematics (algebra, geometry, trigonometry, and calculus) and science (biology, chemistry, and physics), with courses in English, social studies, and humanities. Bachelor's degree programs in engineering typically are designed to last four years, but many students find that it takes between four and five years to complete their studies. In a typical four-year college curriculum, the first two years are spent studying mathematics, basic sciences, introductory engineering, humanities, and social sciences. In the last two years, most courses are in engineering, usually with a concentration in one specialty. Some programs offer a general engineering curriculum; students then specialize on the job or in graduate school.

Some engineering schools have agreements with two-year colleges whereby the college provides the initial engineering education, and the engineering school automatically admits students for their last two years. In addition, a few engineering schools have arrangements that allow students who spend three years in a liberal arts college studying pre-engineering subjects and two years in an engineering school studying core subjects to receive a bachelor's degree from each school. Some colleges and universities offer five-year master's degree programs. Some five-year or even six-year cooperative plans combine classroom study and practical work, permitting students to gain valuable experience and to finance part of their education.

*Licensure.* All 50 states and the District of Columbia require licensure for engineers who offer their services directly to the public. Engineers who are licensed are called professional engineers (PE). This licensure generally requires a degree from an ABET-accredited engineering program, four years of relevant work experience, and successful completion of a state examination. Recent graduates can start the licensing process by taking the examination in two stages. The initial Fundamentals of Engineering (FE) examination can be taken upon graduation. Engineers who pass this examination commonly are called engineers in training (EIT) or engineer interns (EI). After acquiring suitable work experience, EITs can take the second examination, the Principles and Practice of Engineering exam. Several states have imposed mandatory continuing education requirements for relicensure. Most states recognize licensure from other states, provided that the manner in which the initial license was obtained meets or exceeds their own licensure requirements. Many civil, electrical, mechanical, and chemical engineers are licensed PEs. Independent of licensure, various certification programs are offered by professional organizations to demonstrate competency in specific fields of engineering.

*Other qualifications.* Engineers should be creative, inquisitive, analytical, and detail oriented. They should be able to work as part of a team and to communicate well, both orally and in writing. Communication abilities are becoming increasingly important as engineers frequently interact with specialists in a wide range of fields outside engineering.

***Certification and advancement.*** Beginning engineering graduates usually work under the supervision of experienced engineers and, in large companies, also may receive formal classroom or seminar-type training. As new engineers gain knowledge and experience, they are assigned more difficult projects with greater independence to develop designs, solve problems, and make decisions. Engineers may advance to become technical specialists or to supervise a staff or team of engineers and technicians. Some may eventually become engineering managers or enter other managerial or sales jobs. In sales, an engineering background enables them to discuss a product's technical aspects and assist in product planning, installation, and use.

Numerous professional certifications for engineers exist and may be beneficial for advancement to senior technical or managerial positions. Many certification programs are offered by the professional societies listed as sources of additional information for engineering specialties at the end of this statement.

## Employment

In 2006, engineers held about 1.5 million jobs. The distribution of employment by engineering specialty follows.

| | |
|---|---|
| Civil engineers | 256,000 |
| Mechanical engineers | 227,000 |
| Industrial engineers | 201,000 |
| Electrical engineers | 153,000 |
| Electronics engineers, except computer | 138,000 |
| Aerospace engineers | 90,000 |
| Computer hardware engineers | 79,000 |
| Environmental engineers | 54,000 |
| Chemical engineers | 30,000 |
| Health and safety engineers, except mining safety engineers and inspectors | 25,000 |
| Materials engineers | 22,000 |
| Petroleum engineers | 17,000 |
| Nuclear engineers | 15,000 |
| Biomedical engineers | 14,000 |
| Marine engineers and naval architects | 9,200 |
| Mining and geological engineers, including mining safety engineers | 7,100 |
| Agricultural engineers | 3,100 |
| All other engineers | 170,000 |

About 37 percent of engineering jobs were found in manufacturing industries and another 28 percent were in the professional, scientific, and technical services sector, primarily in architectural, engineering, and related services. Many engineers also worked in the construction, telecommunications, and wholesale trade industries.

Federal, state, and local governments employed about 12 percent of engineers in 2006. About half of these were in the federal government, mainly in the U.S. Departments of Defense, Transportation,

Agriculture, Interior, and Energy, and in the National Aeronautics and Space Administration. Most engineers in state and local government agencies worked in highway and public works departments. In 2006, about 3 percent of engineers were self-employed, many as consultants.

Engineers are employed in every state, in small and large cities and in rural areas. Some branches of engineering are concentrated in particular industries and geographic areas—for example, petroleum engineering jobs tend to be located in areas with sizable petroleum deposits, such as Texas, Louisiana, Oklahoma, Alaska, and California. Others, such as civil engineering, are widely dispersed, and engineers in these fields often move from place to place to work on different projects.

Engineers are employed in every major industry. The industries employing the most engineers in each specialty are given in table 1, along with the percent of occupational employment in the industry.

## Job Outlook

Employment of engineers is expected to grow about as fast as the average for all occupations over the next decade, but growth will vary by specialty. Environmental engineers should experience the fastest growth, while civil engineers should see the largest employment increase. Overall job opportunities in engineering are expected to be good.

***Overall employment change.*** Overall engineering employment is expected to grow by 11 percent over the 2006–2016 decade, about as fast as the average for all occupations. Engineers have traditionally been concentrated in slower growing or declining manufacturing industries, in which they will continue to be needed to design, build, test, and improve manufactured products. However, increasing employment of engineers in faster growing service industries should generate most of the employment growth. Job outlook varies by engineering specialty, as discussed later.

Competitive pressures and advancing technology will force companies to improve and update product designs and to optimize their manufacturing processes. Employers will rely on engineers to increase productivity and expand output of goods and services. New technologies continue to improve the design process, enabling engineers to produce and analyze various product designs much more rapidly than in the past. Unlike in some other occupations, however, technological advances are not expected to substantially limit employment opportunities in engineering because engineers will continue to develop new products and processes that increase productivity.

Offshoring of engineering work will likely dampen domestic employment growth to some degree. There are many well-trained, often English-speaking engineers available around the world willing to work at much lower salaries than U.S. engineers. The rise of the Internet has made it relatively easy for part of the engineering work previously done by engineers in this country to be done by engineers in other countries, a factor that will tend to hold down employment growth. Even so, there will always be a need for onsite engineers to interact with other employees and clients.

**Table 1.  Percent concentration of engineering specialty employment in key industries, 2006**

| Specialty | Industry | Percent |
|---|---|---|
| Aerospace engineers | Aerospace product and parts manufacturing | 49 |
| Agricultural engineers | Food manufacturing | 25 |
| | Architectural, engineering, and related services | 15 |
| Biomedical engineers | Medical equipment and supplies manufacturing | 20 |
| | Scientific research and development services | 20 |
| Chemical engineers | Chemical manufacturing | 29 |
| | Architectural, engineering, and related services | 15 |
| Civil engineers | Architectural, engineering, and related services | 49 |
| Computer hardware engineers | Computer and electronic product manufacturing | 41 |
| | Computer systems design and related services | 19 |
| Electrical engineers | Architectural, engineering, and related services | 21 |
| Electronics engineers, except computer | Computer and electronic product manufacturing | 26 |
| | Telecommunications | 15 |
| Environmental engineers | Architectural, engineering, and related services | 29 |
| | State and local government | 21 |
| Health and safety engineers, except mining safety engineers and inspectors | State and local government | 10 |
| Industrial engineers | Transportation equipment manufacturing | 18 |
| | Machinery manufacturing | 8 |
| Marine engineers and naval architects | Architectural, engineering, and related services | 29 |
| Materials engineers | Primary metal manufacturing | 11 |
| | Semiconductor and other electronic component manufacturing | 9 |
| Mechanical engineers | Architectural, engineering, and related services | 22 |
| | Transportation equipment manufacturing | 14 |
| Mining and geological engineers, including mining safety engineers | Mining | 58 |
| Nuclear engineers | Research and development in the physical, engineering, and life sciences | 30 |
| | Electric power generation, transmission, and distribution | 27 |
| Petroleum engineers | Oil and gas extraction | 43 |

*Overall job outlook.* Overall job opportunities in engineering are expected to be good because the number of engineering graduates should be in rough balance with the number of job openings between 2006 and 2016. In addition to openings from job growth, many openings will be created by the need to replace current engineers who retire; transfer to management, sales, or other occupations; or leave engineering for other reasons.

Many engineers work on long-term research and development projects or in other activities that continue even during economic slowdowns. In industries such as electronics and aerospace, however, large cutbacks in defense expenditures and in government funding for research and development have resulted in significant layoffs of engineers in the past. The trend toward contracting for engineering work with engineering services firms, both domestic and foreign, has also made engineers more vulnerable to layoffs during periods of lower demand.

It is important for engineers, as it is for workers in other technical and scientific occupations, to continue their education throughout their careers because much of their value to their employer depends on their knowledge of the latest technology. Engineers in high-technology areas, such as biotechnology or information technology, may find that technical knowledge becomes outdated rapidly. By keeping current in their field, engineers are able to deliver the best solutions and greatest value to their employers. Engineers who have not kept current in their field may find themselves at a disadvantage when seeking promotions or during layoffs.

*Employment change and job outlook by engineering specialty.*

**Aerospace engineers** are expected to have 10 percent growth in employment over the projections decade, about as fast as the average for all occupations. Increases in the number and scope of military aerospace projects likely will generate new jobs. In addition, new technologies expected to be used on commercial aircraft produced during the next decade should spur demand for aerospace engineers. The employment outlook for aerospace engineers appears favorable. The number of degrees granted in aerospace engineering has declined for many years because of a perceived lack of opportunities in this field. Although this trend has reversed, new graduates continue to be needed to replace aerospace engineers who retire or leave the occupation for other reasons.

**Agricultural engineers** are expected to have employment growth of 9 percent over the projections decade, about as fast as the average for all occupations. More engineers will be needed to meet the increasing demand for using biosensors to determine the optimal treatment of crops. Employment growth should also result from the need to increase crop yields to feed an expanding population and produce crops used as renewable energy sources. Moreover, engineers will be needed to develop more efficient agricultural production and conserve resources.

**Biomedical engineers** are expected to have 21 percent employment growth over the projections decade, much faster than the average for all occupations. The aging of the population and the focus on health issues will drive demand for better medical devices and equipment designed by biomedical engineers. Along with the demand for more sophisticated medical equipment and procedures, an increased concern for cost-effectiveness will boost demand for biomedical engineers, particularly in pharmaceutical manufacturing and related industries. However, because of the growing interest in this field, the number of degrees granted in biomedical engineering has increased greatly. Biomedical engineers, particularly those with only a bachelor's degree, may face competition for jobs. Unlike many other engineering specialties, a graduate degree is recommended or required for many entry-level jobs.

**Chemical engineers** are expected to have employment growth of 8 percent over the projections decade, about as fast as the average for all occupations. Although overall employment in the chemical manufacturing industry is expected to decline, chemical companies will continue to research and develop new chemicals and more efficient processes to increase output of existing chemicals. Among manufacturing industries, pharmaceuticals may provide the best opportunities for jobseekers. However, most employment growth for chemical engineers will be in service-providing industries such as professional, scientific, and technical services, particularly for research in energy and the developing fields of biotechnology and nanotechnology.

**Civil engineers** are expected to experience 18 percent employment growth during the projections decade, faster than the average for all occupations. Spurred by general population growth and the related need to improve the nation's infrastructure, more civil engineers will be needed to design and construct or expand transportation, water supply, and pollution control systems and buildings and building complexes. They also will be needed to repair or replace existing roads, bridges, and other public structures. Because construction industries and architectural, engineering and related services employ many civil engineers, employment opportunities will vary by geographic area and may decrease during economic slowdowns, when construction is often curtailed.

**Computer hardware engineers** are expected to have 5 percent employment growth over the projections decade, slower than the average for all occupations. Although the use of information technology continues to expand rapidly, the manufacture of computer hardware is expected to be adversely affected by intense foreign competition. As computer and semiconductor manufacturers contract out more of their engineering needs to both domestic and foreign design firms, much of the growth in employment of hardware engineers is expected in the computer systems design and related services industry.

**Electrical engineers** are expected to have employment growth of 6 percent over the projections decade, slower than the average for all occupations. Although strong demand for electrical devices—including electric power generators, wireless phone transmitters, high-density batteries, and navigation systems—should spur job growth, international competition and the use of engineering services performed in other countries will limit employment growth. Electrical engineers working in firms providing engineering expertise and design services to manufacturers should have better job prospects.

**Electronics engineers, except computer** are expected to have employment growth of 4 percent during the projections decade, slower than the average for all occupations. Although rising demand for electronic goods—including communications equipment, defense-related equipment, medical electronics, and consumer products—should continue to increase demand for electronics engineers, foreign competition in electronic products development and the use of engineering services performed in other countries will limit employment growth. Growth is expected to be fastest in service-providing industries—particularly in firms that provide engineering and design services.

**Environmental engineers** should have employment growth of 25 percent during the projections decade, much faster than the average for all occupations. More environmental engineers will be needed to comply with environmental regulations and to develop methods of cleaning up existing hazards. A shift in emphasis toward preventing problems rather than controlling those that already exist, as well as increasing public health concerns resulting from population growth, also are expected to spur demand for environmental engineers. Because of this employment growth, job opportunities should be good even as more students earn degrees. Even though employment of environmental engineers should be less affected by economic conditions than most other types of engineers, a significant economic downturn could reduce the emphasis on environmental protection, reducing job opportunities.

**Health and safety engineers, except mining safety engineers and inspectors** are projected to experience 10 percent employment growth over the projections decade, about as fast as the average for all occupations. Because health and safety engineers make production processes and products as safe as possible, their services should be in demand as concern increases for health and safety within work environments. As new technologies for production or processing are developed, health and safety engineers will be needed to ensure that they are safe.

**Industrial engineers** are expected to have employment growth of 20 percent over the projections decade, faster than the average for all occupations. As firms look for new ways to reduce costs and raise productivity, they increasingly will turn to industrial engineers to develop more efficient processes and reduce costs, delays, and waste. This should lead to job growth for these engineers, even in manufacturing industries with slowly growing or declining employment overall. Because their work is similar to that done in management occupations, many industrial engineers leave the occupation to become managers. Many openings will be created by the need to replace industrial engineers who transfer to other occupations or leave the labor force.

**Marine engineers and naval architects** are expected to experience employment growth of 11 percent over the projections decade, about as fast as the average for all occupations. Strong demand for naval vessels and recreational small craft should more than offset the long-term decline in the domestic design and construction of large ocean-going vessels. Good prospects are expected for marine engineers and naval architects because of growth in employment, the need to replace workers who retire or take other jobs, and the limited number of students pursuing careers in this occupation.

**Projections data from the National Employment Matrix**

| Occupational Title | SOC Code | Employment, 2006 | Projected employment, 2016 | Change, 2006-2016 | |
|---|---|---|---|---|---|
| | | | | Number | Percent |
| Engineers............................................................................ | 17-2000 | 1,512,000 | 1,671,000 | 160,000 | 11 |
| Aerospace engineers ...................................................... | 17-2011 | 90,000 | 99,000 | 9,200 | 10 |
| Agricultural engineers.................................................... | 17-2021 | 3,100 | 3,400 | 300 | 9 |
| Biomedical engineers...................................................... | 17-2031 | 14,000 | 17,000 | 3,000 | 21 |
| Chemical engineers ........................................................ | 17-2041 | 30,000 | 33,000 | 2,400 | 8 |
| Civil engineers ............................................................... | 17-2051 | 256,000 | 302,000 | 46,000 | 18 |
| Computer hardware engineers ........................................ | 17-2061 | 79,000 | 82,000 | 3,600 | 5 |
| Electrical and electronics engineers.............................. | 17-2070 | 291,000 | 306,000 | 15,000 | 5 |
| Electrical engineers........................................................ | 17-2071 | 153,000 | 163,000 | 9,600 | 6 |
| Electronics engineers, except computer......................... | 17-2072 | 138,000 | 143,000 | 5,100 | 4 |
| Environmental engineers................................................ | 17-2081 | 54,000 | 68,000 | 14,000 | 25 |
| Industrial engineers, including health and safety.......... | 17-2110 | 227,000 | 270,000 | 43,000 | 19 |
| Health and safety engineers, except mining safety engineers and inspectors ......................................... | 17-2111 | 25,000 | 28,000 | 2,400 | 10 |
| Industrial engineers....................................................... | 17-2112 | 201,000 | 242,000 | 41,000 | 20 |
| Marine engineers and naval architects ......................... | 17-2121 | 9,200 | 10,000 | 1,000 | 11 |
| Materials engineers........................................................ | 17-2131 | 22,000 | 22,000 | 900 | 4 |
| Mechanical engineers..................................................... | 17-2141 | 226,000 | 235,000 | 9,400 | 4 |
| Mining and geological engineers, including mining safety engineers ................................................. | 17-2151 | 7,100 | 7,800 | 700 | 10 |
| Nuclear engineers........................................................... | 17-2161 | 15,000 | 16,000 | 1,100 | 7 |
| Petroleum engineers....................................................... | 17-2171 | 17,000 | 18,000 | 900 | 5 |
| Engineers, all other ....................................................... | 17-2199 | 170,000 | 180,000 | 9,400 | 6 |

NOTE: Data in this table are rounded.

**Materials engineers** are expected to have employment growth of 4 percent over the projections decade, slower than the average for all occupations. Although employment is expected to decline in many of the manufacturing industries in which materials engineers are concentrated, growth should be strong for materials engineers working on nanomaterials and biomaterials. As manufacturing firms contract for their materials engineering needs, employment growth is expected in professional, scientific, and technical services industries also.

**Mechanical engineers** are projected to have 4 percent employment growth over the projections decade, slower than the average for all occupations. This is because total employment in manufacturing industries—in which employment of mechanical engineers is concentrated—is expected to decline. Some new job opportunities will be created due to emerging technologies in biotechnology, materials science, and nanotechnology. Additional opportunities outside of mechanical engineering will exist because the skills acquired through earning a degree in mechanical engineering often can be applied in other engineering specialties.

**Mining and geological engineers, including mining safety engineers** are expected to have 10 percent employment growth over the projections decade, about as fast as the average for all occupations. Following a lengthy period of decline, strong growth in demand for minerals and increased use of mining engineers in the oil and gas extraction industry is expected to create some employment growth over the 2006–2016 period. Moreover, many mining engineers currently employed are approaching retirement age, a factor that should create additional job openings. Furthermore, relatively few schools offer mining engineering programs, resulting in good job opportuni-

ties for graduates. The best opportunities may require frequent travel or even living overseas for extended periods of time as mining operations around the world recruit graduates of U.S. mining engineering programs.

**Nuclear engineers** are expected to have employment growth of 7 percent over the projections decade, about as fast as the average for all occupations. Most job growth will be in research and development and engineering services. Although no commercial nuclear power plants have been built in the United States for many years, nuclear engineers will be needed to operate existing plants and design new ones, including researching future nuclear power sources. They also will be needed to work in defense-related areas, to develop nuclear medical technology, and to improve and enforce waste management and safety standards. Nuclear engineers are expected to have good employment opportunities because the small number of nuclear engineering graduates is likely to be in rough balance with the number of job openings.

**Petroleum engineers** are expected to have 5 percent employment growth over the projections decade, more slowly than the average for all occupations. Even though most of the potential petroleum-producing areas in the United States already have been explored, petroleum engineers will increasingly be needed to develop new methods of extracting more resources from existing sources. Favorable opportunities are expected for petroleum engineers because the number of job openings is likely to exceed the relatively small number of graduates. Petroleum engineers work around the world and, in fact, the best employment opportunities may include some work in other countries.

## Earnings

Earnings for engineers vary significantly by specialty, industry, and education. Variation in median earnings and in the earnings distributions for engineers in various specialties is especially significant. Table 2 shows wage-and-salary earnings distributions in May 2006 for engineers in specialties covered in this statement.

In the federal government, mean annual salaries for engineers ranged from $75,144 in agricultural engineering to $107,546 in ceramic engineering in 2007.

As a group, engineers earn some of the highest average starting salaries among those holding bachelor's degrees. Table 3 shows average starting salary offers for engineers, according to a 2007 survey by the National Association of Colleges and Employers.

### Table 2: Earnings distribution by engineering specialty, May 2006

| Specialty | Lowest 10% | Lowest 25% | Median | Highest 25% | Highest 10% |
|---|---|---|---|---|---|
| Aerospace engineers | 59,610 | 71,360 | 87,610 | 106,450 | 124,550 |
| Agricultural engineers | 42,390 | 53,040 | 66,030 | 80,370 | 96,270 |
| Biomedical engineers | 44,930 | 56,420 | 73,930 | 93,420 | 116,330 |
| Chemical engineers | 50,060 | 62,410 | 78,860 | 98,100 | 118,670 |
| Civil engineers | 44,810 | 54,520 | 68,600 | 86,260 | 104,420 |
| Computer hardware engineers | 53,910 | 69,500 | 88,470 | 111,030 | 135,260 |
| Electrical engineers | 49,120 | 60,640 | 75,930 | 94,050 | 115,240 |
| Electronics engineers, except computer | 52,050 | 64,440 | 81,050 | 99,630 | 119,900 |
| Environmental engineers | 43,180 | 54,150 | 69,940 | 88,480 | 106,230 |
| Health and safety engineers, except mining safety engineers and inspectors | 41,050 | 51,630 | 66,290 | 83,240 | 100,160 |
| Industrial engineers | 44,790 | 55,060 | 68,620 | 84,850 | 100,980 |
| Marine engineers and naval architects | 45,200 | 56,280 | 72,990 | 90,790 | 113,320 |
| Materials engineers | 46,120 | 57,850 | 73,990 | 92,210 | 112,140 |
| Mechanical engineers | 45,170 | 55,420 | 69,850 | 87,550 | 104,900 |
| Mining and geological engineers, including mining safety engineers | 42,040 | 54,390 | 72,160 | 94,110 | 128,410 |
| Nuclear engineers | 65,220 | 77,920 | 90,220 | 105,710 | 124,510 |
| Petroleum engineers | 57,960 | 75,880 | 98,380 | 123,130 | 145,600+ |
| All other engineers | 46,080 | 62,710 | 81,660 | 100,320 | 120,610 |

### Table 3: Average starting salary by engineering specialty and degree, 2007

| Curriculum | Bachelor's | Master's | Ph.D. |
|---|---|---|---|
| Aerospace/aeronautical/astronautical | $53,408 | $62,459 | $73,814 |
| Agricultural | 49,764 | — | — |
| Architectual | 48,664 | — | — |
| Bioengineering and biomedical | 51,356 | 59,240 | — |
| Chemical | 59,361 | 68,561 | 73,667 |
| Civil | 48,509 | 48,280 | 62,275 |
| Computer | 56,201 | 60,000 | 92,500 |
| Electrical/electronics and communications | 55,292 | 66,309 | 75,982 |
| Environmental/environmental health | 47,960 | — | — |
| Industrial/manufacturing | 55,067 | 64,759 | 77,364 |
| Materials | 56,233 | — | — |
| Mechanical | 54,128 | 62,798 | 72,763 |
| Mining and mineral | 54,381 | — | — |
| Nuclear | 56,587 | 59,167 | — |
| Petroleum | 60,718 | 57,000 | — |

*Source: National Association of Colleges and Employers*

## Related Occupations

Engineers apply the principles of physical science and mathematics in their work. Other workers who use scientific and mathematical principles include architects, except landscape and naval; engineering and natural sciences managers; computer and information systems managers; computer programmers; computer software engineers; mathematicians; drafters; engineering technicians; sales engineers; science technicians; and physical and life scientists, including agricultural and food scientists, biological scientists, conservation scientists and foresters, atmospheric scientists, chemists and materials scientists, environmental scientists and hydrologists, geoscientists, and physicists and astronomers.

## Sources of Additional Information

Information about careers in engineering is available from:

▸ JETS, 1420 King St., Suite 405, Alexandria, VA 22314. Internet: http://www.jets.org

Information on ABET-accredited engineering programs is available from

▸ ABET, Inc., 111 Market Place, Suite 1050, Baltimore, MD 21202. Internet: http://www.abet.org

Those interested in information on the Professional Engineer licensure should contact

▸ National Council of Examiners for Engineering and Surveying, P.O. Box 1686, Clemson, SC 29633. Internet: http://www.ncees.org

▸ National Society of Professional Engineers, 1420 King St., Alexandria, VA 22314. Internet: http://www.nspe.org

Information on general engineering education and career resources is available from

▸ American Society for Engineering Education, 1818 N St. NW, Suite 600, Washington, DC 20036. Internet: http://www.asee.org

Information on obtaining engineering positions with the federal government is available from the Office of Personnel Management through USAJOBS, the federal government's official employment information system. This resource for locating and applying for job opportunities can be accessed through the Internet at http://www.usajobs.opm.gov or through an interactive voice response telephone system at (703) 724-1850 or TDD (978) 461-8404. These numbers are not toll free, and charges may result. For advice on how to find and apply for federal jobs, see the Occupational Outlook Quarterly article "How to get a job in the Federal Government," online at http://www.bls.gov/opub/ooq/2004/summer/art01.pdf.

For more detailed information on an engineering specialty, contact societies representing the individual branches of engineering. Each can provide information about careers in the particular branch.

Aerospace engineers

▸ Aerospace Industries Association, 1000 Wilson Blvd., Suite 1700, Arlington, VA 22209. Internet: http://www.aia-aerospace.org

▸ American Institute of Aeronautics and Astronautics, Inc., 1801 Alexander Bell Dr., Suite 500, Reston, VA 20191. Internet: http://www.aiaa.org

Agricultural engineers

▸ American Society of Agricultural and Biological Engineers, 2950 Niles Rd., St. Joseph, MI 49085. Internet: http://www.asabe.org

Biomedical engineers

▸ Biomedical Engineering Society, 8401 Corporate Dr., Suite 140, Landover, MD 20785. Internet: http://www.bmes.org

Chemical engineers

▸ American Chemical Society, Department of Career Services, 1155 16th St. NW, Washington, DC 20036. Internet: http://www.chemistry.org

▸ American Institute of Chemical Engineers, 3 Park Ave., New York, NY 10016. Internet: http://www.aiche.org

Civil engineers

▸ American Society of Civil Engineers, 1801 Alexander Bell Dr., Reston, VA 20191. Internet: http://www.asce.org

Computer hardware engineers

▸ IEEE Computer Society, 1730 Massachusetts Ave. NW, Washington, DC 20036. Internet: http://www.computer.org

Electrical and electronics engineers

▸ Institute of Electrical and Electronics Engineers USA, 1828 L St. NW, Suite 1202, Washington, DC 20036. Internet: http://www.ieeeusa.org

Environmental engineers

▸ American Academy of Environmental Engineers, 130 Holiday Court, Suite 100, Annapolis, MD 21401. Internet: http://www.aaee.net

Health and safety engineers

▸ American Society of Safety Engineers, 1800 E Oakton St., Des Plaines, IL 60018. Internet: http://www.asse.org

▸ Board of Certified Safety Professionals, 208 Burwash Ave., Savoy, IL 61874. Internet: http://www.bcsp.org

Industrial engineers

▸ Institute of Industrial Engineers, 3577 Parkway Lane, Suite 200, Norcross, GA 30092. Internet: http://www.iienet.org

Marine engineers and naval architects

▸ Society of Naval Architects and Marine Engineers, 601 Pavonia Ave., Jersey City, NJ 07306. Internet: http://www.sname.org

Materials engineers

▸ ASM International, 9639 Kinsman Rd., Materials Park, OH 44073. Internet: http://www.asminternational.org

▸ Minerals, Metals, and Materials Society, 184 Thorn Hill Rd., Warrendale, PA 15086. Internet: http://www.tms.org

Mechanical engineers

▸ American Society of Heating, Refrigerating, and Air-Conditioning Engineers, Inc., 1791 Tullie Circle NE, Atlanta, GA 30329. Internet: http://www.ashrae.org

▸ American Society of Mechanical Engineers, 3 Park Ave., New York, NY 10016. Internet: http://www.asme.org

▸ SAE International, 400 Commonwealth Dr., Warrendale, PA 15096. Internet: http://www.sae.org

Mining and geological engineers, including mining safety engineers

▸ Society for Mining, Metallurgy, and Exploration, Inc., 8307 Shaffer Parkway, Littleton, CO 80127. Internet: http://www.smenet.org

Nuclear engineers

▸ American Nuclear Society, 555 North Kensington Ave., La Grange Park, IL 60526. Internet: http://www.ans.org

Petroleum engineers

▸ Society of Petroleum Engineers, P.O. Box 833836, Richardson, TX 75083. Internet: http://www.spe.org

# Environmental Scientists and Hydrologists

(O*NET 19-2041.00 and 19-2043.00)

## Significant Points

■ Environmental scientists and hydrologists often work in offices, laboratories, and field sites.

■ Federal, state, and local governments employ 43 percent of all environmental scientists and hydrologists.

■ Although a bachelor's degree in an earth science is adequate for a few entry-level jobs, employers prefer a master's degree; a Ph.D. degree generally is required for research or college teaching positions.

■ Job prospects are expected to be favorable, particularly for hydrologists.

# Nature of the Work

Environmental scientists and hydrologists use their knowledge of the physical makeup and history of the Earth to protect the environment, study the properties of underground and surface waters, locate water and energy resources, predict water-related geologic hazards, and provide environmental site assessments and advice on indoor air quality and hazardous-waste-site remediation.

*Environmental scientists* conduct research to identify, abate, and eliminate hazards that affect people, wildlife, and their environments. These workers analyze measurements or observations of air, food, water, and soil to determine the way to clean and preserve the environment. Understanding the issues involved in protecting the environment—degradation, conservation, recycling, and replenishment—is central to the work of environmental scientists. They often use this understanding to design and monitor waste disposal sites, preserve water supplies, and reclaim contaminated land and water to comply with federal environmental regulations. They also write risk assessments, describing the likely affect of construction and other environmental changes; write technical proposals; and give presentations to managers and regulators.

*Hydrologists* study the quantity, distribution, circulation, and physical properties of bodies of water. Often, they specialize in either underground water or surface water. They examine the form and intensity of precipitation, its rate of infiltration into the soil, its movement through the Earth, and its return to the ocean and atmosphere. Hydrologists use sophisticated techniques and instruments. For example, they may use remote sensing technology, data assimilation, and numerical modeling to monitor the change in regional and global water cycles. Some surface-water hydrologists use sensitive stream-measuring devices to assess flow rates and water quality.

Many environmental scientists and hydrologists work at consulting firms, helping businesses and government agencies comply with environmental policy, particularly with regard to ground-water decontamination and flood control. They are usually hired to solve problems. Most consulting firms fall into two categories: large multidisciplinary engineering companies, the largest of which may employ thousands of workers, and small niche firms that may employ only a few workers. When looking for jobs, environmental scientists and hydrologists should consider the type of firm and the scope of the projects it undertakes. In larger firms, environmental scientists are more likely to engage in large, long-term projects in which they will work with people in other scientific disciplines. In smaller specialty firms, however, they work more often with business professionals and clients in government and the private sector.

Environmental scientists who work on policy formation may help identify ways that human behavior can be modified in the future to avoid such problems as ground-water contamination and depletion of the ozone layer. Some environmental scientists work in managerial positions, usually after spending some time performing research or learning about environmental laws and regulations.

Many environmental scientists do work and have training that is similar to other physical or life scientists, but they focus on environmental issues. Many specialize in subfields such as environmental ecology and conservation, environmental chemistry, environmental biology, or fisheries science. Specialties affect the specific activities that environmental scientists perform, although recent understandings of the interconnectedness of life processes have blurred some traditional classifications. For example, *environmental ecologists* study the relationships between organisms and their environments and the effects of factors such as population size, pollutants, rainfall, temperature, and altitude, on both. They may collect, study, and report data on air, soil, and water using their knowledge of various scientific disciplines. *Ecological modelers* study ecosystems, pollution control, and resource management using mathematical modeling, systems analysis, thermodynamics, and computer techniques. *Environmental chemists* study the toxicity of various chemicals, that is, how those chemicals affect plants, animals, and people.

Environmental scientists and hydrologists in research positions with the federal government or in colleges and universities often have to find funding for their work by writing grant proposals. Consultants face similar pressures to market their skills and write proposals so that they will have steady work.

*Work environment.* Most entry-level environmental scientists and hydrologists spend the majority of their time in the field, while more experienced workers generally devote more time to office or laboratory work. Many beginning hydrologists and some environmental scientists, such as environmental ecologists and environmental chemists, often take field trips that involve physical activity. Environmental scientists and hydrologists in the field may work in warm or cold climates, in all kinds of weather. In their research, they may dig or chip with a hammer, scoop with a net, come in contact with water, and carry equipment. Travel often is required to meet with prospective clients or investors.

Researchers and consultants might face stress when looking for funding. Occasionally, those who write technical reports to business clients and regulators may be under pressure to meet deadlines and thus have to work long hours.

# Training, Other Qualifications, and Advancement

Most environmental scientists and hydrologists need a master's degree. A Ph.D. is usually necessary for jobs in college teaching or research.

*Education and training.* A bachelor's degree in an earth science is adequate for a few entry-level positions, but environmental scientists increasingly need a master's degree in environmental science, hydrology, or a related natural science. A master's degree also is the minimum educational requirement for most entry-level applied research positions in private industry, in state and federal agencies, and at state geological surveys. A doctoral degree generally is necessary for college teaching and most research positions.

Some environmental scientists have a degree in environmental science. Many, however, earn degrees in life science, chemistry, geology, geophysics, atmospheric science, or physics and then apply their education to the environment. They often need research or work experience related to environmental science.

A bachelor's degree in environmental science offers an interdisciplinary approach to the natural sciences, with an emphasis on biology, chemistry, and geology. Undergraduate environmental science majors typically focus on data analysis and physical geography, which are particularly useful in studying pollution abatement, water resources, or ecosystem protection, restoration, and management. Understanding the geochemistry of inorganic compounds is becoming increasingly important in developing remediation goals. Students interested in working in the environmental or regulatory fields, either in environmental consulting firms or for federal or state governments, should take courses in hydrology, hazardous-waste management, environmental legislation, chemistry, fluid mechanics, and geologic logging, which is the gathering of geologic data. An understanding of environmental regulations and government permit issues also is valuable for those planning to work in mining and oil and gas extraction.

Students interested in hydrology should take courses in the physical sciences, geophysics, chemistry, engineering science, soil science, mathematics, aquatic biology, atmospheric science, geology, oceanography, hydrogeology, and the management or conservation of water resources. In some cases, a bachelor's degree in a hydrologic science is sufficient for positions consulting about water quality or wastewater treatment.

For environmental scientists and hydrologists who consult, courses in business, finance, marketing, or economics may be useful. In addition, combining environmental science training with other disciplines such as engineering or business, qualifies these scientists for the widest range of jobs.

*Other qualifications.* Computer skills are essential for prospective environmental scientists and hydrologists. Students who have some experience with computer modeling, data analysis and integration, digital mapping, remote sensing, and Geographic Information Systems (GIS) will be the most prepared to enter the job market. Familiarity with the Global Positioning System (GPS)—a locator system that uses satellites—is vital.

Environmental scientists and hydrologists must have good interpersonal skills, because they usually work as part of a team with other scientists, engineers, and technicians. Strong oral and written communication skills also are essential because writing technical reports and research proposals and communicating results to company managers, regulators, and the public are important aspects of the work. Because international work is becoming increasingly pervasive, knowledge of a second language can be an advantage. Those involved in fieldwork must have physical stamina.

*Certification and advancement.* Environmental scientists and hydrologists often begin their careers in field exploration or, occasionally, as research assistants or technicians in laboratories or offices. They are given more difficult assignments as they gain experience. Eventually, they may be promoted to project leader, program manager, or some other management and research position.

The American Institute of Hydrology offers certification programs in professional hydrology. Certification may be beneficial for those seeking advancement.

## Employment

Environmental scientists and hydrologists held about 92,000 jobs in 2006. Jobs for hydrologists accounted for only 9 percent of the total. Many more individuals held environmental science faculty positions in colleges and universities, but they are classified as postsecondary teachers.

About 35 percent of environmental scientists were employed in state and local governments; 21 percent in management, scientific, and technical consulting services; 15 percent in architectural, engineering and related services; and 8 percent in the federal government. About 2 percent were self-employed.

Among hydrologists, 26 percent were employed in architectural, engineering, and related services, and 18 percent worked for management, scientific, and technical consulting services. In 2006, the federal government employed about 28 percent of hydrologists, mostly within the U.S. Department of the Interior for the U.S. Geological Survey (USGS) and within the U.S. Department of Defense. Another 21 percent worked for state agencies, such as state geological surveys and state departments of conservation. About 2 percent of hydrologists were self-employed, most as consultants to industry or government.

## Job Outlook

Employment of environmental scientists and hydrologists is expected to grow much faster than the average for all occupations. Job prospects are expected to be favorable, particularly for hydrologists.

*Employment change.* Employment of environmental scientists is expected to increase by 25 percent between 2006 and 2016, much faster than the average for all occupations. Over the same period, employment of hydrologists should increase by 24 percent, also much faster than the average. Job growth for environmental scientists and hydrologists should be strongest in private-sector consulting firms. Growth in employment of environmental scientists and hydrologists will be spurred largely by the increasing demands placed on the environment and water resources by population growth. Further demand should result from the need to comply with complex environmental laws and regulations, particularly those regarding ground-water decontamination, clean air, and flood control.

Much job growth will result from a continued need to monitor the quality of the environment, to interpret the impact of human actions on terrestrial and aquatic ecosystems, and to develop strategies for restoring ecosystems. In addition, environmental scientists will be needed to help planners develop and construct buildings, transportation corridors, and utilities that protect water resources and reflect efficient and beneficial land use.

Demand for hydrologists should also be strong as the population increases and moves to more environmentally sensitive locations. As people increasingly migrate toward coastal regions, for example, hydrologists will be needed to assess building sites for potential geologic hazards and to mitigate the effects of natural hazards such as floods, landslides, and hurricanes. Hydrologists also will be needed to study hazardous-waste sites and determine the effect of pollutants on soil and ground water so that engineers can design remediation systems. Increased government regulations, such as those regarding the management of storm water, and issues related to water conservation, deteriorating coastal environments, and rising sea levels also will stimulate employment growth for these workers.

Many environmental scientists and hydrologists work in consulting. Consulting firms have hired these scientists to help businesses and government address issues related to underground tanks, land dis-

**Projections data from the National Employment Matrix**

| Occupational Title | SOC Code | Employment, 2006 | Projected employment, 2016 | Change, 2006-2016 | |
|---|---|---|---|---|---|
| | | | | Number | Percent |
| Environmental scientists and hydrologists......................................... | — | 92,000 | 114,000 | 23,000 | 25 |
|    Environmental scientists and specialists, including health ........... | 19-2041 | 83,000 | 104,000 | 21,000 | 25 |
|    Hydrologists................................................................... | 19-2043 | 8,300 | 10,000 | 2,000 | 24 |

NOTE: Data in this table are rounded.

posal areas, and other hazardous-waste-management facilities. Currently, environmental consulting is evolving from investigations to creating remediation and engineering solutions. At the same time, the regulatory climate is moving from a rigid structure to a more flexible risk-based approach. These factors, coupled with new federal and state initiatives that integrate environmental activities into the business process itself, will result in a greater focus on waste minimization, resource recovery, pollution prevention, and the consideration of environmental effects during product development. This shift in focus to preventive management will provide many new opportunities for environmental scientists and hydrologists in consulting roles.

*Job prospects.* In addition to job openings due to growth, there will be additional demand for new environmental scientists and hydrologists to replace those who retire, advance to management positions, or change careers. Job prospects for hydrologists should be favorable, particularly for those with field experience. Demand for hydrologists who understand both the scientific and engineering aspects of waste remediation should be strong. Few colleges and universities offer programs in hydrology, so the number of qualified workers may be limited.

Job prospects for environmental scientists also will be good, but less favorable than for hydrologists because of the larger number of workers seeking to enter the field.

Funding for federal and state geological surveys depend largely on the political climate and the current budget. Thus, job security for environmental scientists and hydrologists may vary. During periods of economic recession, layoffs of environmental scientists and hydrologists may occur in consulting firms; layoffs are much less likely in government.

# Earnings

Median annual earnings of environmental scientists were $56,100 in May 2006. The middle 50 percent earned between $42,840 and $74,480. The lowest 10 percent earned less than $34,590, and the highest 10 percent earned more than $94,670.

Median annual earnings of hydrologists were $66,260 in 2006, with the middle 50 percent earning between $51,370 and $82,140, the lowest 10 percent earning less than $42,080, and the highest 10 percent earning more than $98,320.

Median annual earnings in the industries employing the largest number of environmental scientists in 2006 were as follows:

Federal executive branch....................................$82,490

Management, scientific, and technical
  consulting services ...........................................57,280

Engineering services ...........................................56,080

Local government ...............................................52,100

State government ...............................................50,590

According to the National Association of Colleges and Employers, beginning salary offers in July 2007 for graduates with bachelor's degrees in an environmental science averaged $38,336 a year.

In 2007, the federal government's average salary for hydrologists was $82,217.

# Related Occupations

Environmental scientists and hydrologists perform investigations for the purpose of abating or eliminating pollutants or hazards that affect the environment or plants, animals, and humans. Many other occupations deal with preserving or researching the natural environment, including conservation scientists and foresters, atmospheric scientists, and some biological scientists, science technicians, and engineering technicians. Environmental scientists and hydrologists have extensive training in physical sciences, and many apply their knowledge of chemistry, physics, biology, and mathematics to the study of the Earth, work closely related to that of geoscientists.

Using problem-solving skills, physicists; chemists; engineers; mathematicians; surveyors, cartographers, photogrammetrists, and surveying technicians; computer systems analysts; and computer scientists and database administrators may also perform similar work related to the environment.

# Sources of Additional Information

Information on training and career opportunities for environmental scientists is available from

▸ American Geological Institute, 4220 King St., Alexandria, VA 22302. Internet: http://www.agiweb.org

For information on careers in hydrology, contact

▸ American Institute of Hydrology, 300 Village Green Circle, Suite #201, Smyrna, GA 30080. Internet: http://www.aihydro.org

Information on obtaining a position as a hydrologist or an environmental protection specialist with the federal government is available from the Office of Personnel Management through USAJOBS, the federal government's official employment information system. This resource for locating and applying for job opportunities can be accessed through the Internet at http://www.usajobs.opm.gov or through an interactive voice response telephone system at (703) 724-1850 or TDD (978) 461-8404. These numbers are not toll free, and charges may result.

# Financial Analysts and Personal Financial Advisors

(O*NET 13-2051.00 and 13-2052.00)

## Significant Points

■ Good interpersonal skills and an aptitude for working with numbers are among the most important qualifications for financial analysts and personal financial advisors.

■ Keen competition is anticipated for these highly paid positions, despite rapid job growth; those who have earned a professional designation or an MBA are expected to have the best opportunities.

■ Almost one third of personal financial advisors are self-employed.

## Nature of the Work

Financial analysts and personal financial advisors provide analysis and guidance to businesses and individuals in making investment decisions. Both types of specialists gather financial information, analyze it, and make recommendations. However, their job duties differ because of the type of investment information they provide and their relationships with investors.

*Financial analysts* assess the economic performance of companies and industries for firms and institutions with money to invest. Also called *securities analysts* and *investment analysts*, they work for investment banks, insurance companies, mutual and pension funds, securities firms, the business media, and other businesses, helping them make investment decisions or recommendations. Financial analysts read company financial statements and analyze commodity prices, sales, costs, expenses, and tax rates in order to determine a company's value and to project its future earnings. They often meet with company officials to gain a better insight into the firm's prospects and to determine its managerial effectiveness.

Financial analysts can usually be divided into two basic types: those who work on the *buy side* and those who work on the *sell side*. Analysts on the buy side work for companies that have a great deal of money to invest. These companies, called institutional investors, include mutual funds, hedge funds, insurance companies, independent money managers, and charitable organizations, such as universities and hospitals, with large endowments. Buy side financial analysts work to devise investment strategies for a company's portfolio. Conversely, analysts on the sell side help securities dealers to sell their products. These companies include investment banks and securities firms. The business media also hire financial advisors that are supposed to be impartial and as such occupy a role somewhere in the middle.

Financial analysts generally focus on a specific industry, region, or type of product. For example, an analyst may focus on the utilities industry, Latin America, or the options market. Firms with larger research departments may divide the work even further so their analysts can maintain sharp focus. Within their areas of specialty, analysts assess current trends in business practices, products, and

competition. They must keep abreast of new regulations or policies that may affect the investments they are watching and monitor the economy to determine its effect on earnings. Some experienced analysts called *portfolio managers* supervise a team of analysts and help guide a company in selecting the right mix of products, industries, and regions for their investment portfolio. Others who manage mutual funds or hedge funds perform a similar role and are generally called *fund managers*. Other analysts, called *risk managers*, analyze portfolio decisions and determine how to maximize profits through diversification and hedging.

Some financial analysts, called *ratings analysts*, evaluate the ability of companies or governments that issue bonds to repay their debts. On the basis of their evaluation, a management team assigns a rating to a company's or government's bonds, which helps them to decide whether to include them in a portfolio. Other financial analysts perform budget, cost, and credit analysis as part of their responsibilities.

Financial analysts use spreadsheet and statistical software packages to analyze financial data, spot trends, and develop forecasts. Analysts also use the data they find to measure the financial risks associated with making a particular investment decision. On the basis of their results, they write reports and make presentations, usually with recommendations to buy or sell particular investments.

*Personal financial advisors* assess the financial needs of individuals. Advisors use their knowledge of investments, tax laws, and insurance to recommend financial options to individuals. They help them to identify and plan to meet short- and long-term goals. Planners help clients with retirement and estate planning, funding the college education of children, and general investment choices. Many also provide tax advice or sell life insurance. Although most planners offer advice on a wide range of topics, some specialize in areas such as retirement and estate planning or risk management.

Personal financial advisors usually work with many clients, and they often must find their own customers. Many personal financial advisors spend a great deal of their time making sales calls and marketing their services. Many advisors also meet potential clients by giving seminars or lectures or through business and social contacts. Finding clients and building a customer base is one of the most important aspects of becoming successful as a financial advisor.

Financial advisors begin work with a client by setting up a consultation. This is usually an in-person meeting where the advisor obtains as much information as possible about the client's finances and goals. The advisor then develops a comprehensive financial plan that identifies problem areas, makes recommendations for improvement, and selects appropriate investments compatible with the client's goals, attitude toward risk, and expectation or need for a return on the investment. Sometimes this plan is written, but more often it is in the form of verbal advice. Advisors sometimes meet with accountants or legal professionals for help.

Financial advisors usually meet with established clients at least once a year to update them on potential investments and adjust their financial plan to any life changes—such as marriage, disability, or retirement. Financial advisors also answer clients' questions regarding changes in benefit plans or the consequences of a change in their jobs or careers. Financial planners must educate their clients about risks and various possible scenarios so that the clients don't harbor unrealistic expectations.

Most personal financial advisors buy and sell financial products, such as securities and life insurance. Fees and commissions from the purchase and sale of securities and life insurance plans are one of the major sources of income for most personal financial advisors.

*Private bankers* or *wealth managers* are personal financial advisors who work for people who have a lot of money to invest. While most investors are simply saving for retirement or their children's college education, these individuals have large amounts of capital and often use the returns on their investments as a major source of income. Because they have so much capital, these clients resemble institutional investors and approach investing differently from the general public. Private bankers manage portfolios for these individuals using the resources of the bank, including teams of financial analysts, accountants, lawyers, and other professionals. Private bankers sell these services to wealthy individuals, generally spending most of their time working with a small number of clients. Unlike most personal financial advisors, private bankers meet with their clients regularly to keep them abreast of financial matters; they often have the responsibility of directly managing customers' finances.

*Work environment.* Financial analysts and personal financial advisors usually work in offices or their own homes. Financial analysts may work long hours, travel frequently to visit companies or potential investors, and face the pressure of deadlines. Much of their research must be done after office hours because their days are filled with telephone calls and meetings.

Personal financial advisors usually work standard business hours, but they also schedule meetings with clients in the evenings or on weekends. Many also teach evening classes or hold seminars in order to bring in more clients. Some personal financial advisors spend a fair amount of their time traveling, usually to attend conferences and training sessions, but also occasionally to visit clients.

Private bankers also generally work during standard business hours, but because they work so closely with their clients, they may have to be available outside normal hours upon request.

# Training, Other Qualifications, and Advancement

Financial analysts and most personal financial advisors must have a bachelor's degree. Many also earn a master's degree in finance or business administration or get professional designations. Because the field is so specialized, workers frequently attend training and seminars to learn the latest developments.

*Education and training.* A bachelor's or graduate degree is required for financial analysts and is strongly preferred for personal financial advisors. Most companies require financial analysts to have at least a bachelor's degree in finance, business administration, accounting, statistics, or economics. Coursework in statistics, economics, and business is required, and knowledge of accounting policies and procedures, corporate budgeting, and financial analysis methods is recommended. A master's degree in finance or business administration also is desirable. Also useful are advanced courses in options pricing or bond valuation and knowledge of risk management.

Employers usually do not require a specific field of study for personal financial advisors, but a bachelor's degree in accounting, finance, economics, business, mathematics, or law provides good preparation for the occupation. Courses in investments, taxes, estate planning, and risk management are also helpful. Programs in financial planning are becoming more widely available in colleges and universities.

*Licensure.* The Financial Industry Regulatory Authority (FINRA) is the main licensing organization for the securities industry. Depending on an individual's work, many different licenses may be required, although buy side analysts are less likely to need licenses. The majority of these licenses require sponsorship by an employer, so companies do not expect individuals to have these licenses before starting a job. Experienced workers who change jobs will need to have their licenses renewed with the new company.

Almost all personal financial advisors need the Series seven and Series 63 or 66 licenses. These licenses give their holders the right to act as a registered representative of a securities firm and to give financial advice. Because the Series 7 license requires sponsorship, self-employed personal financial advisors must maintain a relationship with a large securities firm. This relationship allows them to act as representatives of that firm in the buying and selling of securities.

If personal financial advisors choose to sell insurance, they need additional licenses issued by state licensing boards.

*Other qualifications.* Strong math, analytical, and problem-solving skills are essential qualifications for financial analysts. Good communication skills also are necessary because these workers must present complex financial concepts and strategies. Self-confidence, maturity, and the ability to work independently are important as well. Financial analysts must be detail-oriented; motivated to seek out obscure information; and familiar with the workings of the economy, tax laws, and money markets. Financial analysts should also be very comfortable with computers, as they are frequently used in doing work. Although much of the software they use is proprietary, they must be comfortable working with spreadsheets and statistical packages.

Personal financial advisors need many of the same skills, but they must emphasize customer service. They need strong sales ability, including the ability to make customers feel comfortable. It is important for them to be able to present financial concepts to clients in easy-to-understand language. Personal financial advisors must also be able to interact casually with people from many different backgrounds. Some advisors have experience in a related occupation, such as accountant, auditor, insurance sales agent, or broker.

Private bankers work directly with wealthy individuals, so they must be polished and refined. They should be able to interact comfortably with people who may be well-known in the community.

*Certification and advancement.* Although not required, certification can enhance professional standing and is recommended by many employers.

Financial analysts can earn the Chartered Financial Analyst (CFA) designation, sponsored by the CFA Institute. To qualify for this designation, applicants need a bachelor's degree and four years of work experience in a related field and must pass three examinations. The first exam is administered twice per year, while the second and third

Projections data from the National Employment Matrix

| Occupational Title | SOC Code | Employment, 2006 | Projected employment, 2016 | Change, 2006-16 | |
|---|---|---|---|---|---|
| | | | | Number | Percent |
| Financial analysts and personal financial advisors ........................... | — | 397,000 | 544,000 | 147,000 | 37 |
| Financial analysts......................................................................... | 13-2051 | 221,000 | 295,000 | 75,000 | 34 |
| Personal financial advisors......................................................... | 13-2052 | 176,000 | 248,000 | 72,000 | 41 |

NOTE: Data in this table are rounded.

are administered annually. These exams cover subjects such as accounting, economics, securities analysis, financial markets and instruments, corporate finance, asset valuation, and portfolio management. Increasingly, personal financial advisors, sometimes called wealth managers, working with wealthy individuals have the CFA designation.

Personal financial advisors may obtain the Certified Financial Planner credential, often referred to as CFP. This certification, issued by the Certified Financial Planner Board of Standards, requires three years of relevant experience; the completion of education requirements, including a bachelor's degree; passing a comprehensive examination; and adherence to a code of ethics. The exams test the candidate's knowledge of the financial planning process, insurance and risk management, employee benefits planning, taxes and retirement planning, and investment and estate planning. Candidates are also required to have a working knowledge of debt management, planning liability, emergency fund reserves, and statistical modeling.

Financial analysts advance by moving into positions where they are responsible for larger or more important products. They may also supervise teams of financial analysts. Eventually, they may become portfolio managers or fund managers, directing the investment portfolios of their companies or funds.

Personal financial advisors have several different paths to advancement. Many accumulate clients and manage more assets. Those who work in firms may move into managerial positions. Others may choose to open their own branch offices for large securities firms and serve as independent registered representatives for those firms. In most cases, employees of established firms are barred from keeping their clients after they leave a firm, so an advisor who leaves a firm to establish a new business must find new customers. Many newly independent personal financial advisors sell their services to family and friends, hoping to win business through referrals.

# Employment

Financial analysts and personal financial advisors held 397,000 jobs in 2006, of which financial analysts held 221,000. Many financial analysts work at the headquarters of large financial institutions, most of which are based in New York City or other major financial centers. More than 2 out of 5 financial analysts worked in the finance and insurance industries, including securities and commodity brokers, banks and credit institutions, and insurance carriers. Others worked throughout private industry and government.

Personal financial advisors held 176,000 jobs in 2006. Jobs were spread throughout the country. Much like financial analysts, more than half worked in finance and insurance industries, including

securities and commodity brokers, banks, insurance carriers, and financial investment firms. However, about 30 percent of personal financial advisors were self-employed, operating small investment advisory firms, usually in urban areas.

# Job Outlook

Employment of financial analysts and personal financial advisors is expected to grow much faster than the average for all occupations. Growth will be especially strong for personal financial advisors, which are projected to be among the 10 fastest-growing occupations. Despite strong job growth, keen competition will continue for these well-paid jobs, especially for new entrants.

*Employment change.* As the level of investment increases, overall employment of financial analysts and personal financial advisors is expected to increase by 37 percent during the 2006–2016 decade, which is much faster than the average for all occupations.

Personal financial advisors are projected to grow by 41 percent, which is much faster than the average for all occupations, over the projections decade. Growing numbers of advisors will be needed to assist the millions of workers expected to retire in the next 10 years. As more members of the large baby boom generation reach their peak years of retirement savings, personal investments are expected to increase and more people will seek the help of experts. Many companies also have replaced traditional pension plans with retirement savings programs, so more individuals are managing their own retirements than in the past, creating jobs for advisors. In addition, people are living longer and must plan to finance longer retirements.

Deregulation of the financial services industry also is expected to continue to spur demand for personal financial advisors in the banking industry. In recent years, banks and insurance companies have been allowed to expand into the securities industry. Many firms are adding investment advice to their services and are expected to increase their hiring of personal financial advisors.

Employment of financial analysts is expected to grow by 34 percent between 2006 and 2016, which is also much faster than the average for all occupations. Primary factors for this growth are increasing complexity of investments and growth in the industry. As the number and type of mutual funds and the amount of assets invested in these funds increase, mutual fund companies will need more financial analysts to research and recommend investments.

*Job prospects.* Despite overall employment growth, competition for jobs is expected to be keen in these high-paying occupations. Growth in the industry will create many new positions, but there are still far more people who would like to enter the occupation. For those aspiring to financial analyst jobs, a strong academic background is absolutely essential. Good grades in courses such as finance, accounting, and economics are very important to employers. An MBA or certification is helpful in maintaining employment.

Personal financial advisors will also face competition as many other services compete for customers. Many individuals enter the field by working for a bank or full-service brokerage. Most independent advisories fail within the first year of business, making self-employment challenging. Because the occupation requires sales, people who have strong selling skills will ultimately be most successful. A college degree and certification can lend credibility.

## Earnings

Median annual earnings, including bonuses, of wage and salary financial analysts were $66,590 in May 2006. The middle 50 percent earned between $50,700 and $90,690. The lowest 10 percent earned less than $40,340, and the highest 10 percent earned more than $130,130. The bonuses that many financial analysts receive in addition to their salary can be a significant part of their total earnings. Usually, the bonus is based on how well their predictions compare to the actual performance of a benchmark investment.

Median annual earnings of wage and salary personal financial advisors were $66,120 in May 2006. The middle 50 percent earned between $44,130 and $114,260. The lowest 10 percent earned less than $32,340, and the highest 10 percent earned more than $145,600. Personal financial advisors who work for financial services firms are generally paid a salary plus bonus. Advisors who work for financial investment or planning firms or who are self-employed either charge hourly fees for their services or opt to earn their money through fees on stock and insurance purchases. Advisors generally receive commissions for financial products they sell in addition to charging a fee. Those who manage a client's assets may charge a percentage of those assets. Earnings of self-employed workers are not included in the medians given here.

## Related Occupations

Other jobs requiring expertise in finance and investment or in the sale of financial products include accountants and auditors; financial managers; insurance sales agents; real estate brokers and sales agents; budget analysts; insurance underwriters; actuaries;, and securities, commodities, and financial services sales agents.

## Sources of Additional Information

For general information on securities industry employment, contact

▶ Financial Industry Regulatory Authority (FINRA), 1735 K St. NW, Washington, DC 20006. Internet: http://www.finra.org

▶ Securities Industry and Financial Markets Association, 120 Broadway, 35th Floor, New York, NY 10271. Internet: http://www.sifma.org

For information on financial analyst careers, contact

▶ American Academy of Financial Management, 2 Canal St., Suite 2317, New Orleans, LA 70130. Internet: http://www.aafm.org

▶ CFA Institute, P.O. Box 3668, 560 Ray C. Hunt Dr., Charlottesville, VA 22903. Internet: http://www.cfainstitute.org

For information on personal financial advisor careers, contact

▶ Certified Financial Planner Board of Standards, Inc., 1670 Broadway, Suite 600, Denver, CO 80202. Internet: http://www.cfp.net

▶ Financial Planning Association, 4100 E. Mississippi Ave., Suite 400, Denver, CO 80246-3053. Internet: http://www.fpanet.org

▶ Investment Management Consultants Association, 5619 DTC Parkway, Suite 500, Greenwood Village, CO 80111. Internet: http://www.imca.org

For additional career information, see the *Occupational Outlook Quarterly* article "Financial analysts and personal financial advisors" online at http://www.bls.gov/opub/ooq/2000/summer/art03.pdf and in print at many libraries and career centers.

# Financial Managers

(O*NET 11-3031.00, 11-3031.01, and 11-3031.02)

## Significant Points

■ Jobseekers are likely to face competition.

■ About 3 out of 10 work in finance and insurance industries.

■ A bachelor's degree in finance, accounting, or a related field is the minimum academic preparation, but employers increasingly seek graduates with a master's degree in business administration, economics, finance, or risk management.

■ Experience may be more important than formal education for some financial manager positions—most notably, branch managers in banks.

## Nature of the Work

Almost every firm, government agency, and other type of organization has one or more financial managers. Financial managers oversee the preparation of financial reports, direct investment activities, and implement cash management strategies. Managers also develop strategies and implement the long-term goals of their organization.

The duties of financial managers vary with their specific titles, which include controller, treasurer or finance officer, credit manager, cash manager, risk and insurance manager, and manager of international banking. *Controllers* direct the preparation of financial reports, such as income statements, balance sheets, and analyses of future earnings or expenses, that summarize and forecast the organization's financial position. Controllers also are in charge of preparing special reports required by regulatory authorities. Often, controllers oversee the accounting, audit, and budget departments . *Treasurers* and *finance officers* direct the organization's budgets to meet its financial goals. They oversee the investment of funds, manage associated risks, supervise cash management activities, execute capital-raising strategies to support a firm's expansion, and deal with mergers and acquisitions. *Credit managers* oversee the firm's issuance of credit, establishing credit-rating criteria, determining credit ceilings, and monitoring the collections of past-due accounts.

*Cash managers* monitor and control the flow of cash receipts and disbursements to meet the business and investment needs of the firm. For example, cash flow projections are needed to determine whether loans must be obtained to meet cash requirements or whether surplus cash should be invested in interest-bearing instruments. *Risk* and *insurance managers* oversee programs to minimize risks and losses that might arise from financial transactions and business operations. They also manage the organization's insurance budget. Managers specializing in international finance develop financial and accounting systems for the banking transactions of multinational organizations.

Financial institutions—such as commercial banks, savings and loan associations, credit unions, and mortgage and finance companies—employ additional financial managers who oversee various functions, such as lending, trusts, mortgages, and investments, or programs, including sales, operations, or electronic financial services. These managers may solicit business, authorize loans, and direct the investment of funds, always adhering to federal and state laws and regulations.

Branch managers of financial institutions administer and manage all of the functions of a branch office. Job duties may include hiring personnel, approving loans and lines of credit, establishing a rapport with the community to attract business, and assisting customers with account problems. Branch mangers also are becoming more oriented toward sales and marketing. As a result, it is important that they have substantial knowledge about all types of products that the bank sells. Financial managers who work for financial institutions must keep abreast of the rapidly growing array of financial services and products.

In addition to the preceding duties, all financial managers perform tasks unique to their organization or industry. For example, government financial managers must be experts on the government appropriations and budgeting processes, whereas health care financial managers must be knowledgeable about issues surrounding health care financing. Moreover, financial managers must be aware of special tax laws and regulations that affect their industry.

Financial managers play an increasingly important role in mergers and consolidations and in global expansion and related financing. These areas require extensive, specialized knowledge to reduce risks and maximize profit. Financial managers increasingly are hired on a temporary basis to advise senior managers on these and other matters. In fact, some small firms contract out all their accounting and financial functions to companies that provide such services.

The role of the financial manager, particularly in business, is changing in response to technological advances that have significantly reduced the amount of time it takes to produce financial reports. Financial managers now perform more data analysis and use it to offer senior managers ideas on how to maximize profits. They often work on teams, acting as business advisors to top management. Financial managers need to keep abreast of the latest computer technology to increase the efficiency of their firm's financial operations.

**Work environment.** Working in comfortable offices, often close to top managers and to departments that develop the financial data those managers need, financial managers typically have direct access to state-of-the-art computer systems and information services. They commonly work long hours, often up to 50 or 60 per week. Financial managers generally are required to attend meetings of financial and economic associations and may travel to visit subsidiary firms or to meet customers.

## Training, Other Qualifications, and Advancement

Most financial managers need a bachelor's degree, and many have a master's degree or professional certification. Bank managers often have experience as loan officers. Financial managers also need strong interpersonal and business skills.

**Education and training.** A bachelor's degree in finance, accounting, economics, or business administration is the minimum academic preparation for financial managers. However, many employers now seek graduates with a master's degree, preferably in business administration, economics, finance, or risk management. These academic programs develop analytical skills and teach the latest financial analysis methods and technology.

Experience may be more important than formal education for some financial manager positions—most notably, branch managers in banks. Banks typically fill branch manager positions by promoting experienced loan officers and other professionals who excel at their jobs. Other financial managers may enter the profession through formal management training programs offered by the company. The American Institute of Banking, which is affiliated with the American Bankers Association, sponsors educational and training programs for bank officers at banking schools and educational conferences.

**Other qualifications.** Candidates for financial management positions need many different skills. Interpersonal skills are important because these jobs involve managing people and working as part of a team to solve problems. Financial managers must have excellent communication skills to explain complex financial data. Because financial managers work extensively with various departments in their firm, a broad understanding of business is essential.

Financial managers should be creative thinkers and problem-solvers, applying their analytical skills to business. They must be comfortable with the latest computer technology. Financial managers must have knowledge of international finance because financial operations are increasingly being affected by the global economy. Proficiency in a foreign language also may be important. In addition, a good knowledge of compliance procedures is essential because of the many recent regulatory changes.

**Certification and advancement.** Financial managers may broaden their skills and exhibit their competency by attaining professional certification. Many associations offer professional certification programs. For example, the CFA Institute confers the Chartered Financial Analyst designation on investment professionals who have a bachelor's degree, pass three sequential examinations, and meet work experience requirements. The Association for Financial Professionals confers the Certified Treasury Professional credentials to those who pass a computer-based exam and have a minimum of two years of relevant experience. Continuing education is required to maintain these credentials. Also, financial managers who specialize in accounting sometimes earn the Certified Public Accountant (CPA) or the Certified Management Accountant (CMA) designa-

**Projections data from the National Employment Matrix**

| Occupational Title | SOC Code | Employment, 2006 | Projected employment, 2016 | Change, 2006-16 | |
| --- | --- | --- | --- | --- | --- |
| | | | | Number | Percent |
| Financial managers ........................................................ | 11-3031 | 506,000 | 570,000 | 64,000 | 13 |

NOTE: Data in this table are rounded.

tion. The CMA is offered by the Institute of Management Accountants to its members who have a bachelor's degree and at least two years of work experience and who pass the institute's four-part examination and fulfill continuing education requirements.

Continuing education is vital to financial managers, who must cope with the growing complexity of global trade, changes in federal and state laws and regulations, and the proliferation of new and complex financial instruments. Firms often provide opportunities for workers to broaden their knowledge and skills by encouraging them to take graduate courses at colleges and universities or attend conferences related to their specialty. Financial management, banking, and credit union associations, often in cooperation with colleges and universities, sponsor numerous national and local training programs. Trainees prepare extensively at home and then attend sessions on subjects such as accounting management, budget management, corporate cash management, financial analysis, international banking, and information systems. Many firms pay all or part of the costs for employees who successfully complete the courses. Although experience, ability, and leadership are emphasized for promotion, advancement may be accelerated by this type of special study.

Because financial management is so important to efficient business operations, well-trained, experienced financial managers who display a strong grasp of the operations of various departments within their organization are prime candidates for promotion to top management positions. Some financial managers transfer to closely related positions in other industries. Those with extensive experience and access to sufficient capital may start their own consulting firms.

## Employment

Financial managers held about 506,000 jobs in 2006. Although they can be found in every industry, approximately 3 out of 10 were employed by finance and insurance establishments, such as banks, savings institutions, finance companies, credit unions, insurance carriers, and securities dealers. About 8 percent worked for federal, state, or local government.

## Job Outlook

Employment growth for financial managers is expected is to be about as fast as the average for all occupations. However, applicants will likely face strong competition for jobs. Those with a masters' degree and a certification will have the best opportunities.

*Employment change.* Employment of financial managers over the 2006–2016 decade is expected to grow by 13 percent, which is about as fast as the average for all occupations. Regulatory reforms and the expansion and globalization of the economy will increase the need for financial expertise and drive job growth. As the economy expands, both the growth of established companies and the creation of new businesses will spur demand for financial managers.

Employment of bank branch managers is expected to increase because banks are refocusing on the importance of their existing branches and are creating new branches to service a growing population. However, mergers, acquisitions, and corporate downsizing are likely to restrict the employment growth of financial managers to some extent.

The long-run prospects for financial managers in the securities and commodities industry should be favorable because more people will be needed to handle increasingly complex financial transactions and manage a growing amount of investments. Financial managers also will be needed to handle mergers and acquisitions, raise capital, and assess global financial transactions. Risk managers, who assess risks for insurance and investment purposes, also will be in demand.

Some companies may hire financial managers on a temporary basis to see the organization through a short-term crisis or to offer suggestions for boosting profits. Other companies may contract out all accounting and financial operations. Even in these cases, however, financial managers may be needed to oversee the contracts.

*Job prospects.* As with other managerial occupations, jobseekers are likely to face competition because the number of job openings is expected to be less than the number of applicants. Candidates with expertise in accounting and finance—particularly those with a master's degree and/or certification—should enjoy the best job prospects. Strong computer skills and knowledge of international finance are important, as are excellent communication skills, because financial management involves working on strategic planning teams.

As banks expand the range of products and services they offer to include insurance and investment products, branch managers with knowledge in these areas will be needed. As a result, candidates who are licensed to sell insurance or securities will have the most favorable prospects.

## Earnings

Median annual earnings of wage and salary financial managers were $90,970 in May 2006. The middle 50 percent earned between $66,690 and $125,180. The lowest 10 percent earned less than $50,290, while the top 10 percent earned more than $145,600. Median annual earnings in the industries employing the largest numbers of financial managers were

| | |
| --- | --- |
| Securities and commodity contracts intermediation | $131,730 |
| Management of companies and enterprises | 105,410 |
| Nondepository credit intermediation | 86,340 |
| Local government | 72,790 |
| Depository credit intermediation | 72,580 |

According to a survey by Robert Half International, a staffing services firm specializing in accounting and finance professionals, directors of finance earned between $79,000 and $184,000 in 2007, and corporate controllers earned between $61,250 and $149,250.

Large organizations often pay more than small ones, and salary levels also can depend on the type of industry and location. Many financial managers in both public and private industry receive additional compensation in the form of bonuses, which, like salaries, vary substantially by size of firm. Deferred compensation in the form of stock options is becoming more common, especially for senior-level executives.

## Related Occupations

Financial managers combine formal education with experience in one or more areas of finance, such as asset management, lending, credit operations, securities investment, or insurance risk and loss control. Workers in other occupations requiring similar training and skills include accountants and auditors; budget analysts; financial analysts and personal financial advisors; insurance sales agents; insurance underwriters; loan officers; securities, commodities, and financial services sales agents; and real estate brokers and sales agents.

## Sources of Additional Information

For information about careers and certification in financial management, contact

▸ Financial Management Association International, College of Business Administration, University of South Florida, Tampa, FL 33620. Internet: http://www.fma.org

For information about careers in financial and treasury management and the Certified Treasury Professional program, contact

▸ Association for Financial Professionals, 7315 Wisconsin Ave., Suite 600 West, Bethesda, MD 20814. Internet: http://www.afponline.org

For information about the Chartered Financial Analyst program, contact

▸ CFA Institute, P.O. Box 3668, 560 Ray Hunt Dr., Charlottesville, VA 22903. Internet: http://www.cfainstitute.org

For information on The American Institute of Banking and its programs, contact

▸ American Bankers Association, 1120 Connecticut Ave. NW, Washington, DC 20036.

For information about the Certified in Management Accounting designation, contact

▸ Institute of Management Accountants, 10 Paragon Dr., Montvale, NJ 07645. Internet: http://www.imanet.org

# Fitness Workers

(O*NET 39-9031.00)

## Significant Points

■ Many fitness and personal training jobs are part time, but many workers increase their hours by working at several different facilities or at clients' homes.

■ Night and weekend hours are common.

■ Most fitness workers need to be certified.

■ Job prospects are expected to be good.

## Nature of the Work

Fitness workers lead, instruct, and motivate individuals or groups in exercise activities, including cardiovascular exercise, strength training, and stretching. They work in health clubs, country clubs, hospitals, universities, yoga and Pilates studios, resorts, and clients' homes. Increasingly, fitness workers also are found in workplaces, where they organize and direct health and fitness programs for employees of all ages. Although gyms and health clubs offer a variety of exercise activities such as weightlifting, yoga, cardiovascular training, and karate, fitness workers typically specialize in only a few areas.

*Personal trainers* work one-on-one with clients either in a gym or in the client's home. They help clients assess their level of physical fitness and set and reach fitness goals. Trainers also demonstrate various exercises and help clients improve their exercise techniques. They may keep records of their clients' exercise sessions to monitor clients' progress toward physical fitness. They may also advise their clients on how to modify their lifestyle outside of the gym to improve their fitness.

*Group exercise instructors* conduct group exercise sessions that usually include aerobic exercise, stretching, and muscle conditioning. Cardiovascular conditioning classes are often set to music. Instructors choose and mix the music and choreograph a corresponding exercise sequence. Two increasingly popular conditioning methods taught in exercise classes are Pilates and yoga. In these classes, instructors demonstrate the different moves and positions of the particular method; they also observe students and correct those who are doing the exercises improperly. Group exercise instructors are responsible for ensuring that their classes are motivating, safe, and challenging, yet not too difficult for the participants.

*Fitness directors* oversee the fitness-related aspects of a health club or fitness center. They create and oversee programs that meet the needs of the club's members, including new member orientations, fitness assessments, and workout incentive programs. They also select fitness equipment; coordinate personal training and group exercise programs; hire, train, and supervise fitness staff; and carry out administrative duties.

Fitness workers in smaller facilities with few employees may perform a variety of functions in addition to their fitness duties, such as tending the front desk, signing up new members, giving tours of the fitness center, writing newsletter articles, creating posters and flyers, and supervising the weight training and cardiovascular equipment areas. In larger commercial facilities, personal trainers are often required to sell their services to members and to make a specified number of sales. Some fitness workers may combine the duties of group exercise instructors and personal trainers, and in smaller facilities, the fitness director may teach classes and do personal training.

*Work environment.* Most fitness workers spend their time indoors at fitness centers and health clubs. Fitness directors and supervisors, however, typically spend most of their time in an office. Those in smaller fitness centers may split their time among office work, personal training, and teaching classes. Directors and supervisors generally engage in less physical activity than do lower-level fitness workers. Nevertheless, workers at all levels risk suffering injuries during physical activities.

Since most fitness centers are open long hours, fitness workers often work nights and weekends and even occasional holidays. Some may travel from place to place throughout the day, to different gyms or to clients' homes, to maintain a full work schedule.

Fitness workers generally enjoy a lot of autonomy. Group exercise instructors choreograph or plan their own classes, and personal trainers have the freedom to design and implement their clients' workout routines.

## Training, Other Qualifications, and Advancement

For most fitness workers, certification is critical. Personal trainers usually must have certification to begin working with clients or with members of a fitness facility. Group fitness instructors may begin without a certification, but they are often encouraged or required by their employers to become certified.

*Education and training.* Fitness workers usually do not receive much on-the-job training; they are expected to know how to do their jobs when they are hired. Workers may receive some organizational training to learn about the operations of their new employer. They occasionally receive specialized training if they are expected to teach or lead a specific method of exercise or focus on a particular age or ability group. Because the requirements vary from employer to employer, it may be helpful to contact your local fitness centers or other potential employers to find out what background they prefer before pursuing training.

The education and training required depends on the specific type of fitness work: personal training, group fitness, or a specialization such as Pilates or yoga each need different preparation. Personal trainers often start out by taking classes to become certified. They then may begin by working alongside an experienced trainer before being allowed to train clients alone. Group fitness instructors often get started by participating in exercise classes until they are ready to successfully audition as instructors and begin teaching class. They also may improve their skills by taking training courses or attending fitness conventions. Most employers require instructors to work toward becoming certified.

Training for Pilates and yoga instructors is changing. Because interest in these forms of exercise has exploded in recent years, the demand for teachers has grown faster than the ability to train them properly. However, because inexperienced teachers have contributed to student injuries, there has been a push toward more standardized, rigorous requirements for teacher training.

Pilates and yoga teachers need specialized training in their particular method of exercise. For Pilates, training options range from weekend-long workshops to year-long programs, but the trend is toward requiring more training. The Pilates Method Alliance has established training standards that recommend at least 200 hours of training; the group also has standards for training schools and maintains a list of training schools that meet the requirements. However, some Pilates teachers are certified group exercise instructors who attend short Pilates workshops; currently, many fitness centers hire people with minimal Pilates training if the applicants have a fitness certification and group fitness experience.

Training requirements for yoga teachers are similar to those for Pilates teachers. Training programs range from a few days to more than two years. Many people get their start by taking yoga; eventually, their teachers may consider them ready to assist or to substitute teach. Some students may begin teaching their own classes when their yoga teachers think they are ready; the teachers may even provide letters of recommendation. Those who wish to pursue teaching more seriously usually pursue formal teacher training.

Currently, there are many training programs through the yoga community as well as programs through the fitness industry. The Yoga Alliance has established training standards requiring at least 200 training hours, with a specified number of hours in areas including techniques, teaching methodology, anatomy, physiology, and philosophy. The Yoga Alliance also registers schools that train students to its standards. Because some schools may meet the standards but not be registered, prospective students should check the requirements and decide if particular schools meet them.

An increasing number of employers require fitness workers to have a bachelor's degree in a field related to health or fitness, such as exercise science or physical education. Some employers allow workers to substitute a college degree for certification, but most employers who require a bachelor's degree also require certification.

*Certification and other qualifications.* Most personal trainers must obtain certification in the fitness field to gain employment. Group fitness instructors do not necessarily need certification to begin working. The most important characteristic that an employer looks for in a new fitness instructor is the ability to plan and lead a class that is motivating and safe. However, most organizations encourage their group instructors to become certified over time, and many require it.

In the fitness field, there are many organizations—some of which are listed in the last section of this statement—that offer certification. Becoming certified by one of the top certification organizations is increasingly important, especially for personal trainers. One way to ensure that a certifying organization is reputable is to see that it is accredited by the National Commission for Certifying Agencies.

Most certifying organizations require candidates to have a high school diploma, be certified in cardiopulmonary resuscitation (CPR), and pass an exam. All certification exams have a written component, and some also have a practical component. The exams measure knowledge of human physiology, proper exercise techniques, assessment of client fitness levels, and development of

**Projections data from the National Employment Matrix**

| Occupational Title | SOC Code | Employment, 2006 | Projected employment, 2016 | Change, 2006-16 | |
|---|---|---|---|---|---|
| | | | | Number | Percent |
| Fitness trainers and aerobics instructors ............................................. | 39-9031 | 235,000 | 298,000 | 63,000 | 27 |

NOTE: Data in this table are rounded.

appropriate exercise programs. There is no particular training program required for certifications; candidates may prepare however they prefer. Certifying organizations do offer study materials, including books, CD-ROMs, other audio and visual materials, and exam preparation workshops and seminars, but exam candidates are not required to purchase materials to take exams.

Certification generally is good for two years, after which workers must become recertified by attending continuing education classes or conferences, writing articles, or giving presentations. Some organizations offer more advanced certification, requiring an associate or bachelor's degree in an exercise-related subject for individuals interested in training athletes, working with people who are injured or ill, or advising clients on general health.

Pilates and yoga instructors usually do not need group exercise certifications to maintain employment. It is more important that they have specialized training in their particular method of exercise. However, the Pilates Method Alliance does offer certification.

People planning fitness careers should be outgoing, excellent communicators, good at motivating people, and sensitive to the needs of others. Excellent health and physical fitness are important due to the physical nature of the job. Those who wish to be personal trainers in a large commercial fitness center should have strong sales skills. All personal trainers should have the personality and motivation to attract and retain clients.

*Advancement.* A bachelor's degree in exercise science, physical education, kinesiology (the study of muscles, especially the mechanics of human motion), or a related area, along with experience, usually is required to advance to management positions in a health club or fitness center. Some organizations require a master's degree. As in other occupations, managerial skills are also needed to advance to supervisory or managerial positions. College courses in management, business administration, accounting, and personnel management may be helpful, but many fitness companies have corporate universities in which they train employees for management positions.

Personal trainers may advance to head trainer, with responsibility for hiring and overseeing the personal training staff and for bringing in new personal training clients. Group fitness instructors may be promoted to group exercise director, responsible for hiring instructors and coordinating exercise classes. Later, a worker might become the fitness director, who manages the fitness budget and staff. Workers might also become the general manager, whose main focus is the financial aspects of an organization, particularly setting and achieving sales goals; in a small fitness center, however, the general manager is usually involved with all aspects of running the facility. Some workers go into business for themselves and open their own fitness centers.

## Employment

Fitness workers held about 235,000 jobs in 2006. Almost all personal trainers and group exercise instructors worked in physical fitness facilities, health clubs, and fitness centers, mainly in the amusement and recreation industry or in civic and social organizations. About 8 percent of fitness workers were self-employed; many of these were personal trainers, while others were group fitness instructors working on a contract basis with fitness centers. Many fitness jobs are part time, and many workers hold multiple jobs, teaching or doing personal training at several different fitness centers and at clients' homes.

## Job Outlook

Jobs for fitness workers are expected to increase much faster than the average for all occupations. Fitness workers should have good opportunities due to rapid job growth in health clubs, fitness facilities, and other settings where fitness workers are concentrated.

*Employment change.* Employment of fitness workers is expected to increase 27 percent over the 2006–2016 decade, much faster than the average for all occupations. These workers are expected to gain jobs because an increasing number of people are spending time and money on fitness, and more businesses are recognizing the benefits of health and fitness programs for their employees.

Aging baby boomers are concerned with staying healthy, physically fit, and independent. Moreover, the reduction of physical education programs in schools, combined with parents' growing concern about childhood obesity, has resulted in rapid increases in children's health club membership. Increasingly, parents are also hiring personal trainers for their children, and the number of weight-training gyms for children is expected to continue to grow. Health club membership among young adults also has grown steadily, driven by concern with physical fitness and by rising incomes.

As health clubs strive to provide more personalized service to keep their members motivated, they will continue to offer personal training and a wide variety of group exercise classes. Participation in yoga and Pilates is expected to continue to increase, driven partly by the aging population that demands low-impact forms of exercise and seeks relief from arthritis and other ailments.

*Job prospects.* Opportunities are expected to be good for fitness workers because of rapid job growth in health clubs, fitness facilities, and other settings where fitness workers are concentrated. In addition, many job openings will stem from the need to replace the large numbers of workers who leave these occupations each year. Part-time jobs will be easier to find than full-time jobs.

## Earnings

Median annual earnings of fitness trainers and aerobics instructors in May 2006 were $25,910. The middle 50 percent earned between $18,010 and $41,040. The bottom 10 percent earned less than $14,880, while the top 10 percent earned $56,750 or more. These figures do not include the earnings of the self-employed. Earnings of successful self-employed personal trainers can be much higher. Median annual earnings in the industries employing the largest numbers of fitness workers in 2006 were as follows:

General medical and surgical hospitals ...............$29,640

Local government ..............................................27,720

Fitness and recreational sports centers .................27,200

Other schools and instruction ...........................22,770

Civic and social organizations ...........................22,630

Because many fitness workers work part time, they often do not receive benefits such as health insurance or retirement plans from their employers. They are able to use fitness facilities at no cost, however.

## Related Occupations

Other occupations that focus on physical fitness include athletes, coaches, umpires, and related workers. Physical therapists also do related work when they create exercise plans to improve their patients' flexibility, strength, and endurance. Dietitians and nutritionists advise individuals on improving and maintaining their health, like fitness workers do. Also like fitness workers, many recreation workers lead groups in physical activities.

## Sources of Additional Information

For more information about fitness careers and universities and other institutions offering programs in health and fitness, contact

▸ IDEA Health and Fitness Association, 10455 Pacific Center Court, San Diego, CA 92121-4339.

▸ National Strength and Conditioning Association, 1885 Bob Johnson Drive, Colorado Springs, CO 80906. Internet: http://www.nsca-lift.org

For information about personal trainer and group fitness instructor certifications, contact

▸ American College of Sports Medicine, P.O. Box 1440, Indianapolis, IN 46206-1440. Internet: http://www.acsm.org

▸ American Council on Exercise, 4851 Paramount Dr., San Diego, CA 92123. Internet: http://www.acefitness.org

▸ National Academy of Sports Medicine, 26632 Agoura Rd., Calabasas, CA 91302. Internet: http://www.nasm.org

▸ NSCA Certification Commission, 3333 Landmark Circle, Lincoln, NE 68504. Internet: http://www.nsca-cc.org

For information about Pilates certification and training programs, contact

▸ Pilates Method Alliance, P.O. Box 370906, Miami, FL 33137-0906. Internet: http://www.pilatesmethodalliance.org

For information on yoga teacher training programs, contact

▸ Yoga Alliance, 7801 Old Branch Ave., Suite 400, Clinton, MD 20735. Internet: http://www.yogaalliance.org

To find accredited fitness certification programs, contact

▸ National Commission for Certifying Agencies, 2025 M St. NW, Suite 800, Washington, DC 20036. Internet: http://www.noca.org/ncca/accredorg.htm

For information about health clubs and sports clubs, contact

▸ International Health, Racquet, and Sportsclub Association, 263 Summer St., Boston, MA 02210. Internet: http://www.ihrsa.org

# Food and Beverage Serving and Related Workers

(O*NET 35-3011.00, 35-3021.00, 35-3022.00, 35-3031.00, 35-3041.00, 35-9011.00, 35-9021.00, 35-9031.00, and 35-9099.99)

## Significant Points

■ Most jobs are part time and have few educational requirements, attracting many young people to the occupation—more than one-fifth of these workers are 16 to 19 years old, about five times the proportion for all workers.

■ Job openings are expected to be abundant through 2016, which will create excellent opportunities for jobseekers.

■ Tips comprise a major portion of earnings, so keen competition is expected for jobs in fine dining and more popular restaurants where potential tips are greatest.

## Nature of the Work

Food and beverage serving and related workers are the front line of customer service in restaurants, coffee shops, and other food service establishments. These workers greet customers, escort them to seats and hand them menus, take food and drink orders, and serve food and beverages. They also answer questions, explain menu items and specials, and keep tables and dining areas clean and set for new diners. Most work as part of a team, helping coworkers to improve workflow and customer service.

*Waiters and waitresses*, the largest group of these workers, take customers' orders, serve food and beverages, prepare itemized checks, and sometimes accept payment. Their specific duties vary considerably, depending on the establishment. In coffee shops serving routine, straightforward fare, such as salads, soups, and sandwiches, servers are expected to provide fast, efficient, and courteous service. In fine dining restaurants, where more complicated meals are prepared and often served over several courses, waiters and waitresses provide more formal service emphasizing personal, attentive treatment and a more leisurely pace. They may recommend certain dishes and identify ingredients or explain how various items on the menu are prepared. Some prepare salads, desserts, or other menu items tableside. Additionally, servers may meet with managers and chefs, before each shift to discuss the menu and any new items or specials, review ingredients for any potential food allergies, or talk about any food safety concerns, coordination between the kitchen and the dining room, and any customer service issues from the previous day or shift. Servers usually also check the identification of patrons to ensure they meet the minimum age requirement for the purchase of alcohol and tobacco products wherever those items are sold.

Waiters and waitresses sometimes perform the duties of other food and beverage service workers. These tasks may include escorting guests to tables, serving customers seated at counters, clearing and setting up tables, or operating a cash register. However, full-service restaurants frequently hire other staff, such as hosts and hostesses, cashiers, or dining room attendants, to perform these duties.

*Bartenders* fill drink orders either taken directly from patrons at the bar or through waiters and waitresses who place drink orders for dining room customers. Bartenders check the identification of customers seated at the bar to ensure they meet the minimum age requirement for the purchase of alcohol and tobacco products. They prepare mixed drinks, serve bottled or draught beer, and pour wine or other beverages. Bartenders must know a wide range of drink recipes and be able to mix drinks accurately, quickly, and without waste. Besides mixing and serving drinks, bartenders stock and prepare garnishes for drinks; maintain an adequate supply of ice, glasses, and other bar supplies; and keep the bar area clean for customers. They also may collect payment, operate the cash register, wash glassware and utensils, and serve food to customers who dine at the bar. Bartenders usually are responsible for ordering and maintaining an inventory of liquor, mixes, and other bar supplies.

Most bartenders directly serve and interact with patrons. Bartenders should be friendly and at ease talking with customers. Bartenders at service bars, on the other hand, have less contact with customers. They work in small bars often located off the kitchen in restaurants, hotels, and clubs where only waiters and waitresses place drink orders. Some establishments, especially larger, higher volume ones, use equipment that automatically measures, pours, and mixes drinks at the push of a button. Bartenders who use this equipment, however, still must work quickly to handle a large volume of drink orders and be familiar with the ingredients for special drink requests. Much of a bartender's work still must be done by hand.

*Hosts and hostesses* welcome guests and maintain reservation or waiting lists. They may direct patrons to coatrooms, restrooms, or to a place to wait until their table is ready. Hosts and hostesses assign guests to tables suitable for the size of their group, escort patrons to their seats, and provide menus. They also schedule dining reservations, arrange parties, and organize any special services that are required. In some restaurants, they act as cashiers.

*Dining room and cafeteria attendants and bartender helpers* assist waiters, waitresses, and bartenders by cleaning tables, removing dirty dishes, and keeping serving areas stocked with supplies. Sometimes called backwaiters or runners, they bring meals out of the kitchen and assist waiters and waitresses by distributing dishes to individual diners. They also replenish the supply of clean linens, dishes, silverware, and glasses in the dining room and keep the bar stocked with glasses, liquor, ice, and drink garnishes. Dining room attendants set tables with clean tablecloths, napkins, silverware, glasses, and dishes and serve ice water, rolls, and butter. At the conclusion of meals, they remove dirty dishes and soiled linens from tables. *Cafeteria attendants* stock serving tables with food, trays, dishes, and silverware and may carry trays to dining tables for patrons. Bartender helpers keep bar equipment clean and glasses washed. *Dishwashers* clean dishes, cutlery, and kitchen utensils and equipment.

*Counter attendants* take orders and serve food in cafeterias, coffee shops, and carryout eateries. In cafeterias, they serve food displayed on steam tables, carve meat, dish out vegetables, ladle sauces and soups, and fill beverage glasses. In lunchrooms and coffee shops, counter attendants take orders from customers seated at the counter, transmit orders to the kitchen, and pick up and serve food. They also fill cups with coffee, soda, and other beverages and prepare fountain specialties, such as milkshakes and ice cream sundaes. Counter attendants also take carryout orders from diners and wrap or place items in containers. They clean counters, write itemized bills, and sometimes accept payment. Some counter attendants may prepare short-order items, such as sandwiches and salads.

Some food and beverage serving workers take orders from customers at counters or drive-through windows at fast-food restaurants. They assemble orders, hand them to customers, and accept payment. Many of these are *combined food preparation and serving workers* who also cook and package food, make coffee, and fill beverage cups using drink-dispensing machines.

Other workers serve food to patrons outside of a restaurant environment. They might deliver room service meals in hotels or meals to hospital rooms or act as carhops, bringing orders to parked cars.

*Work environment.* Food and beverage service workers are on their feet most of the time and often carry heavy trays of food, dishes, and glassware. During busy dining periods, they are under pressure to serve customers quickly and efficiently. The work is relatively safe, but care must be taken to avoid slips, falls, and burns.

Part-time work is more common among food and beverage serving and related workers than among workers in almost any other occupation. In 2006, those on part-time schedules included half of all waiters and waitresses and 39 percent of all bartenders.

Food service and drinking establishments typically maintain long dining hours and offer flexible and varied work opportunities. Many food and beverage serving and related workers work evenings, weekends, and holidays. Many students and teenagers seek part time or seasonal work as food and beverage serving and related workers as a first job to gain work experience or to earn spending money. More than one-fifth of all food and beverage serving and related workers were 16 to 19 years old—about five times the proportion for all workers.

## Training, Other Qualifications, and Advancement

Most food and beverage service jobs require little or no previous experience and provide training on the job.

*Education and training.* There are no specific educational requirements for most food and beverage service jobs. Many employers prefer to hire high school graduates for waiter and waitress, bartender, and host and hostess positions, but completion of high school usually is not required for fast-food workers, counter attendants, dishwashers, and dining room attendants and bartender helpers. For many people, a job as a food and beverage service worker serves as a source of immediate income, rather than a career. Many entrants to these jobs are in their late teens or early twenties and have a high school education or less. Usually, they have little or no work experience. Many are full-time students or homemakers. Food and bev-

**Projections data from the National Employment Matrix**

| Occupational Title | SOC Code | Employment, 2006 | Projected employment, 2016 | Change, 2006-16 | |
|---|---|---|---|---|---|
| | | | | Number | Percent |
| Food and beverage serving and related workers ............................... | — | 7,422,000 | 8,415,000 | 993,000 | 13 |
| Food and beverage serving workers............................................ | 35-3000 | 6,081,000 | 6,927,000 | 846,000 | 14 |
| Bartenders ................................................................... | 35-3011 | 495,000 | 551,000 | 56,000 | 11 |
| Fast food and counter workers................................................ | 35-3020 | 3,036,000 | 3,542,000 | 506,000 | 17 |
| Combined food preparation and serving workers, including fast food ................................................................. | 35-3021 | 2,503,000 | 2,955,000 | 452,000 | 18 |
| Counter attendants, cafeteria, food concession, and coffee shop ...................................................................... | 35-3022 | 533,000 | 587,000 | 54,000 | 10 |
| Waiters and waitresses ....................................................... | 35-3031 | 2,361,000 | 2,615,000 | 255,000 | 11 |
| Food servers, nonrestaurant ................................................. | 35-3041 | 189,000 | 219,000 | 30,000 | 16 |
| Other food preparation and serving related workers.................... | 35-9000 | 1,341,000 | 1,488,000 | 147,000 | 11 |
| Dining room and cafeteria attendants and bartender helpers .... | 35-9011 | 416,000 | 466,000 | 49,000 | 12 |
| Dishwashers ................................................................... | 35-9021 | 517,000 | 571,000 | 54,000 | 10 |
| Hosts and hostesses, restaurant, lounge, and coffee shop ........ | 35-9031 | 351,000 | 388,000 | 37,000 | 10 |
| Food preparation and serving related workers, all other........... | 35-9099 | 56,000 | 64,000 | 7,300 | 13 |

NOTE: Data in this table are rounded.

erage service jobs are a major source of part-time employment for high school and college students.

All new employees receive some training from their employer. They learn safe food handling procedures and sanitation practices, for example. Some employers, particularly those in fast-food restaurants, teach new workers using self-study programs, on-line programs, audiovisual presentations, and instructional booklets that explain food preparation and service skills. But most food and beverage serving and related workers pick up their skills by observing and working with more experienced workers. Some full-service restaurants also provide new dining room employees with some form of classroom training that alternates with periods of on-the-job work experience. These training programs communicate the operating philosophy of the restaurant, help establish a personal rapport with other staff, teach formal serving techniques, and instill a desire to work as a team. They also provide an opportunity to discuss customer service situations and the proper ways of handling unpleasant circumstances or unruly patrons.

Some food serving workers can acquire more skills by attending relevant classes offered by public or private vocational schools, restaurant associations, or large restaurant chains. Some bartenders also acquire their skills by attending a bartending or vocational and technical school. These programs often include instruction on state and local laws and regulations, cocktail recipes, proper attire and conduct, and stocking a bar. Some of these schools help their graduates find jobs. Although few employers require any minimum level of educational attainment, some specialized training is usually needed in food handling and legal issues surrounding serving alcoholic beverages. Employers are more likely to hire and promote based on people skills and personal qualities rather than education.

*Other qualifications.* Restaurants rely on good food and quality customer service to retain loyal customers and succeed in a competitive industry. Food and beverage serving and related workers who exhibit excellent personal qualities—such as a neat clean appearance, a well-spoken manner, an ability to work as a part of a team, and a pleasant way with patrons—will be highly sought after. All workers who serve alcoholic beverages must be at least 21 years of age in most jurisdictions and should be familiar with state and local laws concerning the sale of alcoholic beverages. For bartender jobs, many employers prefer to hire people who are 25 or older.

Waiters and waitresses need a good memory to avoid confusing customers' orders and to recall faces, names, and preferences of frequent patrons. These workers also should be comfortable using computers to place orders and generate customers' bills. Some may need to be quick at arithmetic so they can total bills manually. Knowledge of a foreign language is helpful to communicate with a diverse clientele and staff. Prior experience waiting on tables is preferred by restaurants and hotels that have rigid table service standards. Jobs at these establishments often offer higher wages and have greater income potential from tips, but they may also have stiffer employment requirements, such as prior table service experience or higher education than other establishments.

*Advancement.* Due to the relatively small size of most food-serving establishments, opportunities for promotion are limited. After gaining experience, some dining room and cafeteria attendants and bartender helpers advance to waiter, waitress, or bartender jobs. For waiters, waitresses, and bartenders, advancement usually is limited to finding a job in a busier or more expensive restaurant or bar where prospects for tip earnings are better. Some bartenders, hosts and hostesses, and waiters and waitresses advance to supervisory jobs, such as dining room supervisor, *maitre d'hotel*, assistant manager, or restaurant general manager. A few bartenders open their own businesses. In larger restaurant chains, food and beverage service workers who excel often are invited to enter the company's formal management training program.

## Employment

Food and beverage serving and related workers held 7.4 million jobs in 2006. The distribution of jobs among the various food and beverage serving occupations was as follows:

Combined food preparation and serving
   workers, including fast food ..........................2,503,000

Waiters and waitresses .....................................2,361,000

Counter attendants, cafeteria, food concession,
    and coffee shop ............................................533,000
Dishwashers ......................................................517,000
Bartenders ........................................................495,000
Dining room and cafeteria attendants and
    bartender helpers ........................................416,000
Hosts and hostesses, restaurant, lounge, and
    coffee shop ..................................................351,000
Food servers, non restaurant .............................189,000
All other food preparation and serving related
    workers .........................................................56,000

The overwhelming majority of jobs for food and beverage serving and related workers were found in food services and drinking places, such as restaurants, sandwich shops, and catering or contract food service operators. Other jobs were in hotels, motels, and other traveler accommodation establishments; amusement, gambling, and recreation establishments; educational services; grocery stores; nursing care facilities; civic and social organizations; and hospitals.

Jobs are located throughout the country but are typically plentiful in large cities and tourist areas. Vacation resorts offer seasonal employment, and some workers alternate between summer and winter resorts.

## Job Outlook

Average employment growth is expected, and job opportunities should be excellent for food and beverage serving and related workers, but job competition is often keen at upscale restaurants.

***Employment change.*** Overall employment of these workers is expected to increase by 13 percent over the 2006–2016 decade, which is about as fast as the average for all occupations. Food and beverage serving and related workers are projected to have one of the largest numbers of new jobs arise, about 993,000, over this period. The popularity of eating out is expected to increase as the population expands and as customers seek the convenience of restaurants and other dining options. Projected employment growth varies somewhat by job type. Employment of combined food preparation and serving workers, which includes fast-food workers, is expected to increase faster than the average in response to the continuing fast-paced lifestyle of many Americans and the addition of healthier foods at many fast-food restaurants. Average employment growth is expected for waiters and waitresses, hosts and hostesses, and bartenders. Restaurants that offer table service, more varied menus, and an active bar scene are growing in number in response to consumer demands for convenience and to increases in disposable income, especially among families who frequent casual family-oriented restaurants; affluent young professionals, who patronize trendier, more upscale establishments; and retirees and others who dine out as a way to socialize. Employment of dishwashers, dining room and cafeteria attendants, and bartender helpers also will grow about as fast as average.

***Job prospects.*** Job opportunities at most eating and drinking places will be excellent because many people in service sector occupations change jobs frequently and the number of food service outlets need-

ing food service workers will continue to grow. Many of these workers, such as teens, those seeking part-time employment, or multiple jobholders, do so to satisfy short-term income needs before moving on to jobs in other occupations or leaving the workforce. Keen competition is expected, however, for jobs in popular restaurants and fine dining establishments, where potential earnings from tips are greatest.

## Earnings

Food and beverage serving and related workers derive their earnings from a combination of hourly wages and customer tips. Earnings vary greatly, depending on the type of job and establishment. For example, fast-food workers and hosts and hostesses usually do not receive tips, so their wage rates may be higher than those of waiters and waitresses and bartenders in full-service restaurants but their overall earnings might be lower. In many full-service restaurants, tips are higher than wages. In some restaurants, workers contribute all or a portion of their tips to a tip pool, which is distributed among qualifying workers. Tip pools allow workers who don't usually receive tips directly from customers, such as dining room attendants, to feel a part of a team and to share in the rewards of good service.

In May 2006, median hourly wage-and-salary earnings (including tips) of waiters and waitresses were $7.14. The middle 50 percent earned between $6.42 and $9.14. The lowest 10 percent earned less than $5.78, and the highest 10 percent earned more than $12.46 an hour. For most waiters and waitresses, higher earnings are primarily the result of receiving more in tips rather than higher hourly wages. Tips usually average between 10 and 20 percent of guests' checks; waiters and waitresses working in busy, expensive restaurants earn the most.

Bartenders had median hourly wage-and-salary earnings (including tips) of $7.86. The middle 50 percent earned between $6.77 and $10.10. The lowest 10 percent earned less than $6.00, and the highest 10 percent earned more than $13.56 an hour. Like waiters and waitresses, bartenders employed in public bars may receive more than half of their earnings as tips. Service bartenders often are paid higher hourly wages to offset their lower tip earnings.

Median hourly wage-and-salary earnings (including tips) of dining room and cafeteria attendants and bartender helpers were $7.36. The middle 50 percent earned between $6.62 and $8.59. The lowest 10 percent earned less than $5.91, and the highest 10 percent earned more than $10.60 an hour. Most received over half of their earnings as wages; the rest of their income was a share of the proceeds from tip pools.

Median hourly wage-and-salary earnings of hosts and hostesses were $7.78. The middle 50 percent earned between $6.79 and $8.97. The lowest 10 percent earned less than $5.99, and the highest 10 percent earned more than $10.80 an hour. Wages comprised the majority of their earnings. In some cases, wages were supplemented by proceeds from tip pools.

Median hourly wage-and-salary earnings of combined food preparation and serving workers, including fast food, were $7.24. The middle 50 percent earned between $6.47 and $8.46. The lowest 10 percent earned less than $5.79, and the highest 10 percent earned more than $10.16 an hour. Although some combined food preparation and serving workers receive a part of their earnings as tips, fast-food workers usually do not.

Median hourly wage-and-salary earnings of counter attendants in cafeterias, food concessions, and coffee shops (including tips) were $7.76. The middle 50 percent earned between $6.85 and $9.00 an hour. The lowest 10 percent earned less than $6.11, and the highest 10 percent earned more than $10.86 an hour.

Median hourly wage-and-salary earnings of dishwashers were $7.57. The middle 50 percent earned between $6.78 and $8.62. The lowest 10 percent earned less than $6.01, and the highest 10 percent earned more than $10.00 an hour.

Median hourly wage-and-salary earnings of food servers outside of restaurants were $8.70. The middle 50 percent earned between $7.27 and $10.87. The lowest 10 percent earned less than $6.36, and the highest 10 percent earned more than $13.81 an hour.

Many beginning or inexperienced workers earn the federal minimum wage of $5.85 an hour. However, a few states set minimum wages higher than the federal minimum. Under federal law, this wage will increase to $6.55 in the summer of 2008 and to $7.25 in the summer of 2009. Also, various minimum wage exceptions apply under specific circumstances to disabled workers, full-time students, youth under age 20 in their first 90 days of employment, tipped employees, and student-learners. Tipped employees are those who customarily and regularly receive more than $30 a month in tips. The employer may consider tips as part of wages, but the employer must pay at least $2.13 an hour in direct wages.

Many employers provide free meals and furnish uniforms, but some may deduct from wages the cost, or fair value, of any meals or lodging provided. Food and beverage service workers who work full time often receive typical benefits, but part-time workers usually do not. In some large restaurants and hotels, food and beverage serving and related workers belong to unions—principally the Unite HERE and the Service Employees International Union.

## Related Occupations

Other workers who prepare food for diners include chefs, cooks, and food preparation workers. Those whose job involves serving customers and handling money include cashiers, flight attendants, gaming services workers, and retail salespersons.

## Sources of Additional Information

Information about job opportunities may be obtained from local employers and local offices of state employment services agencies.

A guide to careers in restaurants plus a list of two- and four-year colleges offering food service programs and related scholarship information is available from

▸ National Restaurant Association, 1200 17th St. NW, Washington, DC 20036. Internet: http://www.restaurant.org

For general information on hospitality careers, contact

▸ International Council on Hotel, Restaurant, and Institutional Education, 2810 North Parham Rd., Suite 230, Richmond, VA 23294. Internet: http://www.chrie.org

# Food Processing Occupations

(O*NET 51-3011.00, 51-3021.00, 51-3022.00, 51-3023.00, 51-3091.00, 51-3092.00, and 51-3093.00)

## Significant Points

■ Most workers in manual food processing jobs require little or no training prior to being hired.

■ As more jobs involving cutting and processing meat shift from retail stores to food processing plants, job growth will be concentrated among lesser skilled workers, who are employed primarily in manufacturing.

■ Highly skilled bakers should be in demand.

## Nature of the Work

Food processing occupations include many different types of workers who process raw food products into the finished goods sold by grocers, wholesalers, restaurants, or institutional food services. These workers perform a variety of tasks and are responsible for producing many of the food products found in every household. Some of these workers are bakers, others process meat, and still others operate food processing equipment.

*Bakers* mix and bake ingredients according to recipes to produce varying quantities of breads, pastries, and other baked goods. Bakers commonly are employed in grocery stores and specialty shops and produce small quantities of breads, pastries, and other baked goods for consumption on premises or for sale as specialty baked goods. While the quantities are often small, the varieties of bread usually are not. Specialty handcrafted—or artisan—bread, comes with seeds, nuts, fruits, olives, and cheese, which can be included in a crusty loaf, round loaf, flat or even focaccia bread. Bakers can also add a variety of flavors, too, such as rosemary, pecan, fig, garlic, red pepper, sesame, and anise.

In manufacturing, bakers produce goods in large quantities, using high-volume mixing machines, ovens, and other equipment. Goods produced in large quantities usually are available for sale through distributors, grocery stores, supermarkets, or manufacturers' outlets.

Other food processing workers convert animal carcasses into manageable pieces of meat, known as boxed meat or case-ready meat, suitable for sale to wholesalers and retailers. The nature of their jobs varies significantly depending on the stage of the process in which they are involved. Butchers and meat cutters, for example, work primarily in groceries and wholesale establishments that provide meat to restaurants and other retailers; whereas, meat, poultry, and fish cutters and trimmers commonly work in animal slaughtering and processing plants.

In animal slaughtering and processing plants, *slaughterers and meat packers* slaughter cattle, hogs, goats, and sheep, and cut the carcasses into large wholesale cuts, such as rounds, loins, ribs, tenders, and chucks, to facilitate the handling, distribution, marketing, and sale of meat. In most plants, some slaughterers and meat packers further process the large parts into cuts that are ready for retail stores. Retailers and grocers increasingly prefer such prepackaged meat products because a butcher isn't needed to display and sell them. Slaughterers and meat packers also produce hamburger meat and meat trimmings, preparing sausages, luncheon meats, and other fabricated meat products. They usually work on assembly lines, with each individual responsible for only a few of the many cuts needed to process a carcass. Depending on the type of cut, these workers use knives; cleavers; meat saws; band saws; or other potentially dangerous equipment.

*Poultry cutters and trimmers* slaughter and cut up chickens, turkeys, and other types of poultry. Although the poultry processing industry is becoming increasingly automated, many jobs, such as trimming, packing, and deboning, are still done manually. Most poultry cutters and trimmers perform routine cuts on poultry as it moves along production lines.

Meat, poultry, and fish cutters and trimmers also prepare ready-to-heat foods, usually at processing plants. This preparation often entails filleting meat, poultry, or fish; cutting it into bite-sized pieces or tenders; preparing and adding vegetables; and applying sauces and flavorings, marinades, or breading. These case-ready products are gaining in popularity as they offer quick and easy preparation for consumers while, in many cases, also offering a healthier option.

Manufacturing and retail establishments are likely to employ fish cutters and trimmers, also called *fish cleaners*. These workers primarily scale, cut, and dress fish by removing the head, scales, and other inedible portions and cutting the fish into steaks or fillets. In retail markets, these workers may also wait on customers and clean fish to order.

*Butchers and meat cutters* process meat at later stages of production. Those who work for large grocery stores, wholesale establishments that supply meat to restaurants, or institutional food service facilities separate wholesale cuts of meat into retail cuts or smaller pieces, known as primals. These butchers cut meat into steaks and chops, shape and tie roasts, and grind beef for sale as chopped meat. Boneless cuts are prepared using knives, slicers, or power cutters, while band saws and cleavers are required to cut bone-in pieces of meat. Butchers and meat cutters in retail food stores also may weigh, wrap, and label the cuts of meat; arrange them in refrigerated cases for display; and prepare special cuts to fill unique orders by customers.

Others in food processing occupations include *food batchmakers*, who set up and operate equipment that mixes, blends, or cooks ingredients used in the manufacture of food products according to formulas or recipes; *food cooking machine operators and tenders*, who operate or tend cooking equipment, such as steam-cooking vats, deep-fry cookers, pressure cookers, kettles, and boilers to prepare food products, such as meat, sugar, cheese, and grain; and *food and tobacco roasting, baking, and drying machine operators and tenders*, who use equipment to reduce the moisture content of food or tobacco products or to prepare food for canning. The machines they use include hearth ovens, kiln driers, roasters, char kilns, steam ovens, and vacuum drying equipment.

***Work environment.*** Working conditions vary by type and size of establishment. Most traditional bakers work in bakeries, cake shops, hot-bread shops, hotels, restaurants, cafeterias, and in the bakery departments of supermarkets. Bakers may work under hot and noisy conditions. They typically work under strict order deadlines and critical time-sensitive baking requirements, both of which can induce stress.

Although many bakers often work as part of a team, they also may work alone when baking particular items. These workers may supervise assistants and teach apprentices and trainees. Bakers in retail establishments may be required to serve customers. Bakers usually work odd hours in shifts and may work early mornings, evenings, weekends, and holidays.

In animal slaughtering and processing plants and in large retail food establishments, butchers and meat cutters work in large meat cutting rooms equipped with power machines and conveyors. In small retail markets, the butcher or fish cleaner may work in a cramped space behind the meat or fish counter. To prevent viral and bacterial infections, work areas are kept clean and sanitary.

Butchers and meat cutters, poultry and fish cutters and trimmers, and slaughterers and meatpackers often work in cold, damp rooms. Refrigerated work areas prevent meat from spoiling; they are damp because meat cutting generates large amounts of blood, condensation, and fat. Cool, damp floors increase the likelihood of slips and falls. In addition, cool temperatures, long periods of standing, and repetitious physical tasks make the work tiring. As a result, butchers as well as meat, poultry, and fish cutters and trimmers are more susceptible to injury than are most other workers.

Injuries include cuts and occasional amputations, which occur when knives, cleavers, or power tools are used improperly. Also, repetitive slicing and lifting often lead to cumulative trauma injuries, such as carpal tunnel syndrome. To reduce the incidence of cumulative trauma injuries, some employers have reduced employee workloads, added prescribed rest periods, redesigned jobs and tools, and promoted increased awareness of early warning signs as steps to prevent further injury. Nevertheless, workers in the occupation still face the serious threat of disabling injuries.

Workers who operate food processing machinery typically work in production areas that are specially designed for food preservation or processing. Food batchmakers, in particular, work in kitchen-type, assembly-line production facilities. Because this work involves food, work areas must meet governmental sanitary regulations. The ovens, as well as the motors of blenders, mixers, and other equipment, often make work areas very warm and noisy. There are some hazards, such as burns, created by the equipment that these workers use.

Food batchmakers; food and tobacco roasting, baking, and drying machine operators; and food cooking machine operators and tenders spend a great deal of time on their feet and generally work a regular 40-hour week that may include evening and night shifts.

## Training, Other Qualifications, and Advancement

Training varies widely among food processing occupations. However, most manual food processing workers require little or no training before being hired.

***Education and training.*** Bakers often start as apprentices or trainees. Apprentice bakers usually start in craft bakeries, while trainees usually begin in store bakeries, such as those in supermarkets. Bakers need to become skilled in baking, icing, and decorating. Knowledge of bakery products and ingredients, as well as mechanical mixing and baking equipment, is also important. Many apprentice bakers participate in correspondence study and may work towards a certificate in baking. Working as a baker's assistant or at other activities that involve handling food is also a useful way to train.

The skills needed to be a baker are often underestimated. Bakers need to know about ingredients and nutrition, government health and sanitation regulations, business concepts, applied chemistry—including how ingredients combine and how they are affected by heat, and production processes, including how to operate and maintain machinery. Computers often operate high-speed automated equipment typically found in modern food plants.

Most butchers as well as poultry and fish cutters and trimmers acquire their skills through on-the-job training programs. The length of training varies significantly. Simple cutting operations require a few days to learn, while more complicated tasks, such as eviscerating slaughtered animals, generally require several months of training. The training period for highly skilled butchers at the retail level may be one or two years.

Generally, trainees begin by doing less difficult jobs, such as making simple cuts or removing bones. Under the guidance of experienced workers, trainees learn the proper use and care of tools and equipment, while also learning how to prepare various cuts of meat. After demonstrating skill with various meat cutting tools, trainees learn to divide carcasses into wholesale cuts and wholesale cuts into retail and individual portions. Trainees also may learn to roll and tie roasts, prepare sausage, and cure meat. Those employed in retail food establishments often are taught operations, such as inventory control, meat buying, and recordkeeping. In addition, growing concern about food-borne pathogens in meats has led employers to offer numerous safety seminars and extensive training in food safety to employees.

On-the-job training is common among food machine operators and tenders. They learn to run the different types of equipment by watching and helping other workers. Training can last anywhere from a month to a year, depending on the complexity of the tasks and the number of products involved. A degree in an appropriate area—dairy processing for those working in dairy product operations, for example—is helpful for advancement to a lead worker or a supervisory role. Most food batchmakers participate in on-the-job training, usually from about a month to a year. Some food batchmakers learn their trade through an approved apprenticeship program.

*Other qualifications.* Bakers need to be able to follow instructions, have an eye for detail, and communicate well with others.

Meat, poultry, and fish cutters and trimmers need manual dexterity, good depth perception, color discrimination, and good hand-eye coordination. They also need physical strength to lift and move heavy pieces of meat. Butchers and fish cleaners who wait on customers should have a pleasant personality, a neat appearance, and the ability to communicate clearly. In some states, a health certificate is required for employment.

*Certification and advancement.* Bakers have the option of obtaining certification through the Retails Bakers of America. While not mandatory, obtaining certification assures the public and prospec-

tive employers that the baker has sufficient skills and knowledge to work at a retail baking establishment.

The Retail Bakers of America offer certification for four levels of competence with a focus on several broad areas, including baking sanitation, management, retail sales, and staff training. Those who wish to become certified must satisfy a combination of education and experience requirements prior to taking an examination. The education and experience requirements vary by the level of certification desired. For example, a certified journey baker requires no formal education but a minimum of one year of work experience. On the other hand, a certified master baker must have earned the certified baker designation, and must have completed 30 hours of sanitation coursework approved by a culinary school or government agency, 30 hours of professional development courses or workshops, and a minimum of eight years of commercial or retail baking experience.

Food processing workers in retail or wholesale establishments may progress to supervisory jobs, such as department managers or team leaders in supermarkets. A few of these workers may become buyers for wholesalers or supermarket chains. Some food processing workers go on to open their own markets or bakeries. In processing plants, workers may advance to supervisory positions or become team leaders.

## Employment

Food processing workers held 705,000 jobs in 2006. Employment among the various types of food processing occupations was distributed as follows:

| | |
|---|---|
| Bakers | 149,000 |
| Meat, poultry, and fish cutters and trimmers | 144,000 |
| Butchers and meat cutters | 131,000 |
| Slaughterers and meat packers | 122,000 |
| Food batchmakers | 95,000 |
| Food cooking machine operators and tenders | 44,000 |
| Food and tobacco roasting, baking, and drying machine operators and tenders | 19,000 |

Thirty-four percent of all food processing workers were employed in animal slaughtering and processing plants. Grocery stores employed another 24 percent. Most of the remainder worked in other food manufacturing industries. Butchers, meat cutters, and bakers are employed in almost every city and town in the nation, while most other food processing jobs are concentrated in communities with food processing plants.

## Job Outlook

Job opportunities should be available in all food processing specialties due to the need to replace experienced workers who transfer to other occupations or leave the labor force. Overall employment is expected to increase about as fast as average.

*Employment change.* Overall employment in the food processing occupations is projected to increase 8 percent during the 2006–2016 decade, about as fast as the average for all occupations. Increasingly, cheaper meat imports from abroad will have a negative effect on domestic employment in many food processing occupations. As more jobs involving cutting and processing meat shift from retail stores to food processing plants, job growth will be concentrated among lesser skilled workers, who are employed primarily in manufacturing.

As the nation's population grows, the demand for meat, poultry, and seafood should continue to increase. Successful marketing by the poultry industry is likely to increase demand for chicken and ready-to-heat products. Similarly, the development of prepared food products that are lower in fat and more nutritious promises to stimulate the consumption of red meat. The trend toward preparing case-ready meat at the processing level also should contribute to demand for animal slaughterers and meat packers, especially as those products become available at lower prices.

Lesser skilled meat, poultry, and fish cutters and trimmers—who work primarily in animal slaughtering and processing plants—should experience 11 percent growth, about as fast as the average for all occupations, and employment of slaughters and meat packers is expected to increase 13 percent, also about as fast as the average. With the growing popularity of labor-intensive, ready-to-heat poultry products, demand for poultry workers should rise steadily. Potentially offsetting growth will be increased automation and plant efficiency, although some technological breakthroughs may be years away. Fish cutters also will be in demand, as the task of preparing ready-to-heat fish goods gradually shifts from retail stores to processing plants. Advances in fish farming, or "aquaculture," should also help meet the growing demand for fish and produce job growth for fish cutters.

Employment of more highly skilled butchers and meat cutters, who work primarily in large supermarkets, is expected to grow 2 percent, which is considered little or no change in employment. The proliferation of case-ready meat products and automation in the animal slaughtering and processing industries are enabling employers to transfer employment from higher paid butchers to lower wage slaughterers and meat packers in meat packing plants. At present, most red meat arrives at grocery stores partially cut up, but a growing share of meat is being delivered prepackaged with additional fat removed to wholesalers and retailers. This trend is resulting in less work and, thus, fewer jobs for retail butchers.

While high-volume production equipment limits the demand for lesser skilled bakers in manufacturing, overall employment of bakers, particularly highly skilled bakers, should increase 10 percent, about as fast as the average for all occupations, due to growing numbers of bakers in stores, specialty shops, and traditional bakeries. In addition to the growing numbers of cookie, muffin, and cinnamon roll bakeries, the numbers of specialty bread and bagel shops have been growing, spurring demand for artisan bread and pastry bakers.

Employment of food batchmakers and food and tobacco cooking and roasting machine operators and tenders, are expected to grow 11 percent each, about as fast as the average for all occupations. However, as more of this work is being done at the manufacturing level rather than at the retail level, potential employment gains may be offset by productivity gains from automated blending and roasting equipment.

Employment of food cooking machine operators and tenders is expected to decline moderately, about 5 percent, as cooking equipment such as steam vats, deep fryers, kettles, and broilers is increasingly automated.

*Job prospects.* Jobs should be available in all food processing specialties because of the need to replace experienced workers who transfer to other occupations or leave the labor force. Highly skilled bakers should be especially in demand because of growing demand for specialty products and because of the time it takes to learn to make them.

# Earnings

Earnings vary by industry, skill, geographic region, and educational level. Median annual earnings of bakers were $22,030 in May 2006. The middle 50 percent earned between $17,720 and $28,190. The highest 10 percent earned more than $35,380, and the lowest 10 percent earned less than $15,180. Median annual earnings in the industries employing the largest numbers of bakers in May 2006 are given in the following tabulation:

| | |
|---|---|
| Bakeries and tortilla manufacturing | $22,580 |
| Grocery stores | 22,170 |
| Specialty food stores | 21,900 |
| Full-service restaurants | 20,770 |
| Limited-service eating places | 19,990 |

Median annual earnings of butchers and meat cutters were $26,930 in May 2006. The middle 50 percent earned between $20,630 and $35,240. The highest 10 percent earned more than $43,260 annually, while the lowest 10 percent earned less than $16,520. Butchers and meat cutters employed at the retail level typically earn more than those in manufacturing. Median annual earnings in the industries employing the largest numbers of butchers and meat cutters in May 2006 were

| | |
|---|---|
| Other general merchandise stores | $34,190 |
| Grocery stores | 27,830 |
| Grocery and related product wholesalers | 25,690 |
| Specialty food stores | 23,180 |
| Animal slaughtering and processing | 23,080 |

Meat, poultry, and fish cutters and trimmers typically earn less than butchers and meat cutters. In May 2006, median annual earnings for these lower skilled workers were $20,370. The middle 50 percent earned between $17,100 and $24,120. The highest 10 percent earned more than $29,070, while the lowest 10 percent earned less than $14,960. The following tabulation shows median annual earnings in the industries employing the largest numbers of meat, poultry, and fish cutters and trimmers in May 2006:

| | |
|---|---|
| Other general merchandise stores | $25,150 |
| Grocery stores | 20,680 |
| Animal slaughtering and processing | 20,530 |
| Specialty food stores | 19,990 |
| Seafood product preparation and packaging | 18,180 |

Median annual earnings of food batchmakers were $23,100 in May 2006. The middle 50 percent earned between $17,730 and $30,120. The highest 10 percent earned more than $37,930, and the lowest 10 percent earned less than $15,060. The following tabulation presents median annual earnings in the industries employing the largest numbers of food batchmakers in May 2006:

**Projections data from the National Employment Matrix**

| Occupational Title | SOC Code | Employment, 2006 | Projected employment, 2016 | Change, 2006-16 | |
|---|---|---|---|---|---|
| | | | | Number | Percent |
| Food processing occupations ........................................................ | 51-3000 | 705,000 | 764,000 | 59,000 | 8 |
| Bakers ........................................................................................ | 51-3011 | 149,000 | 164,000 | 15,000 | 10 |
| Butchers and other meat, poultry, and fish processing workers.... | 51-3020 | 398,000 | 431,000 | 34,000 | 8 |
| Butchers and meat cutters ................................................... | 51-3021 | 131,000 | 134,000 | 2,500 | 2 |
| Meat, poultry, and fish cutters and trimmers........................... | 51-3022 | 144,000 | 160,000 | 16,000 | 11 |
| Slaughterers and meat packers ............................................. | 51-3023 | 122,000 | 138,000 | 16,000 | 13 |
| Miscellaneous food processing workers .................................... | 51-3090 | 158,000 | 169,000 | 10,000 | 7 |
| Food and tobacco roasting, baking, and drying machine operators and tenders ...................................................... | 51-3091 | 19,000 | 21,000 | 2,000 | 11 |
| Food batchmakers ................................................................ | 51-3092 | 95,000 | 105,000 | 10,000 | 11 |
| Food cooking machine operators and tenders........................... | 51-3093 | 44,000 | 42,000 | -2,100 | -5 |

NOTE: Data in this table are rounded.

Dairy product manufacturing ............................$28,570
Fruit and vegetable preserving and specialty food manufacturing ...........................................25,100
Other food manufacturing....................................23,550
Sugar and confectionery product manufacturing......22,370
Bakeries and tortilla manufacturing ......................21,720

In May 2006, median annual earnings for slaughterers and meat packers were $21,690. The middle 50 percent earned between $18,290 and $25,440. The highest 10 percent earned more than $28,570, and the lowest 10 percent earned less than $15,950. Median annual earnings in animal slaughtering and processing, the industry employing the largest number of slaughterers and meat packers, were $21,730 in May 2006.

Median annual earnings for food cooking machine operators and tenders were $21,280 in May 2006. The middle 50 percent earned between $17,160 and $27,140. The highest 10 percent earned more than $34,350, and the lowest 10 percent earned less than $14,600. Median annual earnings in grocery stores, the industry employing the largest number of food cooking machine operators and tenders, were $19,400 in May 2006.

In May 2006, median annual earnings for food and tobacco roasting, baking, and drying machine operators and tenders were $23,510. The middle 50 percent earned between $18,820 and $31,540. The highest 10 percent earned more than $38,740, and the lowest 10 percent earned less than $15,910.

Food processing workers generally received typical benefits, including pension plans for union members or those employed by grocery stores. However, poultry workers rarely earned substantial benefits. In 2006, 21 percent of all food processing workers were union members or were covered by a union contract. Many food processing workers are members of the United Food and Commercial Workers International Union.

## Related Occupations

Food processing workers must be skilled at both hand and machine work and must have some knowledge of processes and techniques that are involved in handling and preparing food. Other occupations that require similar skills and knowledge include chefs, cooks, and food preparation workers.

## Sources of Additional Information

For information on various levels of certification as a baker, contact

▶ Retail Bakers of America, 8201 Greensboro Dr., Suite 300, McLean, VA, 22102

State employment service offices can provide information about job openings for food processing occupations.

# Gaming Services Occupations

(O*NET 11-9071.00, 39-1011.00, 39-1012.00, 39-3011.00, and 39-3012.00)

## Significant Points

■ Job opportunities are available nationwide and are no longer limited to Nevada and New Jersey.

■ Workers need a license issued by a regulatory agency, such as a state casino control board or commission.

■ Employment is projected to grow much faster than average.

■ Job prospects will be best for those with a degree or certification in gaming or a hospitality-related field, previous training or experience in casino gaming, and strong interpersonal and customer service skills.

## Nature of the Work

Legalized gambling in the United States today includes casino gaming, state lotteries, pari-mutuel wagering on contests such as horse or dog racing, and charitable gaming. Gaming, the playing of games of chance, is a multibillion-dollar industry that is responsible for the creation of a number of unique service occupations.

The majority of all gaming services workers are employed in casinos. Their duties and titles may vary from one establishment to another. Some positions are associated with oversight and direction—supervision, surveillance, and investigation—while others involve working with the games or patrons themselves by tending slot machines, dealing cards or running games, handling money, writing and running tickets, and other activities. In nearly any gaming job, workers interact directly with patrons, and part of their responsibility is to make those interactions enjoyable.

Like nearly every business establishment, casinos have workers who direct and oversee day-to-day operations. *Gaming supervisors* and *gaming managers* oversee the gaming operations and personnel in an assigned area. They circulate among the tables and observe the operations to ensure that all of the stations and games are covered for each shift and workers and gamblers adhere to the rules of the games. Gaming supervisors and gaming managers often explain and interpret the operating rules of the house to patrons who may have difficulty understanding the rules. They also may plan and organize activities to create a friendly atmosphere for the guests staying in casino hotels. Periodically, they address complaints about service.

Gaming managers also have additional responsibilities beyond those of supervisors. For example, gaming managers prepare work schedules and station assignments for their subordinates. They are responsible for interviewing, hiring, training, and evaluating new workers.

Managers supervise a variety of other workers. Some of these workers need specialized skills—dealing blackjack, for example—that are unique to casino work. Others require skills common to most business workers, such as the ability to conduct financial transactions.

*Slot key persons* coordinate and supervise the slot machine department and its workers. Their duties include verifying and handling payoff winnings to patrons, resetting slot machines after completing the payoff, and refilling machines with money. Slot key persons must be familiar with a variety of slot machines and be able to make minor repairs and adjustments to the machines as needed. If major repairs are required, slot key persons determine whether the slot machine should be removed from the floor. Working the floor as frontline personnel, they enforce safety rules and report hazards.

*Gaming and sportsbook writers and runners* assist in the operations of games such as bingo and keno, in addition to taking bets on sporting events. They scan tickets presented by patrons and calculate and distribute winnings. Some writers and runners operate the equipment that randomly selects the numbers. Others may announce numbers selected, pick up tickets from patrons, collect bets, or receive, verify, and record patrons' cash wagers.

*Gaming dealers* operate table games such as craps, blackjack, and roulette. Standing or sitting behind the table, dealers provide dice, dispense cards to players, or run the equipment. Some dealers also monitor the patrons for infractions of casino rules. Gaming dealers must be skilled in customer service and in executing their game. Dealers determine winners, calculate and pay winning bets, and collect losing bets. Because of the fast-paced work environment, most gaming dealers are competent in at least two games, usually blackjack and craps.

**Work environment.** Most casinos are open 24 hours a day, 7 days a week and offer 3 staggered shifts. Employees can be expected to work weekends and holidays. The atmosphere in casinos is generally filled with fun and often considered glamorous. However, casino work can also be physically demanding. Most occupations require that workers stand for long periods; some require the lifting of heavy items. The atmosphere in casinos exposes workers to certain hazards, such as cigarette, cigar, and pipe smoke. Noise from slot machines, gaming tables, and talking workers and patrons may be distracting to some, although workers wear protective headgear in areas where loud machinery is used to count money.

# Training, Other Qualifications, and Advancement

Each casino establishes its own education, training, and experience requirements, but all gaming service workers must obtain a license from a regulatory agency, such as a state casino control board or commission.

*Education and training.* There usually are no minimum educational requirements for entry-level gaming jobs, although most employers prefer workers with at least a high school diploma or GED.

Each casino establishes its own requirements for education, training, and experience. Some of the major casinos and slot manufacturers run their own training schools, and almost all provide some form of in-house training in addition to requiring certification. The type and quantity of classes needed may vary. Many institutions of higher learning give training toward certificates in gaming, as well as offering an associate, bachelor's, or master's degree in a hospitality-related field such as hospitality management, hospitality administration, or hotel management. Some schools offer training in games, gaming supervision, slot attendant and slot repair technician work, slot department management, and surveillance and security.

Slot key persons do not need to meet formal educational requirements to enter the occupation, but completion of slot attendant or slot technician training is helpful. As with most other gaming workers, slot key persons receive on-the-job training during the first several weeks of employment.

Gaming and sports book writers and runners must have at least a high school diploma or GED. Most of these workers receive on-the-job training. Because gaming and sportsbook writers and runners work closely with patrons, they need excellent customer service skills.

Most gaming dealers acquire their skills by attending a dealer school or vocational and technical school. They teach the rules and procedures of the games as well as state and local laws and regulations. Graduation from one of these schools does not guarantee a job at a casino, however, as most casinos also require prospective dealers to audition for open positions. During the audition, personal qualities are assessed along with knowledge of the games.

For most gaming supervisor and gaming manager positions, an associate or bachelor's degree is beneficial, but it is not required. Most employees in these occupations have experience in other gaming occupations, typically as dealers, and have a broad knowledge of casino rules, regulations, procedures, and games.

*Licensure.* Gaming services workers are required to be licensed by a regulatory agency, such as a state casino control board or commission. Applicants for a license must provide photo identification and pay a fee. Some states may require gaming service workers to be residents of that state. Age requirements vary by state. The licensing application process also includes a background investigation and drug test.

*Other qualifications.* In addition to possessing a license, gaming services workers need superior customer service skills. Casino gam-

**Projections data from the National Employment Matrix**

| Occupational Title | SOC Code | Employment, 2006 | Projected employment, 2016 | Change, 2006-16 | |
|---|---|---|---|---|---|
| | | | | Number | Percent |
| Gaming services occupations............................................................ | — | 174,000 | 214,000 | 40,000 | 23 |
| Gaming managers ........................................................... | 11-9071 | 4,000 | 5,000 | 1,000 | 24 |
| First-line supervisors/managers of gaming workers .................... | 39-1010 | 54,000 | 64,000 | 10,000 | 19 |
| Gaming supervisors ............................................... | 39-1011 | 34,000 | 42,000 | 7,900 | 23 |
| Slot key persons ..................................................... | 39-1012 | 20,000 | 22,000 | 2,200 | 11 |
| Gaming dealers ....................................................... | 39-3011 | 84,000 | 104,000 | 20,000 | 24 |
| Gaming and sports book writers and runners .......................... | 39-3012 | 18,000 | 24,000 | 5,200 | 28 |

NOTE: Data in this table are rounded.

ing workers provide entertainment and hospitality to patrons, and the quality of their service contributes to an establishment's success or failure. Therefore, gaming workers need good communication skills, an outgoing personality, and the ability to maintain their composure even when dealing with angry or demanding patrons. Personal integrity also is important because workers handle large amounts of money.

Gaming services workers who manage money should have some experience handling cash or using calculators or computers. For such positions, most casinos administer a math test to assess an applicant's level of competency.

Gaming supervisors and gaming managers must have strong leadership, organizational, and communication skills. Excellent customer service and employee relations skills also are necessary.

*Advancement.* Advancement opportunities in casino gaming depend less on workers' previous casino duties and titles than on their ability and eagerness to learn new jobs. For example, an entry-level gaming worker eventually might advance to become a dealer or card room manager or to assume some other supervisory position.

## Employment

Gaming services occupations provided 174,000 jobs in 2006. Employment among occupational specialties was distributed as follows:

| | |
|---|---|
| Gaming dealers ...................................................... | 84,000 |
| Gaming supervisors ............................................. | 34,000 |
| Slot key persons ................................................. | 20,000 |
| Gaming and sports book writers and runners .......... | 18,000 |
| Gaming managers ................................................ | 4,000 |

Gaming services workers are found mainly in the traveler accommodation and gaming industries. Most are employed in commercial casinos, including riverboat casinos, casino hotels, and pari-mutuel racetracks—known as "racinos"—that in 20 states offer casino games. The largest number work in casinos in Nevada. Mississippi, which boasts the greatest number of riverboat casinos in operation, employs the most workers in that venue. In addition, there are 28 states with Indian casinos. Legal lotteries are held in 41 states and the District of Columbia, and pari-mutuel wagering is legal in 43 states. Forty-seven states and the District of Columbia also allow charitable gaming. Other states are considering legislation to permit gambling, but no casinos have been opened as of yet.

For most workers, gaming licensure requires proof of residency in the state in which gaming workers are employed. But some gaming services workers do not limit themselves to one state or even one country, finding jobs on the small number of casinos located on luxury cruise liners that travel the world. These individuals live and work aboard the vessel.

## Job Outlook

Employment of gaming service workers is expected to grow much faster than the average for all occupations., Opportunities will be best for those with previous casino gaming experience, a degree or technical or vocational training in gaming or a hospitality-related field, and strong customer service skills.

*Employment change.* With demand for gaming showing no sign of waning, employment in gaming services occupations is projected to grow by 23 percent between 2006 and 2016, which is much faster than the average for all occupations. The increasing popularity and prevalence of Indian casinos and racinos will provide substantial new job openings. With many states benefiting from casino gambling in the form of tax revenue or agreements with Indian tribes, additional states are reconsidering their opposition to legalized gambling and will likely approve the construction of more casinos and other gaming establishments during the next decade. Additional job growth will occur in established gaming areas in Nevada and Atlantic City, New Jersey, as they solidify their positions as tourist destinations.

The increase in gaming reflects growth in the population and in its disposable income, both of which are expected to continue. Higher expectations for customer service among gaming patrons also should result in more jobs for gaming services workers. Because of increasing demand in gaming establishments for additional table games, particularly poker, the largest growth is expected among gaming dealers. Conversely, advancements in slot machine technology, such as coinless slot machines—known as "Ticket-in, Ticket-Out machines"—will limit job growth for slot key persons relative to other gaming service occupations. Ticket-in, Ticket-out technology reduces the need for slot key persons to payout jackpots, fill hoppers, and reset machines. Additionally, slot machines linked to a network allow adjustments to be made from a central computer server rather than from the floor by a slot key person. However, there will still be some new jobs for slot key persons because of the casino industry's focus on customer service and the rising popularity of racinos and slot machines in states that have recently legalized gambling or are expected to do so in the future.

*Job prospects.* Job prospects in gaming services occupations will be best for those with previous casino gaming experience, a degree or technical or vocational training in gaming or a hospitality-related field, and strong interpersonal and customer service skills.

In addition to job openings arising from employment growth, opportunities will result from the need to replace workers transferring to other occupations or leaving the labor force. Despite this, keen competition for jobs as gaming dealers is expected. There are generally more applicants than jobs. Experienced dealers who are able to attract new or return business will have the best job prospects.

## Earnings

Wage earnings for gaming services workers vary according to occupation, level of experience, training, location, and size of the gaming establishment. The following were median earnings for various gaming services occupations in May 2006:

| | |
|---|---|
| Gaming managers | $62,820 |
| Gaming supervisors | 41,160 |
| Slot key persons | 22,720 |
| Gaming and sports book writers and runners | 18,800 |
| Gaming dealers | 14,730 |

Gaming dealers generally receive a large portion of their earnings from tokes, which are tips in the form of tokens received from players. Earnings from tokes vary depending on the table games the dealer operates, the personal traits of the dealer, and the pooling policies of the casino.

## Related Occupations

Many other occupations provide hospitality and customer service. Some examples of related occupations are security guards and gaming surveillance officers, sales worker supervisors, cashiers, gaming change persons and booth cashiers, retail salespersons, gaming cage workers, and tellers.

## Sources of Additional Information

For additional information on careers in gaming, visit your public library and your state gaming regulatory agency or casino control commission.

Information on careers in gaming also is available from

▸ American Gaming Association, 1299 Pennsylvania Ave. NW, Suite 1175, Washington, DC 20004. Internet: http://www.americangaming.org

# Grounds Maintenance Workers

(O*NET 37-1012.00, 37-3011.00, 37-3012.00, 37-3013.00, and 37-3019.99)

## Significant Points

- Opportunities should be very good, especially for workers willing to work seasonal or variable schedules, because of significant job turnover and increased demand for landscaping.
- Many beginning jobs have low earnings and are physically demanding.
- Most workers learn through short-term on-the-job training.

## Nature of the Work

Attractively designed, healthy, and well-maintained lawns, gardens, and grounds create a positive impression, establish a peaceful mood, and increase property values. Grounds maintenance workers perform the variety of tasks necessary to achieve a pleasant and functional outdoor environment. They also care for indoor gardens and plantings in commercial and public facilities, such as malls, hotels, and botanical gardens.

These workers use hand tools such as shovels, rakes, pruning and handsaws, hedge and brush trimmers, and axes, as well as power lawnmowers, chain saws, snowblowers, and electric clippers. Some use equipment such as tractors and twin-axle vehicles. Landscaping and groundskeeping workers at parks, schools, cemeteries, and golf courses may lay sod after preparing the ground. Workers at sod farms use sod cutters to harvest sod that will be replanted elsewhere.

Grounds maintenance workers can be divided into landscaping workers and groundskeeping workers, depending on whether they mainly install new landscape elements or maintain existing ones, but their duties often overlap. Other grounds maintenance workers are pesticide handlers and tree trimmers.

*Landscaping workers* install plants and other elements into landscaped areas and often maintain them. They might mow, edge, trim, fertilize, dethatch, water, and mulch lawns and grounds many times during the growing season. They grade property by creating or smoothing hills and inclines, install lighting or sprinkler systems, and build walkways, terraces, patios, decks, and fountains. They also transport and plant new vegetation, and transplant, mulch, fertilize, and water existing plants, trees, and shrubs. A growing number of residential and commercial clients, such as managers of office buildings, shopping malls, multiunit residential buildings, and hotels and motels, favor full-service landscape maintenance.

*Groundskeeping workers*, also called *groundskeepers*, usually focus on maintaining existing grounds. They might work on athletic fields, golf courses, cemeteries, university campuses, and parks. In addition to caring for sod, plants, and trees, they rake and mulch leaves, clear snow from walkways and parking lots, and use irrigation methods to adjust the amount of water consumption and prevent waste. They see to the proper upkeep and repair of sidewalks, parking lots, groundskeeping equipment, pools, fountains, fences, planters, and benches.

Groundskeeping workers who care for athletic fields keep natural and artificial turf in top condition, mark out boundaries, and paint turf with team logos and names before events. They must make sure that the underlying soil on fields with natural turf has the required composition to allow proper drainage and to support the grasses used on the field. Groundskeeping workers mow, water, fertilize, and aerate the fields regularly. In sports venues, they vacuum and disinfect synthetic turf after its use to prevent the growth of harmful bacteria, and they remove the turf and replace the cushioning pad periodically.

Groundskeepers in parks and recreation facilities care for lawns, trees, and shrubs; maintain playgrounds; clean buildings; and keep parking lots, picnic areas, and other public spaces free of litter. They also may erect and dismantle snow fences, and maintain swimming pools. These workers inspect buildings and equipment, make needed repairs, and keep everything freshly painted.

Workers who maintain golf courses are called *greenskeepers*. Greenskeepers do many of the same things as other groundskeepers, but they also periodically relocate the holes on putting greens to prevent uneven wear of the turf and to add interest and challenge to the game. Greenskeepers also keep canopies, benches, ball washers, and tee markers repaired and freshly painted.

Some groundskeepers specialize in caring for cemeteries and memorial gardens. They dig graves to specified depths, generally using a backhoe. They mow grass regularly, apply fertilizers and other chemicals, prune shrubs and trees, plant flowers, and remove debris from graves.

*Pesticide handlers, sprayers, and applicators, vegetation* mix herbicides, fungicides, or insecticides and apply them through sprays, dusts, or vapors into the soil or onto plants. Those working for chemical lawn service firms are more specialized, inspecting lawns for problems and applying fertilizers, pesticides, and other chemicals to stimulate growth and prevent or control weeds, diseases, or insect infestation. Many practice integrated pest-management techniques.

*Tree trimmers and pruners* cut away dead or excess branches from trees or shrubs to clear roads, sidewalks, or utilities' equipment or to improve the appearance, health, and value of trees. Some of these workers also specialize in pruning, trimming and shaping ornamental trees and shrubs for private residences, golf courses, or other institutional grounds. Tree trimmers and pruners use handsaws, pole saws, shears, and clippers. When trimming near power lines, they usually work on truck-mounted lifts and use power pruners.

*Supervisors of landscaping and groundskeeping workers* oversee grounds maintenance work. They prepare cost estimates, schedule work for crews on the basis of weather conditions or the availability of equipment, perform spot checks to ensure the quality of the service, and suggest changes in work procedures. In addition, supervisors train workers in their tasks; keep employees' time records and record work performed; and even assist workers when deadlines are near. Supervisors who own their own business are also known as *landscape contractors*. They also often call themselves *landscape*

*designers* if they create landscape design plans. Landscape designers also design exterior floral displays by planting annual or perennial flowers. Some work with landscape architects. Supervisors of workers on golf courses are known as *superintendents*.

Supervisors of tree trimmers and pruners are called *arborists*. Arborists specialize in the care of individual trees, diagnosing and treating tree diseases and recommending preventative health measures. Some arborists plant trees. Most can recommend types of trees that are appropriate for a specific location, as the wrong tree in the wrong location could lead to future problems with crowding, insects, diseases, or poor growth.

Arborists are employed by cities to improve urban green space, utilities to maintain power distribution networks, companies to care for residential and commercial properties, as well as many other settings.

*Work environment.* Many grounds maintenance jobs are seasonal, available mainly in the spring, summer, and fall, when most planting, mowing, trimming, and cleanup are necessary. Most of the work is performed outdoors in all kinds of weather. It can be physically demanding and repetitive, involving much bending, lifting, and shoveling. Workers in landscaping and groundskeeping may be under pressure to get the job completed, especially when they are preparing for scheduled events such as athletic competitions.

Those who work with pesticides, fertilizers, and other chemicals, as well as dangerous equipment and tools such as power lawnmowers, chain saws, and power clippers, must exercise safety precautions. Workers who use motorized equipment must take care to protect their hearing.

## Training, Other Qualifications, and Advancement

Most grounds maintenance workers learn on-the-job. However, some occupations may require formal training in areas such as landscape design, horticulture, or business management.

*Education and training.* There usually are no minimum educational requirements for entry-level positions in grounds maintenance. In 2006, most workers had a high school education or less. Short-term on-the-job training generally is sufficient to teach new hires how to operate and repair equipment such as mowers, trimmers, leaf blowers, and small tractors and to follow correct safety procedures. They must also learn proper planting and maintenance procedures for their localities. Large institutional employers such as golf courses or municipalities may supplement on-the-job training with coursework in subjects like horticulture or small engine repair for those employees showing ability and willingness to learn.

Landscaping supervisors or contractors who own their own business, arborists, and landscape designers usually need formal training in landscape design, horticulture, arboriculture, or business. A bachelor's degree may be needed for those who want to become specialists or own their own business.

*Licensure.* Most states require licensure or certification for workers who apply pesticides. Requirements vary but usually include passing a test on the proper use and disposal of insecticides, herbicides, and fungicides. Some states require that landscape contractors be licensed.

*Other qualifications.* Employers look for responsible, self-motivated individuals because grounds maintenance workers often work with little supervision. Employers want people who can learn quickly and follow instructions accurately so that time is not wasted and plants are not damaged. Workers who deal directly with customers must get along well with people.

Driving a vehicle is often needed for these jobs. If driving is required, preference is given to applicants with a driver's license, a good driving record, and experience driving a truck.

*Certification and advancement.* The Professional Grounds Management Society offers voluntary certification to grounds managers who have a bachelor's degree in a relevant major with at least four years of experience, including two years as a supervisor; an associate degree in a relevant major with six years of experience, including three years as a supervisor; or eight years of experience including four years as a supervisor, and no degree. Additionally, candidates for certification must pass an examination covering subjects such as equipment management, personnel management, environmental issues, turf care, ornamentals, and circulatory systems. Certification as a grounds technician is also offered by this organization.

The Professional Landcare Network offers six certifications to those who seek to demonstrate specific knowledge in an area of landscaping and grounds maintenance. Obtaining certification may be an asset for career advancement. The Tree Care Industry Association offers four levels of credentials. Currently available credentials include Tree Care Apprentice, Ground Operations Specialist, Tree Climber Specialist, and Tree Care Specialist, as well as a certification program in safety.

Laborers who demonstrate a willingness to work hard and quickly, have good communication skills, and take an interest in the business may advance to crew leader or other supervisory positions. Becoming a grounds manager or landscape contractor usually requires some formal education beyond high school and several years of progressively more responsible experience. Some workers with groundskeeping backgrounds may start their own businesses after several years of experience.

## Employment

Grounds maintenance workers held about 1.5 million jobs in 2006. Employment was distributed as follows:

Landscaping and groundskeeping workers ..........1,220,000

First-line supervisors/managers of landscaping, lawn service, and groundskeeping workers..........202,000

Tree trimmers and pruners ..................................41,000

Pesticide handlers, sprayers, and applicators, vegetation ......................................................31,000

Grounds maintenance workers, all other ...............28,000

More than one-third of the workers in grounds maintenance were employed in companies providing landscaping services to buildings and dwellings. Others worked for amusement and recreation facilities, such as golf courses and racetracks; educational institutions, both public, and private; and property management and real-estate development firms. Some were employed by local governments, installing and maintaining landscaping for parks, hospitals, and other public facilities. Almost 24 percent of grounds maintenance workers were self-employed, providing landscape maintenance directly to customers on a contract basis.

About 14 percent of grounds maintenance workers worked part time; about 9 percent were younger than age twenty.

## Job Outlook

Those interested in grounds maintenance occupations should find very good job opportunities in the future. Employment of grounds maintenance workers is expected to grow faster than average for all occupations through the year 2016.

*Employment change.* Employment of grounds maintenance workers is expected to grow about 18 percent during the 2006–2016 decade. Grounds maintenance workers will have among the largest numbers of new jobs arise, around 270,000 over the 2006–2016 period.

More workers will be needed to keep up with increasing demand by lawn care and landscaping companies. Increased construction of office buildings, shopping malls, and residential housing and of highways and parks is expected to increase demand for grounds maintenance workers. In addition, the upkeep and renovation of existing landscaping and grounds are continuing sources of demand for grounds maintenance workers. Major institutions, such as universities and corporate headquarters, recognize the importance of good landscape design in attracting personnel and clients and are expected to use grounds maintenance services more extensively to maintain and upgrade their properties. Grounds maintenance workers working for state and local governments, however, may face budget cuts, which may affect hiring.

Homeowners are a growing source of demand for grounds maintenance workers. Many two-income households lack the time to take care of their lawns so they increasingly hire people to maintain them. Also, as the population ages, more elderly homeowners will require lawn care services to help maintain their yards. In addition, there is a growing interest by homeowners in their backyards and a desire to make yards more attractive for outdoor entertaining. With many newer homes having more and bigger windows overlooking the property, it is becoming more important to maintain and beautify the grounds.

Job opportunities for tree trimmers and pruners should also increase as utility companies step up pruning of trees around electric lines to prevent power outages. Additionally, tree trimmers and pruners will be needed to help combat infestations caused by new species of insects from other countries. For example, ash trees from Chicago to Washington, D.C. are under threat by a pest from China, and preventative eradication may be employed to control the pest.

*Job prospects.* Jobs for grounds maintenance workers are increasing, and because wages for beginners are low and the work is physically demanding, many employers have difficulty attracting enough workers to fill all openings, creating very good job opportunities.

Job opportunities for nonseasonal work are more numerous in regions with temperate climates, where landscaping and lawn services are required all year. Opportunities may vary with local economic conditions.

**Projections data from the National Employment Matrix**

| Occupational Title | SOC Code | Employment, 2006 | Projected employment, 2016 | Change, 2006-16 | |
|---|---|---|---|---|---|
| | | | | Number | Percent |
| Grounds maintenance workers and related first-line supervisors/ managers ................................................................ | — | 1,521,000 | 1,791,000 | 270,000 | 18 |
| First-line supervisors/managers of landscaping, lawn service, and groundskeeping workers .......................................... | 37-1012 | 202,000 | 237,000 | 36,000 | 18 |
| Grounds maintenance workers........................................... | 37-3000 | 1,319,000 | 1,554,000 | 235,000 | 18 |
| Landscaping and groundskeeping workers ........................... | 37-3011 | 1,220,000 | 1,441,000 | 221,000 | 18 |
| Pesticide handlers, sprayers, and applicators, vegetation ......... | 37-3012 | 31,000 | 35,000 | 4,300 | 14 |
| Tree trimmers and pruners .............................................. | 37-3013 | 41,000 | 45,000 | 4,500 | 11 |
| Grounds maintenance workers, all other.............................. | 37-3019 | 28,000 | 33,000 | 4,600 | 17 |

NOTE: Data in this table are rounded.

# Earnings

Median hourly earnings in May 2006 of grounds maintenance workers were as follows:

First-line supervisors/managers of landscaping,
lawn service, and groundskeeping workers ..........$17.93

Tree trimmers and pruners .....................................13.58

Pesticide handlers, sprayers, and applicators,
vegetation ..............................................................12.84

Landscaping and groundskeeping workers ................10.22

Grounds maintenance workers, all others ..................9.82

Median hourly earnings in the industries employing the largest numbers of landscaping and groundskeeping workers were as follows:

Local government ..............................................$11.64

Services to buildings and dwellings ......................10.17

Landscaping services ...........................................10.17

Other amusement and recreation industries................9.47

Employment services .............................................9.09

# Related Occupations

Grounds maintenance workers perform most of their work outdoors and have some knowledge of plants and soils. Others whose jobs may require that they work outdoors are agricultural workers; farmers, ranchers, and agricultural managers; forest, conservation, and logging workers; landscape architects; and biological scientists.

# Sources of Additional Information

For career and certification information on tree trimmers and pruners, contact

▶ Tree Care Industry Association, 3 Perimeter Rd., Unit I, Manchester, NH 03103-3341. Internet: http://www.treecareindustry.org

▶ International Society of Arboriculture, P.O. Box 3129, Champaign, IL 61826-3129. Internet: http://www.isa-arbor.com/ careersInArboriculture/careers.aspx

For information on work as a landscaping and groundskeeping worker, contact the following organizations:

▶ Professional Grounds Management Society, 720 Light St., Baltimore, MD 21230-3816. Internet: http://www.pgms.org

▶ Professional Landcare Network, 950 Herndon Parkway, Suite 450, Herndon, VA 20170-5528. Internet: http://www.landcarenetwork.org/

For information on becoming a licensed pesticide applicator, contact your state's Department of Agriculture or Department of Environmental Protection or Conservation.

# Health Educators

(O*NET 21-1091.00)

## Significant Points

■ 5 out of 10 health educators work in health care and social assistance and an additional 2 out of 10 work in state and local government.

■ A bachelor's degree is the minimum requirement for entry level jobs, but many employers prefer to hire workers with a master's degree.

■ Rapid job growth is expected, but the relatively small number of jobs in this occupation will limit the number of job openings.

## Nature of the Work

Health educators work to encourage healthy lifestyles and wellness through educating individuals and communities about behaviors that promote healthy living and prevent diseases and other health problems.

They attempt to prevent illnesses by informing and educating individuals and communities about health-related topics, such as proper nutrition, the importance of exercise, how to avoid sexually transmitted diseases, and the habits and behaviors necessary to avoid illness. They begin by assessing the needs of their audience, which includes determining which topics to cover and how to best present the information. For example, they may hold programs on self-examinations for breast cancer to women who are at higher risk or may teach classes on the effects of binge drinking to college students. Health educators must take the cultural norms of their audience into account. For example, programs targeted at the elderly need to be drastically different from those aimed at a college-aged population.

After assessing their audiences' needs, health educators must decide how to meet those needs. Health educators have a lot of options in putting together programs to that end. They may organize a lecture, class, demonstration or health screening, or create a video, pamphlet or brochure. Often, planning a program requires working with other people in a team or on a committee within the organization that employs them. Also, health educators must plan programs that are consistent with the goals and objectives of their employers. For example, many non-profit organizations educate the public about just one disease or health issue and, therefore, limit their programs to cover topics related to that disease or issue.

Next, health educators need to implement their proposed plan. This may require finding funding by applying for grants, writing curriculums for classes, or creating written materials that would be made available to the public. Also, programs may require dealing with basic logistics problems, such as finding speakers or locations for the event.

Generally, after a program is presented, health educators evaluate its success. This could include tracking the absentee rate of employees from work and students from school, surveying participants on their opinions about the program, or other methods of collecting evidence that suggests whether the programs were effective. Through evaluation, they can improve plans for the future by learning from mistakes and capitalizing on strengths.

Although programming is a large part of their job, health educators also serve as a resource on health topics. This may include locating services, reference material and other resources that may be useful to the community they serve and referring individuals or groups to organizations or medical professionals.

The basic goals and duties of health educators are the same but their jobs vary greatly depending on the type of organization in which they work. Most health educators work in medical care settings, colleges and universities, schools, public health departments, nonprofit organizations, and private business.

Within medical care facilities, health educators tend to work one-on-one with patients and their families. Their goal in this setting is to educate individual patients on their diagnosis and how that may change or affect their lifestyle. Often, this includes explaining the necessary procedures or surgeries as well as how patients will need to change their lifestyles in order to manage their illness or return to full health. This may include directing patients to outside resources that may be useful in their transition, such as support groups, home health agencies or social services. Often, health educators work closely with physicians, nurses, and other staff to create educational programs or materials, such as brochures, Web sites, and classes, for other departments. In some cases, health educators train hospital staff about how to better interact with patients.

Health educators in colleges and universities work primarily with the student population. Generally, they create programs on topics that affect young adults, like sexual activity, smoking, and nutrition. They may need to alter their teaching methods to attract audiences to their events. For example, they might show a popular movies followed by a discussion or hold programs in dormitories or cafeterias. They may teach courses for credit or give lectures on health-related topics. Often they train students as peer educators, who then lead their own programs.

Health educators in schools are typically found in secondary schools, where they generally teach health class. They develop lesson plans that are relevant and age appropriate to their students. They may need to cover sensitive topics, like sexually transmitted diseases, alcohol and drugs. They may be required to be able to also teach another subject such as science or physical education. Sometimes they may develop the health education curriculum for the school or the entire school district.

Heath educators in public health are employed primarily by state and local departments of public health and, therefore, administer state-mandated programs. They often serve as members of statewide councils or national committees on topics like aging. As part of this work, they inform other professionals in changes to health policy. They work closely with nonprofit organizations to help them get the resources they need, such as grants, to continue serving the community.

Health educators in nonprofits strive to get information out to the public on various health problems and make people aware of the resources their programs have to help people to the community. While some organizations target a particular audience, others educate the community regarding one disease or health issue. Therefore, in this setting, health educators may be limited in the topics they cover or the population they serve. Work in this setting may include creating print-based material for distribution to the community, often in conjunction with organizing lectures, health screenings, and activities related to increasing awareness.

In private industry, health educators create programs to inform the employees of an entire firm or organization. They organize programs that fit into workers' schedules by arranging lunchtime speakers or daylong health screenings so that workers may come when it is most convenient. Educators in this setting must align their work with the overall goals of their employers. For example, a health educator working for a medical supply company may hold a program related to the company's newest product.

***Work environment.*** Health educators work in various environments based on the industry in which they work. In public health, nonprofit organizations, business work sites, colleges and universities, and medical care settings, they primarily work in offices. However, they may spend a lot of time away from the office implementing and attending programs, meeting with community organizers, speaking with patients, or teaching classes. Health educators in schools spend the majority of their day in classrooms.

Health educators generally work 40 hour weeks. However, when programs, events, or meetings are scheduled they may need to work evening or weekends.

## Training, Other Qualifications, and Advancement

A bachelor's degree is generally required for entry level health educator positions, but some employers prefer a bachelor's degree and some related experience gained through an internship or volunteer work. A master's degree may be required for some positions and is usually required for advancement. In addition, some employers may require candidates to be Certified Health Education Specialists.

**Projections data from the National Employment Matrix**

| Occupational Title | SOC Code | Employment, 2006 | Projected employment, 2016 | Change, 2006-2016 | |
|---|---|---|---|---|---|
| | | | | Number | Percent |
| Health educators............................................................................ | 21-1091 | 62,000 | 78,000 | 16,000 | 26 |

NOTE: Data in this table are rounded.

*Education and training.* Entry level health educator positions generally require a bachelor's degree in health education. Over 250 colleges and universities offer bachelor's programs in health education or a similarly titled major. These programs teach students the theories of health education and develop the skills necessary to implement health education programs. Courses in psychology, human development, and a foreign language are helpful, and experience gained through an internship or other volunteer opportunities can make graduates more appealing to employers.

Graduate health education programs are often offered under titles such as community health education, school health education, or health promotion and lead to a Master of Arts, Master of Science, Master of Education, or a Master of Public Health degree. Many students pursue their master's in health education after majoring or working in another related field, such as nursing or psychology. A master's degree is required for most health educator positions in public health.

Once hired, on-the-job training for health educators varies greatly depending on the type and size of employer. State and local public health departments and other larger offices may have a formal training program, while smaller health education offices and departments may train new employees through less formal means, such as mentoring or working with more experienced staff. Some employers may require and pay for educators to take continuing education courses to keep their skills up-to-date.

*Other qualifications.* Health educators spend much of their time working with people and must be comfortable working with both individuals and large groups. They need to be good communicators and comfortable speaking in public as they may need to teach classes or give presentations. Health educators often work with a very diverse population so they must be sensitive to cultural differences and open to working with people of varied backgrounds. Health educators often create new programs or materials so they should be creative and skilled writers.

*Certification and advancement.* Health educators may choose to become a Certified Health Education Specialist, a credential offered by the National Commission of Health Education Credentialing, Inc. The certification is awarded after passing an examination on the basic areas of responsibility for a health educator. The exam is aimed at entry level educators who have already completed a degree in health education or are within three months of completion. In addition, to maintain certification, health educators must complete 75 hours of approved continuing education courses or seminars over a five-year period. Some employers prefer to hire applicants who are certified and some states require health educators certification to work in a public health department.

A graduate degree is usually required to advance past an entry level position to jobs such as executive director, supervisor, or senior health educator. These positions may spend more time on planning and evaluating programs than on their implementation, but may require supervising other health educators who implement the programs. Health educators at this level may also work with other administrators of related programs. Some health educators pursue a doctoral degree in health education and may transfer to research positions or become professors of health education.

## Employment

Health educators held about 62,000 jobs in 2006. They work primarily in two industries with 20 percent working in state and local government and 53 percent working in health care and social assistance. In addition, a small percent of health educators work in grant-making services and social advocacy organizations.

## Job Outlook

Employment of health educators is expected to grow much faster than the average for all occupations and job prospects are expected to be favorable.

*Employment change.* Employment of health educators is expected to grow by 26 percent, which is much faster than the average for all occupations. Growth will result from the rising cost of health care and the increased recognition of the need for qualified health educators.

The rising cost of healthcare has increased the need for health educators. As health care costs continue to rise, insurance companies, employers and governments are attempting to find ways to curb the cost. One of the more cost effective ways is to employ health educators to teach people how to live healthy lives and avoid costly treatments for illnesses. Awareness of the number of illnesses, such as lung cancer, HIV, heart disease and skin cancer, that may be avoided with lifestyle changes has increased. These diseases may be avoidable if the public better understands the effects of their behavior on their health. In addition, many illnesses, such as breast and testicular cancer are best treated with early detection so it is important for people to understand how to detect possible problems on their own. The need to provide the public with this information will result in state and local governments, hospitals, and businesses employing a growing number of health educators.

The emphasis on health education has been coupled with a growing demand for qualified health educators. In the past, it was thought that anyone could do the job of a health educator and the duties were often given to nurses or other healthcare professionals. However, in recent years, employers have recognized that those trained specifically in health education are better qualified to perform those duties. Therefore, demand for health professionals with a background specifically in health education has increased.

Demand for health educators will increase in most industries, but their employment may decrease in secondary schools. Many schools, facing budget cuts, ask teachers trained in other fields, like science or physical education, to teach the subject of health education.

*Job prospects.* Job prospects for health educators with bachelor's degrees will be favorable, but better for those who have acquired experience through internships or volunteer jobs. A graduate degree is preferred by many employers.

## Earnings

Median annual earnings of health educators was $41,330 in May 2006; the middle 50 percent earned between $31,300 and $56,580. The lowest 10 percent earned less than $24,750, and the highest 10 percent earned more than $72,500.

Median annual earnings in the industries employing the largest numbers of health educators in May 2006 were as follows:

General medical and surgical hospitals ...............$40,890

State government ............................................33,100

Local government ...........................................32,420

Outpatient care centers ...................................27,530

Individual and family services ..........................25,760

## Related Occupations

Health educators work closely with people to alter their behavior. Other professions with similar skills include counselors, social workers, psychologists, teachers, social and human service assistances, and nurses.

## Sources of Additional Information

For further information about health educators, contact

▸ American Association for Health Education, 1900 Association Drive, Reston, VA 20191. Internet: http://www.aahperd.org/aahe/

For information on voluntary credentialing and job opportunities, contact

▸ The National Commission for Health Education Credentialing, Inc., 1541 Alta Drive, Suite 303, Whitehall, PA 18052-5642. Internet: http://www.nchec.org

# Hotel, Motel, and Resort Desk Clerks

(O*NET 43-4081.00)

## Significant Points

■ Job opportunities should be good, because of industry growth and substantial replacement needs.

■ Evening, weekend, and part-time work hours create the potential for flexible schedules.

■ Professional appearance and personality are more important than formal academic training in getting a job.

## Nature of the Work

Hotel, motel, and resort desk clerks are always in the public eye and are usually the first line of customer service for a lodging property. Their attitude and behavior greatly influence the public's impressions of the establishment.

Front-desk clerks perform a variety of services for guests of hotels, motels, and other lodging establishments. Regardless of the type of accommodation, most desk clerks have similar responsibilities. They register arriving guests, assign rooms, and check out guests at the end of their stay. They also keep records of room assignments and other registration-related information on computers. When guests check out, desk clerks prepare and explain the charges and process payments.

Desk clerks answer questions about services, checkout times, the local community, or other matters of public interest. They report problems with guest rooms or public facilities to members of the housekeeping or maintenance staff. In larger hotels or in larger cities, desk clerks may refer queries about area attractions to a concierge and may direct more complicated questions to the appropriate manager.

In some smaller hotels and motels where smaller staffs are employed, clerks may take on a variety of additional responsibilities, such as bringing fresh linens to rooms, and they are often responsible for all front-office operations, information, and services. For example, they may perform the work of a bookkeeper, advance reservation agent, cashier, laundry attendant, and telephone switchboard operator.

*Work environment.* Hotels are open around the clock, creating the need for night and weekend work. About half of all desk clerks work a 40-hour week. Nearly one in five work part-time. Others work full-time, but with varying schedules. Most clerks work in areas that are clean, well lit, and relatively quiet, although lobbies can become crowded and noisy when busy. Many hotels have stringent dress guidelines for desk clerks.

Desk clerks may experience particularly hectic times during check-in and check-out times or when convention guests or large groups arrive at once. Moreover, dealing with irate guests can be stressful. Computer failures can further complicate an already busy time and add to stress levels. Hotel desk clerks may be on their feet most of the time and may occasionally be asked to lift heavy guest luggage.

## Training, Other Qualifications, and Advancement

Employers look for clerks who are friendly and customer-service oriented, well groomed, and display maturity, self confidence, and good judgment.

*Education and training.* Most hotel, motel, and resort desk clerks receive orientation and training on the job. Orientation may include an explanation of the job duties and information about the establishment, such as the arrangement of guest rooms, availability of additional services, such as a business or fitness center, and location of guest services, such as ice and vending machines, restaurants, and nearby retail stores and attractions. New employees learn job tasks under the guidance of a supervisor or an experienced desk clerk.

**Projections data from the National Employment Matrix**

| Occupational Title | SOC Code | Employment, 2006 | Projected employment, 2016 | Change, 2006-16 | |
|---|---|---|---|---|---|
| | | | | Number | Percent |
| Hotel, motel, and resort desk clerks ................................................. | 43-4081 | 219,000 | 257,000 | 38,000 | 17 |

NOTE: Data in this table are rounded.

They often receive additional training on interpersonal or customer service skills and on how to use the computerized reservation, room assignment, and billing systems and equipment. Desk clerks often learn new procedures and company policies after their initial training ends. While postsecondary education is not usually required for this job, formal training in a hospitality management degree or certificate program may be an advantage for getting positions in larger or more upscale properties.

*Other qualifications.* Desk clerks, especially in high-volume and higher-end properties, should be quick-thinking, energetic, and able to work as a member of a team. Hotel managers typically look for these personal characteristics when hiring desk clerks, because personality traits are difficult to teach. A clear speaking voice and fluency in English are essential when talking with guests and using the telephone or public-address systems. Good spelling and computer literacy are also needed because most of the work involves a computer. In addition, speaking a foreign language fluently is increasingly helpful because of the growing international clientele of many properties.

*Advancement.* Large hotel and motel chains may offer better opportunities for advancement than small, independently owned establishments. Large chains have more extensive career ladder programs and may offer desk clerks an opportunity to participate in management training programs. Also, the Educational Institute of the American Hotel and Lodging Association offers home-study or group-study courses in lodging management, which may help some desk clerks obtain promotions more rapidly.

# Employment

Hotel, motel, and resort desk clerks held about 219,000 jobs in 2006. Almost all were in hotels, motels, and other establishments in the accommodation industry.

# Job Outlook

Hotel, motel, and resort desk clerks will experience faster-than-average job growth through the 2006–2016 decade because additional hotel properties continue to be built and more people are expected to travel for business and leisure. Good job opportunities are expected.

*Employment change.* Employment of hotel, motel, and resort desk clerks is expected to grow 17 percent between 2006 and 2016, which is faster than the average for all occupations. As more lodging establishments open and as people and companies have more money and travel more, occupancy rates will increase and create demand for desk clerks.

Employment of hotel and motel desk clerks should benefit from steady or increasing business and leisure travel. Shifts in preferences away from long vacations and toward long weekends and other, more frequent, shorter trips also should boost demand for these

workers. While many lower budget and extended-stay establishments are being built to cater to families and the leisure traveler, many new luxury and resort accommodations also are opening to serve the upscale client. With the increased number of units requiring staff, employment opportunities for desk clerks should be good.

Growth of hotel, motel, and resort desk clerk jobs will be moderated somewhat by technology. Automated check-in and check-out procedures and on-line reservations networks free up staff time for other tasks and reduce the amount of time spent with each guest.

*Job prospects.* In addition to job growth, job opportunities for hotel and motel desk clerks are expected to be good because of the need to replace the many clerks who either transfer to other occupations that offer better pay and advancement opportunities or who leave the workforce altogether. Opportunities for those willing to work a variable schedule should continue to be plentiful.

Employment of desk clerks is sensitive to cyclical swings in the economy. During recessions, vacation and business travel declines, and hotels and motels need fewer desk clerks. Similarly, employment is affected by special events, convention business, and seasonal fluctuations.

# Earnings

Median annual earnings of hotel, motel and resort desk clerks were $18,460 in May 2006. The middle 50 percent earned between $15,930 and $22,220. The lowest 10 percent earned less than $13,690, and the highest 10 percent earned more than $27,030.

Earnings of hotel, motel, and resort desk clerks vary by worker characteristics, season, and geographic factors, such as whether the establishment is in a major metropolitan area or a resort community. Earnings also vary according to the size of the hotel and the level of service offered. For example, luxury hotels that offer guests more personal attention and a greater number of services typically have stricter and more demanding requirements for their desk staff and often provide higher earnings.

# Related Occupations

Lodging managers, particularly at smaller hotels and lodging establishments, may perform some of the same duties as desk clerks. Other occupations that require workers to assist the public include counter and rental clerks, customer service representatives, receptionists and information clerks, and retail salespersons.

# Sources of Additional Information

Information about the hotel and lodging industry and links to state lodging associations may be obtained from

▸ American Hotel & Lodging Association, 1201 New York Ave. NW, #600, Washington, DC 20005.

Information on careers in the lodging industry, as well as information about professional development and training programs, may be obtained from

▶ Educational Institute of the American Hotel and Lodging Association, 800 N. Magnolia Ave., Suite 1800, Orlando, FL 32803. Internet: http://www.ei-ahla.org

# Human Resources, Training, and Labor Relations Managers and Specialists

(O*NET 11-3040.00, 11-3041.00, 11-3042.00, 11-3049.99, 13-1071.00, 13-1071.01, 13-1071.02, 13-1072.00, 13-1073.00, and 13-1079.99)

## Significant Points

■ The educational backgrounds of these workers vary considerably, reflecting the diversity of duties and levels of responsibility.

■ Certification and previous experience are assets for most specialties and are essential for more advanced positions, including managers, arbitrators, and mediators.

■ College graduates who have earned certification should have the best job opportunities.

## Nature of the Work

Every organization wants to attract the most qualified employees and match them to jobs for which they are best suited. However, many enterprises are too large to permit close contact between top management and employees. Human resources, training, and labor relations managers and specialists provide this connection. In the past, these workers performed the administrative function of an organization, such as handling employee benefits questions or recruiting, interviewing, and hiring new staff in accordance with policies established by top management. Today's human resources workers manage these tasks, but, increasingly, they also consult with top executives regarding strategic planning. They have moved from behind-the-scenes staff work to leading the company in suggesting and changing policies.

In an effort to enhance morale and productivity, limit job turnover, and help organizations increase performance and improve business results, these workers also help their firms effectively use employee skills, provide training and development opportunities to improve those skills, and increase employees' satisfaction with their jobs and working conditions. Although some jobs in the human resources field require only limited contact with people outside the human resources office, dealing with people is an important part of the job.

There are many types of human resources, training, and labor relations managers and specialists. In a small organization, a *human resources generalist* may handle all aspects of human resources work and thus require an extensive range of knowledge. The respon-

sibilities of human resources generalists can vary widely, depending on their employer's needs.

In a large corporation, the *director of human resources* may supervise several departments, each headed by an experienced manager who most likely specializes in one human resources activity, such as employment and placement, compensation, and benefits, training and development, or labor relations. The director may report to a top human resources executive.

**Employment and placement.** *Employment and placement managers* supervise the hiring and separation of employees. They also supervise employment, recruitment, and placement specialists, including recruitment specialists and employment interviewers. *Employment, recruitment, and placement specialists* recruit and place workers.

*Recruiters* maintain contacts within the community and may travel considerably, often to college campuses, to search for promising job applicants. Recruiters screen, interview, and occasionally test applicants. They also may check references and extend job offers. These workers must be thoroughly familiar with the organization and its human resources policies in order to discuss wages, working conditions, and promotional opportunities with prospective employees. They also must stay informed about equal employment opportunity (EEO) and affirmative action guidelines and laws, such as the Americans with Disabilities Act.

*Employment interviewers*—whose many job titles include *human resources consultants, human resources development specialists,* and *human resources coordinators*—help to match employers with qualified jobseekers. Similarly, *employer relations representatives,* who usually work in government agencies, maintain working relationships with local employers and promote the use of public employment programs and services.

**Compensation, benefits, and job analysis.** Compensation, benefits, and job analysis specialists conduct compensation programs for employers and may specialize in specific areas, such as pensions or position classifications. For example, *job analysts,* occasionally called *position classifiers,* collect and examine detailed information about job duties in order to prepare job descriptions. These descriptions explain the duties, training, and skills that each job requires. Whenever a large organization introduces a new job or reviews existing jobs, it calls upon the expert knowledge of the job analyst.

*Occupational analysts* conduct research, usually in large firms. They are concerned with occupational classification systems and study the effects of industry and occupational trends on worker relationships. They may serve as technical liaison between the firm and other firms, government, and labor unions.

Establishing and maintaining a firm's pay system is the principal job of the *compensation manager.* Assisted by staff specialists, compensation managers devise ways to ensure fair and equitable pay rates. They may conduct surveys to see how their firm's rates compare with others, and they ensure that the firm's pay scale complies with changing laws and regulations. In addition, compensation managers often manage their firm's performance evaluation system, and they may design reward systems such as pay-for-performance plans.

*Employee benefits managers and specialists* manage the company's employee benefits program, notably its health insurance and pension plans. Expertise in designing and administering benefits programs continues to take on importance as employer-provided benefits account for a growing proportion of overall compensation costs and as benefit plans increase in number and complexity. For example, pension benefits might include a 401 (k) or thrift savings, profit-sharing, and stock ownership plans; health benefits might include long-term catastrophic illness insurance and dental insurance. Familiarity with health benefits is a top priority for employee benefits managers and specialists as more firms struggle to cope with the rising cost of health care for employees and retirees. In addition to health insurance and pension coverage, some firms offer employees life and accidental death and dismemberment insurance; disability insurance; and relatively new benefits designed to meet the needs of a changing workforce, such as parental leave, child and elder care, long-term nursing home care insurance, employee assistance and wellness programs, and flexible benefits plans. Benefits managers must keep abreast of changing federal and state regulations and legislation that may affect employee benefits.

*Employee assistance plan managers*, also called *employee welfare managers*, are responsible for a wide array of programs. These include occupational safety and health standards and practices; health promotion and physical fitness, medical examinations, and minor health treatment, such as first aid; plant security; publications; food service and recreation activities, carpooling and transportation programs, such as transit subsidies; employee suggestion systems; child care and elder care; and counseling services. Child care and elder care are increasingly significant because of growth in the number of dual-income households and the elderly population. Counseling may help employees deal with emotional disorders; alcoholism; or marital, family, consumer, legal, and financial problems. Some employers offer career counseling as well. In large firms, certain programs, such as those dealing with security and safety, may be in separate departments headed by other managers.

**Training and development.** *Training and development managers and specialists* conduct and supervise training and development programs for employees. Increasingly, management recognizes that training offers a way of developing skills, enhancing productivity and quality of work, building worker loyalty to the firm, and most importantly, increasing individual and organizational performance to achieve business results. Training is widely accepted as an employee benefit and a method of improving employee morale, and enhancing employee skills has become a business imperative. Increasingly, managers and leaders realize that the key to business growth and success is through developing the skills and knowledge of its workforce.

Other factors involved in determining whether training is needed include the complexity of the work environment, the rapid pace of organizational and technological change, and the growing number of jobs in fields that constantly generate new knowledge and thus require new skills. In addition, advances in learning theory have provided insights into how adults learn and how training can be organized most effectively for them.

*Training managers* provide worker training either in the classroom or on-site. This includes setting up teaching materials prior to the class, involving the class, and issuing completion certificates at the end of the class. They have the responsibility for the entire learning process, and its environment, to ensure that the course meets its objectives and is measured and evaluated to understand how learning impacts business results.

*Training specialists* plan, organize, and direct a wide range of training activities. Trainers respond to corporate and worker service requests. They consult with on-site supervisors regarding available performance improvement services and conduct orientation sessions and arrange on-the-job training for new employees. They help all employees maintain and improve their job skills and possibly prepare for jobs requiring greater skill. They help supervisors improve their interpersonal skills in order to deal effectively with employees. They may set up individualized training plans to strengthen an employee's existing skills or teach new ones. Training specialists in some companies set up leadership or executive development programs among employees in lower-level positions. These programs are designed to develop leaders, or "groom" them, to replace those leaving the organization and as part of a succession plan. Trainers also lead programs to assist employees with job transitions as a result of mergers and acquisitions, as well as technological changes. In government-supported training programs, training specialists function as case managers. They first assess the training needs of clients and then guide them through the most appropriate training method. After training, clients may either be referred to employer relations representatives or receive job placement assistance.

Planning and program development are essential parts of the training specialist's job. In order to identify and assess training needs within the firm, trainers may confer with managers and supervisors or conduct surveys. They also evaluate training effectiveness to ensure that the training employees receive helps the organization meet its strategic business goals and achieve results.

Depending on the size, goals, and nature of the organization, trainers may differ considerably in their responsibilities and in the methods they use. Training methods include on-the-job training; operating schools that duplicate shop conditions for trainees prior to putting them on the shop floor; apprenticeship training; classroom training; and electronic learning, which may involve interactive Internet-based training, multimedia programs, distance learning, satellite training, other computer-aided instructional technologies, videos, simulators, conferences, and workshops.

**Employee relations.** An organization's *director of industrial relations* forms labor policy, oversees industrial labor relations, negotiates collective bargaining agreements, and coordinates grievance procedures to handle complaints resulting from management disputes with unionized employees. The director of industrial relations also advises and collaborates with the director of human resources, other managers, and members of their staff because all aspects of human resources policy—such as wages, benefits, pensions, and work practices—may be involved in drawing up a new or revised union contract.

*Labor relations managers* and their staffs implement industrial labor relations programs. Labor relations specialists prepare information for management to use during collective bargaining agreement negotiations, a process that requires the specialist to be familiar with economic and wage data and to have extensive knowledge of labor law and collective bargaining trends. The labor relations staff interprets and administers the contract with respect to grievances, wages and salaries, employee welfare, health care, pensions, union and management practices, and other contractual stipulations. As union membership continues to decline in most industries, industrial relations personnel are working more often with employees who are not members of a labor union.

Dispute resolution—attaining tacit or contractual agreements—has become increasingly significant as parties to a dispute attempt to avoid costly litigation, strikes, or other disruptions. Dispute resolution also has become more complex, involving employees, management, unions, other firms, and government agencies. Specialists involved in dispute resolution must be highly knowledgeable and experienced, and they often report to the director of industrial relations. *Conciliators*, or *mediators*, advise and counsel labor and management to prevent and, when necessary, resolve disputes over labor agreements or other labor relations issues. *Arbitrators,* occasionally called umpires or referees, decide disputes that bind both labor and management to specific terms and conditions of labor contracts. Labor relations specialists who work for unions perform many of the same functions on behalf of the union and its members.

*EEO officers, representatives,* or *affirmative action coordinators* handle EEO matters in large organizations. They investigate and resolve EEO grievances, examine corporate practices for possible violations, and compile and submit EEO statistical reports.

Other emerging specialties in human resources include *international human resources managers*, who handle human resources issues related to a company's foreign operations, and *human resources information system specialists*, who develop and apply computer programs to process human resources information, match job seekers with job openings, and handle other human resources matters.

***Work environment.*** Human resources work usually takes place in clean, pleasant, and comfortable office settings. Arbitrators and mediators may work out of their homes.

Although most human resources, training, and labor relations managers and specialists work in the office, some travel extensively. For example, recruiters regularly attend professional meetings and visit college campuses to interview prospective employees; arbitrators and mediators often must travel to the site chosen for negotiations.

Many human resources, training, and labor relations managers and specialists work a standard 35- to 40-hour week. However, longer hours might be necessary for some workers—for example, labor relations managers and specialists, arbitrators, and mediators—when contract agreements are being prepared and negotiated.

# Training, Other Qualifications, and Advancement

The educational backgrounds of human resources, training, and labor relations managers and specialists vary considerably, reflecting the diversity of duties and levels of responsibility. In filling entry-level jobs, many employers seek college graduates who have majored in human resources, human resources administration, or industrial and labor relations. Other employers look for college graduates with a technical or business background or a well-rounded liberal arts education.

***Education and training.*** Many colleges and universities have programs leading to a degree in personnel, human resources, or labor relations. Some offer degree programs in human resources adminis-

tration or human resources management, training and development, or compensation and benefits. Depending on the school, courses leading to a career in human resources management may be found in departments of business administration, education, instructional technology, organizational development, human services, communication, or public administration or within a separate human resources institution or department.

Because an interdisciplinary background is appropriate in this field, a combination of courses in the social sciences, business, and behavioral sciences is useful. Some jobs may require a more technical or specialized background in engineering, science, finance, or law, for example. Most prospective human resources specialists should take courses in compensation, recruitment, training and development, and performance appraisal, as well as courses in principles of management, organizational structure, and industrial psychology. Other relevant courses include business administration, public administration, psychology, sociology, political science, economics, and statistics. Courses in labor law, collective bargaining, labor economics, labor history, and industrial psychology also provide a valuable background for the prospective labor relations specialist. As in many other fields, knowledge of computers and information systems also is useful.

An advanced degree is increasingly important for some jobs. Many labor relations jobs require graduate study in industrial or labor relations. A strong background in industrial relations and law is highly desirable for contract negotiators, mediators, and arbitrators; in fact, many people in these specialties are lawyers. A background in law also is desirable for employee benefits managers and others who must interpret the growing number of laws and regulations. A master's degree in human resources or labor relations or in business administration with a concentration in human resources management is highly recommended for those seeking general and top management positions.

The duties given to entry-level workers will vary, depending on whether the new workers have a degree in human resource management, have completed an internship, or have some other type of human resources–related experience. Entry-level employees commonly learn the profession by performing administrative duties—helping to enter data into computer systems, compiling employee handbooks, researching information for a supervisor, or answering the phone and handling routine questions. Entry-level workers often enter formal or on-the-job training programs in which they learn how to classify jobs, interview applicants, or administer employee benefits. They then are assigned to specific areas in the human resources department to gain experience. Later, they may advance to a managerial position, supervising a major element of the human resources program—compensation or training, for example.

***Other qualifications.*** Previous experience is an asset for many specialties in the human resources field and is essential for more advanced positions, including managers, arbitrators, and mediators. Many employers prefer entry-level workers who have gained some experience through an internship or work-study program while in school. Human resources administration and human resources development require the ability to work with individuals as well as a commitment to organizational goals. This field also demands other skills that people may develop elsewhere—using computers, selling, teaching, supervising, and volunteering, among others. The field offers clerical workers opportunities for advancement to professional positions. Responsible positions occasionally are filled by experienced individuals from other fields, including business, government, education, social services administration, and the military.

The human resources field demands a range of personal qualities and skills. Human resources, training, and labor relations managers and specialists must speak and write effectively. The growing diversity of the workforce requires that they work with or supervise people with various cultural backgrounds, levels of education, and experience. They must be able to cope with conflicting points of view; function under pressure; and demonstrate discretion, integrity, fair-mindedness, and a persuasive and congenial personality.

*Certification and advancement.* Most organizations specializing in human resources offer classes intended to enhance the skills of their members. Some organizations offer certification programs, which are signs of competence and credibility and can enhance one's advancement opportunities. For example, the International Foundation of Employee Benefit Plans confers a designation in three distinct areas of specialization—group benefit, retirement, and compensation—to persons who complete a series of college-level courses and pass exams. Candidates can earn a designation in each of the specialty tracks and, simultaneously, receive credit toward becoming a Certified Employee Benefits Specialist (CEBS). The American Society for Training and Development (ASTD) Certification Institute offers professional certification in the learning and performance field. Addressing nine areas of expertise, it requires passing a knowledge-based exam and successful work experience. In addition, ASTD offers 16 short-term certificate and workshop programs covering a broad range of professional training and development topics. The Society for Human Resource Management offers two levels of certification, including the Professional in Human Resources (PHR) and the Senior Professional in Human Resources (SPHR). Additionally, the organization offers the Global Professional in Human Resources for those with international and cross-border responsibilities and the California Certification in Human Resources for those who plan to work in the state and are unfamiliar with California's labor and human resource laws. All designations require experience and a passing score on a comprehensive exam. World at Work Society of Certified Professionals offers four levels of designations in the areas of compensation, benefits, work life, and total rewards management practices. Through the Society, candidates can obtain the designation of Certified Compensation Professional (CCP), Certified Benefits Professional (CBP), Global Remuneration Professional (GRP), and Work-Life Certified Professional (WLCP).

Exceptional human resources workers may be promoted to director of human resources or industrial relations, which can eventually lead to a top managerial or executive position. Others may join a consulting or outsourcing firm or open their own business. A Ph.D. is an asset for teaching, writing, or consulting work.

## Employment

Human resources, training, and labor relations managers and specialists held about 868,000 jobs in 2006. The following table shows the distribution of jobs by occupational specialty:

| | |
|---|---|
| Training and development specialists | 210,000 |
| Employment, recruitment, and placement specialists | 197,000 |
| Human resources managers | 136,000 |
| Compensation, benefits, and job analysis specialists | 110,000 |
| Human resources, training, and labor relations specialists, all other | 214,000 |

Human resources, training, and labor relations managers and specialists were employed in virtually every industry. About 17,000 managers and specialists were self-employed, working as consultants to public and private employers.

The private sector accounted for nearly 9 out of 10 jobs, including 13 percent in administrative and support services; 10 percent in professional, scientific, and technical services; 9 percent in health care and social assistance; 9 percent in finance and insurance firms; and 7 percent in manufacturing.

Government employed 13 percent of human resources managers and specialists. They handled recruitment, interviewing, job classification, training, salary administration, benefits, employee relations, and other matters related to the nation's public employees.

## Job Outlook

Employment of human resources, training, and labor relations managers and specialists is expected to grow faster than the average for all occupations. College graduates who have earned certification should have the best job opportunities.

*Employment change.* Overall employment is projected to grow by 17 percent between 2006 and 2016, faster than the average for all occupations. Legislation and court rulings setting standards in various areas—occupational safety and health, equal employment opportunity, wages, health care, pensions, and family leave, among others—will increase demand for human resources, training, and labor relations experts. Rising health care costs should continue to spur demand for specialists to develop creative compensation and benefits packages that firms can offer prospective employees.

Employment of labor relations staff, including arbitrators and mediators, should grow as firms become more involved in labor relations and attempt to resolve potentially costly labor-management disputes out of court. Additional job growth may stem from increasing demand for specialists in international human resources management and human resources information systems.

Job growth could be limited by the widespread use of computerized human resources information systems that make workers more productive. Like other workers, employment of human resources, training, and labor relations managers and specialists, particularly in larger firms, may be adversely affected by corporate downsizing, restructuring, and mergers and acquisitions.

Demand may be particularly strong for certain specialists. For example, employers are expected to devote greater resources to job-specific training programs in response to the increasing complexity of many jobs and technological advances that can leave employees with obsolete skills. Additionally, as highly trained and skilled baby boomers retire, there should be strong demand for training and

**Projections data from the National Employment Matrix**

| Occupational Title | SOC Code | Employment, 2006 | Projected employment, 2016 | Change, 2006-16 | |
|---|---|---|---|---|---|
| | | | | Number | Percent |
| Human resources, training, and labor relations managers and specialists ................................................................ | — | 868,000 | 1,015,000 | 147,000 | 17 |
| Compensation and benefits managers ......................................... | 11-3041 | 49,000 | 55,000 | 5,900 | 12 |
| Training and development managers .......................................... | 11-3042 | 29,000 | 33,000 | 4,500 | 16 |
| Human resources managers, all other ........................................ | 11-3049 | 58,000 | 65,000 | 6,600 | 11 |
| Employment, recruitment, and placement specialists.................. | 13-1071 | 197,000 | 233,000 | 36,000 | 18 |
| Compensation, benefits, and job analysis specialists................... | 13-1072 | 110,000 | 130,000 | 20,000 | 18 |
| Training and development specialists ........................................ | 13-1073 | 210,000 | 249,000 | 38,000 | 18 |
| Human resources, training, and labor relations specialists, all other ................................................................................. | 13-1079 | 214,000 | 250,000 | 35,000 | 16 |

NOTE: Data in this table are rounded.

development specialists to impart needed skills to their replacements. In addition, increasing efforts to recruit and retain quality employees should create many jobs for employment, recruitment, and placement specialists.

Among industries, firms involved in management, consulting, and employment services should offer many job opportunities as businesses increasingly contract out human resources functions or hire human resources specialists on a temporary basis in order to deal with the increasing cost and complexity of training and development programs. Demand for specialists also should increase in outsourcing firms that develop and administer complex employee benefits and compensation packages for other organizations.

*Job prospects.* College graduates who have earned certification should have the best job opportunities. Graduates with a bachelor's degree in human resources, human resources administration, or industrial and labor relations should be in demand; those with a technical or business background or a well-rounded liberal arts education also should find opportunities. Demand for human resources, training, and labor relations managers and specialists is governed by the staffing needs of the firms for which they work. A rapidly expanding business is likely to hire additional human resources workers—either as permanent employees or consultants—while a business that has experienced a merger or a reduction in its workforce will require fewer of these workers. Also, as human resources management becomes increasingly important to the success of an organization, some small and medium-size businesses that do not have a human resources department may assign employees various human resources duties together with other unrelated responsibilities.

In addition to human resources management and specialist jobs created over the 2006–2016 projection period, many job openings will arise from the need to replace workers who transfer to other occupations, retire, or leave the labor force for other reasons.

# Earnings

Annual salary rates for human resources workers vary according to occupation, level of experience, training, location, and firm size.

Median annual earnings of compensation and benefits managers were $74,750 in May 2006. The middle 50 percent earned between $55,370 and $99,690. The lowest 10 percent earned less than $42,750, and the highest 10 percent earned more than $132,820. In 2006, median annual earnings were $85,330 in the management of companies and enterprises industry.

Median annual earnings of training and development managers were $80,250 in May 2006. The middle 50 percent earned between $58,770 and $107,450. The lowest 10 percent earned less than $43,530, and the highest 10 percent earned more than $141,140.

Median annual earnings of human resources managers, all other were $88,510 in May 2006. The middle 50 percent earned between $67,710 and $114,860. The lowest 10 percent earned less than $51,810, and the highest 10 percent earned more than $145,600. In May 2006, median annual earnings were $98,400 in the management of companies and enterprises industry.

Median annual earnings of employment, recruitment, and placement specialists were $42,420 in May 2006. The middle 50 percent earned between $32,770 and $58,320. The lowest 10 percent earned less than $26,590, and the highest 10 percent earned more than $81,680. Median annual earnings in the industries employing the largest numbers of employment, recruitment, and placement specialists were

| | |
|---|---|
| Management, scientific, and technical consulting services ......................................................$53,060 | |
| Management of companies and enterprises ............48,360 | |
| Local government ...............................................40,660 | |
| Employment services ..........................................39,720 | |
| State government ...............................................36,320 | |

Median annual earnings of compensation, benefits, and job analysis specialists were $50,230 in May 2006. The middle 50 percent earned between $39,400 and $63,800. The lowest 10 percent earned less than $32,180, and the highest 10 percent earned more than $80,150. Median annual earnings in the industries employing the largest numbers of compensation, benefits, and job analysis specialists were

| | |
|---|---|
| Local government .............................................$53,440 | |
| Management of companies and enterprises ............52,960 | |
| Insurance carriers ..............................................50,510 | |
| Agencies, brokerages, and other insurance related activities..............................................49,100 | |
| State government ...............................................46,100 | |

Median annual earnings of training and development specialists were $47,830 in May 2006. The middle 50 percent earned between $35,980 and $63,200. The lowest 10 percent earned less than $27,450, and the highest 10 percent earned more than $80,630. Median annual earnings in the industries employing the largest numbers of training and development specialists were

Computer systems design and related services ......$60,430
Management of companies and enterprises ...........50,850
Insurance carriers ...............................................50,060
State government ...............................................49,040
Local government ...............................................47,990

The average salary for human resources managers employed by the federal government was $76,503 in 2007; for labor-management relations examiners, $94,927; and for manpower development specialists, $86,071. Salaries were slightly higher in areas where the prevailing local pay level was higher. There are no formal entry-level requirements for managerial positions. Applicants must possess a suitable combination of educational attainment, experience, and record of accomplishment.

According to a July 2007 salary survey conducted by the National Association of Colleges and Employers, bachelor's degree candidates majoring in human resources, including labor and industrial relations, received starting offers averaging $41,680 a year.

## Related Occupations

All human resources occupations are closely related. Other workers with skills and expertise in interpersonal relations include counselors, education administrators, public relations specialists, lawyers, psychologists, social and human service assistants, and social workers.

## Sources of Additional Information

For information about human resource management careers and certification, contact

▸ Society for Human Resource Management, 1800 Duke St., Alexandria, VA 22314. Internet: http://www.shrm.org

For information about careers in employee training and development and certification, contact

▸ American Society for Training and Development, 1640 King St., Box 1443, Alexandria, VA 22313-2043. Internet: http://www.astd.org

For information about careers and certification in employee compensation and benefits, contact

▸ International Foundation of Employee Benefit Plans, 18700 W. Bluemound Rd., P.O. Box 69, Brookfield, WI 53008-0069. Internet: http://www.ifebp.org

▸ World at Work, 14040 N. Northsight Blvd., Scottsdale, AZ 85260. Internet: http://www.worldatwork.org

# Instructional Coordinators

(O*NET 25-9031.00)

## Significant Points

■ Many instructional coordinators have experience as teachers or education administrators.

■ A master's degree is required for positions in public schools and preferred for jobs in other settings.

■ Employment is projected to grow much faster than average, reflecting the need to meet new educational standards, train teachers, and develop new materials.

■ Favorable job prospects are expected.

## Nature of the Work

Instructional coordinators—also known as curriculum specialists, personnel development specialists, instructional coaches, or directors of instructional material—play a large role in improving the quality of education in the classroom. They develop curricula, select textbooks and other materials, train teachers, and assess educational programs for quality and adherence to regulations and standards. They also assist in implementing new technology in the classroom.

At the primary and secondary school level, instructional coordinators often specialize in specific subjects, such as reading, language arts, mathematics, or science. At the postsecondary level, coordinators may work with employers to develop training programs that produce qualified workers.

Instructional coordinators evaluate how well a school or training program's curriculum, or plan of study, meets students' needs. Based on their research and observations of instructional practice, they recommend improvements. They research teaching methods and techniques and develop procedures to ensure that instructors are implementing the curriculum successfully and meeting program goals. To aid in their evaluation, they may meet with members of educational committees and advisory groups to learn about subjects—for example, English, history, or mathematics—and explore how curriculum materials meet students' needs and relate to occupations. Coordinators also may develop questionnaires and interview school staff about the curriculum.

Some instructional coordinators also review textbooks, software, and other educational materials and make recommendations on purchases. They monitor the ways in which teachers use materials in the classroom, and they supervise workers who catalogue, distribute, and maintain a school's educational materials and equipment.

Some instructional coordinators find ways to use technology to enhance student learning. They monitor the introduction of new technology, including the Internet, into a school's curriculum. In addition, instructional coordinators might recommend installing educational software, such as interactive books and exercises designed to enhance student literacy and develop math skills. Instructional coordinators may invite experts—such as computer hardware, software, and library or media specialists—to help integrate technological materials into the curriculum.

**Projections data from the National Employment Matrix**

| Occupational Title | SOC Code | Employment, 2006 | Projected employment, 2016 | Change, 2006-2016 | |
|---|---|---|---|---|---|
| | | | | Number | Percent |
| Instructional coordinators ............................................................ | 25-9031 | 129,000 | 159,000 | 29,000 | 22 |

NOTE: Data in this table are rounded.

In addition to developing curriculum and instructional materials, many instructional coordinators also plan and provide onsite education for teachers and administrators. Instructional coordinators mentor new teachers and train experienced ones in the latest instructional methods. This role becomes especially important when a school district introduces new content, program innovations, or a different organizational structure. For example, when a state or school district introduces standards or tests that students must pass, instructional coordinators often advise teachers on the content of these standards and provide instruction on how to implement them in the classroom.

*Work environment.* Many instructional coordinators work long hours. They often work year round. Some spend much of their time traveling between schools meeting with teachers and administrators. The opportunity to shape and improve instructional curricula and work in an academic environment can be satisfying. However, some instructional coordinators find the work stressful because they are continually accountable to school administrators.

## Training, Other Qualifications, and Advancement

The minimum educational requirement for most instructional coordinator positions in public schools is a master's or higher degree—usually in education—plus a state teacher or administrator license. A master's degree also is preferred for positions in other settings.

*Education and training.* Instructional coordinators should have training in curriculum development and instruction or in the specific field for which they are responsible, such as mathematics or history. Courses in research design teach how to create and implement research studies to determine the effectiveness of a given method of instruction or curriculum and how to measure and improve student performance.

Instructional coordinators usually are also required to take continuing education courses to keep their skills current. Topics may include teacher evaluation techniques, curriculum training, new teacher induction, consulting and teacher support, and observation and analysis of teaching.

*Licensure.* Instructional coordinators must be licensed to work in public schools. Some states require a teaching license, whereas others require an education administrator license.

*Other qualifications.* Instructional coordinators must have a good understanding of how to teach specific groups of students and expertise in developing educational materials. As a result, many people become instructional coordinators after working for several years as teachers. Also beneficial is work experience in an education administrator position, such as a principal or assistant principal, or in another advisory role, such as a master teacher.

Instructional coordinators must be able to make sound decisions about curriculum options and to organize and coordinate work efficiently. They should have strong interpersonal and communication skills. Familiarity with computer technology also is important for instructional coordinators, who are increasingly involved in gathering technical information for students and teachers.

*Advancement.* Depending on experience and educational attainment, instructional coordinators may advance to higher administrative positions in a school system or to management or executive positions in private industry.

## Employment

Instructional coordinators held about 129,000 jobs in 2006. Almost 40 percent worked in public or private elementary and secondary schools, while more than 20 percent worked in public or private junior colleges, colleges and universities, and professional schools. Other employing industries included state and local government; individual and family services; child day care services; scientific research and development services; and management, scientific, and technical consulting services.

## Job Outlook

Much faster-than-average job growth is projected. Job opportunities generally should be favorable, particularly for those with experience in math and reading curriculum development.

*Employment change.* The number of instructional coordinators is expected to grow by 22 percent over the 2006–2016 decade, much faster than the average for all occupations, as they will be instrumental in developing new curricula to meet the demands of a changing society and in training teachers. Although budget constraints may limit employment growth to some extent, a continuing emphasis on improving the quality of education should result in an increasing demand for these workers. The emphasis on accountability also should increase at all levels of government and cause more schools to focus on improving standards of educational quality and student performance. Growing numbers of coordinators will be needed to incorporate the new standards into existing curricula and make sure teachers and administrators are informed of changes.

Additional job growth for instructional coordinators will stem from the increasing emphasis on lifelong learning and on programs for students with special needs, including those for whom English is a second language. These students often require more educational resources and consolidated planning and management within the educational system.

*Job prospects.* Favorable job prospects are expected. Opportunities should be best for those who specialize in subjects targeted for improvement by the No Child Left Behind Act—namely, reading, math, and science. There also will be a need for more instructional coordinators to show teachers how to use technology in the classroom.

## Earnings

Median annual earnings of instructional coordinators in May 2006 were $52,790. The middle 50 percent earned between $38,800 and $70,320. The lowest 10 percent earned less than $29,040, and the highest 10 percent earned more than $87,510.

## Related Occupations

Instructional coordinators are professionals involved in education, training, and development. Occupations with similar characteristics include preschool, kindergarten, elementary, middle, and secondary school teachers; postsecondary teachers; education administrators; counselors; and human resources, training, and labor relations managers and specialists.

## Sources of Additional Information

Information on requirements and job opportunities for instructional coordinators is available from local school systems and state departments of education.

# Insurance Sales Agents

(O*NET 41-3021.00)

## Significant Points

■ In addition to offering insurance policies, agents increasingly sell mutual funds, annuities, and securities and offer comprehensive financial planning services, including retirement and estate planning.

■ Agents must obtain a license in the states where they sell.

■ Job opportunities should be good for college graduates who have sales ability, excellent interpersonal skills, and expertise in a wide range of insurance and financial services.

## Nature of the Work

Most people have their first contact with an insurance company through an insurance sales agent. These workers help individuals, families, and businesses select insurance policies that provide the best protection for their lives, health, and property.

Insurance sales agents, commonly referred to as "producers" in the insurance industry, sell one or more types of insurance, such as property and casualty, life, health, disability, and long-term care. Property and casualty insurance agents sell policies that protect individuals and businesses from financial loss resulting from automobile accidents, fire, theft, storms, and other events that can damage property. For businesses, property and casualty insurance can also cover injured workers' compensation, product liability claims, or medical malpractice claims.

Life insurance agents specialize in selling policies that pay beneficiaries when a policyholder dies. Depending on the policyholder's cir-

cumstances, a cash-value policy can be designed to provide retirement income, funds for the education of children, or other benefits as well. Life insurance agents also sell annuities that promise a retirement income. Health insurance agents sell health insurance policies that cover the costs of medical care and loss of income due to illness or injury. They also may sell dental insurance and short-term and long-term-disability insurance policies. Agents may specialize in any one of these product areas, or function as generalists, providing multiple products to a single customer.

An increasing number of insurance sales agents are offering comprehensive financial planning services to their clients. These services include retirement planning, estate planning, and assistance in setting up pension plans for businesses. As a result, many insurance agents are involved in "cross-selling" or "total account development". Besides offering insurance, these agents may become licensed to sell mutual funds, variable annuities, and other securities. This practice is most common with life insurance agents who already sell annuities, but many property and casualty agents also sell financial products.

Insurance sales agents also prepare reports, maintain records, and seek out new clients. In the event that policy holders experience a loss, agents help them settle their insurance claims. Increasingly, some agents are also offering their clients financial analysis or advice on how to minimize risk.

Insurance sales agents working exclusively for one insurance company are referred to as *captive agents*. Independent insurance agents, or *brokers*, represent several companies and match insurance policies for their clients with the company that offers the best rate and coverage.

Technology has greatly affected the insurance business, making it much more efficient and giving the agent the ability to take on more clients. Agents' computers are now linked directly to insurance carriers via the Internet, making the tasks of obtaining price quotes and processing applications and service requests faster and easier. Computers also allow agents to be better informed about new products that the insurance carriers may be offering.

The growing use of the Internet in the insurance industry has altered the relationship between agent and client. Agents formerly used to devote much of their time to marketing and selling products to new clients. Now, clients are increasingly obtaining insurance quotes from a company's Web site and then contacting the company directly to purchase policies. This interaction gives the client a more active role in selecting their policy, while reducing the amount of time agents spend actively seeking new clients. Insurance sales agents also obtain many new accounts through referrals, so it is important that they maintain regular contact with their clients to ensure that the clients' financial needs are being met. Developing a satisfied clientele that will recommend an agent's services to other potential customers is a key to success for agents.

Increasing competition in the insurance industry has spurred carriers and agents to find new ways to keep their clients satisfied. One solution is to increase the use of call centers, which usually are accessible to clients 24 hours a day, 7 days a week. Insurance carriers and sales agents also are hiring customer service representatives to handle routine tasks such as answering questions, making changes in policies, processing claims, and selling more products to clients.

The opportunity to cross-sell new products to clients will help agents' businesses grow. The use of call centers also allows agents to concentrate their efforts on seeking out new clients and maintaining relationships with old ones.

*Work environment.* Insurance sales agents working as captive agents are usually based in small offices, from which they contact clients and provide information on the policies they sell. Independent insurance agents, or brokers, may work in offices of varying sizes, depending on the size of the agency. However, much of their time may be spent outside their offices, traveling locally to meet with clients, close sales, or investigate claims. Agents usually determine their own hours of work and often schedule evening and weekend appointments for the convenience of clients. Some sales agents may meet with clients during business hours and then spend evenings doing paperwork and preparing presentations to prospective clients. Although most agents work a 40-hour week, some work 60 hours a week or longer.

## Training, Other Qualifications, and Advancement

Every sales agent involved in the solicitation, selling, or negotiation of insurance must have a state issued license. Licensure requirements vary by state but typically require some insurance-related coursework and the passing of several exams. Although some agents are hired right out of college, many are hired by insurance companies as customer service representatives and are later promoted to sales agent.

*Education and training.* For insurance sales agent jobs, many companies and independent agencies prefer to hire college graduates—especially those who have majored in business or economics. High school graduates may be hired if they have proven sales ability or have been successful in other types of work.

College training can help agents grasp the technical aspects of insurance policies as well as the industry fundamentals and operational procedures of selling insurance. Many colleges and universities offer courses in insurance, and a few schools offer a bachelor's degree in the field. College courses in finance, mathematics, accounting, economics, business law, marketing, and business administration enable insurance sales agents to understand how social and economic conditions relate to the insurance industry. Courses in psychology, sociology, and public speaking can prove useful in improving sales techniques. In addition, familiarity with computers and popular software packages has become very important because computers provide instantaneous information on a wide variety of financial products and greatly improve agents' efficiency.

Agents learn many of their job duties on the job from other agents. Many employers have their new agents shadow an experienced agent for a period of time. This allows the agent to learn how to conduct their business, how the agency interacts with clients, and how to write policies.

Employers also are placing greater emphasis on continuing professional education as the diversity of financial products sold by insurance agents increases. It is important for insurance agents to keep up to date on issues concerning clients. Changes in tax laws, government benefits programs, and other state and federal regulations can affect the insurance needs of clients and the way in which agents conduct business. Agents can enhance their selling skills and broaden their knowledge of insurance and other financial services by taking courses at colleges and universities and by attending institutes, conferences, and seminars sponsored by insurance organizations.

*Licensure.* Insurance sales agents must obtain a license in the states where they plan to work. Separate licenses are required for agents to sell life and health insurance and property and casualty insurance. In most states, licenses are issued only to applicants who complete specified prelicensing courses and who pass state examinations covering insurance fundamentals and state insurance laws. The insurance industry is increasingly moving toward uniform state licensing standards and reciprocal licensing, allowing agents who earn a license in one state to become licensed in other states more easily. Most state licensing authorities also have mandatory continuing education requirements focusing on insurance laws, consumer protection, ethics, and the technical details of various insurance policies.

As the demand for financial products and financial planning increases, many insurance agents, especially those involved in life insurance, are choosing to gain the proper licensing and certification to sell securities and other financial products. Doing so, however, requires substantial study and passing an additional examination—either the Series 6 or Series seven licensing exam, both of which are administered by the National Association of Securities Dealers (NASD). The Series 6 exam is for individuals who wish to sell only mutual funds and variable annuities, whereas the Series seven exam is the main NASD series license that qualifies agents as general securities sales representatives.

*Other qualifications.* Previous experience in sales or insurance jobs can be very useful in becoming an insurance sales agent. In fact, many entrants to insurance sales agent jobs transfer from other sales related occupations, such as customer service representative positions. In selling commercial insurance, technical experience in a particular field can help sell policies to those in the same profession. As a result, new agents tend to be older than entrants in many other occupations.

Insurance sales agents should be flexible, enthusiastic, confident, disciplined, hard working, and willing to solve problems. They should communicate effectively and inspire customer confidence. Because they usually work without supervision, sales agents must be able to plan their time well and have the initiative to locate new clients.

*Certification and advancement.* A number of organizations offer professional designation programs that certify agents' expertise in specialties such as life, health, and property and casualty insurance, as well as financial consulting. For example, The National Alliance for Education and Research offers a wide variety of courses in health, life and property, and casualty insurance for independent insurance agents. Although voluntary, such programs assure clients and employers that an agent has a thorough understanding of the relevant specialty. Agents are usually required to complete a specified number of hours of continuing education to retain their designation.

In the area of financial planning, many agents find it worthwhile to demonstrate competency by earning the certified financial planner

**Projections data from the National Employment Matrix**

| Occupational Title | SOC Code | Employment, 2006 | Projected employment, 2016 | Change, 2006-16 | |
|---|---|---|---|---|---|
| | | | | Number | Percent |
| Insurance sales agents ...................................................................... | 41-3021 | 436,000 | 492,000 | 56,000 | 13 |

NOTE: Data in this table are rounded.

or chartered financial consultant designation. The Certified Financial Planner credential, issued by the Certified Financial Planner Board of Standards, requires relevant experience, completion of education requirements, passing a comprehensive examination, and adherence to an enforceable code of ethics. The exam tests the candidate's knowledge of the financial planning process, insurance and risk management, employee benefits planning, taxes and retirement planning, and investment and estate planning.

The Chartered Financial Consultant (ChFC) and the Chartered Life Underwriter (CLU) designations, issued by the American College in Bryn Mawr, Pennsylvania, typically require professional experience and the completion of an eight-course program of study. Many property and casualty insurance agents obtain the Chartered Property Casualty Underwriter (CPCU) designation, offered by the American Institute for Chartered Property Casualty Underwriter. The majority of professional designations in insurance have continuing education requirements.

An insurance sales agent who shows ability and leadership may become a sales manager in a local office. A few advance to agency managerial or executive positions. However, many who have built up a good clientele prefer to remain in sales work. Some—particularly in the property and casualty field—establish their own independent agencies or brokerage firms.

## Employment

Insurance sales agents held about 436,000 jobs in 2006. Almost 50 percent of insurance sales agents work for insurance agencies and brokerages. About 23 percent work directly for insurance carriers. Although most insurance agents specialize in life and health insurance or property and casualty insurance, a growing number of "multiline" agents sell all lines of insurance. A small number of agents work for banks and securities brokerages as a result of the increasing integration of the finance and insurance industries. Approximately 26 percent of insurance sales agents are self employed.

Insurance sales agents are employed throughout the country, but most work in or near large urban centers. Some are employed in the headquarters of insurance companies, but the majority work out of local offices or independent agencies.

## Job Outlook

Employment of insurance sales agents is expected to grow about average for all occupations through 2016, and opportunities will be favorable for persons who are college graduates and who have sales ability, excellent interpersonal skills, and expertise in a wide range of insurance and financial services.

*Employment change.* Employment of insurance sales agents is expected to increase by 13 percent over the 2006–2016 period, which is about as fast as average for all occupations. Future demand for insurance sales agents depends largely on the volume of sales of insurance and other financial products. Sales of health insurance and long-term-care insurance are expected to rise sharply as the population ages. In addition, a growing population will increase demand for insurance for automobiles, homes, and high-priced valuables and equipment. As new businesses emerge and existing firms expand their insurance coverage, sales of commercial insurance also should increase, including coverage such as product liability, workers' compensation, employee benefits, and pollution liability insurance.

Employment of agents will not keep up with the rising level of insurance sales, however. Many insurance carriers are trying to contain costs and are shedding their captive agents—those agents working directly for insurance carriers. Instead carriers are relying more on independent agents or direct marketing through the mail, by phone, or on the Internet.

In many ways, the Internet should not greatly threaten agents' jobs as was widely thought. The automation of policy and claims processing is allowing insurance agents to take on more clients. Most clients value their relationship with their agent and still prefer discussing their policies directly with their agents, rather than through a computer.

Insurance and investments are becoming more complex, and many people and businesses lack the time and expertise to buy insurance without the advice of an agent.

*Job prospects.* Multilingual agents should have good job prospects because they can serve a wider range of customers. Additionally, insurance language tends to be quite technical, so agents who have a firm understanding of relevant technical and legal terms will also be desirable to employers. Many beginning agents fail to earn enough from commissions to meet their income goals and eventually transfer to other careers. Many job openings are likely to result from the need to replace agents who leave the occupation or retire, as a large number of agents are expected to retire over the next decade.

Agents may face increased competition from traditional securities brokers and bankers as they begin to sell insurance policies. Insurance sales agents will need to expand the products and services they offer as consolidation increases among insurance companies, banks, and brokerage firms and as demands increase from clients for more comprehensive financial planning.

Independent agents who incorporate new technology into their existing businesses will remain competitive. Agents who use the Internet to market their products will reach a broader client base and expand their business. Agents who offer better customer service also will remain competitive. Carriers and agencies are increasingly using call centers in an effort to offer better service to customers because they provide greater access to clients' policies and more prompt services.

Most individuals and businesses consider insurance a necessity, regardless of economic conditions, so agents are not likely to face unemployment because of a recession.

## Earnings

The median annual earnings of wage and salary insurance sales agents were $43,870 in May 2006. The middle 50 percent earned between $31,640 and $69,180. The lowest 10 percent had earnings of $24,600 or less, while the highest 10 percent earned more than $115,090. Median annual earnings in May 2006 in the two industries employing the largest number of insurance sales agents were $46,210 for insurance carriers, and $42,950 for agencies, brokerages, and other insurance related activities.

Many independent agents are paid by commission only, whereas sales workers who are employees of an agency or an insurance carrier may be paid in one of three ways: salary only, salary plus commission, or salary plus bonus. In general, commissions are the most common form of compensation, especially for experienced agents. The amount of the commission depends on the type and amount of insurance sold and on whether the transaction is a new policy or a renewal. Bonuses usually are awarded when agents meet their sales goals or when an agency meets its profit goals. Some agents involved with financial planning receive a fee for their services, rather than a commission.

Company-paid benefits to insurance sales agents usually include continuing education, training to qualify for licensing, group insurance plans, office space, and clerical support services. Some companies also may pay for automobile and transportation expenses, attendance at conventions and meetings, promotion and marketing expenses, and retirement plans. Independent agents working for insurance agencies receive fewer benefits, but their commissions may be higher to help them pay for marketing and other expenses.

## Related Occupations

Other workers who provide or sell financial products or services include real estate brokers and sales agents; securities, commodities, and financial services sales agents; financial analysts and personal financial advisors; and financial managers. Occupations with similar sales duties include sales representatives, wholesale and manufacturing; customer service representatives, and advertising sales agents. Other occupations in the insurance industry include insurance underwriters and claims adjusters, examiners, and investigators.

## Sources of Additional Information

Occupational information about insurance sales agents is available from the home office of many insurance companies. Information on state licensing requirements may be obtained from the department of insurance at any state capital.

For information about insurance sales careers and training, contact

▸ Independent Insurance Agents and Brokers of America, 127 S. Peyton St., Alexandria, VA 22314. Internet: http://www.iiaba.org

▸ Insurance Vocational Education Student Training (InVEST), 127 S. Peyton St., Alexandria, VA 22314. Internet: http://www.investprogram.org

▸ National Association of Professional Insurance Agents, 400 N. Washington Street, Alexandria, VA 22314. Internet: http://www.pianet.org

For information about health insurance sales careers, contact

▸ National Association of Health Underwriters, 2000 N. 14th Street, Suite 450, Arlington, VA 22201. Internet: http://www.nahu.org

For general information on the property and casualty field, contact

▸ Insurance Information Institute, 110 William St., New York, NY 10038. Internet: http://www.iii.org

For information about professional designation programs, contact

▸ The American Institute for Chartered Property and Casualty Underwriters/Insurance Institute of America, 720 Providence Rd., P.O. Box 3016, Malvern, PA 19355-0716. Internet: http://www.aicpcu.org

▸ The American College, 270 Bryn Mawr Ave., Bryn Mawr, PA 19010-2195. Internet: http://www.theamericancollege.edu

## Lawyers

(O*NET 23-1011.00)

## Significant Points

■ About 27 percent of lawyers are self-employed, either as partners in law firms or in solo practices.

■ Formal requirements to become a lawyer usually include a 4-year college degree, 3 years of law school, and passing a written bar examination; however, some requirements may vary by state.

■ Competition for admission to most law schools is intense.

■ Competition for job openings should be keen because of the large number of students graduating from law school each year.

## Nature of the Work

The legal system affects nearly every aspect of our society, from buying a home to crossing the street. Lawyers form the backbone of this system, linking it to society in numerous ways. They hold positions of great responsibility and are obligated to adhere to a strict code of ethics.

*Lawyers*, also called *attorneys*, act as both advocates and advisors in our society. As advocates, they represent one of the parties in criminal and civil trials by presenting evidence and arguing in court to support their client. As advisors, lawyers counsel their clients about their legal rights and obligations and suggest particular courses of action in business and personal matters. Whether acting as an advocate or an advisor, all attorneys research the intent of laws and judicial decisions and apply the law to the specific circumstances faced by their clients.

The more detailed aspects of a lawyer's job depend upon his or her field of specialization and position. Although all lawyers are licensed to represent parties in court, some appear in court more frequently than others. Trial lawyers, who specialize in trial work, must be able to think quickly and speak with ease and authority. In addition, familiarity with courtroom rules and strategy is particularly important in trial work. Still, trial lawyers spend the majority of their time outside the courtroom, conducting research, interviewing clients and witnesses, and handling other details in preparation for a trial.

Lawyers may specialize in a number of areas, such as bankruptcy, probate, international, elder, or environmental law. Those specializing in environmental law, for example, may represent interest groups, waste disposal companies, or construction firms in their dealings with the U.S. Environmental Protection Agency and other federal and state agencies. These lawyers help clients prepare and file for licenses and applications for approval before certain activities may occur. Some lawyers specialize in the growing field of intellectual property, helping to protect clients' claims to copyrights, artwork under contract, product designs, and computer programs. Other lawyers advise insurance companies about the legality of insurance transactions, guiding the company in writing insurance policies to conform to the law and to protect the companies from unwarranted claims. When claims are filed against insurance companies, these attorneys review the claims and represent the companies in court.

Most lawyers are in private practice, concentrating on criminal or civil law. In criminal law, lawyers represent individuals who have been charged with crimes and argue their cases in courts of law. Attorneys dealing with civil law assist clients with litigation, wills, trusts, contracts, mortgages, titles, and leases. Other lawyers handle only public-interest cases—civil or criminal—concentrating on particular causes and choosing cases that might have an impact on the way law is applied. Lawyers are sometimes employed full time by a single client. If the client is a corporation, the lawyer is known as "house counsel" and usually advises the company concerning legal issues related to its business activities. These issues might involve patents, government regulations, contracts with other companies, property interests, or collective bargaining agreements with unions.

A significant number of attorneys are employed at the various levels of government. Some work for state attorneys general, prosecutors, and public defenders in criminal courts. At the federal level, attorneys investigate cases for the U.S. Department of Justice and other agencies. Government lawyers also help develop programs, draft and interpret laws and legislation, establish enforcement procedures, and argue civil and criminal cases on behalf of the government.

Other lawyers work for legal aid societies—private, nonprofit organizations established to serve disadvantaged people. These lawyers generally handle civil, rather than criminal, cases.

Lawyers increasingly use various forms of technology to perform more efficiently. Although all lawyers continue to use law libraries to prepare cases, most supplement conventional printed sources with computer sources, such as the Internet and legal databases. Software is used to search this legal literature automatically and to identify legal texts relevant to a specific case. In litigation involving many supporting documents, lawyers may use computers to organize and index material. Lawyers must be geographically mobile and able to reach their clients in a timely matter, so they might use electronic filing, web and videoconferencing, and voice-recognition technology to share information more effectively.

*Work environment.* Lawyers do most of their work in offices, law libraries, and courtrooms. They sometimes meet in clients' homes or places of business and, when necessary, in hospitals or prisons. They may travel to attend meetings, gather evidence, and appear before courts, legislative bodies, and other authorities. They may also face particularly heavy pressure when a case is being tried. Preparation for court includes understanding the latest laws and judicial decisions.

Salaried lawyers usually have structured work schedules. Lawyers who are in private practice may work irregular hours while conducting research, conferring with clients, or preparing briefs during nonoffice hours. Lawyers often work long hours; of those who work full time, about 37 percent work 50 hours or more per week.

## Training, Other Qualifications, and Advancement

Formal requirements to become a lawyer usually include a four-year college degree, three years of law school, and passing a written bar examination; however, some requirements may vary by state. Competition for admission to most law schools is intense. Federal courts and agencies set their own qualifications for those practicing before or in them.

*Education and training.* Becoming a lawyer usually takes seven years of full-time study after high school—four years of undergraduate study, followed by three years of law school. Law school applicants must have a bachelor's degree to qualify for admission. To meet the needs of students who can attend only part time, a number of law schools have night or part-time divisions.

Although there is no recommended "prelaw" undergraduate major, prospective lawyers should develop proficiency in writing and speaking, reading, researching, analyzing, and thinking logically—skills needed to succeed both in law school and in the law. Regardless of major, a multidisciplinary background is recommended. Courses in English, foreign languages, public speaking, government, philosophy, history, economics, mathematics, and computer science, among others, are useful. Students interested in a particular aspect of law may find related courses helpful. For example, prospective patent lawyers need a strong background in engineering or science, and future tax lawyers must have extensive knowledge of accounting.

Acceptance by most law schools depends on the applicant's ability to demonstrate an aptitude for the study of law, usually through undergraduate grades, the Law School Admission Test (LSAT), the quality of the applicant's undergraduate school, any prior work experience, and sometimes, a personal interview. However, law schools vary in the weight they place on each of these and other factors.

All law schools approved by the American Bar Association require applicants to take the LSAT. As of 2006, there were 195 ABA-accredited law schools; others were approved by state authorities only. Nearly all law schools require applicants to have certified transcripts sent to the Law School Data Assembly Service, which then submits the applicants' LSAT scores and their standardized records of college grades to the law schools of their choice. The Law School Admission Council administers both this service and the LSAT. Competition for admission to many law schools—especially the most prestigious ones—is usually intense, with the number of applicants greatly exceeding the number that can be admitted.

During the first year or year and a half of law school, students usually study core courses, such as constitutional law, contracts, property law, torts, civil procedure, and legal writing. In the remaining time, they may choose specialized courses in fields such as tax, labor, or corporate law. Law students often gain practical experience by participating in school-sponsored legal clinics; in the school's moot court competitions, in which students conduct appellate arguments; in practice trials under the supervision of experienced lawyers and judges; and through research and writing on legal issues for the school's law journals.

A number of law schools have clinical programs in which students gain legal experience through practice trials and projects under the supervision of lawyers and law school faculty. Law school clinical programs might include work in legal aid offices, for example, or on legislative committees. Part-time or summer clerkships in law firms, government agencies, and corporate legal departments also provide valuable experience. Such training can lead directly to a job after graduation and can help students decide what kind of practice best suits them. Law school graduates receive the degree of *juris doctor* (J.D.), a first professional degree.

Advanced law degrees may be desirable for those planning to specialize, research, or teach. Some law students pursue joint degree programs, which usually require an additional semester or year of study. Joint degree programs are offered in a number of areas, including business administration or public administration.

After graduation, lawyers must keep informed about legal and nonlegal developments that affect their practices. In 2006, 43 states and jurisdictions required lawyers to participate in mandatory continuing legal education. Many law schools and state and local bar associations provide continuing education courses that help lawyers stay abreast of recent developments. Some states allow continuing education credits to be obtained through participation in seminars on the Internet.

*Licensure.* To practice law in the courts of any state or other jurisdiction, a person must be licensed, or admitted to its bar, under rules established by the jurisdiction's highest court. All states require that applicants for admission to the bar pass a written bar examination; most states also require applicants to pass a separate written ethics examination. Lawyers who have been admitted to the bar in one state occasionally may be admitted to the bar in another without taking another examination if they meet the latter jurisdiction's standards of good moral character and a specified period of legal experience. In most cases, however, lawyers must pass the bar examination in each state in which they plan to practice. Federal courts and agencies set their own qualifications for those practicing before or in them.

To qualify for the bar examination in most states, an applicant must earn a college degree and graduate from a law school accredited by the American Bar Association (ABA) or the proper state authorities. ABA accreditation signifies that the law school, particularly its library and faculty, meets certain standards. With certain exceptions, graduates of schools not approved by the ABA are restricted to taking the bar examination and practicing in the state or other jurisdiction in which the school is located; most of these schools are in California.

Although there is no nationwide bar examination, 48 states, the District of Columbia, Guam, the Northern Mariana Islands, Puerto Rico, and the Virgin Islands require the six-hour Multistate Bar Examination (MBE) as part of their overall bar examination; the MBE is not required in Louisiana or Washington. The MBE covers a broad range of issues, and sometimes a locally prepared state bar examination is given in addition to it. The three-hour Multistate Essay Examination (MEE) is used as part of the bar examination in several states. States vary in their use of MBE and MEE scores.

Many states also require Multistate Performance Testing to test the practical skills of beginning lawyers. Requirements vary by state, although the test usually is taken at the same time as the bar exam and is a one-time requirement.

In 2007, law school graduates in 52 jurisdictions were required to pass the Multistate Professional Responsibility Examination (MPRE), which tests their knowledge of the ABA codes on professional responsibility and judicial conduct. In some states, the MPRE may be taken during law school, usually after completing a course on legal ethics.

***Other qualifications.*** The practice of law involves a great deal of responsibility. Individuals planning careers in law should like to work with people and be able to win the respect and confidence of their clients, associates, and the public. Perseverance, creativity, and reasoning ability also are essential to lawyers, who often analyze complex cases and handle new and unique legal problems.

***Advancement.*** Most beginning lawyers start in salaried positions. Newly hired attorneys usually start as associates and work with more experienced lawyers or judges. After several years, some lawyers are admitted to partnership in their firm, which means they are partial owners of the firm, or go into practice for themselves. Some experienced lawyers are nominated or elected to judgeships. Others become full-time law school faculty or administrators; a growing number of these lawyers have advanced degrees in other fields as well.

Some attorneys use their legal training in administrative or managerial positions in various departments of large corporations. A transfer from a corporation's legal department to another department often is viewed as a way to gain administrative experience and rise in the ranks of management.

# Employment

Lawyers held about 761,000 jobs in 2006. Approximately 27 percent of lawyers were self-employed, practicing either as partners in law firms or in solo practices. Most salaried lawyers held positions in government, in law firms or other corporations, or in nonprofit organizations. Most government-employed lawyers worked at the local level. In the federal government, lawyers worked for many different agencies but were concentrated in the Departments of Justice, Treasury, and Defense. Many salaried lawyers working outside of government were employed as house counsel by public utilities, banks, insurance companies, real estate agencies, manufacturing firms, and other business firms and nonprofit organizations. Some also had part-time independent practices, while others worked part time as lawyers and full time in another occupation.

**Projections data from the National Employment Matrix**

| Occupational Title | SOC Code | Employment, 2006 | Projected employment, 2016 | Change, 2006-2016 | |
|---|---|---|---|---|---|
| | | | | Number | Percent |
| Lawyers............................................................................... | 23-1011 | 761,000 | 844,000 | 84,000 | 11 |

NOTE: Data in this table are rounded.

A relatively small number of trained attorneys work in law schools, and are not included in the employment estimate for lawyers. Most are faculty members who specialize in one or more subjects; however, some serve as administrators. Others work full time in nonacademic settings and teach part time.

## Job Outlook

Average employment growth is projected, but job competition is expected to be keen.

*Employment change.* Employment of lawyers is expected to grow 11 percent during the 2006–2016 decade, about as fast as the average for all occupations. The growth in the population and in the level of business activity is expected create more legal transactions, civil disputes, and criminal cases. Job growth among lawyers also will result from increasing demand for legal services in such areas as health care, intellectual property, venture capital, energy, elder, antitrust, and environmental law. In addition, the wider availability and affordability of legal clinics should result in increased use of legal services by middle-income people. However, growth in demand for lawyers will be constrained as businesses increasingly use large accounting firms and paralegals to perform some of the same functions that lawyers do. For example, accounting firms may provide employee-benefit counseling, process documents, or handle various other services previously performed by a law firm. Also, mediation and dispute resolution increasingly are being used as alternatives to litigation.

Job growth for lawyers will continue to be concentrated in salaried jobs, as businesses and all levels of government employ a growing number of staff attorneys. Most salaried positions are in urban areas where government agencies, law firms, and big corporations are concentrated. The number of self-employed lawyers is expected to grow slowly, reflecting the difficulty of establishing a profitable new practice in the face of competition from larger, established law firms. Moreover, the growing complexity of law, which encourages specialization, along with the cost of maintaining up-to-date legal research materials, favors larger firms.

*Job prospects.* Competition for job openings should continue to be keen because of the large number of students graduating from law school each year. Graduates with superior academic records from highly regarded law schools will have the best job opportunities. Perhaps as a result of competition for attorney positions, lawyers are increasingly finding work in less traditional areas for which legal training is an asset, but not normally a requirement—for example, administrative, managerial, and business positions in banks, insurance firms, real estate companies, government agencies, and other organizations. Employment opportunities are expected to continue to arise in these organizations at a growing rate.

As in the past, some graduates may have to accept positions outside of their field of interest or for which they feel overqualified. Some recent law school graduates who have been unable to find permanent positions are turning to the growing number of temporary staffing firms that place attorneys in short-term jobs. This service allows companies to hire lawyers on an "as-needed" basis and permits beginning lawyers to develop practical skills.

Because of the keen competition for jobs, a law graduate's geographic mobility and work experience assume greater importance. The willingness to relocate may be an advantage in getting a job, but to be licensed in another state, a lawyer may have to take an additional state bar examination. In addition, employers increasingly seek graduates who have advanced law degrees and experience in a specialty, such as tax, patent, or admiralty law.

Job opportunities often are adversely affected by cyclical swings in the economy. During recessions, demand declines for some discretionary legal services, such as planning estates, drafting wills, and handling real estate transactions. Also, corporations are less likely to litigate cases when declining sales and profits restrict their budgets. Some corporations and law firms will not hire new attorneys until business improves, and these establishments may even cut staff to contain costs. Several factors, however, mitigate the overall impact of recessions on lawyers; during recessions, for example, individuals and corporations face other legal problems, such as bankruptcies, foreclosures, and divorces requiring legal action.

For lawyers who wish to work independently, establishing a new practice will probably be easiest in small towns and expanding suburban areas. In such communities, competition from larger, established law firms is likely to be less than in big cities, and new lawyers may find it easier to establish a reputation among potential clients.

## Earnings

In May 2006, the median annual earnings of all wage-and-salaried lawyers were $102,470. The middle half of the occupation earned between $69,910 and $145,600. Median annual earnings in the industries employing the largest numbers of lawyers in May 2006 were

Management of companies and enterprises ........$128,610
Federal government ...........................................119,240
Legal services ..................................................108,100
Local government ...............................................78,810
State government ...............................................75,840

Salaries of experienced attorneys vary widely according to the type, size, and location of their employer. Lawyers who own their own practices usually earn less than those who are partners in law firms.

Lawyers starting their own practice may need to work part time in other occupations to supplement their income until their practice is well established.

Median salaries of lawyers 9 months after graduation from law school in 2005 varied by type of work, as indicated in table 1.

Table 1. Median salaries of lawyers 9 months after graduation, 2005

| Table 1. Median salaries of lawyers 9 months after graduation, 2005 | |
| --- | --- |
| All graduates ................................................. | $60,000 |
| Type of work | |
| Private practice................................... | $85,000 |
| Business ............................................... | 60,000 |
| Government.......................................... | 46,158 |
| Academic/judicial clerkships .............. | 45,000 |
| Source: National Association of Law Placement | |

Most salaried lawyers are provided health and life insurance, and contributions are made to retirement plans on their behalf. Lawyers who practice independently are covered only if they arrange and pay for such benefits themselves.

## Related Occupations

Legal training is necessary in many other occupations, including paralegals and legal assistants; law clerks; title examiners, abstractors, and searchers; and judges, magistrates, and other judicial workers.

## Sources of Additional Information

Information on law schools and a career in law may be obtained from the following organizations:

▸ American Bar Association, 321 North Clark St., Chicago, IL 60610. Internet: http://www.abanet.org

▸ National Association for Law Placement, 1025 Connecticut Ave. NW, Suite 1110, Washington, DC 20036. Internet: http://www.nalp.org

Information on the LSAT, the Law School Data Assembly Service, the law school application process, and financial aid available to law students may be obtained from

▸ Law School Admission Council, P.O. Box 40, Newtown, PA 18940. Internet: http://www.lsac.org

Information on obtaining positions as lawyers with the federal government is available from the Office of Personnel Management through USAJOBS, the federal government's official employment information system. This resource for locating and applying for job opportunities can be accessed through the Internet at http://www.usajobs.opm.gov or through an interactive voice response telephone system at (703) 724-1850 or TDD (978) 461-8404. These numbers are not toll free, and charges may result. For advice on how to find and apply for federal jobs, see the *Occupational Outlook Quarterly* article "How to get a job in the Federal Government," online at http://www.bls.gov/opub/ooq/2004/summer/art01.pdf.

The requirements for admission to the bar in a particular state or other jurisdiction may be obtained at the state capital, from the clerk of the Supreme Court, or from the administrator of the State Board of Bar Examiners.

# Licensed Practical and Licensed Vocational Nurses

(O*NET 29-2061.00)

## Significant Points

■ Most training programs, lasting about 1 year, are offered by vocational or technical schools or community or junior colleges.

■ Overall job prospects are expected to be very good, but job outlook varies by industry.

■ Replacement needs will be a major source of job openings, as many workers leave the occupation permanently.

## Nature of the Work

Licensed practical nurses (LPNs), or licensed vocational nurses (LVNs), care for people who are sick, injured, convalescent, or disabled under the direction of physicians and registered nurses. The nature of the direction and supervision required varies by state and job setting.

LPNs care for patients in many ways. Often, they provide basic bedside care. Many LPNs measure and record patients' vital signs such as height, weight, temperature, blood pressure, pulse, and respiration. They also prepare and give injections and enemas, monitor catheters, dress wounds, and give alcohol rubs and massages. To help keep patients comfortable, they assist with bathing, dressing, and personal hygiene, moving in bed, standing, and walking. They might also feed patients who need help eating. Experienced LPNs may supervise nursing assistants and aides.

As part of their work, LPNs collect samples for testing, perform routine laboratory tests, and record food and fluid intake and output. They clean and monitor medical equipment. Sometimes, they help physicians and registered nurses perform tests and procedures. Some LPNs help to deliver, care for, and feed infants.

LPNs also monitor their patients and report adverse reactions to medications or treatments. LPNs gather information from patients, including their health history and how they are currently feeling. They may use this information to complete insurance forms, pre-authorizations, and referrals, and they share information with registered nurses and doctors to help determine the best course of care for a patient.

LPNs often teach family members how to care for a relative or teach patients about good health habits.

Most LPNs are generalists and work in all areas of health care. However, some work in a specialized setting, such as a nursing home, a doctor's office, or in home health care. LPNs in nursing care facilities help to evaluate residents' needs, develop care plans, and supervise the care provided by nursing aides. In doctors' offices and clinics, they may be responsible for making appointments, keeping records, and performing other clerical duties. LPNs who work in home health care may prepare meals and teach family members simple nursing tasks.

**Projections data from the National Employment Matrix**

| Occupational Title | SOC Code | Employment, 2006 | Projected employment, 2016 | Change, 2006-2016 | |
|---|---|---|---|---|---|
| | | | | Number | Percent |
| Licensed practical and licensed vocational nurses............................ | 29-2061 | 749,000 | 854,000 | 105,000 | 14 |

NOTE: Data in this table are rounded.

In some states, LPNs are permitted to administer prescribed medicines, start intravenous fluids, and provide care to ventilator-dependent patients.

***Work environment.*** Most licensed practical nurses in hospitals and nursing care facilities work a 40-hour week, but because patients need round-the-clock care, some work nights, weekends, and holidays. They often stand for long periods and help patients move in bed, stand, or walk.

LPNs may face hazards from caustic chemicals, radiation, and infectious diseases. They are subject to back injuries when moving patients. They often must deal with the stress of heavy workloads. In addition, the patients they care for may be confused, agitated, or uncooperative.

## Training, Other Qualifications, and Advancement

Most training programs, lasting about one year, are offered by vocational or technical schools or community or junior colleges. LPNs must be licensed to practice. Successful completion of a practical nurse program and passing an examination are required to become licensed.

***Education and training.*** All states and the District of Columbia require LPNs to pass a licensing examination, known as the NCLEX-PN, after completing a state-approved practical nursing program. A high school diploma or its equivalent usually is required for entry, although some programs accept candidates without a diploma, and some programs are part of a high school curriculum.

In 2006, there were more than 1,500 state-approved training programs in practical nursing. Most training programs are available from technical and vocational schools or community and junior colleges. Other programs are available through high schools, hospitals, and colleges and universities.

Most year-long practical nursing programs include both classroom study and supervised clinical practice (patient care). Classroom study covers basic nursing concepts and subjects related to patient care, including anatomy, physiology, medical-surgical nursing, pediatrics, obstetrics, psychiatric nursing, the administration of drugs, nutrition, and first aid. Clinical practice usually is in a hospital but sometimes includes other settings.

***Licensure.*** The NCLEX-PN licensing exam is required in order to obtain licensure as an LPN. The exam is developed and administered by the National Council of State Boards of Nursing. The NCLEX-PN is a computer-based exam and varies in length. The exam covers four major categories: safe and effective care environment, health promotion and maintenance, psychosocial integrity, and physiological integrity.

***Other qualifications.*** LPNs should have a caring, sympathetic nature. They should be emotionally stable because working with the sick and injured can be stressful. They also need to be observant, and to have good decision-making and communication skills. As part of a health-care team, they must be able to follow orders and work under close supervision.

***Advancement.*** In some employment settings, such as nursing homes, LPNs can advance to become charge nurses who oversee the work of other LPNs and of nursing aides. Some LPNs also choose to become registered nurses through numerous LPN-to-RN training programs.

## Employment

Licensed practical nurses held about 749,000 jobs in 2006. About 26 percent of LPNs worked in hospitals, 26 percent in nursing care facilities, and another 12 percent in offices of physicians. Others worked for home health care services; employment services; residential care facilities; community care facilities for the elderly; outpatient care centers; and federal, state, and local government agencies. About 19 percent worked part time.

## Job Outlook

Employment of LPNs is projected to grow faster than average. Overall job prospects are expected to be very good, but job outlook varies by industry. The best job opportunities will occur in nursing care facilities and home health care services, while applicants for jobs in hospitals may face competition.

***Employment change.*** Employment of LPNs is expected to grow 14 percent between 2006 and 2016, faster than the average for all occupations, in response to the long-term care needs of an increasing elderly population and the general increase in demand for health care services.

Many procedures once performed only in hospitals are being performed in physicians' offices and in outpatient care centers such as ambulatory surgical and emergency medical centers, largely because of advances in technology. LPNs care for patients who undergo these and other procedures, so employment of LPNs is projected to decline in traditional hospitals, but is projected to grow faster than average in most settings outside of hospitals. However, some hospitals are assigning a larger share of nursing duties to LPNs, which will temper the employment decline in the industry.

Employment of LPNs is expected to grow much faster than average in home health care services. Home health care agencies will offer a large number of new jobs for LPNs because of an increasing number of older people with functional disabilities, consumer preference for care in the home, and technological advances that make it possible to bring increasingly complex treatments into the home.

Employment of LPNs in nursing care facilities is expected to grow faster than average, and provide the most new jobs for LPNs, because of the growing number of people who are aged and disabled and in need of long-term care. In addition, LPNs in nursing care facilities will be needed to care for the increasing number of patients who have been discharged from the hospital but who have not recovered enough to return home.

*Job prospects.* Replacement needs will be a major source of job openings, as many workers leave the occupation permanently. Very good job opportunities are expected. Rapid employment growth is projected in most health care industries, with the best job opportunities occurring in nursing care facilities and in home health care services. However, applicants for jobs in hospitals may face competition as the number of hospital jobs for LPNs declines.

## Earnings

Median annual earnings of licensed practical nurses were $36,550 in May 2006. The middle 50 percent earned between $31,080 and $43,640. The lowest 10 percent earned less than $26,380, and the highest 10 percent earned more than $50,480. Median annual earnings in the industries employing the largest numbers of licensed practical nurses in May 2006 were

| | |
|---|---|
| Employment services | $42,110 |
| Nursing care facilities | 38,320 |
| Home health care services | 37,880 |
| General medical and surgical hospitals | 35,000 |
| Offices of physicians | 32,710 |

## Related Occupations

LPNs work closely with people while helping them. So do emergency medical technicians and paramedics; medical assistants; nursing, psychiatric, and home health aides; registered nurses; athletic trainers; social and human service assistants; pharmacy technicians; pharmacy aides; and surgical technologists.

## Sources of Additional Information

For information about practical nursing, contact the following organizations:

▸ National Association for Practical Nurse Education and Service, Inc., P.O. Box 25647, Alexandria, VA 22313. Internet: http://www.napnes.org

▸ National Federation of Licensed Practical Nurses, Inc., 605 Poole Dr., Garner, NC 27529. Internet: http://www.nflpn.org

▸ National League for Nursing, 61 Broadway, New York, NY 10006. Internet: http://www.nln.org

Information on the NCLEX-PN licensing exam is available from

▸ National Council of State Boards of Nursing, 111 East Wacker Dr., Suite 2900, Chicago, IL 60611. Internet: http://www.ncsbn.org

A list of state-approved LPN programs is available from individual state boards of nursing.

# Loan Officers

(O*NET 13-2072.00)

## Significant Points

■ About 9 out of 10 loan officers work for commercial banks, savings institutions, credit unions, and related financial institutions.

■ Loan officers usually need a bachelor's degree in finance, economics, or a related field; training or experience in banking, lending, or sales is advantageous.

■ Earnings often fluctuate with the number of loans generated, rising substantially when the economy is good and interest rates are low.

## Nature of the Work

For many individuals, taking out a loan is the only way to buy a house, car, or college education. For businesses, loans likewise are essential to start many companies, purchase inventory, or invest in capital equipment. *Loan officers* facilitate this lending by finding potential clients and helping them to apply for loans. Loan officers also gather personal information about clients and businesses to ensure an informed decision regarding their creditworthiness and the probability of repayment. Loan officers may also provide guidance to prospective borrowers who have problems qualifying for traditional loans. For example, loan officers might determine the most appropriate type of loan for a particular customer and explain specific requirements and restrictions associated with the loan.

Loan officers guide clients through the process of applying for a loan. The process begins with a meeting or telephone call with a prospective client, during which the loan officer obtains basic information about the purpose of the loan and explains the different types of loans and credit terms available to the applicant. Loan officers answer questions about the process and sometimes assist clients in filling out the application.

After a client completes the application, the loan officer begins the process of analyzing and verifying the information on the application to determine the client's creditworthiness. Often, loan officers can quickly access the client's credit history by computer and obtain a credit "score," representing a software program's assessment of the client's creditworthiness. When a credit history is not available or when unusual financial circumstances are present, the loan officer may request additional financial information from the client or, in the case of commercial loans, copies of the company's financial statements. Loan officers include such information and their written comments in a loan file, which is used to analyze whether the prospective loan meets the lending institution's requirements. Loan officers then decide, in consultation with their managers, whether to grant the loan. If the loan is approved, a repayment schedule is arranged with the client.

Loan officers usually specialize in commercial, consumer, or mortgage loans. Commercial or business loans help companies pay for new equipment or expand operations; consumer loans include home equity, automobile, and personal loans; mortgage loans are made to purchase real estate or to refinance an existing mortgage. As banks and other financial institutions begin to offer new types of loans and a growing variety of financial services, loan officers will have to learn about these new product lines.

In many instances, loan officers act as salespeople. Commercial loan officers, for example, contact firms to determine their needs for loans. If a firm is seeking new funds, the loan officer will try to persuade the company to obtain the loan from his or her institution. Similarly, mortgage loan officers develop relationships with commercial and residential real estate agencies so that, when an individual or firm buys a property, the real estate agent might recommend contacting a specific loan officer for financing.

Some loan officers, called loan underwriters, specialize in evaluating a client's creditworthiness and may conduct a financial analysis or other risk assessment.

Other loan officers, referred to as *loan collection officers*, contact borrowers with delinquent loan accounts to help them find a method of repayment to avoid their defaulting on the loan. If a repayment plan cannot be developed, the loan collection officer initiates collateral liquidation, a process in which the lender seizes the collateral used to secure the loan—a home or car, for example—and sells it to repay the loan.

*Work environment.* Working as a loan officer usually involves considerable travel. For example, commercial and mortgage loan officers frequently work away from their offices and rely on laptop computers, cellular telephones, and pagers to keep in contact with their employers and clients. Mortgage loan officers often work out of their home or car, visiting offices or homes of clients to complete loan applications. Commercial loan officers sometimes travel to other cities to prepare complex loan agreements. Consumer loan officers, however, are likely to spend most of their time in an office.

Most loan officers work a standard 40-hour week, but many work longer, depending on the number of clients and the demand for loans. Mortgage loan officers can work especially long hours because they are free to take on as many customers as they choose. Loan officers are especially busy when interest rates are low, causing a surge in loan applications.

## Training, Other Qualifications, and Advancement

Loan officers usually need a bachelor's degree in finance, economics, or a related field. Previous banking, lending, or sales experience is also highly valued by employers.

*Education and training.* Loan officer positions generally require a bachelor's degree in finance, economics, or a related field. Loan officers without a college degree often advance to their positions after gaining several years of work experience in various other related occupations, such as teller or customer service representative.

*Licensure.* There are currently no specific licensing requirements for loan officers working in banks or credit unions. Training and licensing requirements for loan officers who work in mortgage banks or brokerages vary by state and may include continuing education requirements. As the types of mortgages offered to prospective homebuyers increases, licensing requirements may become more stringent as regulators and lawmakers become more leery of possible predatory lending.

*Other qualifications.* People planning a career as a loan officer should be good at working with others, confident in their abilities, and highly motivated. Loan officers must be willing to attend community events as representatives of their employer. Sales ability, good interpersonal and communication skills, and a strong desire to succeed also are important qualities for loan officers. Most employers also prefer applicants who are familiar with computers and their applications in banking.

*Certification and advancement.* Capable loan officers may advance to larger branches of their firms or to managerial positions. Some loan officers advance to supervise other loan officers and clerical staff.

Various banking associations and private schools offer courses and programs for students interested in lending and for experienced loan officers who want to keep their skills current. For example, the Bank Administration Institute, an affiliate of the American Banker's Association, offers the Loan Review Certificate Program for people who review and approve loans. This program enhances the quality of reviews and improves the early detection of deteriorating loans, thereby contributing to the safety and soundness of the loan portfolio.

The Mortgage Bankers Association offers the Certified Mortgage Banker (CMB) designation to loan officers in real estate finance. The association offers three CMB designations—residential, commerce, and masters—to candidates who have three years of experience, earn educational credits, and pass an exam. Completion of these courses and programs generally enhances employment and advancement opportunities.

## Employment

Loan officers held about 373,000 jobs in 2006. About 9 out of 10 loan officers were employed by commercial banks, savings institutions, credit unions, and related financial institutions. Loan officers are employed throughout the nation, but most work in urban and suburban areas. At some banks, particularly in rural areas, the branch or assistant manager often handles the loan application process.

## Job Outlook

Loan officers can expect average employment growth. Job opportunities will be best for people with a college education and related experience.

*Employment change.* Employment of loan officers is projected to increase 11 percent between 2006 and 2016, which is about as fast as the average for all occupations. Employment growth stemming from economic expansion and population increases—factors that generate demand for loans—will be partially offset by increased automation that speeds the lending process and by the growing use of the Internet to apply for and obtain loans.

The use of credit scoring has made the loan evaluation process much simpler than in the past and even unnecessary in some cases. Credit scoring allows loan officers—particularly loan underwriters—to evaluate many more loans in less time than previously. In addition,

**Projections data from the National Employment Matrix**

| Occupational Title | SOC Code | Employment, 2006 | Projected employment, 2016 | Change, 2006-16 | |
|---|---|---|---|---|---|
| | | | | Number | Percent |
| Loan officers ................................................................... | 13-2072 | 373,000 | 415,000 | 43,000 | 11 |

NOTE: Data in this table are rounded.

the mortgage application process has become highly automated and standardized, a simplification that has enabled mortgage loan vendors to offer their services over the Internet. Online vendors accept loan applications from customers over the Internet and determine which lenders have the best interest rates for particular loans. With this knowledge, customers can go directly to the lending institution, thereby bypassing mortgage loan brokers. Shopping for loans on the Internet, especially for mortgages, is expected to become more common in the future and to slow job growth for loan officers.

*Job prospects.* Besides openings arising from growth, additional job openings will result from the need to replace workers who retire or otherwise leave the occupation permanently.

College graduates and those with banking, lending, or sales experience should have the best job prospects.

Job opportunities for loan officers are influenced by the volume of applications, which is determined largely by interest rates and by the overall level of economic activity. Although loans remain a major source of revenue for banks, demand for new loans fluctuates and affects the income and employment opportunities of loan officers. An upswing in the economy or a decline in interest rates often results in a surge in real estate buying and mortgage refinancing, requiring loan officers to work long hours processing applications and inducing lenders to hire additional loan officers. Loan officers often are paid by commission on the value of the loans they place, and when the real estate market slows, they often suffer a decline in earnings and may even be subject to layoffs. The same applies to commercial loan officers, whose workloads increase during good economic times as companies seek to invest more in their businesses. In difficult economic conditions, an increase in the number of delinquent loans results in more demand for loan collection officers.

## Earnings

Median annual earnings of wage and salary loan officers were $51,760 in May 2006. The middle 50 percent earned between $37,590 and $73,630. The lowest 10 percent earned less than $29,590, while the top 10 percent earned more than $107,040. Median annual earnings in the industries employing the largest numbers of loan officers were as follows:

Activities related to credit intermediation ............$54,880

Other nondepository credit intermediation ............52,250

Nondepository credit intermediation......................52,100

Depository credit intermediation ..........................48,900

The form of compensation for loan officers varies. Most are paid a commission based on the number of loans they originate. Some institutions pay only salaries, while others pay their loan officers a salary plus a commission or bonus based on the number of loans originated. Loan officers who are paid on commission usually earn

more than those who earn only a salary, and those who work for smaller banks generally earn less than those employed by larger institutions.

According to a salary survey conducted by Robert Half International, a staffing services firm specializing in accounting and finance, consumer loan officers, referred to as personal bankers, with 1 to 3 years of experience earned between $30,750 and $36,250 in 2007, and commercial loan officers with 1 to 3 years of experience made between $45,750 and $70,250. Commercial loan officers with more than 3 years of experience made between $61,750 and $100,750, and consumer loan officers earned between $36,250 and $51,250. Earnings of loan officers with graduate degrees or professional certifications are higher.

Banks and other lenders sometimes may offer their loan officers free checking privileges and somewhat lower interest rates on personal loans.

## Related Occupations

Loan officers help people manage financial assets and secure loans. Occupations that involve similar functions include those of securities, commodities, and financial services sales agents; financial analysts and personal financial advisors; real estate brokers and sales agents; insurance underwriters; insurance sales agents; and loan counselors.

## Sources of Additional Information

Information about a career as a mortgage loan officer can be obtained from

▸ Mortgage Bankers Association, 1919 Pennsylvania Ave. NW, Washington, DC 20006. Internet: http://www.mortgagebankers.org

State bankers' associations can furnish specific information about job opportunities in their state. Also, individual banks can supply information about job openings and the activities, responsibilities, and preferred qualifications of their loan officers.

# Maintenance and Repair Workers, General

(O*NET 49-9042.00)

## Significant Points

■ General maintenance and repair workers are employed in almost every industry.

■ Many workers learn their skills informally on the job.

■ Job growth and turnover in this large occupation should result in excellent job opportunities, especially for people with experience in maintenance and related fields.

**Projections data from the National Employment Matrix**

| Occupational Title | SOC Code | Employment, 2006 | Projected employment, 2016 | Change, 2006-16 | |
| --- | --- | --- | --- | --- | --- |
| | | | | Number | Percent |
| Maintenance and repair workers, general ......................................... | 49-9042 | 1,391,000 | 1,531,000 | 140,000 | 10 |

NOTE: Data in this table are rounded.

## Nature of the Work

Most craft workers specialize in one kind of work, such as plumbing or carpentry. General maintenance and repair workers, however, have skills in many different crafts. They repair and maintain machines, mechanical equipment, and buildings and work on plumbing, electrical, and air-conditioning and heating systems. They build partitions, make plaster or drywall repairs, and fix or paint roofs, windows, doors, floors, woodwork, and other parts of building structures. They also maintain and repair specialized equipment and machinery found in cafeterias, laundries, hospitals, stores, offices, and factories.

Typical duties include troubleshooting and fixing faulty electrical switches, repairing air-conditioning motors, and unclogging drains. New buildings sometimes have computer-controlled systems that allow maintenance workers to make adjustments in building settings and monitor for problems from a central location. For example, they can remotely control light sensors that turn off lights automatically after a set amount of time or identify a broken ventilation fan that needs to be replaced.

General maintenance and repair workers inspect and diagnose problems and determine the best way to correct them, frequently checking blueprints, repair manuals, and parts catalogs. They obtain supplies and repair parts from distributors or storerooms. Using common hand and power tools such as screwdrivers, saws, drills, wrenches, and hammers, as well as specialized equipment and electronic testing devices, these workers replace or fix worn or broken parts, where necessary, or make adjustments to correct malfunctioning equipment and machines.

General maintenance and repair workers also perform routine preventive maintenance and ensure that machines continue to run smoothly, building systems operate efficiently, and the physical condition of buildings does not deteriorate. Following a checklist, they may inspect drives, motors, and belts, check fluid levels, replace filters, and perform other maintenance actions. Maintenance and repair workers keep records of their work.

Employees in small establishments, where they are often the only maintenance worker, make all repairs, except for very large or difficult jobs. In larger establishments, duties may be limited to the maintenance of everything in a workshop or a particular area.

*Work environment.* General maintenance and repair workers often carry out several different tasks in a single day, at any number of locations. They may work inside a single building or in several different buildings. They may have to stand for long periods, lift heavy objects, and work in uncomfortably hot or cold environments, in awkward and cramped positions, or on ladders. Those employed in small establishments often work with only limited supervision. Those in larger establishments frequently work under the direct supervision of an experienced worker. Some tasks put workers at risk of electrical shock, burns, falls, cuts, and bruises.

Most general maintenance workers work a 40-hour week. Some work evening, night, or weekend shifts or are on call for emergency repairs.

## Training, Other Qualifications, and Advancement

Many general maintenance and repair workers learn their skills informally on the job as helpers to other repairers or to carpenters, electricians, and other construction workers.

*Education and training.* General maintenance and repair workers often learn their skills informally on the job. They start as helpers, watching and learning from skilled maintenance workers. Helpers begin by doing simple jobs, such as fixing leaky faucets and replacing light bulbs, and progress to more difficult tasks, such as overhauling machinery or building walls. Some learn their skills by working as helpers to other types of repair or construction workers, including machinery repairers, carpenters, or electricians.

Several months of on-the-job training are required to become fully qualified, depending on the skill level required. Some jobs require a year or more to become fully qualified. Because a growing number of new buildings rely on computers to control their systems, general maintenance and repair workers may need basic computer skills, such as how to log onto a central computer system and navigate through a series of menus. Companies that install computer-controlled equipment usually provide on-site training for general maintenance and repair workers.

Many employers prefer to hire high school graduates. High school courses in mechanical drawing, electricity, woodworking, blueprint reading, science, mathematics, and computers are useful. Because of the wide variety of tasks performed by maintenance and repair workers, technical education is an important part of their training. Maintenance and repair workers often need to do work that involves electrical, plumbing, and heating and air-conditioning systems, or painting and roofing tasks. Although these basic tasks may not require a license to do the work, a good working knowledge of many repair and maintenance tasks is required. Many maintenance and repair workers learn some of these skills in high school shop classes and postsecondary trade or vocational schools or community colleges.

*Licensure.* Licensing requirements vary by state and locality. In some cases, workers may need to be licensed in a particular specialty such as electrical or plumbing work.

*Other qualifications.* Mechanical aptitude, the ability to use shop mathematics, and manual dexterity are important. Good health is necessary because the job involves much walking, standing, reaching, and heavy lifting. Difficult jobs require problem-solving ability, and many positions require the ability to work without direct supervision.

*Advancement.* Many general maintenance and repair workers in large organizations advance to maintenance supervisor or become craftworkers such as electricians, heating and air-conditioning mechanics, or plumbers. Within small organizations, promotion opportunities may be limited.

## Employment

General maintenance and repair workers held 1.4 million jobs in 2006. They were employed in almost every industry. Around 19 percent worked in manufacturing industries, almost evenly distributed through all sectors, while about 10 percent worked for federal, state, and local governments. Others worked for wholesale and retail firms and for real estate firms that operate office and apartment buildings.

## Job Outlook

Average employment growth is expected. Job growth and the need to replace those who leave this large occupation should result in excellent job opportunities, especially for those with experience in maintenance and related fields.

*Employment change.* Employment of general maintenance and repair workers is expected to grow 10 percent during the 2006–2016 decade, about as fast as the average for all occupations. Employment is related to the number of buildings—for example, office and apartment buildings, stores, schools, hospitals, hotels, and factories—and the amount of equipment needing maintenance and repair. One factor limiting job growth is that computers allow buildings to be monitored more efficiently, partially reducing the need for workers.

*Job prospects.* Job opportunities should be excellent, especially for those with experience in maintenance or related fields. General maintenance and repair is a large occupation, generating many job openings due to growth and the need to replace those who leave the occupation. Many job openings are expected to result from the retirement of experienced maintenance workers over the next decade.

## Earnings

Median hourly earnings of general maintenance and repair workers were $15.34 in May 2006. The middle 50 percent earned between $11.66 and $19.90. The lowest 10 percent earned less than $9.20, and the highest 10 percent earned more than $24.44. Median hourly earnings in the industries employing the largest numbers of general maintenance and repair workers in May 2006 are shown in the following tabulation:

| | |
|---|---|
| Local government | $15.85 |
| Elementary and secondary schools | 15.76 |
| Activities related to real estate | 13.44 |
| Lessors of real estate | 13.06 |
| Traveler accommodation | 11.76 |

Some general maintenance and repair workers are members of unions including the American Federation of State, County, and Municipal Employees and the United Auto Workers.

## Related Occupations

Some duties of general maintenance and repair workers are similar to those of carpenters; pipelayers, plumbers, pipefitters, and steamfitters; electricians; and heating, air-conditioning, and refrigeration mechanics. Other duties are similar to those of coin, vending, and amusement machine servicers and repairers; electrical and electronics installers and repairers; electronic home entertainment equipment installers and repairers; and radio and telecommunications equipment installers and repairers.

## Sources of Additional Information

Information about job opportunities may be obtained from local employers and local offices of the state.

For information related to maintenance managers, contact

▸ International Maintenance Institute, P.O. Box 751896, Houston, TX 77275-1896. Internet: http://www.imionline.org

# Management Analysts

(O*NET 13-1111.00)

## Significant Points

■ Despite much-faster-than-average employment growth, keen competition is expected for jobs; opportunities should be best for those with a graduate degree, specialized expertise, and a talent for salesmanship and public relations.

■ About 27 percent, over three times the average for all occupations, are self-employed.

■ A bachelor's degree is sufficient for many entry-level government jobs; many positions in private industry require a master's degree, specialized expertise, or both.

## Nature of the Work

As business becomes more complex, firms are continually faced with new challenges. They increasingly rely on management analysts to help them remain competitive amidst these changes. Management analysts, often referred to as *management consultants* in private industry, analyze and propose ways to improve an organization's structure, efficiency, or profits.

For example, a small but rapidly growing company might employ a consultant who is an expert in just-in-time inventory management to help improve its inventory-control system. In another case, a large company that has recently acquired a new division may hire management analysts to help reorganize the corporate structure and eliminate duplicate or nonessential jobs. In recent years, information technology and electronic commerce have provided new opportunities for management analysts. Companies hire consultants to develop strategies for entering and remaining competitive in the new electronic marketplace.

Management analysts might be single practitioners or part of large international organizations employing thousands of other consultants. Some analysts and consultants specialize in a specific industry, such as health care or telecommunications, while others specialize by type of business function, such as human resources, marketing, logistics, or information systems. In government, management analysts tend to specialize by type of agency. The work of management analysts and consultants varies with each client or employer and from project to project. Some projects require a team of consultants, each specializing in one area. In other projects, consultants work independently with the organization's managers. In all cases, analysts and consultants collect, review, and analyze information in order to make recommendations to managers.

Both public and private organizations use consultants for a variety of reasons. Some lack the internal resources needed to handle a project, while others need a consultant's expertise to determine what resources will be required and what problems may be encountered if they pursue a particular opportunity. To retain a consultant, a company first solicits proposals from a number of consulting firms specializing in the area in which it needs assistance. These proposals include the estimated cost and scope of the project, staffing requirements, references from a number of previous clients, and a completion deadline. The company then selects the proposal that best suits its needs. Some firms, however, employ internal management consulting groups rather than hiring outside consultants.

After obtaining an assignment or contract, management analysts first define the nature and extent of the problem that they have been asked to solve. During this phase, they analyze relevant data—which may include annual revenues, employment, or expenditures—and interview managers and employees while observing their operations. The analysts or consultants then develop solutions to the problem. While preparing their recommendations, they take into account the nature of the organization, the relationship it has with others in the industry, and its internal organization and culture. Insight into the problem often is gained by building and solving mathematical models, such as one that shows how inventory levels affect costs and product delivery times.

Once they have decided on a course of action, consultants report their findings and recommendations to the client. Their suggestions usually are submitted in writing, but oral presentations regarding findings also are common. For some projects, management analysts are retained to help implement the suggestions they have made.

Like their private-sector colleagues, management analysts in government agencies try to increase efficiency and worker productivity and to control costs. For example, if an agency is planning to purchase personal computers, it must first determine which type to buy, given its budget and data-processing needs. In this case, management analysts would assess the prices and characteristics of various machines and determine which ones best meet the agency's goals. Analysts may manage contracts for a wide range of goods and services to ensure quality performance and to prevent cost overruns.

*Work environment.* Management analysts usually divide their time between their offices and the client's site. In either situation, much of an analyst's time is spent indoors in clean, well-lit offices. Because they must spend a significant portion of their time with clients, analysts travel frequently.

Analysts and consultants generally work at least 40 hours a week. Uncompensated overtime is common, especially when project dead-

lines are approaching. Analysts may experience a great deal of stress when trying to meet a client's demands, often on a tight schedule.

Self-employed consultants can set their workload and hours and work at home. On the other hand, their livelihood depends on their ability to maintain and expand their client base. Salaried consultants also must impress potential clients to get and keep clients for their company.

## Training, Other Qualifications, and Advancement

Entry requirements for management analysts vary. For some entry-level positions, a bachelor's degree is sufficient. For others, a master's degree, specialized expertise, or both is required.

*Education and training.* Educational requirements for entry-level jobs in this field vary between private industry and government. Many employers in private industry generally seek individuals with a master's degree in business administration or a related discipline. Some employers also require additional years of experience in the field or industry in which the worker plans to consult. Other firms hire workers with a bachelor's degree as research analysts or associates and promote them to consultants after several years. Some government agencies require experience, graduate education, or both, but many also hire people with a bachelor's degree and little work experience for entry-level management analyst positions.

Few universities or colleges offer formal programs in management consulting; however, many fields of study provide a suitable educational background for this occupation because of the wide range of areas addressed by management analysts. Common fields of study include business, management, accounting, marketing, economics, statistics, computer and information science, and engineering. Most analysts also have years of experience in management, human resources, information technology, or other specialties. Analysts also routinely attend conferences to keep abreast of current developments in their field.

*Other qualifications.* Management analysts often work with minimal supervision, so they need to be self-motivated and disciplined. Analytical skills, the ability to get along with a wide range of people, strong oral and written communication skills, good judgment, time-management skills, and creativity are other desirable qualities. The ability to work in teams also is an important attribute as consulting teams become more common.

*Certification and advancement.* As consultants gain experience, they often become solely responsible for specific projects, taking on more responsibility and managing their own hours. At the senior level, consultants may supervise teams working on more complex projects and become more involved in seeking out new business. Those with exceptional skills may eventually become partners in the firm, focusing on attracting new clients and bringing in revenue. Senior consultants who leave their consulting firms often move to senior management positions at non-consulting firms. Others with entrepreneurial ambition may open their own firms.

A high percentage of management consultants are self-employed, partly because business startup and overhead costs are low. Since many small consulting firms fail each year because of lack of managerial expertise and clients, persons interested in opening their own

**Projections data from the National Employment Matrix**

| Occupational Title | SOC Code | Employment, 2006 | Projected employment, 2016 | Change, 2006-16 | |
|---|---|---|---|---|---|
| | | | | Number | Percent |
| Management analysts................................................................. | 13-1111 | 678,000 | 827,000 | 149,000 | 22 |

NOTE: Data in this table are rounded.

firm must have good organizational and marketing skills. Several years of consulting experience are also helpful.

The Institute of Management Consultants USA, Inc. offers the Certified Management Consultant (CMC) designation to those who meet minimum levels of education and experience, submit client reviews, and pass an interview and exam covering the IMC USA's Code of Ethics. Management consultants with a CMC designation must be recertified every three years. Certification is not mandatory for management consultants, but it may give a jobseeker a competitive advantage.

## Employment

Management analysts held about 678,000 jobs in 2006. About 27 percent of these workers, over three times the average for all occupations, were self-employed. Management analysts are found throughout the country, but employment is concentrated in large metropolitan areas. Management analysts work in a range of industries, including management, scientific, and technical consulting firms; computer systems design and related services firms; and federal, state, and local governments.

## Job Outlook

Employment of management analysts is expected to grow much faster than average. Despite projected rapid employment growth, keen competition is expected for jobs as management analysts because of the independent and challenging nature of the work and the high earnings potential that make this occupation attractive to many.

*Employment change.* Employment of management analysts is expected to grow 22 percent over the 2006–2016 decade, much faster than the average for all occupations, as industry and government increasingly rely on outside expertise to improve the performance of their organizations. Job growth is projected in very large consulting firms with international expertise and in smaller consulting firms that specialize in specific areas, such as biotechnology, health care, information technology, human resources, engineering, and marketing. Growth in the number of individual practitioners may be hindered by increasing use of consulting teams that are often more versatile.

Job growth for management analysts has been driven by a number of changes in the business environment that have forced firms to take a closer look at their operations. These changes include regulatory changes, developments in information technology, and the growth of electronic commerce. Firms hire consultants to help them adapt to new business regulations, such as the Sarbanes-Oxley Act, which tightened financial reporting rules. Traditional companies hire analysts to help design intranets or company Web sites or to establish online businesses. New Internet startup companies hire analysts not only to design Web sites but also to advise them in traditional business practices, such as pricing strategies, marketing, and inventory and human resource management.

To offer clients better quality and a wider variety of services, consulting firms are partnering with traditional computer software and technology firms. Also, many computer firms are developing consulting practices of their own to take advantage of this expanding market. Although information technology consulting should remain one of the fastest-growing consulting areas, employment in the computer services industry can be volatile, so the most successful management analysts may also consult in other business areas.

The growth of international business also has contributed to an increase in demand for management analysts. As U.S. firms expand their business abroad, many will hire management analysts to help them form the right strategy for entering the market; to advise them on legal matters pertaining to specific countries; or to help them with organizational, administrative, and other issues, especially if the U.S. company is involved in a partnership or merger with a local firm. These trends provide management analysts with more opportunities to travel or work abroad but also require them to have a more comprehensive knowledge of international business and foreign cultures and languages. Just as globalization creates new opportunities for management analysts, it also allows U.S. firms to hire management analysts in other countries; however, because international work is expected to increase the total amount of work, this development is not expected to adversely affect employment in this occupation.

Furthermore, as international and domestic markets have become more competitive, firms have needed to use resources more efficiently. Management analysts increasingly are sought to help reduce costs, streamline operations, and develop marketing strategies. As this process continues and businesses downsize, even more opportunities will be created for analysts to perform duties that previously were handled internally. Finally, more management analysts also will be needed in the public sector as federal, state, and local government agencies seek ways to become more efficient.

*Job prospects.* Despite rapid employment growth, keen competition is expected. The pool of applicants from which employers can draw is quite large since analysts can have very diverse educational backgrounds and work experience. Furthermore, the independent and challenging nature of the work, combined with high earnings potential, makes this occupation attractive to many. Job opportunities are expected to be best for those with a graduate degree, specialized expertise, and a talent for salesmanship and public relations.

Economic downturns also can have adverse effects on employment for some management consultants. In these times, businesses look to cut costs, and consultants may be considered an excess expense. On the other hand, some consultants might experience an increase in work during recessions because they advise businesses on how to cut costs and remain profitable.

# Earnings

Salaries for management analysts vary widely by years of experience and education, geographic location, specific expertise, and size of employer. Generally, management analysts employed in large firms or in metropolitan areas have the highest salaries. Median annual earnings of wage and salary management analysts in May 2006 were $68,050. The middle 50 percent earned between $50,860 and $92,390. The lowest 10 percent earned less than $39,840, and the highest 10 percent earned more than $128,330. Median annual earnings in the industries employing the largest numbers of management analysts were

| | |
|---|---|
| Management, scientific, and technical consulting services | $76,600 |
| Computer systems design and related services | 76,130 |
| Federal executive branch | 73,800 |
| Management of companies and enterprises | 68,660 |
| State government | 50,270 |

Salaried management analysts usually receive common benefits, such as health and life insurance, a retirement plan, vacation, and sick leave, as well as less common benefits, such as profit sharing and bonuses for outstanding work. In addition, all travel expenses usually are reimbursed by the employer. Self-employed consultants have to maintain their own office and provide their own benefits.

# Related Occupations

Management analysts collect, review, and analyze data; make recommendations; and implement their ideas. Occupations with similar duties include accountants and auditors, budget analysts, cost estimators, financial analysts and personal financial advisors, operations research analysts, economists, and market and survey researchers. Some management analysts specialize in information technology and work with computers, as do computer systems analysts and computer scientists and database administrators. Most management analysts also have managerial experience similar to that of administrative services managers; advertising, marketing, promotions, public relations, and sales managers; financial managers; human resources, training, and labor relations managers and specialists; industrial production managers; or top executives.

# Sources of Additional Information

Information about career opportunities in management consulting is available from

▸ Association of Management Consulting Firms, 380 Lexington Ave., Suite 1700, New York, NY 10168. Internet: http://www.amcf.org

Information about the Certified Management Consultant designation can be obtained from

▸ Institute of Management Consultants USA, Inc., 2025 M St. NW, Suite 800, Washington, DC 20036. Internet: http://www.imcusa.org

Information on obtaining a management analyst position with the federal government is available from the Office of Personnel Management (OPM) through USAJOBS, the federal government's official employment information system. This resource for locating and applying for job opportunities can be accessed through the Internet at http://www.usajobs.opm.gov or through an interactive voice response telephone system at (703) 724-1850 or TDD (978) 461-8404. These numbers are not toll free, and charges may result. For advice on how to find and apply for federal jobs, see the *Occupational Outlook Quarterly* article "How to get a job in the Federal Government," online at http://www.bls.gov/opub/ooq/2004/summer/art01.pdf.

# Market and Survey Researchers

(O*NET 19-3021.00 and 19-3022.00)

## Significant Points

- Market and survey researchers need at least a bachelor's degree.
- Continuing education and keeping current with the latest methods of developing, conducting, and analyzing surveys and other data is important for advancement.
- Employment is expected to grow faster than average.
- Job opportunities should be best for those with a master's or Ph.D. degree in marketing or a related field and with strong quantitative skills.

## Nature of the Work

Market and survey researchers gather information about what people think. *Market*, or *marketing, research analysts* help companies understand what types of products people want and at what price. They also help companies market their products to the people most likely to buy them. Gathering statistical data on competitors and examining prices, sales, and methods of marketing and distribution, they analyze data on past sales to predict future sales.

Market research analysts devise methods and procedures for obtaining the data they need. Often, they design surveys to assess consumer preferences through Internet, telephone, or mail responses. They conduct some surveys as personal interviews, going door-to-door, leading focus group discussions, or setting up booths in public places such as shopping malls. Trained interviewers usually conduct the surveys under the market research analyst's direction.

After compiling and evaluating the data, market research analysts make recommendations to their client or employer. They provide a company's management with information needed to make decisions on the promotion, distribution, design, and pricing of products or services. The information also may be used to determine the advisability of adding new lines of merchandise, opening branches of the company in a new location, or otherwise diversifying the company's operations. Market research analysts also might develop advertising brochures and commercials, sales plans, and product promotions such as rebates and giveaways.

*Survey researchers* also gather information about people and their opinions, but these workers focus exclusively on designing and conducting surveys. They work for a variety of clients, such as corporations, government agencies, political candidates, and providers of

**Projections data from the National Employment Matrix**

| Occupational Title | SOC Code | Employment, 2006 | Projected employment, 2016 | Change, 2006-2016 | |
|---|---|---|---|---|---|
| | | | | Number | Percent |
| Market and survey researchers........................................................ | 19-3020 | 261,000 | 313,000 | 51,000 | 20 |
|   Market research analysts.............................................................. | 19-3021 | 234,000 | 281,000 | 47,000 | 20 |
|   Survey researchers ...................................................................... | 19-3022 | 27,000 | 31,000 | 4,300 | 16 |

NOTE: Data in this table are rounded.

various services. The surveys collect information that is used in performing research, making fiscal or policy decisions, measuring the effectiveness of those decisions, or improving customer satisfaction. Analysts may conduct opinion research to determine public attitudes on various issues; the research results may help political or business leaders to measure public support for their electoral prospects or social policies. Like market research analysts, survey researchers may use a variety of mediums to conduct surveys, such as the Internet, personal or telephone interviews, or questionnaires sent through the mail. They also may supervise interviewers who conduct surveys in person or over the telephone.

Survey researchers design surveys in many different formats, depending upon the scope of their research and the method of collection. Interview surveys, for example, are common because they can increase participation rates. Survey researchers may consult with economists, statisticians, market research analysts, or other data users in order to design surveys. They also may present survey results to clients.

*Work environment.* Market and survey researchers generally have structured work schedules. They often work alone, writing reports, preparing statistical charts, and using computers, but they also may be an integral part of a research team. Market researchers who conduct personal interviews have frequent contact with the public. Most work under pressure of deadlines and tight schedules, which may require overtime. Travel may be necessary.

## Training, Other Qualifications, and Advancement

A bachelor's degree is usually sufficient for entry-level market and survey research positions. Higher degrees may be required for some positions, however. Continuing education and keeping current with the latest methods of developing, conducting, and analyzing surveys and other data also is important for advancement.

*Education and training.* A bachelor's degree is the minimum educational requirement for many market and survey research jobs. However, a master's degree may be required, especially for technical positions.

In addition to completing courses in business, marketing, and consumer behavior, prospective market and survey researchers should take other liberal arts and social science courses, including economics, psychology, English, and sociology. Because of the importance of quantitative skills to market and survey researchers, courses in mathematics, statistics, sampling theory and survey design, and computer science are extremely helpful. Market and survey researchers often earn advanced degrees in business administration, marketing, statistics, communications, or other closely related disciplines.

While in college, aspiring market and survey researchers should gain experience gathering and analyzing data, conducting interviews or surveys, and writing reports on their findings. This experience can prove invaluable later in obtaining a full-time position in the field, because much of the initial work may center on these duties. Some schools help graduate students find internships or part-time employment in government agencies, consulting firms, financial institutions, or marketing research firms prior to graduation.

*Other qualifications.* Market and survey researchers spend a lot of time performing precise data analysis, so those considering careers in the occupation should be able to pay attention to detail. Patience and persistence are also necessary qualities because these workers must spend long hours on independent study and problem solving. At the same time, they must work well with others; often, market and survey researchers oversee the interviewing of a wide variety of individuals. Communication skills are important, too, because researchers must be able to present their findings well both orally and in writing.

*Certification and advancement.* The Marketing Research Association (MRA) offers a certification program for professional researchers who wish to demonstrate their expertise. Certification is based on education and experience and requires ongoing continuing education.

Researchers and analysts often begin by assisting others. With experience, market and survey analysts are eventually are assigned their own research projects. Continuing education and advanced degrees will be helpful to those looking to advance to more responsible positions in this occupation. It also is important to keep current with the latest methods of developing, conducting, and analyzing surveys and other data.

Some people with expertise in marketing or survey research choose to teach others these skills. A master's degree usually is the minimum educational requirement for a job as a marketing or survey research instructor in junior and community colleges. In most colleges and universities, however, a Ph.D. is necessary for appointment as an instructor. A Ph.D. and extensive publications in academic journals are required for professorship, tenure, and promotion. Others advance to supervisory or managerial positions. Many corporation and government executives have a strong background in marketing.

## Employment

Market and survey researchers held about 261,000 jobs in 2006, most of which—234,000—were held by market research analysts. Because of the applicability of market research to many industries, market research analysts are employed throughout the economy. The industries that employ the largest number of market research analysts were management of companies and enterprises; management, scientific, and technical consulting services; insurance carriers; computer systems design and related services; and other professional, scientific, and technical services—which includes marketing research and public opinion polling.

Survey researchers held about 27,000 jobs in 2006. Survey researchers were employed primarily by firms in other professional, scientific, and technical services—which include market research and public opinion polling; scientific research and development services; and management, scientific, and technical consulting services. Colleges, universities, and professional schools also provided many jobs for survey researchers.

A number of market and survey researchers combine a full-time job in government, academia, or business with part-time consulting work in another setting. About seven percent of market and survey researchers are self-employed.

Besides holding the previously mentioned jobs, many people who do market and survey research work held faculty positions in colleges and universities. These workers are counted as postsecondary teachers rather than market and survey researchers.

## Job Outlook

Employment growth of market and survey researchers is projected to be faster than average. Bachelor's degree holders may face competition for employment in these occupations. Job opportunities should be best for jobseekers with a master's or Ph.D. degree in marketing or a related field and with strong quantitative skills.

*Employment change.* Employment of market and survey researchers is projected to grow 20 percent from 2006 to 2016, faster than the average for all occupations. As companies seek to expand their market and as consumers become better informed, the need for marketing professionals will increase. In addition, globalization of the marketplace creates a need for more market and survey researchers to analyze foreign markets and competition.

Marketing research provides organizations valuable feedback from purchasers, allowing companies to evaluate consumer satisfaction and plan more effectively for the future. Survey researchers also will be needed to meet the growing demand for market and opinion research as an increasingly competitive economy requires businesses to allocate advertising funds more effectively and efficiently.

*Job prospects.* Bachelor's degree holders may face competition for jobs, as many positions, especially the more technical ones, require a master's or doctorate degree. Among bachelor's degree holders, those with good quantitative skills, including a strong background in mathematics, statistics, survey design, and computer science, will have the best opportunities. Job opportunities should be best for jobseekers with a master's or Ph.D. degree in marketing or a related field and with strong quantitative skills. Ph.D. holders in marketing and related fields should have a range of opportunities in many industries, especially in consulting firms. Like those in many other disciplines, however, Ph.D. holders probably will face keen competition for tenured teaching positions in colleges and universities.

Market research analysts should have the best opportunities in consulting firms and marketing research firms as companies find it more profitable to contract for market research services rather than support their own marketing department. However, other organizations, including computer systems design companies, software publishers, financial services organizations, health care institutions, advertising firms, and insurance companies, may also offer job opportunities for market research analysts. Increasingly, market research analysts not only collect and analyze information, but also help clients implement analysts' ideas and recommendations.

There will be fewer job opportunities for survey researchers since it is a relatively smaller occupation. The best prospects will come from growth in the market research and public opinion polling industry, which employs many survey researchers.

## Earnings

Median annual earnings of market research analysts in May 2006 were $58,820. The middle 50 percent earned between $42,190 and $84,070. The lowest 10 percent earned less than $32,250, and the highest 10 percent earned more than $112,510. Median annual earnings in the industries employing the largest numbers of market research analysts in May 2006 were

| | |
|---|---|
| Computer systems design and related services | $76,220 |
| Management of companies and enterprises | 62,680 |
| Other professional, scientific, and technical services | 57,520 |
| Management, scientific, and technical consulting services | 54,040 |
| Insurance carriers | 53,430 |

Median annual earnings of survey researchers in May 2006 were $33,360. The middle 50 percent earned between $22,150 and $50,960. The lowest 10 percent earned less than $16,720, and the highest 10 percent earned more than $73,630. Median annual earnings of survey researchers in other professional, scientific, and technical services were $27,440.

## Related Occupations

Market and survey researchers perform research to find out how well the market will receive products, services, and ideas. Such research may include planning, implementing, and analyzing surveys to determine the needs and preferences of people. Other jobs using these skills include economists, psychologists, sociologists, statisticians, operations research analysts, management analysts, and urban and regional planners. Market and survey researchers often work closely with advertising, marketing, promotions, public relations, and sales managers. When analyzing data, market and survey researchers must use quantitative skills similar to those of mathematicians, cost estimators, and actuaries. Also, market and survey researchers often are concerned with public opinion, as are public relations specialists.

## Sources of Additional Information

For information about careers and certification in market research, contact

▸ Marketing Research Association, 110 National Dr., Glastonbury, CT 06033. Internet: http://www.mra-net.org

For information about careers in survey research, contact

▸ Council of American Survey Research Organizations, 170 North Country Rd., Suite 4, Port Jefferson, NY 11777. Internet: http://www.casro.org

# Medical and Health Services Managers

(O*NET 11-9111.00)

## Significant Points

■ Job opportunities will be good, especially for applicants with work experience in health care and strong business and management skills.

■ A master's degree is the standard credential, although a bachelor's degree is adequate for some entry-level positions.

■ Medical and health services managers typically work long hours and may be called at all hours to deal with problems.

## Nature of the Work

Health care is a business and, like every business, it needs good management to keep it running smoothly. Medical and health services managers, also referred to as *health-care executives* or *health-care administrators*, plan, direct, coordinate, and supervise the delivery of health care. These workers are either specialists in charge of a specific clinical department or generalists who manage an entire facility or system.

The structure and financing of health care are changing rapidly. Future medical and health services managers must be prepared to deal with the integration of health-care delivery systems, technological innovations, an increasingly complex regulatory environment, restructuring of work, and an increased focus on preventive care. They will be called on to improve efficiency in health-care facilities and the quality of the care provided.

Large facilities usually have several assistant administrators who aid the top administrator and handle daily decisions. Assistant administrators direct activities in clinical areas such as nursing, surgery, therapy, medical records, or health information.

In smaller facilities, top administrators handle more of the details of daily operations. For example, many nursing home administrators manage personnel, finances, facility operations, and admissions while also providing resident care.

Clinical managers have training or experience in a specific clinical area and, accordingly, have more specific responsibilities than do generalists. For example, directors of physical therapy are experienced physical therapists, and most health information and medical record administrators have a bachelor's degree in health information or medical record administration. Clinical managers establish and implement policies, objectives, and procedures for their departments; evaluate personnel and work quality; develop reports and budgets; and coordinate activities with other managers.

Health information managers are responsible for the maintenance and security of all patient records. Recent regulations enacted by the federal government require that all health-care providers maintain electronic patient records and that these records be secure. As a result, health information managers must keep up with current computer and software technology and with legislative requirements. In addition, as patient data become more frequently used for quality management and in medical research, health information managers ensure that databases are complete, accurate, and available only to authorized personnel.

In group medical practices, managers work closely with physicians. Whereas an office manager might handle business affairs in small medical groups, leaving policy decisions to the physicians themselves, larger groups usually employ a full-time administrator to help formulate business strategies and coordinate day-to-day business.

A small group of 10 to 15 physicians might employ 1 administrator to oversee personnel matters, billing and collection, budgeting, planning, equipment outlays, and patient flow. A large practice of 40 to 50 physicians might have a chief administrator and several assistants, each responsible for different areas.

Medical and health services managers in managed care settings perform functions similar to those of their counterparts in large group practices, except that they could have larger staffs to manage. In addition, they might do more community outreach and preventive care than do managers of a group practice.

Some medical and health services managers oversee the activities of a number of facilities in health systems. Such systems might contain both inpatient and outpatient facilities and offer a wide range of patient services.

*Work environment.* Some managers work in comfortable, private offices; others share space with other staff. Most medical and health services managers work long hours. Nursing care facilities and hospitals operate around the clock; administrators and managers may be called at all hours to deal with problems. They also travel to attend meetings or inspect satellite facilities.

## Training, Other Qualifications, and Advancement

A master's degree in one of a number of fields is the standard credential for most generalist positions as a medical or health-care manager. A bachelor's degree is sometimes adequate for entry-level positions in smaller facilities and departments. In physicians' offices and some other facilities, on-the-job experience may substitute for formal education.

*Education and training.* Medical and health services managers must be familiar with management principles and practices. A master's degree in health services administration, long-term care administration, health sciences, public health, public administration, or business administration is the standard credential for most generalist positions in this field. However, a bachelor's degree is adequate for some entry-level positions in smaller facilities, at the departmental level within health-care organizations, and in health information management. Physicians' offices and some other facilities hire those with on-the-job experience instead of formal education.

Bachelor's, master's, and doctoral degree programs in health administration are offered by colleges; universities; and schools of public health, medicine, allied health, public administration, and business administration. In 2007, 72 schools had accredited programs leading to the master's degree in health services administration, according to the Commission on Accreditation of Healthcare Management Education.

For people seeking to become heads of clinical departments, a degree in the appropriate field and work experience may be sufficient early in their career. However, a master's degree in health services administration or a related field might be required to advance. For example, nursing service administrators usually are chosen from among supervisory registered nurses with administrative abilities and graduate degrees in nursing or health services administration.

Health information managers require a bachelor's degree from an accredited program. In 2007, there were 42 accredited bachelor's degree programs and three master's degree programs in health information management, according to the Commission on Accreditation for Health Informatics and Information Management Education.

Some graduate programs seek students with undergraduate degrees in business or health administration; however, many graduate programs prefer students with a liberal arts or health profession background. Candidates with previous work experience in health care also may have an advantage. Competition for entry into these programs is keen, and applicants need above-average grades to gain admission. Graduate programs usually last between two and three years. They may include up to one year of supervised administrative experience and coursework in areas such as hospital organization and management, marketing, accounting and budgeting, human resources administration, strategic planning, law and ethics, biostatistics or epidemiology, health economics, and health information systems. Some programs allow students to specialize in one type of facility—hospitals, nursing care facilities, mental health facilities, or medical groups. Other programs encourage a generalist approach to health administration education.

*Licensure.* All states and the District of Columbia require nursing care facility administrators to have a bachelor's degree, pass a licensing examination, complete a state-approved training program, and pursue continuing education. Some states also require licenses for administrators in assisted living facilities. A license is not required in other areas of medical and health services management.

*Certification and other qualifications.* Medical and health services managers often are responsible for facilities and equipment worth millions of dollars and for hundreds of employees. To make effective decisions, they need to be open to different opinions and good at analyzing contradictory information. They must understand finance and information systems and be able to interpret data. Motivating others to implement their decisions requires strong leadership abilities. Tact, diplomacy, flexibility, and communication skills are essential because medical and health services managers spend most of their time interacting with others.

Health information managers who have a bachelor's degree or postbaccalaureate from an approved program and who pass an exam can earn certification as a Registered Health Information Administrator from the American Health Information Management Association.

*Advancement.* Medical and health services managers advance by moving into more responsible and higher-paying positions, such as assistant or associate administrator, department head, or chief executive officer, or by moving to larger facilities. Some experienced managers also may become consultants or professors of health-care management.

New graduates with master's degrees in health services administration may start as department managers or as supervisory staff. The level of the starting position varies with the experience of the applicant and the size of the organization. Hospitals and other health facilities offer postgraduate residencies and fellowships, which usually are staff positions. Graduates from master's degree programs also take jobs in large medical group practices, clinics, mental health facilities, nursing care corporations, and consulting firms.

Graduates with bachelor's degrees in health administration usually begin as administrative assistants or assistant department heads in larger hospitals. They also may begin as department heads or assistant administrators in small hospitals or nursing care facilities.

## Employment

Medical and health services managers held about 262,000 jobs in 2006. About 37 percent worked in hospitals, and another 22 percent worked in offices of physicians or in nursing and residential care facilities. Most of the remainder worked in home health care services, federal government health care facilities, outpatient care centers, insurance carriers, and community care facilities for the elderly.

## Job Outlook

Employment of medical and health services managers is expected to grow faster than average. Job opportunities should be good, especially for applicants with work experience in the health care field and strong business management skills.

*Employment change.* Employment of medical and health services managers is expected to grow 16 percent from 2006 to 2016, faster than the average for all occupations. The health care industry will continue to expand and diversify, requiring managers to help ensure smooth business operations.

Managers in all settings will be needed to improve the quality and efficiency of health care while controlling costs, as insurance companies and Medicare demand higher levels of accountability. Managers also will be needed to oversee the computerization of patient records and to ensure their security as required by law. Additional demand for managers will stem from the need to recruit workers and increase employee retention, to comply with changing regulations, to implement new technology, and to help improve the health of their communities by emphasizing preventive care.

Hospitals will continue to employ the most medical and health services managers over the 2006–2016 decade. However, the number of new jobs created is expected to increase at a slower rate in hospitals than in many other industries because of the growing use of clinics and other outpatient care sites. Despite relatively slow employment growth, a large number of new jobs will be created because of the industry's large size.

Employment will grow fastest in practitioners' offices and in home health care agencies. Many services previously provided in hospitals will continue to shift to these settings, especially as medical tech-

**Projections data from the National Employment Matrix**

| Occupational Title | SOC Code | Employment, 2006 | Projected employment, 2016 | Change, 2006-16 | |
| --- | --- | --- | --- | --- | --- |
| | | | | Number | Percent |
| Medical and health services managers............................................. | 11-9111 | 262,000 | 305,000 | 43,000 | 16 |

NOTE: Data in this table are rounded.

nologies improve. Demand in medical group practice management will grow as medical group practices become larger and more complex.

Medical and health services managers also will be employed by health-care management companies that provide management services to hospitals and other organizations and to specific departments such as emergency, information management systems, managed care contract negotiations, and physician recruiting.

*Job prospects.* Job opportunities will be good, and applicants with work experience in the health care field and strong business management skills should have the best opportunities. Medical and health services managers with experience in large hospital facilities will enjoy an advantage in the job market as hospitals become larger and more complex. Competition for jobs at the highest management levels will be keen because of the high pay and prestige.

## Earnings

Median annual earnings of wage and salary medical and health services managers were $73,340 in May 2006. The middle 50 percent earned between $57,240 and $94,780. The lowest 10 percent earned less than $45,050, and the highest 10 percent earned more than $127,830. Median annual earnings in the industries employing the largest numbers of medical and health services managers in May 2006 were

| | |
| --- | --- |
| General medical and surgical hospitals | $78,660 |
| Outpatient care centers | 67,920 |
| Offices of physicians | 67,540 |
| Nursing care facilities | 66,730 |
| Home health care services | 66,720 |

Earnings of medical and health services managers vary by type and size of the facility and by level of responsibility. For example, the Medical Group Management Association reported that, in 2006, median salaries for administrators were $72,875 in practices with 6 or fewer physicians, $95,766 in practices with 7 to 25 physicians, and $132,955 in practices with 26 or more physicians.

According to a survey by the Professional Association of Health Care Office Management, 2006 average total compensation for office managers in specialty physicians' practices was $70,474 in gastroenterology, $70,599 in dermatology, $76,392 in cardiology, $67,317 in ophthalmology, $67,222 in obstetrics and gynecology, $77,621 in orthopedics, $62,125 in pediatrics, $66,853 in internal medicine, and $60,040 in family practice.

## Related Occupations

Medical and health services managers have training or experience in both health and management. Other occupations requiring knowledge of both fields are insurance underwriters and social and community service managers.

## Sources of Additional Information

Information about undergraduate and graduate academic programs in this field is available from

▶ Association of University Programs in Health Administration, 2000 North 14th St., Suite 780, Arlington, VA 22201. Internet: http://www.aupha.org

For a list of accredited graduate programs in medical and health services administration, contact

▶ Commission on Accreditation of Healthcare Management Education, 2000 North 14th St., Suite 780, Arlington, VA 22201. Internet: http://www.cahme.org

For information about career opportunities in health care management, contact

▶ American College of Healthcare Executives, One N. Franklin St., Suite 1700, Chicago, IL 60606. Internet: http://www.healthmanagementcareers.org

For information about career opportunities in long-term care administration, contact

▶ American College of Health Care Administrators, 300 N. Lee St., Suite 301, Alexandria, VA 22314. Internet: http://www.achca.org

For information about career opportunities in medical group practices and ambulatory care management, contact

▶ Medical Group Management Association, 104 Inverness Terrace East, Englewood, CO 80112. Internet: http://www.mgma.org

For information about medical and health care office managers, contact

▶ Professional Association of Health Care Office Management, 461 East Ten Mile Rd., Pensacola, FL 32534.

For information about career opportunities in health information management, contact

▶ American Health Information Management Association, 233 N. Michigan Ave., Suite 2150, Chicago, IL 60601. Internet: http://www.ahima.org

## Medical Assistants

(O*NET 31-9092.00)

## Significant Points

■ About 62 percent of medical assistants work in offices of physicians.

■ Some medical assistants are trained on the job, but many complete 1-year or 2-year programs.

■ Employment is projected to grow much faster than average, ranking medical assistants among the fastest growing occupations over the 2006–2016 decade.

■ Job prospects should be excellent.

## Nature of the Work

Medical assistants perform administrative and clinical tasks to keep the offices of physicians, podiatrists, chiropractors, and other health practitioners running smoothly. They should not be confused with Physician assistants, who examine, diagnose, and treat patients under the direct supervision of a physician.

The duties of medical assistants vary from office to office, depending on the location and size of the practice and the practitioner's specialty. In small practices, medical assistants usually do many different kinds of tasks, handling both administrative and clinical duties and reporting directly to an office manager, physician, or other health practitioner. Those in large practices tend to specialize in a particular area, under the supervision of department administrators.

Medical assistants who perform administrative tasks have many duties. They update and file patients' medical records, fill out insurance forms, and arrange for hospital admissions and laboratory services. They also perform tasks less specific to medical settings, such as answering telephones, greeting patients, handling correspondence, scheduling appointments, and handling billing and bookkeeping.

For clinical medical assistants, duties vary according to what is allowed by state law. Some common tasks include taking medical histories and recording vital signs, explaining treatment procedures to patients, preparing patients for examinations, and assisting physicians during examinations. Medical assistants collect and prepare laboratory specimens and sometimes perform basic laboratory tests on the premises, dispose of contaminated supplies, and sterilize medical instruments. They might instruct patients about medications and special diets, prepare and administer medications as directed by a physician, authorize drug refills as directed, telephone prescriptions to a pharmacy, draw blood, prepare patients for x-rays, take electrocardiograms, remove sutures, and change dressings.

Medical assistants also may arrange examining room instruments and equipment, purchase and maintain supplies and equipment, and keep waiting and examining rooms neat and clean.

*Ophthalmic medical assistants*, *optometric assistants*, and *podiatric medical assistants* are examples of specialized assistants who have additional duties. Ophthalmic medical assistants help ophthalmologists provide eye care. They conduct diagnostic tests, measure and record vision, and test eye muscle function. They also show patients how to insert, remove, and care for contact lenses, and they apply eye dressings. Under the direction of the physician, ophthalmic medical assistants may administer eye medications. They also maintain optical and surgical instruments and may assist the ophthalmologist in surgery. Optometric assistants also help provide eye care, working with optometrists. They provide chair-side assistance, instruct patients about contact lens use and care, conduct preliminary tests on patients, and otherwise provide assistance while working directly with an optometrist. Podiatric medical assistants make castings of feet, expose and develop x rays, and assist podiatrists in surgery.

*Work environment.* Medical assistants work in well-lighted, clean environments. They constantly interact with other people and may have to handle several responsibilities at once. Most full-time medical assistants work a regular 40-hour week. However, many medical assistants work part time, evenings, or weekends.

## Training, Other Qualifications, and Advancement

Some medical assistants are trained on the job, but many complete one-year or two-year programs.

*Education and training.* Postsecondary medical assisting programs are offered in vocational-technical high schools, postsecondary vocational schools, and community and junior colleges. Programs usually last either one year and result in a certificate or diploma, or two years and result in an associate degree. Courses cover anatomy, physiology, and medical terminology, as well as typing, transcription, recordkeeping, accounting, and insurance processing. Students learn laboratory techniques, clinical and diagnostic procedures, pharmaceutical principles, the administration of medications, and first aid. They study office practices, patient relations, medical law, and ethics. There are various organizations that accredit medical assisting programs. Accredited programs often include an internship that provides practical experience in physicians' offices, hospitals, or other health care facilities.

Formal training in medical assisting, while generally preferred, is not always required. Some medical assistants are trained on the job, although this practice is less common than in the past. Applicants usually need a high school diploma or the equivalent. Recommended high school courses include mathematics, health, biology, typing, bookkeeping, computers, and office skills. Volunteer experience in the health care field also is helpful. Medical assistants who are trained on the job usually spend their first few months attending training sessions and working closely with more experienced workers.

Some states allow medical assistants to perform more advanced procedures, such as giving injections, after passing a test or taking a course.

*Certification and other qualifications.* Employers prefer to hire experienced workers or those who are certified. Although not required, certification indicates that a medical assistant meets certain standards of competence. There are various associations—some listed in the sources of information below—that award certification credentials to medical assistants, and the certification process varies. It also is possible to become certified in a specialty, such as podiatry, optometry, or ophthalmology.

Medical assistants deal with the public; therefore, they must be neat and well groomed and have a courteous, pleasant manner and they must be able to put patients at ease and explain physicians' instructions. They must respect the confidential nature of medical information. Clinical duties require a reasonable level of manual dexterity and visual acuity.

*Advancement.* Medical assistants may advance to other occupations through experience or additional training. For example, some may go on to teach medical assisting, and others pursue additional education to become nurses or other health care workers. Administrative medical assistants may advance to office manager, or qualify for a variety of administrative support occupations.

**Projections data from the National Employment Matrix**

| Occupational Title | SOC Code | Employment, 2006 | Projected employment, 2016 | Change, 2006-16 | |
| --- | --- | --- | --- | --- | --- |
| | | | | Number | Percent |
| Medical assistants ............................................................................... | 31-9092 | 417,000 | 565,000 | 148,000 | 35 |

NOTE: Data in this table are rounded.

# Employment

Medical assistants held about 417,000 jobs in 2006. About 62 percent worked in offices of physicians; 12 percent worked in public and private hospitals, including inpatient and outpatient facilities; and 11 percent worked in offices of other health practitioners, such as chiropractors, optometrists, and podiatrists. Most of the remainder worked in other health care industries such as outpatient care centers and nursing and residential care facilities.

# Job Outlook

Employment is projected to grow much faster than average, ranking medical assistants among the fastest growing occupations over the 2006–2016 decade. Job opportunities should be excellent, particularly for those with formal training or experience, and certification.

***Employment change.*** Employment of medical assistants is expected to grow 35 percent from 2006 to 2016, much faster than the average for all occupations. As the health care industry expands because of technological advances in medicine and the growth and aging of the population, there will be an increased need for all health care workers. Increasing use of medical assistants in the rapidly growing health care industry will further stimulate job growth.

Helping to drive job growth is the increasing number of group practices, clinics, and other health care facilities that need a high proportion of support personnel, particularly medical assistants who can handle both administrative and clinical duties. In addition, medical assistants work primarily in outpatient settings, a rapidly growing sector of the health care industry.

***Job prospects.*** Job seekers who want to work as a medical assistant should find excellent job prospects. Medical assistants are projected to account for a very large number of new jobs, and many other opportunities will come from the need to replace workers leaving the occupation. Those with formal training or experience—particularly those with certification—should have the best job opportunities.

# Earnings

The earnings of medical assistants vary, depending on their experience, skill level, and location. Median annual earnings of wage-and-salary medical assistants were $26,290 in May 2006. The middle 50 percent earned between $21,970 and $31,210. The lowest 10 percent earned less than $18,860, and the highest 10 percent earned more than $36,840. Median annual earnings in the industries employing the largest numbers of medical assistants in May 2006 were

| | |
| --- | --- |
| General medical and surgical hospitals ................ | $27,340 |
| Outpatient care centers ...................................... | 26,840 |
| Offices of physicians .......................................... | 26,620 |
| Offices of chiropractors ..................................... | 22,940 |
| Offices of optometrists....................................... | 22,850 |

# Related Occupations

Medical assistants perform work similar to the tasks completed by other workers in medical support occupations. Administrative medical assistants do work similar to that of medical secretaries, medical transcriptionists, and medical records and health information technicians. Clinical medical assistants perform duties similar to those of dental assistants; dental hygienists; occupational therapist assistants and aides; pharmacy aides; licensed practical and licensed vocational nurses; surgical technologists; physical therapist assistants and aides; and nursing, psychiatric, and home health aides.

# Sources of Additional Information

Information about career opportunities and certification for medical assistants is available from

▶ American Association of Medical Assistants, 20 North Wacker Dr., Suite 1575, Chicago, IL 60606. Internet: http://www.aama-ntl.org

▶ American Medical Technologists, 10700 West Higgins Rd., Suite 150, Rosemont, IL 60018. Internet: http://www.amt1.com

▶ National Healthcareer Association, 7 Ridgedale Ave., Suite 203, Cedar Knolls, NJ 07927.

Information about career opportunities, training programs, and certification for ophthalmic medical personnel is available from

▶ Joint Commission on Allied Health Personnel in Ophthalmology, 2025 Woodlane Dr., St. Paul, MN 55125. Internet: http://www.jcahpo.org/newsite/index.htm

Information about career opportunities, training programs and certification for optometric assistants is available from

▶ American Optometric Association, 243 N. Lindbergh Blvd., St. Louis, MO 63141. Internet: http://www.aoa.org

Information about certification for podiatric assistants is available from

▶ American Society of Podiatric Medical Assistants, 2124 South Austin Blvd., Cicero, IL 60804. Internet: http://www.aspma.org

For lists of accredited educational programs in medical assisting, contact

▶ Accrediting Bureau of Health Education Schools, 7777 Leesburg Pike, Suite 314 N, Falls Church, VA 22043. Internet: http://www.abhes.org

▶ Commission on Accreditation of Allied Health Education Programs, 1361 Park St., Clearwater, FL 33756. Internet: http://www.caahep.org

# Medical Records and Health Information Technicians

(O*NET 29-2071.00)

## Significant Points

- Employment is expected to grow faster than average.
- Job prospects should be very good; technicians with a strong background in medical coding will be in particularly high demand.
- Entrants usually have an associate degree.
- This is one of the few health occupations in which there is little or no direct contact with patients.

## Nature of the Work

Every time a patient receives health care, a record is maintained of the observations, medical or surgical interventions, and treatment outcomes. This record includes information that the patient provides concerning his or her symptoms and medical history, the results of examinations, reports of x rays and laboratory tests, diagnoses, and treatment plans. Medical records and health information technicians organize and evaluate these records for completeness and accuracy.

Technicians assemble patients' health information, making sure that patients' initial medical charts are complete, that all forms are completed and properly identified and authenticated, and that all necessary information is in the computer. They regularly communicate with physicians and other health care professionals to clarify diagnoses or to obtain additional information. Technicians regularly use computer programs to tabulate and analyze data to improve patient care, better control cost, provide documentation for use in legal actions, or use in research studies.

Medical records and health information technicians' duties vary with the size of the facility where they work. In large to medium size facilities, technicians might specialize in one aspect of health information or might supervise health information clerks and transcriptionists while a medical records and health information administrator manages the department. In small facilities, a credentialed medical records and health information technician may have the opportunity to manage the department.

Some medical records and health information technicians specialize in coding patients' medical information for insurance purposes. Technicians who specialize in coding are called *health information coders, medical record coders, coder/abstractors*, or *coding specialists*. These technicians assign a code to each diagnosis and procedure, relying on their knowledge of disease processes. Technicians then use classification systems software to assign the patient to one of several hundred "diagnosis-related groups," or DRGs. The DRG determines the amount for which the hospital will be reimbursed if the patient is covered by Medicare or other insurance programs using the DRG system. In addition to the DRG system, coders use other coding systems, such as those required for ambulatory settings, physician offices, or long-term care.

Medical records and health information technicians also may specialize in cancer registry. *Cancer* (or tumor) *registrars* maintain facility, regional, and national databases of cancer patients. Registrars review patient records and pathology reports and assign codes for the diagnosis and treatment of different cancers and selected benign tumors. Registrars conduct annual followups on all patients in the registry to track their treatment, survival, and recovery. Physicians and public health organizations then use this information to calculate survivor rates and success rates of various types of treatment, locate geographic areas with high incidences of certain cancers, and identify potential participants for clinical drug trials. Public health officials also use cancer registry data to target areas for the allocation of resources to provide intervention and screening.

*Work environment.* Medical records and health information technicians work in pleasant and comfortable offices. This is one of the few health-related occupations in which there is little or no direct contact with patients. Because accuracy is essential in their jobs, technicians must pay close attention to detail. Technicians who work at computer monitors for prolonged periods must guard against eyestrain and muscle pain.

Medical records and health information technicians usually work a 40-hour week. Some overtime may be required. In hospitals—where health information departments often are open 24 hours a day, 7 days a week—technicians may work day, evening, and night shifts.

## Training, Other Qualifications, and Advancement

Medical records and health information technicians entering the field usually have an associate degree from a community or junior college. Many employers favor technicians who have become Registered Health Information Technicians (RHIT). Advancement opportunities for medical record and health information technicians are typically achieved by specialization or promotion to a management position.

*Education and training.* Medical records and health information technicians generally obtain an associate degree from a community or junior college. Typically, community and junior colleges offer flexible course scheduling or online distance learning courses. In addition to general education, coursework includes medical terminology, anatomy and physiology, legal aspects of health information, health data standards, coding and abstraction of data, statistics, database management, quality improvement methods, and computer science. Applicants can improve their chances of admission into a program by taking biology, math, chemistry, health, and computer science courses in high school.

*Certification and other qualifications.* Most employers prefer to hire Registered Health Information Technicians (RHIT), who must pass a written examination offered by the American Health Information Management Association (AHIMA). To take the examination, a person must graduate from a two-year associate degree program accredited by the Commission on Accreditation for Health Informatics and Information Management Education (CAHIIM). Technicians trained in non-CAHIIM-accredited programs or trained on the job are not eligible to take the examination. In 2007, there were about 245 CAHIIM accredited programs in Health Informatics and Information Management Education.

**Projections data from the National Employment Matrix**

| Occupational Title | SOC Code | Employment, 2006 | Projected employment, 2016 | Change, 2006-2016 | |
|---|---|---|---|---|---|
| | | | | Number | Percent |
| Medical records and health information technicians ....................... | 29-2071 | 170,000 | 200,000 | 30,000 | 18 |

NOTE: Data in this table are rounded.

Some employers prefer candidates with experience in a health care setting. Experience is valuable in demonstrating certain skills or desirable qualities. It is beneficial for health information technicians to possess good communication skills, as they often serve as a liaison between health care facilities, insurance companies, and other establishments. Accuracy is also essential to technicians because they must pay close attention to detail. A candidate who exhibits proficiency with computers will become more valuable as health care facilities continue to adopt electronic medical records.

*Certification and advancement.* Experienced medical records and health information technicians usually advance in one of two ways—by specializing or by moving into a management position. Many senior technicians specialize in coding, in cancer registry, or in privacy and security. Most coding and registry skills are learned on the job. A number of schools offer certificate programs in coding or include coding as part of the associate degree program for health information technicians, although there are no formal degree programs in coding. For cancer registry, there are a few formal two-year certificate programs approved by the National Cancer Registrars Association (NCRA). Some schools and employers offer intensive one- to two-week training programs in either coding or cancer registry.

Certification in coding is available from several organizations. Coding certification within specific medical specialty areas is available from the Board of Medical Specialty Coding and the Professional Association of Healthcare Coding Specialist (PAHCS). The American Academy of Professional Coders (AAPC) offers three distinct certification programs in coding. The AHIMA also offers certification for Certified Healthcare Privacy and Security because of growing concerns for the security of electronic medical records. Certification in cancer registry is available from the NCRA. Continuing education units are typically required to renew credentials.

In large medical records and health information departments, experienced technicians may advance to section supervisor, overseeing the work of the coding, correspondence, or discharge sections, for example. Senior technicians with RHIT credentials may become director or assistant director of a medical records and health information department in a small facility. However, in larger institutions, the director usually is an administrator with a bachelor's degree in medical records and health information administration.

Hospitals sometimes advance promising health information clerks to jobs as medical records and health information technicians, although this practice may be less common in the future. Advancement usually requires two to four years of job experience and completion of a hospital's in-house training program.

## Employment

Medical records and health information technicians held about 170,000 jobs in 2006. About 2 out of 5 jobs were in hospitals. The rest were mostly in offices of physicians, nursing care facilities, outpatient care centers, and home health care services. Insurance firms that deal in health matters employ a small number of health information technicians to tabulate and analyze health information. Public health departments also employ technicians to supervise data collection from health care institutions and to assist in research.

## Job Outlook

Employment is expected to grow faster than average. Job prospects should be very good; technicians with a strong background in medical coding will be in particularly high demand.

*Employment change.* Employment of medical records and health information technicians is expected to increase by 18 percent through 2016—faster than the average for all occupations—because of rapid growth in the number of medical tests, treatments, and procedures that will be increasingly scrutinized by health insurance companies, regulators, courts, and consumers. Also, technicians will be needed to enter patient information into computer databases to comply with federal legislation mandating the use of electronic medical records.

New jobs are expected in offices of physicians as a result of increasing demand for detailed records, especially in large group practices. New jobs also are expected in home health care services, outpatient care centers, and nursing and residential care facilities. Although employment growth in hospitals will not keep pace with growth in other health care industries, many new jobs will, nevertheless, be created.

Cancer registrars should experience job growth. As the population continues to age, the incidence of cancer may increase.

*Job prospects.* Job prospects should be very good. In addition to job growth, openings will result from the need to replace technicians who retire or leave the occupation permanently.

Technicians with a strong background in medical coding will be in particularly high demand. Changing government regulations and the growth of managed care have increased the amount of paperwork involved in filing insurance claims. Additionally, health care facilities are having some difficulty attracting qualified workers, primarily because employers prefer trained and experienced technicians prepared to work in an increasingly electronic environment with the integration of electronic health records. Job opportunities may be especially good for coders employed through temporary help agencies or by professional services firms.

## Earnings

Median annual earnings of medical records and health information technicians were $28,030 in May 2006. The middle 50 percent earned between $22,420 and $35,990. The lowest 10 percent earned less than $19,060, and the highest 10 percent earned more than $45,260. Median annual earnings in the industries employing the largest numbers of medical records and health information technicians in May 2006 were

General medical and surgical hospitals ................$29,400
Nursing care facilities .........................................28,410
Outpatient care centers ......................................26,680
Offices of physicians ..........................................24,170

## Related Occupations

Medical records and health information technicians need a strong clinical background to analyze the contents of medical records. Medical secretaries and medical transcriptionists also must be knowledgeable about medical terminology, anatomy, and physiology even though they have little or no direct contact with patients.

## Sources of Additional Information

Information on careers in medical records and health information technology, and a list of accredited training programs is available from

▸ American Health Information Management Association, 233 N. Michigan Ave., Suite 2150, Chicago, IL 60601-5800. Internet: http://www.ahima.org

Information on training and certification for medical coders is available from

▸ American Academy of Professional Coders, 2480 South 3850 West, Suite B, Salt Lake City, UT 84120. Internet: http://www.aapc.com

Information on cancer registrars is available from

▸ National Cancer Registrars Association, 1340 Braddock Place, Suite 203, Alexandria, VA 22314. Internet: http://www.ncra-usa.org

## Medical Scientists

(O*NET 19-1041.00 and 19-1042.00)

## Significant Points

■ Most medical scientists need a Ph.D. in a biological science; some hold a medical degree.

■ Epidemiologists typically need a master's degree in public health or, in some cases, a Ph.D. or medical degree.

■ Competition is expected for most positions; however, those with both a Ph.D. and M.D. are likely to have very good opportunities.

## Nature of the Work

Medical scientists research human diseases to improve human health. Most medical scientists conduct biomedical research and development to advance knowledge of life processes and living organisms, including viruses, bacteria, and other infectious agents. Past research has resulted in advances in diagnosis, treatment, and prevention of many diseases. Basic medical research continues to build the foundation for new vaccines, drugs, and treatment procedures. Medical scientists engage in laboratory research, clinical investigation, technical writing, drug application review, and related activities.

Medical scientists study biological systems to understand the causes of disease and other health problems. They develop treatments and design research tools and techniques that have medical applications. Some try to identify changes in cells or in chromosomes that signal the development of medical problems. For example, medical scientists involved in cancer research may formulate a combination of drugs that will lessen the effects of the disease. Medical scientists who are also physicians can administer these drugs to patients in clinical trials, monitor their reactions, and observe the results. They may draw blood, excise tissue, or perform other invasive procedures. Those who are not physicians normally collaborate with physicians who deal directly with patients. Medical scientists examine the results of clinical trials and adjust the dosage levels to reduce negative side effects or to induce better results. In addition to developing treatments for medical conditions, medical scientists attempt to discover ways to prevent health problems. For example, they may study the link between smoking and lung cancer or between alcoholism and liver disease.

Medical scientists who work in applied research or product development use knowledge discovered through basic research to develop new drugs and medical treatments. They usually have less autonomy than basic medical researchers do to choose the emphasis of their research. They spend more time working on marketable treatments to meet the business goals of their employers. Medical scientists doing applied research and product development in private industry may also be required to explain their research plans or results to nonscientists who are in a position to reject or approve their ideas. These scientists must consider the business effects of their work. Scientists increasingly work as part of teams, interacting with engineers, scientists of other disciplines, business managers, and technicians.

Swift advances in basic medical knowledge related to genetics and organic molecules have spurred growth in the field of biotechnology. Discovery of important drugs, including human insulin and growth hormone, is the result of research using biotechnology techniques, such as recombining DNA. Many other substances not previously available in large quantities are now produced by biotechnological means; some may one day be useful in treating diseases such as Parkinson's or Alzheimer's. Today, many medical scientists are involved in the science of genetic engineering—isolating, identifying, and sequencing human genes to determine their functions. This work continues to lead to the discovery of genes associated with specific diseases and inherited health risks, such as sickle cell anemia. These advances in biotechnology have opened up research opportunities in almost all areas of medical science.

Some medical scientists specialize in epidemiology. This branch of medical science investigates and describes the causes and spread of disease and develops the means for prevention or control. Epidemiologists may study many different illnesses, often focusing on major infectious diseases such as influenza or cholera. Epidemiologists can be separated into two groups—research and clinical.

*Research epidemiologists* conduct research in an effort to eradicate or control infectious diseases. Many work on illnesses that affect the entire body, such as AIDS or typhus, while others focus on localized infections such as those of the brain, lungs, or digestive tract. Research epidemiologists work at colleges and universities, schools of public health, medical schools, and independent research firms. For example, federal government agencies, such as the U.S. Department of Defense, may contract with a research firm to evaluate the incidence of malaria in certain parts of the world. Other research epidemiologists may work as college and university faculty and are counted as postsecondary teachers.

*Clinical epidemiologists* work primarily in consulting roles at hospitals, informing the medical staff of infectious outbreaks and providing containment solutions. These epidemiologists sometimes are referred to as infection control professionals, and some of them are also physicians. Clinical epidemiologists who are not also physicians often collaborate with physicians to find ways to contain outbreaks of diseases. In addition to traditional duties of studying and controlling diseases, clinical epidemiologists also may be required to develop standards and guidelines for the treatment and control of communicable diseases. Some clinical epidemiologists may work in outpatient settings.

*Work environment.* Many medical scientists work independently in private industry, university, or government laboratories, exploring new areas of research or expanding on specialized research that they began in graduate school. Medical scientists working in colleges and universities, hospitals, and nonprofit medical research organizations typically submit grant proposals to obtain funding for their projects. Colleges and universities, private industry, and federal government agencies—particularly the National Institutes of Health and the National Science Foundation—provide the primary support for researchers whose proposals are determined to be financially feasible and to have the potential to advance new ideas or processes. Medical scientists who rely on grant money may be under pressure to meet deadlines and to conform to rigid grant-writing specifications when preparing proposals to seek new or extended funding.

Medical scientists who conduct research usually work in laboratories and use a wide variety of equipment. Some may work directly with individual patients or larger groups as they administer drugs and monitor patients during clinical trials. Often, these medical scientists also spend time working in clinics and hospitals.

Medical scientists usually are not exposed to unsafe or unhealthy conditions; however, those scientists who work with dangerous organisms or toxic substances must follow strict safety procedures to avoid contamination.

Medical scientists typically work regular hours in offices or laboratories, but longer hours are not uncommon. Researchers may be required to work odd hours in laboratories or other locations, depending on the nature of their research. On occasion, epidemiologists may be required to travel to meetings and hearings for medical investigations.

## Training, Other Qualifications, and Advancement

A Ph.D. in a biological science is the minimum education required for most prospective medical scientists, except epidemiologists. However, some medical scientists pursue medical degrees to perform clinical work. Epidemiologists typically need at least a master's degree in public health, but some work requires a Ph.D. or medical degree. A period of postdoctoral work in the laboratory of a senior researcher is becoming increasingly common for medical scientists.

*Education and training.* A Ph.D. typically qualifies people to research basic life processes or particular medical problems and to analyze the results of experiments. Some medical scientists obtain a medical degree instead of a Ph.D., but some do not become licensed physicians because they prefer research to clinical practice. It is particularly helpful for medical scientists to earn both a Ph.D. and a medical degree.

Students planning careers as medical scientists should have a bachelor's degree in a biological science. In addition to required courses in chemistry and biology, undergraduates should study allied disciplines, such as mathematics, engineering, physics, and computer science, or courses in their field of interest. Once they have completed undergraduate studies, they can then select a specialty for their advanced degree, such as cytology, bioinformatics, genomics, or pathology.

The minimum educational requirement for epidemiologists is a master's degree from a school of public health. Some jobs may require a Ph.D. or medical degree, depending on the work performed. Epidemiologists who work in hospitals and health care centers often must have a medical degree with specific training in infectious diseases. Some employees in research epidemiology positions are required to be licensed physicians because they must administer drugs in clinical trials.

Few students select epidemiology for undergraduate study. Undergraduates, nonetheless, should study biological sciences and should have a solid background in chemistry, mathematics, and computer science. Once a student is prepared for graduate studies, he or she can choose a specialty within epidemiology. For example, those interested in studying environmental epidemiology should focus on environmental coursework, such as water pollution, air pollution, pesticide use, toxicology, and molecular biology. Other specialties include occupational epidemiology, infection processes, infection control precautions, surveillance methodology, and outbreak investigation. Some epidemiologists begin their careers in other health care occupations, such as registered nurse or medical technologist.

In addition to formal education, medical scientists usually spend some time in a postdoctoral position before they apply for permanent jobs. Postdoctoral work provides valuable laboratory experience, including experience in specific processes and techniques such as gene splicing, which is transferable to other research projects. In some institutions, the postdoctoral position can lead to a permanent job.

*Licensure.* Medical scientists who administer drug or gene therapy to human patients, or who otherwise interact medically with patients—drawing blood, excising tissue, or performing other invasive procedures—must be licensed physicians. To be licensed, physicians must graduate from an accredited medical school, pass a licensing examination, and complete one to seven years of graduate medical education.

Epidemiologists who perform laboratory tests often require the knowledge and expertise of a licensed physician to administer drugs to patients in clinical trials. Epidemiologists who are not physicians frequently work closely with one.

*Other qualifications.* Medical scientists should be able to work independently or as part of a team and be able to communicate clearly and concisely, both orally and in writing. Those in private industry, especially those who aspire to consulting and administrative positions, should possess strong communication skills so that they can provide instruction and advice to physicians and other health care professionals.

*Certification and advancement.* The Association for Professionals in Infection Control and Epidemiology offers continuing education courses and certification programs in infection prevention and control and applied epidemiology. To become certified as an infection control professional, applicants must pass an examination. Certification can be an advantage for those seeking advancement in this rapidly evolving field.

Advancement among medical scientists usually takes the form of greater independence in their work, larger budgets, or tenure in university positions. Others choose to move into managerial positions and become natural science managers. Those who pursue management careers spend more time preparing budgets and schedules.

# Employment

Medical scientists held about 92,000 jobs in 2006. Epidemiologists accounted for only 5 percent of that total. In addition, many medical scientists held faculty positions in colleges and universities, but they are classified as college or university faculty.

About 34 percent of medical scientists, except epidemiologists, were employed in colleges and universities. About 28 percent were employed in scientific research and development services firms; 12 percent were employed in pharmaceutical and medicine manufacturing; 9 percent were employed in hospitals; and most of the remainder were employed in private educational services and ambulatory health care services.

Among epidemiologists, 57 percent were employed in government; 12 percent were employed in hospitals; 11 percent were employed in colleges and universities; and 9 percent were employed in scientific research and development services.

# Job Outlook

Medical scientists can expect to face competition for most jobs, in part because of the attractiveness of the career. However, those with both a Ph.D. and M.D. are likely to experience very good opportunities.

*Employment change.* Employment of medical scientists is expected to increase 20 percent over the 2006–2016 decade, faster than the average for all occupations. The federal government funds much

basic research and development, including many areas of medical research. Although previous budget increases at the National Institutes of Health have led to large increases in the number of grants awarded to researchers, the increase in expenditures has slowed significantly, causing expected future employment growth to be more modest than in the past despite the faster than average projected growth.

Medical scientists enjoyed rapid gains in employment since the 1980s—reflecting, in part, the growth of biotechnology companies. Job growth should be dampened somewhat as fewer new biotechnology firms are founded and as existing firms merge or are absorbed by larger biotechnology or pharmaceutical firms. Some companies may conduct a portion of their research and development in other lower-wage countries, further limiting employment growth. However, much of the basic medical research done in recent years has resulted in new knowledge, including the isolation and identification of new genes. Medical scientists will be needed to take this knowledge to the next stage—understanding how certain genes function within an entire organism—so that medical treatments can be developed for various diseases. Even pharmaceutical and other firms not solely engaged in biotechnology have largely adopted biotechnology techniques, thus creating employment for medical scientists.

Employment growth should also occur as a result of the expected expansion in research related to illnesses such as AIDS, cancer, and avian influenza, along with growing treatment problems such as antibiotic resistance. Moreover, environmental conditions such as overcrowding and the increasing frequency of international travel will tend to spread existing diseases and give rise to new ones. Medical scientists will continue to be needed because they greatly contribute to the development of treatments and medicines that improve human health.

An increasing focus on monitoring patients at hospitals and health care centers to ensure positive patient outcomes will contribute to job growth for epidemiologists. In addition, a heightened awareness of bioterrorism and rare, but infectious diseases such as West Nile Virus or severe acute respiratory syndrome (SARS) should spur demand for these workers. As hospitals enhance their infection control programs, many will seek to boost the quality and quantity of their staff.

*Job prospects.* Besides job openings due to employment growth, openings will arise as workers leave the labor force or transfer to other occupations. However, doctoral degree holders can expect to face considerable competition for basic research positions and for research grants. If the number of advanced degrees awarded continues to grow, applicants are likely to face even more competition.

Although medical scientists can expect competition for jobs, those with both doctoral and medical degrees are likely to experience very good opportunities. As funding for research becomes more difficult to obtain, those with both a biological and professional medical background will have a distinct advantage. Opportunities in epidemiology also should be highly competitive, as the number of available positions will continue to be limited.

Medical scientists and epidemiologists are less likely to lose their jobs during recessions than are those in many other occupations because they are employed on long-term research projects. How-

**Projections data from the National Employment Matrix**

| Occupational Title | SOC Code | Employment, 2006 | Projected employment, 2016 | Change, 2006-2016 | |
| --- | --- | --- | --- | --- | --- |
| | | | | Number | Percent |
| Medical scientists............................................................... | 19-1040 | 92,000 | 110,000 | 18,000 | 20 |
| Epidemiologists............................................................. | 19-1041 | 4,500 | 5,100 | 600 | 14 |
| Medical scientists, except epidemiologists ............................... | 19-1042 | 87,000 | 105,000 | 18,000 | 20 |

NOTE: Data in this table are rounded.

ever, a recession could influence the amount of money allocated to new research and development, particularly in areas of risky or innovative medical research. A recession also could limit extensions or renewals of existing projects.

## Earnings

Median annual earnings of wage and salary medical scientists, except epidemiologists, were $61,680 in May 2006. The middle 50 percent of these workers earned between $44,830 and $88,130. The lowest 10 percent earned less than $35,490, and the highest 10 percent earned more than $117,520. Median annual earnings in the industries employing the largest numbers of medical scientists were

Pharmaceutical and medicine manufacturing ........$82,640

Research and development in the physical,
engineering, and life sciences...........................71,490

Offices of physicians ........................................70,000

General medical and surgical hospitals .................64,700

Colleges, universities, and professional schools ......44,600

Median annual earnings of wage and salary epidemiologists were $56,670 in May 2006. The middle 50 percent earned between $45,220 and $71,080. The lowest 10 percent earned less than $36,920, and the highest 10 percent earned more than $87,300.

## Related Occupations

Many other occupations deal with living organisms and require a level of training similar to that of medical scientists. These occupations include biological scientists, agricultural and food scientists, pharmacists, engineering and natural sciences managers, and health occupations such as physicians and surgeons, dentists, and veterinarians.

## Sources of Additional Information

For information on pharmaceutical scientists, contact

▶ American Association of Pharmaceutical Scientists (AAPS), 2107 Wilson Blvd., Suite 700, Arlington, VA 22201. Internet: http://www.aapspharmaceutica.org

For information on careers in microbiology, contact

▶ American Society for Microbiology, Career Information—Education Department, 1752 N St. NW, Washington, DC 20036. Internet: http://www.asm.org

For information on infectious diseases training programs, contact

▶ Infectious Diseases Society of America, Guide to Training Programs, 66 Canal Center Plaza, Suite 600, Alexandria, VA 22314. Internet: http://www.idsociety.org

Information on obtaining a medical scientist position with the federal government is available from the Office of Personnel Management through USAJOBS, the federal government's official employment information system. This resource for locating and applying for job opportunities can be accessed through the Internet at http://www.usajobs.opm.gov or through an interactive voice response telephone system at (703) 724-1850 or TDD (978) 461-8404. These numbers are not toll free, and charges may result. For advice on how to find and apply for federal jobs, see the *Occupational Outlook Quarterly* article "How to get a job in the Federal Government," online at http://www.bls.gov/opub/ooq/2004/summer/art01.pdf.

# Nursing, Psychiatric, and Home Health Aides

(O*NET 31-1011.00, 31-1012.00, and 31-1013.00)

## Significant Points

■ Numerous job openings and excellent job opportunities are expected.

■ Most jobs are in nursing and residential care facilities, hospitals, and home health care services.

■ This occupation is characterized by modest entry requirements, low pay, high physical and emotional demands, and limited advancement opportunities.

## Nature of the Work

Nursing and psychiatric aides help care for physically or mentally ill, injured, disabled, or infirm individuals in hospitals, nursing care facilities, and mental health settings. Home health aides have duties that are similar, but they work in patients' homes or residential care facilities. Nursing aides and home health aides are among the occupations commonly referred to as direct care workers, due to their role in working with patients who need long-term care. The specific care they give depends on their specialty.

*Nursing aides* also known as nurse aides, nursing assistants, certified nursing assistants, geriatric aides, unlicensed assistive personnel, orderlies, or hospital attendants provide hands-on care and perform routine tasks under the supervision of nursing and medical staff. Specific tasks vary, with aides handling many aspects of a patient's care. They often help patients to eat, dress, and bathe. They also answer calls for help, deliver messages, serve meals, make beds, and tidy up rooms. Aides sometimes are responsible for taking a patient's temperature, pulse rate, respiration rate, or blood pressure. They also may help provide care to patients by helping them get into and out of bed and walk, escorting them to operating and examining rooms, or providing skin care. Some aides help other medical staff by setting up equipment, storing and moving supplies, and assisting with some procedures. Aides also observe patients' physical, mental, and emotional conditions and report any change to the nursing or medical staff.

Nurse aides employed in nursing care facilities often are the principal caregivers, having far more contact with residents than do other members of the staff. Because some residents may stay in a nursing care facility for months or even years, aides develop ongoing relationships with them and interact with them in a positive, caring way.

*Home health aides* help elderly, convalescent, or disabled persons live in their own homes instead of health care facilities. Under the direction of nursing or medical staff, they provide health-related services, such as administering oral medications. Like nursing aides, home health aides may check patients' pulse rate, temperature, and respiration rate; help with simple prescribed exercises; and help patients to get in and out of bed, bathe, dress, and groom. Occasionally, they change nonsterile dressings, give massages and provide skin care, or assist with braces and artificial limbs. Experienced home health aides, with training, also may assist with medical equipment such as ventilators, which help patients breathe.

Most home health aides work with elderly or disabled persons who need more extensive care than family or friends can provide. Some help discharged hospital patients who have relatively short-term needs.

In home health agencies, a registered nurse, physical therapist, or social worker usually assigns specific duties to and supervises home health aides, who keep records of the services they perform and record each patient's condition and progress. The aides report changes in a patient's condition to the supervisor or case manager.

*Psychiatric aides*, also known as mental health assistants or psychiatric nursing assistants, care for mentally impaired or emotionally disturbed individuals. They work under a team that may include psychiatrists, psychologists, psychiatric nurses, social workers, and therapists. In addition to helping patients to dress, bathe, groom themselves, and eat, psychiatric aides socialize with them and lead them in educational and recreational activities. Psychiatric aides may play card games or other games with patients, watch television with them, or participate in group activities, such as playing sports or going on field trips. They observe patients and report any physical or behavioral signs that might be important for the professional staff to know. They accompany patients to and from therapy and treatment. Because they have such close contact with patients, psychiatric aides can have a great deal of influence on their outlook and treatment.

***Work environment.*** Work as an aide can be physically demanding. Aides spend many hours standing and walking, and they often face heavy workloads. Aides must guard against back injury because they may have to move patients into and out of bed or help them to stand or walk. It is important for aides to be trained in and to follow the proper procedures for lifting and moving patients. Aides also may face hazards from minor infections and major diseases, such as hepatitis, but can avoid infections by following proper procedures.

Aides also perform tasks that some may consider unpleasant, such as emptying bedpans and changing soiled bed linens. The patients they care for may be disoriented, irritable, or uncooperative. Psychiatric aides must be prepared to care for patients whose illness may cause violent behavior. Although their work can be emotionally demanding, many aides gain satisfaction from assisting those in need.

Home health aides may go to the same patient's home for months or even years. However, most aides work with a number of different patients, each job lasting a few hours, days, or weeks. Home health aides often visit multiple patients on the same day.

Home health aides generally work alone, with periodic visits from their supervisor. They receive detailed instructions explaining when to visit patients and what services to perform. Aides are individually responsible for getting to patients' homes, and they may spend a good portion of the working day traveling from one patient to another. Because mechanical lifting devices available in institutional settings are not as frequently available in patients' homes, home health aides must take extra care to avoid injuries resulting from overexertion when they assist patients.

Most full-time aides work about 40 hours per week, but because patients need care 24 hours a day, some aides work evenings, nights, weekends, and holidays. In 2006, 23 percent of aides worked part time compared with 15 percent of all workers.

## Training, Other Qualifications, and Advancement

In many cases, a high school diploma or equivalent is necessary for a job as a nursing or psychiatric aide. However, a high school diploma generally is not required for jobs as home health aides. Specific qualifications vary by occupation, state laws, and work setting. Advancement opportunities are limited.

***Education and training.*** Nursing and psychiatric aide training is offered in high schools, vocational-technical centers, some nursing care facilities, and some community colleges. Courses cover body mechanics, nutrition, anatomy and physiology, infection control, communication skills, and resident rights. Personal care skills, such as how to help patients to bathe, eat, and groom themselves, also are taught. Hospitals may require previous experience as a nursing aide or home health aide. Some states also require psychiatric aides to complete a formal training program. However, most psychiatric aides learn their skills on the job from experienced workers.

Home health aides are generally not required to have a high school diploma. They usually are trained on the job by registered nurses, licensed practical nurses, or experienced aides. Also, clients may prefer that tasks are done a certain way, and make those suggestions to the home health aide. A competency evaluation may be required to ensure the aide can perform the required tasks.

Some employers provide classroom instruction for newly hired aides, while others rely exclusively on informal on-the-job instruction by a licensed nurse or an experienced aide. Such training may last from several days to a few months. Aides also may attend lectures, workshops, and in-service training.

***Licensure and certification.*** The federal government has guidelines for home health aides whose employers receive reimbursement from

**Projections data from the National Employment Matrix**

| Occupational Title | SOC Code | Employment, 2006 | Projected employment, 2016 | Change, 2006-16 | |
|---|---|---|---|---|---|
| | | | | Number | Percent |
| Nursing, psychiatric, and home health aides ................................... | 31-1000 | 2,296,000 | 2,944,000 | 647,000 | 28 |
| Home health aides......................................................................... | 31-1011 | 787,000 | 1,171,000 | 384,000 | 49 |
| Nursing aides, orderlies, and attendants ..................................... | 31-1012 | 1,447,000 | 1,711,000 | 264,000 | 18 |
| Psychiatric aides.......................................................................... | 31-1013 | 62,000 | 62,000 | 0 | 0 |

NOTE: Data in this table are rounded.

Medicare. Federal law requires home health aides to pass a competency test covering a wide range of areas. A home health aide may receive training before taking the competency test. In addition, the National Association for Home Care and Hospice offers voluntary certification for home health aides. Some states also require aides to be licensed.

Similar federal requirements exist for nurse aides who work in nursing care facilities. These aides must complete a minimum of 75 hours of state-approved training and pass a competency evaluation. Aides who complete the program are known as certified nurse assistants (CNAs) and are placed on the state registry of nurse aides.

*Other qualifications.* Aides must be in good health. A physical examination, including state-regulated tests such as those for tuberculosis, may be required. A criminal background check also is usually required for employment.

Applicants should be tactful, patient, understanding, emotionally stable, and dependable and should have a desire to help people. They also should be able to work as part of a team, have good communication skills, and be willing to perform repetitive, routine tasks. Home health aides should be honest and discreet because they work in private homes. They also will need access to a car or public transportation to reach patients' homes.

*Advancement.* Opportunities for advancement within these occupations are limited. Aides generally need additional formal training or education to enter other health occupations. The most common health care occupations for former aides are licensed practical nurse, registered nurse, and medical assistant.

For some individuals, these occupations serve as entry-level jobs. For example, some high school and college students gain experience working in these occupations while attending school. In addition, experience as an aide can help individuals decide whether to pursue a career in health care.

## Employment

Nursing, psychiatric, and home health aides held about 2.3 million jobs in 2006. Nursing aides held the most jobs—approximately 1.4 million. Home health aides held roughly 787,000 jobs, and psychiatric aides held about 62,000 jobs. About 52 percent of nursing aides worked in nursing and residential care facilities and another 29 percent worked in hospitals. Home health aides were mainly employed by home health care services, nursing and residential care facilities and social assistance agencies. About 47 percent of all psychiatric aides worked in hospitals, primarily in psychiatric and substance abuse hospitals, although some also worked in the psychiatric units of general medical and surgical hospitals. Others were employed in state government agencies; residential mental retardation, mental

health, and substance abuse facilities; and nursing and residential care facilities.

## Job Outlook

Excellent job opportunities for nursing, psychiatric, and home health aides will arise from a combination of rapid employment growth and the need to replace the many workers who leave the occupation each year.

*Employment change.* Overall employment of nursing, psychiatric, and home health aides is projected to grow 28 percent between 2006 and 2016, much faster than the average for all occupations. However, growth will vary for the individual occupations. Home health aides are expected to gain jobs faster than other aides as a result of growing demand for home services from an aging population and efforts to contain costs by moving patients out of hospitals and nursing care facilities as quickly as possible. Consumer preference for care in the home and improvements in medical technologies for in-home treatment also will contribute to much-faster-than-average employment growth for home health aides.

Nursing aide employment will not grow as fast as home health aide employment, largely because nursing aides are concentrated in relatively slower-growing industries. Employment of nursing aides is expected to grow faster than the average for all occupations through 2016, in response to the long-term care needs of an increasing elderly population. Financial pressures on hospitals to discharge patients as soon as possible should boost admissions to nursing care facilities. As a result, job openings will be more numerous in nursing and residential care facilities than in hospitals. Modern medical technology also will drive demand for nursing aides because as the technology saves and extends more lives, it increases the need for long-term care provided by aides.

Little or no change is expected in employment of psychiatric aides—the smallest of the three occupations. Most psychiatric aides currently work in hospitals, but the industries most likely to see growth will be residential facilities for people with developmental disabilities, mental illness, and substance abuse problems. There is a long-term trend toward treating psychiatric patients outside of hospitals because it is more cost effective and allows patients to live more independent lives. Demand for psychiatric aides in residential facilities will rise in response to the increase in the number of older persons, many of whom will require mental health services. Growing demand for these workers also rests on an increasing number of mentally disabled adults who were formerly cared for by their elderly parents and who will continue to need care. Job growth also could be affected by changes in government funding of programs for the mentally ill.

*Job prospects.* High replacement needs for nursing, psychiatric, and home health aides reflect modest entry requirements, low pay, high physical and emotional demands, and limited opportunities for advancement within the occupation. For these same reasons, the number of people looking to enter the occupation will be limited. Many aides leave the occupation to attend training programs for other health care occupations. Therefore, people who are interested in, and suited for, this work should have excellent job opportunities.

## Earnings

Median hourly earnings of nursing aides, orderlies, and attendants were $10.67 in May 2006. The middle 50 percent earned between $9.09 and $12.80 an hour. The lowest 10 percent earned less than $7.78, and the highest 10 percent earned more than $14.99 an hour. Median hourly earnings in the industries employing the largest numbers of nursing aides, orderlies, and attendants in May 2006 were

Local government .............................................$12.15

Employment services ...........................................11.47

General medical and surgical hospitals ...................11.06

Nursing care facilities ..........................................10.37

Community care facilities for the elderly..................10.07

Nursing and psychiatric aides in hospitals generally receive at least 1 week of paid vacation after 1 year of service. Paid holidays and sick leave, hospital and medical benefits, extra pay for late-shift work, and pension plans also are available to many hospital employees and to some nursing care facility employees.

Median hourly earnings of home health aides were $9.34 in May 2006. The middle 50 percent earned between $7.99 and $10.90 an hour. The lowest 10 percent earned less than $7.06, and the highest 10 percent earned more than $13.00 an hour. Median hourly earnings in the industries employing the largest numbers of home health aides in May 2006 were

Nursing care facilities ...........................................$9.76

Residential mental retardation facilities ....................9.34

Services for the elderly and persons with disabilities ..9.26

Home health care services ......................................9.14

Community care facilities for the elderly ..................8.87

Home health aides receive slight pay increases with experience and added responsibility. Usually, they are paid only for the time worked in the home, not for travel time between jobs, and must pay for their travel costs from their earnings. Most employers hire only on-call hourly workers and provide no benefits.

Median hourly earnings of psychiatric aides were $11.49 in May 2006. The middle 50 percent earned between $9.20 and $14.46 an hour. The lowest 10 percent earned less than $7.75, and the highest 10 percent earned more than $17.32 an hour. Median hourly earnings in the industries employing the largest numbers of psychiatric aides in May 2006 were

State government ...............................................$13.27

General medical and surgical hospitals ...................12.31

Psychiatric and substance abuse hospitals ..............11.76

Residential mental health and substance abuse
   facilities ..............................................................9.65

Residential mental retardation facilities ...................8.80

## Related Occupations

Nursing, psychiatric, and home health aides help people who need routine care or treatment. So do child care workers, licensed practical and licensed vocational nurses, medical assistants, occupational therapist assistants and aides, personal and home care aides, physical therapist assistants and aides, radiation therapists, and registered nurses. Social and human service assistants, who sometimes work with mental health patients, do work similar to that of psychiatric aides.

## Sources of Additional Information

Information about employment opportunities may be obtained from local hospitals, nursing care facilities, home health care agencies, psychiatric facilities, state boards of nursing, and local offices of the state employment service.

Information on licensing requirements for nursing and home health aides, and lists of state-approved nursing aide programs are available from state departments of public health, departments of occupational licensing, boards of nursing, and home care associations.

For more information on training and requirements for home health aides, contact

▶ National Association for Home Care and Hospice, 228 7th St. SE, Washington, DC 20003. Internet: http://www.nahc.org

For more information on the home health care industry, contact

▶ Visiting Nurse Associations of America, 8403 Colesville Rd., Suite 1550, Silver Spring, MD 20910-6374. Internet: http://www.vnaa.org

For more information on the health care workforce, contact

▶ The Center for the Health Professions, 3333 California St., San Francisco, CA 94118. Internet: http://www.futurehealth.ucsf.edu

## Occupational Therapists

(O*NET 29-1122.00)

## Significant Points

■ Employment is expected to grow much faster than average and job opportunities should be good, especially for therapists treating the elderly.

■ Occupational therapists must be licensed, requiring a master's degree in occupational therapy, 6 months of supervised fieldwork, and passing scores on national and state examinations.

■ Occupational therapists are increasingly taking on supervisory roles, allowing assistants and aides to work more closely with clients under the guidance of a therapist.

■ More than a quarter of occupational therapists work part time.

# Nature of the Work

Occupational therapists help patients improve their ability to perform tasks in living and working environments. They work with individuals who suffer from a mentally, physically, developmentally, or emotionally disabling condition. Occupational therapists use treatments to develop, recover, or maintain the daily living and work skills of their patients. The therapist helps clients not only to improve their basic motor functions and reasoning abilities, but also to compensate for permanent loss of function. The goal is to help clients have independent, productive, and satisfying lives.

Occupational therapists help clients to perform all types of activities, from using a computer to caring for daily needs such as dressing, cooking, and eating. Physical exercises may be used to increase strength and dexterity, while other activities may be chosen to improve visual acuity or the ability to discern patterns. For example, a client with short-term memory loss might be encouraged to make lists to aid recall, and a person with coordination problems might be assigned exercises to improve hand-eye coordination. Occupational therapists also use computer programs to help clients improve decision-making, abstract-reasoning, problem-solving, and perceptual skills, as well as memory, sequencing, and coordination—all of which are important for independent living.

Patients with permanent disabilities, such as spinal cord injuries, cerebral palsy, or muscular dystrophy, often need special instruction to master certain daily tasks. For these individuals, therapists demonstrate the use of adaptive equipment, including wheelchairs, orthoses, eating aids, and dressing aids. They also design or build special equipment needed at home or at work, including computer-aided adaptive equipment. They teach clients how to use the equipment to improve communication and control various situations in their environment.

Some occupational therapists treat individuals whose ability to function in a work environment has been impaired. These practitioners might arrange employment, evaluate the work space, plan work activities, and assess the client's progress. Therapists also may collaborate with the client and the employer to modify the work environment so that the client can successfully complete the work.

Assessing and recording a client's activities and progress is an important part of an occupational therapist's job. Accurate records are essential for evaluating clients, for billing, and for reporting to physicians and other health care providers.

Occupational therapists may work exclusively with individuals in a particular age group or with a particular disability. In schools, for example, they evaluate children's capabilities, recommend and provide therapy, modify classroom equipment, and help children participate in school activities. A therapist may work with children individually, lead small groups in the classroom, consult with a teacher, or serve on an administrative committee. Some therapists provide early intervention therapy to infants and toddlers who have, or are at risk of having, developmental delays. Therapies may include facilitating the use of the hands and promoting skills for listening, following directions, social play, dressing, or grooming.

Other occupational therapists work with elderly patients. These therapists help the elderly lead more productive, active, and independent lives through a variety of methods. Therapists with specialized training in driver rehabilitation assess an individual's ability to drive using both clinical and on-the-road tests. The evaluations allow the therapist to make recommendations for adaptive equipment, training to prolong driving independence, and alternative transportation options. Occupational therapists also work with clients to assess their homes for hazards and to identify environmental factors that contribute to falls.

Occupational therapists in mental health settings treat individuals who are mentally ill, developmentally challenged, or emotionally disturbed. To treat these problems, therapists choose activities that help people learn to engage in and cope with daily life. Activities might include time management skills, budgeting, shopping, homemaking, and the use of public transportation. Occupational therapists also work with individuals who are dealing with alcoholism, drug abuse, depression, eating disorders, or stress-related disorders.

*Work environment.* In large rehabilitation centers, therapists may work in spacious rooms equipped with machines, tools, and other devices generating noise. The work can be tiring because therapists are on their feet much of the time. Those providing home health care services may spend time driving from appointment to appointment. Therapists also face hazards such as back strain from lifting and moving clients and equipment.

Occupational therapists in hospitals and other health care and community settings usually work a 40-hour week. Those in schools may participate in meetings and other activities during and after the school day. In 2006, more than a quarter of occupational therapists worked part time.

# Training, Other Qualifications, and Advancement

Occupational therapists must be licensed, requiring a master's degree in occupational therapy, six months of supervised fieldwork, and passing scores on national and state examinations.

*Education and training.* A master's degree or higher in occupational therapy is the minimum requirement for entry into the field. In 2007, 124 master's degree programs offered entry-level education, 66 programs offered a combined bachelor's and master's degree, and five offered an entry-level doctoral degree. Most schools have full-time programs, although a growing number are offering weekend or part-time programs as well. Coursework in occupational therapy programs include the physical, biological, and behavioral sciences as well as the application of occupational therapy theory and skills. Programs also require the completion of six months of supervised fieldwork.

People considering this profession should take high school courses in biology, chemistry, physics, health, art, and the social sciences. College admissions offices also look favorably on paid or volunteer experience in the health care field. Relevant undergraduate majors include biology, psychology, sociology, anthropology, liberal arts, and anatomy.

*Licensure.* All states, Puerto Rico, Guam, and the District of Columbia regulate the practice of occupational therapy. To obtain a license, applicants must graduate from an accredited educational program and pass a national certification examination. Those who pass the exam are awarded the title "Occupational Therapist Registered (OTR)." Some states have additional requirements for therapists

**Projections data from the National Employment Matrix**

| Occupational Title | SOC Code | Employment, 2006 | Projected employment, 2016 | Change, 2006-16 | |
|---|---|---|---|---|---|
| | | | | Number | Percent |
| Occupational therapist assistants and aides ..................................... | 31-2010 | 33,000 | 41,000 | 8,200 | 25 |
| Occupational therapist assistants ................................................. | 31-2011 | 25,000 | 31,000 | 6,400 | 25 |
| Occupational therapist aides ...................................................... | 31-2012 | 8,200 | 10,000 | 1,800 | 22 |

NOTE: Data in this table are rounded.

who work in schools or early intervention programs. These requirements may include education-related classes, an education practice certificate, or early intervention certification.

*Other qualifications.* Occupational therapists need patience and strong interpersonal skills to inspire trust and respect in their clients. Patience is necessary because many clients may not show rapid improvement. Ingenuity and imagination in adapting activities to individual needs are assets. Those working in home health care services also must be able to adapt to a variety of settings.

*Advancement.* Occupational therapists are expected to continue their professional development by participating in continuing education courses and workshops. In fact, a number of states require continuing education as a condition of maintaining licensure.

Therapists are increasingly taking on supervisory roles. Because of rising health care costs, third-party payers are beginning to encourage occupational therapist assistants and aides to take more hands-on responsibility for clients. Occupational therapists can choose to advance their careers by taking on administrative duties and supervising assistants and aides.

Occupational therapists also can advance by specializing in a clinical area and gaining expertise in treating a certain type of patient or ailment. Therapists have specialized in gerontology, mental health, pediatrics, and physical rehabilitation. In addition, some occupational therapists choose to teach classes in accredited occupational therapy educational programs.

# Employment

Occupational therapists held about 99,000 jobs in 2006. About 1 in 10 occupational therapists held more than one job. The largest number of jobs was in hospitals. Other major employers were offices of other health practitioners (including offices of occupational therapists), public and private educational services, and nursing care facilities. Some occupational therapists were employed by home health care services, outpatient care centers, offices of physicians, individual and family services, community care facilities for the elderly, and government agencies.

A small number of occupational therapists were self-employed in private practice. These practitioners treated clients referred by other health professionals. They also provided contract or consulting services to nursing care facilities, schools, adult day care programs, and home health care agencies.

# Job Outlook

Employment of occupational therapists is expected to grow much faster than the average for all occupations. Job opportunities should be good, especially for occupational therapists treating the elderly.

*Employment change.* Employment of occupational therapists is expected to increase 23 percent between 2006 and 2016, much faster than the average for all occupations. The increasing elderly population will drive growth in the demand for occupational therapy services. In the short run, the impact of proposed federal legislation imposing limits on reimbursement for therapy services may adversely affect the job market for occupational therapists. However, over the long run, the demand for occupational therapists should continue to rise as a result of the increasing number of individuals with disabilities or limited function who require therapy services. The baby-boom generation's movement into middle age, a period when the incidence of heart attack and stroke increases, will spur demand for therapeutic services. Growth in the population 75 years and older—an age group that suffers from high incidences of disabling conditions—also will increase demand for therapeutic services. In addition, medical advances now enable more patients with critical problems to survive—patients who ultimately may need extensive therapy.

Hospitals will continue to employ a large number of occupational therapists to provide therapy services to acutely ill inpatients. Hospitals also will need occupational therapists to staff their outpatient rehabilitation programs.

Employment growth in schools will result from the expansion of the school-age population, the extension of services for disabled students, and an increasing prevalence of sensory disorders in children. Therapists will be needed to help children with disabilities prepare to enter special education programs.

*Job prospects.* Job opportunities should be good for licensed occupational therapists in all settings, particularly in acute hospital, rehabilitation, and orthopedic settings because the elderly receive most of their treatment in these settings. Occupational therapists with specialized knowledge in a treatment area also will have increased job prospects. Driver rehabilitation and fall-prevention training for the elderly are emerging practice areas for occupational therapy.

# Earnings

Median annual earnings of occupational therapists were $60,470 in May 2006. The middle 50 percent earned between $50,450 and $73,710. The lowest 10 percent earned less than $40,840, and the highest 10 percent earned more than $89,450. Median annual earnings in the industries employing the largest numbers of occupational therapists in May 2006 were

Home health care services...................................$67,600

Nursing care facilities .........................................64,750

Offices of physical, occupational and speech
 therapists, and audiologists ..............................62,290

General medical and surgical hospitals ..................61,610
Elementary and secondary schools ........................54,260

## Related Occupations

Occupational therapists use specialized knowledge to help individuals perform daily living skills and achieve maximum independence. Other workers performing similar duties include athletic trainers, audiologists, chiropractors, physical therapists, recreational therapists, rehabilitation counselors, respiratory therapists, and speech-language pathologists.

## Sources of Additional Information

For more information on occupational therapy as a career, contact

▶ American Occupational Therapy Association, 4720 Montgomery Lane, Bethesda, MD 20824-1220. Internet: http://www.aota.org

For information regarding the requirements to practice as an occupational therapist in schools, contact the appropriate occupational therapy regulatory agency for your state.

# Office Clerks, General

(O*NET 43-9061.00)

## Significant Points

- Employment growth and high replacement needs in this large occupation will result in numerous job openings.

- Prospects should be best for those with knowledge of basic computer applications and office machinery as well as good communication skills.

- Part-time and temporary positions are common.

## Nature of the Work

Rather than performing a single specialized task, general office clerks have responsibilities that often change daily with the needs of the specific job and the employer. Some clerks spend their days filing or keyboarding. Others enter data at a computer terminal. They also operate photocopiers, fax machines, and other office equipment; prepare mailings; proofread documents; and answer telephones and deliver messages.

The specific duties assigned to a clerk vary significantly, depending on the type of office in which he or she works. An office clerk in a doctor's office, for example, would not perform the same tasks that a clerk in a large financial institution or in the office of an auto parts wholesaler would. Although all clerks may sort checks, keep payroll records, take inventory, and access information, they also perform duties unique to their employer, such as organizing medications in a doctor's office, preparing materials for presentations in a corporate office, or filling orders received by fax machine for a wholesaler.

Clerks' duties also vary by level of experience. Whereas inexperienced employees make photocopies, stuff envelopes, or record inquiries, experienced clerks usually are given additional responsibilities. For example, they may maintain financial or other records, set up spreadsheets, verify statistical reports for accuracy and completeness, handle and adjust customer complaints, work with vendors, make travel arrangements, take inventory of equipment and supplies, answer questions on departmental services and functions, or help prepare invoices or budgetary requests. Senior office clerks may be expected to monitor and direct the work of lower level clerks.

*Work environment.* For the most part, general office clerks work in comfortable office settings. Those on full-time schedules usually work a standard 40-hour week; however, some work shifts or overtime during busy periods. About 26 percent of clerks work part time in 2006. Many clerks also work in temporary positions.

## Training, Other Qualifications, and Advancement

Office clerks often need to know how to use word processing and other business software and office equipment. Experience working in an office is helpful, but office clerks also learn skills on the job.

*Education and training.* Although most office clerk jobs are entry-level positions, employers may prefer or require previous office or business experience. Employers usually require a high school diploma or equivalent, and some require basic computer skills, including familiarity with word processing software, as well as other general office skills.

Training for this occupation is available through business education programs offered in high schools, community and junior colleges, and postsecondary vocational schools. Courses in office practices, word processing, and other computer applications are particularly helpful.

*Other qualifications.* Because general office clerks usually work with other office staff, they should be cooperative and able to work as part of a team. Employers prefer individuals who can perform a variety of tasks and satisfy the needs of the many departments within a company. In addition, applicants should have good communication skills, be detail oriented, and adaptable.

*Advancement.* General office clerks who exhibit strong communication, interpersonal, and analytical skills may be promoted to supervisory positions. Others may move into different, more senior administrative jobs, such as receptionist, secretary, or administrative assistant. After gaining some work experience or specialized skills, many workers transfer to jobs with higher pay or greater advancement potential. Advancement to professional occupations within an organization normally requires additional formal education, such as a college degree.

## Employment

General office clerks held about 3.2 million jobs in 2006. Most are employed in relatively small businesses. Although they work in every sector of the economy, about 43 percent worked in local government, health care and social assistance, administrative and support services, finance and insurance, or professional, scientific, and technical services industries.

**Projections data from the National Employment Matrix**

| Occupational Title | SOC Code | Employment, 2006 | Projected employment, 2016 | Change, 2006-16 | |
|---|---|---|---|---|---|
| | | | | Number | Percent |
| Office clerks, general ......................................................... | 43-9061 | 3,200,000 | 3,604,000 | 404,000 | 13 |

NOTE: Data in this table are rounded.

## Job Outlook

Employment growth and high replacement needs in this large occupation is expected to result in numerous job openings for general office clerks.

*Employment change.* Employment of general office clerks is expected to grow 13 percent between 2006 and 2016, which is about as fast as the average for all occupations. The employment outlook for these workers will continue to be affected by the increasing use of technology, expanding office automation, and the consolidation of administrative support tasks. These factors have led to a consolidation of administrative support staffs and a diversification of job responsibilities. However, this consolidation will increase the demand for general office clerks because they perform a variety of administrative support tasks, as opposed to clerks with very specific functions. It will become increasingly common within businesses, especially those smaller in size, to find only general office clerks in charge of all administrative support work.

*Job prospects.* Many job openings for general office clerks are expected to be for full-time jobs; there will also be a demand for part-time and temporary positions. Prospects should be best for those who have good writing and communication skills and knowledge of basic computer applications and office machinery—such as fax machines, telephone systems, and scanners. As general administrative support duties continue to be consolidated, employers will increasingly seek well-rounded individuals with highly developed communication skills and the ability to perform multiple tasks.

Job opportunities may vary from year to year because the strength of the economy affects demand for general office clerks. Companies tend to employ more workers when the economy is strong. Industries least likely to be affected by economic fluctuations tend to be the most stable places for employment.

## Earnings

Median annual earnings of general office clerks were $23,710 in May 2006; the middle 50 percent earned between $18,640 and $30,240 annually. The lowest 10 percent earned less than $14,850, and the highest 10 percent earned more than $37,600. Median annual salaries in the industries employing the largest numbers of general office clerks in May 2006 were

| | |
|---|---|
| Local government .............................................. | $26,590 |
| General medical and surgical hospitals .................. | 26,050 |
| Elementary and secondary schools ........................ | 24,230 |
| Colleges, universities, and professional schools ...... | 23,980 |
| Employment services ......................................... | 21,890 |

## Related Occupations

The duties of general office clerks can include a combination of bookkeeping, keyboarding, office machine operation, and filing. Other office and administrative support workers who perform similar duties include bookkeeping, accounting, and auditing clerks; communications equipment operators; customer service representatives; data entry and information processing workers; order clerks; receptionists and information clerks; secretaries and administrative assistants; stock clerks and order fillers; and tellers. Nonclerical entry-level workers include cashiers; counter and rental clerks; and food and beverage serving and related workers.

## Sources of Additional Information

State employment service offices and agencies can provide information about job openings for general office clerks.

For information related to administrative occupations, including educational programs and certified designations, contact

▸ International Association of Administrative Professionals, 10502 NW Ambassador Dr., P.O. Box 20404, Kansas City, MO 64195-0404. Internet: http://www.iaap-hq.org

▸ American Management Association, 1601 Broadway, New York, NY 10019. Internet: http://www.amanet.org

# Painters and Paperhangers

(U*NET 47-2141.00 and 47-2142.00)

## Significant Points

■ Employment prospects for painters should be excellent due to the large numbers of workers who leave the occupation for other jobs; paperhangers will face very limited opportunities.

■ Most workers learn informally on the job as helpers, but some experts recommend completion of an apprenticeship program.

■ About 42 percent of painters and paperhangers are self-employed.

## Nature of the Work

Paint and wall coverings make surfaces clean, attractive, and bright. In addition, paints and other sealers protect exterior surfaces from wear caused by exposure to the weather.

*Painters* apply paint, stain, varnish, and other finishes to buildings and other structures. They choose the right paint or finish for the surface to be covered, taking into account durability, ease of handling, method of application, and customers' wishes. Painters first prepare the surfaces to be covered, so that the paint will adhere properly. This may require removing the old coat of paint by stripping, sanding, wire brushing, burning, or water and abrasive blasting. Painters also wash walls and trim to remove dirt and grease, fill nail holes and cracks, sandpaper rough spots, and brush off dust. On new surfaces, they apply a primer or sealer to prepare the surface for the finish coat. Painters also mix paints and match colors, relying on knowledge of paint composition and color harmony. In large paint shops or hardware stores, mixing and matching are automated.

There are several ways to apply paint and similar coverings. Painters must be able to choose the right paint applicator for each job, depending on the surface to be covered, the characteristics of the finish, and other factors. Some jobs need only a good bristle brush with a soft, tapered edge; others require a dip or fountain pressure roller; still others are best done using a paint sprayer. Many jobs need several types of applicators. In fact, painters may use an assortment of brushes, edgers, and rollers for a single job. The right tools speed the painter's work and also produce the most attractive surface.

Some painting artisans specialize in creating unique finishes by using one of many decorative techniques. These techniques often involve "broken color," a process created by applying one or more colors in broken layers over a different base coat to produce a mottled or textured effect. Often these techniques employ glazes or washes applied over a solid colored background. Glazes are made of oil-based paints and give a sleek glow to walls. Washes are made of latex-based paints that have been thinned with water and can add a greater sense of depth and texture. Other decorative painting techniques include sponging, rag-rolling, stippling, sheen striping, dragging, distressing, color blocking, marbling, and faux finishes.

Some painters specialize in painting industrial structures to prevent deterioration. One example is applying a protective coating to steel bridges to fight corrosion. The coating most commonly used is a waterborne acrylic solvent that is easy to apply and environmentally friendly, but other specialized and sometimes difficult-to-apply coatings may be used. Painters may also coat interior and exterior manufacturing facilities and equipment such as storage tanks, plant buildings, lockers, piping, structural steel, and ships.

When painting any industrial structure, workers must take necessary safety precautions depending on their project. Those who specialize in interior applications such as painting the inside of storage tanks, for example, must wear a full-body protective suit. When working on bridges, painters are often suspended by cables and may work at extreme heights. When working on tall buildings, painters erect scaffolding, including "swing stages," scaffolds suspended by ropes, or cables attached to roof hooks. When painting steeples and other conical structures, they use a bosun's chair, a swing-like device.

*Paperhangers* cover walls and ceilings with decorative wall coverings made of paper, vinyl, or fabric. They first prepare the surface to be covered by applying "sizing," which seals the surface and makes the covering adhere better. When redecorating, they may first remove the old covering by soaking, steaming, or applying solvents. When necessary, they patch holes and take care of other imperfections before hanging the new wall covering.

After the surface has been prepared, paperhangers must prepare the paste or other adhesive, unless they are using pretreated paper. They then measure the area to be covered, check the covering for flaws, cut the covering into strips of the proper size, and closely examine the pattern in order to match it when the strips are hung. Much of this process can now be handled by specialized equipment.

The next step is to brush or roll the adhesive onto the back of the covering, if needed, and to then place the strips on the wall or ceiling, making sure the pattern is matched, the strips are straight, and the edges are butted together to make tight, closed seams. Finally, paperhangers smooth the strips to remove bubbles and wrinkles, trim the top and bottom with a razor knife, and wipe off any excess adhesive.

*Work environment.* Most painters and paperhangers work 40 hours a week or less; about 24 percent have variable schedules or work part time. Painters and paperhangers must stand for long periods, often working from scaffolding and ladders. Their jobs also require a considerable amount of climbing, bending, and stretching. These workers must have stamina because much of the work is done with their arms raised overhead. Painters, especially industrial painters, often work outdoors, almost always in dry, warm weather. Those who paint bridges or building infrastructure may be exposed to extreme heights and uncomfortable positions; some painters work suspended with ropes or cables.

Some painting jobs can leave a worker covered with paint. Drywall dust created by electric sanders prior to painting requires workers to wear protective safety glasses and a dust mask. Painters and paperhangers sometimes work with materials that are hazardous or toxic, such as when they are required to remove lead-based paints. In the most dangerous situations, painters work in a sealed self-contained suit to prevent inhalation of or contact with hazardous materials. Although workers are subject to falls from ladders, the occupation is not as hazardous as some other construction occupations.

## Training, Other Qualifications, and Advancement

Painting and paperhanging is learned mostly on the job, but some experts recommend completion of an apprenticeship program.

*Education and training.* Most painters and paperhangers learn through on-the-job training and by working as a helper to an experienced painter. However, there are a number of formal and informal training programs that provide more thorough instruction and a better career foundation. In general, the more formal the training received, the more likely the individual will enter the profession at a higher level. There are limited informal training opportunities for paperhangers because there are fewer paperhangers and helpers are usually not required.

If available, apprenticeships generally provide a mixture of classroom instruction and paid on-the-job training. Apprenticeships for painters and paperhangers consist of two to four years of on-the-job training, supplemented by a minimum of 144 hours of related classroom instruction each year. A high school education or its equivalent, with courses in mathematics, usually is required to enter an apprenticeship program. Apprentices receive instruction in color harmony, use and care of tools and equipment, surface preparation, application techniques, paint mixing and matching, characteristics of different finishes, blueprint reading, wood finishing, and safety.

**Projections data from the National Employment Matrix**

| Occupational Title | SOC Code | Employment, 2006 | Projected employment, 2016 | Change, 2006-16 | |
|---|---|---|---|---|---|
| | | | | Number | Percent |
| Painters and paperhangers.................................................... | 47-2140 | 473,000 | 526,000 | 53,000 | 11 |
| Painters, construction and maintenance ......................... | 47-2141 | 463,000 | 517,000 | 54,000 | 12 |
| Paperhangers ................................................................... | 47-2142 | 9,900 | 8,700 | -1,200 | -12 |

NOTE: Data in this table are rounded.

Besides apprenticeships, some workers gain skills by attending technical schools that offer training prior to employment. These schools can take about a year to complete. Others receive training through local vocational high schools.

Whether a painter learns the trade through a formal apprenticeship or informally as a helper, on-the-job instruction covers similar skill areas. Under the direction of experienced workers, trainees carry supplies, erect scaffolds, and do simple painting and surface preparation tasks while they learn about paint and painting equipment. As they gain experience, trainees learn to prepare surfaces for painting and paperhanging, to mix paints, and to apply paint and wall coverings efficiently and neatly. Near the end of their training, they may learn decorating concepts, color coordination, and cost-estimating techniques. In addition to learning craft skills, painters must become familiar with safety and health regulations so that their work complies with the law.

*Other qualifications.* Painters and paperhangers should have good manual dexterity, vision, and color sense. They also need physical stamina and balance to work on ladders and platforms. Apprentices or helpers generally must be at least 18 years old and in good physical condition, in addition to the high school diploma or equivalent that most apprentices need.

*Certification and advancement.* Some organizations offer training and certification to enhance the skills of their members. People interested in industrial painting, for example, can earn several designations from the National Association of Corrosion Engineers in several areas of specialization, including one for coating applicators, called Protective Coating Specialist. Courses range from one day to several weeks depending on the certification program and specialty.

Painters and paperhangers may advance to supervisory or estimating jobs with painting and decorating contractors. Many establish their own painting and decorating businesses. For those who would like to advance, it is increasingly important to be able to communicate in both English and Spanish in order to relay instructions and safety precautions to workers with limited English skills; Spanish-speaking workers make up a large part of the construction workforce in many areas. Painting contractors need good English skills to deal with clients and subcontractors.

## Employment

Painters and paperhangers held about 473,000 jobs in 2006; about 98 percent were painters. Around 38 percent of painters and paperhangers work for painting and wall covering contractors engaged in new construction, repair, restoration, or remodeling work. In addition, organizations that own or manage large buildings—such as apartment complexes—may employ painters, as do some schools, hospitals, factories, and government agencies.

Self-employed independent painting contractors accounted for 42 percent of all painters and paperhangers, significantly greater than the 20 percent of all construction trades workers combined.

## Job Outlook

Employment of painters and paperhangers is expected to grow about as fast as the average for all occupations, reflecting increases in the stock of buildings and other structures that require maintenance and renovation. Excellent employment opportunities are expected for painters due to the need to replace the large number of workers who leave the occupation; paperhangers will have very limited opportunities.

*Employment change.* Overall employment is expected to grow by 11 percent between 2006 and 2016, about as fast as the average for all occupations. Driving employment growth will be retiring baby boomers who either purchase second homes or otherwise leave their existing homes that then require interior painting. Investors who sell properties or rent them out will also require the services of painters prior to completing a transaction. The relatively short life of exterior paints in residential homes as well as changing color and application trends will continue to support demand for painters. Painting is labor-intensive and not susceptible to technological changes that might make workers more productive and slow employment growth.

Growth of industrial painting will be driven by the need to prevent corrosion and deterioration of the many industrial structures by painting or coating them. Applying a protective coating to steel bridges, for example, is cost effective and can add years to the life expectancy of a bridge.

Employment of paperhangers should decline rapidly as many homeowners take advantage of easy application materials and resort to cheaper alternatives, such as painting.

*Job prospects.* Job prospects for painters should be excellent because of the need to replace workers who leave the occupation for other jobs. There are no strict training requirements for entry into these jobs, so many people with limited skills work as painters or helpers for a relatively short time and then move on to other types of work with higher pay or better working conditions.

Opportunities for industrial painters should be excellent as the positions available should be greater than the pool of qualified individuals to fill them. While industrial structures that require painting are located throughout the nation, the best employment opportunities should be in the petrochemical industry in the Gulf Coast region, where strong demand and the largest concentration of workers exists.

Very few openings will arise for paperhangers because the number of these jobs is comparatively small and cheaper, more modern decorative finishes such as faux effects and sponging have gained in popularity at the expense of paper, vinyl, or fabric wall coverings.

Jobseekers considering these occupations should expect some periods of unemployment, especially until they gain experience. Many construction projects are of short duration, and construction activity is cyclical in nature. Remodeling, restoration, and maintenance projects, however, should continue as homeowners undertake renovation projects and hire painters even in economic downturns. Nonetheless, workers in these trades may experience periods of unemployment when the overall level of construction falls. On the other hand, shortages of these workers may occur in some areas during peak periods of building activity.

## Earnings

In May 2006, median hourly earnings of wage and salary painters, construction and maintenance, were $15.00, not including the earnings of the self-employed. The middle 50 percent earned between $12.19 and $19.51. The lowest 10 percent earned less than $9.97, and the highest 10 percent earned more than $25.62. Median hourly earnings in the industries employing the largest numbers of painters were as follows:

| | |
|---|---|
| Local government | $20.11 |
| Drywall and insulation contractors | 16.18 |
| Nonresidential building construction | 15.68 |
| Residential building construction | 15.04 |
| Painting and wall covering contractors | 14.62 |

In May 2006, median earnings for wage and salary paperhangers were $16.21. The middle 50 percent earned between $13.12 and $20.62. The lowest 10 percent earned less than $10.34, and the highest 10 percent earned more than $26.77.

Earnings for painters may be reduced on occasion because of bad weather and the short-term nature of many construction jobs. Hourly wage rates for apprentices usually start at 40 to 50 percent of the rate for experienced workers and increase periodically.

Some painters and paperhangers are members of the International Brotherhood of Painters and Allied Trades. Some painters are members of other unions.

## Related Occupations

Painters and paperhangers apply various coverings to decorate and protect wood, drywall, metal, and other surfaces. Other construction occupations in which workers do finishing work include carpenters; carpet, floor, and tile installers and finishers; drywall installers, ceiling tile installers, and tapers; painting and coating workers, except construction and maintenance; and plasterers and stucco masons.

## Sources of Additional Information

For details about painting and paperhanging apprenticeships or work opportunities, contact local painting and decorating contractors, local trade organizations, a local of the International Union of Painters and Allied Trades, a local joint union-management apprenticeship committee, or an office of the state apprenticeship agency or employment service.

For information about the work of painters and paperhangers and training opportunities, contact

▸ Associated Builders and Contractors, Workforce Development Department, 4250 North Fairfax Dr., 9th Floor, Arlington, VA 22203. Internet: http://www.trytools.org

▸ International Union of Painters and Allied Trades, 1750 New York Ave. NW, Washington, DC 20006. Internet: http://www.iupat.org

▸ National Center for Construction Education and Research, P.O. Box 141104, Gainesville, FL 32614. Internet: http://www.nccer.org

▸ Painting and Decorating Contractors of America, 1801 Park 270 Dr., Suite 220, St. Louis, MO 63146. Internet: http://www.pdca.org

For general information about the work of industrial painters and opportunities for training and certification as a protective coating specialist, contact

▸ National Association of Corrosion Engineers, 1440 South Creek Dr., Houston, TX 77084. Internet: http://www.nace.org

# Paralegals and Legal Assistants

(O*NET 23-2011.00)

## Significant Points

■ Most entrants have an associate degree in paralegal studies, or a bachelor's degree coupled with a certificate in paralegal studies.

■ About 7 out of 10 work for law firms; others work for corporate legal departments and government agencies.

■ Employment is projected to grow much faster than average, as employers try to reduce costs by hiring paralegals to perform tasks once done by lawyers.

■ Competition for jobs should continue; experienced, formally trained paralegals should have the best employment opportunities.

## Nature of the Work

While lawyers assume ultimate responsibility for legal work, they often delegate many of their tasks to paralegals. In fact, paralegals—also called legal assistants—are continuing to assume a growing range of tasks in legal offices and perform many of the same tasks as lawyers. Nevertheless, they are explicitly prohibited from carrying out duties considered to be the practice of law, such as setting legal fees, giving legal advice, and presenting cases in court.

One of a paralegal's most important tasks is helping lawyers prepare for closings, hearings, trials, and corporate meetings. Paralegals might investigate the facts of cases and ensure that all relevant information is considered. They also identify appropriate laws, judicial decisions, legal articles, and other materials that are relevant to assigned cases. After they analyze and organize the information, paralegals may prepare written reports that attorneys use in determining how cases should be handled. If attorneys decide to file lawsuits on behalf of clients, paralegals may help prepare the legal arguments, draft pleadings and motions to be filed with the court, obtain affidavits, and assist attorneys during trials. Paralegals also organize and track files of all important case documents and make them available and easily accessible to attorneys.

In addition to this preparatory work, paralegals perform a number of other functions. For example, they help draft contracts, mortgages, and separation agreements. They also may assist in preparing tax returns, establishing trust funds, and planning estates. Some paralegals coordinate the activities of other law office employees and maintain financial office records.

Computer software packages and the Internet are used to search legal literature stored in computer databases and on CD-ROM. In litigation involving many supporting documents, paralegals usually use computer databases to retrieve, organize, and index various materials. Imaging software allows paralegals to scan documents directly into a database, while billing programs help them to track hours billed to clients. Computer software packages also are used to perform tax computations and explore the consequences of various tax strategies for clients.

Paralegals are found in all types of organizations, but most are employed by law firms, corporate legal departments, and various government offices. In these organizations, they can work in many different areas of the law, including litigation, personal injury, corporate law, criminal law, employee benefits, intellectual property, labor law, bankruptcy, immigration, family law, and real estate. As the law becomes more complex, paralegals become more specialized. Within specialties, functions are often broken down further. For example, paralegals specializing in labor law may concentrate exclusively on employee benefits. In small and medium-size law firms, duties are often more general.

The tasks of paralegals differ widely according to the type of organization for which they work. A corporate paralegal often assists attorneys with employee contracts, shareholder agreements, stock-option plans, and employee benefit plans. They also may help prepare and file annual financial reports, maintain corporate minutes' record resolutions, and prepare forms to secure loans for the corporation. Corporate paralegals often monitor and review government regulations to ensure that the corporation is aware of new requirements and is operating within the law. Increasingly, experienced corporate paralegals or paralegal managers are assuming additional supervisory responsibilities such as overseeing team projects.

The duties of paralegals who work in the public sector usually vary by agency. In general, litigation paralegals analyze legal material for internal use, maintain reference files, conduct research for attorneys, and collect and analyze evidence for agency hearings. They may prepare informative or explanatory material on laws, agency regulations, and agency policy for general use by the agency and the public. Paralegals employed in community legal-service projects help the poor, the aged, and others who are in need of legal assistance. They file forms, conduct research, prepare documents, and, when authorized by law, may represent clients at administrative hearings.

*Work environment.* Paralegals handle many routine assignments, particularly when they are inexperienced. As they gain experience, paralegals usually assume more varied tasks with additional responsibility. Paralegals do most of their work in offices and law libraries. Occasionally, they travel to gather information and perform other duties.

Paralegals employed by corporations and government usually work a standard 40-hour week. Although most paralegals work year round, some are temporarily employed during busy times of the year and then released. Paralegals who work for law firms sometimes work very long hours when under pressure to meet deadlines.

## Training, Other Qualifications, and Advancement

Most entrants have an associate degree in paralegal studies, or a bachelor's degree coupled with a certificate in paralegal studies. Some employers train paralegals on the job.

*Education and training.* There are several ways to become a paralegal. The most common is through a community college paralegal program that leads to an associate degree. Another common method of entry, mainly for those who already have a college degree, is earning a certificate in paralegal studies. A small number of schools offer a bachelor's and master's degree in paralegal studies. Finally, some employers train paralegals on the job.

Associate and bachelor's degree programs usually combine paralegal training with courses in other academic subjects. Certificate programs vary significantly, with some only taking a few months to complete. Most certificate programs provide intensive paralegal training for individuals who already hold college degrees.

About 1,000 colleges and universities, law schools, and proprietary schools offer formal paralegal training programs. Approximately 260 paralegal programs are approved by the American Bar Association (ABA). Although many employers do not require such approval, graduation from an ABA-approved program can enhance employment opportunities. Admission requirements vary. Some require certain college courses or a bachelor's degree, while others accept high school graduates or those with legal experience. A few schools require standardized tests and personal interviews.

The quality of paralegal training programs varies; some programs may include job placement services. If possible, prospective students should examine the experiences of recent graduates before enrolling in a paralegal program. Any training program usually includes courses in legal research and the legal applications of computers. Many paralegal training programs also offer an internship in which students gain practical experience by working for several months in a private law firm, the office of a public defender or attorney general, a corporate legal department, a legal aid organization, a bank, or a government agency. Internship experience is an asset when one is seeking a job after graduation.

Some employers train paralegals on the job, hiring college graduates with no legal experience or promoting experienced legal secretaries. Other entrants have experience in a technical field that is useful to law firms, such as a background in tax preparation or criminal justice. Nursing or health administration experience is valuable in personal injury law practices.

*Certification and other qualifications.* Although most employers do not require certification, earning a voluntary certification from a professional society may offer advantages in the labor market. The National Association of Legal Assistants (NALA), for example, has established standards for certification requiring various combinations of education and experience. Paralegals who meet these

**Projections data from the National Employment Matrix**

| Occupational Title | SOC Code | Employment, 2006 | Projected employment, 2016 | Change, 2006-2016 | |
|---|---|---|---|---|---|
| | | | | Number | Percent |
| Paralegals and legal assistants........................................................ | 23-2011 | 238,000 | 291,000 | 53,000 | 22 |

NOTE: Data in this table are rounded.

standards are eligible to take a two-day examination. Those who pass the exam may use the Certified Legal Assistant (CLA) or Certified Paralegal (CP) credential. The NALA also offers the Advanced Paralegal Certification for experienced paralegals who want to specialize. The Advanced Paralegal Certification program is a curriculum based program offered on the Internet.

The American Alliance of Paralegals, Inc. offers the American Alliance Certified Paralegal (AACP) credential, a voluntary certification program. Paralegals seeking the AACP certification must possess at least five years of paralegal experience and meet one of the three educational criteria. Certification must be renewed every two years, including the completion 18 hours of continuing education.

In addition, the National Federation of Paralegal Association offers the Registered Paralegal (RP) designation to paralegals with a bachelor's degree and at least two years of experience who pass an exam. To maintain the credential, workers must complete 12 hours of continuing education every two years. The National Association for Legal Professionals offers the Professional Paralegal (PP) certification to those who pass a four-part exam. Recertification requires 75 hours of continuing education.

Paralegals must be able to document and present their findings and opinions to their supervising attorney. They need to understand legal terminology and have good research and investigative skills. Familiarity with the operation and applications of computers in legal research and litigation support also is important. Paralegals should stay informed of new developments in the laws that affect their area of practice. Participation in continuing legal education seminars allows paralegals to maintain and expand their knowledge of the law. In fact, all paralegals in California must complete four hours of mandatory continuing education in either general law or in a specialized area of law.

Because paralegals frequently deal with the public, they should be courteous and uphold the ethical standards of the legal profession. The National Association of Legal Assistants, the National Federation of Paralegal Associations, and a few states have established ethical guidelines for paralegals to follow.

*Advancement.* Paralegals usually are given more responsibilities and require less supervision as they gain work experience. Experienced paralegals who work in large law firms, corporate legal departments, or government agencies may supervise and delegate assignments to other paralegals and clerical staff. Advancement opportunities also include promotion to managerial and other law-related positions within the firm or corporate legal department. However, some paralegals find it easier to move to another law firm when seeking increased responsibility or advancement.

## Employment

Paralegals and legal assistants held about 238,000 jobs in 2006. Private law firms employed 7 out of 10 paralegals and legal assistants; most of the remainder worked for corporate legal departments and various levels of government. Within the federal government, the U.S. Department of Justice is the largest employer, followed by the Social Security Administration and the U.S. Department of the Treasury. A small number of paralegals own their own businesses and work as freelance legal assistants, contracting their services to attorneys or corporate legal departments.

## Job Outlook

Despite projected rapid employment growth, competition for jobs is expected to continue as many people seek to go into this profession; experienced, formally trained paralegals should have the best employment opportunities.

*Employment change.* Employment of paralegals and legal assistants is projected to grow 22 percent between 2006 and 2016, much faster than the average for all occupations. Employers are trying to reduce costs and increase the availability and efficiency of legal services by hiring paralegals to perform tasks once done by lawyers. Paralegals are performing a wider variety of duties, making them more useful to businesses.

Demand for paralegals also is expected to grow as an expanding population increasingly requires legal services, especially in areas such as intellectual property, health care, international law, elder issues, criminal law, and environmental law. The growth of prepaid legal plans also should contribute to the demand for legal services.

Private law firms will continue to be the largest employers of paralegals, but a growing array of other organizations, such as corporate legal departments, insurance companies, real estate and title insurance firms, and banks also hire paralegals. Corporations in particular are expected to increase their in-house legal departments to cut costs. In part because of the range of tasks they can perform, paralegals are also increasingly employed in small and medium-size establishments of all types.

*Job prospects.* In addition to new jobs created by employment growth, more job openings will arise as people leave the occupation. There will be demand for paralegals who specialize in areas such as real estate, bankruptcy, medical malpractice, and product liability. Community legal service programs, which provide assistance to the poor, elderly, minorities, and middle-income families, will employ additional paralegals to minimize expenses and serve the most people. Job opportunities also are expected in federal, state, and local government agencies, consumer organizations, and the courts. However, this occupation attracts many applicants, creating competition for jobs. Experienced, formally trained paralegals should have the best job prospects.

To a limited extent, paralegal jobs are affected by the business cycle. During recessions, demand declines for some discretionary legal services, such as planning estates, drafting wills, and handling real estate transactions. Corporations are less inclined to initiate certain types of litigation when falling sales and profits lead to fiscal belt tightening. As a result, full-time paralegals employed in offices adversely affected by a recession may be laid off or have their work hours reduced. However, during recessions, corporations and individuals are more likely to face problems that require legal assistance, such as bankruptcies, foreclosures, and divorces. Paralegals, who provide many of the same legal services as lawyers at a lower cost, tend to fare relatively better in difficult economic conditions.

## Earnings

Earnings of paralegals and legal assistants vary greatly. Salaries depend on education, training, experience, the type and size of employer, and the geographic location of the job. In general, paralegals who work for large law firms or in large metropolitan areas earn more than those who work for smaller firms or in less populated regions. In May 2006, full-time wage-and-salary paralegals and legal assistants had median annual earnings, including bonuses, of $43,040. The middle 50 percent earned between $33,920 and $54,690. The top 10 percent earned more than $67,540, and the bottom 10 percent earned less than $27,450. Median annual earnings in the industries employing the largest numbers of paralegals were

| | |
|---|---|
| Federal government | $56,080 |
| Management of companies and enterprises | 52,220 |
| Local government | 42,170 |
| Legal services | 41,460 |
| State government | 38,020 |

In addition to earning a salary, many paralegals receive bonuses, in part, to compensate them for sometimes having to work long hours. Paralegals also receive vacation, paid sick leave, a 401 savings plan, life insurance, personal paid time off, dental insurance, and reimbursement for continuing legal education.

## Related Occupations

Among the other occupations that call for a specialized understanding of the law but do not require the extensive training of a lawyer, are law clerks; title examiners, abstractors, and searchers; claims adjusters, appraisers, examiners, and investigators; and occupational health and safety specialists and technicians.

## Sources of Additional Information

General information on a career as a paralegal can be obtained from

▸ Standing Committee on Paralegals, American Bar Association, 321 North Clark St., Chicago, IL 60610. Internet: http://www.abanet.org/legalservices/paralegals

For information on the Certified Legal Assistant exam, schools that offer training programs in a specific state, and standards and guidelines for paralegals, contact

▸ National Association of Legal Assistants, Inc., 1516 South Boston St., Suite 200, Tulsa, OK 74119. Internet: http://www.nala.org

Information on the Paralegal Advanced Competency Exam, paralegal careers, paralegal training programs, job postings, and local associations is available from

▸ National Federation of Paralegal Associations, PO Box 2016, Edmonds, WA 98020. Internet: http://www.paralegals.org

Information on paralegal training programs, including the pamphlet *How to Choose a Paralegal Education Program*, may be obtained from

▸ American Association for Paralegal Education, 19 Mantua Rd., Mt. Royal, NJ 08061. Internet: http://www.aafpe.org

Information on paralegal careers, certification, and job postings is available from

▸ American Alliance of Paralegals, Inc., 16815 East Shea Boulevard, Suite 110, No. 101, Fountain Hills, Arizona, 85268. Internet: http://www.aapipara.org

For information on the Professional Paralegal exam, schools that offer training programs in a specific state, and standards and guidelines for paralegals, contact

▸ NALS, 314 E. 3rd St., Suite 210, Tulsa, OK 74120. Internet: http://www.nals.org

Information on obtaining positions as a paralegal or legal assistant with the federal government is available from the Office of Personnel Management through USAJOBS, the federal government's official employment information system. This resource for locating and applying for job opportunities can be accessed through the Internet at http://www.usajobs.opm.gov or through an interactive voice response telephone system at (703) 724-1850 or TDD (978) 461-8404. These numbers are not toll free, and charges may result. For advice on how to find and apply for federal jobs, see the *Occupational Outlook Quarterly* article "How to get a job in the Federal Government," online at http://www.bls.gov/opub/ooq/2004/summer/art01.pdf.

# Personal and Home Care Aides

(O*NET 39-9021.00)

## Significant Points

■ Job opportunities are expected to be excellent because of rapid growth in home health care and high replacement needs.

■ Skill requirements are low, as is the pay.

■ About 1 out of 3 personal and home care aides work part time; most aides work with a number of different clients, each job lasting a few hours, days, or weeks.

## Nature of the Work

Personal and home care aides help people who are elderly, disabled, ill, and/or mentally disabled to live in their own homes or in residential care facilities instead of in health facilities or institutions. Most personal and home care aides work with elderly or physically or mentally disabled clients who need more extensive personal and home care than family or friends can provide. Some aides work with families in which a parent is incapacitated and small children need care. Others help discharged hospital patients who have relatively short-term needs.

Personal and home care aides—also called *homemakers, caregivers, companions*, and *personal attendants*—provide housekeeping and routine personal care services. They clean clients' houses, do laundry, and change bed linens. Aides may plan meals (including special diets), shop for food, and cook. Aides also may help clients get out of bed, bathe, dress, and groom. Some accompany clients to doctors' appointments or on other errands.

Personal and home care aides provide instruction and psychological support to their patients. They may advise families and patients on nutrition, cleanliness, and household tasks. Aides also may assist in toilet training a severely mentally handicapped child, or they may just listen to clients talk.

In home health care agencies, a registered nurse, physical therapist, or social worker assigns specific duties and supervises personal and home care aides. Aides keep records of services performed and of clients' condition and progress. They report changes in the client's condition to the supervisor or case manager. In carrying out their work, aides cooperate with health care professionals, including registered nurses, therapists, and other medical staff.

The personal and home care aide's daily routine may vary. Aides may go to the same home every day for months or even years. Aides often visit four or five clients on the same day. However, some aides may work solely with one client who is in need of more care and attention. In some situations, this may involve working with other aides in shifts so the client has an aide throughout the day and night.

Personal and home care aides generally work on their own, with periodic visits by their supervisor. They receive detailed instructions explaining when to visit clients and what services to perform for them.

Aides are individually responsible for getting to the client's home. They may spend a good portion of the work day traveling from one client to another. Aides must be careful to avoid over-exertion or injury when they assist clients.

*Work environment.* Surroundings differ from case to case. Some homes are neat and pleasant, whereas others are untidy and depressing. Some clients are pleasant and cooperative; others are angry, abusive, depressed, or otherwise difficult. Aides may spend a large portion of each day traveling between clients' homes.

About 33 percent of aides work part time, and some work weekends or evenings to suit the needs of their clients.

## Training, Other Qualifications, and Advancement

In some states, the only requirement for employment is on-the-job training, which generally is provided by employers. Other states may require formal training, which is available from community colleges, vocational schools, elder care programs, and home health care agencies.

*Education and training.* Most personal and home care aides receive short term on-the-job training in a range of job functions. Aides are instructed on how to properly cook for a client, which includes information on nutrition and special diets. Furthermore, they may be trained on basic housekeeping tasks, such as making a bed and keeping the home sanitary and safe for the client. Generally, they are taught how to respond to an emergency situation, learning basic safety techniques. Employers may also train aides to conduct themselves in a professional and courteous manner while in a clients' home.

*Other qualifications.* Personal and home care aides should have a desire to help people and not mind hard work. They should be responsible, compassionate, patient, emotionally stable, and cheerful. In addition, aides should be tactful, honest, and discreet because they work in private homes. Aides also must be in good health. A physical examination, including state-mandated tests for tuberculosis and other diseases, may be required. A criminal background check, credit check, and good driving record may also be required for employment. Additionally, personal and home care aides are responsible for their own transportation to reach patients' homes.

*Certification and advancement.* The National Association for Home Care and Hospice (NAHC) offers national certification for personal and home care aides. Certification is a voluntary demonstration that the individual has met industry standards. Certification requires the completion of a 75-hour course, observation and documentation of 17 skills for competency assessed by a registered nurse and passing a written exam developed by NAHC.

Advancement for personal and home care aides is limited. In some agencies, workers start out performing homemaker duties, such as cleaning. With experience and training, they may take on more personal care duties. Some aides choose to receive additional training to become nursing and home health aides, licensed practical nurses, or registered nurses. Some experienced personal and home care aides may start their own home care agency or work as a self-employed aide. Self-employed aides have no agency affiliation or supervision and accept clients, set fees, and arrange work schedules on their own.

## Employment

Personal and home care aides held about 767,000 jobs in 2006. The majority of jobs were in home health care services; individual and family services; residential care facilities; and private households. In 2006, about 8 percent of personal and home care aides were self-employed.

## Job Outlook

Excellent job opportunities are expected for this occupation because rapid employment growth and high replacement needs are projected to produce a large number of job openings.

*Employment change.* Employment of personal and home care aides is projected to grow by 51 percent between 2006 and 2016, which is much faster than the average for all occupations. This occupation will be amongst the occupations adding the most new jobs, growing by about 389,000 jobs. The expected growth is due, in large part, to the projected rise in the number of elderly people, an age group that

**Projections data from the National Employment Matrix**

| Occupational Title | SOC Code | Employment, 2006 | Projected employment, 2016 | Change, 2006-16 | |
|---|---|---|---|---|---|
| | | | | Number | Percent |
| Personal and home care aides ....................................................... | 39-9021 | 767,000 | 1,156,000 | 389,000 | 51 |

NOTE: Data in this table are rounded.

often has mounting health problems and that needs some assistance with daily activities. The elderly and other patients, such as the mentally disabled, increasingly rely on home care.

This trend reflects several developments. Inpatient care in hospitals and nursing homes can be extremely expensive, so more patients return to their homes from these facilities as quickly as possible to contain costs. Patients who need assistance with everyday tasks and household chores rather than medical care can reduce medical expenses by returning to their homes. Furthermore, most patients—particularly the elderly—increasingly prefer care in their homes rather than in nursing homes or other in-patient facilities. This trend is aided by the realization that treatment can be more effective in familiar surroundings. Finally, home care has become easier and more feasible with the development of better medical technologies for in-home treatment.

*Job prospects.* In addition to job openings created by the increased demand for these workers, replacement needs are expected to lead to many openings. The relatively low skill requirements, low pay, and high emotional demands of the work result in high replacement needs. For these same reasons, many people are reluctant to seek jobs in the occupation. Therefore, persons who are interested in and suited for this work—particularly those with experience or training as personal care, home health, or nursing aides—should have excellent job prospects.

## Earnings

Median hourly earnings of wage-and-salary personal and home care aides were $8.54 in May 2006. The middle 50 percent earned between $7.09 and $10.19 an hour. The lowest 10 percent earned less than $6.05, and the highest 10 percent earned more than $11.60 an hour. Median hourly earnings in the industries employing the largest numbers of personal and home care aides were as follows:

Residential mental retardation facilities ..................$9.54

Services for the elderly and persons with disabilities ..9.18

Home health care services ......................................7.19

Most employers give slight pay increases with experience and added responsibility. Aides usually are paid only for the time they work in the home, not for travel time between jobs. Employers often hire on-call hourly workers and provide no benefits.

## Related Occupations

Personal and home care aides combine the duties of caregivers and social service workers. Workers in related occupations that involve personal contact to help others include childcare workers; nursing, psychiatric, and home health aides; occupational therapist assistants and aides; physical therapist assistants and aides; and social and human service assistants.

## Sources of Additional Information

Information about employment opportunities may be obtained from local hospitals, nursing care facilities, home health care agencies, psychiatric facilities, residential mental health facilities, social assistance agencies, and local offices of the state employment service.

For information about voluntary credentials for personal and home care aides, contact

▸ National Association for Homecare and Hospice, 228 Seventh St. SE, Washington, DC 20003. Internet: http://www.nahc.org

## Pharmacists

(O*NET 29-1051.00)

## Significant Points

■ Excellent job opportunities are expected.

■ Earnings are high, but some pharmacists are required to work nights, weekends, and holidays.

■ Pharmacists are becoming more involved in counseling patients and planning drug therapy programs.

■ A license is required; the prospective pharmacist must graduate from an accredited college of pharmacy and pass a series of examinations.

## Nature of the Work

Pharmacists distribute prescription drugs to individuals. They also advise their patients, as well as physicians and other health practitioners, on the selection, dosages, interactions, and side effects of medications. Pharmacists monitor the health and progress of patients to ensure the safe and effective use of medication. Compounding—the actual mixing of ingredients to form medications—is a small part of a pharmacist's practice, because most medicines are produced by pharmaceutical companies in a standard dosage and drug delivery form. Most pharmacists work in a community setting, such as a retail drugstore, or in a health care facility, such as a hospital, nursing home, mental health institution, or neighborhood health clinic.

Pharmacists in community pharmacies dispense medications, counsel patients on the use of prescription and over-the-counter medications, and advise physicians about patients' medication therapy. They also advise patients about general health topics such as diet, exercise, and stress management, and provide information on products such as durable medical equipment or home health care supplies. In addition, they may complete third-party insurance forms and other paperwork. Those who own or manage community pharmacies may sell non-health-related merchandise, hire and supervise personnel, and oversee the general operation of the pharmacy. Some community pharmacists provide specialized services to help patients with conditions such as diabetes, asthma, smoking cessation, or high blood pressure; others also are trained to administer vaccinations.

Pharmacists in health care facilities dispense medications and advise the medical staff on the selection and effects of drugs. They may make sterile solutions to be administered intravenously. They also plan, monitor and evaluate drug programs or regimens. They may counsel hospitalized patients on the use of drugs before the patients are discharged.

Pharmacists who work in home health care monitor drug therapy and prepare infusions—solutions that are injected into patients—and other medications for use in the home.

Some pharmacists specialize in specific drug therapy areas, such as intravenous nutrition support, oncology (cancer), nuclear pharmacy (used for chemotherapy), geriatric pharmacy, and psychiatric pharmacy (the use of drugs to treat mental disorders).

Most pharmacists keep confidential computerized records of patients' drug therapies to prevent harmful drug interactions. Pharmacists are responsible for the accuracy of every prescription that is filled, but they often rely upon Pharmacy technicians and pharmacy aides to assist them in the dispensing process. Thus, the pharmacist may delegate prescription-filling and administrative tasks and supervise their completion. Pharmacists also frequently oversee pharmacy students serving as interns.

Increasingly, pharmacists are pursuing nontraditional pharmacy work. Some are involved in research for pharmaceutical manufacturers, developing new drugs and testing their effects. Others work in marketing or sales, providing clients with expertise on the use, effectiveness, and possible side effects of drugs. Some pharmacists work for health insurance companies, developing pharmacy benefit packages and carrying out cost-benefit analyses on certain drugs. Other pharmacists work for the government, managed care organizations, public health care services, the armed services, or pharmacy associations. Finally, some pharmacists are employed full time or part time as college faculty, teaching classes and performing research in a wide range of areas.

*Work environment.* Pharmacists work in clean, well-lighted, and well-ventilated areas. Many pharmacists spend most of their workday on their feet. When working with sterile or dangerous pharmaceutical products, pharmacists wear gloves, masks, and other protective equipment.

Most full-time salaried pharmacists work approximately 40 hours a week, and about 10 percent work more than 50 hours. Many community and hospital pharmacies are open for extended hours or around the clock, so pharmacists may be required to work nights, weekends, and holidays. Consultant pharmacists may travel to nursing homes or other facilities to monitor patients' drug therapy. About 16 percent of pharmacists worked part time in 2006.

# Training, Other Qualifications, and Advancement

A license is required in all states, the District of Columbia, and all U.S. territories. In order to obtain a license, pharmacists must earn a Doctor of Pharmacy (Pharm.D.) degree from a college of pharmacy and pass several examinations.

*Education and training.* Pharmacists must earn a Pharm.D. degree from an accredited college or school of pharmacy. The Pharm.D. degree has replaced the Bachelor of Pharmacy degree, which is no longer being awarded. To be admitted to a Pharm.D. program, an applicant must have completed at least two years of postsecondary study, although most applicants have completed three or more years. Other entry requirements usually include courses in mathematics and natural sciences, such as chemistry, biology, and physics, as well as courses in the humanities and social sciences. In 2007, 92 colleges and schools of pharmacy were accredited to confer degrees by the Accreditation Council for Pharmacy Education (ACPE). About 70 percent of Pharm.D. programs require applicants to take the Pharmacy College Admissions Test (PCAT).

Courses offered at colleges of pharmacy are designed to teach students about all aspects of drug therapy. In addition, students learn how to communicate with patients and other health care providers about drug information and patient care. Students also learn professional ethics, concepts of public health, and medication distribution systems management. In addition to receiving classroom instruction, students in Pharm.D. programs spend about one-forth of their time in a variety of pharmacy practice settings under the supervision of licensed pharmacists.

In the 2006–2007 academic year, 70 colleges of pharmacy also awarded the master-of-science degree or the Ph.D. degree. Both degrees are awarded after the completion of a Pharm.D. degree and are designed for those who want additional clinical, laboratory, and research experience. Areas of graduate study include pharmaceutics and pharmaceutical chemistry (physical and chemical properties of drugs and dosage forms), pharmacology (effects of drugs on the body), and pharmacy administration. Many master's and Ph.D. degree holders go on to do research for a drug company or teach at a university.

Other options for pharmacy graduates who are interested in further training include one-year or two-year residency programs or fellowships. Pharmacy residencies are postgraduate training programs in pharmacy practice and usually require the completion of a research project. These programs are often mandatory for pharmacists who wish to work in hospitals. Pharmacy fellowships are highly individualized programs that are designed to prepare participants to work in a specialized area of pharmacy, such clinical practice or research laboratories. Some pharmacists who own their own pharmacy obtain a master's degree in business administration (MBA). Others may obtain a degree in public administration or public health.

*Licensure.* A license to practice pharmacy is required in all states, the District of Columbia, and all U.S. territories. To obtain a license, a prospective pharmacist must graduate from a college of pharmacy that is accredited by the ACPE and pass a series of examinations. All states, U.S. territories, and the District of Columbia require the North American Pharmacist Licensure Exam (NAPLEX), which tests pharmacy skills and knowledge. Forty-four states and the District of Columbia also require the Multistate Pharmacy Jurisprudence Exam (MPJE), which tests pharmacy law. Both exams are administered by the National Association of Boards of Pharmacy (NABP). Each of the eight states and territories that do not require the MJPE has its own pharmacy law exam. In addition to the NAPLEX and MPJE, some states and territories require additional exams that are unique to their jurisdiction.

**Projections data from the National Employment Matrix**

| Occupational Title | SOC Code | Employment, 2006 | Projected employment, 2016 | Change, 2006-2016 | |
|---|---|---|---|---|---|
| | | | | Number | Percent |
| Pharmacists .................................................... | 29-1051 | 243,000 | 296,000 | 53,000 | 22 |

NOTE: Data in this table are rounded.

All jurisdictions except California currently grant license transfers to qualified pharmacists who already are licensed by another jurisdiction. Many pharmacists are licensed to practice in more than one jurisdiction. Most jurisdictions require continuing education for license renewal. Persons interested in a career as a pharmacist should check with individual jurisdiction boards of pharmacy for details on license renewal requirements and license transfer procedures.

Graduates of foreign pharmacy schools may also qualify for licensure in some U.S. states and territories. These individuals must apply for certification from the Foreign Pharmacy Graduate Examination Committee (FPGEC). Once certified, they must pass the Foreign Pharmacy Graduate Equivalency Examination (FPGEE), Test of English as a Foreign Language (TOEFL) exam, and Test of Spoken English (TSE) exam. They then must pass all of the exams required by the licensing jurisdiction, such as the NAPLEX and MJPE. Applicants who graduated from programs accredited by the Canadian Council for Accreditation of Pharmacy Programs (CCAPP) between 1993 and 2004 are exempt from FPGEC certification and examination requirements.

*Other qualifications.* Prospective pharmacists should have scientific aptitude, good interpersonal skills, and a desire to help others. They also must be conscientious and pay close attention to detail, because the decisions they make affect human lives.

*Advancement.* In community pharmacies, pharmacists usually begin at the staff level. Pharmacists in chain drugstores may be promoted to pharmacy supervisor or manager at the store level, then to manager at the district or regional level, and later to an executive position within the chain's headquarters. Hospital pharmacists may advance to supervisory or administrative positions. After they gain experience and secure the necessary capital, some pharmacists become owners or part owners of independent pharmacies. Pharmacists in the pharmaceutical industry may advance in marketing, sales, research, quality control, production, or other areas.

## Employment

Pharmacists held about 243,000 jobs in 2006. About 62 percent worked in community pharmacies that were either independently owned or part of a drugstore chain, grocery store, department store, or mass merchandiser. Most community pharmacists were salaried employees, but some were self-employed owners. About 23 percent of pharmacists worked in hospitals. A small proportion worked in mail-order and Internet pharmacies, pharmaceutical wholesalers, offices of physicians, and the federal government.

## Job Outlook

Employment is expected to increase much faster than the average through 2016. As a result of rapid growth and the need to replace workers who leave the occupation, job prospects should be excellent.

*Employment change.* Employment of pharmacists is expected to grow by 22 percent between 2006 and 2016, which is much faster than the average for all occupations. The increasing numbers of middle-aged and elderly people—who use more prescription drugs than younger people—will continue to spur demand for pharmacists throughout the projection period. Other factors likely to increase the demand for pharmacists include scientific advances that will make more drug products available and the coverage of prescription drugs by a greater number of health insurance plans and Medicare.

As the use of prescription drugs increases, demand for pharmacists will grow in most practice settings, such as community pharmacies, hospital pharmacies, and mail-order pharmacies. As the population ages, assisted living facilities and home care organizations should see particularly rapid growth. Demand will also increase as cost conscious insurers, in an attempt to improve preventative care, use pharmacists in areas such as patient education and vaccination administration.

Demand is also increasing in managed care organizations where pharmacists analyze trends and patterns in medication use, and in pharmacoeconomics—the cost and benefit analysis of different drug therapies. New jobs also are being created in disease management—the development of new methods for curing and controlling diseases—and in sales and marketing. Rapid growth is also expected in pharmacy informatics—the use of information technology to improve patient care.

*Job prospects.* Excellent opportunities are expected for pharmacists over the 2006 to 2016 period. Job openings will result from rapid employment growth, and from the need to replace workers who retire or leave the occupation for other reasons.

## Earnings

Median annual of wage-and-salary pharmacists in May 2006 were $94,520. The middle 50 percent earned between $83,180 and $108,140 a year. The lowest 10 percent earned less than $67,860, and the highest 10 percent earned more than $119,480 a year. Median annual earnings in the industries employing the largest numbers of pharmacists in May 2006 were

| | |
|---|---|
| Department stores ............................................... | $99,050 |
| Grocery stores ..................................................... | 95,600 |
| Pharmacies and drug stores ................................. | 94,640 |
| General medical and surgical hospitals ................. | 93,640 |

According to a 2006 survey by *Drug Topics Magazine*, pharmacists in retail settings earned an average of $92,291 per year, while pharmacists in institutional settings earned an average of $97,545. Full-time pharmacists earned an average of $102,336, while part-time pharmacists earned an average of $55,589.

## Related Occupations

Pharmacy technicians and pharmacy aides also work in pharmacies. Persons in other professions who may work with pharmaceutical compounds include biological scientists, medical scientists, and chemists and materials scientists. Increasingly, pharmacists are involved in patient care and therapy, work that they have in common with physicians and surgeons.

## Sources of Additional Information

For information on pharmacy as a career, preprofessional and professional requirements, programs offered by colleges of pharmacy, and student financial aid, contact

▸ American Association of Colleges of Pharmacy, 1426 Prince St., Alexandria, VA 22314. Internet: http://www.aacp.org

General information on careers in pharmacy is available from

▸ American Society of Health-System Pharmacists, 7272 Wisconsin Ave., Bethesda, MD 20814. Internet: http://www.ashp.org

▸ National Association of Chain Drug Stores, 413 N. Lee St., P.O. Box 1417-D49, Alexandria, VA 22313-1480. Internet: http://www.nacds.org

▸ Academy of Managed Care Pharmacy, 100 North Pitt St., Suite 400, Alexandria, VA 22314. Internet: http://www.amcp.org

▸ American Pharmacists Association, 1100 15th Street NW, Suite 400, Washington, DC 20005. Internet: http://www.aphanet.org

Information on the North American Pharmacist Licensure Exam (NAPLEX) and the Multistate Pharmacy Jurisprudence Exam (MPJE) is available from

▸ National Association of Boards of Pharmacy, 1600 Feehanville Dr., Mount Prospect, IL 60056. Internet: http://www.nabp.net

State licensure requirements are available from each state's board of pharmacy. Information on specific college entrance requirements, curriculums, and financial aid is available from any college of pharmacy.

# Pharmacy Technicians

(O*NET 29-2052.00)

## Significant Points

■ Job opportunities are expected to be good, especially for those with certification or previous work experience.

■ Many technicians work evenings, weekends, and holidays.

■ About 71 percent of jobs are in retail pharmacies, grocery stores, department stores, or mass retailers.

## Nature of the Work

Pharmacy technicians help licensed pharmacists provide medication and other health care products to patients. Technicians usually perform routine tasks to help prepare prescribed medication, such as counting tablets and labeling bottles. They also perform administrative duties, such as answering phones, stocking shelves, and operating cash registers. Technicians refer any questions regarding prescriptions, drug information, or health matters to a *pharmacist*.

Pharmacy technicians who work in retail or mail-order pharmacies have varying responsibilities, depending on state rules and regulations. Technicians receive written prescriptions or requests for prescription refills from patients. They also may receive prescriptions sent electronically from the doctor's office. They must verify that information on the prescription is complete and accurate. To prepare the prescription, technicians must retrieve, count, pour, weigh, measure, and sometimes mix the medication. Then, they prepare the prescription labels, select the type of prescription container, and affix the prescription and auxiliary labels to the container. Once the prescription is filled, technicians price and file the prescription, which must be checked by a pharmacist before it is given to the patient. Technicians may establish and maintain patient profiles, prepare insurance claim forms, and stock and take inventory of prescription and over-the-counter medications.

In hospitals, nursing homes, and assisted-living facilities, technicians have added responsibilities, including reading patients' charts and preparing the appropriate medication. After the pharmacist checks the prescription for accuracy, the pharmacy technician may deliver it to the patient. The technician then copies the information about the prescribed medication onto the patient's profile. Technicians also may assemble a 24-hour supply of medicine for every patient. They package and label each dose separately. The packages are then placed in the medicine cabinets of patients until the supervising pharmacist checks them for accuracy, and only then is the medication given to the patients.

*Pharmacy aides* work closely with pharmacy technicians. They often are clerks or cashiers who primarily answer telephones, handle money, stock shelves, and perform other clerical duties. Pharmacy technicians usually perform more complex tasks than pharmacy aides, although in some states their duties and job titles may overlap.

*Work environment.* Pharmacy technicians work in clean, organized, well-lighted, and well-ventilated areas. Most of their workday is spent on their feet. They may be required to lift heavy boxes or to use stepladders to retrieve supplies from high shelves.

Technicians work the same hours that pharmacists work. These may include evenings, nights, weekends, and holidays, particularly in facilities that are open 24 hours a day such as hospitals and some retail pharmacies. As their seniority increases, technicians often acquire increased control over the hours they work. There are many opportunities for part-time work in both retail and hospital settings.

## Training, Other Qualifications, and Advancement

Most pharmacy technicians are trained on-the-job, but employers favor applicants who have formal training, certification, or previous experience. Strong customer service skills also are important. Pharmacy technicians may become supervisors, may move into specialty positions or into sales, or may become pharmacists.

*Education and training.* Although most pharmacy technicians receive informal on-the-job training, employers favor those who have completed formal training and certification. However, there are currently few state and no federal requirements for formal training or certification of pharmacy technicians. Employers who have insuf-

**Projections data from the National Employment Matrix**

| Occupational Title | SOC Code | Employment, 2006 | Projected employment, 2016 | Change, 2006-2016 | |
|---|---|---|---|---|---|
| | | | | Number | Percent |
| Pharmacy technicians...................................................... | 29-2052 | 285,000 | 376,000 | 91,000 | 32 |

NOTE: Data in this table are rounded.

ficient resources to give on-the-job training often seek formally educated pharmacy technicians. Formal education programs and certification emphasize the technician's interest in and dedication to the work. In addition to the military, some hospitals, proprietary schools, vocational or technical colleges, and community colleges offer formal education programs.

Formal pharmacy technician education programs require classroom and laboratory work in a variety of areas, including medical and pharmaceutical terminology, pharmaceutical calculations, pharmacy recordkeeping, pharmaceutical techniques, and pharmacy law and ethics. Technicians also are required to learn medication names, actions, uses, and doses. Many training programs include internships, in which students gain hands-on experience in actual pharmacies. After completion, students receive a diploma, a certificate, or an associate's degree, depending on the program.

Prospective pharmacy technicians with experience working as an aide in a community pharmacy or volunteering in a hospital may have an advantage. Employers also prefer applicants with experience managing inventories, counting tablets, measuring dosages, and using computers. In addition, a background in chemistry, English, and health education may be beneficial.

*Certification and other qualifications.* Two organizations, the Pharmacy Technician Certification Board and the Institute for the Certification of Pharmacy Technicians, administer national certification examinations. Certification is voluntary in most states, but is required by some states and employers. Some technicians are hired without formal training, but under the condition that they obtain certification within a specified period of time. To be eligible for either exam, candidates must have a high school diploma or GED, no felony convictions of any kind within five years of applying, and no drug or pharmacy related felony convictions at any point. Employers, often pharmacists, know that individuals who pass the exam have a standardized body of knowledge and skills. Many employers also will reimburse the costs of the exam.

Under both programs, technicians must be recertified every two years. Recertification requires 20 hours of continuing education within the two-year certification period. At least one hour must be in pharmacy law. Continuing education hours can be earned from several different sources, including colleges, pharmacy associations, and pharmacy technician training programs. Up to 10 hours of continuing education can be earned on the job under the direct supervision and instruction of a pharmacist.

Strong customer service and teamwork skills are needed because pharmacy technicians interact with patients, coworkers, and health care professionals. Mathematics, spelling, and reading skills also are important. Successful pharmacy technicians are alert, observant, organized, dedicated, and responsible. They should be willing and able to take directions, but be able to work independently without constant instruction. They must be precise; details are sometimes a matter of life and death. Candidates interested in becoming pharmacy technicians cannot have prior records of drug or substance abuse.

*Advancement.* In large pharmacies and health systems, pharmacy technicians with significant training, experience and certification can be promoted to supervisory positions, mentoring and training pharmacy technicians with less experience. Some may advance into specialty positions such as chemotherapy technician and nuclear pharmacy technician. Others move into sales. With a substantial amount of formal training, some pharmacy technicians go on to become pharmacists.

## Employment

Pharmacy technicians held about 285,000 jobs in 2006. About 71 percent of jobs were in retail pharmacies, either independently owned or part of a drugstore chain, grocery store, department store, or mass retailer. About 18 percent of jobs were in hospitals and a small proportion was in mail-order and Internet pharmacies, offices of physicians, pharmaceutical wholesalers, and the federal government.

## Job Outlook

Employment is expected to increase much faster than the average through 2016, and job opportunities are expected to be good.

*Employment change.* Employment of pharmacy technicians is expected to increase by 32 percent from 2006 to 2016, which is much faster than the average for all occupations. The increased number of middle-aged and elderly people—who use more prescription drugs than younger people—will spur demand for technicians throughout the projection period. In addition, as scientific advances bring treatments for an increasing number of conditions, more pharmacy technicians will be needed to fill a growing number of prescriptions.

As cost-conscious insurers begin to use pharmacies as patient-care centers, pharmacy technicians will assume responsibility for some of the more routine tasks previously performed by pharmacists. In addition, they will adopt some of the administrative duties that were previously performed by pharmacy aides, such as answering phones and stocking shelves.

Reducing the need for pharmacy technicians to some degree, however, will be the growing use of drug dispensing machines. These machines increase productivity by completing some of the pharmacy technician's duties, namely counting pills and placing them into prescription containers. These machines are only used for the most common medications, however, and their effect on employment should be minimal.

Almost all states have legislated the maximum number of technicians who can safely work under a pharmacist at one time. Changes in these laws could directly affect employment.

*Job prospects.* Good job opportunities are expected for full-time and part-time work, especially for technicians with formal training or previous experience. Job openings for pharmacy technicians will result from employment growth, and from the need to replace workers who transfer to other occupations or leave the labor force.

## Earnings

Median hourly earnings of wage-and-salary pharmacy technicians in May 2006 were $12.32. The middle 50 percent earned between $10.10 and $14.92. The lowest 10 percent earned less than $8.56, and the highest 10 percent earned more than $17.65. Median hourly earnings in the industries employing the largest numbers of pharmacy technicians in May 2006 were

General medical and surgical hospitals ...................$13.86
Grocery stores.....................................................12.78
Pharmacies and drug stores ...............................11.50

Certified technicians may earn more. Shift differentials for working evenings or weekends also can increase earnings. Some technicians belong to unions representing hospital or grocery store workers.

## Related Occupations

This occupation is most closely related to pharmacists and pharmacy aides. Workers in other medical support occupations include dental assistants, medical transcriptionists, medical records and health information technicians, occupational therapist assistants and aides, and physical therapist assistants and aides.

## Sources of Additional Information

For information on pharmacy technician certification programs, contact

▶ Pharmacy Technician Certification Board, 2215 Constitution Ave. NW, Washington, DC 20037-2985. Internet: http://www.ptcb.org

▶ Institute for the Certification of Pharmacy Technicians, 2536 S. Old Hwy 94, Suite 214, St. Charles, MO 63303. Internet: http://www.nationaltechexam.org

For a list of accredited pharmacy technician training programs, contact

▶ American Society of Health-System Pharmacists, 7272 Wisconsin Ave., Bethesda, MD 20814. Internet: http://www.ashp.org

For pharmacy technician career information, contact

▶ National Pharmacy Technician Association, P.O. Box 683148, Houston, TX 77268. Internet: http://www.pharmacytechnician.org

# Physical Therapist Assistants and Aides

(O*NET 31-2021.00 and 31-2022.00)

## Significant Points

■ Employment is projected to increase much faster than average.

■ Assistants should have very good job prospects; on the other hand, aides may face keen competition from the large pool of qualified applicants.

■ Aides usually learn skills on the job, while assistants generally have an associate degree; some states require licensing for assistants.

■ About 71 percent of jobs are in offices of physical therapists or in hospitals.

## Nature of the Work

Physical therapist assistants and aides help physical therapists to provide treatment that improves patient mobility, relieves pain, and prevents or lessens physical disabilities of patients. A physical therapist might ask an assistant to help patients exercise or learn to use crutches, for example, or an aide to gather and prepare therapy equipment. Patients include accident victims and individuals with disabling conditions such as lower-back pain, arthritis, heart disease, fractures, head injuries, and cerebral palsy.

*Physical therapist assistants* perform a variety of tasks. Under the direction and supervision of physical therapists, they provide part of a patient's treatment. This might involve exercises, massages, electrical stimulation, paraffin baths, hot and cold packs, traction, and ultrasound. Physical therapist assistants record the patient's responses to treatment and report the outcome of each treatment to the physical therapist.

*Physical therapist aides* help make therapy sessions productive, under the direct supervision of a physical therapist or physical therapist assistant. They usually are responsible for keeping the treatment area clean and organized and for preparing for each patient's therapy. When patients need assistance moving to or from a treatment area, aides push them in a wheelchair or provide them with a shoulder to lean on. Because they are not licensed, aides do not perform the clinical tasks of a physical therapist assistant in states where licensure is required.

The duties of aides include some clerical tasks, such as ordering depleted supplies, answering the phone, and filling out insurance forms and other paperwork. The extent to which an aide or an assistant performs clerical tasks depends on the size and location of the facility.

*Work environment.* Physical therapist assistants and aides need a moderate degree of strength because of the physical exertion required in assisting patients with their treatment. In some cases, assistants and aides need to lift patients. Frequent kneeling, stooping, and standing for long periods also are part of the job.

The hours and days that physical therapist assistants and aides work vary with the facility. About 23 percent of all physical therapist assistants and aides work part time. Many outpatient physical therapy offices and clinics have evening and weekend hours, to coincide with patients' personal schedules.

## Training, Other Qualifications, and Advancement

Most physical therapist aides are trained on the job, but most physical therapist assistants earn an associate degree from an accredited physical therapist assistant program. Some states require licensing for physical therapist assistants.

*Education and training.* Employers typically require physical therapist aides to have a high school diploma. They are trained on the job, and most employers provide clinical on-the-job training.

In many states, physical therapist assistants are required by law to hold at least an associate degree. According to the American Physical Therapy Association, there were 233 accredited physical therapist assistant programs in the United States as of 2006. Accredited programs usually last two years, or four semesters, and culminate in an associate degree.

Programs are divided into academic study and hands-on clinical experience. Academic course work includes algebra, anatomy and physiology, biology, chemistry, and psychology. Clinical work includes certifications in CPR and other first aid and field experience in treatment centers. Both educators and prospective employers view clinical experience as essential to ensuring that students understand the responsibilities of a physical therapist assistant.

*Licensure.* Licensing is not required to practice as a physical therapist aide. However, some states require licensure or registration in order to work as a physical therapist assistant. states that require licensure stipulate specific educational and examination criteria. Additional requirements may include certification in cardiopulmonary resuscitation (CPR) and other first aid and a minimum number of hours of clinical experience. Complete information on regulations can be obtained from state licensing boards.

*Other qualifications.* Physical therapist assistants and aides should be well-organized, detail oriented, and caring. They usually have strong interpersonal skills and a desire to help people in need.

*Advancement.* Some physical therapist aides advance to become therapist assistants after gaining experience and, often, additional education. Sometimes, this education is required by law.

Some physical therapist assistants advance by specializing in a clinical area. They gain expertise in treating a certain type of patient, such as geriatric or pediatric, or a type of ailment, such as sports injuries. Many physical therapist assistants advance to administration positions. These positions might include organizing all the assistants in a large physical therapy organization or acting as the director for a specific department such as sports medicine. Other assistants go on to teach in an accredited physical therapist assistant academic program, lead health risk reduction classes for the elderly, or organize community activities related to fitness and risk reduction.

## Employment

Physical therapist assistants and aides held about 107,000 jobs in 2006. Physical therapist assistants held about 60,000 jobs; physical therapist aides, approximately 46,000. Both work with physical therapists in a variety of settings. About 71 percent of jobs were in offices of physical therapists or in hospitals. Others worked primarily in nursing care facilities, offices of physicians, home health care services, and outpatient care centers.

## Job Outlook

Employment is expected to grow much faster than average because of increasing consumer demand for physical therapy services. Job prospects for physical therapist assistants are expected to be very good. Aides should experience keen competition for jobs.

*Employment change.* Employment of physical therapist assistants and aides is expected to grow by 29 percent over the 2006–2016 decade, much faster than the average for all occupations. The impact of federal limits on Medicare and Medicaid reimbursement for therapy services may adversely affect the short-term job outlook for physical therapist assistants and aides. However, long-term demand for physical therapist assistants and aides will continue to rise, as the number of individuals with disabilities or limited function grows.

The increasing number of people who need therapy reflects, in part, the increasing elderly population. The elderly population is particularly vulnerable to chronic and debilitating conditions that require therapeutic services. These patients often need additional assistance in their treatment, making the roles of assistants and aides vital. In addition, the large baby-boom generation is entering the prime age for heart attacks and strokes, further increasing the demand for cardiac and physical rehabilitation. Moreover, future medical developments should permit an increased percentage of trauma victims to survive, creating added demand for therapy services.

Physical therapists are expected to increasingly use assistants to reduce the cost of physical therapy services. Once a patient is evaluated and a treatment plan is designed by the physical therapist, the physical therapist assistant can provide many parts of the treatment, as approved by the therapist.

*Job prospects.* Opportunities for individuals interested in becoming physical therapist assistants are expected to be very good. Physical therapist aides may face keen competition from the large pool of qualified individuals. In addition to employment growth, job openings will result from the need to replace workers who leave the occupation permanently. Physical therapist assistants and aides with prior experience working in a physical therapy office or other health care setting will have the best job opportunities.

## Earnings

Median annual earnings of physical therapist assistants were $41,360 in May 2006. The middle 50 percent earned between $33,840 and $49,010. The lowest 10 percent earned less than $26,190, and the highest 10 percent earned more than $57,220. Median annual earnings in the industries employing the largest numbers of physical therapist assistants in May 2006 were

Home health care services....................................$46,390
Nursing care facilities ........................................44,460

Offices of physical, occupational and speech
therapists, and audiologists .............................40,780

General medical and surgical hospitals .................40,670

Offices of physicians ........................................39,290

Median annual earnings of physical therapist aides were $22,060 in May 2006. The middle 50 percent earned between $18,550 and $26,860. The lowest 10 percent earned less than $15,850, and the highest 10 percent earned more than $32,600. Median annual earnings in the industries employing the largest numbers of physical therapist aides in May 2006 were

Nursing care facilities.......................................$24,170

Offices of physicians ........................................22,680

General medical and surgical hospitals .................22,680

Offices of physical, occupational and speech
therapists, and audiologists .............................21,230

## Related Occupations

Physical therapist assistants and aides work under the supervision of physical therapists. Other workers in the health care field who work under similar supervision include dental assistants; medical assistants; occupational therapist assistants and aides; pharmacy aides; pharmacy technicians; nursing, psychiatric, and home health aides; personal and home care aides; and social and human service assistants.

## Sources of Additional Information

Career information on physical therapist assistants and a list of schools offering accredited programs can be obtained from

▸ The American Physical Therapy Association, 1111 North Fairfax St., Alexandria, VA 22314-1488. Internet: http://www.apta.org

## Physical Therapists

(O*NET 29-1123.00)

## Significant Points

■ Employment is expected to increase much faster than average.

■ Job opportunities should be good, particularly in acute hospital, rehabilitation, and orthopedic settings.

■ Physical therapists need a master's degree from an accredited physical therapy program and a state license, requiring passing scores on national and state examinations.

■ About 6 out of 10 physical therapists work in hospitals or in offices of physical therapists.

## Nature of the Work

Physical therapists provide services that help restore function, improve mobility, relieve pain, and prevent or limit permanent physical disabilities of patients suffering from injuries or disease. They restore, maintain, and promote overall fitness and health. Their patients include accident victims and individuals with disabling conditions such as low-back pain, arthritis, heart disease, fractures, head injuries, and cerebral palsy.

Therapists examine patients' medical histories and then test and measure the patients' strength, range of motion, balance and coordination, posture, muscle performance, respiration, and motor function. Next, physical therapists develop plans describing a treatment strategy and its anticipated outcome.

Treatment often includes exercise, especially for patients who have been immobilized or who lack flexibility, strength, or endurance. Physical therapists encourage patients to use their muscles to increase their flexibility and range of motion. More advanced exercises focus on improving strength, balance, coordination, and endurance. The goal is to improve how an individual functions at work and at home.

Physical therapists also use electrical stimulation, hot packs or cold compresses, and ultrasound to relieve pain and reduce swelling. They may use traction or deep-tissue massage to relieve pain and improve circulation and flexibility. Therapists also teach patients to use assistive and adaptive devices, such as crutches, prostheses, and wheelchairs. They also may show patients how to do exercises at home to expedite their recovery.

As treatment continues, physical therapists document the patient's progress, conduct periodic examinations, and modify treatments when necessary.

Physical therapists often consult and practice with a variety of other professionals, such as physicians, dentists, nurses, educators, social workers, occupational therapists, speech-language pathologists, and audiologists.

Some physical therapists treat a wide range of ailments; others specialize in areas such as pediatrics, geriatrics, orthopedics, sports medicine, neurology, and cardiopulmonary physical therapy.

*Work environment.* Physical therapists practice in hospitals, clinics, and private offices that have specially equipped facilities. They also treat patients in hospital rooms, homes, or schools. These jobs can be physically demanding because therapists often have to stoop, kneel, crouch, lift, and stand for long periods. In addition, physical therapists move heavy equipment and lift patients or help them turn, stand, or walk.

In 2006, most full-time physical therapists worked a 40-hour week; some worked evenings and weekends to fit their patients' schedules. About 1 in 5 physical therapists worked part time.

## Training, Other Qualifications, and Advancement

Physical therapists need a master's degree from an accredited physical therapy program and a state license, requiring passing scores on national and state examinations.

*Education and training.* According to the American Physical Therapy Association, there were 209 accredited physical therapist education programs in 2007. Of the accredited programs, 43 offered master's degrees and 166 offered doctoral degrees. Only master's degree and doctoral degree programs are accredited, in accordance with the Commission on Accreditation in Physical Therapy Education. In the future, a doctoral degree might be the required entry-

**Projections data from the National Employment Matrix**

| Occupational Title | SOC Code | Employment, 2006 | Projected employment, 2016 | Change, 2006-2016 | |
|---|---|---|---|---|---|
| | | | | Number | Percent |
| Physical therapists............................................................... | 29-1123 | 173,000 | 220,000 | 47,000 | 27 |

NOTE: Data in this table are rounded.

level degree. Master's degree programs typically last two years, and doctoral degree programs last three years.

Physical therapist education programs start with basic science courses such as biology, chemistry, and physics and then introduce specialized courses, including biomechanics, neuroanatomy, human growth and development, manifestations of disease, examination techniques, and therapeutic procedures. Besides getting classroom and laboratory instruction, students receive supervised clinical experience.

Among the undergraduate courses that are useful when one applies to a physical therapist education program are anatomy, biology, chemistry, social science, mathematics, and physics. Before granting admission, many programs require volunteer experience in the physical therapy department of a hospital or clinic. For high school students, volunteering with the school athletic trainer is a good way to gain experience.

*Licensure.* All states require physical therapists to pass national and state licensure exams before they can practice. They must also graduate from an accredited physical therapist education program.

*Other qualifications.* Physical therapists should have strong interpersonal skills so that they can educate patients about their physical therapy treatments and communicate with patients' families. Physical therapists also should be compassionate and possess a desire to help patients.

*Advancement.* Physical therapists are expected to continue their professional development by participating in continuing education courses and workshops. In fact, a number of states require continuing education as a condition of maintaining licensure.

## Employment

Physical therapists held about 173,000 jobs in 2006. The number of jobs is greater than the number of practicing physical therapists because some physical therapists hold two or more jobs. For example, some may work in a private practice, but also work part time in another health care facility.

About 6 out of 10 physical therapists worked in hospitals or in offices of physical therapists. Other jobs were in the home health care services industry, nursing care facilities, outpatient care centers, and offices of physicians. Some physical therapists were self-employed in private practices, seeing individual patients and contracting to provide services in hospitals, rehabilitation centers, nursing care facilities, home health care agencies, adult day care programs, and schools. Physical therapists also teach in academic institutions and conduct research.

## Job Outlook

Employment of physical therapists is expected to grow much faster than average. Job opportunities will be good, especially in acute hospital, rehabilitation, and orthopedic settings.

*Employment change.* Employment of physical therapists is expected to grow 27 percent from 2006 to 2016, much faster than the average for all occupations. The impact of proposed federal legislation imposing limits on reimbursement for therapy services may adversely affect the short-term job outlook for physical therapists. However, the long-run demand for physical therapists should continue to rise as new treatments and techniques expand the scope of physical therapy practices. Moreover, demand will be spurred by the increasing numbers of individuals with disabilities or limited function.

The increasing elderly population will drive growth in the demand for physical therapy services. The elderly population is particularly vulnerable to chronic and debilitating conditions that require therapeutic services. Also, the baby-boom generation is entering the prime age for heart attacks and strokes, increasing the demand for cardiac and physical rehabilitation. And increasing numbers of children will need physical therapy as technological advances save the lives of a larger proportion of newborns with severe birth defects.

Future medical developments also should permit a higher percentage of trauma victims to survive, creating additional demand for rehabilitative care. In addition, growth may result from advances in medical technology that could permit the treatment of an increasing number of disabling conditions that were untreatable in the past.

Widespread interest in health promotion also should increase demand for physical therapy services. A growing number of employers are using physical therapists to evaluate worksites, develop exercise programs, and teach safe work habits to employees.

*Job prospects.* Job opportunities will be good for licensed physical therapists in all settings. Job opportunities should be particularly good in acute hospital, rehabilitation, and orthopedic settings, where the elderly are most often treated. Physical therapists with specialized knowledge of particular types of treatment also will have excellent job prospects.

## Earnings

Median annual earnings of physical therapists were $66,200 in May 2006. The middle 50 percent earned between $55,030 and $78,080. The lowest 10 percent earned less than $46,510, and the highest 10 percent earned more than $94,810. Median annual earnings in the industries employing the largest numbers of physical therapists in May 2006 were

Home health care services....................................$70,920

Nursing care facilities .......................................68,650

General medical and surgical hospitals ..................66,630

Offices of physicians .........................................65,900

Offices of physical, occupational and speech
 therapists, and audiologists ............................65,150

## Related Occupations

Physical therapists rehabilitate people with physical disabilities. Others who work in the rehabilitation field include audiologists, chiropractors, occupational therapists, recreational therapists, rehabilitation counselors, respiratory therapists, and speech-language pathologists.

## Sources of Additional Information

Additional career information and a list of accredited educational programs in physical therapy are available from

▶ American Physical Therapy Association, 1111 North Fairfax St., Alexandria, VA 22314-1488. Internet: http://www.apta.org

# Physician Assistants

(O*NET 29-1071.00)

## Significant Points

■ Physician assistant programs usually last at least 2 years; admission requirements vary by program, but many require at least 2 years of college and some health care experience.

■ All states require physician assistants to complete an accredited education program and to pass a national exam in order to obtain a license.

■ Employment is projected to grow much faster than average as health care establishments increasingly use physician assistants to contain costs.

■ Job opportunities should be good, particularly in rural and inner-city clinics.

## Nature of the Work

Physician assistants (PAs) practice medicine under the supervision of physicians and surgeons. They should not be confused with Medical assistants, who perform routine clinical and clerical tasks. PAs are formally trained to provide diagnostic, therapeutic, and preventive health care services, as delegated by a physician. Working as members of the health care team, they take medical histories, examine and treat patients, order and interpret laboratory tests and x rays, and make diagnoses. They also treat minor injuries, by suturing, splinting, and casting. PAs record progress notes, instruct and counsel patients, and order or carry out therapy. In 48 states and the District of Columbia, physician assistants may prescribe some medications. In some establishments, a PA is responsible for managerial duties, such as ordering medical supplies or equipment and supervising technicians and assistants.

Physician assistants work under the supervision of a physician. However, PAs may be the principal care providers in rural or inner city clinics where a physician is present for only one or two days each week. In such cases, the PA confers with the supervising physician and other medical professionals as needed and as required by law. PAs also may make house calls or go to hospitals and nursing care facilities to check on patients, after which they report back to the physician.

The duties of physician assistants are determined by the supervising physician and by state law. Aspiring PAs should investigate the laws and regulations in the states in which they wish to practice.

Many PAs work in primary care specialties, such as general internal medicine, pediatrics, and family medicine. Other specialty areas include general and thoracic surgery, emergency medicine, orthopedics, and geriatrics. PAs specializing in surgery provide preoperative and postoperative care and may work as first or second assistants during major surgery.

*Work environment.* Although PAs usually work in a comfortable, well-lighted environment, those in surgery often stand for long periods. At times, the job requires a considerable amount of walking. Schedules vary according to the practice setting, and often depend on the hours of the supervising physician. The work week of hospital-based PAs may include weekends, nights, or early morning hospital rounds to visit patients. These workers also may be on call. PAs in clinics usually work a 40-hour week.

## Training, Other Qualifications, and Advancement

Physician assistant programs usually last at least two years. Admission requirements vary by program, but many require at least two years of college and some health care experience. All states require that PAs complete an accredited, formal education program and pass a national exam to obtain a license.

*Education and training.* Physician assistant education programs usually last at least two years and are full time. Most programs are in schools of allied health, academic health centers, medical schools, or four-year colleges; a few are in community colleges, the military, or hospitals. Many accredited PA programs have clinical teaching affiliations with medical schools.

In 2007, 136 education programs for physician assistants were accredited or provisionally accredited by the American Academy of Physician Assistants. More than 90 of these programs offered the option of a master's degree, and the rest offered either a bachelor's degree or an associate degree. Most applicants to PA educational programs already have a bachelor's degree.

Admission requirements vary, but many programs require two years of college and some work experience in the health care field. Students should take courses in biology, English, chemistry, mathematics, psychology, and the social sciences. Many PAs have prior experience as registered nurses, and others come from varied backgrounds, including military corpsman or medics and allied health occupations such as respiratory therapists, physical therapists, and emergency medical technicians and paramedics.

PA education includes classroom instruction in biochemistry, pathology, human anatomy, physiology, microbiology, clinical pharmacology, clinical medicine, geriatric and home health care, disease prevention, and medical ethics. Students obtain supervised clinical

**Projections data from the National Employment Matrix**

| Occupational Title | SOC Code | Employment, 2006 | Projected employment, 2016 | Change, 2006-2016 | |
|---|---|---|---|---|---|
| | | | | Number | Percent |
| Physician assistants ................................................................ | 29-1071 | 66,000 | 83,000 | 18,000 | 27 |

NOTE: Data in this table are rounded.

training in several areas, including family medicine, internal medicine, surgery, prenatal care and gynecology, geriatrics, emergency medicine, psychiatry, and pediatrics. Sometimes, PA students serve one or more of these rotations under the supervision of a physician who is seeking to hire a PA. The rotations often lead to permanent employment.

*Licensure.* All states and the District of Columbia have legislation governing the qualifications or practice of physician assistants. All jurisdictions require physician assistants to pass the Physician Assistant National Certifying Examination, administered by the National Commission on Certification of Physician Assistants (NCCPA) and open only to graduates of accredited PA education programs. Only those successfully completing the examination may use the credential "Physician Assistant-Certified." To remain certified, PAs must complete 100 hours of continuing medical education every two years. Every six years, they must pass a recertification examination or complete an alternative program combining learning experiences and a take-home examination.

*Other qualifications.* Physician assistants must have a desire to serve patients and be self-motivated. PAs also must have a good bedside manner, emotional stability, and the ability to make decisions in emergencies. Physician assistants must be willing to study throughout their career to keep up with medical advances.

*Certification and advancement.* Some PAs pursue additional education in a specialty such as surgery, neonatology, or emergency medicine. PA postgraduate educational programs are available in areas such as internal medicine, rural primary care, emergency medicine, surgery, pediatrics, neonatology, and occupational medicine. Candidates must be graduates of an accredited program and be certified by the NCCPA.

As they attain greater clinical knowledge and experience, PAs can advance to added responsibilities and higher earnings. However, by the very nature of the profession, clinically practicing PAs always are supervised by physicians.

## Employment

Physician assistants held about 66,000 jobs in 2006. The number of jobs is greater than the number of practicing PAs because some hold two or more jobs. For example, some PAs work with a supervising physician, but also work in another practice, clinic, or hospital. According to the American Academy of Physician Assistants, about 15 percent of actively practicing PAs worked in more than one clinical job concurrently in 2006.

More than half of jobs for PAs were in the offices of physicians. About a quarter were in hospitals, public or private. The rest were mostly in outpatient care centers, including health maintenance organizations; the federal government; and public or private colleges, universities, and professional schools. A few were self-employed.

## Job Outlook

Employment is expected to grow much faster than the average as health care establishments increasingly use physician assistants to contain costs. Job opportunities for PAs should be good, particularly in rural and inner city clinics, as these settings typically have difficulty attracting physicians.

*Employment change.* Employment of physician assistants is expected to grow 27 percent from 2006 to 2016, much faster than the average for all occupations. Projected rapid job growth reflects the expansion of health care industries and an emphasis on cost containment, which results in increasing use of PAs by health care establishments.

Physicians and institutions are expected to employ more PAs to provide primary care and to assist with medical and surgical procedures because PAs are cost-effective and productive members of the health care team. Physician assistants can relieve physicians of routine duties and procedures. Telemedicine—using technology to facilitate interactive consultations between physicians and physician assistants—also will expand the use of physician assistants.

Besides working in traditional office-based settings, PAs should find a growing number of jobs in institutional settings such as hospitals, academic medical centers, public clinics, and prisons. PAs also may be needed to augment medical staffing in inpatient teaching hospital settings as the number of hours physician residents are permitted to work is reduced, encouraging hospitals to use PAs to supply some physician resident services.

*Job prospects.* Job opportunities for PAs should be good, particularly in rural and inner-city clinics because those settings have difficulty attracting physicians. In addition to job openings from employment growth, openings will result from the need to replace physician assistants who retire or leave the occupation permanently during the 2006–2016 decade. Opportunities will be best in states that allow PAs a wider scope of practice, such as allowing PAs to prescribe medications.

## Earnings

Median annual earnings of wage-and-salary physician assistants were $74,980 in May 2006. The middle 50 percent earned between $62,430 and $89,220. The lowest 10 percent earned less than $43,100, and the highest 10 percent earned more than $102,230. Median annual earnings in the industries employing the largest numbers of physician assistants in May 2006 were

Outpatient care centers ......................................$80,960

General medical and surgical hospitals ..................76,710

Offices of physicians ..........................................74,160

According to the American Academy of Physician Assistants, median income for physician assistants in full-time clinical practice was $80,356 in 2006; median income for first-year graduates was $69,517. Income varies by specialty, practice setting, geographical location, and years of experience. Employers often pay for their employees' liability insurance, registration fees with the Drug Enforcement Administration, state licensing fees, and credentialing fees.

## Related Occupations

Other health care workers who provide direct patient care that requires a similar level of skill and training include audiologists, occupational therapists, physical therapists, registered nurses, and speech-language pathologists.

## Sources of Additional Information

For information on a career as a physician assistant, including a list of accredited programs, contact

▸ American Academy of Physician Assistants Information Center, 950 North Washington St., Alexandria, VA 22314. Internet: http://www.aapa.org

For eligibility requirements and a description of the Physician Assistant National Certifying Examination, contact

▸ National Commission on Certification of Physician Assistants, Inc., 12000 Findley Rd., Suite 200, Duluth, GA 30097. Internet: http://www.nccpa.net

# Physicians and Surgeons

(O*NET 29-1061.00, 29-1062.00, 29-1063.00, 29-1064.00, 29-1065.00, 29-1066.00, 29-1067.00, and 29-1069.99)

## Significant Points

■ Many physicians and surgeons work long, irregular hours; more than one-third of full-time physicians worked 60 hours or more a week in 2006.

■ Acceptance to medical school is highly competitive.

■ Formal education and training requirements are among the most demanding of any occupation, but earnings are among the highest.

■ Job opportunities should be very good, particularly in rural and low-income areas.

## Nature of the Work

Physicians and surgeons diagnose illnesses and prescribe and administer treatment for people suffering from injury or disease. Physicians examine patients, obtain medical histories, and order, perform, and interpret diagnostic tests. They counsel patients on diet, hygiene, and preventive health care.

There are two types of physicians: M.D.—Doctor of Medicine—and D.O.—Doctor of Osteopathic Medicine. M.D.s also are known as allopathic physicians. While both M.D.s and D.O.s may use all accepted methods of treatment, including drugs and surgery, D.O.s place special emphasis on the body's musculoskeletal system, preventive medicine, and holistic patient care. D.O.s are most likely to

be primary care specialists although they can be found in all specialties. About half of D.O.s practice general or family medicine, general internal medicine, or general pediatrics.

Physicians work in one or more of several specialties, including, but not limited to, anesthesiology, family and general medicine, general internal medicine, general pediatrics, obstetrics and gynecology, psychiatry, and surgery.

*Anesthesiologists* focus on the care of surgical patients and pain relief. Like other physicians, they evaluate and treat patients and direct the efforts of their staffs. Through continual monitoring and assessment, these critical care specialists are responsible for maintenance of the patient's vital life functions—heart rate, body temperature, blood pressure, breathing—during surgery. They also work outside of the operating room, providing pain relief in the intensive care unit, during labor and delivery, and for those who suffer from chronic pain. Anesthesiologists confer with other physicians and surgeons about appropriate treatments and procedures before, during, and after operations.

*Family and general practitioners* often provide the first point of contact for people seeking health care, by acting as the traditional family doctor. They assess and treat a wide range of conditions, from sinus and respiratory infections to broken bones. Family and general practitioners typically have a base of regular, long-term patients. These doctors refer patients with more serious conditions to specialists or other health care facilities for more intensive care.

*General internists* diagnose and provide nonsurgical treatment for a wide range of problems that affect internal organ systems, such as the stomach, kidneys, liver, and digestive tract. Internists use a variety of diagnostic techniques to treat patients through medication or hospitalization. Like general practitioners, general internists commonly act as primary care specialists. They treat patients referred from other specialists, and, in turn they refer patients to other specialists when more complex care is required.

*General pediatricians* care for the health of infants, children, teenagers, and young adults. They specialize in the diagnosis and treatment of a variety of ailments specific to young people and track patients' growth to adulthood. Like most physicians, pediatricians work with different health care workers, such as nurses and other physicians, to assess and treat children with various ailments. Most of the work of pediatricians involves treating day-to-day illnesses—minor injuries, infectious diseases, and immunizations—that are common to children, much as a general practitioner treats adults. Some pediatricians specialize in pediatric surgery or serious medical conditions, such as autoimmune disorders or serious chronic ailments.

*Obstetricians and gynecologists* (OB/GYNs) specialize in women's health. They are responsible for women's general medical care, and they also provide care related to pregnancy and the reproductive system. Like general practitioners, OB/GYNs attempt to prevent, diagnose, and treat general health problems, but they focus on ailments specific to the female anatomy, such as cancers of the breast or cervix, urinary tract and pelvic disorders, and hormonal disorders. OB/GYNs also specialize in childbirth, treating and counseling women throughout their pregnancy, from giving prenatal diagnoses to assisting with delivery and providing postpartum care.

*Psychiatrists* are the primary caregivers in the area of mental health. They assess and treat mental illnesses through a combination of psychotherapy, psychoanalysis, hospitalization, and medication. Psychotherapy involves regular discussions with patients about their problems; the psychiatrist helps them find solutions through changes in their behavioral patterns, the exploration of their past experiences, or group and family therapy sessions. Psychoanalysis involves long-term psychotherapy and counseling for patients. In many cases, medications are administered to correct chemical imbalances that cause emotional problems. Psychiatrists also may administer electroconvulsive therapy to those of their patients who do not respond to, or who cannot take, medications.

*Surgeons* specialize in the treatment of injury, disease, and deformity through operations. Using a variety of instruments, and with patients under anesthesia, a surgeon corrects physical deformities, repairs bone and tissue after injuries, or performs preventive surgeries on patients with debilitating diseases or disorders. Although a large number perform general surgery, many surgeons choose to specialize in a specific area. One of the most prevalent specialties is orthopedic surgery: the treatment of the musculoskeletal system. Others include neurological surgery (treatment of the brain and nervous system), cardiovascular surgery, otolaryngology (treatment of the ear, nose, and throat), and plastic or reconstructive surgery. Like other physicians, surgeons also examine patients, perform and interpret diagnostic tests, and counsel patients on preventive health care.

*Other physicians and surgeons* work in a number of other medical and surgical specialists, including allergists, cardiologists, dermatologists, emergency physicians, gastroenterologists, ophthalmologists, pathologists, and radiologists.

**Work environment.** Many physicians—primarily general and family practitioners, general internists, pediatricians, OB/GYNs, and psychiatrists—work in small private offices or clinics, often assisted by a small staff of nurses and other administrative personnel. Increasingly, physicians are practicing in groups or health care organizations that provide backup coverage and allow for more time off. Physicians in a group practice or health care organization often work as part of a team that coordinates care for a number of patients; they are less independent than the solo practitioners of the past. Surgeons and anesthesiologists usually work in well-lighted, sterile environments while performing surgery and often stand for long periods. Most work in hospitals or in surgical outpatient centers.

Many physicians and surgeons work long, irregular hours. Over one-third of full-time physicians and surgeons worked 60 hours or more a week in 2006. Only 8 percent of all physicians and surgeons worked part-time, compared with 15 percent for all occupations. Physicians and surgeons must travel frequently between office and hospital to care for their patients. While on call, a physician will deal with many patients' concerns over the phone and make emergency visits to hospitals or nursing homes.

# Training, Other Qualifications, and Advancement

The common path to practicing as a physician requires eight years of education beyond high school and three to eight additional years

of internship and residency. All states, the District of Columbia, and U.S. territories license physicians.

**Education and training.** Formal education and training requirements for physicians are among the most demanding of any occupation—four years of undergraduate school, four years of medical school, and three to eight years of internship and residency, depending on the specialty selected. A few medical schools offer combined undergraduate and medical school programs that last six years rather than the customary eight years.

Premedical students must complete undergraduate work in physics, biology, mathematics, English, and inorganic and organic chemistry. Students also take courses in the humanities and the social sciences. Some students volunteer at local hospitals or clinics to gain practical experience in the health professions.

The minimum educational requirement for entry into medical school is three years of college; most applicants, however, have at least a bachelor's degree, and many have advanced degrees. There are 146 medical schools in the United States—126 teach allopathic medicine and award a Doctor of Medicine (M.D.) degree; 20 teach osteopathic medicine and award the Doctor of Osteopathic Medicine (D.O.) degree.

Acceptance to medical school is highly competitive. Applicants must submit transcripts, scores from the Medical College Admission Test, and letters of recommendation. Schools also consider an applicant's character, personality, leadership qualities, and participation in extracurricular activities. Most schools require an interview with members of the admissions committee.

Students spend most of the first two years of medical school in laboratories and classrooms, taking courses such as anatomy, biochemistry, physiology, pharmacology, psychology, microbiology, pathology, medical ethics, and laws governing medicine. They also learn to take medical histories, examine patients, and diagnose illnesses. During their last two years, students work with patients under the supervision of experienced physicians in hospitals and clinics, learning acute, chronic, preventive, and rehabilitative care. Through rotations in internal medicine, family practice, obstetrics and gynecology, pediatrics, psychiatry, and surgery, they gain experience in the diagnosis and treatment of illness.

Following medical school, almost all M.D.s enter a residency—graduate medical education in a specialty that takes the form of paid on-the-job training, usually in a hospital. Most D.O.s serve a 12-month rotating internship after graduation and before entering a residency, which may last two to six years.

A physician's training is costly. According to the Association of American Medical Colleges, in 2004 more than 80 percent of medical school graduates were in debt for educational expenses.

**Licensure and certification.** All states, the District of Columbia, and U.S. territories license physicians. To be licensed, physicians must graduate from an accredited medical school, pass a licensing examination, and complete one to seven years of graduate medical education. Although physicians licensed in one state usually can get a license to practice in another without further examination, some states limit reciprocity. Graduates of foreign medical schools generally can qualify for licensure after passing an examination and completing a U.S. residency.

M.D.s and D.O.s seeking board certification in a specialty may spend up to seven years in residency training, depending on the specialty. A final examination immediately after residency or after one or two years of practice also is necessary for certification by a member board of the American Board of Medical Specialists (ABMS) or the American Osteopathic Association (AOA). The ABMS represents 24 boards related to medical specialties ranging from allergy and immunology to urology. The AOA has approved 18 specialty boards, ranging from anesthesiology to surgery. For certification in a subspecialty, physicians usually need another one to two years of residency.

*Other qualifications.* People who wish to become physicians must have a desire to serve patients, be self-motivated, and be able to survive the pressures and long hours of medical education and practice. Physicians also must have a good bedside manner, emotional stability, and the ability to make decisions in emergencies. Prospective physicians must be willing to study throughout their career to keep up with medical advances.

*Advancement.* Some physicians and surgeons advance by gaining expertise in specialties and subspecialties and by developing a reputation for excellence among their peers and patients. Many physicians and surgeons start their own practice or join a group practice. Others teach residents and other new doctors, and some advance to supervisory and managerial roles in hospitals, clinics, and other settings.

## Employment

Physicians and surgeons held about 633,000 jobs in 2006; approximately 15 percent were self-employed. About half of wage–and–salary physicians and surgeons worked in offices of physicians, and 18 percent were employed by hospitals. Others practiced in federal, state, and local governments, including colleges, universities, and professional schools; private colleges, universities, and professional schools; and outpatient care centers.

According to 2005 data from the American Medical Association (AMA), about one half of physicians in patient care were in primary care, but not in a subspecialty of primary care. (See table 1.)

### Table 1. Percent distribution of active physicians in patient care by specialty, 2005

|  | Percent |
| --- | --- |
| Total | 100.0 |
| Primary care | 40.4 |
|   Family medicine and general practice | 12.3 |
|   Internal medicine | 15.0 |
|   Obstetrics & gynecology | 5.5 |
|   Pediatrics | 7.5 |
| Specialties | 59.6 |
|   Anesthesiology | 5.2 |
|   Psychiatry | 5.1 |
|   Surgical specialties, selected | 10.8 |
|   All other specialties | 38.5 |

SOURCE: American Medical Association, Physician Characteristics and Distribution in the US, 2007.

A growing number of physicians are partners or wage-and-salary employees of group practices. Organized as clinics or as associations of physicians, medical groups can more easily afford expensive medical equipment, can share support staff, and benefit from other business advantages.

According to the AMA, the New England and Middle Atlantic states have the highest ratio of physicians to population; the South Central and Mountain states have the lowest. D.O.s are more likely than M.D.s to practice in small cities and towns and in rural areas. M.D.s tend to locate in urban areas, close to hospitals and education centers.

## Job Outlook

Employment of physicians and surgeons is expected to grow faster than the average for all occupations. Job opportunities should be very good, especially for physicians and surgeons willing to practice in specialties—including family practice, internal medicine, and OB/GYN—or in rural and low-income areas where there is a perceived shortage of medical practitioners.

*Employment change.* Employment of physicians and surgeons is projected to grow 14 percent from 2006 to 2016, faster than the average for all occupations. Job growth will occur because of continued expansion of health care related industries. The growing and aging population will drive overall growth in the demand for physician services, as consumers continue to demand high levels of care using the latest technologies, diagnostic tests, and therapies.

Demand for physicians' services is highly sensitive to changes in consumer preferences, health care reimbursement policies, and legislation. For example, if changes to health coverage result in consumers facing higher out-of-pocket costs, they may demand fewer physician services. Patients relying more on other health care providers—such as physician assistants, nurse practitioners, optometrists, and nurse anesthetists—also may temper demand for physician services. In addition, new technologies will increase physician productivity. These technologies include electronic medical records, test and prescription orders, billing, and scheduling.

*Job prospects.* Opportunities for individuals interested in becoming physicians and surgeons are expected to be very good. In addition to job openings from employment growth, numerous openings will result from the need to replace physicians and surgeons who retire over the 2006–2016 decade.

Unlike their predecessors, newly trained physicians face radically different choices of where and how to practice. New physicians are much less likely to enter solo practice and more likely to take salaried jobs in group medical practices, clinics, and health networks.

Reports of shortages in some specialties, such as general or family practice, internal medicine, and OB/GYN, or in rural or low-income areas should attract new entrants, encouraging schools to expand programs and hospitals to increase available residency slots. However, because physician training is so lengthy, employment change happens gradually. In the short term, to meet increased demand, experienced physicians may work longer hours, delay retirement, or take measures to increase productivity, such as using more support staff to provide services. Opportunities should be particularly good

**Projections data from the National Employment Matrix**

| Occupational Title | SOC Code | Employment, 2006 | Projected employment, 2016 | Change, 2006-2016 Number | Change, 2006-2016 Percent |
|---|---|---|---|---|---|
| Physicians and surgeons................................................ | 29-1060 | 633,000 | 723,000 | 90,000 | 14 |

NOTE: Data in this table are rounded.

in rural and low-income areas, as some physicians find these areas unattractive because of less control over work hours, isolation from medical colleagues, or other reasons.

## Earnings

Earnings of physicians and surgeons are among the highest of any occupation. The Medical Group Management Association's Physician Compensation and Production Survey, reports that median total compensation for physicians in 2005 varied by specialty, as shown in table 2. Total compensation for physicians reflects the amount reported as direct compensation for tax purposes, plus all voluntary salary reductions. Salary, bonus and incentive payments, research stipends, honoraria, and distribution of profits were included in total compensation.

Self-employed physicians—those who own or are part owners of their medical practice—generally have higher median incomes than salaried physicians. Earnings vary according to number of years in practice, geographic region, hours worked, skill, personality, and professional reputation. Self-employed physicians and surgeons must provide for their own health insurance and retirement.

**Table 2. Median compensation for physicians, 2005**

| Specialty | Less than two years in specialty | Over one year in specialty |
|---|---|---|
| Anesthesiology.................................... | $259,948 | $321,686 |
| Surgery: General ............................... | 228,839 | 282,504 |
| Obstetrics/gynecology: General.......... | 203,270 | 247,348 |
| Psychiatry: General ........................... | 173,922 | 180,000 |
| Internal medicine: General................. | 141,912 | 166,420 |
| Pediatrics: General ............................ | 132,953 | 161,331 |
| Family practice (without obstetrics) ... | 137,119 | 156,010 |

SOURCE: Medical Group Management Association, Physician Compensation and Production Report, 2005.

## Related Occupations

Physicians work to prevent, diagnose, and treat diseases, disorders, and injuries. Other health care practitioners who need similar skills and who exercise critical judgment include chiropractors, dentists, optometrists, physician assistants, podiatrists, registered nurses, and veterinarians.

## Sources of Additional Information

For a list of medical schools and residency programs, as well as general information on premedical education, financial aid, and medicine as a career, contact

▸ American Association of Colleges of Osteopathic Medicine, 5550 Friendship Blvd., Suite 310, Chevy Chase, MD 20815. Internet: http://www.aacom.org

▸ Association of American Medical Colleges, Section for Student Services, 2450 N St. NW, Washington, DC 20037. Internet: http://www.aamc.org/students

For general information on physicians, contact

▸ American Medical Association, 515 N. State St., Chicago, IL 60610. Internet: http://www.ama-assn.org

▸ American Osteopathic Association, Department of Communications, 142 East Ontario St., Chicago, IL 60611. Internet: http://www.osteopathic.org

For information about various medical specialties, contact

▸ American Academy of Family Physicians, Resident Student Activities Department, 11400 Tomahawk Creek Pkwy., Leawood, KS 66211. Internet: http://fmignet.aafp.org

▸ American Academy of Pediatrics, 141 Northwest Point Blvd., Elk Grove Village, IL 60007. Internet: http://www.aap.org

▸ American Board of Medical Specialties, 1007 Church St., Suite 404, Evanston, IL 60201. Internet: http://www.abms.org

▸ American College of Obstetricians and Gynecologists, 409 12th St. SW, P.O. Box 96920, Washington, DC 20090. Internet: http://www.acog.org

▸ American College of Physicians, 190 North Independence Mall West, Philadelphia, PA 19106. Internet: http://www.acponline.org

▸ American College of Surgeons, Division of Education, 633 North Saint Clair St., Chicago, IL 60611. Internet: http://www.facs.org

▸ American Psychiatric Association, 1000 Wilson Blvd., Suite 1825, Arlington, VA 22209. Internet: http://www.psych.org

▸ American Society of Anesthesiologists, 520 N. Northwest Hwy., Park Ridge, IL 60068. Internet: http://www.asahq.org/career/homepage.htm

Information on federal scholarships and loans is available from the directors of student financial aid at schools of medicine. Information on licensing is available from state boards of examiners.

# Pipelayers, Plumbers, Pipefitters, and Steamfitters

(O*NET 47-2151.00, 47-2152.00, 47-2152.01, and 47-2152.02)

## Significant Points

■ Job opportunities should be very good, especially for workers with welding experience.

■ Pipelayers, plumbers, pipefitters, and steamfitters comprise one of the largest and highest paid construction occupations.

■ Most states and localities require plumbers to be licensed.

■ Apprenticeship programs generally provide the most comprehensive training, but many workers train in career or technical schools or community colleges.

## Nature of the Work

Most people are familiar with plumbers who come to their home to unclog a drain or install an appliance. In addition to these activities, however, pipelayers, plumbers, pipefitters, and steamfitters install, maintain, and repair many different types of pipe systems. For example, some systems move water to a municipal water treatment plant and then to residential, commercial, and public buildings. Other systems dispose of waste, provide gas to stoves and furnaces, or provide for heating and cooling needs. Pipe systems in powerplants carry the steam that powers huge turbines. Pipes also are used in manufacturing plants to move material through the production process. Specialized piping systems are very important in both pharmaceutical and computer-chip manufacturing.

Although pipelaying, plumbing, pipefitting, and steamfitting sometimes are considered a single trade, workers generally specialize in one of five areas. *Pipelayers* lay clay, concrete, plastic, or cast-iron pipe for drains, sewers, water mains, and oil or gas lines. Before laying the pipe, pipelayers prepare and grade the trenches either manually or with machines. After laying the pipe, they weld, glue, cement, or otherwise join the pieces together. *Plumbers* install and repair the water, waste disposal, drainage, and gas systems in homes and commercial and industrial buildings. Plumbers also install plumbing fixtures—bathtubs, showers, sinks, and toilets—and appliances such as dishwashers and water heaters. *Pipefitters* install and repair both high-pressure and low-pressure pipe systems used in manufacturing, in the generation of electricity, and in the heating and cooling of buildings. They also install automatic controls that are increasingly being used to regulate these systems. Some pipefitters specialize in only one type of system. *Steamfitters* install pipe systems that move liquids or gases under high pressure. *Sprinklerfitters* install automatic fire sprinkler systems in buildings.

Pipelayers, plumbers, pipefitters, and steamfitters use many different materials and construction techniques, depending on the type of project. Residential water systems, for example, incorporate copper, steel, and plastic pipe that can be handled and installed by one or two plumbers. Municipal sewerage systems, on the other hand, are made of large cast-iron pipes; installation normally requires crews of pipefitters. Despite these differences, all pipelayers, plumbers,

pipefitters, and steamfitters must be able to follow building plans or blueprints and instructions from supervisors, lay out the job, and work efficiently with the materials and tools of their trade. Computers and specialized software are used to create blueprints and plan layouts.

When construction plumbers install piping in a new house, for example, they work from blueprints or drawings that show the planned location of pipes, plumbing fixtures, and appliances. Recently, plumbers have become more involved in the design process. Their knowledge of codes and the operation of plumbing systems can cut costs. They first lay out the job to fit the piping into the structure of the house with the least waste of material. Then they measure and mark areas in which pipes will be installed and connected. Construction plumbers also check for obstructions such as electrical wiring and, if necessary, plan the pipe installation around the problem.

Sometimes, plumbers have to cut holes in walls, ceilings, and floors of a house. For some systems, they may hang steel supports from ceiling joists to hold the pipe in place. To assemble a system, plumbers—using saws, pipe cutters, and pipe-bending machines—cut and bend lengths of pipe. They connect lengths of pipe with fittings, using methods that depend on the type of pipe used. For plastic pipe, plumbers connect the sections and fittings with adhesives. For copper pipe, they slide a fitting over the end of the pipe and solder it in place with a torch.

After the piping is in place in the house, plumbers install the fixtures and appliances and connect the system to the outside water or sewer lines. Finally, using pressure gauges, they check the system to ensure that the plumbing works properly.

***Work environment.*** Pipefitters and steamfitters most often work in industrial and power plants. Plumbers work in commercial and residential settings where water and septic systems need to be installed and maintained. Pipelayers work outdoors, sometime in remote areas, as they build the pipelines that connect sources of oil, gas, and chemicals with the users of these materials. Sprinklerfitters work in all buildings that require the use of fire sprinkler systems.

Because pipelayers, plumbers, pipefitters, and steamfitters frequently must lift heavy pipes, stand for long periods, and sometimes work in uncomfortable or cramped positions, they need physical strength and stamina. They also may have to work outdoors in inclement weather. In addition, they are subject to possible falls from ladders, cuts from sharp tools, and burns from hot pipes or soldering equipment.

Pipelayers, plumbers, pipefitters, and steamfitters engaged in construction generally work a standard 40-hour week; those involved in maintaining pipe systems, including those who provide maintenance services under contract, may have to work evening or weekend shifts and work on call. These maintenance workers may spend a lot of time traveling to and from worksites.

## Training, Other Qualifications, and Advancement

Most pipelayers, plumbers, pipefitters, and steamfitters train in career or technical schools or community colleges, and on the job through apprenticeships.

*Education and training.* Pipelayers, plumbers, pipefitters, and steamfitters enter into the occupation in a variety of ways. Most residential and industrial plumbers get their training in career and technical schools and community colleges and from on-the-job training. Pipelayers, plumbers, pipefitters, and steamfitters who work for nonresidential enterprises are usually trained through formal apprenticeship programs.

Apprenticeship programs generally provide the most comprehensive training available for these jobs. They are administered either by union locals and their affiliated companies or by nonunion contractor organizations. Organizations that sponsor apprenticeships include: the United Association of Journeymen and Apprentices of the Plumbing and Pipefitting Industry of the United States and Canada; local employers of either the Mechanical Contractors Association of America or the National Association of Plumbing-Heating-Cooling Contractors; a union associated with a member of the National Fire Sprinkler Association; the Associated Builders and Contractors; the National Association of Plumbing-Heating-Cooling Contractors; the American Fire Sprinkler Association, or the Home Builders Institute of the National Association of Home Builders.

Apprenticeships—both union and nonunion—consist of four or five years of paid on-the-job training and at least 144 hours of related classroom instruction per year. Classroom subjects include drafting and blueprint reading, mathematics, applied physics and chemistry, safety, and local plumbing codes and regulations. On the job, apprentices first learn basic skills, such as identifying grades and types of pipe, using the tools of the trade, and safely unloading materials. As apprentices gain experience, they learn how to work with various types of pipe and how to install different piping systems and plumbing fixtures. Apprenticeship gives trainees a thorough knowledge of all aspects of the trade. Although most pipelayers, plumbers, pipefitters, and steamfitters are trained through apprenticeship, some still learn their skills informally on the job.

*Licensure.* Although there are no uniform national licensing requirements, most states and communities require plumbers to be licensed. Licensing requirements vary, but most localities require workers to have two to five years of experience and to pass an examination that tests their knowledge of the trade and of local plumbing codes before working independently. Several states require a special license to work on gas lines. A few states require pipe fitters to be licensed. These licenses usually require a test, experience, or both.

*Other qualifications.* Applicants for union or nonunion apprentice jobs must be at least 18 years old and in good physical condition. A drug test may be required. Apprenticeship committees may require applicants to have a high school diploma or its equivalent. Armed Forces training in pipelaying, plumbing, and pipefitting is considered very good preparation. In fact, people with this background may be given credit for previous experience when entering a civilian apprenticeship program. High school or postsecondary courses in shop, plumbing, general mathematics, drafting, blueprint reading, computers, and physics also are good preparation.

*Advancement.* With additional training, some pipelayers, plumbers, pipefitters, and steamfitters become supervisors for mechanical and plumbing contractors. Others, especially plumbers, go into business for themselves, often starting as a self-employed plumber working from home. Some eventually become owners of businesses employing many workers and may spend most of their time as managers rather than as plumbers. Others move into closely related areas such as construction management or building inspection.

For those who would like to advance, it is increasingly important to be able to communicate in both English and Spanish in order to relay instructions and safety precautions to workers with limited understanding of English; Spanish-speaking workers make up a large part of the construction workforce in many areas. Supervisors and contractors need good communication skills to deal with clients and subcontractors.

## Employment

Pipelayers, plumbers, pipefitters, and steamfitters constitute one of the largest construction occupations, holding about 569,000 jobs in 2006. About 55 percent worked for plumbing, heating, and air-conditioning contractors engaged in new construction, repair, modernization, or maintenance work. Others did maintenance work for a variety of industrial, commercial, and government employers. For example, pipefitters were employed as maintenance personnel in the petroleum and chemical industries, both of which move liquids and gases through pipes. About 12 percent of pipelayers, plumbers, pipefitters, and steamfitters were self-employed.

## Job Outlook

Average employment growth is projected. Job opportunities are expected to be very good, especially for workers with welding experience.

*Employment change.* Employment of pipelayers, plumbers, pipefitters, and steamfitters is expected to grow 10 percent between 2006 and 2016, about as fast as the average for all occupations. Demand for plumbers will stem from new construction and building renovation. Bath remodeling, in particular, is expected to continue to grow and create more jobs for plumbers. In addition, repair and maintenance of existing residential systems will keep plumbers employed. Demand for pipefitters and steamfitters will be driven by maintenance and construction of places such as powerplants, water and wastewater treatment plants, office buildings, and factories, with extensive pipe systems. Growth of pipelayer jobs will stem from the building of new water and sewer lines and pipelines to new oil and gas fields. Demand for sprinklerfitters will increase because of changes to state and local rules for fire protection in homes and businesses.

*Job prospects.* Job opportunities are expected to be very good, as demand for skilled pipelayers, plumbers, pipefitters, and steamfitters is expected to outpace the supply of workers well trained in this craft in some areas. Some employers report difficulty finding workers with the right qualifications. In addition, many people currently working in these trades are expected to retire over the next 10 years, which will create additional job openings. Workers with welding experience should have especially good opportunities.

Traditionally, many organizations with extensive pipe systems have employed their own plumbers or pipefitters to maintain equipment and keep systems running smoothly. But, to reduce labor costs, many of these firms no longer employ full-time, in-house plumbers

**Projections data from the National Employment Matrix**

| Occupational Title | SOC Code | Employment, 2006 | Projected employment, 2016 | Change, 2006-16 | |
|---|---|---|---|---|---|
| | | | | Number | Percent |
| Pipelayers, plumbers, pipefitters, and steamfitters............................ | 47-2150 | 569,000 | 628,000 | 59,000 | 10 |
| Pipelayers............................................................................. | 47-2151 | 67,000 | 72,000 | 5,800 | 9 |
| Plumbers, pipefitters, and steamfitters ............................................ | 47-2152 | 502,000 | 555,000 | 53,000 | 11 |

NOTE: Data in this table are rounded.

or pipefitters. Instead, when they need a plumber, they rely on workers provided under service contracts by plumbing and pipefitting contractors.

Construction projects generally provide only temporary employment. When a project ends, some pipelayers, plumbers, pipefitters, and steamfitters may be unemployed until they can begin work on a new project, although most companies are trying to limit these periods of unemployment to retain workers. In addition, the jobs of pipelayers, plumbers, pipefitters, and steamfitters are generally less sensitive to changes in economic conditions than jobs in other construction trades. Even when construction activity declines, maintenance, rehabilitation, and replacement of existing piping systems, as well as the increasing installation of fire sprinkler systems, provide many jobs for pipelayers, plumbers, pipefitters, and steamfitters.

## Earnings

Pipelayers, plumbers, pipefitters, and steamfitters are among the highest paid construction occupations. Median hourly earnings of wage and salary plumbers, pipefitters, and steamfitters were $20.56. The middle 50 percent earned between $15.62 and $27.54. The lowest 10 percent earned less than $12.30, and the highest 10 percent earned more than $34.79. Median hourly earnings in the industries employing the largest numbers of plumbers, pipefitters, and steamfitters were

Natural gas distribution ........................................$24.91

Nonresidential building construction ......................21.30

Plumbing, heating, and air-conditioning
    contractors ....................................................20.44

Utility system construction...................................19.18

Local government ...............................................17.86

In May 2006, median hourly earnings of wage and salary pipelayers were $14.58. The middle 50 percent earned between $11.75 and $19.76. The lowest 10 percent earned less than $9.73, and the highest 10 percent earned more than $25.73.

Apprentices usually begin at about 50 percent of the wage rate paid to experienced workers. Wages increase periodically as skills improve. After an initial waiting period, apprentices receive the same benefits as experienced pipelayers, plumbers, pipefitters, and steamfitters.

About 30 percent of pipelayers, plumbers, pipefitters, and steamfitters belonged to a union. Many of these workers are members of the United Association of Journeymen and Apprentices of the Plumbing and Pipefitting Industry of the United States and Canada.

## Related Occupations

Other workers who install and repair mechanical systems in buildings include boilermakers; electricians; elevator installers and repairers; heating, air-conditioning, and refrigeration mechanics and installers; industrial machinery mechanics and maintenance workers; millwrights; sheet metal workers; and stationary engineers and boiler operators. Other related occupations include construction managers and construction and building inspectors.

## Sources of Additional Information

For information about apprenticeships or work opportunities in pipelaying, plumbing, pipefitting, and steamfitting, contact local plumbing, heating, and air-conditioning contractors; a local or state chapter of the National Association of Plumbing, Heating, and Cooling Contractors; a local chapter of the Mechanical Contractors Association; a local chapter of the United Association of Journeymen and Apprentices of the Plumbing and Pipefitting Industry of the United States and Canada; or the nearest office of your state employment service or apprenticeship agency. Apprenticeship information is also available from the U.S. Department of Labor's toll-free helpline: 1 (877) 872-5627.

For information about apprenticeship opportunities for pipelayers, plumbers, pipefitters, and steamfitters, contact

▸ United Association of Journeymen and Apprentices of the Plumbing and Pipefitting Industry, 901 Massachusetts Ave. NW, Washington, DC 20001. Internet: http://www.ua.org

For more information about training programs for pipelayers, plumbers, pipefitters, and steamfitters, contact

▸ Associated Builders and Contractors, Workforce Development Department, 4250 North Fairfax Dr., 9th Floor, Arlington, VA 22203. Internet: http://www.trytools.org

▸ Home Builders Institute, National Association of Home Builders, 1201 15th St. NW, Washington, DC 20005. Internet: http://www.hbi.org

For general information about the work of pipelayers, plumbers, and pipefitters, contact

▸ Mechanical Contractors Association of America, 1385 Piccard Dr., Rockville, MD 20850. Internet: http://www.mcaa.org

▸ National Center for Construction Education and Research, 3600 NW 43rd St., Bldg. G, Gainesville, FL 32606. Internet: http://www.nccer.org

▸ Plumbing-Heating-Cooling Contractors—National Association, 180 S. Washington St, Falls Church, VA 22040. Internet: http://www.phccweb.org

For general information about the work of sprinklerfitters, contact

▸ American Fire Sprinkler Association, Inc., 12750 Merit Dr., Suite 350, Dallas, TX 75251. Internet: http://www.firesprinkler.org

▸ National Fire Sprinkler Association, 40 Jon Barrett Rd., Patterson, NY 12563. Internet: http://www.nfsa.org

For general information on apprenticeships and how to get them, see the *Occupational Outlook Quarterly* article "Apprenticeships: Career training, credentials—and a paycheck in your pocket," online at http://www.bls.gov/opub/ooq/2002/summer/art01.pdf and in print at many libraries and career centers.

# Police and Detectives

(O*NET 33-1012.00, 33-3021.00, 33-3021.01, 33-3021.02, 33-3021.03, 33-3021.04, 33-3021.05, 33-3031.00, 33-3051.00, 33-3051.01, 33-3051.02, 33-3051.03, and 33-3052.00)

## Significant Points

■ Police work can be dangerous and stressful.

■ Education requirements range from a high school diploma to a college degree or higher.

■ Job opportunities in most local police departments will be excellent for qualified individuals, while competition is expected for jobs in state and federal agencies.

■ Applicants with college training in police science or military police experience will have the best opportunities.

## Nature of the Work

People depend on police officers and detectives to protect their lives and property. Law enforcement officers, some of whom are state or federal special agents or inspectors, perform these duties in a variety of ways depending on the size and type of their organization. In most jurisdictions, they are expected to exercise authority when necessary, whether on or off duty.

Police and detectives pursue and apprehend individuals who break the law and then issue citations or give warnings. A large proportion of their time is spent writing reports and maintaining records of incidents they encounter. Most police officers patrol their jurisdictions and investigate any suspicious activity they notice. Detectives, who are often called agents or special agents, perform investigative duties such as gathering facts and collecting evidence.

The daily activities of police and detectives differ depending on their occupational specialty—such as police officer, game warden, or detective—and whether they are working for a local, state, or federal agency. Duties also differ substantially among various federal agencies, which enforce different aspects of the law. Regardless of job duties or location, police officers and detectives at all levels must write reports and maintain meticulous records that will be needed if they testify in court.

*Uniformed police officers* have general law enforcement duties, including maintaining regular patrols and responding to calls for service. Much of their time is spent responding to calls and doing paperwork. They may direct traffic at the scene of an accident, investigate a burglary, or give first aid to an accident victim. In large police departments, officers usually are assigned to a specific type of duty. Many urban police agencies are involved in community policing—a practice in which an officer builds relationships with the citizens of local neighborhoods and mobilizes the public to help fight crime.

Police agencies are usually organized into geographic districts, with uniformed officers assigned to patrol a specific area such as part of the business district or outlying residential neighborhoods. Officers may work alone, but in large agencies, they often patrol with a partner. While on patrol, officers attempt to become thoroughly familiar with their patrol area and remain alert for anything unusual. Suspicious circumstances and hazards to public safety are investigated or noted, and officers are dispatched to individual calls for assistance within their district. During their shift, they may identify, pursue, and arrest suspected criminals; resolve problems within the community; and enforce traffic laws.

Some agencies have special geographic jurisdictions and enforcement responsibilities. Public college and university police forces, public school district police, and agencies serving transportation systems and facilities are examples. Most law enforcement workers in special agencies are uniformed officers; a smaller number are investigators.

Some police officers specialize in a particular field, such as chemical and microscopic analysis, training and firearms instruction, or handwriting and fingerprint identification. Others work with special units, such as horseback, bicycle, motorcycle, or harbor patrol; canine corps; special weapons and tactics (SWAT); or emergency response teams. A few local and special law enforcement officers primarily perform jail-related duties or work in courts.

*Sheriffs and deputy sheriffs* enforce the law on the county level. Sheriffs are usually elected to their posts and perform duties similar to those of a local or county police chief. Sheriffs' departments tend to be relatively small, most having fewer than 50 sworn officers. Deputy sheriffs have law enforcement duties similar to those of officers in urban police departments. Police and sheriffs' deputies who provide security in city and county courts are sometimes called bailiffs.

*State police officers*, sometimes called *state troopers* or *highway patrol officers*, arrest criminals statewide and patrol highways to enforce motor vehicle laws and regulations. State police officers often issue traffic citations to motorists. At the scene of accidents, they may direct traffic, give first aid, and call for emergency equipment. They also write reports used to determine the cause of the accident. State police officers are frequently called upon to render assistance to other law enforcement agencies, especially those in rural areas or small towns.

State law enforcement agencies operate in every state except Hawaii. Most full-time sworn personnel are uniformed officers who regularly patrol and respond to calls for service. Others work as investigators, perform court-related duties, or carry out administrative or other assignments.

*Detectives* are plainclothes investigators who gather facts and collect evidence for criminal cases. Some are assigned to interagency task forces to combat specific types of crime. They conduct interviews, examine records, observe the activities of suspects, and participate in raids or arrests. Detectives and state and federal agents and inspectors usually specialize in investigating one type of violation, such as homicide or fraud. They are assigned cases on a rotating basis and work on them until an arrest and conviction is made or until the case is dropped.

*Fish and game wardens* enforce fishing, hunting, and boating laws. They patrol hunting and fishing areas, conduct search and rescue operations, investigate complaints and accidents, and aid in prosecuting court cases.

The federal government works in many areas of law enforcement. *Federal Bureau of Investigation (FBI) agents* are the government's principal investigators, responsible for investigating violations of more than 200 categories of federal law and conducting sensitive national security investigations. Agents may conduct surveillance, monitor court-authorized wiretaps, examine business records, investigate white-collar crime, or participate in sensitive undercover assignments. The FBI investigates a wide range of criminal activity, including organized crime, public corruption, financial crime, bank robbery, kidnapping, terrorism, espionage, drug trafficking, and cyber crime.

There are many other federal agencies that enforce particular types of laws. *U.S. Drug Enforcement Administration (DEA) agents* enforce laws and regulations relating to illegal drugs. *U.S. marshals and deputy marshals* protect the federal courts and ensure the effective operation of the judicial system. *Bureau of Alcohol, Tobacco, Firearms, and Explosives agents* enforce and investigate violations of federal firearms and explosives laws, as well as federal alcohol and tobacco tax regulations. The U.S. Department of State *Bureau of Diplomatic Security special agents* are engaged in the battle against terrorism.

The *Department of Homeland Security* also employs numerous law enforcement officers within several different agencies, including Customs and Border Protection, Immigration and Customs Enforcement, and the U.S. Secret Service. *U.S. Border Patrol agents* protect more than 8,000 miles of international land and water boundaries. *Immigration inspectors* interview and examine people seeking entrance to the United States and its territories. *Customs inspectors* enforce laws governing imports and exports by inspecting cargo, baggage, and articles worn or carried by people, vessels, vehicles, trains, and aircraft entering or leaving the United States. *Federal Air Marshals* provide air security by guarding against attacks targeting U.S. aircraft, passengers, and crews. *U.S. Secret Service special agents* and U.S. *Secret Service uniformed officers* protect the President, Vice President, their immediate families, and other public officials. Secret Service special agents also investigate counterfeiting, forgery of Government checks or bonds, and fraudulent use of credit cards.

Other federal agencies employ police and special agents with sworn arrest powers and the authority to carry firearms. These agencies include the Postal Service, the Bureau of Indian Affairs Office of Law Enforcement, the Forest Service, and the National Park Service.

*Work environment.* Police and detective work can be very dangerous and stressful. In addition to the obvious dangers of confrontations with criminals, police officers and detectives need to be constantly alert and ready to deal appropriately with a number of other threatening situations. Many law enforcement officers witness death and suffering resulting from accidents and criminal behavior. A career in law enforcement may take a toll on their private lives.

The jobs of some federal agents such as U.S. Secret Service and DEA special agents require extensive travel, often on very short notice. They may relocate a number of times over the course of their careers. Some special agents in agencies such as the U.S. Border Patrol work outdoors in rugged terrain for long periods and in all kinds of weather.

Uniformed officers, detectives, agents, and inspectors are usually scheduled to work 40-hour weeks, but paid overtime is common. Shift work is necessary because protection must be provided around the clock. Junior officers frequently work weekends, holidays, and nights. Police officers and detectives are required to work whenever they are needed and may work long hours during investigations. Officers in most jurisdictions, whether on or off duty, are expected to be armed and to exercise their authority when necessary.

## Training, Other Qualifications, and Advancement

Most police and detectives learn much of what they need to know on the job, often in their agency's police academy. Civil service regulations govern the appointment of police and detectives in most states, large municipalities, and special police agencies, as well as in many smaller jurisdictions. Candidates must be U.S. citizens, usually at least 20 years old, and must meet rigorous physical and personal qualifications.

*Education and training.* Applicants usually must have at least a high school education, and some departments require one or two years of college coursework or, in some cases, a college degree.

Law enforcement agencies encourage applicants to take courses or training related to law enforcement subjects after high school. Many entry-level applicants for police jobs have completed some formal postsecondary education, and a significant number are college graduates. Many junior colleges, colleges, and universities offer programs in law enforcement or administration of justice.

Physical education classes and participating in sports are also helpful in developing the competitiveness, stamina, and agility needed for many law enforcement positions. Knowledge of a foreign language is an asset in many federal agencies and urban departments.

Many agencies pay all or part of the tuition for officers to work toward degrees in criminal justice, police science, administration of justice, or public administration and pay higher salaries to those who earn such a degree.

Before their first assignments, officers usually go through a period of training. In state and large local police departments, recruits get training in their agency's police academy, often for 12 to 14 weeks. In small agencies, recruits often attend a regional or state academy. Training includes classroom instruction in constitutional law and civil rights, state laws and local ordinances, and accident investigation. Recruits also receive training and supervised experience in patrol, traffic control, the use of firearms, self-defense, first aid, and emergency response. Police departments in some large cities hire high school graduates who are still in their teens as police cadets or trainees. They do clerical work and attend classes, usually for one to two years, until they reach the minimum age requirement and can be appointed to the regular force.

**Projections data from the National Employment Matrix**

| Occupational Title | SOC Code | Employment, 2006 | Projected employment, 2016 | Change, 2006-16 | |
|---|---|---|---|---|---|
| | | | | Number | Percent |
| Police and detectives ............................................... | — | 861,000 | 959,000 | 97,000 | 11 |
| First-line supervisors/managers of police and detectives ............. | 33-1012 | 93,000 | 102,000 | 8,500 | 9 |
| Detectives and criminal investigators........................................... | 33-3021 | 106,000 | 125,000 | 18,000 | 17 |
| Fish and game wardens ................................................................ | 33-3031 | 8,000 | 8,000 | 0 | 0 |
| Police officers............................................................................... | 33-3050 | 654,000 | 724,000 | 70,000 | 11 |
| Police and sheriff's patrol officers .......................................... | 33-3051 | 648,000 | 719,000 | 70,000 | 11 |
| Transit and railroad police ....................................................... | 33-3052 | 5,600 | 5,900 | 400 | 6 |

NOTE: Data in this table are rounded.

To be considered for appointment as an FBI agent, an applicant must be a college graduate and have at least three years of professional work experience, or have an advanced degree plus two years of professional work experience. An applicant who meets these criteria must also have one of the following: a college major in accounting, electrical engineering, information technology, or computer science; fluency in a foreign language; a degree from an accredited law school; or three years of related full-time work experience. All new FBI agents undergo 18 weeks of training at the FBI Academy on the U.S. Marine Corps base in Quantico, Virginia.

Most other federal law enforcement agencies require either a bachelor's degree or related work experience or a combination of the two. Federal law enforcement agents undergo extensive training, usually at the U.S. Marine Corps base in Quantico, Virginia, or the Federal Law Enforcement Training Center in Glynco, Georgia. The educational requirements, qualifications, and training information for a particular federal agency can be found on the agency's Web site, most of which are listed in the last section of this statement.

Fish and game wardens also must meet specific requirements. Most states require at least two years of college study. Once hired, fish and game wardens attend a training academy lasting from three to 12 months, sometimes followed by further training in the field.

*Other qualifications.* Civil service regulations govern the appointment of police and detectives in most states, large municipalities, and special police agencies, as well as in many smaller jurisdictions. Candidates must be U.S. citizens, usually at least 20 years old, and must meet rigorous physical and personal qualifications. Physical examinations for entrance into law enforcement often include tests of vision, hearing, strength, and agility. Eligibility for appointment usually depends on performance in competitive written examinations and previous education and experience.

Candidates should enjoy working with people and meeting the public. Because personal characteristics such as honesty, sound judgment, integrity, and a sense of responsibility are especially important in law enforcement, candidates are interviewed by senior officers, and their character traits and backgrounds are investigated. In some agencies, candidates are interviewed by a psychiatrist or a psychologist or given a personality test. Most applicants are subjected to lie detector examinations or drug testing. Some agencies subject sworn personnel to random drug testing as a condition of continuing employment.

*Advancement.* Police officers usually become eligible for promotion after a probationary period ranging from six months to three years. In large departments, promotion may enable an officer to become a detective or to specialize in one type of police work, such as working with juveniles. Promotions to corporal, sergeant, lieutenant, and captain usually are made according to a candidate's position on a promotion list, as determined by scores on a written examination and on-the-job performance.

Continuing training helps police officers, detectives, and special agents improve their job performance. Through police department academies, regional centers for public safety employees established by the states, and federal agency training centers, instructors provide annual training in self-defense tactics, firearms, use-of-force policies, sensitivity and communications skills, crowd-control techniques, relevant legal developments, and advances in law enforcement equipment.

## Employment

Police and detectives held about 861,000 jobs in 2006. Seventy-nine percent were employed by local governments. State police agencies employed about 11 percent, and various federal agencies employed about 7 percent. A small proportion worked for educational services, rail transportation, and contract investigation and security services.

According to the U.S. Bureau of Justice Statistics, police and detectives employed by local governments primarily worked in cities with more than 25,000 inhabitants. Some cities have very large police forces, while thousands of small communities employ fewer than 25 officers each.

## Job Outlook

Job opportunities in most local police departments will be excellent for qualified individuals, while competition is expected for jobs in state and federal agencies. Average employment growth is expected.

*Employment change.* Employment of police and detectives is expected to grow 11 percent over the 2006–2016 decade, about as fast as the average for all occupations. A more security-conscious society and population growth will contribute to the increasing demand for police services.

*Job prospects.* Overall opportunities in local police departments will be excellent for individuals who meet the psychological, personal, and physical qualifications. In addition to openings from employment growth, many openings will be created by the need to replace workers who retire and those who leave local agencies for federal jobs and private sector security jobs. There will be more competition for jobs in federal and state law enforcement agencies than for jobs in local agencies. Less competition for jobs will occur in depart-

ments that offer relatively low salaries or those in urban communities where the crime rate is relatively high. Applicants with military experience or college training in police science will have the best opportunities in local and state departments. Applicants with a bachelor's degree and several years of law enforcement or military experience, especially investigative experience, will have the best opportunities in federal agencies.

The level of government spending determines the level of employment for police and detectives. The number of job opportunities, therefore, can vary from year to year and from place to place. Layoffs, on the other hand, are rare because retirements enable most staffing cuts to be handled through attrition. Trained law enforcement officers who lose their jobs because of budget cuts usually have little difficulty finding jobs with other agencies.

## Earnings

Police and sheriff's patrol officers had median annual earnings of $47,460 in May 2006. The middle 50 percent earned between $35,600 and $59,880. The lowest 10 percent earned less than $27,310, and the highest 10 percent earned more than $72,450. Median annual earnings were $43,510 in federal government, $52,540 in state government, and $47,190 in local government.

In May 2006, median annual earnings of police and detective supervisors were $69,310. The middle 50 percent earned between $53,900 and $83,940. The lowest 10 percent earned less than $41,260, and the highest 10 percent earned more than $104,410. Median annual earnings were $85,170 in federal government, $68,990 in state government, and $68,670 in local government.

In May 2006, median annual earnings of detectives and criminal investigators were $58,260. The middle 50 percent earned between $43,920 and $76,350. The lowest 10 percent earned less than $34,480, and the highest 10 percent earned more than $92,590. Median annual earnings were $69,510 in federal government, $49,370 in state government, and $52,520 in local government.

Federal law provides special salary rates to federal employees who serve in law enforcement. Additionally, federal special agents and inspectors receive law enforcement availability pay (LEAP)—equal to 25 percent of the agent's grade and step—awarded because of the large amount of overtime that these agents are expected to work. For example, in 2007, FBI agents entered federal service as GS-10 employees on the pay scale at a base salary of $48,159, yet they earned about $60,199 a year with availability pay. They could advance to the GS-13 grade level in field nonsupervisory assignments at a base salary of $75,414, which was worth $94,268 with availability pay. FBI supervisory, management, and executive positions in grades GS-14 and GS-15 paid a base salary of about $89,115 and $104,826 a year, respectively, which amounted to $111,394 or $131,033 per year including availability pay. Salaries were slightly higher in selected areas where the prevailing local pay level was higher. Because federal agents may be eligible for a special law enforcement benefits package, applicants should ask their recruiter for more information.

Total earnings for local, state, and special police and detectives frequently exceed the stated salary because of payments for overtime, which can be significant.

According to the International City-County Management Association's annual Police and Fire Personnel, Salaries, and Expenditures Survey, average salaries for sworn full-time positions in 2006 were

| Rank | Minimum annual base salary | Maximum annual base salary |
| --- | --- | --- |
| Police chief | $78,547 | $99,698 |
| Deputy chief | 68,797 | 87,564 |
| Police captain | 65,408 | 81,466 |
| Police lieutenant | 59,940 | 72,454 |
| Police sergeant | 53,734 | 63,564 |
| Police corporal | 44,160 | 55,183 |

In addition to the common benefits—paid vacation, sick leave, and medical and life insurance—most police and sheriffs' departments provide officers with special allowances for uniforms. Because police officers usually are covered by liberal pension plans, many retire at half-pay after 25 or 30 years of service.

## Related Occupations

Police and detectives maintain law and order, collect evidence and information, and conduct investigations and surveillance. Workers in related occupations include correctional officers, private detectives and investigators, probation officers and correctional treatment specialists, and security guards and gaming surveillance officers. Like police and detectives, firefighters and emergency medical technicians and paramedics provide public safety services and respond to emergencies.

## Sources of Additional Information

Information about entrance requirements may be obtained from federal, state, and local law enforcement agencies.

For general information about sheriffs and to learn more about the National Sheriffs' Association scholarship, contact

▸ National Sheriffs' Association, 1450 Duke St., Alexandria, VA 22314. Internet: http://www.sheriffs.org

▸ Information about qualifications for employment as a FBI Special Agent is available from the nearest state FBI office. The address and phone number are listed in the local telephone directory. Internet: http://www.fbi.gov

▸ Information on career opportunities, qualifications, and training for U.S. Secret Service Special Agents and Uniformed Officers is available from the Secret Service Personnel Division at (202) 406-5800, (888) 813-877, or (888) 813-USSS. Internet: http://www.secretservice.gov/join

▸ Information about qualifications for employment as a DEA Special Agent is available from the nearest DEA office, or call (800) DEA-4288. Internet: http://www.usdoj.gov/dea

Information about career opportunities, qualifications, and training to become a deputy marshal is available from

▸ U.S. Marshals Service, Human Resources Division—Law Enforcement Recruiting, Washington, DC 20530-1000. Internet: http://www.usmarshals.gov

For information on operations and career opportunities in the U.S. Bureau of Alcohol, Tobacco, Firearms, and Explosives, contact

▶ U.S. Bureau of Alcohol, Tobacco, Firearms, and Explosives, Office of Governmental and Public Affairs, 650 Massachusetts Ave. NW, Room 8290, Washington, D.C. 20226. Internet: http://www.atf.gov

Information about careers in U.S. Customs and Border Protection is available from

▶ U.S. Customs and Border Protection, 1300 Pennsylvania Ave. NW, Washington, DC 20229. Internet: http://www.cbp.gov

Information about law enforcement agencies within the Department of Homeland Security is available from

▶ U.S. Department of Homeland Security, Washington, DC 20528. Internet: http://www.dhs.gov

To find federal, state, and local law enforcement job fairs and other recruiting events across the country, contact

▶ National Law Enforcement Recruiters Association, 2045 15th St. North, Suite 210, Arlington, VA 22201. Internet: http://www.nlera.org

# Property, Real Estate, and Community Association Managers

(O*NET 11-9141.00)

## Significant Points

■ Opportunities should be best for those with college degrees in business administration, real estate, or related fields and those with professional designations.

■ Particularly good opportunities are expected for those with experience managing housing for older people or those with experience running a health unit.

■ More than half of property, real estate, and community association managers are self-employed.

## Nature of the Work

To businesses and investors, properly managed real estate is a source of income and profits; to homeowners, well-managed property is a way to preserve and enhance resale values and increase comfort. Property, real estate, and community association managers maintain and increase the value of real estate investments by handling the logistics of running a property. *Property and real estate managers* oversee the performance of income-producing commercial or residential properties and ensure that real estate investments achieve their expected revenues. *Community association managers* manage the common property and services of condominiums, cooperatives, and planned communities through their homeowner or community associations.

When owners of apartments, office buildings, or retail or industrial properties lack the time or expertise needed for the day-to-day management of their real estate investments or homeowner associations, they often hire a property or real estate manager or a community association manager. The manager is employed either directly by the owner or indirectly through a contract with a property management firm.

Generally, property and real estate managers handle the financial operations of the property, ensuring that rent is collected and that mortgages, taxes, insurance premiums, payroll, and maintenance bills are paid on time. In community associations, homeowners pay no rent and pay their own real estate taxes and mortgages, but community association managers collect association dues. Some property managers, usually senior-level property managers, supervise the preparation of financial statements and periodically report to the owners on the status of the property, occupancy rates, expiration dates of leases, and other matters.

Often, property managers negotiate contracts for janitorial, security, groundskeeping, trash removal, and other services. When contracts are awarded competitively, managers solicit bids from several contractors and advise the owners on which bid to accept. They monitor the performance of contractors and investigate and resolve complaints from residents and tenants when services are not properly provided. Managers also purchase supplies and equipment for the property and make arrangements with specialists for repairs that cannot be handled by regular property maintenance staff.

In addition to fulfilling these duties, property managers must understand and comply with relevant legislation, such as the Americans with Disabilities Act, the Federal Fair Housing Amendment Act, and local fair housing laws. They must ensure that their renting and advertising practices are not discriminatory and that the property itself complies with all of the local, state, and federal regulations and building codes.

On-site property managers are responsible for the day-to-day operations of a single property, such as an office building, a shopping center, a community association, or an apartment complex. To ensure that the property is safe and properly maintained, on-site managers routinely inspect the grounds, facilities, and equipment to determine whether repairs or maintenance are needed. In handling requests for repairs or trying to resolve complaints, they meet not only with current residents, but also with prospective residents or tenants to show vacant apartments or office space. On-site managers also are responsible for enforcing the terms of rental or lease agreements, such as rent collection, parking and pet restrictions, and termination-of-lease procedures. Other important duties of on-site managers include keeping accurate, up-to-date records of income and expenditures from property operations and submitting regular expense reports to the senior-level property manager or owners.

Property managers who do not work on-site act as a liaison between the on-site manager and the owner. They also market vacant space to prospective tenants by hiring a leasing agent, advertising, or other means, and they establish rental rates in accordance with prevailing local economic conditions.

Some property and real estate managers, often called *real estate asset managers*, act as the property owners' agent and adviser for the property. They plan and direct the purchase, development, and disposition of real estate on behalf of the business and investors. These managers focus on long-term strategic financial planning rather than on day-to-day operations of the property.

In deciding to acquire property, real estate asset managers consider several factors, such as property values, taxes, zoning, population growth, transportation, and traffic volume and patterns. Once a site is selected, they negotiate contracts for the purchase or lease of the property, securing the most beneficial terms. Real estate asset managers review their company's real estate holdings periodically and identify properties that are no longer financially profitable. They then negotiate the sale of, or terminate the lease on, such properties.

Community association managers, on the other hand, do work that more closely parallels that of on-site property managers. They collect monthly assessments, prepare financial statements and budgets, negotiate with contractors, and help to resolve complaints. In other respects, however, the work of association managers differs from that of other residential property and real estate managers because they interact with homeowners and other residents on a daily basis. Usually hired by a volunteer board of directors of the association, they administer the daily affairs and oversee the maintenance of property and facilities that the homeowners own and use jointly through the association. They also assist the board and owners in complying with association and government rules and regulations.

Some associations encompass thousands of homes and employ their own on-site staff and managers. In addition to administering the associations' financial records and budget, managers may be responsible for the operation of community pools, golf courses, and community centers and for the maintenance of landscaping and parking areas. Community association managers also may meet with the elected boards of directors to discuss and resolve legal issues or disputes that may affect the owners, as well as to review any proposed changes or improvements by homeowners to their properties, to make sure that they comply with community guidelines.

*Work environment.* The offices of most property, real estate, and community association managers are clean, modern, and well lighted. However, many managers spend a major portion of their time away from their desks. On-site managers, in particular, may spend a large portion of their workday away from their offices, visiting the building engineer, showing apartments, checking on the janitorial and maintenance staff, or investigating problems reported by tenants. Property and real estate managers frequently visit the properties they oversee, sometimes daily when contractors are doing major repair or renovation work. Real estate asset managers may spend time away from home while traveling to company real estate holdings or searching for properties to acquire.

Property, real estate, and community association managers often must attend evening meetings with residents, property owners, community association boards of directors, or civic groups. Not surprisingly, many managers put in long work weeks, especially before financial and tax reports are due and before board and annual meetings. Some apartment managers are required to live in the apartment complexes where they work so that they are available to handle emergencies even when they are off duty. They usually receive compensatory time off for working nights or weekends. Many apartment managers receive time off during the week so that they are available on weekends to show apartments to prospective residents.

## Training, Other Qualifications, and Advancement

Employers increasingly are hiring college graduates with a bachelor's or master's degree in business administration, accounting,

finance, or real estate even if they don't have much practical experience.

*Education and training.* Most employers prefer to hire college graduates for property management positions. In fact, employers increasingly are hiring inexperienced college graduates with a bachelor's or master's degree in business administration, accounting, finance, real estate, or public administration for these positions. Those with degrees in the liberal arts also may qualify, especially if they have relevant coursework. Many people entering jobs such as assistant property manager have on-site management experience.

*Licensure.* Managers of public housing subsidized by the federal government are required to be certified, but many property, real estate, and community association managers who work with all types of property choose to earn a professional designation voluntarily because it represents formal recognition of their achievements and affords status in the occupation. Real estate managers who buy or sell property are required to be licensed by the state in which they practice. In a few states, property association managers must be licensed.

*Other qualifications.* Previous employment as a real estate sales agent may be an asset to on-site managers because it provides experience that is useful in showing apartments or office space. In the past, those with backgrounds in building maintenance have advanced to on-site manager positions on the strength of their knowledge of building mechanical systems, but this path is becoming less common as employers place greater emphasis on administrative, financial, and communication abilities for managerial jobs.

People most commonly enter real estate asset manager jobs by transferring from positions as property managers or real estate brokers. Real estate asset managers must be good negotiators, adept at persuading and working with people, and good at analyzing data in order to assess the fair market value of property or its development potential. Resourcefulness and creativity in arranging financing are essential for managers who specialize in land development.

Good speaking, writing, computer, and financial skills, as well as an ability to deal tactfully with people, are essential in all areas of property management.

*Certification and advancement.* Many people begin property management careers as assistants. Assistants work closely with a property manager and learn how to prepare budgets, analyze insurance coverage and risk options, market property to prospective tenants, and collect overdue rent payments. In time, many assistants advance to property manager positions.

Some people start as on-site managers of apartment buildings, office complexes, or community associations. As they acquire experience, often working under the direction of a more experienced property manager, they may advance to positions of greater responsibility. Those who excel as on-site managers often transfer to assistant off-site property manager positions in which they can acquire experience handling a broad range of property management responsibilities.

The responsibilities and compensation of property, real estate, and community association managers increase as these workers manage more and larger properties. Most property managers, often called portfolio managers, are responsible for several properties at a time. As their careers advance, they gradually are entrusted with larger

**Projections data from the National Employment Matrix**

| Occupational Title | SOC Code | Employment, 2006 | Projected employment, 2016 | Change, 2006-16 | |
|---|---|---|---|---|---|
| | | | | Number | Percent |
| Property, real estate, and community association managers............. | 11-9141 | 329,000 | 379,000 | 50,000 | 15 |

NOTE: Data in this table are rounded.

properties that are more complex to manage. Many specialize in the management of one type of property, such as apartments, office buildings, condominiums, cooperatives, homeowners' associations, or retail properties. Managers who excel at marketing properties to tenants might specialize in managing new properties, while those who are particularly knowledgeable about buildings and their mechanical systems might specialize in the management of older properties requiring renovation or more frequent repairs. Some experienced managers open their own property management firms.

Many employers encourage attendance at short-term formal training programs conducted by various professional and trade associations that are active in the real estate field. Employers send managers to these programs to improve their management skills and expand their knowledge of specialized subjects, such as the operation and maintenance of building mechanical systems, the enhancement of property values, insurance and risk management, personnel management, business and real estate law, community association risks and liabilities, tenant relations, communications, accounting and financial concepts, and reserve funding. Managers also participate in these programs to prepare themselves for positions of greater responsibility in property management. The completion of these programs, plus related job experience and a satisfactory score on a written examination, can lead to certification, or the formal award of a professional designation, by the sponsoring association. (Some organizations offering certifications are listed as sources of additional information at the end of this statement.) Some associations also require their members to adhere to a specific code of ethics.

## Employment

Property, real estate, and community association managers held about 329,000 jobs in 2006. About 36 percent worked for real estate agents and brokers, for lessors of real estate, or in activities related to real estate. Others worked for real estate development companies, government agencies that manage public buildings, and corporations with extensive holdings of commercial properties. More than half of property, real estate, and community association managers are self-employed.

## Job Outlook

Faster-than-average employment growth is expected. Opportunities should be best for jobseekers with a college degree in business administration, real estate, or a related field and for those who attain a professional designation. Particularly good opportunities are expected for those with experience managing housing for older people or with experience running a health unit.

*Employment change.* Employment of property, real estate, and community association managers is projected to increase by 15 percent during the 2006–16 decade, faster than the average for all occupations. Job growth among on-site property managers in

commercial real estate is expected to accompany the projected expansion of the real estate and rental and leasing industry. An increase in the nation's stock of apartments, houses, and offices also should require more property managers. Developments of new homes are increasingly being organized with community or homeowner associations that provide community services and oversee jointly owned common areas requiring professional management. To help properties become more profitable or to enhance the resale values of homes, more commercial and residential property owners are expected to place their investments in the hands of professional managers. Moreover, the number of older people will grow during the 2006–16 projection period, increasing the need for specialized housing, such as assisted-living facilities and retirement communities that require management.

*Job prospects.* In addition to openings from job growth, a number of openings are expected as managers transfer to other occupations or leave the labor force. Opportunities should be best for jobseekers with a college degree in business administration, real estate, or a related field and for those who attain a professional designation. Because of the expected increase in assisted-living and retirement communities, particularly good opportunities are expected for those with experience managing housing for older people or with experience running a health unit.

## Earnings

Median annual earnings of salaried property, real estate, and community association managers were $43,070 in May 2006. The middle 50 percent earned between $28,700 and $64,200 a year. The lowest 10 percent earned less than $20,140, and the highest 10 percent earned more than $95,170 a year. Median annual earnings of salaried property, real estate, and community association managers in the largest industries that employed them in May 2006 were

| | |
|---|---|
| Land subdivision | $78,040 |
| Local government | 55,210 |
| Activities related to real estate | 40,590 |
| Offices of real estate agents and brokers | 40,500 |
| Lessors of real estate | 37,480 |

Many resident apartment managers and on-site association managers receive the use of an apartment as part of their compensation package. Managers often are reimbursed for the use of their personal vehicles, and managers employed in land development often receive a small percentage of ownership in the projects that they develop.

## Related Occupations

Property, real estate, and community association managers plan, organize, staff, and manage the real estate operations of businesses. Workers who perform similar functions in other fields include administrative services managers, education administrators, food service managers, lodging managers, medical and health services managers, real estate brokers and sales agents, and urban and regional planners.

## Sources of Additional Information

For information about education and careers in property management, as well as information about professional designation and certification programs in both residential and commercial property management, contact

▸ Institute of Real Estate Management, 430 N. Michigan Ave., Chicago, IL 60611. Internet: http://www.irem.org

For information on careers and certification programs in commercial property management, contact

▸ Building Owners and Managers Institute, 1521 Ritchie Hwy., Arnold, MD 21012. Internet: http://www.bomi.org

For information on careers and professional designation and certification programs in residential property management and community association management, contact

▸ Community Associations Institute, 225 Reinekers Ln., Suite 300, Alexandria, VA 22314. Internet: http://www.caionline.org

▸ National Board of Certification for Community Association Managers, 225 Reinekers Ln., Suite 310, Alexandria, VA 22314. Internet: http://www.nbccam.org

# Public Relations Specialists

(O*NET 27-3031.00)

## Significant Points

■ Although employment is projected to grow faster than average, keen competition is expected for entry-level jobs.

■ Opportunities should be best for college graduates who combine a degree in public relations, journalism, or another communications-related field with a public relations internship or other related work experience.

■ The ability to communicate effectively is essential.

## Nature of the Work

An organization's reputation, profitability, and even its continued existence can depend on the degree to which its targeted "publics" support its goals and policies. Public relations specialists—also referred to as communications specialists and media specialists, among other titles—serve as advocates for businesses, nonprofit associations, universities, hospitals, and other organizations, and build and maintain positive relationships with the public. As managers recognize the importance of good public relations to the success of their organizations, they increasingly rely on public relations specialists for advice on the strategy and policy of such programs.

Public relations specialists handle organizational functions such as media, community, consumer, industry, and governmental relations; political campaigns; interest-group representation; conflict mediation; and employee and investor relations. They do more than "tell the organization's story." They must understand the attitudes and concerns of community, consumer, employee, and public interest groups and establish and maintain cooperative relationships with them and with representatives from print and broadcast journalism.

Public relations specialists draft press releases and contact people in the media who might print or broadcast their material. Many radio or television special reports, newspaper stories, and magazine articles start at the desks of public relations specialists. Sometimes the subject is an organization and its policies toward its employees or its role in the community. Often the subject is a public issue, such as health, energy, or the environment, and what an organization does to advance that issue.

Public relations specialists also arrange and conduct programs to keep up contact between organization representatives and the public. For example, they set up speaking engagements and often prepare speeches for company officials. These media specialists represent employers at community projects; make film, slide, or other visual presentations at meetings and school assemblies; and plan conventions. In addition, they are responsible for preparing annual reports and writing proposals for various projects.

In government, public relations specialists—who may be called press secretaries, information officers, public affairs specialists, or communication specialists—keep the public informed about the activities of agencies and officials. For example, public affairs specialists in the U.S. Department of State keep the public informed of travel advisories and of U.S. positions on foreign issues. A press secretary for a member of Congress keeps constituents aware of the representative's accomplishments.

In large organizations, the key public relations executive, who often is a vice president, may develop overall plans and policies with other executives. In addition, public relations departments employ public relations specialists to write, research, prepare materials, maintain contacts, and respond to inquiries.

People who handle publicity for an individual or who direct public relations for a small organization may deal with all aspects of the job. They contact people, plan and research, and prepare materials for distribution. They also may handle advertising or sales promotion work to support marketing efforts.

*Work environment.* Public relations specialists work in busy offices. The pressures of deadlines and tight work schedules can be stressful.

Some public relations specialists work a standard 35- to 40-hour week, but unpaid overtime is common and work schedules can be irregular and frequently interrupted. Occasionally, they must be at the job or on call around the clock, especially if there is an emergency or crisis. Schedules often have to be rearranged so that workers can meet deadlines, deliver speeches, attend meetings and community activities, and travel.

## Training, Other Qualifications, and Advancement

There are no defined standards for entry into a public relations career. A college degree in a communications-related field combined with public relations experience is excellent preparation for public relations work.

*Education and training.* Many entry-level public relations specialists have a college degree in public relations, journalism, advertis-

**Projections data from the National Employment Matrix**

| Occupational Title | SOC Code | Employment, 2006 | Projected employment, 2016 | Change, 2006-2016 | |
|---|---|---|---|---|---|
| | | | | Number | Percent |
| Public relations specialists .............................................................. | 27-3031 | 243,000 | 286,000 | 43,000 | 18 |

NOTE: Data in this table are rounded.

ing, or communication. Some firms seek college graduates who have worked in electronic or print journalism. Other employers seek applicants with demonstrated communication skills and training or experience in a field related to the firm's business—information technology, health care, science, engineering, sales, or finance, for example.

Many colleges and universities offer bachelor's and postsecondary degrees in public relations, usually in a journalism or communications department. In addition, many other colleges offer at least one course in this field. A common public relations sequence includes courses in public relations principles and techniques; public relations management and administration, including organizational development; writing, emphasizing news releases, proposals, annual reports, scripts, speeches, and related items; visual communications, including desktop publishing and computer graphics; and research, emphasizing social science research and survey design and implementation. Courses in advertising, journalism, business administration, finance, political science, psychology, sociology, and creative writing also are helpful. Specialties are offered in public relations for business, government, and nonprofit organizations.

Many colleges help students gain part-time internships in public relations that provide valuable experience and training. Membership in local chapters of the Public Relations Student Society of America (affiliated with the Public Relations Society of America) or in student chapters of the International Association of Business Communicators provides an opportunity for students to exchange views with public relations specialists and to make professional contacts that may help them find a job in the field. A portfolio of published articles, television or radio programs, slide presentations, and other work is an asset in finding a job. Writing for a school publication or television or radio station provides valuable experience and material for one's portfolio.

Some organizations, particularly those with large public relations staffs, have formal training programs for new employees. In smaller organizations, new employees work under the guidance of experienced staff members. Beginners often maintain files of material about company activities, scan newspapers and magazines for appropriate articles to clip, and assemble information for speeches and pamphlets. They also may answer calls from the press and the public, work on invitation lists and details for press conferences, or escort visitors and clients. After gaining experience, they write news releases, speeches, and articles for publication or plan and carry out public relations programs. Public relations specialists in smaller firms usually get all-around experience, whereas those in larger firms tend to be more specialized.

*Other qualifications.* Public relations specialists must show creativity, initiative, and good judgment and have the ability to communicate thoughts clearly and simply. Decision-making, problem-solving, and research skills also are important. People who choose public relations as a career need an outgoing personality, self-confidence, an understanding of human psychology, and an enthusiasm for motivating people. They should be competitive, yet able to function as part of a team and be open to new ideas.

*Certification and advancement.* The Universal Accreditation Board accredits public relations specialists who are members of the Public Relations Society of America and who participate in the Examination for Accreditation in Public Relations process. This process includes both a readiness review and an examination, which are designed for candidates who have at least five years of full-time work or teaching experience in public relations and who have earned a bachelor's degree in a communications-related field. The readiness review includes a written submission by each candidate, a portfolio review, and dialogue between the candidate and a three-member panel. Candidates who successfully advance through readiness review and pass the computer-based examination earn the Accredited in Public Relations (APR) designation.

The International Association of Business Communicators (IABC) also has an accreditation program for professionals in the communications field, including public relations specialists. Those who meet all the requirements of the program earn the Accredited Business Communicator (ABC) designation. Candidates must have at least five years of experience and a bachelor's degree in a communications field and must pass written and oral examinations. They also must submit a portfolio of work samples demonstrating involvement in a range of communications projects and a thorough understanding of communications planning.

Employers may consider professional recognition through accreditation as a sign of competence in this field, which could be especially helpful in a competitive job market.

Promotion to supervisory jobs may come to public relations specialists who show that they can handle more demanding assignments. In public relations firms, a beginner might be hired as a research assistant or account coordinator and be promoted to account executive, senior account executive, account manager, and eventually vice president. A similar career path is followed in corporate public relations, although the titles may differ.

Some experienced public relations specialists start their own consulting firms.

## Employment

Public relations specialists held about 243,000 jobs in 2006. They are concentrated in service-providing industries such as advertising and related services; health care and social assistance; educational services; and government. Others work for communications firms, financial institutions, and government agencies.

Public relations specialists are concentrated in large cities, where press services and other communications facilities are readily available and many businesses and trade associations have their headquarters. Many public relations consulting firms, for example, are in New York, Los Angeles, San Francisco, Chicago, and Washington, DC. There is a trend, however, for public relations jobs to be dispersed throughout the nation, closer to clients.

## Job Outlook

Employment is projected to grow faster than average; however, keen competition is expected for entry-level jobs.

*Employment change.* Employment of public relations specialists is expected to grow by 18 percent from 2006 to 2016, faster than average for all occupations. The need for good public relations in an increasingly competitive business environment should spur demand for these workers in organizations of all types and sizes. Those with additional language capabilities also are in great demand.

Employment in public relations firms should grow as firms hire contractors to provide public relations services rather than support full-time staff.

Among detailed industries, the largest job growth will continue to be in advertising and related services.

*Job prospects.* Keen competition likely will continue for entry-level public relations jobs, as the number of qualified applicants is expected to exceed the number of job openings. Many people are attracted to this profession because of the high profile nature of the work. Opportunities should be best for college graduates who combine a degree in journalism, public relations, advertising, or another communications-related field with a public relations internship or other related work experience. Applicants without the appropriate educational background or work experience will face the toughest obstacles.

Additional job opportunities should result from the need to replace public relations specialists who retire or leave the occupation for other reasons.

## Earnings

Median annual earnings for salaried public relations specialists were $47,350 in May 2006. The middle 50 percent earned between $35,600 and $65,310; the lowest 10 percent earned less than $28,080, and the top 10 percent earned more than $89,220. Median annual earnings in the industries employing the largest numbers of public relations specialists in May 2006 were

Management of companies and enterprises ..........$52,940

Business, professional, labor, political, and
    similar organizations .........................................51,400

Advertising and related services .........................49,980

Local government ...............................................47,550

Colleges, universities, and professional schools ......43,330

## Related Occupations

Public relations specialists create favorable attitudes among various organizations, interest groups, and the public through effective communication. Other workers with similar jobs include advertising, marketing, promotions, public relations, and sales managers; demonstrators, product promoters, and models; news analysts,

reporters, and correspondents; lawyers; market and survey researchers; sales representatives, wholesale and manufacturing; and police and detectives involved in community relations.

## Sources of Additional Information

A comprehensive directory of schools offering degree programs, a sequence of study in public relations, a brochure on careers in public relations, and an online brochure entitled *Where Shall I Go to Study Advertising and Public Relations?*, are available from

▸ Public Relations Society of America, Inc., 33 Maiden Lane, New York, NY 10038-5150. Internet: http://www.prsa.org

For information on accreditation for public relations professionals and the IABC Student Web site, contact

▸ International Association of Business Communicators, One Hallidie Plaza, Suite 600, San Francisco, CA 94102.

# Real Estate Brokers and Sales Agents

(O*NET 41-9021.00 and 41-9022.00)

## Significant Points

■ Real estate brokers and sales agents often work evenings and weekends and usually are on call to suit the needs of clients.

■ A license is required in every state and the District of Columbia.

■ Although gaining a job may be relatively easy, beginning workers face competition from well-established, more experienced agents and brokers.

■ Employment is sensitive to swings in the economy, especially interest rates; during periods of declining economic activity and rising interest rates, the volume of sales and the resulting demand for sales workers fall.

## Nature of the Work

One of the most complex and significant financial events in peoples' lives is the purchase or sale of a home or investment property. Because of this complexity and significance, people typically seek the help of real estate brokers and sales agents when buying or selling real estate.

Real estate brokers and sales agents have a thorough knowledge of the real estate market in their communities. They know which neighborhoods will best fit clients' needs and budgets. They are familiar with local zoning and tax laws and know where to obtain financing. Agents and brokers also act as intermediaries in price negotiations between buyers and sellers.

When selling property, brokers and agents arrange for title searches to verify ownership and for meetings between buyers and sellers during which they agree to the details of the transactions and in a final meeting, the new owners take possession of the property. They also may help to arrange favorable financing from a lender for the prospective buyer; often, this makes the difference between success and failure in closing a sale. In some cases, brokers and agents assume primary responsibility for closing sales; in others, lawyers or lenders do.

Agents and brokers spend a significant amount of time looking for properties to sell. They obtain listings—agreements by owners to place properties for sale with the firm. When listing a property for sale, agents and brokers compare the listed property with similar properties that recently sold, in order to determine a competitive market price for the property. Following the sale of the property, both the agent who sold it and the agent who obtained the listing receive a portion of the commission. Thus, agents who sell a property that they themselves have listed can increase their commission.

Before showing residential properties to potential buyers, agents meet with them to get an idea of the type of home the buyers would like. In this prequalifying phase, the agent determines how much the buyers can afford to spend. In addition, the agent and the buyer usually sign a loyalty contract, which states that the agent will be the only one to show houses to the buyer. An agent or broker then generates lists of properties for sale, their location and description, and available sources of financing. In some cases, agents and brokers use computers to give buyers a virtual tour of properties that interest them.

Agents may meet several times with prospective buyers to discuss and visit available properties. Agents identify and emphasize the most pertinent selling points. To a young family looking for a house, for example, they may emphasize the convenient floor plan, the area's low crime rate, and the proximity to schools and shopping. To a potential investor, they may point out the tax advantages of owning a rental property and the ease of finding a renter. If bargaining over price becomes necessary, agents must follow their client's instructions carefully and may have to present counteroffers to get the best possible price.

Once the buyer and seller have signed a contract, the real estate broker or agent must make sure that all special terms of the contract are met before the closing date. The agent must make sure that any legally mandated or agreed-upon inspections, such as termite and radon inspections, take place. In addition, if the seller agrees to any repairs, the broker or agent ensures they are made. Increasingly, brokers and agents are handling environmental problems as well, by making sure that the properties they sell meet environmental regulations. For example, they may be responsible for dealing with lead paint on the walls. Loan officers, attorneys, or other people handle many details, but the agent must ensure that they are carried out.

Most real estate brokers and sales agents sell residential property. A small number—usually employed in large or specialized firms—sell commercial, industrial, agricultural, or other types of real estate. Every specialty requires knowledge of that particular type of property and clientele. Selling or leasing business property requires an understanding of leasing practices, business trends, and the location of the property. Agents who sell or lease industrial properties must know about the region's transportation, utilities, and labor supply. Whatever the type of property, the agent or broker must know how to meet the client's particular requirements.

Brokers and agents do the same type of work, but brokers are licensed to manage their own real estate businesses. Agents must work with a broker. They usually provide their services to a licensed real estate broker on a contract basis. In return, the broker pays the agent a portion of the commission earned from the agent's sale of the property. Brokers, as independent businesspeople, often sell real estate owned by others; they also may rent or manage properties for a fee.

***Work environment.*** Advances in telecommunications and the ability to retrieve data about properties over the Internet allow many real estate brokers and sales agents to work out of their homes instead of real estate offices. Even with this convenience, workers spend much of their time away from their desks—showing properties to customers, analyzing properties for sale, meeting with prospective clients, or researching the real estate market.

Agents and brokers often work more than a standard 40-hour week. They usually work evenings and weekends and are usually on call to respond to the needs of clients. Although the hours are long and frequently irregular, most agents and brokers have the freedom to determine their own schedule. They can arrange their work so that they have time off when they want it. Business usually is slower during the winter season.

## Training, Other Qualifications, and Advancement

In every state and the District of Columbia, real estate brokers and sales agents must be licensed. Prospective agents must be high school graduates, be at least 18 years old, and pass a written test.

***Education and training.*** Agents and brokers must be high school graduates. In fact, as real estate transactions have become more legally complex, many firms have turned to college graduates to fill positions. A large number of agents and brokers have some college training. College courses in real estate, finance, business administration, statistics, economics, law, and English are helpful. For those who intend to start their own company, business courses such as marketing and accounting are as important as courses in real estate or finance.

More than 1,000 universities, colleges, and community colleges offer courses in real estate. Most offer an associate or bachelor's degree in real estate; some offer graduate degrees. Many local real estate associations that are members of the National Association of Realtors sponsor courses covering the fundamentals and legal aspects of the field. Advanced courses in mortgage financing, property development and management, and other subjects also are available.

Many firms offer formal training programs for both beginners and experienced agents. Larger firms usually offer more extensive programs than smaller firms do.

***Licensure.*** In every state and the District of Columbia, real estate brokers and sales agents must be licensed. Prospective brokers and agents must pass a written examination. The examination—more comprehensive for brokers than for agents—includes questions on basic real estate transactions and laws affecting the sale of property. Most states require candidates for the general sales license to complete between 30 and 90 hours of classroom instruction. To get a broker's license an individual needs between 60 and 90 hours of formal training and a specific amount of experience selling real estate,

**Projections data from the National Employment Matrix**

| Occupational Title | SOC Code | Employment, 2006 | Projected employment, 2016 | Change, 2006-16 | |
|---|---|---|---|---|---|
| | | | | Number | Percent |
| Real estate brokers and sales agents ................................................. | 41-9020 | 564,000 | 624,000 | 60,000 | 11 |
| Real estate brokers ..................................................................... | 41-9021 | 131,000 | 146,000 | 15,000 | 11 |
| Real estate sales agents ............................................................ | 41-9022 | 432,000 | 478,000 | 46,000 | 11 |

NOTE: Data in this table are rounded.

usually one to three years. Some states waive the experience requirements for the broker's license for applicants who have a bachelor's degree in real estate.

State licenses typically must be renewed every one or two years; usually, no examination is needed. However, many states require continuing education for license renewals. Prospective agents and brokers should contact the real estate licensing commission of the state in which they wish to work to verify the exact licensing requirements.

*Other qualifications.* Personality traits are as important as academic background. Brokers look for agents who have a pleasant personality, honesty, and a neat appearance. Maturity, good judgment, trustworthiness, and enthusiasm for the job are required to attract prospective customers in this highly competitive field. Agents should be well organized, be detail oriented, and have a good memory for names, faces, and business particulars. They must be at least 18 years old.

Those interested in jobs as real estate agents often begin in their own communities. Their knowledge of local neighborhoods is a clear advantage. Under the direction of an experienced agent, beginners learn the practical aspects of the job, including the use of computers to locate or list available properties and identify sources of financing.

*Advancement.* As agents gain knowledge and expertise, they become more efficient in closing a greater number of transactions and increase their earnings. In many large firms, experienced agents can advance to sales manager or general manager. People who earn their broker's license may open their own offices. Others with experience and training in estimating property value may become real estate appraisers, and people familiar with operating and maintaining rental properties may become property managers. Experienced agents and brokers with a thorough knowledge of business conditions and property values in their localities may enter mortgage financing or real estate investment counseling.

## Employment

In 2006, real estate brokers and sales agents held about 564,000 jobs; real estate sales agents held approximately 77 percent of these jobs.

Many real estate brokers and sales agents worked part time, combining their real estate activities with other careers. About 61 percent real estate brokers and sales agents were self-employed. Real estate is sold in all areas, but employment is concentrated in large urban areas and in rapidly growing communities.

Most real estate firms are relatively small; indeed, some are one-person businesses. By contrast, some large real estate firms have sev-

eral hundred agents operating out of numerous branch offices. Many brokers have franchise agreements with national or regional real estate organizations. Under this type of arrangement, the broker pays a fee in exchange for the privilege of using the more widely known name of the parent organization. Although franchised brokers often receive help in training sales staff and running their offices, they bear the ultimate responsibility for the success or failure of their firms.

## Job Outlook

Average employment growth is expected because of the increasing housing needs of a growing population, as well as the perception that real estate is a good investment. Beginning agents and brokers face competition from their well-established, more experienced counterparts.

*Employment change.* Employment of real estate brokers and sales agents is expected to grow 11 percent during the 2006–2016 projection decade—about as fast as the average for all occupations. Relatively low interest rates and the perception that real estate usually is a good investment may continue to stimulate sales of real estate, resulting in the need for more agents and brokers. However, job growth will be somewhat limited by the increasing use of technology, which is improving the productivity of agents and brokers. For example, prospective customers often can perform their own searches for properties that meet their criteria by accessing real estate information on the Internet. The increasing use of technology is likely to be more detrimental to part-time or temporary real estate agents than to full-time agents because part-time agents generally are not able to compete with full-time agents who have invested in new technology. Changing legal requirements, such as disclosure laws, also may dissuade some who are not serious about practicing full time from continuing to work part time.

*Job prospects.* In addition to job growth, a large number of job openings will arise from the need to replace workers who transfer to other occupations or leave the labor force. Real estate brokers and sales agents are older, on average, than are most other workers. Historically, many homemakers and retired people were attracted to real estate sales by the flexible and part-time work schedules characteristic of the field. These individuals could enter, leave, and later return to the occupation, depending on the strength of the real estate market, their family responsibilities, or other personal circumstances. Recently, however, the attractiveness of part-time real estate work has declined, as increasingly complex legal and technological requirements are raising startup costs associated with becoming an agent.

Employment of real estate brokers and sales agents often is sensitive to swings in the economy, especially interest rates. During periods of declining economic activity and rising interest rates, the volume of sales and the resulting demand for sales workers falls. As a result, the earnings of agents and brokers decline, and many work fewer hours or leave the occupation altogether.

This occupation is relatively easy to enter and is attractive because of its flexible working conditions; the high interest in, and familiarity with, local real estate markets that entrants often have; and the potential for high earnings. Therefore, although gaining a job as a real estate agent or broker may be relatively easy, beginning agents and brokers face competition from their well-established, more experienced counterparts in obtaining listings and in closing an adequate number of sales.

Well-trained, ambitious people who enjoy selling—particularly those with extensive social and business connections in their communities—should have the best chance for success.

## Earnings

The median annual earnings, including commissions, of salaried real estate sales agents were $39,760 in May 2006. The middle 50 percent earned between $26,790 and $65,270 a year. The lowest 10 percent earned less than $20,170, and the highest 10 percent earned more than $111,500. Median annual earnings in the industries employing the largest number of real estate sales agents in May 2006 were

Residential building construction .........................$53,390

Land subdivision ..................................................49,230

Offices of real estate agents and brokers................39,930

Activities related to real estate ...........................36,510

Lessors of real estate .........................................32,580

Median annual earnings, including commissions, of salaried real estate brokers were $60,790 in May 2006. The middle 50 percent earned between $37,800 and $102,180 a year. Median annual earnings in the industries employing the largest number of real estate brokers in May 2006 were

Offices of real estate agents and brokers..............$64,350

Lessors of real estate ...........................................61,030

Activities related to real estate ............................48,250

Commissions on sales are the main source of earnings of real estate agents and brokers. The rate of commission varies according to whatever the agent and broker agree on, the type of property, and its value. The percentage paid on the sale of farm and commercial properties or unimproved land is typically higher than the percentage paid for selling a home.

Commissions may be divided among several agents and brokers. The broker or agent who obtains a listing usually shares the commission with the broker or agent who sells the property and with the firms that employ each of them. Although an agent's share varies greatly from one firm to another, often it is about half of the total amount received by the firm. Agents who both list and sell a property maximize their commission.

Income usually increases as an agent gains experience, but individual motivation, economic conditions, and the type and location of the property affect earnings, too. Sales workers who are active in

community organizations and in local real estate associations can broaden their contacts and increase their earnings. A beginner's earnings often are irregular because a few weeks or even months may go by without a sale. Although some brokers allow an agent to draw against future earnings from a special account, the practice is not common with new employees. The beginner, therefore, should have enough money to live for about 6 months or until commissions increase.

## Related Occupations

Selling expensive items such as homes requires maturity, tact, and a sense of responsibility. Other sales workers who find these character traits important in their work include insurance sales agents; retail salespersons; sales representatives, wholesale and manufacturing; and securities, commodities, and financial services sales agents. Although not involving sales, others who need an understanding of real estate include property, real estate, and community association managers, as well as appraisers and assessors of real estate.

## Sources of Additional Information

Information on licensing requirements for real estate brokers and sales agents is available from most local real estate organizations or from the state real estate commission or board.

More information about opportunities in real estate is available on the Internet site of the following organization:

▸ National Association of Realtors. Internet: http://www.realtor.org

# Receptionists and Information Clerks

(O*NET 43-4171.00)

## Significant Points

■ Good interpersonal skills are critical.

■ A high school diploma or its equivalent is the most common educational requirement.

■ Employment is expected to grow faster than average for all occupations.

## Nature of the Work

Receptionists and information clerks are charged with a responsibility that may affect the success of an organization: making a good first impression. Receptionists and information clerks answer telephones, route and screen calls, greet visitors, respond to inquiries from the public, and provide information about the organization. Some are responsible for the coordination of all mail into and out of the office. In addition, they contribute to the security of an organization by helping to monitor the access of visitors—a function that has become increasingly important.

Whereas some tasks are common to most receptionists and information clerks, their specific responsibilities vary with the type of establishment in which they work. For example, receptionists and

**Projections data from the National Employment Matrix**

| Occupational Title | SOC Code | Employment, 2006 | Projected employment, 2016 | Change, 2006-16 | |
|---|---|---|---|---|---|
| | | | | Number | Percent |
| Receptionists and information clerks............................................. | 43-4171 | 1,173,000 | 1,375,000 | 202,000 | 17 |

NOTE: Data in this table are rounded.

information clerks in hospitals and in doctors' offices may gather patients' personal and insurance information and direct them to the proper waiting rooms. In corporate headquarters, they may greet visitors and manage the scheduling of the board room or common conference area. In beauty or hair salons, they arrange appointments, direct customers to the hairstylist, and may serve as cashiers. In factories, large corporations, and government offices, receptionists and information clerks may provide identification cards and arrange for escorts to take visitors to the proper office. Those working for bus and train companies respond to inquiries about departures, arrivals, stops, and other related matters.

Increasingly, receptionists and information clerks use multiline telephone systems, personal computers, and fax machines. Despite the widespread use of automated answering systems or voice mail, many receptionists and clerks still take messages and inform other employees of visitors' arrivals or cancellation of an appointment. When they are not busy with callers, most workers are expected to perform a variety of office duties, including opening and sorting mail, collecting and distributing parcels, and transmitting and delivering facsimiles. Other duties include updating appointment calendars, preparing travel vouchers, and performing basic bookkeeping, word processing, and filing.

*Work environment.* Receptionists and information clerks who greet customers and visitors usually work in areas that are highly visible and designed and furnished to make a good impression. Most work stations are clean, well lighted, and relatively quiet. The work performed by some receptionists and information clerks may be tiring, repetitive, and stressful as they may spend all day answering continuously ringing telephones and sometimes encounter difficult or irate callers. The work environment, however, may be very friendly and motivating for individuals who enjoy greeting customers face to face and making them feel comfortable.

## Training, Other Qualifications, and Advancement

A high school diploma or its equivalent is the most common educational requirement, although hiring requirements for receptionists and information clerks vary by industry. Good interpersonal skills and being technologically proficient also are important to employers.

*Education and training.* Receptionists and information clerks generally need a high school diploma or equivalent as most of their training is received on the job. However, employers often look for applicants who already possess certain skills, such as prior computer experience or answering telephones. Some employers also may prefer some formal office education or training. On the job, they learn how to operate the telephone system and computers. They also learn the proper procedures for greeting visitors and for distributing mail, fax messages, and parcels. While many of these skills can be learned

quickly, those who are charged with relaying information to visitors or customers may need several months to learn details about the organization.

*Other qualifications.* Good interpersonal and customer service skills—being courteous, professional, and helpful—are critical for this job. Being an active listener often is a key quality needed by receptionists and information clerks that requires the ability to listen patiently to the points being made, to wait to speak until others have finished, and to ask appropriate questions when necessary. In addition, the ability to relay information accurately to others is important.

The ability to operate a wide range of office technology also is helpful, as receptionists and information clerks are often asked to work on other assignments during the day.

*Advancement.* Advancement for receptionists generally comes about either by transferring to an occupation with more responsibility or by being promoted to a supervisory position. Receptionists with especially strong computer skills may advance to a better paying job as a secretary or an administrative assistant.

## Employment

Receptionists and information clerks held about 1.2 million jobs in 2006. The health care and social assistance industries—including offices of physicians, hospitals, nursing homes, and outpatient care facilities—employed about 33 percent of all receptionists and information clerks. Manufacturing, wholesale and retail trade, government, and real estate industries also employed large numbers of receptionists and information clerks. More than 3 of every 10 receptionists and information clerks work part time.

## Job Outlook

Employment of receptionists and information clerks is expected to grow faster than average for all occupations. Receptionists and information clerks will have a very large number of new jobs arise, more than 200,000 over the 2006–2016 period. Additional job opportunities will result from the need to replace workers who transfer to other occupations or leave the labor force.

*Employment change.* Receptionists and information clerks are expected to increase by 17 percent from 2006 to 2016, which is faster than the average for all occupations. Employment growth will result from rapid growth in the following industries: offices of physicians, legal services, employment services, and management and technical consulting.

Technology will have conflicting effects on employment growth for receptionists and information clerks. The increasing use of voice mail and other telephone automation reduces the need for receptionists by allowing one receptionist to perform work that formerly required several. At the same time, however, the increasing use of other technology has caused a consolidation of clerical responsibilities and growing demand for workers with diverse clerical and technical skills. Because receptionists and information clerks may perform a wide variety of clerical tasks, they should continue to be in demand. Further, they perform many tasks that are interpersonal in nature and are not easily automated, ensuring continued demand for their services in a variety of establishments.

*Job prospects.* In addition to job growth, numerous job opportunities will be created as receptionists and information clerks transfer to other occupations or leave the labor force altogether. Opportunities should be best for persons with a wide range of clerical and technical skills, particularly those with related work experience.

## Earnings

Median hourly earnings of receptionists and information clerks in May 2006 were $11.01. The middle 50 percent earned between $9.06 and $13.51. The lowest 10 percent earned less than $7.54, and the highest 10 percent earned more than $16.23. Median hourly earnings in the industries employing the largest number of receptionists and information clerks in May 2006 were

| | |
|---|---|
| Offices of dentists | $12.89 |
| General medical and surgical hospitals | 11.74 |
| Offices of physicians | 11.44 |
| Employment services | 10.72 |
| Personal care services | 8.57 |

## Related Occupations

Receptionists deal with the public and often direct people to others who can assist them. Other workers who perform similar duties include dispatchers, secretaries and administrative assistants, and customer service representatives.

## Sources of Additional Information

State employment offices can provide information on job openings for receptionists.

## Recreation Workers

(O*NET 39-9032.00)

## Significant Points

- The recreation field offers an unusually large number of part-time and seasonal job opportunities.
- Educational requirements range from a high school diploma to a graduate degree.
- Opportunities for part-time, seasonal, and temporary recreation jobs will be good, but competition will remain keen for full-time career positions.

## Nature of the Work

People spend much of their leisure time participating in a wide variety of organized recreational activities, such as arts and crafts, the performing arts, camping, and sports. Recreation workers plan, organize, and direct these activities in local playgrounds and recreation areas, parks, community centers, religious organizations, camps, theme parks, and tourist attractions. Increasingly, recreation workers also are found in businesses where they organize and direct leisure activities for employees.

Recreation workers hold a variety of positions at different levels of responsibility. Workers who provide instruction and coaching in art, music, drama, swimming, tennis, or other activities may be called *activity specialists.*

*Camp counselors* lead and instruct children and teenagers in outdoor recreation, such as swimming, hiking, horseback riding, and camping. In addition, counselors teach campers special subjects such as archery, boating, music, drama, gymnastics, tennis, and computers. In residential camps, counselors also provide guidance and supervise daily living and socialization. *Camp directors* typically supervise camp counselors, plan camp activities or programs, and perform the various administrative functions of a camp.

*Recreation leaders*, who are responsible for a recreation program's daily operation, primarily organize and direct participants. They may lead and give instruction in dance, drama, crafts, games, and sports; schedule the use of facilities; keep records of equipment use; and ensure that recreation facilities and equipment are used properly.

*Recreation supervisors* oversee recreation leaders and plan, organize, and manage recreational activities to meet the needs of a variety of populations. These workers often serve as liaisons between the director of the park or recreation center and the recreation leaders. Recreation supervisors with more specialized responsibilities also may direct special activities or events or oversee a major activity, such as aquatics, gymnastics, or performing arts.

*Directors of recreation and parks* develop and manage comprehensive recreation programs in parks, playgrounds, and other settings. Directors usually serve as technical advisors to state and local recreation and park commissions and may be responsible for recreation and park budgets.

*Work environment.* Recreation workers may work in a variety of settings—for example, a cruise ship, a woodland recreational park, a summer camp, or a playground in the center of a large urban community. Regardless of the setting, most recreation workers spend much of their time outdoors and may work in a variety of weather conditions. Recreation directors and supervisors, however, typically spend most of their time in an office, planning programs and special events. Directors and supervisors generally engage in less physical activity than do lower level recreation workers. Nevertheless, recreation workers at all levels risk suffering injuries during physical activities.

Some recreation workers work about 40 hours a week. However, many people entering this field, such as camp counselors, may have some night and weekend work, irregular hours, and seasonal employment.

Projections data from the National Employment Matrix

| Occupational Title | SOC Code | Employment, 2006 | Projected employment, 2016 | Change, 2006-16 | |
|---|---|---|---|---|---|
| | | | | Number | Percent |
| Recreation workers ................................................................ | 39-9032 | 320,000 | 360,000 | 41,000 | 13 |

NOTE: Data in this table are rounded.

## Training, Other Qualifications, and Advancement

The educational and training requirements for recreation workers vary widely depending on the type of job. Full-time career positions usually require a college degree. Many jobs, however, can be learned with only a short period of on-the-job training.

*Education and training.* Educational requirements for recreation workers range from a high school diploma—or sometimes less for those seeking summer jobs—to graduate degrees for some administrative positions in large public recreation systems. Full-time career professional positions usually require a college degree with a major in parks and recreation or leisure studies, but a bachelor's degree in any liberal arts field may be sufficient for some jobs in the private sector. In industrial recreation, or "employee services" as it is more commonly called, companies prefer to hire those with a bachelor's degree in recreation or leisure studies and a background in business administration. Some college students work part time as recreation workers while earning degrees.

Employers seeking candidates for some administrative positions favor those with at least a master's degree in parks and recreation, business administration, or public administration. Most required at least an associate degree in recreation studies or a related field.

An associate or bachelor's degree in a recreation-related discipline and experience are preferred for most recreation supervisor jobs and are required for most higher level administrative jobs. Graduates of associate degree programs in parks and recreation, social work, and other human services disciplines also enter some career recreation positions. High school graduates occasionally enter career positions, but this is not common.

Programs leading to an associate or bachelor's degree in parks and recreation, leisure studies, or related fields are offered at several hundred colleges and universities. Many also offer master's or doctoral degrees in the field. In 2006, about 100 bachelor's degree programs in parks and recreation were accredited by the National Recreation and Park Association (NRPA). Accredited programs provide broad exposure to the history, theory, and practice of park and recreation management. Courses offered include community organization; supervision and administration; recreational needs of special populations, such as the elderly or disabled; and supervised fieldwork. Students may specialize in areas such as therapeutic recreation, park management, outdoor recreation, industrial or commercial recreation, or camp management.

Specialized training or experience in a particular field, such as art, music, drama, or athletics, is an asset for many jobs. Some jobs also require certification. For example, a lifesaving certificate is a prerequisite for teaching or coaching water-related activities.

The large number of seasonal and part-time workers learn through on-the-job training.

*Licensure and certification.* The NRPA certifies individuals for professional and technical jobs. Certified Park and Recreation Professionals must pass an exam; earn a bachelor's degree with a major in recreation, park resources, or leisure services from a program accredited by the NRPA or earn a bachelor's degree and have at least five years of relevant full-time work experience. Continuing education is necessary to remain certified.

Many areas require lifeguards to be certified. Training and certification details vary from state to state and county to county. Information on lifeguards is available from your local Parks and Recreation Department.

*Other qualifications.* People planning recreation careers should be outgoing, good at motivating people, and sensitive to the needs of others. Excellent health and physical fitness are often required, due to the physical nature of some jobs. Volunteer experience, part-time work during school, or a summer job can lead to a full-time career as a recreation worker.

*Advancement.* Recreation workers with experience and managerial skills may advance to supervisory or managerial positions.

## Employment

Recreation workers held about 320,000 jobs in 2006, and many additional workers held summer jobs in the occupation. About 32 percent of recreation workers worked for local governments, primarily in park and recreation departments. About 16 percent of recreation workers were employed by nursing and residential care facilities and another 10 percent were employed in civic and social organizations, such as the Boy Scouts or Girl Scouts or the Red Cross.

## Job Outlook

Jobs opportunities for part-time, seasonal, and temporary recreation workers will be good, but competition will remain keen for career positions as recreation workers. Average growth is expected.

*Employment change.* Overall employment of recreation workers is projected to increase by 13 percent between 2006 and 2016, which is about as fast as the average for all occupations. Although people will spend more time and money on recreation, budget restrictions in state and local government will moderate the number of jobs added. Many of the new jobs will be in social assistance organizations and in nursing and residential care facilities.

Growth will be driven by retiring baby boomers who, with more leisure time, high disposable income, and concern for health and fitness, are expected to increase the demand for recreation services.

*Job prospects.* Applicants for part-time, seasonal, and temporary recreation jobs should have good opportunities, but competition will remain keen for career positions because the recreation field attracts many applicants and because the number of career positions is limited compared with the number of lower-level seasonal jobs. Opportunities for staff positions should be best for people with formal training and experience in part-time or seasonal recreation jobs. Those with graduate degrees should have the best opportunities for supervisory or administrative positions. Job openings will stem from growth and the need to replace the large numbers of workers who leave the occupation each year.

## Earnings

In May 2006, median annual earnings of recreation workers who worked full time were $20,470. The middle 50 percent earned between $16,360 and $27,050. The lowest-paid 10 percent earned less than $14,150, while the highest-paid 10 percent earned $35,780 or more. However, earnings of recreation directors and others in supervisory or managerial positions can be substantially higher. Most public and private recreation agencies provide full-time recreation workers with typical benefits; part-time workers receive few, if any, benefits. In May 2006, median annual earnings in the industries employing the largest numbers of recreation workers were as follows:

Nursing care facilities........................................$21,510
Individual and family services .............................20,410
Local government ...............................................20,100
Other amusement and recreation industries ............18,810
Civic and social organizations .............................17,920

The large numbers of temporary, seasonal jobs in the recreation field typically are filled by high school or college students, generally do not have formal education requirements, and are open to anyone with the desired personal qualities. Employers compete for a share of the vacationing student labor force, and although salaries in recreation often are lower than those in other fields, the nature of the work and the opportunity to work outdoors are attractive to many.

Part-time, seasonal, and volunteer jobs in recreation include summer camp counselors, craft specialists, and after-school and weekend recreation program leaders. In addition, many teachers and college students accept jobs as recreation workers when school is not in session. The vast majority of volunteers serve as activity leaders at local day camp programs, or in youth organizations, camps, nursing homes, hospitals, senior centers, and other settings.

## Related Occupations

Recreation workers must exhibit leadership and sensitivity when dealing with people. Other occupations that require similar personal qualities include counselors; probation officers and correctional treatment specialists; psychologists; recreational therapists; teachers—self enrichment education; athletes, coaches, umpires, and related workers; and social workers.

## Sources of Additional Information

For information on jobs in recreation, contact employers such as local government departments of parks and recreation, nursing and personal care facilities, the Boy Scouts or Girl Scouts, or local social or religious organizations.

For career, certification, and academic program information in parks and recreation, contact

▸ National Recreation and Park Association, 22377 Belmont Ridge Rd., Ashburn, VA 20148-4501. Internet: http://www.nrpa.org

For career information about camp counselors, contact

▸ American Camping Association, 5000 State Road 67 North, Martinsville, IN 46151-7902. Internet: http://www.acacamps.org

## Registered Nurses

(O*NET 29-1111.00)

## Significant Points

■ Registered nurses constitute the largest health care occupation, with 2.5 million jobs.

■ About 59 percent of jobs are in hospitals.

■ The three major educational paths to registered nursing are a bachelor's degree, an associate degree, and a diploma from an approved nursing program.

■ Registered nurses are projected to generate about 587,000 new jobs over the 2006–2016 period, one of the largest numbers among all occupations; overall job opportunities are expected to be excellent, but may vary by employment setting.

## Nature of the Work

Registered nurses (RNs), regardless of specialty or work setting, treat patients, educate patients and the public about various medical conditions, and provide advice and emotional support to patients' family members. RNs record patients' medical histories and symptoms, help perform diagnostic tests and analyze results, operate medical machinery, administer treatment and medications, and help with patient follow-up and rehabilitation.

RNs teach patients and their families how to manage their illness or injury, explaining post-treatment home care needs; diet, nutrition, and exercise programs; and self-administration of medication and physical therapy. Some RNs work to promote general health by educating the public on warning signs and symptoms of disease. RNs also might run general health screening or immunization clinics, blood drives, and public seminars on various conditions.

When caring for patients, RNs establish a plan of care or contribute to an existing plan. Plans may include numerous activities, such as administering medication, including careful checking of dosages and avoiding interactions; starting, maintaining, and discontinuing intravenous (IV) lines for fluid, medication, blood, and blood products; administering therapies and treatments; observing the patient and recording those observations; and consulting with physicians and other health care clinicians. Some RNs provide direction to licensed practical nurses and nursing aids regarding patient care. RNs with advanced educational preparation and training may perform diagnostic and therapeutic procedures and may have prescriptive authority.

RNs can specialize in one or more areas of patient care. There generally are four ways to specialize. RNs can choose a particular work setting or type of treatment, such as perioperative nurses, who work in operating rooms and assist surgeons. RNs also may choose to specialize in specific health conditions, as do diabetes management nurses, who assist patients to manage diabetes. Other RNs specialize in working with one or more organs or body system types, such as dermatology nurses, who work with patients who have skin disorders. RNs also can choose to work with a well-defined population, such as geriatric nurses, who work with the elderly. Some RNs may combine specialties. For example, pediatric oncology nurses deal with children and adolescents who have cancer.

There are many options for RNs who specialize in a work setting or type of treatment. *Ambulatory care nurses* provide preventive care and treat patients with a variety of illnesses and injuries in physicians' offices or in clinics. Some ambulatory care nurses are involved in telehealth, providing care and advice through electronic communications media such as videoconferencing, the Internet, or by telephone. *Critical care nurses* provide care to patients with serious, complex, and acute illnesses or injuries that require very close monitoring and extensive medication protocols and therapies. Critical care nurses often work in critical or intensive care hospital units. *Emergency*, or *trauma, nurses* work in hospital or stand-alone emergency departments, providing initial assessments and care for patients with life-threatening conditions. Some emergency nurses may become qualified to serve as *transport nurses*, who provide medical care to patients who are transported by helicopter or airplane to the nearest medical facility. *Holistic nurses* provide care such as acupuncture, massage and aroma therapy, and biofeedback, which are meant to treat patients' mental and spiritual health in addition to their physical health. *Home health care nurses* provide at-home nursing care for patients, often as follow-up care after discharge from a hospital or from a rehabilitation, long-term care, or skilled nursing facility. *Hospice and palliative care nurses* provide care, most often in home or hospice settings, focused on maintaining quality of life for terminally ill patients. *Infusion nurses* administer medications, fluids, and blood to patients through injections into patients' veins. *Long- term care nurses* provide health care services on a recurring basis to patients with chronic physical or mental disorders, often in long-term care or skilled nursing facilities. *Medical-surgical nurses* provide health promotion and basic medical care to patients with various medical and surgical diagnoses. *Occupational health nurses* seek to prevent job-related injuries and illnesses, provide monitoring and emergency care services, and help employers implement health and safety standards. *Perianesthesia nurses* provide preoperative and postoperative care to patients undergoing anesthesia during surgery or other procedure. *Perioperative nurses* assist surgeons by selecting and handling instruments, controlling bleeding, and suturing incisions. Some of these nurses also can specialize in plastic and reconstructive surgery. *Psychiatric-mental health nurses* treat patients with personality and mood disorders. *Radiology nurses* provide care to patients undergoing diagnostic radiation procedures such as ultrasounds, magnetic resonance imaging, and radiation therapy for oncology diagnoses. *Rehabilitation nurses* care for patients with temporary and permanent disabilities. *Transplant nurses* care for both transplant recipients and living donors and monitor signs of organ rejection.

RNs specializing in a particular disease, ailment, or health care condition are employed in virtually all work settings, including physicians' offices, outpatient treatment facilities, home health care agencies, and hospitals. *Addictions nurses* care for patients seeking help with alcohol, drug, tobacco, and other addictions. *Intellectual and developmental disabilities nurses* provide care for patients with physical, mental, or behavioral disabilities; care may include help with feeding, controlling bodily functions, sitting or standing independently, and speaking or other communication. *Diabetes management nurses* help diabetics to manage their disease by teaching them proper nutrition and showing them how to test blood sugar levels and administer insulin injections. *Genetics nurses* provide early detection screenings, counseling, and treatment of patients with genetic disorders, including cystic fibrosis and Huntington's disease. *HIV/AIDS nurses* care for patients diagnosed with HIV and AIDS. *Oncology nurses* care for patients with various types of cancer and may assist in the administration of radiation and chemotherapies and follow-up monitoring. *Wound, ostomy, and continence nurses* treat patients with wounds caused by traumatic injury, ulcers, or arterial disease; provide postoperative care for patients with openings that allow for alternative methods of bodily waste elimination; and treat patients with urinary and fecal incontinence.

RNs specializing in treatment of a particular organ or body system usually are employed in hospital specialty or critical care units, specialty clinics, and outpatient care facilities. *Cardiovascular nurses* treat patients with coronary heart disease and those who have had heart surgery, providing services such as postoperative rehabilitation. *Dermatology nurses* treat patients with disorders of the skin, such as skin cancer and psoriasis. *Gastroenterology nurses* treat patients with digestive and intestinal disorders, including ulcers, acid reflux disease, and abdominal bleeding. Some nurses in this field also assist in specialized procedures such as endoscopies, which look inside the gastrointestinal tract using a tube equipped with a light and a camera that can capture images of diseased tissue. *Gynecology nurses* provide care to women with disorders of the reproductive system, including endometriosis, cancer, and sexually transmitted diseases. *Nephrology nurses* care for patients with kidney disease caused by diabetes, hypertension, or substance abuse. *Neuroscience nurses* care for patients with dysfunctions of the nervous system, including brain and spinal cord injuries and seizures. *Ophthalmic nurses* provide care to patients with disorders of the eyes, including blindness and glaucoma, and to patients undergoing eye surgery. *Orthopedic nurses* care for patients with muscular and skeletal problems, including arthritis, bone fractures, and muscular dystrophy. *Otorhinolaryngology nurses* care for patients with ear, nose, and throat disorders, such as cleft palates, allergies, and sinus disorders. *Respiratory nurses* provide care to patients with respiratory disorders such as asthma, tuberculosis, and cystic fibrosis. *Urology nurses* care for patients with disorders of the kidneys, urinary tract, and male reproductive organs, including infections, kidney and bladder stones, and cancers.

RNs who specialize by population provide preventive and acute care in all health care settings to the segment of the population in which they specialize, including newborns (neonatology), children and adolescents (pediatrics), adults, and the elderly (gerontology or geriatrics). RNs also may provide basic health care to patients outside of health care settings in such venues as including correctional facilities, schools, summer camps, and the military. Some RNs travel around the United States and abroad providing care to patients in areas with shortages of health care workers.

Most RNs work as staff nurses as members of a team providing critical health care . However, some RNs choose to become advanced practice nurses, who work independently or in collaboration with physicians, and may focus on the provision of primary care services. *Clinical nurse specialists* provide direct patient care and expert consultations in one of many nursing specialties, such as psychiatric-mental health. *Nurse anesthetists* provide anesthesia and related care before and after surgical, therapeutic, diagnostic and obstetrical procedures. They also provide pain management and emergency services, such as airway management. *Nurse-midwives* provide primary care to women, including gynecological exams, family planning advice, prenatal care, assistance in labor and delivery, and neonatal care. *Nurse practitioners* serve as primary and specialty care providers, providing a blend of nursing and health care services to patients and families. The most common specialty areas for nurse practitioners are family practice, adult practice, women's health, pediatrics, acute care, and geriatrics. However, there are a variety of other specialties that nurse practitioners can choose, including neonatology and mental health. Advanced practice nurses can prescribe medications in all states and in the District of Columbia.

Some nurses have jobs that require little or no direct patient care, but still require an active RN license. *Case managers* ensure that all of the medical needs of patients with severe injuries and severe or chronic illnesses are met. *Forensics nurses* participate in the scientific investigation and treatment of abuse victims, violence, criminal activity, and traumatic accident. *Infection control nurses* identify, track, and control infectious outbreaks in health care facilities and develop programs for outbreak prevention and response to biological terrorism. *Legal nurse consultants* assist lawyers in medical cases by interviewing patients and witnesses, organizing medical records, determining damages and costs, locating evidence, and educating lawyers about medical issues. *Nurse administrators* supervise nursing staff, establish work schedules and budgets, maintain medical supply inventories, and manage resources to ensure high-quality care. *Nurse educators* plan, develop, implement, and evaluate educational programs and curricula for the professional development of student nurses and RNs. *Nurse informaticists* manage and communicate nursing data and information to improve decision making by consumers, patients, nurses, and other health care providers. RNs also may work as health care consultants, public policy advisors, pharmaceutical and medical supply researchers and salespersons, and medical writers and editors.

*Work environment.* Most RNs work in well-lighted, comfortable health care facilities. Home health and public health nurses travel to patients' homes, schools, community centers, and other sites. RNs may spend considerable time walking, bending, stretching, and standing. Patients in hospitals and nursing care facilities require 24-hour care; consequently, nurses in these institutions may work nights, weekends, and holidays. RNs also may be on call—available to work on short notice. Nurses who work in offices, schools, and other settings that do not provide 24-hour care are more likely to work regular business hours. About 21 percent of RNs worked part time in 2006, and 7 percent held more than one job.

Nursing has its hazards, especially in hospitals, nursing care facilities, and clinics, where nurses may be in close contact with individuals who have infectious diseases and with toxic, harmful, or potentially hazardous compounds, solutions, and medications. RNs must observe rigid, standardized guidelines to guard against disease and other dangers, such as those posed by radiation, accidental needle sticks, chemicals used to sterilize instruments, and anesthetics. In addition, they are vulnerable to back injury when moving patients, shocks from electrical equipment, and hazards posed by compressed gases. RNs also may suffer emotional strain from caring for patients suffering unrelieved intense pain, close personal contact with patients' families, the need to make critical decisions, and ethical dilemmas and concerns.

## Training, Other Qualifications, and Advancement

The three major educational paths to registered nursing are a bachelor's degree, an associate degree, and a diploma from an approved nursing program. Nurses most commonly enter the occupation by completing an associate degree or bachelor's degree program. Individuals then must complete a national licensing examination in order to obtain a nursing license. Further training or education can qualify nurses to work in specialty areas, and may help improve advancement opportunities.

*Education and training.* There are three major educational paths to registered nursing—a bachelor's of science degree in nursing (BSN), an associate degree in nursing (ADN), and a diploma. BSN programs, offered by colleges and universities, take about four years to complete. In 2006, 709 nursing programs offered degrees at the bachelor's level. ADN programs, offered by community and junior colleges, take about two to three years to complete. About 850 RN programs granted associate degrees. Diploma programs, administered in hospitals, last about three years. Only about 70 programs offered diplomas. Generally, licensed graduates of any of the three types of educational programs qualify for entry-level positions.

Many RNs with an ADN or diploma later enter bachelor's programs to prepare for a broader scope of nursing practice. Often, they can find an entry-level position and then take advantage of tuition reimbursement benefits to work toward a BSN by completing an RN-to-BSN program. In 2006, there were 629 RN-to-BSN programs in the United States. Accelerated master's degree in nursing (MSN) programs also are available by combining one year of an accelerated BSN program with two years of graduate study. In 2006, there were 149 RN-to-MSN programs.

Accelerated BSN programs also are available for individuals who have a bachelor's or higher degree in another field and who are interested in moving into nursing. In 2006, 197 of these programs were available. Accelerated BSN programs last 12 to 18 months and provide the fastest route to a BSN for individuals who already hold a degree. MSN programs also are available for individuals who hold a bachelor's or higher degree in another field.

Individuals considering nursing should carefully weigh the advantages and disadvantages of enrolling in a BSN or MSN program because, if they do, their advancement opportunities usually are broader. In fact, some career paths are open only to nurses with a bachelor's or master's degree. A bachelor's degree often is necessary for administrative positions and is a prerequisite for admission to graduate nursing programs in research, consulting, and teaching, and all four advanced practice nursing specialties—clinical nurse specialists, nurse anesthetists, nurse-midwives, and nurse practitioners. Individuals who complete a bachelor's receive more training in areas such as communication, leadership, and critical thinking, all of which are becoming more important as nursing care becomes more complex. Additionally, bachelor's degree programs offer more clinical experience in nonhospital settings. Education beyond a bachelor's degree can also help students looking to enter certain fields or increase advancement opportunities. In 2006, 448 nursing schools offered master's degrees, 108 offered doctoral degrees, and 58 offered accelerated BSN-to-doctoral programs.

All four advanced practice nursing specialties require at least a master's degree. Most programs include about two years of full-time study and require a BSN degree for entry; some programs require at least one to two years of clinical experience as an RN for admission. In 2006, there were 342 master's and post-master's programs offered for nurse practitioners, 230 master's and post-master's programs for clinical nurse specialists, 106 programs for nurse anesthetists, and 39 programs for nurse-midwives.

All nursing education programs include classroom instruction and supervised clinical experience in hospitals and other health care facilities. Students take courses in anatomy, physiology, microbiology, chemistry, nutrition, psychology and other behavioral sciences, and nursing. Coursework also includes the liberal arts for ADN and BSN students.

Supervised clinical experience is provided in hospital departments such as pediatrics, psychiatry, maternity, and surgery. A growing number of programs include clinical experience in nursing care facilities, public health departments, home health agencies, and ambulatory clinics.

*Licensure and certification.* In all states, the District of Columbia, and U.S. territories, students must graduate from an approved nursing program and pass a national licensing examination, known as the NCLEX-RN, in order to obtain a nursing license. Nurses may be licensed in more than one state, either by examination or by the endorsement of a license issued by another state. The Nurse Licensure Compact Agreement allows a nurse who is licensed and permanently resides in one of the member states to practice in the other member states without obtaining additional licensure. In 2006, 20 states were members of the Compact, while two more were pending membership. All states require periodic renewal of licenses, which may require continuing education.

Certification is common, and sometimes required, for the four advanced practice nursing specialties—clinical nurse specialists, nurse anesthetists, nurse-midwives, and nurse practitioners. Upon completion of their educational programs, most advanced practice nurses become nationally certified in their area of specialty. Certification also is available in specialty areas for all nurses. In some states, certification in a specialty is required in order to practice that specialty.

Foreign-educated and foreign-born nurses wishing to work in the United States must obtain a work visa. To obtain the visa, nurses must undergo a federal screening program to ensure that their education and licensure are comparable to that of a U.S. educated nurse,

that they have proficiency in written and spoken English, and that they have passed either the Commission on Graduates of Foreign Nursing Schools (CGFNS) Qualifying Examination or the NCLEX-RN. CGFNS administers the VisaScreen Program. (The Commission is an immigration-neutral, nonprofit organization that is recognized internationally as an authority on credentials evaluation in the health care field.) Nurses educated in Australia, Canada (except Quebec), Ireland, New Zealand, and the United Kingdom, or foreign-born nurses who were educated in the United States, are exempt from the language proficiency testing. In addition to these national requirements, foreign-born nurses must obtain state licensure in order to practice in the United States. Each state has its own requirements for licensure.

*Other qualifications.* Nurses should be caring, sympathetic, responsible, and detail oriented. They must be able to direct or supervise others, correctly assess patients' conditions, and determine when consultation is required. They need emotional stability to cope with human suffering, emergencies, and other stresses.

*Advancement.* Some RNs start their careers as licensed practical nurses or nursing aides, and then go back to school to receive their RN degree. Most RNs begin as staff nurses in hospitals, and with experience and good performance often move to other settings or are promoted to more responsible positions. In management, nurses can advance from assistant unit manger or head nurse to more senior-level administrative roles of assistant director, director, vice president, or chief nurse. Increasingly, management-level nursing positions require a graduate or an advanced degree in nursing or health services administration. Administrative positions require leadership, communication and negotiation skills, and good judgment.

Some nurses move into the business side of health care. Their nursing expertise and experience on a health care team equip them to manage ambulatory, acute, home-based, and chronic care. Employers—including hospitals, insurance companies, pharmaceutical manufacturers, and managed care organizations, among others—need RNs for health planning and development, marketing, consulting, policy development, and quality assurance. Other nurses work as college and university faculty or conduct research.

# Employment

As the largest health care occupation, registered nurses held about 2.5 million jobs in 2006. Hospitals employed the majority of RNs, with 59 percent of jobs. Other industries also employed large shares of workers. About 8 percent of jobs were in offices of physicians, 5 percent in home health care services, 5 percent in nursing care facilities, 4 percent in employment services, and 3 percent in outpatient care centers. The remainder worked mostly in government agencies, social assistance agencies, and educational services. About 21 percent of RNs worked part time.

# Job Outlook

Overall job opportunities for registered nurses are expected to be excellent, but may vary by employment and geographic setting. Employment of RNs is expected to grow much faster than the average for all occupations through 2016 and, because the occupation is

**Projections data from the National Employment Matrix**

| Occupational Title | SOC Code | Employment, 2006 | Projected employment, 2016 | Change, 2006-2016 | |
|---|---|---|---|---|---|
| | | | | Number | Percent |
| Registered nurses ............................................................... | 29-1111 | 2,505,000 | 3,092,000 | 587,000 | 23 |

NOTE: Data in this table are rounded.

very large, many new jobs will result. In fact, registered nurses are projected to generate 587,000 new jobs, among the largest number of new jobs for any occupation. Additionally, hundreds of thousands of job openings will result from the need to replace experienced nurses who leave the occupation.

*Employment change.* Employment of registered nurses is expected to grow 23 percent from 2006 to 2016, much faster than the average for all occupations. Growth will be driven by technological advances in patient care, which permit a greater number of health problems to be treated, and by an increasing emphasis on preventive care. In addition, the number of older people, who are much more likely than younger people to need nursing care, is projected to grow rapidly.

However, employment of RNs will not grow at the same rate in every industry. The projected growth rates for RNs in the industries with the highest employment of these workers are:

Offices of physicians .................................................39%

Home health care services .........................................39

Outpatient care centers, except mental health
and substance abuse .............................................34

Employment services.................................................27

General medical and surgical hospitals, public
and private ............................................................22

Nursing care facilities ...............................................20

Employment is expected to grow more slowly in hospitals—health care's largest industry—than in most other health care industries. While the intensity of nursing care is likely to increase, requiring more nurses per patient, the number of inpatients (those who remain in the hospital for more than 24 hours) is not likely to grow by much. Patients are being discharged earlier, and more procedures are being done on an outpatient basis, both inside and outside hospitals. Rapid growth is expected in hospital outpatient facilities, such as those providing same-day surgery, rehabilitation, and chemotherapy.

More and more sophisticated procedures, once performed only in hospitals, are being performed in physicians' offices and in outpatient care centers, such as freestanding ambulatory surgical and emergency centers. Accordingly, employment is expected to grow very fast in these places as health care in general expands.

Employment in nursing care facilities is expected to grow because of increases in the number of elderly, many of whom require long-term care. However, this growth will be relatively slower than in other health care industries because of the desire of patients to be treated at home or in residential care facilities, and the increasing availability of that type of care. The financial pressure on hospitals to discharge patients as soon as possible should produce more admissions to nursing and residential care facilities and to home health care. Job growth also is expected in units that provide special-ized long-term rehabilitation for stroke and head injury patients, as well as units that treat Alzheimer's victims.

Employment in home health care is expected to increase rapidly in response to the growing number of older persons with functional disabilities, consumer preference for care in the home, and technological advances that make it possible to bring increasingly complex treatments into the home. The type of care demanded will require nurses who are able to perform complex procedures.

Rapid employment growth in employment services industry is expected as hospitals, physician's offices, and other health care establishments utilize temporary workers to fill short-term staffing needs. And as the demand for nurses grows, temporary nurses will be needed more often, further contributing to employment growth in this industry.

*Job prospects.* Overall job opportunities are expected to be excellent for registered nurses. Employers in some parts of the country and in certain employment settings report difficulty in attracting and retaining an adequate number of RNs, primarily because of an aging RN workforce and a lack of younger workers to fill positions. Enrollments in nursing programs at all levels have increased more rapidly in the past few years as students seek jobs with stable employment. However, many qualified applicants are being turned away because of a shortage of nursing faculty. The need for nursing faculty will only increase as many instructors near retirement. Many employers also are relying on foreign-educated nurses to fill vacant positions.

Even though overall employment opportunities for all nursing specialties are expected to be excellent, they can vary by employment setting. Despite the slower employment growth in hospitals, job opportunities should still be excellent because of the relatively high turnover of hospital nurses. RNs working in hospitals frequently work overtime and night and weekend shifts and also treat seriously ill and injured patients, all of which can contribute to stress and burnout. Hospital departments in which these working conditions occur most frequently—critical care units, emergency departments, and operating rooms—generally will have more job openings than other departments. To attract and retain qualified nurses, hospitals may offer signing bonuses, family-friendly work schedules, or subsidized training. A growing number of hospitals also are experimenting with online bidding to fill open shifts, in which nurses can volunteer to fill open shifts at premium wages. This can decrease the amount of mandatory overtime that nurses are required to work.

Although faster employment growth is projected in physicians' offices and outpatient care centers, RNs may face greater competition for these positions because they generally offer regular working hours and more comfortable working environments. There also may be some competition for jobs in employment services, despite a high rate of employment growth, because a large number of workers are attracted by the industry's relatively high wages and the flexibility of the work in this industry.

Generally, RNs with at least a bachelor's degree will have better job prospects than those without a bachelor's. In addition, all four advanced practice specialties—clinical nurse specialists, nurse practitioners, nurse-midwives, and nurse anesthetists—will be in high demand, particularly in medically underserved areas such as inner cities and rural areas. Relative to physicians, these RNs increasingly serve as lower-cost primary care providers.

## Earnings

Median annual earnings of registered nurses were $57,280 in May 2006. The middle 50 percent earned between $47,710 and $69,850. The lowest 10 percent earned less than $40,250, and the highest 10 percent earned more than $83,440. Median annual earnings in the industries employing the largest numbers of registered nurses in May 2006 were

| | |
|---|---|
| Employment services | $64,260 |
| General medical and surgical hospitals | 58,550 |
| Home health care services | 54,190 |
| Offices of physicians | 53,800 |
| Nursing care facilities | 52,490 |

Many employers offer flexible work schedules, child care, educational benefits, and bonuses.

## Related Occupations

Because of the number of specialties for registered nurses, and the variety of responsibilities and duties, many other health care occupations are similar in some aspect of the job. Other occupations that deal directly with patients when providing care include licensed practical and licensed vocational nurses, physicians and surgeons, athletic trainers, respiratory therapists, massage therapists, dietitians and nutritionists, occupational therapists, physical therapists, and emergency medical technicians and paramedics. Other occupations that use advanced medical equipment to treat patients include cardiovascular technologists and technicians, diagnostic medical sonographers, radiologic technologists and technicians, radiation therapists, and surgical technologists. Workers who also assist other health care professionals in providing care include nursing, psychiatric, and home health aides; physician assistants; and dental hygienists. Some nurses take on a management role, similar to medical and health services managers.

## Sources of Additional Information

For information on a career as a registered nurse and nursing education, contact

▸ National League for Nursing, 61 Broadway, New York, NY 10006. Internet: http://www.nln.org

For information on baccalaureate and graduate nursing education, nursing career options, and financial aid, contact

▸ American Association of Colleges of Nursing, 1 Dupont Circle NW, Suite 530, Washington, DC 20036. Internet: http://www.aacn.nche.edu

For additional information on registered nurses, including credentialing, contact

▸ American Nurses Association, 8515 Georgia Ave., Suite 400, Silver Spring, MD 20910. Internet: http://nursingworld.org

For information on the NCLEX-RN exam and a list of individual state boards of nursing, contact

▸ National Council of State Boards of Nursing, 111 E. Wacker Dr., Suite 2900, Chicago, IL 60611. Internet: http://www.ncsbn.org

For information on the nursing population, including workforce shortage facts, contact

▸ Bureau of Health Professions, 5600 Fishers Lane, Room 8-05, Rockville, MD 20857. Internet: http://bhpr.hrsa.gov

For information on obtaining U.S. certification and work visas for foreign-educated nurses, contact

▸ Commission on Graduates of Foreign Nursing Schools, 3600 Market St., Suite 400, Philadelphia, PA 19104. Internet: http://www.cgfns.org

For a list of accredited clinical nurse specialist programs, contact

▸ National Association of Clinical Nurse Specialists, 2090 Linglestown Rd., Suite 107, Harrisburg, PA 17110. Internet: http://www.nacns.org

For information on nurse anesthetists, including a list of accredited programs, contact

▸ American Association of Nurse Anesthetists, 222 Prospect Ave., Park Ridge, IL 60068.

For information on nurse-midwives, including a list of accredited programs, contact

▸ American College of Nurse-Midwives, 8403 Colesville Rd., Suite 1550, Silver Spring, MD 20910. Internet: http://www.midwife.org

For information on nurse practitioners, including a list of accredited programs, contact

▸ American Academy of Nurse Practitioners, P.O. Box 12846, Austin, TX 78711. Internet: http://www.aanp.org

For information on nurse practitioners education, contact

▸ National Organization of Nurse Practitioner Faculties, 1522 K St. NW, Suite 702, Washington, DC 20005. Internet: http://www.nonpf.org

For information on critical care nurses, contact

▸ American Association of Critical-Care Nurses, 101 Columbia, Aliso Viejo, CA 92656. Internet: http://www.aacn.org

For additional information on registered nurses in all fields and specialties, contact

▸ American Society of Registered Nurses, 1001 Bridgeway, Suite 411, Sausalito, CA 94965. Internet: http://www.asrn.org

# Retail Salespersons

(O*NET 41-2031.00)

## Significant Points

■ Good employment opportunities are expected because of the need to replace the large number of workers who leave the occupation each year.

■ Most salespersons work evenings and weekends, particularly during sales and other peak retail periods.

■ Employers look for people who enjoy working with others and who have tact, patience, an interest in sales work, a neat appearance, and the ability to communicate clearly.

## Nature of the Work

Consumers spend millions of dollars every day on merchandise and often rely on a store's sales force for help. Whether selling shoes, computer equipment, or automobiles, retail salespersons assist customers in finding what they are looking for and try to interest them in buying the merchandise. Most are able to describe a product's features, demonstrate its use, or show various models and colors.

In addition to selling, most retail salespersons—especially those who work in department and apparel stores—make out sales checks; receive cash, checks, debit, and charge payments; bag or package purchases; and give change and receipts. Depending on the hours they work, retail salespersons may have to open or close cash registers. This work may include counting the money in the register; separating charge slips, coupons, and exchange vouchers; and making deposits at the cash office. Salespersons often are held responsible for the contents of their registers, and repeated shortages are cause for dismissal in many organizations.

Retailers stress the importance of providing courteous and efficient service to remain competitive. For example, when a customer wants an item that is not on the sales floor, the salesperson may check the stockroom, place a special order, or call another store to locate the item.

For some sales jobs, particularly those involving expensive and complex items, retail salespersons need special knowledge or skills. For example, salespersons who sell automobiles must be able to explain the features of various models, the manufacturers' specifications, the types of options and financing available, and the warranty.

Salespersons also may handle returns and exchanges of merchandise, wrap gifts, and keep their work areas neat. In addition, they may help stock shelves or racks, arrange for mailing or delivery of purchases, mark price tags, take inventory, and prepare displays.

Frequently, salespersons must be aware of special sales and promotions. They also must recognize security risks and thefts and know how to handle or prevent such situations.

*Work environment.* Most salespersons in retail trade work in clean, comfortable, well-lit stores. However, they often stand for long periods and may need supervisory approval to leave the sales floor. They also may work outdoors if they sell items such as cars, plants, or lumber yard materials.

The Monday-through-Friday, 9-to-5 work week is the exception rather than the rule in retail trade. Most salespersons work evenings and weekends, particularly during sales and other peak retail periods. The end-of-year holiday season is the busiest time for most retailers. As a result, many employers limit the use of vacation time between Thanksgiving and the beginning of January.

This occupation offers many opportunities for part-time work and is especially appealing to students, retirees, and others seeking to supplement their income. More than 32 percent of retail salespersons worked part-time in 2006. However, most of those selling big-ticket items work full time and have substantial experience.

## Training, Other Qualifications, and Advancement

Retail salespeople typically learn their skills through on-the-job training. Although advancement opportunities are limited, having a college degree or a great deal of experience may help retail salespersons move into management positions.

*Education and training.* There usually are no formal education requirements for this type of work, although a high school diploma or the equivalent is often preferred. A college degree may be required for management trainee positions, especially in larger retail establishments.

In most small stores, an experienced employee or the store owner instructs newly hired sales personnel in making out sales checks and operating cash registers. In large stores, training programs are more formal and are usually conducted over several days. Topics discussed often include customer service, security, the store's policies and procedures, and how to work a cash register. Depending on the type of product they are selling, employees may be given additional specialized training by sales representatives. For example, those working in cosmetics receive instruction on the types of products the store offers and for whom the cosmetics would be most beneficial. Likewise, salespersons employed by motor vehicle dealers may be instructed on the technical details of standard and optional equipment available on new vehicle models. Since providing the best possible service to customers is a high priority for many employers, employees often are given periodic training to update and refine their skills.

*Other qualifications.* Employers look for people who enjoy working with others and who have the tact and patience to deal with difficult customers. Among other desirable characteristics are an interest in sales work, a neat appearance, and the ability to communicate clearly and effectively. The ability to speak more than one language may be helpful for employment in communities where people from various cultures live and shop. Before hiring a salesperson, some employers may conduct a background check, especially for a job selling high-priced items.

*Advancement.* Opportunities for advancement vary. In some small establishments, advancement is limited because one person—often the owner—does most of the managerial work. In others, some salespersons are promoted to assistant manager. Large retail businesses usually prefer to hire college graduates as management trainees, making a college education increasingly important. However, motivated and capable employees without college degrees still may advance to administrative or supervisory positions in large establishments.

As salespersons gain experience and seniority, they usually move to positions of greater responsibility and may be given their choice of departments in which to work. This often means moving to areas with higher potential earnings and commissions. The highest earnings potential usually lies in selling "big-ticket" items—such as cars, jewelry, furniture, and electronic equipment—although doing so often requires extensive knowledge of the product and an extraordinary talent for persuasion.

Retail selling experience may be an asset when applying for sales positions with larger retailers or in nonretail industries, such as financial services, wholesale trade, or manufacturing.

## Employment

Retail salespersons held about 4.5 million jobs in 2006. They worked in stores ranging from small specialty shops employing a few workers to giant department stores with hundreds of salespersons. In addition, some were self-employed representatives of direct-sales companies and mail-order houses. The largest employers of retail salespersons are department stores, clothing and clothing accessories stores, building material and garden equipment and supplies dealers, other general merchandise stores, and motor vehicle and parts dealers.

Because retail stores are found in every city and town, employment is distributed geographically in much the same way as the population.

## Job Outlook

Due to the high level of turnover in this occupation, opportunities are expected to be good. The average projected employment growth in this occupation reflects the expansion of the economy and consumer spending.

*Employment change.* Employment is expected to grow by 12 percent over the 2006–2016 decade, which is about as fast as the average for all occupations. In fact, due to the size of this occupation, retail salespersons will have one of the largest numbers of new jobs arise, about 557,000 over the projections decade. This growth reflects rising retail sales stemming from a growing population. Many retail establishments will continue to expand in size and number, leading to new retail sales positions. Since retail salespeople must be available to assist customers in person, this is not an occupation that will suffer negative effects from advancements in technology. To the contrary, software that integrates purchase transactions, inventory management, and purchasing has greatly changed retailing, but retail salespersons continue to be essential in dealing with customers. There will also be an increased demand for retail salespersons in warehouse clubs and supercenters, which sell a wide assortment of goods at low prices, since they continue to grow as many consumers prefer these stores.

Despite the growing popularity of electronic commerce, the impact of electronic commerce on employment of retail salespersons is expected to be minimal. Internet sales have not decreased the need for retail salespersons. Retail stores commonly use an online presence to complement their in-store sales; there are a limited number of Internet-only apparel and specialty stores. Retail salespersons will remain important in assuring customers, providing specialized service, and increasing customer satisfaction. Most shoppers continue to prefer to make their purchases in stores, and growth of retail sales will continue to generate employment growth in various retail establishments.

*Job prospects.* As in the past, employment opportunities for retail salespersons are expected to be good because of the need to replace the large number of workers who transfer to other occupations or leave the labor force each year. Warehouse clubs and supercenters are expected to have excellent job prospects as they continue to grow in popularity with consumers. In addition, many new jobs will be created for retail salespersons as businesses seek to expand operations and enhance customer service.

Opportunities for part-time work should be abundant, and demand will be strong for temporary workers during peak selling periods, such as the end-of-year holiday season. The availability of part-time and temporary work attracts many people seeking to supplement their income.

During economic downturns, sales volumes and the resulting demand for sales workers usually decline. Purchases of costly items, such as cars, appliances, and furniture, tend to be postponed during difficult economic times. In areas of high unemployment, sales of many types of goods decline. However, because many retail salespersons constantly transfer to other occupations in search of better pay or career opportunities, employers often can adjust employment levels simply by not replacing all those who leave.

## Earnings

Median hourly earnings of retail salespersons, including commissions, were $9.50 in May 2006. The middle 50 percent earned between $7.81 and $12.83 an hour. The lowest 10 percent earned less than $6.79, and the highest 10 percent earned more than $18.48 an hour. Median hourly earnings in the industries employing the largest numbers of retail salespersons in May 2006 were as follows:

Automobile dealers ...........................................$18.70

Building material and supplies dealers ....................11.37

Other general merchandise stores ...........................8.79

Department stores................................................8.70

Clothing stores ....................................................8.53

Many beginning or inexperienced workers earn the federal minimum wage of $5.85 an hour, but many states set minimum wages higher than the federal minimum. Under federal law, this wage will increase to $6.55 in the summer of 2008 and to $7.25 in the summer of 2009. In areas where employers have difficulty attracting and retaining workers, wages tend to be higher than the legislated minimum.

Compensation systems can vary by type of establishment and merchandise sold. Salespersons receive hourly wages, commissions, or a combination thereof. Under a commission system, salespersons receive a percentage of the sales they make. This system offers sales workers the opportunity to increase their earnings considerably, but they may find that their earnings strongly depend on their ability to sell their product and on the ups and downs of the economy.

**Projections data from the National Employment Matrix**

| Occupational Title | SOC Code | Employment, 2006 | Projected employment, 2016 | Change, 2006-16 | |
|---|---|---|---|---|---|
| | | | | Number | Percent |
| Retail salespersons ............................................................. | 41-2031 | 4,477,000 | 5,034,000 | 557,000 | 12 |

NOTE: Data in this table are rounded.

Benefits may be limited in smaller stores, but benefits in large establishments usually are comparable to those offered by other employers. In addition, nearly all salespersons are able to buy their store's merchandise at a discount, with the savings depending on the type of merchandise. Also, to bolster revenue, employers may use incentive programs such as awards, banquets, bonuses, and profit-sharing plans to promote teamwork among the sales staff.

## Related Occupations

Salespersons use sales techniques, coupled with their knowledge of merchandise, to assist customers and encourage purchases. Workers in other occupations who use these same skills include sales representatives, wholesale and manufacturing; securities, commodities, and financial services sales agents; counter and rental clerks; real estate brokers and sales agents; purchasing managers, buyers, and purchasing agents; insurance sales agents; sales engineers; and cashiers.

## Sources of Additional Information

Information on careers in retail sales may be obtained from the personnel offices of local stores or from state merchants' associations.

General information about retailing is available from

‣ National Retail Federation, 325 7th St. NW, Suite 1100, Washington, DC 20004.

Information about training for a career in automobile sales is available from

‣ National Automobile Dealers Association, Public Relations Department, 8400 Westpark Dr., McLean, VA 22102-3591. Internet: http://www.nada.org

# Roofers

(O*NET 47-2181.00)

## Significant Points

■ Most roofers learn their skills informally on the job; some roofers train through 3-year apprenticeships.

■ Most job openings will arise from the need to replace those who leave the occupation because the work is hot, strenuous, and dirty, causing many people to switch to jobs in other construction trades.

■ Demand for roofers is less susceptible to downturns in the economy than demand for other construction trades because most roofing work consists of repair and reroofing.

## Nature of the Work

A leaky roof can damage ceilings, walls, and furnishings. Roofers repair and install roofs made of tar or asphalt and gravel; rubber or thermoplastic; metal; or shingles to protect buildings and their contents from water damage. Repair and reroofing—replacing old roofs on existing buildings—makes up the majority of work for roofers.

There are two types of roofs—low-slope and steep-slope. Low-slope roofs rise 4 inches per horizontal foot or less and are installed in layers. Steep-slope roofs rise more than 4 inches per horizontal foot and are usually covered in shingles. Most commercial, industrial, and apartment buildings have low-slope roofs. Most houses have steep-slope roofs. Some roofers work on both types; others specialize.

Most low-slope roofs are covered with several layers of materials. Roofers first put a layer of insulation on the roof deck. Over the insulation, they often spread a coat of molten bitumen, a tarlike substance. Next, they install partially overlapping layers of roofing felt—a fabric saturated in bitumen—over the surface. Roofers use a mop to spread hot bitumen over the felt before adding another layer of felt. This seals the seams and makes the surface watertight. Roofers repeat these steps to build up the desired number of layers, called "plies." The top layer is glazed to make a smooth finish or has gravel embedded in the hot bitumen to create a rough surface.

An increasing number of low-slope roofs are covered with a single-ply membrane of waterproof rubber or thermoplastic compounds. Roofers roll these sheets over the roof's insulation and seal the seams. Adhesive, mechanical fasteners, or stone ballast hold the sheets in place. Roofers must make sure the building is strong enough to hold the stone ballast.

A small but growing number of buildings now have "green" roofs that incorporate plants. A "green" roof begins with a single or multiply waterproof layer. After it is proven to be leak free, roofers put a root barrier over it, and then layers of soil, in which trees and grass are planted. Roofers are usually responsible for making sure the roof is watertight and can withstand the weight and water needs of the plants.

Most residential steep-slope roofs are covered with shingles. To apply shingles, roofers first lay, cut, and tack 3-foot strips of roofing felt over the entire roof. Starting from the bottom edge, the roofer then staples or nails overlapping rows of shingles to the roof. Roofers measure and cut the felt and shingles to fit intersecting roof surfaces and to fit around vent pipes and chimneys. Wherever two roof surfaces intersect, or shingles reach a vent pipe or chimney, roofers cement or nail flashing-strips of metal or shingle over the joints to make them watertight. Finally, roofers cover exposed nail-heads with roofing cement or caulking to prevent water leakage. Roofers who use tile, metal shingles, or shakes (rough wooden shingles) follow a similar process.

Roofers also install equipment that requires cutting through roofs, such as ventilation ducts and attic fans. Some roofers are expert in waterproofing; some waterproof and dampproof masonry and concrete walls, floors, and foundations. To prepare surfaces for waterproofing, they hammer and chisel away rough spots or remove them with a rubbing brick, before applying a coat of liquid waterproofing compound. They also may paint or spray surfaces with a waterproofing material or attach waterproofing membrane to surfaces. Roofers usually spray a bitumen-based coating on interior or exterior surfaces when dampproofing.

*Work environment.* Roofing work is strenuous. It involves heavy lifting, as well as climbing, bending, and kneeling. Roofers work outdoors in all types of weather, particularly when making repairs. However, they rarely work when it rains or in very cold weather as ice can be dangerous. In northern states, roofing work is generally not performed during winter months. During the summer, roofers may work overtime to complete jobs quickly, especially before forecasted rainfall.

Workers risk slips or falls from scaffolds, ladders, or roofs or burns from hot bitumen, but safety precautions, can prevent most accidents. In addition, roofs can become extremely hot during the summer, causing heat-related illnesses. In 2005, the rate of injuries for roofing contractors in construction was almost twice that of workers overall.

## Training, Other Qualifications, and Advancement

Most roofers learn their skills informally by working as helpers for experienced roofers and by taking classes, including safety training, offered by their employers; some complete three-year apprenticeships.

*Education and training.* A high school education, or its equivalent, is helpful and so are courses in mechanical drawing and basic mathematics. Although most workers learn roofing as helpers for experienced workers, some roofers train through three-year apprenticeship programs administered by local union-management committees representing roofing contractors and locals of the United Union of Roofers, Waterproofers, and Allied Workers. Apprenticeship programs usually include at least 2,000 hours of paid on-the-job training each year, plus a minimum of 144 hours of classroom instruction a year in tools and their use, arithmetic, safety, and other topics. On-the-job training for apprentices is similar to the training given to helpers, but an apprenticeship program is more structured and comprehensive. Apprentices, for example, learn to dampproof and waterproof walls.

Trainees start by carrying equipment and material and erecting scaffolds and hoists. Within two or three months, they are taught to measure, cut, and fit roofing materials and, later, to lay asphalt or fiberglass shingles. Because some roofing materials are used infrequently, it can take several years to get experience working on all types of roofing.

*Other qualifications.* Good physical condition and good balance are essential for roofers. They cannot be afraid of heights. Experience with metal-working is helpful for workers who install metal roofing. Usually, apprentices must be at least 18 years old.

*Advancement.* Roofers may advance to become supervisors or estimators for a roofing contractor or become contractors themselves.

## Employment

Roofers held about 156,000 jobs in 2006. Almost all salaried roofers worked for roofing contractors. About 20 percent of roofers were self-employed. Many self-employed roofers specialized in residential work.

## Job Outlook

Most job openings will arise from turnover, because the work is hot, strenuous, and dirty, causing many people to switch to jobs in other construction trades. Faster-than-average employment growth is expected.

*Employment change.* Employment of roofers is expected to grow 14 percent between 2006 and 2016, which is faster than the average for all occupations. Roofs deteriorate faster than most other parts of buildings, and they need to be repaired or replaced more often. So as the number of buildings continues to increase, demand for roofers is expected to grow. In addition to repair work, the need to install roofs on new buildings is also expected to add to the demand for roofers.

*Job prospects.* Job opportunities for roofers will arise primarily because of the need to replace workers who leave the occupation. The proportion of roofers who leave the occupation each year is higher than in most construction trades—roofing work is hot, strenuous, and dirty, and a significant number of workers treat roofing as a temporary job until they find other work. Some roofers leave the occupation to go into other construction trades. Jobs should be easiest to find during spring and summer.

Employment of roofers who install new roofs, like that of many other construction workers, is sensitive to the fluctuations of the economy. Workers in these trades may experience periods of unemployment when the overall level of construction falls. On the other hand, shortages of these workers may occur in some areas during peak periods of building activity. Nevertheless, roofing is more heavily concentrated on repair and replacement rather than new installation, making demand for roofers less susceptible to the business cycle than it is for some other construction trades.

## Earnings

In May 2006, median hourly earnings of wage and salary roofers were $15.51. The middle 50 percent earned between $12.12 and $20.79. The lowest 10 percent earned less than $9.81, and the highest 10 percent earned more than $26.79. The median hourly earnings of roofers in the foundation, structure, and building exterior contractors industry were $15.54. Earnings may be reduced on occasion when poor weather limits the time roofers can work.

Apprentices usually start earning about 40 percent to 50 percent of the rate paid to experienced roofers. They receive periodic raises as they master the skills of the trade.

Some roofers are members of the United Union of Roofers, Waterproofers, and Allied Workers. Hourly wages and fringe benefits are generally higher for union workers.

**Projections data from the National Employment Matrix**

| Occupational Title | SOC Code | Employment, 2006 | Projected employment, 2016 | Change, 2006-16 | |
|---|---|---|---|---|---|
| | | | | Number | Percent |
| Roofers | 47-2181 | 156,000 | 179,000 | 22,000 | 14 |

NOTE: Data in this table are rounded.

## Related Occupations

Roofers use shingles, bitumen and gravel, single-ply plastic or rubber sheets, or other materials to waterproof building surfaces. Workers in other occupations who cover surfaces with special materials for protection and decoration include carpenters; carpet, floor, and tile installers and finishers; cement masons, concrete finishers, segmental pavers, and terrazzo workers; drywall installers, ceiling tile installers, and tapers; plasterers and stucco masons; and sheet metal workers.

## Sources of Additional Information

For information about apprenticeships or job opportunities in roofing, contact local roofing contractors, a local chapter of the roofers union, a local joint union-management apprenticeship committee, or the nearest office of your state employment service or apprenticeship agency. You can also find information on the registered apprenticeship system with links to state apprenticeship programs on the U.S. Department of Labor's Web site: http://www.doleta.gov/atels_bat. Apprenticeship information is also available from the U.S. Department of Labor's toll free helpline: 1 (877) 872-5627.

For information about the work of roofers, contact

▸ National Roofing Contractors Association, 10255 W. Higgins Rd., Suite 600, Rosemont, IL 60018-5607. Internet: http://www.nrca.net

▸ United Union of Roofers, Waterproofers, and Allied Workers, 1660 L St. NW, Suite 800, Washington, DC 20036. Internet: http://www.unionroofers.org

For general information on apprenticeships and how to get them, see the *Occupational Outlook Quarterly* article "Apprenticeships: Career training, credentials—and a paycheck in your pocket," online at http://www.bls.gov/opub/ooq/2002/summer/art01.pdf and in print at many libraries and career centers.

# Sales Representatives, Wholesale and Manufacturing

(O*NET 41-4011.00 and 41-4012.00)

## Significant Points

■ Competition for jobs is expected, but opportunities will be best for those with a college degree, the appropriate technical expertise, and the personal traits necessary for successful selling.

■ Job prospects for sales representatives will be better for those working with essential goods, since the demand for these products do not fluctuate with the economy.

■ Earnings of sales representatives are relatively high and usually are based on a combination of salary and commission.

## Nature of the Work

Sales representatives are an important part of manufacturers' and wholesalers' success. Regardless of the type of product they sell, sales representatives' primary duties are to make wholesale and retail buyers and purchasing agents interested in their merchandise and to address any of their clients' questions and concerns. Sales representatives demonstrate their products and explain how using those products can reduce costs and increase sales.

Sales representatives may represent one or several manufacturers or wholesale distributors by selling one product or a complementary line of products. The clients of sales representatives span almost every industry and include other manufacturers, wholesale and retail establishments, construction contractors, and government agencies.

The process of promoting and selling products can take up to several months. Sales representatives present their products to a customer and negotiate the sale. Whether in person or over the phone, they can make a persuasive sales pitch and often will immediately answer technical and non-technical questions about the products. They may also record any interactions with clients and their respective sales to better match their future needs and sales potential.

There are two major categories of products that sales representatives work with: technical and scientific products and all products except technical and scientific products. Technical and scientific products may include anything from agricultural and mechanical equipment to electrical and pharmaceutical goods. Products included in the later category are more everyday items, including goods such as food, office supplies, and apparel.

Sales representatives stay abreast of new products and the changing needs of their customers in a variety of ways. They attend trade shows at which new products and technologies are showcased. They also attend conferences and conventions to meet other sales representatives and clients and discuss new product developments. In addition, the entire sales force may participate in company-sponsored meetings to review sales performance, product development, sales goals, and profitability.

Frequently, sales representatives who lack the necessary expertise about a given product may team with a technical expert. In this arrangement, the technical expert—sometimes a sales engineer—attends the sales presentation to explain the product and answer questions or concerns. The sales representative makes the preliminary contact with customers, introduces the company's product, and closes the sale. The representative is then able to spend more time maintaining and soliciting accounts and less time acquiring technical knowledge. After the sale, representatives may make follow-up visits to ensure that the equipment is functioning properly and may even help train customers' employees to operate and maintain new equipment. Those selling technical goods may also help set up the installation. Those selling consumer goods often suggest how and where merchandise should be displayed. When working with retailers, they may help arrange promotional programs, store displays, and advertising.

Obtaining new accounts is an important part of the job for all sales representatives. Sales representatives follow leads from other clients, track advertisements in trade journals, participate in trade shows and conferences, and may visit potential clients unannounced. In addition, they may spend time meeting with and entertaining prospective clients during evenings and weekends.

Sales representatives have several duties beyond selling products. They analyze sales statistics; prepare reports; and handle administrative duties, such as filing expense accounts, scheduling appointments, and making travel plans. They also read about new and existing products and monitor the sales, prices, and products of their competitors.

Sales representatives, regardless of where they are employed, may work in either inside sales or outside "field" sales. *Inside sales representatives* may spend a lot of their time on the phone, taking orders and resolving any problems or complaints about the merchandise. These sales representatives typically do not leave the office. *Outside sales representatives* spend much of their time traveling to and visiting with current clients and prospective buyers. During a sales call, they discuss the client's needs and suggest how their merchandise or services can meet those needs. They may show samples or catalogs that describe items their company stocks and inform customers about prices, availability, and ways in which their products can save money and boost productivity. Given that a number of manufacturers and wholesalers sell similar products, sales representatives must emphasize any unique qualities of their products and services. Since many sales representatives sell several complementary products made by different manufacturers, they may take a broad approach to their customers' business. For example, sales representatives may help install new equipment and train employees in its use.

Sales representatives working at an independent sales agency usually sell several products from multiple manufacturers. Additionally, these firms may only cover a certain territory, ranging from local areas to several states. These independent firms are called "manufacturers' representative companies" because their selling is on behalf of the manufacturers.

Depending on where they work, sales representatives may have different job titles. *Manufacturers' agents* or *manufacturers' representatives*, for example, are self-employed sales workers who own independent firms which contract their services to all types of manufacturing companies.

*Work environment.* Some sales representatives have large territories and travel considerably. Because a sales region may cover several states, representatives may be away from home for several days or weeks at a time. Others work near their home base and travel mostly by car. Sales representatives often are on their feet for long periods and may carry heavy sample products, necessitating some physical stamina.

Sales representatives may work more than 40 hours per week because of the nature of the work and the amount of travel. Since sales calls take place during regular working hours, most of the planning and paperwork involved with sales must be completed during the evening and on the weekends. Although the hours are long and often irregular, many sales representatives working for independent sales companies have the freedom to determine their own schedules.

Dealing with different types of people can be stimulating but demanding. Sales representatives often face competition from representatives of other companies. Companies usually set goals or quotas that representatives are expected to meet. Because their earnings depend on commissions, manufacturers' representatives are also under the added pressure to maintain and expand their clientele.

# Training, Other Qualifications, and Advancement

Many employers hire individuals with previous sales experience who lack a college degree, but hiring candidates with a college degree is becoming increasingly common. Regardless of educational background, factors such as personality, the ability to sell, and familiarity with brands are essential to being a successful sales representative.

*Education and training.* Since there is no formal educational requirement for sales representative, their levels of education varies. Having a bachelor's degree can be highly desirable, especially for sales representatives who work with technical and scientific products. This is because technological advances result in new and more complex products. Additionally, manufacturers' representatives who start their own independent sales company might have an MBA. As shown in the tabulation below, in 2006 many sales representatives had a bachelor's degree, and many others had some college classes. Some, however, had no degree or formal training, but these workers often had sales experience or potential.

High school graduate or less ....................................27%
Some college, no degree.........................................19
Associate's degree ................................................9
Bachelor's degree ...............................................38
Graduate degree .................................................6

Many sales representatives attend seminars in sales techniques or take courses in marketing, economics, communication, or even a foreign language to provide the extra edge needed to make sales. Often, companies have formal training programs for beginning sales representatives lasting up to two years. However, most businesses accelerate these programs to reduce costs and expedite the returns from training. In some programs, trainees rotate among jobs in plants and offices to learn all phases of production, installation, and distribution of the product. In others, trainees take formal classroom instruction at the plant, followed by on-the-job training under the supervision of a field sales manager.

Regardless of where they work, new employees may get training by accompanying experienced workers on their sales calls. As they gain familiarity with the firm's products and clients, the new workers are given increasing responsibility until they are eventually assigned their own territory. As businesses experience greater competition, representatives face more pressure to produce sales.

*Other qualifications.* For sales representative jobs, companies seek the best and brightest individuals who have the personality and desire to sell. Those who want to become sales representatives should be goal oriented, persuasive, and able to work well both independently and as part of a team. A pleasant personality and appearance, the ability to communicate well with people, and problem-solving skills are highly valued. Patience and perseverance are also keys to completing a sale, which can take up to several months. Sales representatives also need to be able to work with computers since computers are increasingly used to place and track orders and to monitor inventory levels.

Manufacturers' representatives who operate a sales agency must also manage their business. This requires organizational and general business skills, as well as knowledge of accounting, marketing, and administration. Usually, however, sales representatives gain experience and recognition with a manufacturer or wholesaler before becoming self-employed.

*Certification and advancement.* Certifications are available that provide formal recognition of the skills of sales representatives, wholesale and manufacturing. Many obtaining certification in this profession have either the Certified Professional Manufacturers' Representative (CPMR) or the Certified Sales Professional (CSP), offered by the Manufacturers' Representatives Education Research Foundation. Certification typically involves completion of formal training and passing an examination.

Frequently, promotion takes the form of an assignment to a larger account or territory where commissions are likely to be greater. Those who have good sales records and leadership ability may advance to higher level positions such as sales supervisor, district manager, or vice president of sales. Others find opportunities in purchasing, advertising, or marketing research.

Advancement opportunities typically depend on whether the sales representatives are working directly for a manufacturer or wholesaler or if they are working with an independent sales agency. Experienced sales representatives working directly for a manufacturer or wholesaler may move into jobs as sales trainers and instruct new employees on selling techniques and company policies and procedures. Some leave the manufacturer or wholesaler and start their own independent sales company. Those working for an independent

sales company can also advance by going into business for themselves or by receiving higher pay.

## Employment

Manufacturers' and wholesale sales representatives held about 2 million jobs in 2006. About 21 percent worked with technical and scientific products. Almost 60 percent of all representatives worked in wholesale trade. Others were employed in manufacturing, retail trade, information, and construction. Because of the diversity of products and services sold, employment opportunities are available throughout the country in a wide range of industries. In addition to those working directly for a firm, some sales representatives are self-employed manufacturers' agents. They often form small sales firms that may start with just themselves and gradually grow to employ a small staff.

## Job Outlook

Job growth of sales representatives, wholesale and manufacturing, is expected to be average, but keen competition is expected for these highly paid sales jobs.

*Employment change.* Employment of sales representatives, wholesale and manufacturing, is expected to grow by 9 percent between 2006 and 2016, which is about as fast as the average for all occupations. Given the size of this occupation, a large number of new jobs, about 182,000 will arise over the projections decade. This is primarily because of continued growth in the variety and number of goods sold throughout the economy. Technological progress will also have an impact on job growth. Sales representatives can help ensure that retailers offer the latest technology available to their customers or that businesses acquire the right technical products that will increase their efficiency in operations. Advances in technology will therefore lead to more products being demanded and sold, and thus growth in the sales representative profession.

At the same time, however, computers and other information technology are also making sales representatives more effective and productive, allowing sales representatives to handle more clients, and thus hindering job growth somewhat.

Employment growth will be greatest in independent sales companies as manufacturers and wholesalers continue to outsource sales activities to independent agents rather than using in-house or direct sales workers. Independent agent companies are paid only if they sell, a practice that reduces the overhead cost to their clients. Also, by using agents who usually contract their services to more than one company, companies can share costs of the agents with each other. As the customers of independent agents continue to merge with other companies, independent agent companies and other wholesale trade firms will also merge with each other in response to better serve their clients.

*Job prospects.* Earnings of sales representatives, wholesale and manufacturing are relatively high, especially for those selling technical and scientific products, so keen competition is likely for jobs. Prospects will be best for those with a solid technical background and the personal traits necessary for successful selling. Opportunities will be better for sales representatives working for an independent sales company as opposed to working directly for a

**Projections data from the National Employment Matrix**

| Occupational Title | SOC Code | Employment, 2006 | Projected employment, 2016 | Change, 2006-16 | |
|---|---|---|---|---|---|
| | | | | Number | Percent |
| Sales representatives, wholesale and manufacturing ........................ | 41-4000 | 1,973,000 | 2,155,000 | 182,000 | 9 |
| Sales representatives, wholesale and manufacturing, technical and scientific products ................................................................. | 41-4011 | 411,000 | 462,000 | 51,000 | 12 |
| Sales representatives, wholesale and manufacturing, except technical and scientific products ............................................. | 41-4012 | 1,562,000 | 1,693,000 | 131,000 | 8 |

NOTE: Data in this table are rounded.

manufacturer because manufacturers are expected to continue contracting out field sales duties.

Opportunities for sales representatives in manufacturing are likely to be best for those selling products for which there is strong demand. Jobs will be most plentiful in small wholesale and manufacturing firms because a growing number of these companies will rely on agents to market their products as a way to control their costs and expand their customer base.

Employment opportunities and earnings may fluctuate from year to year because sales are affected by changing economic conditions, legislative issues, and consumer preferences. Also, many job openings will result from the need to replace workers who transfer to other occupations or leave the labor force.

## Earnings

Median annual earnings of wage and salary sales representatives, wholesale and manufacturing, technical and scientific products, were $64,440, including commissions, in May 2006. The middle 50 percent earned between $45,630 and $91,090 a year. The lowest 10 percent earned less than $33,410, and the highest 10 percent earned more than $121,850 a year. Median annual earnings in the industries employing the largest numbers of sales representatives, technical and scientific products, were as follows:

Computer systems design and related services ......$75,240

Wholesale electronic markets and agents
and brokers ...................................................69,510

Professional and commercial equipment and
supplies merchant wholesalers ..........................67,700

Drugs and druggists' sundries merchant
wholesalers ...................................................66,210

Electrical and electronic goods merchant
wholesalers ...................................................61,000

Median annual earnings of wage and salary sales representatives, wholesale and manufacturing, except technical and scientific products, were $49,610, including commission, in May 2006. The middle 50 percent earned between $35,460 and $71,650 a year. The lowest 10 percent earned less than $26,030, and the highest 10 percent earned more than $101,030 a year. Median annual earnings in the industries employing the largest numbers of sales representatives, except technical and scientific products, were as follows:

Wholesale electronic markets and agents
and brokers ..................................................$54,900

Professional and commercial equipment and
supplies merchant wholesalers ..........................49,730

Machinery, equipment, and supplies merchant
wholesalers ...................................................48,620

Grocery and related product wholesalers ...............46,150

Miscellaneous nondurable goods merchant
wholesalers ...................................................42,530

Compensation methods for those representatives working for an independent sales company vary significantly by the type of firm and the product sold. Most employers use a combination of salary and commissions or salary plus bonus. Commissions usually are based on the amount of sales, whereas bonuses may depend on individual performance, on the performance of all sales workers in the group or district, or on the company's performance. Unlike those working directly for a manufacturer or wholesaler, sales representatives working for an independent sales company usually are not reimbursed for expenses. Depending on the type of product or products they are selling, their experience in the field, and the number of clients they have, they can earn significantly more or less than those working in direct sales for a manufacturer or wholesaler.

In addition to their earnings, sales representatives working directly for a manufacturer or wholesaler usually are reimbursed for expenses such as transportation costs, meals, hotels, and entertaining customers. They often receive benefits such as health and life insurance, pension plans, vacation and sick leave, personal use of a company car, and frequent flyer mileage. Some companies offer incentives such as free vacation trips or gifts for outstanding sales workers.

## Related Occupations

Sales representatives, wholesale and manufacturing, must have sales ability and knowledge of the products they sell. Other occupations that require similar skills include advertising, marketing, promotions, public relations, and sales managers; insurance sales agents; purchasing managers, buyers, and purchasing agents; real estate brokers and sales agents; retail salespersons; sales engineers; and securities, commodities, and financial services sales agents.

## Sources of Additional Information

Information on careers for manufacturers' representatives and sales agents is available from

▸ Manufacturers' Agents National Association, One Spectrum Pointe, Suite 150, Lake Forest, CA 92630. Internet: http://www.manaonline.org

▸ Manufacturers' Representatives Educational Research Foundation, 8329 Cole St., Arvada, CO 80005. Internet: http://www.mrerf.org

# Sales Worker Supervisors

(O*NET 41-1011.00 and 41-1012.00)

## Significant Points

- Overall employment is projected to grow more slowly than average.
- Applicants with retail experience should have the best job opportunities.
- Long, irregular hours, including evenings and weekends, are common.

## Nature of the Work

Sales worker supervisors oversee the work of sales and related workers, such as retail salespersons, cashiers, customer service representatives, stock clerks and order fillers, sales engineers, and wholesale sales representatives. Sales worker supervisors are responsible for interviewing, hiring, and training employees. They also may prepare work schedules and assign workers to specific duties. Many of these supervisors hold job titles such as *sales manager* or *department manager*. Under the occupational classification system used in this book, however, workers who mainly supervise workers and who do not focus on broader managerial issues of planning and strategy are classified as *supervisors*.

In retail establishments, sales worker supervisors ensure that customers receive satisfactory service and quality goods. They also answer customers' inquiries, deal with complaints, and sometimes handle purchasing, budgeting, and accounting.

Responsibilities vary with the size and type of establishment. As the size of retail stores and the types of goods and services increase, supervisors tend to specialize in one department or one aspect of merchandising. Sales worker supervisors in large retail establishments are often referred to as department supervisors or managers. They provide day-to-day oversight of individual departments, such as shoes, cosmetics, or housewares in department stores; produce or meat in grocery stores; and car sales in automotive dealerships. Department supervisors establish and implement policies, goals, and procedures for their specific departments; coordinate activities with other department heads; and strive for smooth operations within their departments. They supervise employees who price and ticket goods and place them on display; clean and organize shelves, displays, and inventories in stockrooms; and inspect merchandise to ensure that nothing is outdated. Sales worker supervisors also review inventory and sales records, develop merchandising techniques, and coordinate sales promotions. In addition, they may greet and assist customers and promote sales and good public relations.

Sales worker supervisors in non-retail establishments oversee and coordinate the activities of sales workers who sell industrial products, insurance policies, or services such as advertising, financial, or Internet services. They may prepare budgets, make personnel decisions, devise sales-incentive programs, and approve sales contracts.

In small or independent companies and retail stores, sales worker supervisors not only directly supervise sales associates, but they also are responsible for the operation of the entire company or store. Some are self-employed business or store owners.

*Work environment.* Most sales worker supervisors have offices. In retail trade, their offices are within the stores, usually close to the areas they oversee. Although they spend some time in the office completing merchandise orders or arranging work schedules, a large portion of their workday is spent on the sales floor, supervising employees or selling.

Work hours of supervisors vary greatly among establishments because work schedules usually depend on customers' needs. Supervisors generally work at least 40 hours a week. Long, irregular hours are common, particularly during sales, holidays, and busy shopping seasons and at times when inventory is taken. Supervisors are expected to work some evenings and weekends but usually are given a day off during the week. Hours can change weekly, and supervisors sometimes must report to work on short notice, especially when employees are absent. Independent owners often can set their own schedules, but hours must be convenient to customers.

## Training, Other Qualifications, and Advancement

Sales worker supervisors usually gain knowledge of management principles and practices through work experience. Many supervisors begin their careers on the sales floor as salespersons, cashiers, or customer service representatives. These workers should be patient, decisive, and sales-oriented.

*Education and training.* The educational backgrounds of sales worker supervisors vary widely. Supervisors who have postsecondary education often hold associate or bachelor's degrees in liberal arts, social sciences, business, or management. Recommended high school or college courses include those related to business, such as accounting, marketing, management, and sales, and those related to social science, such as psychology, sociology, and communication. Supervisors also must know how to use computers because almost all cash registers, inventory control systems, and sales quotes and contracts are computerized. To gain experience, many college students participate in internship programs that usually are developed jointly by schools and businesses.

Having previous sales experience is usually a requirement for becoming a sales worker supervisor. Most sales worker supervisors have retail sales experience or experience as a customer service representative. In these positions, they learn merchandising, customer service, and the basic policies and procedures of the company.

The type and amount of training available to supervisors varies by company. Many national retail chains and companies have formal training programs for management trainees that include both classroom and on-site training. Training time may be as brief as one week or may last more than one year, giving trainees experience during all sales seasons.

Ordinarily, classroom training includes topics such as interviewing, customer service skills, inventory management, employee relations, and scheduling. Management trainees may work in one specific department while training on the job, or they may rotate through several departments to gain a well-rounded knowledge of the company's operation. Training programs for retail franchises are gener-

**Projections data from the National Employment Matrix**

| Occupational Title | SOC Code | Employment, 2006 | Projected employment, 2016 | Change, 2006-16 | |
|---|---|---|---|---|---|
| | | | | Number | Percent |
| Supervisors, sales workers ................................................................ | 41-1000 | 2,206,000 | 2,296,000 | 91,000 | 4 |
| First-line supervisors/managers of retail sales workers ............... | 41-1011 | 1,676,000 | 1,747,000 | 71,000 | 4 |
| First-line supervisors/managers of non-retail sales workers ......... | 41-1012 | 530,000 | 549,000 | 19,000 | 4 |

NOTE: Data in this table are rounded.

ally extensive, covering all functions of the company's operation, including budgeting, marketing, management, finance, purchasing, product preparation, human resource management, and compensation. College graduates usually can enter management training programs directly, without much experience.

*Other qualifications.* Sales worker supervisors must get along with all types of people. They need initiative, self-discipline, good judgment, and decisiveness. Patience and a conciliatory temperament are necessary when dealing with demanding customers. Supervisors also must be able to motivate, organize, and direct the work of subordinates and communicate clearly and persuasively with customers and other supervisors.

*Advancement.* Supervisors who display leadership and team-building skills, self-confidence, motivation, and decisiveness become candidates for promotion to assistant manager or manager. A postsecondary degree may speed their advancement into management because employers view it as a sign of motivation and maturity—qualities deemed important for promotion to more responsible positions. In many retail establishments, managers are promoted from within the company. In small retail establishments, where the number of positions is limited, advancement to a higher management position may come slowly. Large establishments often have extensive career ladder programs and may offer supervisors the opportunity to transfer to another store in the chain or to the central office. Although promotions may occur more quickly in large establishments, some managers may need to relocate every several years in order to advance.

Supervisors also can become advertising, marketing, promotions, public relations, and sales managers—workers who coordinate marketing plans, monitor sales, and propose advertisements and promotions—or purchasing managers, buyers, or purchasing agents—workers who purchase goods and supplies for their organization or for resale.

Some supervisors who have worked in their industry for a long time open their own stores or sales firms. However, retail trade and sales occupations are highly competitive, and although many independent owners succeed, some fail to cover expenses and eventually go out of business. To prosper, owners usually need good business sense and strong customer service and public relations skills.

# Employment

Sales worker supervisors held about 2.2 million jobs in 2006. Approximately 37 percent were self-employed, most of whom were store owners. About 44 percent of sales worker supervisors were wage-and-salary workers employed in the retail sector; some of the largest employers were grocery stores, department stores, motor vehicle and parts dealers, and clothing and clothing accessory stores.

The remaining sales worker supervisors worked in non-retail establishments.

# Job Outlook

Despite slower than average growth, retail sales worker supervisors with previous experience in sales are expected to have good job prospects because of the large size of the occupation and the need to replace workers who leave their positions.

*Employment change.* Employment of sales worker supervisors is expected to grow by 4 percent between 2006 and 2016, which is more slowly than the average for all occupations. Growth in the occupation will be limited as retail companies increase the responsibilities of retail salespersons and existing sales worker supervisors.

The Internet and electronic commerce are creating new opportunities to reach and communicate with potential customers. Some firms are hiring Internet sales supervisors, who are in charge of maintaining an Internet site and answering inquiries relating to the product, to prices, and to the terms of delivery. However, Internet sales and electronic commerce may reduce the number of additional sales workers needed in stores, thus reducing the total number of additional supervisors required. Overall, the impact of electronic commerce on employment of sales worker supervisors should be minimal.

Projected employment growth of sales worker supervisors will mirror, in part, the patterns of employment growth in the industries in which they work. For example, faster-than-average employment growth is expected in many of the rapidly growing service-providing industries. In contrast, the number of self-employed sales worker supervisors is expected to grow slowly as independent retailers face increasing competition from national chains.

Unlike mid-level and top-level managers, retail store managers generally will not be affected by the restructuring and consolidation taking place at the corporate headquarters of many retail chains.

*Job prospects.* Candidates who have retail experience—as a salesperson, cashier, or customer service representative, for example—will have the best opportunities for jobs as supervisors, especially in retail establishments. Stronger competition for supervisory jobs is expected in non-retail establishments, particularly those with the most attractive earnings and work environment.

Some of the job openings over the next decade will occur as experienced supervisors move into higher levels of management, transfer to other occupations, or leave the labor force. However, these job openings will not be great in number since, as with other supervisory and managerial occupations, the separation rate is low. This is the case especially for non-retail sales worker supervisors.

## Earnings

Salaries of sales worker supervisors vary substantially, depending on a worker's level of responsibility and length of service and the type, size, and location of the firm.

Salaried supervisors of retail sales workers had median annual earnings of $33,960, including commissions, in May 2006. The middle 50 percent earned between $26,490 and $44,570 a year. The lowest 10 percent earned less than $21,420, and the highest 10 percent earned more than $59,710 a year. Median annual earnings in the industries employing the largest numbers of salaried supervisors of retail sales workers were as follows:

| | |
|---|---|
| Building material and supplies dealers | $35,820 |
| Grocery stores | 33,390 |
| Clothing stores | 33,140 |
| Gasoline stations | 29,270 |
| Other general merchandise stores | 28,870 |

Salaried supervisors of nonretail sales workers had median annual earnings of, $65,510, including commissions, in May 2006. The middle 50 percent earned between $48,900 and $94,670 a year. The lowest 10 percent earned less than $34,840, and the highest 10 percent earned more than $135,270 a year. Median annual earnings in the industries employing the largest numbers of salaried supervisors of nonretail sales workers were as follows:

| | |
|---|---|
| Professional and commercial equipment and supplies merchant wholesalers | $80,650 |
| Wholesale electronic markets and agents and brokers | 78,260 |
| Machinery, equipment, and supplies merchant wholesalers | 65,660 |
| Postal service | 58,640 |
| Business support services | 45,490 |

Compensation systems vary by type of establishment and by merchandise sold. Many supervisors receive a commission or a combination of salary and commission. Under a commission system, supervisors receive a percentage of department or store sales. Thus, these supervisors' earnings depend on their ability to sell their product and the condition of the economy. Those who sell large amounts of merchandise or exceed sales goals often receive bonuses or other awards.

## Related Occupations

Sales worker supervisors serve customers, supervise workers, and direct and coordinate the operations of an establishment. Workers with similar responsibilities include financial managers, food service managers, lodging managers, office and administrative support worker supervisors and managers, and medical and health services managers.

## Sources of Additional Information

Information on employment opportunities for sales worker supervisors may be obtained from the employment offices of various retail establishments or from state employment service offices.

General information on management careers in retail establishments is available from

▶ National Retail Federation, 325 7th St. NW, Suite 1100, Washington, DC 20004.

Information about management careers and training programs in the motor vehicle dealers industry is available from

▶ National Automobile Dealers Association, Public Relations Dept., 8400 Westpark Dr., McLean, VA 22102-3591. Internet: http://www.nada.org

Information about management careers in convenience stores is available from

▶ National Association of Convenience Stores, 1600 Duke St., Alexandria, VA 22314-3436.

# Science Technicians

(O*NET 19-4011.00, 19-4011.01, 19-4011.02, 19-4021.00, 19-4031.00, 19-4041.00, 19-4041.01, 19-4041.02, 19-4051.00, 19-4051.01, 19-4051.02, 19-4091.00, 19-4092.00, 19-4093.00, and 19-4099.99)

## Significant Points

■ Science technicians in production jobs can be employed on day, evening, or night shifts; other technicians work outdoors, sometimes in remote locations.

■ Most science technicians need an associate degree or a certificate in applied science or science-related technology; biological and forensic science technicians usually need a bachelor's degree.

■ Projected job growth varies among occupational specialties; for example, forensic science technicians will grow much faster than average, while chemical technicians will grow more slowly than average.

■ Job opportunities are expected to be best for graduates of applied science technology programs who are well trained on equipment used in laboratories or production facilities.

## Nature of the Work

Science technicians use the principles and theories of science and mathematics to solve problems in research and development and to help invent and improve products and processes. However, their jobs are more practically oriented than those of scientists. Technicians set up, operate, and maintain laboratory instruments, monitor experiments, make observations, calculate and record results, and often develop conclusions. They must keep detailed logs of all of their work. Those who perform production work monitor manufacturing processes and may ensure quality by testing products for proper proportions of ingredients, for purity, or for strength and durability.

As laboratory instrumentation and procedures have become more complex, the role of science technicians in research and development has expanded. In addition to performing routine tasks, many technicians, under the direction of scientists, now develop and adapt laboratory procedures to achieve the best results, interpret data, and devise solutions to problems. Technicians must develop expert knowledge of laboratory equipment so that they can adjust settings when necessary and recognize when equipment is malfunctioning.

Most science technicians specialize, learning their skills and working in the same disciplines in which scientists work. Occupational titles, therefore, tend to follow the same structure as those for scientists.

*Agricultural and food science technicians* work with related scientists to conduct research, development, and testing on food and other agricultural products. Agricultural technicians are involved in food, fiber, and animal research, production, and processing. Some conduct tests and experiments to improve the yield and quality of crops or to increase the resistance of plants and animals to disease, insects, or other hazards. Other agricultural technicians breed animals for the purpose of investigating nutrition. Food science technicians assist food scientists and technologists in research and development, production technology, and quality control. For example, food science technicians may conduct tests on food additives and preservatives to ensure compliance with Food and Drug Administration regulations regarding color, texture, and nutrients. These technicians analyze, record, and compile test results; order supplies to maintain laboratory inventory; and clean and sterilize laboratory equipment.

*Biological technicians* work with biologists studying living organisms. Many assist scientists who conduct medical research—helping to find a cure for cancer or AIDS, for example. Those who work in pharmaceutical companies help develop and manufacture medicine. Those working in the field of microbiology generally work as laboratory assistants, studying living organisms and infectious agents. Biological technicians also analyze organic substances, such as blood, food, and drugs. Biological technicians working in biotechnology apply knowledge and techniques gained from basic research, including gene splicing and recombinant DNA, and apply them to product development.

*Chemical technicians* work with chemists and chemical engineers, developing and using chemicals and related products and equipment. Generally, there are two types of chemical technicians: research technicians who work in experimental laboratories and process control technicians who work in manufacturing or other industrial plants. Many chemical technicians working in research and development conduct a variety of laboratory procedures, from routine process control to complex research projects. For example, they may collect and analyze samples of air and water to monitor pollution levels, or they may produce compounds through complex organic synthesis. Most *process technicians* work in manufacturing, testing packaging for design, integrity of materials, and environmental acceptability. Often, process technicians who work in plants focus on quality assurance, monitoring product quality or production processes and developing new production techniques. A few work in shipping to provide technical support and expertise.

*Environmental science and protection technicians* perform laboratory and field tests to monitor environmental resources and determine the contaminants and sources of pollution in the environment. They may collect samples for testing or be involved in abating and controlling sources of environmental pollution. Some are responsible for waste management operations, control and management of hazardous materials inventory, or general activities involving regu-

latory compliance. Many environmental science technicians employed at private consulting firms work directly under the supervision of an environmental scientist.

*Forensic science technicians* investigate crimes by collecting and analyzing physical evidence. Often, they specialize in areas such as DNA analysis or firearm examination, performing tests on weapons or on substances such as fiber, glass, hair, tissue, and body fluids to determine their significance to the investigation. Proper collection and storage methods are important to protect the evidence. Forensic science technicians also prepare reports to document their findings and the laboratory techniques used, and they may provide information and expert opinions to investigators. When criminal cases come to trial, forensic science technicians often give testimony as expert witnesses on laboratory findings by identifying and classifying substances, materials, and other evidence collected at the scene of a crime. Some forensic science technicians work closely with other experts or technicians. For example, a forensic science technician may consult either a medical expert about the exact time and cause of a death or another technician who specializes in DNA typing in hopes of matching a DNA type to a suspect.

*Forest and conservation technicians* compile data on the size, content, and condition of forest land. These workers usually work in a forest under the supervision of a forester, doing specific tasks such as measuring timber, supervising harvesting operations, assisting in road building operations, and locating property lines and features. They also may gather basic information, such as data on populations of trees, disease and insect damage, tree seedling mortality, and conditions that may pose a fire hazard. In addition, forest and conservation technicians train and lead forest and conservation workers in seasonal activities, such as planting tree seedlings, and maintaining recreational facilities. Increasing numbers of forest and conservation technicians work in urban forestry—the study of individual trees in cities—and other nontraditional specialties, rather than in forests or rural areas.

*Geological and petroleum technicians* measure and record physical and geologic conditions in oil or gas wells, using advanced instruments lowered into the wells or analyzing the mud from the wells. In oil and gas exploration, technicians collect and examine geological data or test geological samples to determine their petroleum content and their mineral and element composition. Some petroleum technicians, called scouts, collect information about oil well and gas well drilling operations, geological and geophysical prospecting, and land or lease contracts.

*Nuclear technicians* operate nuclear test and research equipment, monitor radiation, and assist nuclear engineers and physicists in research. Some also operate remote controlled equipment to manipulate radioactive materials or materials exposed to radioactivity. Workers who control nuclear reactors are classified as *nuclear power reactor operators* and are not included in this statement.

Other science technicians perform a wide range of activities. Some collect weather information or assist oceanographers; others work as laser technicians or radiographers.

**Work environment.** Science technicians work under a wide variety of conditions. Most work indoors, usually in laboratories, and have regular hours. Some occasionally work irregular hours to monitor experiments that cannot be completed during regular working hours.

Production technicians often work in 8-hour shifts around the clock. Others, such as agricultural, forest and conservation, geological and petroleum, and environmental science and protection technicians, perform much of their work outdoors, sometimes in remote locations.

Advances in automation and information technology require technicians to operate more sophisticated laboratory equipment. Science technicians make extensive use of computers, electronic measuring equipment, and traditional experimental apparatus.

Some science technicians may be exposed to hazards from equipment, chemicals, or toxic materials. Chemical technicians sometimes work with toxic chemicals or radioactive isotopes; nuclear technicians may be exposed to radiation, and biological technicians sometimes work with disease-causing organisms or radioactive agents. Forensic science technicians often are exposed to human body fluids and firearms. However, these working conditions pose little risk if proper safety procedures are followed. For forensic science technicians, collecting evidence from crime scenes can be distressing and unpleasant.

## Training, Other Qualifications, and Advancement

Most science technicians need an associate degree or a certificate in applied science or science-related technology. Biological and forensic science technicians usually need a bachelor's degree. Science technicians with a high school diploma and no college degree typically begin work as trainees under the direct supervision of a more experienced technician, and eventually earn a two-year degree in science technology.

*Education and training.* There are several ways to qualify for a job as a science technician. Many employers prefer applicants who have at least two years of specialized training or an associate degree in applied science or science-related technology. Because employers' preferences vary, however, some science technicians have a bachelor's degree in chemistry, biology, or forensic science or have completed several science and math courses at a four-year college.

Most biological technician jobs, for example, require a bachelor's degree in biology or a closely related field. Forensic science positions also typically require a bachelor's degree to work in the field. Knowledge and understanding of legal procedures also can be helpful. Chemical technician positions in research and development also often have a bachelor's degree, but most chemical process technicians have a two-year degree instead, usually an associate degree in process technology. In some cases, a high school diploma is sufficient. These workers usually receive additional on-the-job training. Entry-level workers whose college training encompasses extensive hands-on experience with a variety of diagnostic laboratory equipment generally require less on-the-job training.

Whatever their degree, science technicians usually need hands-on training either in school or on the job. Most can get good career preparation through two-year formal training programs that combine the teaching of scientific principles and theory with practical hands-on application in a laboratory setting with up-to-date equipment. Graduates of bachelor's degree programs in science who have considerable experience in laboratory-based courses, have completed internships, or have held summer jobs in laboratories also are well qualified for science technician positions and are preferred by some employers.

Job candidates who have extensive hands-on experience with a variety of laboratory equipment, including computers and related equipment, usually require a short period of on-the-job training. Those with a high school diploma and no college degree typically begin work as trainees under the direct supervision of a more experienced technician. Many with a high school diploma eventually earn a two-year degree in science technology, often paid for by their employer.

Many technical and community colleges offer associate degrees in a specific technology or more general education in science and mathematics. A number of associate degree programs are designed to provide easy transfer to bachelor's degree programs at colleges or universities. Technical institutes usually offer technician training, but they provide less theory and general education than do community colleges. The length of programs at technical institutes varies, although one-year certificate programs and two-year associate degree programs are common. Prospective forestry and conservation technicians can choose from more than 20 associate degree programs in forest technology accredited by the Society of American Foresters.

Approximately 30 colleges and universities offer a bachelor's degree program in forensic science; about another 25 schools offer a bachelor's degree in a natural science with an emphasis on forensic science or criminology; a few additional schools offer a bachelor's degree with an emphasis in a specialty area, such as criminology, pathology, jurisprudence, investigation, odontology, toxicology, or forensic accounting.

Some schools offer cooperative-education or internship programs, allowing students the opportunity to work at a local company or some other workplace while attending classes during alternate terms. Participation in such programs can significantly enhance a student's employment prospects.

People interested in careers as science technicians should take as many high school science and math courses as possible. Science courses taken beyond high school, in an associate or bachelor's degree program, should be laboratory oriented, with an emphasis on bench skills. A solid background in applied chemistry, physics, and math is vital.

*Other qualifications.* Communication skills are important because technicians are often required to report their findings both orally and in writing. In addition, technicians should be able to work well with others. Because computers often are used in research and development laboratories, technicians should also have strong computer skills, especially in computer modeling. Organizational ability, an eye for detail, and skill in interpreting scientific results are important as well, as are a high mechanical aptitude, attention to detail, and analytical thinking.

*Advancement.* Technicians usually begin work as trainees in routine positions under the direct supervision of a scientist or a more experienced technician. As they gain experience, technicians take on more responsibility and carry out assignments under only general supervision, and some eventually become supervisors. However, technicians employed at universities often have job prospects tied to those of particular professors; when those professors retire or leave, these technicians face uncertain employment prospects.

## Employment

Science technicians held about 267,000 jobs in 2006. As indicated by the following tabulation, chemical and biological technicians accounted for 52 percent of all jobs:

Biological technicians .........................................79,000

Chemical technicians ..........................................61,000

Environmental science and protection technicians, including health .............................................37,000

Forest and conservation technicians......................34,000

Agricultural and food science technicians ..............26,000

Forensic science technicians ...............................13,000

Geological and petroleum technicians....................12,000

Nuclear technicians ...............................................6,500

About 30 percent of biological technicians worked in professional, scientific, or technical services firms; most other biological technicians worked in educational services, federal, state, and local governments, or pharmaceutical and medicine manufacturing. Chemical technicians held jobs in a wide range of manufacturing and service-providing industries. About 39 percent worked in chemical manufacturing and another 30 percent worked in professional, scientific, or technical services firms. Most environmental science and protection technicians worked for state and local governments and professional, scientific, and technical services firms. About 76 percent of forest and conservation technicians held jobs in the federal government, mostly in the Forest Service; another 17 percent worked for state governments. Around 32 percent of agricultural and food science technicians worked in educational services and 20 percent worked for food processing companies; most of the rest were employed in agriculture. Forensic science technicians worked primarily for state and local governments. Approximately 37 percent of all geological and petroleum technicians worked for oil and gas extraction companies and 49 percent of nuclear technicians worked for utilities.

## Job Outlook

Employment of science technicians is projected to grow about as fast as the average, although employment change will vary by specialty. Job opportunities are expected to be best for graduates of applied science technology programs who are well trained on equipment used in laboratories or production facilities.

*Employment change.* Overall employment of science technicians is expected to grow 12 percent during the 2006–2016 decade, about as fast as the average for all occupations. The continued growth of scientific and medical research—particularly research related to biotechnology—will be the primary driver of employment growth, but the development and production of technical products should also stimulate demand for science technicians in many industries.

Employment of biological technicians should increase faster than the average, as the growing number of agricultural and medicinal products developed with the use of biotechnology techniques boosts demand for these workers. Also, an aging population and stronger competition among pharmaceutical companies are expected to contribute to the need for innovative and improved drugs, further spurring demand. Most growth in employment will be in professional, scientific, and technical services and in educational services.

Job growth for chemical technicians is projected to grow more slowly than the average. The chemical manufacturing industry, except pharmaceutical and medicine manufacturing, is anticipated to experience a decline in overall employment as companies downsize and turn to outside contractors to provide specialized services. Some of these contractors will be in other countries with lower average wages, further limiting employment growth. An increasing focus on quality assurance will require a greater number of process technicians, however, stimulating demand for these workers.

Employment of environmental science and protection technicians is expected to grow much faster than the average; these workers will be needed to help regulate waste products; to collect air, water, and soil samples for measuring levels of pollutants; to monitor compliance with environmental regulations; and to clean up contaminated sites. Over 80 percent of this growth is expected to be in professional, scientific, and technical services as environmental monitoring, management, and regulatory compliance increase.

An expected decline in employment of forest and conservation technicians within the federal government will lead to little or no change in employment in this specialty, due to budgetary constraints and continued reductions in demand for timber management on federal lands. However, opportunities at state and local governments within specialties such as urban forestry may provide some new jobs. In addition, an increased emphasis on specific conservation issues, such as environmental protection, preservation of water resources, and control of exotic and invasive pests, may provide some employment opportunities.

Employment of agricultural and food science technicians is projected to grow about as fast as the average. Research in biotechnology and other areas of agricultural science will increase as it becomes more important to balance greater agricultural output with protection and preservation of soil, water, and the ecosystem. In particular, research will be needed to combat insects and diseases as they adapt to pesticides and as soil fertility and water quality continue to need improvement.

Jobs for forensic science technicians are expected to increase much faster than the average. Employment growth in state and local government should be driven by the increasing application of forensic science to examine, solve, and prevent crime. Crime scene technicians who work for state and county crime labs should experience favorable employment prospects resulting from strong job growth.

Average employment growth is expected for geological and petroleum technicians. Job growth should be strongest in professional, scientific, and technical services firms because geological and petroleum technicians will be needed to assist environmental scientists and geoscientists as they provide consultation services for companies regarding environmental policy and federal government mandates, such as those requiring lower sulfur emissions.

Nuclear technicians should grow about as fast as the average as more are needed to monitor the nation's aging fleet of nuclear reactors and research future advances in nuclear power. Although no new nuclear powerplants have been built for decades in the United

**Projections data from the National Employment Matrix**

| Occupational Title | SOC Code | Employment, 2006 | Projected employment, 2016 | Change, 2006-2016 | |
|---|---|---|---|---|---|
| | | | | Number | Percent |
| Science technicians ................................................................. | — | 267,000 | 300,000 | 33,000 | 12 |
|   Agricultural and food science technicians .................................... | 19-4011 | 26,000 | 28,000 | 1,700 | 7 |
|   Biological technicians .................................................................. | 19-4021 | 79,000 | 91,000 | 13,000 | 16 |
|   Chemical technicians .................................................................. | 19-4031 | 61,000 | 65,000 | 3,600 | 6 |
|   Geological and petroleum technicians ........................................ | 19-4041 | 12,000 | 13,000 | 1,000 | 9 |
|   Nuclear technicians .................................................................... | 19-4051 | 6,500 | 6,900 | 400 | 7 |
|   Environmental science and protection technicians, including health.......................................................................................... | 19-4091 | 37,000 | 47,000 | 10,000 | 28 |
|   Forensic science technicians ...................................................... | 19-4092 | 13,000 | 17,000 | 4,000 | 31 |
|   Forest and conservation technicians .......................................... | 19-4093 | 34,000 | 33,000 | -700 | -2 |

NOTE: Data in this table are rounded.

States, energy demand has recently renewed interest in this form of electricity generation and may lead to future construction. Technicians also will be needed to work in defense-related areas, to develop nuclear medical technology, and to improve and enforce waste management and safety standards.

*Job prospects.* In addition to job openings created by growth, many openings should arise from the need to replace technicians who retire or leave the labor force for other reasons. Job opportunities are expected to be best for graduates of applied science technology programs who are well trained on equipment used in laboratories or production facilities. As the instrumentation and techniques used in industrial research, development, and production become increasingly more complex, employers will seek individuals with highly developed technical skills. Good communication skills are also increasingly sought by employers.

Job opportunities vary by specialty. The best opportunities for agricultural and food science technicians will be in agricultural biotechnology, specifically in research and development on biofuels. Geological and petroleum technicians should experience little competition for positions because of the relatively small number of new entrants. Forensic science technicians with a bachelor's degree in a forensic science will enjoy much better opportunities than those with an associate degree. During periods of economic recession, science technicians may be laid off.

# Earnings

Median hourly earnings of science technicians in May 2006 were as follows:

| | |
|---|---|
| Nuclear technicians | $31.49 |
| Geological and petroleum technicians | 22.19 |
| Forensic science technicians | 21.79 |
| Chemical technicians | 18.87 |
| Environmental science and protection technicians, including health | 18.31 |
| Biological technicians | 17.17 |
| Agricultural and food science technicians | 15.26 |
| Forest and conservation technicians | 14.84 |

In 2007, the average annual salary in the federal government was $40,629 for biological science technicians; $53,026 for physical sci-ence technicians; $40,534 for forestry technicians; $54,081 for geodetic technicians; $50,337 for hydrologic technicians; and $63,396 for meteorological technicians.

# Related Occupations

Other technicians who apply scientific principles and who usually have a 2-year associate degree include engineering technicians, broadcast and sound engineering technicians and radio operators, drafters, and health technologists and technicians—especially clinical laboratory technologists and technicians, diagnostic medical sonographers, and radiologic technologists and technicians.

# Sources of Additional Information

For information about a career as a chemical technician, contact

▸ American Chemical Society, Education Division, Career Publications, 1155 16th St. NW, Washington, DC 20036. Internet: http://www.acs.org

For career information and a list of undergraduate, graduate, and doctoral programs in forensic sciences, contact

▸ American Academy of Forensic Sciences, P.O. Box 669, Colorado Springs, CO 80901. Internet: http://www.aafs.org

For general information on forestry technicians and a list of schools offering education in forestry, send a self-addressed, stamped business envelope to

▸ Society of American Foresters, 5400 Grosvenor Ln., Bethesda, MD 20814. Internet: http://www.safnet.org

# Secretaries and Administrative Assistants

(O*NET 43-6011.00, 43-6012.00, 43-6013.00, and 43-6014.00)

## Significant Points

- This occupation is expected to be among those with the largest number of new jobs.

- Opportunities should be best for applicants with extensive knowledge of software applications.

- Secretaries and administrative assistants today perform fewer clerical tasks and are increasingly taking on the roles of information and communication managers.

## Nature of the Work

As the reliance on technology continues to expand in offices, the role of the office professional has greatly evolved. Office automation and organizational restructuring have led secretaries and administrative assistants to assume responsibilities once reserved for managerial and professional staff. In spite of these changes, however, the core responsibilities for secretaries and administrative assistants have remained much the same: Performing and coordinating an office's administrative activities and storing, retrieving, and integrating information for dissemination to staff and clients.

Secretaries and administrative assistants perform a variety of administrative and clerical duties necessary to run an organization efficiently. They serve as information and communication managers for an office; plan and schedule meetings and appointments; organize and maintain paper and electronic files; manage projects; conduct research; and disseminate information by using the telephone, mail services, Web sites, and e-mail. They also may handle travel and guest arrangements.

Secretaries and administrative assistants use a variety of office equipment, such as fax machines, photocopiers, scanners, and videoconferencing and telephone systems. In addition, secretaries and administrative assistants often use computers to do tasks previously handled by managers and professionals, such as: create spreadsheets; compose correspondence; manage databases; and create presentations, reports, and documents using desktop publishing software and digital graphics. They also may negotiate with vendors, maintain and examine leased equipment, purchase supplies, manage areas such as stockrooms or corporate libraries, and retrieve data from various sources. At the same time, managers and professionals have assumed many tasks traditionally assigned to secretaries and administrative assistants, such as keyboarding and answering the telephone. Because secretaries and administrative assistants do less dictation and word processing, they now have time to support more members of the executive staff. In a number of organizations, secretaries and administrative assistants work in teams to work flexibly and share their expertise.

Many secretaries and administrative assistants now provide training and orientation for new staff, conduct research on the Internet, and operate and troubleshoot new office technologies.

Specific job duties vary with experience and titles. *Executive secretaries and administrative assistants* provide high-level administrative support for an office and for top executives of an organization. Generally, they perform fewer clerical tasks than do secretaries and more information management. In addition to arranging conference calls and supervising other clerical staff, they may handle more complex responsibilities such as reviewing incoming memos, submissions, and reports in order to determine their significance and to plan for their distribution. They also prepare agendas and make arrangements for meetings of committees and executive boards. They also may conduct research and prepare statistical reports.

Some secretaries and administrative assistants, such as legal and medical secretaries, perform highly specialized work requiring knowledge of technical terminology and procedures. For instance, *legal secretaries* prepare correspondence and legal papers such as summonses, complaints, motions, responses, and subpoenas under the supervision of an attorney or a paralegal. They also may review legal journals and assist with legal research—for example, by verifying quotes and citations in legal briefs. Additionally, legal secretaries often teach newly minted lawyers how to prepare documents for submission to the courts. *Medical secretaries* transcribe dictation, prepare correspondence, and assist physicians or medical scientists with reports, speeches, articles, and conference proceedings. They also record simple medical histories, arrange for patients to be hospitalized, and order supplies. Most medical secretaries need to be familiar with insurance rules, billing practices, and hospital or laboratory procedures. Other technical secretaries who assist engineers or scientists may prepare correspondence, maintain their organization's technical library, and gather and edit materials for scientific papers.

Secretaries employed in elementary schools and high schools perform important administrative functions for the school. They are responsible for handling most of the communications between parents, the community, and teachers and administrators who work at the school. As such, they are required to know details about registering students, immunizations, and bus schedules, for example. They schedule appointments, keep track of students' academic records, and make room assignments for classes. Those who work directly for principals screen inquiries from parents and handle those matters not needing a principal's attention. They also may set a principal's calendar to help set her or his priorities for the day.

*Work environment.* Secretaries and administrative assistants usually work in schools, hospitals, corporate settings, government agencies, or legal and medical offices. Their jobs often involve sitting for long periods. If they spend a lot of time keyboarding, particularly at a computer monitor, they may encounter problems of eyestrain, stress, and repetitive motion ailments such as carpal tunnel syndrome.

Almost one-fifth of secretaries work part time and many others work in temporary positions. A few participate in job-sharing arrangements, in which two people divide responsibility for a single job. The majority of secretaries and administrative assistants, however, are full-time employees who work a standard 40-hour week.

# Training, Other Qualifications, and Advancement

Word processing, writing, and communication skills are essential for all secretaries and administrative assistants. However, employers increasingly require extensive knowledge of software applications, such as desktop publishing, project management, spreadsheets, and database management.

*Education and training.* High school graduates who have basic office skills may qualify for entry-level secretarial positions. They can acquire these skills in various ways. Training ranges from high school vocational education programs that teach office skills and typing to one- and two-year programs in office administration offered by business and vocational-technical schools, and community colleges. Many temporary placement agencies also provide formal training in computer and office skills. Most medical and legal secretaries must go through specialized training programs that teach them the language of the industry.

Employers of executive secretaries increasingly are seeking candidates with a college degree, as these secretaries work closely with top executives. A degree related to the business or industry in which a person is seeking employment may provide the job seeker with an advantage in the application process.

Most secretaries and administrative assistants, once hired, tend to acquire more advanced skills through on-the-job instruction by other employees or by equipment and software vendors. Others may attend classes or participate in online education to learn how to operate new office technologies, such as information storage systems, scanners, or new updated software packages. As office automation continues to evolve, retraining and continuing education will remain integral parts of secretarial jobs.

*Other qualifications.* Secretaries and administrative assistants should be proficient in typing and good at spelling, punctuation, grammar, and oral communication. Employers also look for good customer service and interpersonal skills because secretaries and administrative assistants must be tactful in their dealings with people. Discretion, good judgment, organizational or management ability, initiative, and the ability to work independently are especially important for higher-level administrative positions. Changes in the office environment have increased the demand for secretaries and administrative assistants who are adaptable and versatile.

*Certification and advancement.* Testing and certification for proficiency in office skills are available through organizations such as the International Association of Administrative Professionals; National Association of Legal Secretaries (NALS), Inc.; and Legal Secretaries International, Inc. As secretaries and administrative assistants gain experience, they can earn several different designations. Prominent designations include the Certified Professional Secretary (CPS) and the Certified Administrative Professional (CAP), which can be earned by meeting certain experience or educational requirements and passing an examination. Similarly, those with one year of experience in the legal field, or who have concluded an approved training course and who want to be certified as a legal support professional, can acquire the Accredited Legal Secretary (ALS) designation through a testing process administered by NALS.

NALS offers two additional designations: Professional Legal Secretary (PLS), considered an advanced certification for legal support professionals, and a designation for proficiency as a paralegal. Legal Secretaries International confers the Certified Legal Secretary Specialist (CLSS) designation in areas such as intellectual property, criminal law, civil litigation, probate, and business law to those who have five years of legal experience and pass an examination. In some instances, certain requirements may be waived.

Secretaries and administrative assistants generally advance by being promoted to other administrative positions with more responsibilities. Qualified administrative assistants who broaden their knowledge of a company's operations and enhance their skills may be promoted to senior or executive secretary or administrative assistant, clerical supervisor, or office manager. Secretaries with word processing or data entry experience can advance to jobs as word processing or data entry trainers, supervisors, or managers within their own firms or in a secretarial, word processing, or data entry service bureau. Secretarial and administrative support experience also can lead to jobs such as instructor or sales representative with manufacturers of software or computer equipment. With additional training, many legal secretaries become paralegals.

# Employment

Secretaries and administrative assistants held more than 4.2 million jobs in 2006, ranking it among the largest occupations in the U.S. economy. The following tabulation shows the distribution of employment by secretarial specialty:

| | |
|---|---|
| Secretaries, except legal, medical, and executive | 1,940,000 |
| Executive secretaries and administrative assistants | 1,618,000 |
| Medical secretaries | 408,000 |
| Legal secretaries | 275,000 |

Secretaries and administrative assistants are employed in organizations of every type. Around 9 out of 10 secretaries and administrative assistants are employed in service providing industries, ranging from education and health care to government and retail trade. Most of the rest work for firms engaged in manufacturing or construction.

# Job Outlook

Employment of secretaries and administrative assistants is expected to grow about as fast as average for all occupations. Secretaries and administrative assistants will have among the largest numbers of new jobs arise, about 362,000 over the 2006–2016 period. Additional opportunities will result from the need to replace workers who transfer to other occupations or leave this occupation.

*Employment change.* Employment of secretaries and administrative assistants is expected to increase about 9 percent, which is about as fast as average for all occupations, between 2006 and 2016. Projected employment varies by occupational specialty. Above average employment growth in the health care and social assistance industry should lead to faster than average growth for medical secretaries, while moderate growth in legal services is projected to lead to average growth in employment of legal secretaries. Employment of

**Projections data from the National Employment Matrix**

| Occupational Title | SOC Code | Employment, 2006 | Projected employment, 2016 | Change, 2006-16 | |
|---|---|---|---|---|---|
| | | | | Number | Percent |
| Secretaries and administrative assistants ......................................... | 43-6000 | 4,241,000 | 4,603,000 | 362,000 | 9 |
| Executive secretaries and administrative assistants ..................... | 43-6011 | 1,618,000 | 1,857,000 | 239,000 | 15 |
| Legal secretaries.................................................................... | 43-6012 | 275,000 | 308,000 | 32,000 | 12 |
| Medical secretaries................................................................ | 43-6013 | 408,000 | 477,000 | 68,000 | 17 |
| Secretaries, except legal, medical, and executive ....................... | 43-6014 | 1,940,000 | 1,962,000 | 22,000 | 1 |

NOTE: Data in this table are rounded.

executive secretaries and administrative assistants is projected to grow faster than average for all occupations. Growing industries—such as administrative and support services; health care and social assistance; and professional, scientific, and technical services—will continue to generate the most new jobs. Little or no change in employment is expected for secretaries, except legal, medical, or executive, who account for about 46 percent of all secretaries and administrative assistants.

Increasing office automation and organizational restructuring will continue to make secretaries and administrative assistants more productive in coming years. Computers, e-mail, scanners, and voice message systems will allow secretaries and administrative assistants to accomplish more in the same amount of time. The use of automated equipment also is changing the distribution of work in many offices. In some cases, traditional secretarial duties as typing, filing, photocopying, and bookkeeping are being done by clerks in other departments or by the professionals themselves. For example, professionals and managers increasingly do their own word processing and data entry, and handle much of their own correspondence. Also, in some law and medical offices, paralegals and medical assistants are assuming some tasks formerly done by secretaries.

Developments in office technology are certain to continue. However, many secretarial and administrative duties are of a personal, interactive nature and, therefore, are not easily automated. Responsibilities such as planning conferences, working with clients, and instructing staff require tact and communication skills. Because technology cannot substitute for these personal skills, secretaries and administrative assistants will continue to play a key role in most organizations.

As paralegals and medical assistants assume more of the duties traditionally assigned to secretaries, there is a trend in many offices for professionals and managers to replace the traditional arrangement of one secretary per manager with secretaries and administrative assistants who support the work of systems, departments, or units. This approach often means that secretaries and administrative assistants assume added responsibilities and are seen as valuable members of a team.

*Job prospects.* In addition to jobs created from growth, numerous job opportunities will arise from the need to replace secretaries and administrative assistants who transfer to other occupations, especially exceptionally skilled executive secretaries and administrative assistants who often move into professional occupations. Job opportunities should be best for applicants with extensive knowledge of software applications and for experienced secretaries and administrative assistants. Opportunities also should be very good for those

with advanced communication and computer skills. Applicants with a bachelor's degree will be in great demand to act more as managerial assistants and to perform more complex tasks.

# Earnings

Median annual earnings of secretaries, except legal, medical, and executive, were $27,450 in May 2006. The middle 50 percent earned between $21,830 and $34,250. The lowest 10 percent earned less than $17,560, and the highest 10 percent earned more than $41,550. Median annual earnings in the industries employing the largest numbers of secretaries, except legal, medical, and executive in May 2006 were

Local government ............................................$30,350
General medical and surgical hospitals .................28,810
Colleges, universities, and professional schools ......28,700
Elementary and secondary schools ........................28,120
Employment services ........................................26,810

Median annual earnings of executive secretaries and administrative assistants were $37,240 in May 2006. The middle 50 percent earned between $30,240 and $46,160. The lowest 10 percent earned less than $25,190, and the highest 10 percent earned more than $56,740. Median annual earnings in the industries employing the largest numbers of executive secretaries and administrative assistants in May 2006 were

Management of companies and enterprises ..........$41,570
Local government ............................................38,670
Colleges, universities, and professional schools ......36,510
State government ............................................35,830
Employment services ........................................31,600

Median annual earnings of legal secretaries were $38,190 in May 2006. The middle 50 percent earned between $29,650 and $48,520. The lowest 10 percent earned less than $23,870, and the highest 10 percent earned more than $58,770. Medical secretaries earned a median annual salary of $28,090 in May 2006. The middle 50 percent earned between $23,250 and $34,210. The lowest 10 percent earned less than $19,750, and the highest 10 percent earned more than $40,870.

Salaries vary a great deal, however, reflecting differences in skill, experience, and level of responsibility. Certification in this field may be rewarded by a higher salary.

## Related Occupations

Workers in a number of other occupations also type, record information, and process paperwork. Among them are bookkeeping, accounting, and auditing clerks; receptionists and information clerks; communications equipment operators; court reporters; human resources assistants, except payroll and timekeeping; computer operators; data entry and information processing workers; paralegals and legal assistants; medical assistants; and medical records and health information technicians. A growing number of secretaries and administrative assistants share in managerial and human resource responsibilities. Occupations requiring these skills include office and administrative support worker supervisors and managers; computer and information systems managers; administrative services managers; and human resources, training, and labor relations managers and specialists.

## Sources of Additional Information

State employment offices provide information about job openings for secretaries and administrative assistants.

For information on the latest trends in the profession, career development advice, and the CPS or CAP designations, contact

▸ International Association of Administrative Professionals, 10502 NW Ambassador Dr., P.O. Box 20404, Kansas City, MO 64195-0404. Internet: http://www.iaap-hq.org

▸ Association of Executive and Administrative Professionals, Suite G-13, 900 South Washington Street, Falls Church, VA 22406-4009. Internet: http://www.theaeap.com

Information on the CLSS designation can be obtained from

▸ Legal Secretaries International Inc., 2302 Fannin Street, Suite 500, Houston, TX 77002-9136. Internet: http://www.legalsecretaries.org

Information on the ALS, PLS, and paralegal certifications are available from

▸ National Association of Legal Secretaries, Inc., 314 East Third St., Suite 210, Tulsa, OK 74120. Internet: http://www.nals.org

## Securities, Commodities, and Financial Services Sales Agents

(O*NET 41-3031.00, 41-3031.01, and 41-3031.02)

## Significant Points

■ A college degree, sales ability, good interpersonal and communication skills, and a strong desire to succeed are important qualifications.

■ Competition for entry-level jobs usually is keen, especially in investment banks; opportunities should be better in smaller firms.

■ Many people leave the occupation because of underperformance, but those who are successful have a very strong attachment to their occupation because of high earnings and considerable investment in training.

## Nature of the Work

Each day, hundreds of billions of dollars change hands on the major United States securities exchanges. This money is used to purchase stocks, bonds, mutual funds, and other financial instruments, called securities. Securities are bought and sold by large institutional investors, wealthy individuals, mutual funds and pension plans, and the general public. In fact, about half of American households own stock. Most securities trades are arranged through securities, commodities, and financial services sales agents, whether they are between individuals with a few hundred dollars to invest or between large institutions having millions of dollars. The duties of sales agents vary greatly depending on occupational specialty.

The most common type of securities sales agent is called a *broker* or *stock broker*. These are the people who sell securities to everyday people, also known as retail investors. Although only about 2 out of every 10 equities are held by small investors, most investors fall into this category. Because there are so many retail investors, they must work through a broker rather than trading directly on an exchange. First, the investor speaks with the broker, discussing the terms of the trade. Then, the broker relays this information to a *trader* at the company's headquarters. Because most securities companies are very large, they can often find other company clients who are willing to buy or sell the same security. Otherwise, the stock trader places an order with a floor broker at an exchange, or trades the stock on an electronic network. The broker charges a fee for this service, and may also make money by finding a lower price for the security than was arranged with the investor.

The most important part of a broker's job is finding clients and building a customer base. Thus, beginning securities and commodities sales agents spend much of their time searching for customers, often relying heavily on telephone solicitation. They also may meet clients through business and social contacts. Agents also join civic organizations and other social groups to expand their networks of possible clients. Many find it useful to contact potential clients by teaching adult education investment courses or by giving lectures at libraries or social clubs. Brokerage firms may give sales agents lists of people with whom the firm has done business in the past. Some agents inherit the clients of agents who have retired. After an agent is established, referrals from satisfied clients are an important source of new business.

*Investment bankers* are sales agents who connect businesses that need money to finance their operations or expansion plans with investors who are interested in providing that funding in exchange for debt (in the form of bonds) or equity (in the form of stock). This process is called underwriting, and it is the main function of the investment bank. Investment bankers have to sell twice: first, they sell their advisory services to help companies set up issuing new stock or bonds, and second, they then sell the securities they issue to investors.

Perhaps the most important advisory service provided by investment banks is to help companies new to the public investment arena issue stock for the first time. This process, known as an initial public offering, or IPO, can take a great deal of effort because private companies must meet stringent requirements to become public or be allowed to issue stocks and bonds. Corporate finance departments also help private companies sell stock to institutional investors or wealthy individuals. They also advise companies that are interested in funding their operations by taking on debt. This debt can be issued in the form of bonds. Unlike a stock, which entitles its holder to partial ownership of a company, a bond entitles its holder to be repaid with a pre-determined rate of interest.

Another important advisory service is provided by the mergers and acquisitions department. Bankers in this area advise companies that are interested in merging with or purchasing other companies. They also help companies that would like to be acquired. Once a potential seller or buyer is found, bankers advise their client on how to execute the agreement. Generally both buyers and sellers have investment banks working for them to make sure that the transaction goes smoothly.

*Investment banking sales agents* and *traders* sell stocks and bonds to investors. Instead of selling their services to companies for fees, salespeople and traders sell securities to customers for commissions. These sales agents generally work by telephone, calling customers and their agents to discuss new stock and bond issues. When an investor decides to make a purchase, the order goes to the trading floor. Traders execute buy and sell orders from clients and make trades on behalf of the bank itself. Because markets fluctuate so much, trading is a split-second decision making process. If a trader cannot secure the promised price on an exchange, millions of dollars could potentially be lost. On the other hand, if a trader finds a better deal, the bank could make millions more.

A small but powerful group of sales agents work directly on the floor of a stock or commodities exchange. When a firm or investor wishes to buy or sell a security or commodity, sales agents relay the order through their firm's computers to the floor of the exchange. There, *floor brokers* negotiate the price with other floor brokers, make the sale, and forward the purchase price to the sales agents. In addition to floor brokers, who work for individual securities dealers, there are also *independent brokers*. These are similar to floor brokers, except that they are not buyers for specific firms. Instead, they can buy and sell stocks for their own accounts, or corporate accounts that they manage,, or they can sell their services to floor brokers who are too busy to execute all of the trades they are responsible for making. *Specialists* or *market makers* also work directly on the exchange floor, and there is generally one for each security or commodity being traded. They facilitate the trading process by quoting prices and by buying or selling shares when there are too many or too few available.

*Financial services sales agents* sell a wide variety of banking, accounting, securities, insurance, tax preparation, and other related services. They contact potential customers to explain their services and to ascertain customers' banking and other financial needs. They also may solicit businesses to participate in consumer credit card programs.

**Work environment.** Most securities and commodities sales agents work in offices under fairly stressful conditions. The pace of work is very fast, and managers tend to be very demanding of their workers since both commissions and advancement are tied to sales.

Stock brokers and investment advisors generally work somewhat more than 40 hours a week, but they may not work at traditional times. Evening and weekend work is often necessary, as many of their clients work during the day. A growing number of securities

sales agents, employed mostly by discount or online brokerage firms, work in call-center environments. In these centers, hundreds of agents spend much of the day on the telephone taking orders from clients or offering advice and information on different securities. Often, such call centers operate 24 hours a day, requiring agents to work in shifts.

Investment bankers in corporate finance or mergers and acquisitions typically work long hours and endure extreme stress, especially at the junior levels. Evening and weekend work is common. Because banks work with companies all over the world, extensive travel is often part of the job. With some experience, the workload becomes more manageable, but since higher-level workers generally have more contact with clients, they also tend to travel more.

Sales and trading departments typically work somewhat more than 40 hours a week, but not nearly as much as their counterparts in investment banking. They also travel less, and many only travel a few times a year for conferences or training. On the other hand, their jobs are incredibly stressful. For sales agents, every minute of the day that is wasted means they might have made another sale. Since both commissions and advancement are tied to sales, this can be very stressful. Traders have perhaps the most stressful jobs of all, as split second decisions can lead to millions of dollars being won or lost. Trading floors are very busy and often very loud. Exchange workers, much like traders, have highly stressful jobs because the bulk of their work takes place on the floor of the exchanges. However, exchange traders and workers typically work shorter hours than many other agents since most of their work is done while the market is open.

Exchange workers, much like traders, have highly stressful jobs, but the bulk of their work takes place on the floor of the exchanges, so hours are not very long. Trading floors of exchanges are even busier and louder than those inside of investment banks. Stress is very high, as millions of dollars are on the line for almost every trade, but workers who have made it to this level are generally up to the task.

Financial services sales agents normally work 40 hours a week in a comfortable, less stressful office environment. They may spend considerable time outside the office, meeting with current and prospective clients, attending civic functions, and participating in trade association meetings. Some financial services sales agents work exclusively inside banks, providing service to walk-in customers.

## Training, Other Qualifications, and Advancement

Most positions require a bachelor's degree, although few require a specific major. An MBA or professional certification can also be very helpful. Advancement is often very difficult, but those who are successful can have extremely lucrative careers.

*Education and training.* A college education is important for securities and commodities sales agents, especially in larger firms, because they must be knowledgeable about economic conditions and trends. Most workers have a bachelor's degree in business, finance, accounting, or economics, although this is not necessarily a requirement. Many firms hire summer interns before their last year of college and those who are most successful are offered full-time jobs after they graduate.

After working for a few years, many agents get Master's degrees in Business Administration (MBA). This degree is a requirement for many of the high-level positions in the securities industry. Because the MBA is a professional degree designed to expose students to real-world business practices, it is considered to be a major asset for jobseekers. Employers often reward MBA-holders with higher-level positions, better compensation, and even large signing bonuses.

Most employers provide intensive on-the-job training, especially for entry-level employees. While college coursework is helpful, most firms have a specialized business model which employees must learn. New employees must also come to know the large number of products and services offered by most firms. Trainees in large firms may receive classroom instruction in securities analysis, effective speaking, and the finer points of selling. Firms often rotate their trainees among various departments, to give them a broad perspective of the securities business. In small firms, sales agents often receive training in outside institutions and on the job.

Securities and commodities sales agents must keep up with new products and services and other developments. Because of this, brokers regularly attend conferences and training seminars.

*Licensure.* Brokers and investment advisors must register as representatives of their firm with the Financial Industry Regulatory Authority (FINRA). Before beginners can qualify as registered representatives, they must be an employee of a registered firm for at least four months and pass the General Securities Registered Representative Examination—known as the Series seven Exam—administered by FINRA. The exam takes six hours and contains 250 multiple-choice questions; a passing score is above 70 percent.

Most states require a second examination—the Uniform Securities Agents state Law Examination (Series 63 or 66). This test measures the prospective representative's knowledge of the securities business in general, customer protection requirements, and recordkeeping procedures. Most firms offer training to help their employees pass these exams.

There are many other licenses available, each of which gives the holder the right to sell different products and services. Most experienced representatives have several. Traders and some other workers also need licenses, although these vary greatly by firm and specialization. Financial services sales agents may also need to be licensed, especially if they sell securities or insurance.

Registered representatives must attend periodic continuing education classes to maintain their licenses. Courses consist of computer-based training in regulatory matters and company training on new products and services.

*Other qualifications.* Many employers consider personal qualities and skills more important than academic training. Employers seek applicants who have excellent interpersonal and communication skills, a strong work ethic, the ability to work in a team, and a desire to succeed. The ability to understand and analyze numbers is also especially important. Because securities, commodities, and financial services sales agents are entrusted with large sums of money and personal information, employers also make sure that applicants have a good credit history and a clean record. Self-confidence and an ability to handle frequent rejection are important ingredients for success.

Maturity and the ability to work independently are important so many employers prefer to hire those who have achieved success in other jobs. Most firms prefer candidates with sales experience, particularly those who have worked on commission in areas such as real estate or insurance. Other firms prefer to hire workers right out of college, with the intention of molding them to their corporate image.

*Advancement.* The principal form of advancement for brokers, investment advisors, and financial services sales agents is an increase in the number and size of the accounts they handle. Although beginners usually service the accounts of individual investors, they may eventually handle very large institutional accounts, such as those of banks and pension funds. After taking a series of tests, some brokers become portfolio managers and have greater authority to make investment decisions regarding an account. Some experienced sales agents become branch office managers and supervise other sales agents while continuing to provide services for their own customers. A few agents advance to top management positions or become partners in their firms.

*Investment bankers* who enter the occupation directly after college generally start as analysts. At this level, employees have some contact with clients but spend most of their time producing "pitchbooks," information booklets used to sell products. They also receive intensive training. After two to three years, top analysts may be promoted to an associate position or asked to leave. Recent graduates from MBA programs can start as associates, which is similar to the analyst position, but with more responsibilities. Associate may lead a group of analysts and tend to have more contact with clients. After two to three years, associates are promoted or terminated. Successful associates can become vice presidents, who manage the work of analysts and associates and have a great deal of contact with clients. Vice presidents may advance to become directors, sometimes called executive directors.

## Employment

Securities, commodities, and financial services sales agents held about 320,000 jobs in 2006. More than half of jobs were in the securities, commodity contracts, and other financial investments and related activities industry. One in 5 worked in the depository and nondepository credit intermediation industries, which include commercial banks, savings institutions, and credit unions. About 1 out of 6 securities, commodities, and financial services sales agents were self-employed.

Although securities and commodities sales agents are employed by firms in all parts of the country, about 1 in 10 jobs were located in New York City, including the majority of those in investment banking. Because of their close relationship to stock exchanges and large banking operations, most of the major investment banks in the United States are based in New York City. Smaller investment banks can be found in many major American cities and some major investment banks have operations in other cities, although most of their business remains in New York.

**Projections data from the National Employment Matrix**

| Occupational Title | SOC Code | Employment, 2006 | Projected employment, 2016 | Change, 2006-16 | |
|---|---|---|---|---|---|
| | | | | Number | Percent |
| Securities, commodities, and financial services sales agents............ | 41-3031 | 320,000 | 399,000 | 79,000 | 25 |

NOTE: Data in this table are rounded.

## Job Outlook

Securities, commodities, and financial services sales agent jobs are projected to grow rapidly over the next decade, especially in the banking industry. However, the number of applicants will continue to far exceed the number of job openings in this high-paying occupation.

***Employment change.*** Employment of securities, commodities, and financial services sales agents is expected to grow 25 percent during the 2006–2016 decade, which is much faster than the average for all occupations. The replacement of traditional pension plans with self-directed retirement accounts has led more Americans to hold stock in recent years. This change means that where companies were making investments to secure their employees' retirements in the past, individuals now save money for their own retirements. About half of American households now own stock, and the number of new investors grows daily. While these individual investors are still only a small part of the total, the nationwide interest in owning securities will greatly increase the number of brokers and investment advisors.

Members of the baby boomer generation, in their peak savings years, will fuel much of this increase in investment. As they begin to retire, the number of transactions they make will go up, fueling the need for more investment advisors and brokers. The growing demand for brokers will also stem from the increasing number and complexity of investment products, as well as the effects of globalization. As the public and businesses become more sophisticated about investing, they are venturing into the options and futures markets. Also, markets for investment are expanding with the increase in global trading of stocks and bonds.

The deregulation of financial markets has broken down the barriers between investment activities and banking. The result is that banks now compete with securities companies on all levels. Many of the major investment banks are now owned by large banks and most major banks also have brokerages, which allow their customers to quickly and easily transfer money between their personal banking and investment accounts. This will lead to increased employment of financial services sales agents in banks as they expand their product offerings in order to compete directly with other investment firms.

***Job prospects.*** Despite job growth, competition for jobs in this occupation usually is keen with more applicants than jobs, especially in larger companies. Jobs in brokerages are competitive but are accessible to graduates who have first-rate résumés, strong interpersonal skills, and good grades. Opportunities for beginning sales agents should be better in smaller firms. Investment banking is especially known for its competitive hiring process. Having a degree from a prestigious undergraduate institution is very helpful, as are excellent grades in finance, economics, accounting, and business courses. Competition is even greater for positions working in exchanges.

Employment in the securities industry is closely connected with market conditions and the state of the overall economy and is highly volatile during recessionary periods. Turnover is high for newcomers, who face difficult prospects no matter when they join the industry. Once established, however, securities and commodities sales agents have a very strong attachment to their profession because of their high earnings and considerable investment in training.

## Earnings

The median annual wage-and-salary earnings of securities, commodities, and financial services sales agents were $68,500 in May 2006. The middle half earned between $42,630 and $126,290. The lowest 10 percent earned less than $31,170, and the highest 10 percent made more than $145,600.

Median annual earnings in the industries employing the largest numbers of securities, commodities, and financial services sales agents were

Other financial investment activities...................$103,640

Security and commodity contracts
  intermediation and brokerage ...........................81,050

Activities related to credit intermediation..............67,080

Other nondepository credit intermediation ............53,750

Nondepository credit intermediation......................52,100

Because this is a sales occupation, many workers are paid a commission based on the amount of stocks, bonds, mutual funds, insurance, and other products they sell. Earnings from commissions are likely to be high when there is much buying and selling, and low when there is a slump in market activity. Most firms provide sales agents with a steady income by paying a "draw against commission"—a minimum salary based on commissions they can be expected to earn. Trainee brokers usually are paid a salary until they develop a client base. The salary gradually decreases in favor of commissions as the broker gains clients.

Investment bankers in corporate finance and mergers and acquisitions are generally paid a base salary with the opportunity to earn a substantial bonus. At the higher levels, bonuses far exceed base salary. This arrangement works similarly to commissions but gives banks greater flexibility to reward members of the team who were more effective. Since investment bankers in sales and trading departments generally work alone, they generally work on commissions.

Brokers who work for discount brokerage firms that promote the use of telephone and online trading services usually are paid a salary, sometimes boosted by bonuses that reflect the profitability of the office. Financial services sales agents usually are paid a salary also, although bonuses or commissions from sales are starting to account for a larger share of their income.

Benefits in the securities industry are generally very good. They normally include health care, retirement, and life insurance. Securities firms may also give discounts to employees on financial services that they sell to customers. Other benefits may include paid lunches with clients, paid dinners for employees who work late, and often extensive travel opportunities

## Related Occupations

Other jobs requiring knowledge of finance and an ability to sell include insurance sales agents, real estate brokers and sales agents, financial analysts and personal financial advisors, and loan officers.

## Sources of Additional Information

For information on securities industry employment, contact

▸ American Academy of Financial Management, 245 Glendale Dr., Metairie, LA 70001. Internet: http://www.aafm.org

▸ Securities Industry and Financial Markets Association, 120 Broadway, 35th Floor, New York, NY 10271. Internet: http://www.sifma.org

For information on licensing, contact

▸ Financial Industry Regulatory Authority (FINRA). 1735 K St. NW, Washington, DC 20006. Internet: http://www.finra.org

## Security Guards and Gaming Surveillance Officers

(O*NET 33-9031.00 and 33-9032.00)

## Significant Points

▪ Jobs should be plentiful, but competition is expected for higher paying positions at facilities requiring longer periods of training and a high level of security, such as nuclear power plants and weapons installations.

▪ Because of limited formal training requirements and flexible hours, this occupation attracts many individuals seeking a second or part-time job.

▪ Some positions, such as those of armored car guards, are hazardous.

## Nature of the Work

Security guards, also called *security officers*, patrol and inspect property to protect against fire, theft, vandalism, terrorism, and illegal activity. These workers protect their employer's investment, enforce laws on the property, and deter criminal activity and other problems. They use radio and telephone communications to call for assistance from police, fire, or emergency medical services as the situation dictates. Security guards write comprehensive reports outlining their observations and activities during their assigned shift. They also may interview witnesses or victims, prepare case reports, and testify in court.

Although all security guards perform many of the same duties, their specific tasks depend on whether they work in a "static" security position or on a mobile patrol. Guards assigned to static security positions usually stay at one location for a specified length of time. These guards must become closely acquainted with the property and people associated with their station and must often monitor alarms

and closed-circuit TV cameras. In contrast, guards assigned to mobile patrol drive or walk from one location to another and conduct security checks within an assigned geographical zone. They may detain or arrest criminal violators, answer service calls concerning criminal activity or problems, and issue traffic violation warnings.

The security guard's job responsibilities also vary with the size, type, and location of the employer. In department stores, guards protect people, records, merchandise, money, and equipment. They often work with undercover store detectives to prevent theft by customers or employees, and help apprehend shoplifting suspects prior to the arrival of the police. Some shopping centers and theaters have officers who patrol their parking lots to deter car thefts and robberies. In office buildings, banks, and hospitals, guards maintain order and protect the institution's customers, staff and property. At air, sea, and rail terminals and other transportation facilities, guards protect people, freight, property, and equipment. Using metal detectors and high-tech equipment, they may screen passengers and visitors for weapons and explosives, ensure that nothing is stolen while a vehicle is being loaded or unloaded, and watch for fires and criminals.

Guards who work in public buildings such as museums or art galleries protect paintings and exhibits by inspecting people and packages entering and leaving the building. In factories, laboratories, government buildings, data processing centers, and military bases, security officers protect information, products, computer codes, and defense secrets and check the credentials of people and vehicles entering and leaving the premises. Guards working at universities, parks, and sports stadiums perform crowd control, supervise parking and seating, and direct traffic. Security guards stationed at the entrance to bars and nightclubs, prevent access by minors, collect cover charges at the door, maintain order among customers, and protect patrons and property.

*Armored car guards* protect money and valuables during transit. In addition, they protect individuals responsible for making commercial bank deposits from theft or injury. They pick up money or other valuables from businesses to transport to another location. Carrying money between the truck and the business can be extremely hazardous. As a result, armored car guards usually wear bulletproof vests.

*Gaming surveillance officers*, also known as *surveillance agents*, and *gaming investigators* act as security agents for casino managers and patrons. Using primarily audio and video equipment in an observation room, they observe casino operations for irregular activities, such as cheating or theft, and monitor compliance to rules, regulations and laws. They maintain and organize recordings from security cameras as they are sometimes used as evidence in police investigations. Some casinos use a catwalk over one-way mirrors located above the casino floor to augment electronic surveillance equipment. Surveillance agents occasionally leave the surveillance room and walk the casino floor.

All security officers must show good judgment and common sense, follow directions, testify accurately in court, and follow company policy and guidelines. In an emergency, they must be able to take charge and direct others to safety. In larger organizations, a security manager might oversee a group of security officers. In smaller organizations, however, a single worker may be solely responsible for all security.

*Work environment.* Most security guards and gaming surveillance officers spend considerable time on their feet, either assigned to a specific post or patrolling buildings and grounds. Guards may be stationed at a guard desk inside a building to monitor electronic security and surveillance devices or to check the credentials of people entering or leaving the premises. They also may be stationed at a guardhouse outside the entrance to a gated facility or community and may use a portable radio or cellular telephone to be in constant contact with a central station. The work usually is routine, but guards must be constantly alert for threats to themselves and the property they are protecting. Guards who work during the day may have a great deal of contact with other employees and the public. Gaming surveillance officers often work behind a bank of monitors controlling numerous cameras in a casino and thus can develop eyestrain.

Guards usually work shifts of 8 hours or longer for 40 hours per week and are often on call in case of an emergency. Some employers offer three shifts, and guards rotate to divide daytime, weekend, and holiday work equally. Guards usually eat on the job instead of taking a regular break away from the site. In 2006, about 15 percent of guards worked part time, and some held a second job as a guard to supplement their primary earnings.

## Training, Other Qualifications, and Advancement

Generally, there are no specific education requirements for security guards, but employers usually prefer to fill armed guard positions with people who have at least a high school diploma. Gaming surveillance officers often need some education beyond high school. In most states, guards must be licensed.

*Education and training.* Many employers of unarmed guards do not have any specific educational requirements. For armed guards, employers usually prefer individuals who are high school graduates or who hold an equivalent certification.

Many employers give newly hired guards instruction before they start the job and provide on-the-job training. The amount of training guards receive varies. Training is more rigorous for armed guards because their employers are legally responsible for any use of force. Armed guards receive formal training in areas such as weapons retention and laws covering the use of force. They may be periodically tested in the use of firearms.

An increasing number of states are making ongoing training a legal requirement for retention of licensure. Guards may receive training in protection, public relations, report writing, crisis deterrence, first aid, and specialized training relevant to their particular assignment.

The American Society for Industrial Security International has written voluntary training guidelines that are intended to provide regulating bodies consistent minimum standards for the quality of security services. These guidelines recommend that security guards receive at least 48 hours of training within the first 100 days of employment. The guidelines also suggest that security guards be required to pass a written or performance examination covering topics such as sharing information with law enforcement, crime prevention, handling evidence, the use of force, court testimony, report writing, interpersonal and communication skills, and emergency response procedures. In addition, they recommend annual retraining and additional firearms training for armed officers.

Guards who are employed at establishments that place a heavy emphasis on security usually receive extensive formal training. For example, guards at nuclear power plants undergo several months of training before going on duty—and even then, they perform their tasks under close supervision for a significant period of time. They are taught to use firearms, administer first aid, operate alarm systems and electronic security equipment, and spot and deal with security problems.

Gaming surveillance officers and investigators usually need some training beyond high school but not usually a bachelor's degree. Several educational institutes offer certification programs. Classroom training usually is conducted in a casino-like atmosphere and includes the use of surveillance camera equipment. Previous security experience is a plus. Employers prefer either individuals with casino experience and significant knowledge of casino operations or those with law enforcement and investigation experience.

*Licensure.* Most states require that guards be licensed. To be licensed as a guard, individuals must usually be at least 18 years old, pass a background check, and complete classroom training in such subjects as property rights, emergency procedures, and detention of suspected criminals. Drug testing often is required and may be random and ongoing.

Guards who carry weapons must be licensed by the appropriate government authority, and some receive further certification as special police officers, allowing them to make limited types of arrests while on duty. Armed guard positions have more stringent background checks and entry requirements than those of unarmed guards.

*Other qualifications.* Most jobs require a driver's license. For positions as armed guards, employers often seek people who have had responsible experience in other occupations.

Rigorous hiring and screening programs consisting of background, criminal record, and fingerprint checks are becoming the norm in the occupation. Applicants are expected to have good character references, no serious police record, and good health. They should be mentally alert, emotionally stable, and physically fit to cope with emergencies. Guards who have frequent contact with the public should communicate well.

Like security guards, gaming surveillance officers and gaming investigators must have keen observation skills and excellent verbal and writing abilities to document violations or suspicious behavior. They also need to be physically fit and have quick reflexes because they sometimes must detain individuals until local law enforcement officials arrive.

*Advancement.* Compared with unarmed security guards, armed guards and special police usually enjoy higher earnings and benefits, greater job security, and more potential for advancement. Because many people do not stay long in this occupation, opportunities for advancement are good for those who make a career in security. Most large organizations use a military type of ranking that offers the possibility of advancement in both position and salary. Some guards may advance to supervisor or security manager positions. Guards with management skills may open their own contract security guard agencies. Guards can also move to an organization with more stringent security and higher pay.

**Projections data from the National Employment Matrix**

| Occupational Title | SOC Code | Employment, 2006 | Projected employment, 2016 | Change, 2006-16 | |
|---|---|---|---|---|---|
| | | | | Number | Percent |
| Security guards and gaming surveillance officers............................ | 33-9030 | 1,049,000 | 1,227,000 | 178,000 | 17 |
| Gaming surveillance officers and gaming investigators .............. | 33-9031 | 8,700 | 12,000 | 2,900 | 34 |
| Security guards.................................................................. | 33-9032 | 1,040,000 | 1,216,000 | 175,000 | 17 |

NOTE: Data in this table are rounded.

# Employment

Security guards and gaming surveillance officers held over 1 million jobs in 2006. More than half of all jobs for security guards were in investigation and security services, including guard and armored car services. These organizations provide security on a contract basis, assigning their guards to buildings and other sites as needed. Most other security officers were employed directly by educational services, hospitals, food services and drinking places, traveler accommodation (hotels), department stores, manufacturing firms, lessors of real estate (residential and nonresidential buildings), and governments. Guard jobs are found throughout the country, most commonly in metropolitan areas.

Gaming surveillance officers work primarily in gambling industries; traveler accommodation, which includes casino hotels; and local government. They are employed only in those states and on those Indian reservations where gambling is legal.

A significant number of law enforcement officers work as security guards when they are off duty, in order to supplement their incomes. Often working in uniform and with the official cars assigned to them, they add a high-profile security presence to the establishment with which they have contracted. At construction sites and apartment complexes, for example, their presence often deters crime.

# Job Outlook

Opportunities for security guards and gaming surveillance officers should be favorable. Numerous job openings will stem from employment growth, driven by the demand for increased security, and from the need to replace those who leave this large occupation each year.

*Employment change.* Employment of security guards is expected to grow by 17 percent between 2006 and 2016, which is faster than the average for all occupations. This occupation will have a very large number of new jobs arise, about 175,000 over the projections decade. Concern about crime, vandalism, and terrorism continues to increase the need for security. Demand for guards also will grow as private security firms increasingly perform duties—such as providing security at public events and in residential neighborhoods—that were formerly handled by police officers.

Employment of gaming surveillance officers is expected to grow by 34 percent between 2006 and 2016, which is much faster than the average for all occupations. Casinos will continue to hire more surveillance officers as more states legalize gambling and as the number of casinos increases in states where gambling is already legal. In addition, casino security forces will employ more technically trained personnel as technology becomes increasingly important in thwarting casino cheating and theft.

*Job prospects.* Job prospects for security guards should be excellent because of growing demand for these workers and the need to replace experienced workers who leave the occupation. In addition to full-time job opportunities, the limited training requirements and flexible hours attract many people seeking part-time or second jobs. However, competition is expected for higher paying positions that require longer periods of training; these positions usually are found at facilities that require a high level of security, such as nuclear power plants or weapons installations. Job prospects for gaming surveillance officers should be good, but they will be better for those with experience in the gaming industry.

# Earnings

Median annual wage-and-salary earnings of security guards were $21,530 in May 2006. The middle 50 percent earned between $17,620 and $27,430. The lowest 10 percent earned less than $15,030, and the highest 10 percent earned more than $35,840. Median annual earnings in the industries employing the largest numbers of security guards were

| | |
|---|---|
| General medical and surgical hospitals | $26,610 |
| Elementary and secondary schools | 26,290 |
| Local government | 24,950 |
| Investigation, guard and armored car services | 20,280 |

Gaming surveillance officers and gaming investigators had median annual wage-and-salary earnings of $27,130 in May 2006. The middle 50 percent earned between $21,600 and $35,970. The lowest 10 percent earned less than $18,720, and the highest 10 percent earned more than $45,940.

# Related Occupations

Guards protect property, maintain security, and enforce regulations and standards of conduct in the establishments at which they work. Related security and protective service occupations include correctional officers, police and detectives, private detectives and investigators, and gaming services occupations.

# Sources of Additional Information

Further information about work opportunities for guards is available from local security and guard firms and state employment service offices. Information about licensing requirements for guards may be obtained from the state licensing commission or the state police department. In states where local jurisdictions establish licensing requirements, contact a local government authority such as the sheriff, county executive, or city manager.

# Social and Human Service Assistants

(O*NET 21-1093.00)

## Significant Points

- A bachelor's degree usually is not required for these jobs, but employers increasingly seek individuals with relevant work experience or education beyond high school.

- Employment is projected to grow much faster than average for all occupations.

- Job opportunities should be excellent, particularly for applicants with appropriate postsecondary education, but wages remain low.

## Nature of the Work

Social and human service assistants help social workers, health care workers, and other professionals to provide services to people. Social and human service assistant is a generic term for workers with a wide array of job titles, including human service worker, case management aide, social work assistant, community support worker, mental health aide, community outreach worker, life skills counselor, or gerontology aide. They usually work under the direction of workers from a variety of fields, such as nursing, psychiatry, psychology, rehabilitative or physical therapy, or social work. The amount of responsibility and supervision they are given varies a great deal. Some have little direct supervision—they may run a group home, for example. Others work under close direction.

Social and human service assistants provide services to clients to help them improve their quality of life. They assess clients' needs, investigate their eligibility for benefits and services such as food stamps, Medicaid, or welfare, and help to obtain them. They also arrange for transportation and escorts, if necessary, and provide emotional support. Social and human service assistants monitor and keep case records on clients and report progress to supervisors and case managers.

Social and human service assistants play a variety of roles in a community. They may organize and lead group activities, assist clients in need of counseling or crisis intervention, or administer food banks or emergency fuel programs, for example. In halfway houses, group homes, and government-supported housing programs, they assist adults who need supervision with personal hygiene and daily living skills. They review clients' records, ensure that they take their medication, talk with family members, and confer with medical personnel and other caregivers to provide insight into clients' needs. Social and human service assistants also give emotional support and help clients become involved in community recreation programs and other activities.

In psychiatric hospitals, rehabilitation programs, and outpatient clinics, social and human service assistants work with psychiatrists, psychologists, social workers, and others to help clients master everyday living skills, communicate more effectively, and live well with others. They support the client's participation in a treatment plan, such as individual or group counseling or occupational therapy.

The work, while satisfying, can be emotionally draining. Understaffing and relatively low pay may add to the pressure.

***Work environment.*** Working conditions of social and human service assistants vary. Some work in offices, clinics, and hospitals, while others work in group homes, shelters, sheltered workshops, and day programs. Traveling to see clients is also required for some jobs. Sometimes working with clients can be dangerous even though most agencies do everything they can to ensure their workers' safety. Most assistants work 40 hours a week; some work in the evening and on weekends.

## Training, Other Qualifications, and Advancement

A bachelor's degree is not required for most jobs in this occupation, but employers increasingly seek individuals with relevant work experience or education beyond high school.

***Education and training.*** Many employers prefer to hire people with some education beyond high school. Certificates or associate degrees in subjects such as human services, gerontology or one of the social or behavioral sciences meet many employers' requirements. Some jobs may require a bachelor's or master's degree in human services or a related field, such as counseling, rehabilitation, or social work.

Human services degree programs have a core curriculum that trains students to observe patients and record information, conduct patient interviews, implement treatment plans, employ problem-solving techniques, handle crisis intervention matters, and use proper case management and referral procedures. Many programs utilize field work to give students hands-on experience. General education courses in liberal arts, sciences, and the humanities also are part of most curriculums. Most programs also offer specialized courses related to addictions, gerontology, child protection, and other areas. Many degree programs require completion of a supervised internship.

The level of education workers have often influence the kind of work they are assigned and the degree of responsibility that is given to them. For example, workers with no more than a high school education are likely to receive extensive on-the-job training to work in direct-care services, helping clients to fill out paperwork, for example. Workers with a college degree, however, might do supportive counseling, coordinate program activities, or manage a group home. Social and human service assistants with proven leadership ability, especially from paid or volunteer experience in social services, often have greater autonomy in their work. Regardless of the academic or work background of employees, most employers provide some form of in-service training to their employees such as seminars and workshops.

***Other qualifications.*** These workers should have a strong desire to help others, effective communication skills, a sense of responsibility, and the ability to manage time effectively. Many human services jobs involve direct contact with people who are vulnerable to exploitation or mistreatment; so patience and understanding are also highly valued characteristics.

**Projections data from the National Employment Matrix**

| Occupational Title | SOC Code | Employment, 2006 | Projected employment, 2016 | Change, 2006-2016 | |
|---|---|---|---|---|---|
| | | | | Number | Percent |
| Social and human service assistants ................................................. | 21-1093 | 339,000 | 453,000 | 114,000 | 34 |

NOTE: Data in this table are rounded.

It is becoming more common for employers to require a criminal background check, and in some settings, workers may be required to have a valid driver's license.

*Advancement.* Formal education is almost always necessary for advancement. In general, advancement to case management, rehabilitation, or social work jobs requires a bachelor's or master's degree in human services, counseling, rehabilitation, social work, or a related field.

## Employment

Social and human service assistants held about 339,000 jobs in 2006. Over 60 percent were employed in the health care and social assistance industries. Nearly 3 in 10 were employed by state and local governments, primarily in public welfare agencies and facilities for mentally disabled and developmentally challenged individuals.

## Job Outlook

Employment of social and human service assistants is expected to grow by nearly 34 percent through 2016. Job prospects are expected to be excellent, particularly for applicants with appropriate postsecondary education.

*Employment change.* The number of social and human service assistants is projected to grow by nearly 34 percent between 2006 and 2016, which is much faster than the average for all occupations. This occupation will have a very large number of new jobs arise, about 114,000 over the projections decade. Faced with rapid growth in the demand for social and human services, many employers increasingly rely on social and human service assistants.

Demand for social services will expand with the growing elderly population, who are more likely to need adult day care, meal delivery programs, support during medical crises, and other services. In addition, more social and human service assistants will be needed to provide services to pregnant teenagers, people who are homeless, people who are mentally disabled or developmentally challenged, and people who are substance abusers.

Job training programs are also expected to require additional social and human service assistants. As social welfare policies shift focus from benefit-based programs to work-based initiatives, there will be more demand for people to teach job skills to the people who are new to, or returning to, the workforce.

Residential care establishments should face increased pressures to respond to the needs of the mentally and physically disabled. The number of people who are disabled is increasing, and many need help to care for themselves. More community-based programs and supportive independent-living sites are expected to be established to house and assist the homeless and the mentally and physically dis-

abled. Furthermore, as substance abusers are increasingly being sent to treatment programs instead of prison, employment of social and human service assistants in substance abuse treatment programs also will grow.

Opportunities are expected to be good in private social service agencies. Employment in private agencies will grow as state and local governments continue to contract out services to the private sector in an effort to cut costs. Also, some private agencies have been employing more social and human service assistants in place of social workers, who are more educated and more highly paid.

The number of jobs for social and human service assistants in local governments will grow but not as fast as employment for social and human service assistants in other industries. Employment in the public sector may fluctuate with the level of funding provided by state and local governments and with the number of services contracted out to private organizations.

*Job prospects.* Job prospects for social and human service assistants are expected to be excellent, particularly for individuals with appropriate education after high school. Job openings will come from job growth, but also from the need to replace workers who advance into new positions, retire, or leave the workforce for other reasons. There will be more competition for jobs in urban areas than in rural ones, but qualified applicants should have little difficulty finding employment.

## Earnings

Median annual earnings of social and human service assistants were $25,580 in May 2006. The middle 50 percent earned between $20,350 and $32,440. The top 10 percent earned more than $40,780, while the lowest 10 percent earned less than $16,180.

Median annual earnings in the industries employing the largest numbers of social and human service assistants in May 2006 were

| | |
|---|---|
| Local government | ............................................$30,510 |
| State government | .............................................29,810 |
| Individual and family services | ............................24,490 |
| Vocational rehabilitation services | .........................22,530 |
| Residential mental retardation, mental health and substance abuse facilities | ............................22,380 |

## Related Occupations

Workers in other occupations that require skills similar to those of social and human service assistants include social workers, clergy, counselors, child care workers; occupational therapist assistants and aides, physical therapist assistants and aides, and nursing, psychiatric, and home health aides.

## Sources of Additional Information

For information on programs and careers in human services, contact

▸ Council for Standards in Human Services Education, PMB 703, 1050 Larrabee Avenue, Suite 104, Bellingham, WA 98225-7367. Internet: http://www.cshse.org

▸ National Organization for Human Services, 90 Madison Street, Suite 206, Denver, CO 80206. Internet: http://www.nationalhumanservices.org

Information on job openings may be available from state employment service offices or directly from city, county, or state departments of health, mental health and mental retardation, and human resources.

# Social Workers

(O*NET 21-1021.00, 21-1022.00, 21-1023.00, and 21-1029.99)

## Significant Points

■ Employment is projected to grow much faster than average.

■ About 5 out of 10 jobs are in health care and social assistance industries and 3 in 10 work for state and local government agencies.

■ While a bachelor's degree is the minimum requirement, a master's degree in social work or a related field has become the standard for many positions.

■ Competition for jobs is expected in cities, but opportunities should be good in rural areas.

## Nature of the Work

Social work is a profession for those with a strong desire to help improve people's lives. Social workers assist people by helping them cope with issues in their everyday lives, deal with their relationships, and solve personal and family problems. Some social workers help clients who face a disability or a life-threatening disease or a social problem, such as inadequate housing, unemployment, or substance abuse. Social workers also assist families that have serious domestic conflicts, sometimes involving child or spousal abuse. Some social workers conduct research, advocate for improved services, engage in systems design or are involved in planning or policy development. Many social workers specialize in serving a particular population or working in a specific setting.

*Child, family, and school social workers* provide social services and assistance to improve the social and psychological functioning of children and their families and to maximize the well-being of families and the academic functioning of children. They may assist single parents, arrange adoptions, or help find foster homes for neglected, abandoned, or abused children. Some specialize in services for senior citizens. These social workers may run support groups for the children of aging parents; advise elderly people or family members about housing, transportation, long-term care, and other services; and coordinate and monitor these services. Through employee assistance programs, social workers may help people cope with job-related pressures or with personal problems that affect the quality of their work.

In schools, social workers often serve as the link between students' families and the school, working with parents, guardians, teachers, and other school officials to ensure students reach their academic and personal potential. In addition, they address problems such as misbehavior, truancy, and teenage pregnancy and advise teachers on how to cope with difficult students. Increasingly, school social workers teach workshops to entire classes.

Child, family, and school social workers may also be known as child welfare social workers, family services social workers, child protective services social workers, occupational social workers, or gerontology social workers. They often work for individual and family services agencies, schools, or state or local governments.

*Medical and public health social workers* provide psychosocial support to people, families, or vulnerable populations so they can cope with chronic, acute, or terminal illnesses, such as Alzheimer's disease, cancer, or AIDS. They also advise family caregivers, counsel patients, and help plan for patients' needs after discharge from hospitals. They may arrange for at-home services, such as meals-on-wheels or home care. Some work on interdisciplinary teams that evaluate certain kinds of patients—geriatric or organ transplant patients, for example. Medical and public health social workers may work for hospitals, nursing and personal care facilities, individual and family services agencies, or local governments.

*Mental health and substance abuse social workers* assess and treat individuals with mental illness or substance abuse problems, including abuse of alcohol, tobacco, or other drugs. Such services include individual and group therapy, outreach, crisis intervention, social rehabilitation, and teaching skills needed for everyday living. They also may help plan for supportive services to ease clients' return to the community. Mental health and substance abuse social workers are likely to work in hospitals, substance abuse treatment centers, individual and family services agencies, or local governments. These social workers may be known as clinical social workers.

Other types of social workers include social work administrators, planners and policymakers, who develop and implement programs to address issues such as child abuse, homelessness, substance abuse, poverty, and violence. These workers research and analyze policies, programs, and regulations. They identify social problems and suggest legislative and other solutions. They may help raise funds or write grants to support these programs.

***Work environment.*** Social workers usually spend most of their time in an office or residential facility, but they also may travel locally to visit clients, meet with service providers, or attend meetings. Some may meet with clients in one of several offices within a local area. Social work, while satisfying, can be challenging. Understaffing and large caseloads add to the pressure in some agencies. To tend to patient care or client needs, many hospitals and long-term care facilities employ social workers on teams with a broad mix of occupations, including clinical specialists, registered nurses, and health aides. Full-time social workers usually work a standard 40-hour week, but some occasionally work evenings and weekends to meet with clients, attend community meetings, and handle emergencies. Some work part time, particularly in voluntary nonprofit agencies.

## Training, Other Qualifications, and Advancement

A bachelor's degree is the minimum requirement for entry into the occupation, but many positions require an advanced degree. All states and the District of Columbia have some licensure, certification, or registration requirement, but the regulations vary.

*Education and training.* A bachelor's degree in social work (BSW) is the most common minimum requirement to qualify for a job as a social worker; however, majors in psychology, sociology, and related fields may qualify for some entry-level jobs, especially in small community agencies. Although a bachelor's degree is sufficient for entry into the field, an advanced degree has become the standard for many positions. A master's degree in social work (MSW) is typically required for positions in health settings and is required for clinical work as well. Some jobs in public and private agencies also may require an advanced degree, such as a master's degree in social services policy or administration. Supervisory, administrative, and staff training positions usually require an advanced degree. College and university teaching positions and most research appointments normally require a doctorate in social work (DSW or Ph.D.).

As of 2006, the Council on Social Work Education accredited 458 bachelor's programs and 181 master's programs. The Group for the Advancement of Doctoral Education listed 74 doctoral programs in social work (DSW or Ph. D.) in the United States. Bachelor's degree programs prepare graduates for direct service positions, such as caseworker, and include courses in social work values and ethics, dealing with a culturally diverse clientele and at-risk populations, promotion of social and economic justice, human behavior and the social environment, social welfare policy and services, social work practice, social research methods, and field education. Accredited programs require a minimum of 400 hours of supervised field experience.

Master's degree programs prepare graduates for work in their chosen field of concentration and continue to develop the skills required to perform clinical assessments, manage large caseloads, take on supervisory roles, and explore new ways of drawing upon social services to meet the needs of clients. Master's programs last two years and include a minimum of 900 hours of supervised field instruction or internship. A part-time program may take four years. Entry into a master's program does not require a bachelor's degree in social work, but courses in psychology, biology, sociology, economics, political science, and social work are recommended. In addition, a second language can be very helpful. Most master's programs offer advanced standing for those with a bachelor's degree from an accredited social work program.

*Licensure.* All states and the District of Columbia have licensing, certification, or registration requirements regarding social work practice and the use of professional titles. Although standards for licensing vary by state, a growing number of states are placing greater emphasis on communications skills, professional ethics, and sensitivity to cultural diversity issues. Most states require two years (3,000 hours) of supervised clinical experience for licensure of clinical social workers.

*Other qualifications.* Social workers should be emotionally mature, objective, and sensitive to people and their problems. They must be able to handle responsibility, work independently, and maintain good working relationships with clients and coworkers. Volunteer or paid jobs as a social work aide can help people test their interest in this field.

*Certification and advancement.* The National Association of Social Workers offers voluntary credentials. Social workers with a master's degree in social work may be eligible for the Academy of Certified Social Workers (ACSW), the Qualified Clinical Social Worker (QCSW), or the Diplomate in Clinical Social Work (DCSW) credential, based on their professional experience. Credentials are particularly important for those in private practice; some health insurance providers require social workers to have them in order to be reimbursed for services.

Advancement to supervisor, program manager, assistant director, or executive director of a social service agency or department usually requires an advanced degree and related work experience. Other career options for social workers include teaching, research, and consulting. Some of these workers also help formulate government policies by analyzing and advocating policy positions in government agencies, in research institutions, and on legislators' staffs.

Some social workers go into private practice. Most private practitioners are clinical social workers who provide psychotherapy, usually paid for through health insurance or by the client themselves. Private practitioners must have at least a master's degree and a period of supervised work experience. A network of contacts for referrals also is essential. Many private practitioners split their time between working for an agency or hospital and working in their private practice. They may continue to hold a position at a hospital or agency in order to receive health and life insurance.

## Employment

Social workers held about 595,000 jobs in 2006. About 5 out of 10 jobs were in health care and social assistance industries and 3 out of 10 are employed by state and local government agencies, primarily in departments of health and human services. Although most social workers are employed in cities or suburbs, some work in rural areas. Employment by type of social worker in 2006, follows:

Child, family, and school social workers ..............282,000

Medical and public health social workers..............124,000

Mental health and substance abuse social
   workers ......................................................122,000

Social workers, all other ......................................66,000

## Job Outlook

Employment for social workers is expected grow much faster than the average for all occupations through 2016. Job prospects are expected to be favorable, particularly for social workers who specialize in the aging population or work in rural areas.

*Employment change.* Employment of social workers is expected to increase by 22 percent during the 2006–2016 decade, which is much faster than the average for all occupations. The growing elderly population and the aging baby boom generation will create greater

**Projections data from the National Employment Matrix**

| Occupational Title | SOC Code | Employment, 2006 | Projected employment, 2016 | Change, 2006-2016 | |
|---|---|---|---|---|---|
| | | | | Number | Percent |
| Social workers.............................................................................. | 21-1020 | 595,000 | 727,000 | 132,000 | 22 |
| Child, family, and school social workers ...................................... | 21-1021 | 282,000 | 336,000 | 54,000 | 19 |
| Medical and public health social workers.................................... | 21-1022 | 124,000 | 154,000 | 30,000 | 24 |
| Mental health and substance abuse social workers...................... | 21-1023 | 122,000 | 159,000 | 37,000 | 30 |
| Social workers, all other................................................................ | 21-1029 | 66,000 | 78,000 | 12,000 | 18 |

NOTE: Data in this table are rounded.

demand for health and social services, resulting in rapid job growth among gerontology social workers. Employment of social workers in private social service agencies also will increase. However, agencies increasingly will restructure services and hire more social and human service assistants, who are paid less, instead of social workers. Employment in state and local government agencies may grow somewhat in response to growing needs for public welfare, family services, and child protective services, but many of these services will be contracted out to private agencies. Employment levels in public and private social services agencies may fluctuate, depending on need and government funding levels.

Opportunities for social workers in private practice will expand, but growth may be somewhat hindered by restrictions that managed care organizations put on mental health services. The growing popularity of employee assistance programs is expected to spur demand for private practitioners, some of whom provide social work services to corporations on a contractual basis. However, the popularity of employee assistance programs will fluctuate with the business cycle because businesses are not likely to offer these services during recessions.

Employment of child, family and school social workers is expected to grow by 19 percent, which is faster than the average for all occupations. One of the major contributing factors is the rise in the elderly population. Social workers, particularly family social workers, will be needed to assist in finding the best care for the aging and to support their families. Furthermore, demand for school social workers will increase and lead to more jobs as efforts are expanded to respond to rising student enrollments as well as the continued emphasis on integrating disabled children into the general school population. There could be competition for school social work jobs in some areas because of the limited number of openings. The availability of federal, state, and local funding will be a major factor in determining the actual job growth in schools. The demand for child and family social workers may also be tied to the availability of government funding.

Mental health and substance abuse social workers will grow by 29 percent, which is much faster than the average, over the 2006–2016 decade. In particular, social workers specializing in substance abuse will experience strong demand. Substance abusers are increasingly being placed into treatment programs instead of being sentenced to prison. Also, growing numbers of the substance abusers sentenced to prison or probation are, increasingly being required by correctional systems to have substance abuse treatment added as a condition to their sentence or probation. As this trend grows, demand will strengthen for treatment programs and social workers to assist abusers on the road to recovery.

Growth of medical and public health social workers is expected to be 24 percent, which is much faster than the average for all occupations. Hospitals continue to limit the length of patient stays, so the demand for social workers in hospitals will grow more slowly than in other areas. But hospitals are releasing patients earlier than in the past, so social worker employment in home health care services is growing. However, the expanding senior population is an even larger factor. Employment opportunities for social workers with backgrounds in gerontology should be good in the growing numbers of assisted-living and senior-living communities. The expanding senior population also will spur demand for social workers in nursing homes, long-term care facilities, and hospices. However, in these settings other types of workers are often being given tasks that were previously done by social workers.

*Job prospects.* Job prospects are generally expected to be favorable. Many job openings will stem from growth and the need to replace social workers who leave the occupation. However, competition for social worker jobs is expected in cities, where training programs for social workers are prevalent. Opportunities should be good in rural areas, which often find it difficult to attract and retain qualified staff. By specialty, job prospects may be best for those social workers with a background in gerontology and substance abuse treatment.

# Earnings

Median annual earnings of child, family, and school social workers were $37,480 in May 2006. The middle 50 percent earned between $29,590 and $49,060. The lowest 10 percent earned less than $24,480, and the top 10 percent earned more than $62,530. Median annual earnings in the industries employing the largest numbers of child, family, and school social workers in May 2006 were

| | |
|---|---|
| Elementary and secondary schools | $48,360 |
| Local government | 43,500 |
| State government | 39,000 |
| Individual and family services | 32,680 |
| Other residential care facilities | 32,590 |

Median annual earnings of medical and public health social workers were $43,040 in May 2006. The middle 50 percent earned between $34,110 and $53,740. The lowest 10 percent earned less than $27,280, and the top 10 percent earned more than $64,070. Median annual earnings in the industries employing the largest numbers of medical and public health social workers in May 2006 were

| | |
|---|---|
| General medical and surgical hospitals | $48,420 |
| Home health care services | 44,470 |
| Local government | 41,590 |

Nursing care facilities .........................................38,550

Individual and family services .............................35,510

Median annual earnings of mental health and substance abuse social workers were $35,410 in May 2006. The middle 50 percent earned between $27,940 and $45,720. The lowest 10 percent earned less than $22,490, and the top 10 percent earned more than $57,630. Median annual earnings in the industries employing the largest numbers of mental health and substance abuse social workers in May 2006 were

Local government ...........................................$39,550

Psychiatric and substance abuse hospitals..............39,240

Individual and family services .............................34,920

Residential mental retardation, mental health
and substance abuse facilities...........................30,590

Outpatient mental health and substance
abuse centers ................................................34,290

Median annual earnings of social workers, all other were $43,580 in May 2006. The middle 50 percent earned between $32,530 and $56,420. The lowest 10 percent earned less than $25,540, and the top 10 percent earned more than $68,500. Median annual earnings in the industries employing the largest numbers of social workers, all other in May 2006 were

Local government ...........................................$46,330

State government .............................................45,070

Individual and family services .............................35,150

About 20 percent of social workers are members of a union. Many belong to the union that represents workers in other occupations at their place of employment.

## Related Occupations

Through direct counseling or referral to other services, social workers help people solve a range of personal problems. Workers in occupations with similar duties include the clergy, counselors, probation officers and correctional treatment specialists, psychologists, and social and human services assistants.

## Sources of Additional Information

For information about career opportunities in social work and voluntary credentials for social workers, contact

▶ National Association of Social Workers, 750 First St. N.E., Suite 700, Washington, DC 20002-4241. Internet: http://www.socialworkers.org

For a listing of accredited social work programs, contact

▶ Council on Social Work Education, 1725 Duke St., Suite 500, Alexandria, VA 22314-3457. Internet: http://www.cswe.org

Information on licensing requirements and testing procedures for each state may be obtained from state licensing authorities, or from

▶ Association of Social Work Boards, 400 South Ridge Pkwy., Suite B, Culpeper, VA 22701. Internet: http://www.aswb.org

# Surgical Technologists

(O*NET 29-2055.00)

## Significant Points

■ Employment is expected to grow much faster than average.

■ Job opportunities will be best for technologists who are certified.

■ Training programs last 9 to 24 months and lead to a certificate, diploma, or associate degree.

■ Hospitals will continue to be the primary employer, although much faster employment growth is expected in other health care industries.

## Nature of the Work

Surgical technologists, also called scrubs and surgical or operating room technicians, assist in surgical operations under the supervision of surgeons, registered nurses, or other surgical personnel. Surgical technologists are members of operating room teams, which most commonly include surgeons, anesthesiologists, and circulating nurses.

Before an operation, surgical technologists help prepare the operating room by setting up surgical instruments and equipment, sterile drapes, and sterile solutions. They assemble both sterile and nonsterile equipment, as well as check and adjust it to ensure it is working properly. Technologists also get patients ready for surgery by washing, shaving, and disinfecting incision sites. They transport patients to the operating room, help position them on the operating table, and cover them with sterile surgical drapes. Technologists also observe patients' vital signs, check charts, and help the surgical team put on sterile gowns and gloves.

During surgery, technologists pass instruments and other sterile supplies to surgeons and surgeon assistants. They may hold retractors, cut sutures, and help count sponges, needles, supplies, and instruments. Surgical technologists help prepare, care for, and dispose of specimens taken for laboratory analysis and help apply dressings. Some operate sterilizers, lights, or suction machines, and help operate diagnostic equipment.

After an operation, surgical technologists may help transfer patients to the recovery room and clean and restock the operating room.

Certified surgical technologists with additional specialized education or training also may act in the role of the surgical first assistant or circulator. The surgical first assistant, as defined by the American College of Surgeons (ACS), provides aid in exposure, hemostasis (controlling blood flow and stopping or preventing hemorrhage), and other technical functions under the surgeon's direction that help the surgeon carry out a safe operation. A circulating technologist is the "unsterile" member of the surgical team who interviews the patient before surgery; prepares the patient; helps with anesthesia; obtains and opens packages for the "sterile" people to remove the sterile contents during the procedure; keeps a written account of the surgical procedure; and answers the surgeon's questions about the patient during the surgery.

Projections data from the National Employment Matrix

| Occupational Title | SOC Code | Employment, 2006 | Projected employment, 2016 | Change, 2006-2016 | |
|---|---|---|---|---|---|
| | | | | Number | Percent |
| Surgical technologists ................................................................ | 29-2055 | 86,000 | 107,000 | 21,000 | 24 |

NOTE: Data in this table are rounded.

***Work environment.*** Surgical technologists work in clean, well-lighted, cool environments. They must stand for long periods and remain alert during operations. At times, they may be exposed to communicable diseases and unpleasant sights, odors, and materials.

Most surgical technologists work a regular 40-hour week, although they may be on call or work nights, weekends, and holidays on a rotating basis.

# Training, Other Qualifications, and Advancement

Training programs last nine to 24 months and lead to a certificate, diploma, or associate degree. Professional certification can help in getting jobs and promotions.

***Education and training.*** Surgical technologists receive their training in formal programs offered by community and junior colleges, vocational schools, universities, hospitals, and the military. In 2006, the Commission on Accreditation of Allied Health Education Programs (CAAHEP) recognized more than 400 accredited training programs. Programs last from nine to 24 months and lead to a certificate, diploma, or associate degree. High school graduation normally is required for admission. Recommended high school courses include health, biology, chemistry, and mathematics.

Programs provide classroom education and supervised clinical experience. Students take courses in anatomy, physiology, microbiology, pharmacology, professional ethics, and medical terminology. Other topics covered include the care and safety of patients during surgery, sterile techniques, and surgical procedures. Students also learn to sterilize instruments; prevent and control infection; and handle special drugs, solutions, supplies, and equipment.

***Certification and other qualifications.*** Most employers prefer to hire certified technologists. Technologists may obtain voluntary professional certification from the Liaison Council on Certification for the Surgical Technologist by graduating from a CAAHEP-accredited program and passing a national certification examination. They may then use the Certified Surgical Technologist (CST) designation. Continuing education or reexamination is required to maintain certification, which must be renewed every four years.

Certification also may be obtained from the National Center for Competency Testing (NCCT). To qualify to take the exam, candidates follow one of three paths: complete an accredited training program; undergo a two-year hospital on-the-job training program; or acquire seven years of experience working in the field. After passing the exam, individuals may use the designation Tech in Surgery-Certified, TS-C (NCCT). This certification must be renewed every five years through either continuing education or reexamination.

Surgical technologists need manual dexterity to handle instruments quickly. They also must be conscientious, orderly, and emotionally stable to handle the demands of the operating room environment.

Technologists must respond quickly and must be familiar with operating procedures in order to have instruments ready for surgeons without having to be told. They are expected to keep abreast of new developments in the field.

***Advancement.*** Technologists advance by specializing in a particular area of surgery, such as neurosurgery or open heart surgery. They also may work as circulating technologists. With additional training, some technologists advance to first assistant. Some surgical technologists manage central supply departments in hospitals, or take positions with insurance companies, sterile supply services, and operating equipment firms.

# Employment

Surgical technologists held about 86,000 jobs in 2006. About 70 percent of jobs for surgical technologists were in hospitals, mainly in operating and delivery rooms. Other jobs were in offices of physicians or dentists who perform outpatient surgery and in outpatient care centers, including ambulatory surgical centers. A few technologists, known as private scrubs, are employed directly by surgeons who have special surgical teams, like those for liver transplants.

# Job Outlook

Employment of surgical technologists is expected to grow much faster than the average for all occupations. Job opportunities will be best for technologists who are certified.

***Employment change.*** Employment of surgical technologists is expected to grow 24 percent between 2006 and 2016, much faster than the average for all occupations, as the volume of surgeries increases. The number of surgical procedures is expected to rise as the population grows and ages. Older people, including the baby boom generation, who generally require more surgical procedures, will account for a larger portion of the general population. In addition, technological advances, such as fiber optics and laser technology, will permit an increasing number of new surgical procedures to be performed and also will allow surgical technologists to assist with a greater number of procedures.

Hospitals will continue to be the primary employer of surgical technologists, although much faster employment growth is expected in offices of physicians and in outpatient care centers, including ambulatory surgical centers.

***Job prospects.*** Job opportunities will be best for technologists who are certified.

# Earnings

Median annual earnings of wage-and-salary surgical technologists were $36,080 in May 2006. The middle 50 percent earned between $30,300 and $43,560. The lowest 10 percent earned less than

$25,490, and the highest 10 percent earned more than $51,140. Median annual earnings in the industries employing the largest numbers of surgical technologists were

| | |
|---|---|
| Offices of physicians | $37,300 |
| Outpatient care centers | 37,280 |
| General medical and surgical hospitals | 35,840 |
| Offices of dentists | 34,160 |

Benefits provided by most employers include paid vacation and sick leave, health, medical, vision, dental insurance and life insurance, and retirement program. A few employers also provide tuition reimbursement and child care benefits.

## Related Occupations

Other health occupations requiring approximately 1 year of training after high school include dental assistants, licensed practical and licensed vocational nurses, clinical laboratory technologists and technicians, and medical assistants.

## Sources of Additional Information

For additional information on a career as a surgical technologist and a list of CAAHEP-accredited programs, contact

▸ Association of Surgical Technologists, 6 West Dry Creek Circle, Suite 200, Littleton, CO 80120. Internet: http://www.ast.org

For information on becoming a Certified Surgical Technologist, contact

▸ Liaison Council on Certification for the Surgical Technologist, 6 West Dry Creek Circle, Suite 100, Littleton, CO 80120. Internet: http://www.lcc-st.org

For information on becoming a Tech in Surgery-Certified, contact

▸ National Center for Competency Testing, 7007 College Blvd., Suite 705, Overland Park, KS 66211.

# Surveyors, Cartographers, Photogrammetrists, and Surveying and Mapping Technicians

(O*NET 17-1021.00, 17-1022.00, 17-3031.00, 17-3031.01, and 17-3031.02)

## Significant Points

- About 7 out of 10 jobs are in architectural, engineering, and related services.

- Opportunities will be best for surveyors, cartographers, and photogrammetrists who have a bachelor's degree and strong technical skills.

- Overall employment of surveyors, cartographers, photogrammetrists, and surveying technicians is expected to grow much faster than the average for all occupations through the year 2016.

## Nature of the Work

Surveyors, cartographers, and photogrammetrists are responsible for measuring and mapping the Earth's surface. *Surveyors* establish official land, airspace, and water boundaries. They write descriptions of land for deeds, leases, and other legal documents; define airspace for airports; and take measurements of construction and mineral sites. Other surveyors provide data about the shape, contour, location, elevation, or dimension of land or land features. *Cartographers and photogrammetrists* collect, analyze, interpret, and map geographic information from surveys and from data and photographs collected using airplanes and satellites. *Surveying and mapping technicians* assist these professionals by collecting data in the field, making calculations, and helping with computer-aided drafting. Collectively, these occupations play key roles in the field of geospatial information.

Surveyors measure distances, directions, and angles between points and elevations of points, lines, and contours on, above, and below the Earth's surface. In the field, they select known survey reference points and determine the precise location of important features in the survey area using specialized equipment. Surveyors also research legal records, look for evidence of previous boundaries, and analyze data to determine the location of boundary lines. They are sometimes called to provide expert testimony in court about their work. Surveyors also record their results, verify the accuracy of data, and prepare plots, maps, and reports.

Some surveyors perform specialized functions closer to those of cartographers and photogrammetrists than to those of traditional surveyors. For example, *geodetic surveyors* use high-accuracy techniques, including satellite observations, to measure large areas of the earth's surface. *Geophysical prospecting surveyors* mark sites for subsurface exploration, usually to look for petroleum. *Marine or hydrographic surveyors* survey harbors, rivers, and other bodies of water to determine shorelines, the topography of the bottom, water depth, and other features.

Surveyors use the Global Positioning System (GPS) to locate reference points with a high degree of precision. To use this system, a surveyor places a satellite signal receiver—a small instrument mounted on a tripod—on a desired point, and another receiver on a point for which the geographic position is known. The receiver simultaneously collects information from several satellites to establish a precise position. The receiver also can be placed in a vehicle for tracing out road systems. Because receivers now come in different sizes and shapes, and because the cost of receivers has fallen, much more surveying work can be done with GPS. Surveyors then interpret and check the results produced by the new technology.

Field measurements are often taken by a survey party that gathers the information needed by the surveyor. A typical survey party consists of a party chief and one or more surveying technicians and helpers. The party chief, who may be either a surveyor or a senior surveying technician, leads day-to-day work activities. Surveying technicians assist the party chief by adjusting and operating surveying instruments, such as the total station, which measures and records angles and distances simultaneously. Surveying technicians or assistants position and hold the vertical rods, or targets, that the operator sights on to measure angles, distances, or elevations. They may hold measuring tapes if electronic distance-measuring equipment is not used. Surveying technicians compile notes, make sketches, and enter the data obtained from surveying instruments into computers either in the field or at the office. Survey parties also may include laborers or helpers who perform less-skilled duties, such as clearing brush from sight lines, driving stakes, or carrying equipment.

Photogrammetrists and cartographers measure, map, and chart the Earth's surface. Their work involves everything from performing geographical research and compiling data to producing maps. They collect, analyze, and interpret both spatial data—such as latitude, longitude, elevation, and distance—and nonspatial data—for example, population density, land-use patterns, annual precipitation levels, and demographic characteristics. Their maps may give both physical and social characteristics of the land. They prepare maps in either digital or graphic form, using information provided by geodetic surveys and remote sensing systems including aerial cameras, satellites, and LIDAR.

LIDAR—light-imaging detection and ranging—uses lasers attached to planes and other equipment to digitally map the topography of the Earth. It is often more accurate than traditional surveying methods and also can be used to collect other forms of data, such as the location and density of forests. Data developed by LIDAR can be used by surveyors, cartographers, and photogrammetrists to provide spatial information to specialists in geology, seismology, forestry, and construction, and other fields.

Geographic Information Systems (GIS) have become an integral tool for surveyors, cartographers and photogrammetrists, and surveying and mapping technicians. Workers use GIS to assemble, integrate, analyze, and display data about location in a digital format. They also use GIS to compile information from a variety of sources. GIS typically are used to make maps which combine information useful for environmental studies, geology, engineering, planning, business marketing, and other disciplines. As more of these systems are developed, many mapping specialists are being called *geographic information specialists.*

*Work environment.* Surveyors and surveying technicians usually work an 8-hour day, 5 days a week and may spend a lot of time outdoors. Sometimes, they work longer hours during the summer, when weather and light conditions are most suitable for fieldwork. Construction-related work may be limited during times of inclement weather.

Surveyors and technicians engage in active, sometimes strenuous, work. They often stand for long periods, walk considerable distances, and climb hills with heavy packs of instruments and other equipment. They also can be exposed to all types of weather. Traveling is sometimes part of the job, and land surveyors and technicians may commute long distances, stay away from home overnight, or temporarily relocate near a survey site. Surveyors also work indoors while planning surveys, searching court records for deed information, analyzing data, and preparing reports and maps.

Cartographers and photogrammetrists spend most of their time in offices using computers. However, certain jobs may require extensive field work to verify results and acquire data.

# Training, Other Qualifications, and Advancement

Most surveyors, cartographers, and photogrammetrists have a bachelor's degree in surveying or a related field. Every state requires that surveyors be licensed.

*Education and training.* In the past, many people with little formal training started as members of survey crews and worked their way up to become licensed surveyors, but this has become increasingly difficult to do. Now, most surveyors need a bachelor's degree. A number of universities offer bachelor's degree programs in surveying, and many community colleges, technical institutes, and vocational schools offer one-, two-, and three-year programs in surveying or surveying technology.

Cartographers and photogrammetrists usually have a bachelor's degree in cartography, geography, surveying, engineering, forestry, computer science, or a physical science, although a few enter these positions after working as technicians. With the development of GIS, cartographers and photogrammetrists need more education and stronger technical skills—including more experience with computers—than in the past.

Most cartographic and photogrammetric technicians also have specialized postsecondary education. High school students interested in surveying and cartography should take courses in algebra, geometry, trigonometry, drafting, mechanical drawing, and computer science.

*Licensure.* All 50 states and all U.S. territories license surveyors. For licensure, most state licensing boards require that individuals pass a written examination given by the National Council of Examiners for Engineering and Surveying (NCEES). Most states also require surveyors to pass a written examination prepared by the state licensing board.

Licensing happens in stages. After passing a first exam, the Fundamentals of Surveying, most candidates work under the supervision of an experienced surveyor for four years and then for licensure take a second exam, the Principles and Practice of Surveyors.

Specific requirements for training and education vary among the states. An increasing number of states require a bachelor's degree in surveying or in a closely related field, such as civil engineering or forestry, regardless of the number of years of experience. Some states require the degree to be from a school accredited by the Accreditation Board for Engineering and Technology. Many states also have a continuing education requirement.

Additionally a number of states require cartographers and photogrammetrists to be licensed as surveyors, and some states have specific licenses for photogrammetrists.

*Other qualifications.* Surveyors, cartographers, and photogrammetrists should be able to visualize objects, distances, sizes, and abstract forms. They must work with precision and accuracy because mistakes can be costly.

Members of a survey party must be in good physical condition because they work outdoors and often carry equipment over difficult terrain. They need good eyesight, coordination, and hearing to communicate verbally and using hand signals. Surveying is a cooperative operation, so good interpersonal skills and the ability to work as part of a team is important. Good office skills also are essential

**Projections data from the National Employment Matrix**

| Occupational Title | SOC Code | Employment, 2006 | Projected employment, 2016 | Change, 2006-2016 | |
|---|---|---|---|---|---|
| | | | | Number | Percent |
| Surveyors, cartographers, photogrammetrists, and surveying technicians............................................................................. | — | 148,000 | 179,000 | 31,000 | 21 |
| Cartographers and photogrammetrists ......................................... | 17-1021 | 12,000 | 15,000 | 2,500 | 20 |
| Surveyors ............................................................................ | 17-1022 | 60,000 | 74,000 | 14,000 | 24 |
| Surveying and mapping technicians ........................................... | 17-3031 | 76,000 | 90,000 | 15,000 | 19 |

NOTE: Data in this table are rounded.

because surveyors must be able to research old deeds and other legal papers and prepare reports that document their work.

***Certification and advancement.*** High school graduates with no formal training in surveying usually start as apprentices. Beginners with postsecondary school training in surveying usually can start as technicians or assistants. With on-the-job experience and formal training in surveying—either in an institutional program or from a correspondence school—workers may advance to senior survey technician, then to party chief. Depending on state licensing requirements, in some cases they may advance to licensed surveyor.

The National Society of Professional Surveyors, a member organization of the American Congress on Surveying and Mapping, has a voluntary certification program for surveying technicians. Technicians are certified at four levels requiring progressive amounts of experience and the passing of written examinations. Although not required for state licensure, many employers require certification for promotion to positions with greater responsibilities.

The American Society for Photogrammetry and Remote Sensing has voluntary certification programs for technicians and professionals in photogrammetry, remote sensing, and GIS. To qualify for these professional distinctions, individuals must meet work experience and training standards and pass a written examination. The professional recognition these certifications can help workers gain promotions.

## Employment

Surveyors, cartographers, photogrammetrists, and surveying technicians held about 148,000 jobs in 2006. Employment was distributed by occupational specialty as follows:

Surveying and mapping technicians ......................76,000

Surveyors .............................................................60,000

Cartographers and photogrammetrists....................12,000

The architectural, engineering, and related services industry—including firms that provided surveying and mapping services to other industries on a contract basis—provided 7 out of 10 jobs for these workers. Federal, state, and local governmental agencies provided about 14 percent of these jobs. Major federal government employers are the U.S. Geological Survey (USGS), the Bureau of Land Management (BLM), the National Geodetic Survey, the National Geospatial Intelligence Agency, and the Army Corps of Engineers. Most surveyors in state and local government work for highway departments or urban planning and redevelopment agencies. Construction, mining and utility companies also employ surveyors, cartographers, photogrammetrists, and surveying technicians.

## Job Outlook

Surveyors, cartographers, photogrammetrists, and surveying and mapping technicians should have favorable job prospects. These occupations should experience much faster than average employment growth.

***Employment change.*** Overall employment of surveyors, cartographers, photogrammetrists, and surveying and mapping technicians is expected to increase by 21 percent from 2006 to 2016, which is much faster than the average for all occupations. Increasing demand for fast, accurate, and complete geographic information will be the main source of growth for these occupations.

An increasing number of firms are interested in geographic information and its applications. For example, GIS can be used to create maps and information used in emergency planning, security, marketing, urban planning, natural resource exploration, construction, and other applications. Also, the increased popularity of online mapping systems has created a higher demand for and awareness of geographic information among consumers.

***Job prospects.*** In addition to openings from growth, job openings will continue to arise from the need to replace workers who transfer to other occupations or who leave the labor force altogether. Many of the workers in these occupations are approaching retirement age.

Opportunities for surveyors, cartographers, and photogrammetrists should remain concentrated in engineering, surveying, mapping, building inspection, and drafting services firms. However, employment may fluctuate from year to year with construction activity or with mapping needs for land and resource management.

Opportunities should be stronger for professional surveyors than for surveying and mapping technicians. Advancements in technology, such as total stations and GPS, have made surveying parties smaller than they once were. Additionally, cartographers, photogrammetrists, and technicians who produce more basic GIS data may face competition for jobs from offshore firms and contractors.

As technologies become more complex, opportunities will be best for surveyors, cartographers, and photogrammetrists who have a bachelor's degree and strong technical skills. Increasing demand for geographic data, as opposed to traditional surveying services, will mean better opportunities for cartographers and photogrammetrists who are involved in the development and use of geographic and land information systems.

## Earnings

Median annual earnings of cartographers and photogrammetrists were $48,240 in May 2006. The middle 50 percent earned between

$37,480 and $65,240. The lowest 10 percent earned less than $30,910 and the highest 10 percent earned more than $80,520.

Median annual earnings of surveyors were $48,290 in May 2006. The middle 50 percent earned between $35,720 and $63,990. The lowest 10 percent earned less than $26,690 and the highest 10 percent earned more than $79,910. Median annual earnings of surveyors employed in architectural, engineering, and related services were $47,570 in May 2006.

Median annual earnings of surveying and mapping technicians were $32,340 in May 2006. The middle 50 percent earned between $25,070 and $42,230. The lowest 10 percent earned less than $20,020, and the highest 10 percent earned more than $53,310. Median annual earnings of surveying and mapping technicians employed in architectural, engineering, and related services were $30,670 in May 2006, while those employed by local governments had median annual earnings of $37,550.

## Related Occupations

Surveying is related to the work of civil engineers, architects, and landscape architects because an accurate survey is the first step in land development and construction projects. Cartographic and geodetic surveying are related to the work of environmental scientists and geoscientists, who study the earth's internal composition, surface, and atmosphere. Cartography also is related to the work of geographers and urban and regional planners, who study and decide how the earth's surface is being and may be used.

## Sources of Additional Information

For career information on surveyors, cartographers, photogrammetrists, and surveying technicians, contact

▶ American Congress on Surveying and Mapping, Suite 403, 6 Montgomery Village Ave., Gaithersburg, MD 20879. Internet: http://www.acsm.net

Information about career opportunities, licensure requirements, and the surveying technician certification program is available from

▶ National Society of Professional Surveyors, Suite 403, 6 Montgomery Village Ave., Gaithersburg, MD 20879.

For information on a career as a geodetic surveyor, contact

▶ American Association of Geodetic Surveying (AAGS), Suite 403, 6 Montgomery Village Ave., Gaithersburg, MD 20879.

For career information on photogrammetrists, photogrammetric technicians, remote sensing scientists and image-based cartographers or geographic information system specialists, contact

▶ ASPRS: Imaging and Geospatial Information Society, 5410 Grosvenor Lane, Suite 210, Bethesda, MD 20814-2160. Internet: http://www.asprs.org

General information on careers in photogrammetry, mapping, and surveying is available from

▶ MAPPS: Management Association for Private Photogrammetric Surveyors, 1760 Reston Parkway, Suite 515, Reston, VA 20190. Internet: http://www.mapps.org

Information on about careers in remote sensing, photogrammetry, surveying, GIS, and other geography-related disciplines also is available from the Spring 2005 *Occupational Outlook Quarterly* article, "Geography Jobs", available online at http://www.bls.gov/opub/ooq/2005/spring/art01.pdf

## Taxi Drivers and Chauffeurs

(O*NET 53-3041.00)

## Significant Points

■ Taxi drivers and chauffeurs may work any schedule, including full-time, part-time, night, evening, weekend, and on a seasonal basis.

■ Many taxi drivers like the independent, unsupervised work of driving their automobile.

■ Local governments set license standards for driving experience and training; many taxi and limousine companies set higher standards.

■ Job opportunities should be plentiful; applicants with good driving records, good customer service instincts, and the ability to work flexible schedules should have the best prospects.

## Nature of the Work

Anyone who has been in a large city knows the importance of taxi and limousine services. *Taxi drivers* and *chauffeurs* take passengers to and from their homes, workplaces, and recreational pursuits, such as dining, entertainment, and shopping, and to and from business-related events. These professional drivers also help out-of-town business people and tourists get around in unfamiliar surroundings. Some drivers offer sight-seeing services around their city.

Drivers must be alert to conditions on the road, especially in heavy and congested traffic or in bad weather. They must take precautions to prevent accidents and avoid sudden stops, turns, and other driving maneuvers that would jar passengers.

Taxi drivers. At the beginning of their driving shift, taxi drivers usually report to a taxicab service or garage where they are assigned a vehicle, most frequently a large, conventional automobile modified for commercial passenger transport. They record their name, the date, and the cab's identification number on a trip sheet. Drivers check the cab's fuel and oil levels and make sure that the lights, brakes, and windshield wipers are in good working order. Drivers adjust rear and side mirrors and their seat for comfort. Any equipment or part not in good working order is reported to the dispatcher or company mechanic.

Taxi drivers pick up passengers by "cruising" for fares, prearranging pickups, and picking up passengers from taxistands in high-traffic areas. In urban areas, many passengers flag down drivers cruising the streets. Customers also may prearrange a pickup by calling a cab company and giving a location, approximate pickup time, and destination. The cab company dispatcher then relays the information to a driver by two-way radio, cellular telephone, or onboard computer. Outside of urban areas, the majority of trips are dispatched in this manner. Drivers also pick up passengers waiting at cabstands or in taxi lines at airports, train stations, hotels, restaurants, and other places where people frequently seek taxis.

Some taxi commissions force cabs to specialize in either cruising or prearranged pick ups. In other cases, not all drivers are allowed to pick up riders in certain parts of a city (a business district) or at certain landmarks (a convention center or airport). These restrictions aim to make taxis available to people in areas that drivers find less profitable.

Good drivers are familiar with streets in the areas they serve so they can choose the most efficient route to destinations. They know the locations of frequently requested destinations, such as airports, bus and railroad terminals, convention centers, hotels, and other points of interest. In case of emergency, drivers should know the location of fire and police stations as well as hospitals.

Upon reaching the destination, drivers determine the fare and announce it to their riders. Each jurisdiction determines the rate and structure of the fare system covering licensed taxis. In many cabs, a taximeter measures the fare based on the distance covered and the amount of time the trip took. Drivers turn on the meter when passengers enter the cab and turn it off when they reach the final destination. The fare also may include surcharges to help cover fuel costs as well as fees for additional passengers, tolls, handling luggage, and a drop charge—an additional flat fee added for use of the cab. In some cases, fares are determined by a system of zones through which the taxi passes during a trip.

Passengers usually add a tip or gratuity to the fare. The amount of the gratuity depends, in part, on the passengers' satisfaction with the quality and efficiency of the ride and the courtesy of the driver.

Drivers issue receipts upon request by the passenger. They enter onto the trip sheet all information regarding the trip, including the place and time of pickup and drop off and the total fee; these logs help taxi company management check drivers' activity and efficiency. Drivers also must fill out accident reports when necessary.

Some drivers transport individuals with special needs, such as those with disabilities and the elderly. These drivers, known as *paratransit drivers*, operate specially equipped vehicles designed to accommodate a variety of needs in non-emergency situations. Although special certification is not necessary, some additional training on the equipment and passenger needs may be required.

Chauffeurs. Chauffeurs operate limousines, vans, and private cars for limousine companies, private businesses, government agencies, and wealthy individuals. Chauffeur service differs from taxi service in that all trips are prearranged. Many chauffeurs transport customers in large vans between hotels and airports, bus terminals, or train stations. Others drive luxury automobiles, such as limousines, to business events, entertainment venues, and social events. Still others provide full-time personal transportation for wealthy families and private companies.

At the beginning of the workday, chauffeurs prepare their automobiles or vans for use. They inspect the vehicle for cleanliness and, when needed, clean the interior and wash the exterior body, windows, and mirrors. They check fuel and oil levels and make sure the lights, tires, brakes, and windshield wipers work. Chauffeurs may perform routine maintenance and make minor repairs, such as changing tires or adding oil and other fluids. If a vehicle requires a more complicated repair, they take it to a professional mechanic.

Chauffeurs cater to passengers by providing attentive customer service and paying attention to detail. They help riders into the car by holding open doors, holding umbrellas when it is raining, and loading packages and luggage into the trunk of the car. Chauffeurs may perform errands for their employers such as delivering packages or picking up clients arriving at airports. To ensure a pleasurable ride in their limousines, many chauffeurs offer conveniences and luxuries such as newspapers, magazines, music, drinks, televisions, and telephones. Increasingly, chauffeurs work as full-service executive assistants, simultaneously acting as driver, secretary, and itinerary planner.

*Work environment.* Taxi drivers and chauffeurs occasionally have to load and unload heavy luggage and packages. Driving for long periods can be tiring and uncomfortable, especially in densely populated urban areas. Taxi drivers risk robbery because they work alone and often carry large amounts of cash.

Design improvements in newer cars have reduced the stress and increased the comfort and efficiency of drivers. Many regulatory bodies overseeing taxi and chauffeur services require standard amenities such as air-conditioning and general upkeep of the vehicles. Some modern taxicabs also are equipped with sophisticated tracking devices, fare meters, and dispatching equipment. Satellites and tracking systems link many of these state-of-the-art vehicles with company headquarters. In a matter of seconds, dispatchers can deliver directions, traffic advisories, weather reports, and other important communications to drivers anywhere in the area. The satellite link also allows dispatchers to track vehicle location, fuel consumption, and engine performance. Automated dispatch systems help dispatchers locate the closest driver to a customer in order to minimize individual wait time and increase the quality of service. Drivers easily can communicate with dispatchers to discuss delivery schedules and courses of action if there are mechanical problems. When threatened with crime or violence, drivers may have special "trouble lights" to alert authorities of emergencies.

Work hours of taxi drivers and chauffeurs vary greatly. Some jobs offer full-time or part-time employment with work hours that can change from day to day or remain the same. It is often necessary for drivers to report to work on short notice. Chauffeurs who work for a single employer may be on call much of the time. Evening and weekend work is common for drivers and chauffeurs employed by limousine and taxicab services.

Whereas the needs of the client or employer dictate the work schedule for chauffeurs, the work of taxi drivers is much less structured. Working free of supervision, they may break for a meal or a rest whenever their vehicle is unoccupied. Many taxi drivers like the independent, unsupervised work of driving.

This occupation is attractive to individuals, such as college and postgraduate students, seeking flexible work schedules and to anyone seeking a second source of income. Other service workers, such as ambulance drivers and police officers, sometimes moonlight as taxi drivers or chauffeurs.

Full-time taxi drivers usually work one shift a day, which may last 8 to 12 hours. Part-time drivers may work half a shift each day, or

**Projections data from the National Employment Matrix**

| Occupational Title | SOC Code | Employment, 2006 | Projected employment, 2016 | Change, 2006-16 | |
|---|---|---|---|---|---|
| | | | | Number | Percent |
| Taxi drivers and chauffeurs ............................................................. | 53-3041 | 229,000 | 258,000 | 30,000 | 13 |

NOTE: Data in this table are rounded.

work a full shift once or twice a week. Drivers may work shifts at all times of the day and night because most taxi companies offer services 24 hours a day. Early morning and late night shifts are not uncommon. Drivers work long hours during holidays, weekends, and other special times when demand for their services is heavier. Independent drivers set their own hours and schedules.

## Training, Other Qualifications, and Advancement

Local governments set licensing standards and requirements for taxi drivers and chauffeurs, which may include minimum amounts of driving experience and training. Many taxi and limousine companies set higher standards than those required by law. It is common for companies to review an applicant's medical, credit, criminal, and driving record. In addition, many companies require an applicant to be at least 21 years old, which is higher than the age typically required by law. Most companies also prefer that an applicant be a high school graduate.

*Education and training.* Little formal education is needed for taxi drivers or chauffeurs, but most have at least a high school diploma, GED, or its equivalent. Drivers need to be able to communicate effectively, use basic math, and often need knowledge of basic mechanics. Beyond having these skills, most drivers take a course offered by the government or their employer.

Some taxi and limousine companies give new drivers on-the-job training. This training typically is informal and often lasts only about a week. Companies show drivers how to operate the taximeter and communications equipment and how to complete paperwork. Other topics covered may include driver safety and the best routes to popular sightseeing and entertainment destinations. Many companies have contracts with social service agencies and transportation services to transport elderly and disabled citizens in non-emergency situations. To support these services, new drivers may get special training in how to handle wheelchair lifts and other mechanical devices.

*Licensure.* People interested in driving a taxicab or a limousine first must have a regular automobile driver's license. Usually, applicants then must get a taxi driver or chauffeur's license, commonly called a "hack" license. Some states require only a passenger endorsement, which allows the driver to carry passengers in the vehicle, on a regular driver's license; some require only that drivers be certified by their employer; but the federal government requires a commercial driver's license with a passenger endorsement for drivers transporting 16 or more passengers.

While states set licensing requirements, local regulatory bodies usually set other terms and conditions. These often include requirements for training, which can vary greatly. Some localities require new drivers to enroll in up to 80 hours of classroom instruction, to take an exam, or both before they are allowed to work, Applicants must know local geography, motor vehicle laws, safe driving practices, and relevant regulations. Often, they must also display some aptitude for customer service. Some localities require an English proficiency test, usually in the form of listening comprehension; applicants who do not pass the English exam must take an English course in addition to any formal driving programs.

Some classroom instruction includes route management, map reading, and service for passengers with disabilities. Many taxicab or limousine companies sponsor applicants, giving them a temporary permit that allows them to drive before they have finished the training program and passed the test. Some jurisdictions, such as New York City, have discontinued this practice and now require driver applicants to complete the licensing process before operating a taxi or limousine.

*Other qualifications.* Taxi drivers and chauffeurs work almost exclusively with the public, and should be able to get along with many different types of people. They must be patient when waiting for passengers and when dealing with rude customers. It also is helpful for drivers to be tolerant and level-headed when driving in heavy and congested traffic. Drivers should be dependable since passengers expect to be picked up at a prearranged time and taken to the correct destination. To be successful, drivers must be responsible and self-motivated because they work with little supervision. Increasingly, companies encourage drivers to develop their own loyal customer base, so as to improve their business.

Many municipalities and taxicab and chauffeur companies require drivers to have a neat appearance. Many chauffeurs wear formal attire, such as a tuxedo, a coat and tie, a dress, or a uniform and cap.

*Advancement.* Taxi drivers and chauffeurs have limited advancement opportunities. Experienced drivers may obtain preferred routes or shifts. Some advance to become lead drivers, who help to train new drivers. Others take dispatching and managerial positions. Many managers start their careers as drivers. Some people start their own limousine companies.

In small and medium-size communities, drivers sometimes are able to buy their own taxi, limousine, or other type of automobile and go into business for themselves. These independent owner-drivers require an additional permit allowing them to operate their vehicle as a company. Some big cities limit the number of operating permits. In these cities, drivers become owner-drivers by buying permits from owner-drivers who leave the business, or by purchasing or leasing them from the city. Although many owner-drivers are successful, some fail to cover expenses and eventually lose their permits and automobiles. Individuals starting their own taxi company face many obstacles because of the difficulty in running a small fleet. The lack of dispatch and maintenance facilities often is hard for an owner to overcome. Chauffeurs often have a good deal of success and many companies begin as an individually owned and operated business.

For both taxi and limousine service owners, good business sense and courses in accounting, business, and business arithmetic can help an owner-driver to be successful. Knowledge of mechanics enables owner-drivers to perform their own routine maintenance and minor repairs to cut expenses.

## Employment

Taxi drivers and chauffeurs held about 229,000 jobs in 2006. About 30 percent of taxi drivers and chauffeurs were self-employed.

## Job Outlook

Employment is expected to grow about as fast as average. Job opportunities should be plentiful because of the need to replace the many people who work in this occupation for short periods and then leave. Applicants with good driving records, good customer service instincts, and the ability to work flexible schedules should have the best prospects.

*Employment change.* Employment of taxi drivers and chauffeurs is expected to grow 13 percent during the 2006–2016 projection period—about as fast as the average for all occupations—as local and suburban travel increases. Job growth also will stem from federal legislation requiring increased services for people with disabilities. Demand for paratransit drivers will grow in response to the increase in the number of elderly people, who often have difficulty driving and using public transportation.

*Job prospects.* People seeking jobs as taxi drivers and chauffeurs are expected to have plentiful opportunities because of the need to replace the many people who work in this occupation for short periods and then transfer to other occupations or leave the labor force. Earnings, work hours, and working conditions vary greatly, depending on economic and regulatory conditions. Applicants with good driving records, good customer service instincts, and the ability to work flexible schedules should have the best prospects.

The number of job opportunities can fluctuate with the overall movements of the economy because the demand for taxi and limousine transportation depends on travel and tourism. During economic slowdowns, drivers seldom are laid off, but they may have to increase their work hours, and earnings may decline. When the economy is strong, job prospects are numerous as many drivers transfer to other occupations. Extra drivers may be hired during holiday seasons as well as during peak travel and tourist times.

Rapidly growing metropolitan areas and cities experiencing economic growth should offer the best job opportunities.

## Earnings

Earnings of taxi drivers and chauffeurs vary greatly, depending on factors such as the number of hours worked, regulatory conditions, customers' tips, and geographic location. Hybrid vehicles, which have improved gas mileage, offer taxi drivers better earnings because drivers pay for their gas out of pocket. Median hourly earnings of salaried taxi drivers and chauffeurs, including tips, were $9.78 in May 2006. The middle 50 percent earned between $8.00 and $12.19 an hour. The lowest 10 percent earned less than $6.85,

and the highest 10 percent earned more than $15.80 an hour. Median hourly earnings in the industries employing the largest numbers of taxi drivers and chauffeurs were

| | |
|---|---|
| Taxi and limousine service | $10.62 |
| Other transit and ground passenger transportation | 9.32 |
| Traveler accommodation | 9.09 |
| Individual and family services | 8.94 |
| Automobile dealers | 8.86 |

Many taxi drivers and chauffeurs are *lease drivers*. These drivers pay a daily, weekly, or monthly fee to the company allowing them to lease their vehicles. In the case of limousines, leasing also permits the driver access to the company's dispatch system. The fee also may include charges for vehicle maintenance, insurance, and a deposit on the vehicle. Lease drivers may take their cars home with them when they are not on duty.

Most taxi drivers and chauffeurs do not receive benefits. This is unlikely to change because companies have little incentive to offer them. However, a few cities have made an attempt to provide health insurance for drivers.

## Related Occupations

Other workers who have similar jobs include bus drivers and truck drivers and driver/sales workers.

## Sources of Additional Information

Information on necessary permits and the registration of taxi drivers and chauffeurs is available from local government agencies that regulate taxicabs. Questions regarding licensing should be directed to your state motor vehicle administration. For information about work opportunities as a taxi driver or chauffeur, contact local taxi or limousine companies or state employment service offices in your area.

For general information about the work of taxi drivers, chauffeurs, and paratransit drivers, contact

▸ Taxicab, Limousine and Paratransit Association, 3849 Farragut Ave., Kensington, MD 20895.

For general information about the work of limousine drivers, contact

▸ National Limousine Association, 49 South Maple Ave., Marlton, NJ 08053. Internet: http://www.limo.org

## Teacher Assistants

(O*NET 25-9041.00)

## Significant Points

■ Almost 4 in 10 teacher assistants work part time.

■ Educational requirements range from a high school diploma to some college training.

■ Favorable job prospects are expected.

■ Opportunities should be best for those with at least 2 years of formal postsecondary education, those with experience in helping special education students, or those who can speak a foreign language.

Projections data from the National Employment Matrix

| Occupational Title | SOC Code | Employment, 2006 | Projected employment, 2016 | Change, 2006-2016 | |
| --- | --- | --- | --- | --- | --- |
| | | | | Number | Percent |
| Teacher assistants ............................................................. | 25-9041 | 1,312,000 | 1,449,000 | 137,000 | 10 |

NOTE: Data in this table are rounded.

## Nature of the Work

Teacher assistants provide instructional and clerical support for classroom teachers, allowing teachers more time for lesson planning and teaching. They support and assist children in learning class material using the teacher's lesson plans, providing students with individualized attention. Teacher assistants also supervise students in the cafeteria, schoolyard, and hallways, or on field trips; they record grades, set up equipment, and help prepare materials for instruction. Teacher assistants also are called teacher aides or instructional aides. Some assistants refer to themselves as paraeducators or paraprofessionals.

Some teacher assistants perform exclusively noninstructional or clerical tasks, such as monitoring nonacademic settings. Playground and lunchroom attendants are examples of such assistants. Most teacher assistants, however, perform a combination of instructional and clerical duties. They generally provide instructional reinforcement to children, under the direction and guidance of teachers. They work with students individually or in small groups—listening while students read, reviewing or reinforcing class lessons, or helping them find information for reports. At the secondary school level, teacher assistants often specialize in a certain subject, such as math or science. Teacher assistants often take charge of special projects and prepare equipment or exhibits, such as for a science demonstration. Some assistants work in computer laboratories, helping students to use computers and educational software programs.

In addition to instructing, assisting, and supervising students, teacher assistants may grade tests and papers, check homework, keep health and attendance records, do typing and filing, and duplicate materials. They also stock supplies, operate audiovisual equipment, and keep classroom equipment in order.

Many teacher assistants work extensively with special education students. As schools become more inclusive and integrate special education students into general education classrooms, teacher assistants in both general education and special education classrooms increasingly assist students with disabilities. They attend to the physical needs of students with disabilities, including feeding, teaching good grooming habits, or assisting students riding the school bus. They also provide personal attention to students with other special needs, such as those who speak English as a second language or those who need remedial education. Some work with young adults to help them obtain a job or to apply for community services to support them after schooling. Teacher assistants help assess a student's progress by observing performance and recording relevant data.

While the majority of teacher assistants work in primary and secondary educational settings, others work in preschools and other child care centers. Often one or two assistants will work with a lead teacher in order to better provide the individual attention that young children require. In addition to assisting in educational instruction, they also supervise the children at play and assist in feeding and other basic care activities.

Teacher assistants also work with infants and toddlers who have developmental delays or other disabilities. Under the guidance of a teacher or therapist, teacher assistants perform exercises or play games to help the child develop physically and behaviorally.

*Work environment.* Teacher assistants work in a variety of settings—including preschools, child care centers, and religious and community centers, where they work with young adults—but most work in classrooms in elementary, middle, and secondary schools. They also work outdoors supervising recess when weather allows, and they spend much of their time standing, walking, or kneeling.

Approximately 4 in 10 teacher assistants work part time. However, even among full-time workers, about 17 percent work less than 40 hours per week. Most assistants who provide educational instruction work the traditional 9-month to 10-month school year.

Seeing students develop and gain appreciation of the joy of learning can be very rewarding. However, working closely with students can be both physically and emotionally tiring. Teacher assistants who work with special education students often perform more strenuous tasks, including lifting, as they help students with their daily routine. Those who perform clerical work may tire of administrative duties, such as copying materials or entering data.

## Training, Other Qualifications, and Advancement

Training requirements for teacher assistants vary by state or school district and range from a high school diploma to some college training. Increasingly, employers prefer applicants with some related college coursework.

*Education and training.* Many teacher assistants need only a high school diploma and on-the-job training. A college degree or related coursework in child development improves job opportunities, however. In fact, teacher assistants who work in Title 1 schools—those with a large proportion of students from low-income households—must have college training or proven academic skills. They face new federal requirements as of 2006: Assistants must hold a two-year or higher degree, have a minimum of two years of college, or pass a rigorous state or local assessment.

A number of colleges offer associate degrees or certificate programs that either prepare graduates to work as teacher assistants or provide additional training for current teacher assistants.

All teacher assistants receive some on-the-job training. Teacher assistants need to become familiar with the school system and with the operation and rules of the school. Those who tutor and review lessons with students, must learn and understand the class materials and instructional methods used by the teacher. Teacher assistants also must know how to operate audiovisual equipment, keep records, and prepare instructional materials, as well as have adequate computer skills.

*Other qualifications.* Many schools require previous experience in working with children and a valid driver's license. Some schools may require the applicant to pass a background check. Teacher assistants should enjoy working with children from a wide range of cultural backgrounds and be able to handle classroom situations with fairness and patience. Teacher assistants also must demonstrate initiative and a willingness to follow a teacher's directions. They must have good writing skills and be able to communicate effectively with students and teachers. Teacher assistants who speak a second language, especially Spanish, are in great demand for communicating with growing numbers of students and parents whose primary language is not English.

*Advancement.* Advancement for teacher assistants—usually in the form of higher earnings or increased responsibility—comes primarily with experience or additional education. Some school districts provide time away from the job or tuition reimbursement so that teacher assistants can earn their bachelor's degrees and pursue licensed teaching positions. In return for tuition reimbursement, assistants are often required to teach for a certain length of time in the school district.

## Employment

Teacher assistants held 1.3 million jobs in 2006. About 3 out of 4 worked for public and private elementary and secondary schools. Child care centers and religious organizations employed most of the rest.

## Job Outlook

Many job openings are expected for teacher assistants due to turnover and average employment growth in this large occupation, resulting in favorable job prospects.

*Employment change.* Employment of teacher assistants is expected to grow by 10 percent between 2006 and 2016, about as fast as the average for all occupations. A large number of new jobs, 137,000, will arise over the 2006–2016 period because of the size of the occupation. School enrollments are projected to increase slowly over the next decade, but faster growth is expected among special education students and students for whom English is a second language, and they will increase as a share of the total school-age population. These students are the ones who most need teacher assistants.

Legislation requires students with disabilities and non-native English speakers to receive an education equal to that of other students, so it will continue to generate jobs for teacher assistants, who help to accommodate these students' special needs. Children with special needs require much personal attention, and teachers rely heavily on teacher assistants to provide much of that attention. An increasing number of after-school programs and summer programs also will create new opportunities for teacher assistants.

The greater focus on school quality and accountability in recent years also is likely to lead to an increased demand for teacher assistants. Growing numbers of teacher assistants may be needed to help teachers prepare students for standardized testing and to provide extra assistance to students who perform poorly on these tests. Job

growth of assistants may be moderated, however, if schools are encouraged to hire more full-fledged teachers for instructional purposes.

*Job prospects.* Favorable job prospects are expected. Opportunities for teacher assistant jobs should be best for those with at least 2 years of formal postsecondary education, those with experience in helping special education students, or those who can speak a foreign language. Demand is expected to vary by region of the country. Regions in which the population and school enrollments are expected to grow faster, such as many communities in the South and West, should have rapid growth in the demand for teacher assistants.

In addition to job openings stemming from employment growth, numerous openings will arise as assistants leave their jobs and must be replaced. Many assistant jobs require limited formal education and offer relatively low pay so many workers transfer to other occupations or leave the labor force to assume family responsibilities, to return to school, or for other reasons.

## Earnings

Median annual earnings of teacher assistants in May 2006 were $20,740. The middle 50 percent earned between $16,430 and $26,160. The lowest 10 percent earned less than $13,910, and the highest 10 percent earned more than $31,610.

Full-time workers usually receive health coverage and other benefits. Teacher assistants who work part time ordinarily do not receive benefits. In 2006, about 3 out of 10 teacher assistants belonged to unions—mainly the American Federation of Teachers and the National Education Association—which bargain with school systems over wages, hours, and the terms and conditions of employment.

## Related Occupations

Teacher assistants who instruct children have duties similar to those of preschool, kindergarten, elementary, middle, and secondary school teachers, as well as special education teachers. However, teacher assistants do not have the same level of responsibility or training. The support activities of teacher assistants and their educational backgrounds are similar to those of childcare workers, library technicians, and library assistants. Teacher assistants who work with children with disabilities perform many of the same functions as occupational therapist assistants and aides.

## Sources of Additional Information

For information on teacher assistants, including training and certification, contact

▸ American Federation of Teachers, Paraprofessional and School Related Personnel Division, 555 New Jersey Ave. NW, Washington, DC 20001.

▸ National Education Association, Educational Support Personnel Division, 1201 16th Street NW, Washington, DC 20036.

▸ National Resource Center for Paraprofessionals, 6526 Old Main Hill, Utah State University, Logan, UT 84322. Internet: http://www.nrcpara.org

Human resource departments of school systems, school administrators, and state departments of education also can provide details about employment opportunities and required qualifications for teacher assistant jobs.

## Teachers—Postsecondary

(O*NET 25-1011.00, 25-1021.00, 25-1022.00, 25-1031.00, 25-1032.00, 25-1041.00, 25-1042.00, 25-1043.00, 25-1051.00, 25-1052.00, 25-1053.00, 25-1054.00, 25-1061.00, 25-1062.00, 25-1063.00, 25-1064.00, 25-1065.00, 25-1066.00, 25-1067.00, 25-1069.99, 25-1071.00, 25-1072.00, 25-1081.00, 25-1082.00, 25-1111.00, 25-1112.00, 25-1113.00, 25-1121.00, 25-1122.00, 25-1123.00, 25-1124.00, 25-1125.00, 25-1126.00, 25-1191.00, 25-1192.00, 25-1193.00, 25-1194.00, and 25-1199.99)

## Significant Points

- Educational qualifications range from expertise in a particular field to a Ph.D., depending on the subject taught and the type of educational institution.

- Job opportunities are expected to be very good, but many new openings will be for part-time or non-tenure-track positions.

- Prospects will be better and earnings higher in rapidly growing fields that offer many nonacademic career options.

## Nature of the Work

Postsecondary teachers instruct students in a wide variety of academic and vocational subjects beyond the high school level. Most of theses students are working toward a degree, but many others are studying for a certificate or certification to improve their knowledge or career skills. Postsecondary teachers include college and university faculty, postsecondary career and technical education teachers, and graduate teaching assistants. Teaching in any venue involves forming a lesson plan, presenting material to students, responding to students learning needs, and evaluating student progress. In addition to instruction, postsecondary teachers, particularly those at 4-year colleges and universities, also perform a significant amount of research in the subject they teach. They must also keep up with new developments in their field and may consult with government, business, nonprofit, and community organizations.

*College and university faculty* make up the majority of postsecondary teachers. Faculty usually are organized into departments or divisions, based on academic subject or field. They typically teach several different related courses in their subject—algebra, calculus, and statistics, for example. They may instruct undergraduate or graduate students, or both. College and university faculty may give lectures to several hundred students in large halls, lead small seminars, or supervise students in laboratories. They prepare lectures, exercises, and laboratory experiments; grade exams and papers; and advise and work with students individually. In universities, they also supervise graduate students' teaching and research. College faculty work with an increasingly varied student population made up of growing shares of part-time, older, and culturally and racially diverse students.

Faculty keep up with developments in their field by reading current literature, talking with colleagues, and participating in professional conferences. They also are encouraged to do their own research to expand knowledge in their field by performing experiments; collecting and analyzing data; or examining original documents, literature, and other source material. They publish their findings in scholarly journals, books, and electronic media.

Most postsecondary teachers extensively use computer technology, including the Internet, e-mail, and software programs. They may use computers in the classroom as teaching aids and may post course content, class notes, class schedules, and other information on the Internet. The use of e-mail, chat rooms, and other techniques has greatly improved communications between students and teachers and among students.

Some instructors use the Internet to teach courses to students at remote sites. These so-called "distance learning" courses are an increasingly popular option for students who work while attending school. Faculty who teach these courses must be able to adapt existing courses to make them successful online or design a new course that takes advantage of the format.

Most full-time faculty members serve on academic or administrative committees that deal with the policies of their institution, departmental matters, academic issues, curricula, budgets, equipment purchases, and hiring. Some work with student and community organizations. Department chairpersons are faculty members who usually teach some courses but have heavier administrative responsibilities.

The proportion of time spent on research, teaching, administrative, and other duties varies by individual circumstance and type of institution. Faculty members at universities normally spend a significant part of their time doing research; those in 4-year colleges, somewhat less; and those in 2-year colleges, relatively little. The teaching load, however, often is heavier in 2-year colleges and somewhat lighter at 4-year institutions. At all types of institutions, full professors—those that have reached the highest level in their field—usually spend a larger portion of their time conducting research than do assistant professors, instructors, and lecturers.

In addition to traditional 2- and 4-year institutions, an increasing number of postsecondary educators work in alternative schools or in programs aimed at providing career-related education for working adults. Courses are usually offered online or on nights and weekends. Instructors at these programs generally work part time and are only responsible for teaching, with little to no administrative and research responsibilities.

*Postsecondary vocational education teachers,* also known as *postsecondary career and technical education teachers*, provide instruction for occupations that require specialized training but not usually a 4-year degree. They may teach classes in welding, dental hygienics, x-ray technician techniques, auto mechanics, or cosmetology, for example. Classes often are taught in an industrial or laboratory setting where students are provided hands-on experience. For example, welding instructors show students various welding techniques and essential safety practices, watch them use tools and equipment, and have them repeat procedures until they meet the specific standards required by the trade. Increasingly, career and technical education teachers are integrating academic and vocational curriculums so that students obtain a variety of skills that can be applied on the job. In addition, career and technical education teachers at community colleges and career and technical schools also often play a key role in students' transition from school to work by helping to establish internship programs for students and by facilitating contact between students and prospective employers.

*Graduate teaching assistants*, often referred to as *graduate TAs*, assist faculty, department chairs, or other professional staff at colleges and universities by performing teaching or teaching-related duties. In addition to their work responsibilities, assistants have their own school commitments, as they are also students who are working towards earning a graduate degree, such as a Ph.D. Some teaching assistants have full responsibility for teaching a course—usually one that is introductory—which can include preparation of lectures and exams, and assigning final grades to students. Others help faculty members, which may include doing a variety of tasks such as grading papers, monitoring exams, holding office hours or help-sessions for students, conducting laboratory sessions, or administering quizzes to the class. Teaching assistants generally meet initially with the faculty member whom they are going to assist to determine exactly what is expected of them, as each faculty member may have his or her own needs. For example, some faculty members prefer assistants to sit in on classes, but others assign them other tasks to do during class time. Graduate teaching assistants may work one-on-one with a faculty member or, for large classes, they may be one of several assistants.

***Work environment.*** Many postsecondary teachers find the environment intellectually stimulating and rewarding because they are surrounded by others who enjoy their subject. The ability to share their expertise with others is also appealing to many.

Most postsecondary teachers have flexible schedules. They must be present for classes, usually 12 to 16 hours per week, and for faculty and committee meetings. Most establish regular office hours for student consultations, usually 3 to 6 hours per week. Otherwise, teachers are free to decide when and where they will work, and how much time to devote to course preparation, grading, study, research, graduate student supervision, and other activities.

Classes are typically scheduled during weekdays, although some occur at night or during the weekend. This is particularly true for teachers at 2-year community colleges or institutions with large enrollments of older students who have full-time jobs or family responsibilities. Most colleges and universities require teachers to work 9 months of the year, which allows them time during the summer and school holidays to teach additional courses, do research, travel, or pursue nonacademic interests.

About 30 percent of college and university faculty worked part time in 2006. Some part-timers, known as "adjunct faculty," have primary jobs outside of academia—in government, private industry, or nonprofit research—and teach "on the side." Others may have multiple part-time teaching positions at different institutions. Most graduate teaching assistants work part time while working on their graduate studies. The number of hours that they work may vary, depending on their assignments.

University faculty may experience a conflict between their responsibilities to teach students and the pressure to do research and publish their findings. This may be a particular problem for young

faculty seeking advancement in 4-year research universities. Also, recent cutbacks in support workers and the hiring of more part-time faculty have put a greater administrative burden on full-time faculty. Requirements to teach online classes also have added greatly to the workloads of postsecondary teachers. Many find that developing the courses to put online is very time-consuming, especially when learning how to operate the technology and answering large amounts of e-mail.

Graduate TAs usually have flexibility in their work schedules like college and university faculty, but they also must spend a considerable amount of time pursuing their own academic coursework and studies. Work may be stressful, particularly when assistants are given full responsibility for teaching a class. However, these types of positions allow graduate students the opportunity to gain valuable teaching experience, which is especially helpful for those who seek to become college faculty members after completing their degree.

## Training, Other Qualifications, and Advancement

The education and training required of postsecondary teachers varies widely, depending on the subject taught and educational institution employing them. Educational requirements for teachers are generally highest at research universities, where a Ph.D. is the most commonly held degree; at career and technical institutes, experience and expertise in a related occupation is the principal qualification.

***Education and training.*** Four-year colleges and universities usually require candidates for full-time, tenure-track positions, to hold a doctoral degree. However, they may hire master's degree holders or doctoral candidates for certain disciplines, such as the arts, or for part-time and temporary jobs.

Doctoral programs take an average of six years of full-time study beyond the bachelor's degree; this includes time spent completing a master's degree and a dissertation. Some programs, such as those in the humanities, may take longer to complete; others, such as those in engineering, usually are shorter. Candidates specialize in a subfield of a discipline, for example, organic chemistry, counseling psychology, or European history, and also take courses covering the entire discipline. Programs typically include 20 or more increasingly specialized courses and seminars plus comprehensive examinations on all major areas of the field. Candidates also must complete a dissertation—a written report on original research in the candidate's major field of study. The dissertation sets forth an original hypothesis or proposes a model and tests it. Students in the natural sciences and engineering usually do laboratory work; in the humanities, they study original documents and other published material. The dissertation is done under the guidance of one or more faculty advisors and usually takes one or two years of full-time work.

In two-year colleges, master's degree holders fill most full-time teaching positions. However, in certain fields where there may be more applicants than available jobs, institutions can be more selective in their hiring practices. In these fields, master's degree holders may be passed over in favor of candidates holding Ph.Ds. Many two-year institutions increasingly prefer job applicants to have some teaching experience or experience with distance learning. Preference also may be given to those holding dual master's degrees, especially at smaller institutions, because they can teach more subjects.

Training requirements for postsecondary career and technical education teachers vary by state and subject. In general, career and technical education teachers need a bachelor's or graduate degree, plus at least three years of work experience in their field. In some fields, a license or certificate that demonstrates one's qualifications may be all that is required. These teachers may need to update their skills through continuing education to maintain certification. They must also maintain ongoing dialogue with businesses to determine the skills most needed in the current workplace.

*Other qualifications.* Postsecondary teachers should communicate and relate well with students, enjoy working with them, and be able to motivate them. They should have inquiring and analytical minds, and a strong desire to pursue and disseminate knowledge. Additionally, they must be self-motivated and able to work in an environment in which they receive little direct supervision.

Obtaining a position as a graduate teaching assistant is a good way to gain college teaching experience. To qualify, candidates must be enrolled in a graduate school program. In addition, some colleges and universities require teaching assistants to attend classes or take some training prior to being given responsibility for a course.

Although graduate teaching assistants usually work at the institution and in the department where they are earning their degree, teaching or internship positions for graduate students at institutions that do not grant a graduate degree have become more common in recent years. For example, a program called Preparing Future Faculty, administered by the Association of American Colleges and Universities and the Council of Graduate Schools, has led to the creation of many programs that are now independent. These programs offer graduate students at research universities the opportunity to work as teaching assistants at other types of institutions, such as liberal arts or community colleges. Working with a mentor, the graduate students teach classes and learn how to improve their teaching techniques. They may attend faculty and committee meetings, develop a curriculum, and learn how to balance the teaching, research, and administrative roles that faculty play. These programs provide valuable learning opportunities for graduate students interested in teaching at the postsecondary level, and also help to make these students aware of the differences among the various types of institutions at which they may someday work.

Some degree holders, particularly those who studied in the natural sciences, spend additional years after earning their graduate degree on postdoctoral research and study before taking a faculty position. Some Ph.D.s are able to extend postdoctoral appointments, or take new ones, if they are unable to find a faculty job. Most of these appointments offer a nominal salary.

*Advancement.* For faculty, a major goal in the traditional academic career is attaining tenure. The process of attaining tenure can take approximately seven years with faculty moving up the ranks in tenure-track positions as they meet specific criteria. The ranks are instructor, assistant professor, associate professor, and professor. Colleges and universities usually hire new tenure-track faculty as instructors or assistant professors under term contracts. At the end of the period, their record of teaching, research, and overall contribution to the institution is reviewed and tenure may be granted if the review is favorable. Those denied tenure usually must leave the institution. Tenured professors cannot be fired without just cause and due process. Tenure protects the faculty's academic freedom—

the ability to teach and conduct research without fear of being fired for advocating controversial or unpopular ideas. It also gives both faculty and institutions the stability needed for effective research and teaching, and provides financial security for faculty. Some institutions have adopted post-tenure review policies to encourage ongoing evaluation of tenured faculty.

The number of tenure-track positions is declining as institutions seek flexibility in dealing with financial matters and changing student interests. Institutions rely more heavily on limited term contracts and part-time, or adjunct, faculty, thus shrinking the total pool of tenured faculty. Limited-term contracts—typically two- to five years, may be terminated or extended when they expire but generally do not lead to the granting of tenure. In addition, some institutions have limited the percentage of faculty who can be tenured.

For tenured postsecondary teachers, further advancement involves a move into administrative and managerial positions, such as departmental chairperson, dean, and president. At four-year institutions, such advancement requires a doctoral degree. At two-year colleges, a doctorate is helpful but not usually required, except for advancement to some top administrative positions.

# Employment

Postsecondary teachers held nearly 1.7 million jobs in 2006. Most were employed in 4-year colleges and universities and in 2-year community colleges. Other postsecondary teachers are employed by schools and institutes that specialize in training people in a specific field, such as technology centers or culinary schools, or work for businesses that provide professional development courses to employees of companies. Some career and technical education teachers work for state and local governments and job training facilities. The following tabulation shows postsecondary teaching jobs in specialties having 20,000 or more jobs in 2006:

| | |
|---|---|
| Health specialties teachers | 145,000 |
| Graduate teaching assistants | 144,000 |
| Vocational education teachers | 119,000 |
| Art, drama, and music teachers | 88,000 |
| Business teachers | 82,000 |
| English language and literature teachers | 72,000 |
| Education teachers | 67,000 |
| Biological science teachers | 65,000 |
| Mathematical science teachers | 54,000 |
| Nursing instructors and teachers | 46,000 |
| Computer science teachers | 44,000 |
| Engineering teachers | 40,000 |
| Psychology teachers | 37,000 |
| Foreign language and literature teachers | 30,000 |
| Communications teachers | 29,000 |
| History teachers | 26,000 |
| Philosophy and religion teachers | 25,000 |
| Chemistry teachers | 24,000 |
| Recreation and fitness studies teachers | 20,000 |

**Projections data from the National Employment Matrix**

| Occupational Title | SOC Code | Employment, 2006 | Projected employment, 2016 | Change, 2006-2016 | |
|---|---|---|---|---|---|
| | | | | Number | Percent |
| Postsecondary teachers ................................................................... | 25-1000 | 1,672,000 | 2,054,000 | 382,000 | 23 |

NOTE: Data in this table are rounded.

## Job Outlook

Employment of postsecondary teachers is expected to grow much faster than average as student enrollments continue to increase. However, a significant proportion of these new jobs will be part-time and non-tenure-track positions. Retirements of current postsecondary teachers should create numerous openings for all types of postsecondary teachers, so job opportunities are generally expected to be very good, although they will vary by the subject taught and the type of educational institution.

*Employment change.* Postsecondary teachers are expected to grow by 23 percent between 2006 and 2016, much faster than the average for all occupations. Because of the size of this occupation and its much faster than average growth rate, postsecondary teachers will account for 382,000 new jobs, which is among the largest number of new jobs for an occupation. Projected growth in the occupation will be primarily due to increases in college and university enrollment over the next decade. This enrollment growth stems mainly from the expected increase in the population of 18- to 24-year-olds, who constitute the majority of students at postsecondary institutions, and from the increasing number of high school graduates who choose to attend these institutions. Adults returning to college to enhance their career prospects or to update their skills also will continue to create new opportunities for postsecondary teachers, particularly at community colleges and for-profit institutions that cater to working adults. However, many postsecondary educational institutions receive a significant portion of their funding from state and local governments, so expansion of public higher education will be limited by state and local budgets.

*Job prospects.* A significant number of openings in this occupation will be created by growth in enrollments and the need to replace the large numbers of postsecondary teachers who are likely to retire over the next decade. Many postsecondary teachers were hired in the late 1960s and the 1970s to teach members of the baby boom generation, and they are expected to retire in growing numbers in the years ahead. As a result, Ph.D. recipients seeking jobs as postsecondary teachers will experience favorable job prospects over the next decade.

Although competition will remain tight for tenure-track positions at 4-year colleges and universities, there will be available a considerable number of part-time or renewable, term appointments at these institutions and at community colleges. Opportunities for master's degree holders are also expected to be favorable because there will be considerable growth at community colleges, career education programs, and other institutions that employ them.

Opportunities for graduate teaching assistants are expected to be very good, reflecting expectations of higher undergraduate enrollments coupled with more modest increases in graduate student enrollment. Constituting almost 9 percent of all postsecondary teachers, graduate teaching assistants play an integral role in the postsecondary education system, and they are expected to continue to do so in the future.

Opportunities will also be excellent for postsecondary vocational teachers due to an increased emphasis on career and technical education at the postsecondary level. Job growth, combined with a large number of expected retirements, will result in many job openings for these workers. Prospects will be best for instructors in specialties that pay well outside of the teaching field, such as the construction trades and manufacturing technology.

One of the main reasons why students attend postsecondary institutions is to prepare themselves for careers, so the best job prospects for postsecondary teachers are likely to be in rapidly growing fields that offer many nonacademic career options. These will include fields such as business, nursing and other health specialties, and biological sciences. Community colleges and other institutions offering career and technical education have been among the most rapidly growing, and these institutions are expected to offer some of the best opportunities for postsecondary teachers.

## Earnings

Median annual earnings of all postsecondary teachers in 2006 were $56,120. The middle 50 percent earned between $39,610 and $80,390. The lowest 10 percent earned less than $27,590, and the highest 10 percent earned more than $113,450.

Earnings for college faculty vary according to rank and type of institution, geographic area, and field. According to a 2006-07 survey by the American Association of University Professors, salaries for full-time faculty averaged $73,207. By rank, the average was $98,974 for professors, $69,911 for associate professors, $58,662 for assistant professors, $42,609 for instructors, and $48,289 for lecturers. Faculty in 4-year institutions earn higher salaries, on average, than do those in 2-year schools. In 2006-07, faculty salaries averaged $84,249 in private independent institutions, $71,362 in public institutions, and $66,118 in religiously affiliated private colleges and universities. In fields with high-paying nonacademic alternatives—medicine, law, engineering, and business, among others—earnings exceed these averages. In other fields, such as the humanities and education, earnings are lower. Earnings for postsecondary career and technical education teachers vary widely by subject, academic credentials, experience, and region of the country.

Many faculty members have significant earnings in addition to their base salary from consulting, teaching additional courses, research, writing for publication, or other employment. In addition, many college and university faculty enjoy unique benefits, including access to campus facilities, tuition waivers for dependents, housing and travel allowances, and paid leave for sabbaticals. Part-time faculty and instructors usually have fewer benefits than full-time faculty.

## Related Occupations

Postsecondary teaching requires the ability to communicate ideas well, motivate students, and be creative. Workers in other occupations that require these skills are preschool, kindergarten, elementary, middle, and secondary school teachers; education administrators; librarians; counselors; writers and editors; public relations specialists; and management analysts. Faculty research activities often are similar to those of life, physical, and social scientists, as well as to those of managers and administrators in industry, government, and nonprofit research organizations.

## Sources of Additional Information

Professional societies related to a field of study often provide information on academic and nonacademic employment opportunities.

Special publications on higher education, such as *The Chronicle of Higher Education*, list specific employment opportunities for faculty. These publications are available in libraries.

For information on the Preparing Future Faculty program, contact

▶ Council of Graduate Schools, One Dupont Circle NW, Suite 430, Washington, DC 20036-1173. Internet: http://www.preparing-faculty.org

For information on postsecondary career and technical education teaching positions, contact state departments of career and technical education. General information on adult and career and technical education is available from

▶ Association for Career and Technical Education, 1410 King St., Alexandria, VA 22314. Internet: http://www.acteonline.org

# Teachers—Preschool, Kindergarten, Elementary, Middle, and Secondary

(O*NET 25-2011.00, 25-2012.00, 25-2021.00, 25-2022.00, 25-2023.00, 25-2031.00, and 25-2032.00)

## Significant Points

■ Public school teachers must be licensed, which typically requires a bachelor's degree and completion of an approved teacher education program.

■ Many states offer alternative licensing programs to attract people into teaching, especially for hard-to-fill positions.

■ Job prospects should be favorable; opportunities will vary by geographic area and subject taught.

## Nature of the Work

Teachers play an important role in fostering the intellectual and social development of children during their formative years. The education that teachers impart plays a key role in determining the future prospects of their students. Whether in preschools or high schools or in private or public schools, teachers provide the tools and the environment for their students to develop into responsible adults.

Teachers act as facilitators or coaches, using classroom presentations or individual instruction to help students learn and apply concepts in subjects such as science, mathematics, or English. They plan, evaluate, and assign lessons; prepare, administer, and grade tests; listen to oral presentations; and maintain classroom discipline. Teachers observe and evaluate a student's performance and potential and increasingly are asked to use new assessment methods. For example, teachers may examine a portfolio of a student's artwork or writing in order to judge the student's overall progress. They then can provide additional assistance in areas in which a student needs help. Teachers also grade papers, prepare report cards, and meet with parents and school staff to discuss a student's academic progress or personal problems.

Many teachers use a "hands-on" approach that uses "props" or "manipulatives" to help children understand abstract concepts, solve problems, and develop critical thought processes. For example, they teach the concepts of numbers or of addition and subtraction by playing board games. As the children get older, teachers use more sophisticated materials, such as science apparatus, cameras, or computers. They also encourage collaboration in solving problems by having students work in groups to discuss and solve problems together. To be prepared for success later in life, students must be able to interact with others, adapt to new technology, and think through problems logically.

*Preschool, kindergarten, and elementary school teachers* play a vital role in the development of children. What children learn and experience during their early years can shape their views of themselves and the world and can affect their later success or failure in school, work, and their personal lives. Preschool, kindergarten, and elementary school teachers introduce children to mathematics, language, science, and social studies. They use games, music, artwork, films, books, computers, and other tools to teach basic skills.

Preschool children learn mainly through play and interactive activities. *Preschool teachers* capitalize on children's play to further language and vocabulary development (using storytelling, rhyming games, and acting games), improve social skills (having the children work together to build a neighborhood in a sandbox), and introduce scientific and mathematical concepts (showing the children how to balance and count blocks when building a bridge or how to mix colors when painting). Thus, a less structured approach, including small-group lessons, one-on-one instruction, and learning through creative activities such as art, dance, and music, is adopted to teach preschool children. Play and hands-on teaching also are used by *kindergarten teachers*, but academics begin to take priority in kindergarten classrooms. Letter recognition, phonics, numbers, and awareness of nature and science, introduced at the preschool level, are taught primarily in kindergarten.

Most *elementary school teachers* instruct one class of children in several subjects. In some schools, two or more teachers work as a team and are jointly responsible for a group of students in at least one subject. In other schools, a teacher may teach one special subject—usually music, art, reading, science, arithmetic, or physical education—to a number of classes. A small but growing number of teachers instruct multilevel classrooms, with students at several different learning levels.

*Middle school teachers* and *secondary school teachers* help students delve more deeply into subjects introduced in elementary school and expose them to more information about the world. Middle and secondary school teachers specialize in a specific subject, such as English, Spanish, mathematics, history, or biology. They also may teach subjects that are career oriented. *Vocational education teachers*, also referred to as career and technical or career-technology teachers, instruct and train students to work in a wide variety of fields, such as healthcare, business, auto repair, communications, and, increasingly, technology. They often teach courses that are in high demand by area employers, who may provide input into the curriculum and offer internships to students. Many vocational teachers play an active role in building and overseeing these partnerships. Additional responsibilities of middle and secondary school teachers may include career guidance and job placement, as well as follow-ups with students after graduation.

In addition to conducting classroom activities, teachers oversee study halls and homerooms, supervise extracurricular activities, and accompany students on field trips. They may identify students with physical or mental problems and refer the students to the proper authorities. Secondary school teachers occasionally assist students in choosing courses, colleges, and careers. Teachers also participate in education conferences and workshops.

Computers play an integral role in the education teachers provide. Resources such as educational software and the Internet expose students to a vast range of experiences and promote interactive learning. Through the Internet, students can communicate with other students anywhere in the world, allowing them to share experiences and differing viewpoints. Students also use the Internet for individual research projects and to gather information. Computers are used in other classroom activities as well, from solving math problems to learning English as a second language. Teachers also may use computers to record grades and perform other administrative and clerical duties. They must continually update their skills so that they can instruct and use the latest technology in the classroom.

Teachers often work with students from varied ethnic, racial, and religious backgrounds. With growing minority populations in most parts of the country, it is important for teachers to work effectively with a diverse student population. Accordingly, some schools offer training to help teachers enhance their awareness and understanding of different cultures. Teachers may also include multicultural programming in their lesson plans, to address the needs of all students, regardless of their cultural background.

In recent years, site-based management, which allows teachers and parents to participate actively in management decisions regarding school operations, has gained popularity. In many schools, teachers are increasingly involved in making decisions regarding the budget, personnel, textbooks, curriculum design, and teaching methods.

*Work environment.* Seeing students develop new skills and gain an appreciation of knowledge and learning can be very rewarding. However, teaching may be frustrating when one is dealing with unmotivated or disrespectful students. Occasionally, teachers must cope with unruly behavior and violence in the schools. Teachers may experience stress in dealing with large classes, heavy workloads, or old schools that are run down and lack many modern amenities. Accountability standards also may increase stress levels, with teachers expected to produce students who are able to exhibit satisfactory performance on standardized tests in core subjects. Many teachers, particularly in public schools, are also frustrated by the lack of control they have over what they are required to teach.

Teachers in private schools generally enjoy smaller class sizes and more control over establishing the curriculum and setting standards for performance and discipline. Their students also tend to be more motivated, since private schools can be selective in their admissions processes.

Teachers are sometimes isolated from their colleagues because they work alone in a classroom of students. However, some schools allow teachers to work in teams and with mentors to enhance their professional development.

Including school duties performed outside the classroom, many teachers work more than 40 hours a week. Part-time schedules are more common among preschool and kindergarten teachers. Although most school districts have gone to all-day kindergartens, some kindergarten teachers still teach two kindergarten classes a day. Most teachers work the traditional 10-month school year with a 2-month vacation during the summer. During the vacation break, those on the 10-month schedule may teach in summer sessions, take other jobs, travel, or pursue personal interests. Many enroll in college courses or workshops to continue their education. Teachers in districts with a year-round schedule typically work 8 weeks, are on vacation for 1 week, and have a 5-week midwinter break. Preschool teachers working in day care settings often work year round.

Most states have tenure laws that prevent public school teachers from being fired without just cause and due process. Teachers may obtain tenure after they have satisfactorily completed a probationary period of teaching, normally 3 years. Tenure does not absolutely guarantee a job, but it does provide some security.

## Training, Other Qualifications, and Advancement

The traditional route to becoming a public school teacher involves completing a bachelor's degree from a teacher education program and then obtaining a license. However, most states now offer alternative routes to licensure for those who have a college degree in other fields. Private school teachers do not have to be licensed but still need a bachelor's degree. A bachelor's degree may not be needed by preschool teachers and vocational education teachers, who need experience in their field rather than a specific degree.

*Education and training.* Traditional education programs for kindergarten and elementary school teachers include courses designed specifically for those preparing to teach. These courses include mathematics, physical science, social science, music, art, and literature, as well as prescribed professional education courses, such as philosophy of education, psychology of learning, and teaching methods. Aspiring secondary school teachers most often major in the subject they plan to teach while also taking a program of study in teacher preparation. Many four-year colleges require students to wait until their sophomore year before applying for admission to teacher education programs. To maintain their accreditation, teacher education programs are now required to include classes in the use of computers and other technologies. Most programs require students to perform a student-teaching internship. Teacher education programs are accredited by the National Council for Accreditation of Teacher Education and the Teacher Education Accreditation Council. Graduation from an accredited program is not necessary to become a teacher, but it may make fulfilling licensure requirements easier.

Many states now offer professional development schools, which are partnerships between universities and elementary or secondary schools. Professional development schools merge theory with practice and allow the student to experience a year of teaching firsthand, under professional guidance. Students enter these one-year programs after completion of their bachelor's degree.

*Licensure and certification.* All 50 states and the District of Columbia require public school teachers to be licensed. Licensure is not required for teachers in most private schools. Usually licensure is granted by the state Board of Education or a licensure advisory committee. Teachers may be licensed to teach the early childhood grades (usually preschool through grade 3); the elementary grades (grades 1 through 6 or 8); the middle grades (grades 5 through 8); a secondary-education subject area (usually grades seven through 12); or a special subject, such as reading or music (usually grades kindergarten through 12).

Requirements for regular licenses to teach kindergarten through grade 12 vary by state. However, all states require general education teachers to have a bachelor's degree and to have completed an approved teacher training program with a prescribed number of subject and education credits, as well as supervised practice teaching. Some states also require technology training and the attainment of a minimum grade point average. A number of states require that teachers obtain a master's degree in education within a specified period after they begin teaching.

Almost all states require applicants for a teacher's license to be tested for competency in basic skills, such as reading and writing, and in teaching. Almost all also require teachers to exhibit proficiency in their subject. Many school systems are presently moving toward implementing performance-based systems for licensure, which usually require teachers to demonstrate satisfactory teaching performance over an extended period in order to obtain a provisional license, in addition to passing an examination in their subject. Most states require teachers to complete a minimum number of hours of continuing education to renew their license. Many states have reciprocity agreements that make it easier for teachers licensed in one state to become licensed in another.

Licensing requirements for preschool teachers also vary by state. Requirements for public preschool teachers are generally more stringent than those for private preschool teachers. Some states require a bachelor's degree in early childhood education, while others require an associate's degree, and still others require certification by a nationally recognized authority. The Child Development Associate (CDA) credential, the most common type of certification, requires a mix of classroom training and experience working with children, along with an independent assessment of the teacher's competence.

Nearly all states now also offer alternative licensure programs for teachers who have a bachelor's degree in the subject they will teach, but who lack the necessary education courses required for a regular license. Many of these alternative licensure programs are designed to ease shortages of teachers of certain subjects, such as mathemat-

ics and science. Other programs provide teachers for urban and rural schools that have difficulty filling positions with teachers from traditional licensure programs. Alternative licensure programs are intended to attract people into teaching who do not fulfill traditional licensing standards, including recent college graduates who did not complete education programs and those changing from another career to teaching. In some programs, individuals begin teaching quickly under provisional licensure under the close supervision of experienced educators while taking education courses outside school hours. If they progress satisfactorily, they receive regular licensure after working for one or two years. In other programs, college graduates who do not meet licensure requirements take only those courses that they lack and then become licensed. This approach may take one or two semesters of full-time study. The coursework for alternative certification programs often leads to a master's degree. In extreme circumstances, when schools cannot attract enough qualified teachers to fill positions, states may issue emergency licenses to individuals who do not meet the requirements for a regular license that let them begin teaching immediately.

In many states, vocational teachers have many of the same licensure requirements as other teachers. However, knowledge and experience in a particular field are important, so some states will license vocational education teachers without a bachelor's degree, provided they can demonstrate expertise in their field. A minimum number of hours in education courses may also be required.

Private schools are generally exempt from meeting state licensing standards. For secondary school teacher jobs, they prefer candidates who have a bachelor's degree in the subject they intend to teach, or in childhood education for elementary school teachers. They seek candidates among recent college graduates as well as from those who have established careers in other fields.

*Other qualifications.* In addition to being knowledgeable about the subjects they teach, teachers must have the ability to communicate, inspire trust and confidence, and motivate students, as well as understand the students' educational and emotional needs. Teachers must be able to recognize and respond to individual and cultural differences in students and employ different teaching methods that will result in higher student achievement. They should be organized, dependable, patient, and creative. Teachers also must be able to work cooperatively and communicate effectively with other teachers, support staff, parents, and members of the community. Private schools associated with religious institutions also desire candidates who share the values that are important to the institution.

*Additional certifications and advancement.* In some cases, teachers of kindergarten through high school may attain professional certification in order to demonstrate competency beyond that required for a license. The National Board for Professional Teaching Standards offers a voluntary national certification. To become nationally certified, experienced teachers must prove their aptitude by compiling a portfolio showing their work in the classroom and by passing a written assessment and evaluation of their teaching knowledge. Currently, teachers may become certified in a variety of areas, on the basis of the age of the students and, in some cases, the subject taught. For example, teachers may obtain a certificate for teaching English language arts to early adolescents (aged 11 to 15), or they may become certified as early childhood generalists. All states recognize national certification, and many states and school districts

**Projections data from the National Employment Matrix**

| Occupational Title | SOC Code | Employment, 2006 | Projected employment, 2016 | Change, 2006-2016 | |
|---|---|---|---|---|---|
| | | | | Number | Percent |
| Teachers—preschool, kindergarten, elementary, middle, and secondary ................................................................ | — | 3,954,000 | 4,433,000 | 479,000 | 12 |
| Preschool and kindergarten teachers........................................... | 25-2010 | 607,000 | 750,000 | 143,000 | 23 |
| Preschool teachers, except special education.......................... | 25-2011 | 437,000 | 552,000 | 115,000 | 26 |
| Kindergarten teachers, except special education .................... | 25-2012 | 170,000 | 198,000 | 28,000 | 16 |
| Elementary and middle school teachers...................................... | 25-2020 | 2,214,000 | 2,496,000 | 282,000 | 13 |
| Elementary school teachers, except special education.............. | 25-2021 | 1,540,000 | 1,749,000 | 209,000 | 14 |
| Middle school teachers, except special and vocational education ............................................................................. | 25-2022 | 658,000 | 732,000 | 74,000 | 11 |
| Vocational education teachers, middle school ........................ | 25-2023 | 16,000 | 15,000 | -800 | -5 |
| Secondary school teachers ........................................................ | 25-2030 | 1,133,000 | 1,187,000 | 54,000 | 5 |
| Secondary school teachers, except special and vocational education ............................................................................. | 25-2031 | 1,038,000 | 1,096,000 | 59,000 | 6 |
| Vocational education teachers, secondary school .................... | 25-2032 | 96,000 | 91,000 | -4,400 | -5 |

NOTE: Data in this table are rounded.

provide special benefits to teachers who earn certification. Benefits typically include higher salaries and reimbursement for continuing education and certification fees. In addition, many states allow nationally certified teachers to carry a license from one state to another.

With additional preparation, teachers may move into such positions as school librarians, reading specialists, instructional coordinators, or guidance counselors. Teachers may become administrators or supervisors, although the number of these positions is limited and competition for them can be intense. In some systems, highly qualified, experienced teachers can become senior or mentor teachers, with higher pay and additional responsibilities. They guide and assist less experienced teachers while keeping most of their own teaching responsibilities. Preschool teachers usually work their way up from assistant teacher, to teacher, to lead teacher—who may be responsible for the instruction of several classes—and, finally, to director of the center. Preschool teachers with a bachelor's degree frequently are qualified to teach kindergarten through grade 3 as well. Teaching at these higher grades often results in higher pay.

## Employment

Preschool, kindergarten, elementary school, middle school, and secondary school teachers, except special education, held about 4.0 million jobs in 2006. Of the teachers in those jobs, about 1.5 million are elementary school teachers, 1.1 million are secondary school teachers, 673,000 are middle school teachers, 437,000 are preschool teachers, and 170,000 are kindergarten teachers. The vast majority work in elementary and secondary schools. Preschool teachers, except special education, are most often employed in child daycare services (59 percent), public and private educational services (16 percent), and religious organizations (15 percent). Employment of teachers is geographically distributed much the same as the population.

## Job Outlook

Employment of preschool, kindergarten, elementary, middle, and secondary school teachers is projected to grow about as fast as aver-

age. Job prospects are expected to be favorable, with particularly good prospects for teachers in high-demand fields like math, science, and bilingual education, or in less desirable urban or rural school districts.

***Employment change.*** Employment of school teachers is expected to grow by 12 percent between 2006 and 2016, about as fast as the average for all occupations. However, because of the size of the occupations in this group, this growth will create 479,000 additional teacher positions, more than all but a few occupations.

Through 2016, overall student enrollments in elementary, middle, and secondary schools—a key factor in the demand for teachers—are expected to rise more slowly than in the past as children of the baby boom generation leave the school system. This will cause employment of teachers from kindergarten through the secondary grades to grow as fast as the average. Projected enrollments will vary by region. Fast-growing states in the South and West—led by Nevada, Arizona, Texas, and Georgia—will experience the largest enrollment increases. Enrollments in the Midwest are expected to hold relatively steady, while those in the Northeast are expected to decline. Teachers who are geographically mobile and who obtain licensure in more than one subject should have a distinct advantage in finding a job.

The number of teachers employed is dependent on state and local expenditures for education and on the enactment of legislation to increase the quality and scope of public education. At the federal level, there has been a large increase in funding for education, particularly for the hiring of qualified teachers in lower income areas. Also, some states are instituting programs to improve early childhood education, such as offering full day kindergarten and universal preschool. These programs, along with projected higher enrollment growth for preschool age children, will create many new jobs for preschool teachers, which are expected to grow much faster than the average for all occupations.

***Job prospects.*** Job opportunities for teachers over the next 10 years will vary from good to excellent, depending on the locality, grade level, and subject taught. Most job openings will result from the need to replace the large number of teachers who are expected to retire over the 2006–2016 period. Also, many beginning teachers decide to leave teaching for other careers after a year or two—especially those employed in poor, urban schools—creating additional job openings for teachers.

The job market for teachers also continues to vary by school location and by subject taught. Job prospects should be better in inner cities and rural areas than in suburban districts. Many inner cities—often characterized by overcrowded, ill-equipped schools and higher-than-average poverty rates—and rural areas—characterized by their remote location and relatively low salaries—have difficulty attracting and retaining enough teachers. Currently, many school districts have difficulty hiring qualified teachers in some subject areas—most often mathematics, science (especially chemistry and physics), bilingual education, and foreign languages. Increasing enrollments of minorities, coupled with a shortage of minority teachers, should cause efforts to recruit minority teachers to intensify. Also, the number of non-English-speaking students will continue to grow, creating demand for bilingual teachers and for those who teach English as a second language. Qualified vocational teachers also are currently in demand in a variety of fields at both the middle school and secondary school levels. Specialties that have an adequate number of qualified teachers include general elementary education, physical education, and social studies.

The supply of teachers is expected to increase in response to reports of improved job prospects, better pay, more teacher involvement in school policy, and greater public interest in education. In addition, more teachers may be drawn from a reserve pool of career changers, substitute teachers, and teachers completing alternative certification programs. In recent years, the total number of bachelor's and master's degrees granted in education has been increasing slowly. But many states have implemented policies that will encourage even more students to become teachers because of a shortage of teachers in certain locations and in anticipation of the loss of a number of teachers to retirement.

## Earnings

Median annual earnings of kindergarten, elementary, middle, and secondary school teachers ranged from $43,580 to $48,690 in May 2006; the lowest 10 percent earned $28,590 to $33,070; the top 10 percent earned $67,490 to $76,100. Median earnings for preschool teachers were $22,680.

According to the American Federation of Teachers, beginning teachers with a bachelor's degree earned an average of $31,753 in the 2004–05 school year. The estimated average salary of all public elementary and secondary school teachers in the 2004–05 school year was $47,602.

In 2006, more than half of all elementary, middle, and secondary school teachers belonged to unions—mainly the American Federation of Teachers and the National Education Association—that bargain with school systems over salaries, hours, and other terms and conditions of employment. Fewer preschool and kindergarten teachers were union members—about 17 percent in 2006.

Teachers can boost their earnings in a number of ways. In some schools, teachers receive extra pay for coaching sports and working with students in extracurricular activities. Getting a master's degree or national certification often results in a raise in pay, as does acting as a mentor. Some teachers earn extra income during the summer by teaching summer school or performing other jobs in the school system. Although private school teachers generally earn less than public school teachers, they may be given other benefits, such as free or subsidized housing.

## Related Occupations

Preschool, kindergarten, elementary school, middle school, and secondary school teaching requires a variety of skills and aptitudes, including a talent for working with children; organizational, administrative, and recordkeeping abilities; research and communication skills; the power to influence, motivate, and train others; patience; and creativity. Workers in other occupations requiring some of these aptitudes include teachers—postsecondary; counselors; teacher assistants; education administrators; librarians; childcare workers; public relations specialists; social workers; and athletes, coaches, umpires, and related workers.

## Sources of Additional Information

Information on licensure or certification requirements and approved teacher training institutions is available from local school systems and state departments of education.

Information on teachers' unions and education-related issues may be obtained from the following sources:

▶ American Federation of Teachers, 555 New Jersey Ave. NW, Washington, DC 20001.

▶ National Education Association, 1201 16th St. NW, Washington, DC 20036.

A list of institutions with accredited teacher education programs can be obtained from

▶ National Council for Accreditation of Teacher Education, 2010 Massachusetts Ave. NW, Suite 500, Washington, DC 20036-1023. Internet: http://www.ncate.org

▶ Teacher Education Accreditation Council, Suite 300, One Dupont Circle, Washington, DC 20036. Internet: http://www.teac.org

Information on alternative certification programs can be obtained from

▶ National Center for Alternative Certification, 1901 Pennsylvania Ave NW, Suite 201, Washington, DC 20006. Internet: http://www.teach-now.org

Information on National Board Certification can be obtained from

▶ National Board for Professional Teaching Standards, 1525 Wilson Blvd., Suite 500, Arlington, VA 22209. Internet: http://www.nbpts.org

For information on vocational education and vocational education teachers, contact

▶ Association for Career and Technical Education, 1410 King St., Alexandria, VA 22314. Internet: http://www.acteonline.org

For information on careers in educating children and issues affecting preschool teachers, contact either of the following organizations:

▶ National Association for the Education of Young Children, 1509 16th St. NW, Washington, DC 20036. Internet: http://www.naeyc.org

▶ Council for Professional Recognition, 2460 16th St. NW, Washington, DC 20009-3575. Internet: http://www.cdacouncil.org

# Teachers—Self-Enrichment Education

(O*NET 25-3021.00)

## Significant Points

- Many self-enrichment teachers are self-employed or work part time.
- Teachers should have knowledge and enthusiasm for their subject, but little formal training is required.
- Employment is projected to grow much faster than average, and job prospects should be favorable; opportunities may vary by subject taught.

## Nature of the Work

Self-enrichment teachers provide instruction in a wide variety of subjects that students take for fun or self-improvement. Some teach a series of classes that provide students with useful life skills, such as cooking, personal finance, and time management. Others provide group instruction intended solely for recreation, such as photography, pottery, and painting. Many others provide one-on-one instruction in a variety of subjects, including dance, singing, or playing a musical instrument. Some teachers conduct courses on academic subjects, such as literature, foreign language, and history, in a nonacademic setting. The classes self-enrichment teachers give seldom lead to a degree and attendance is voluntary, but dedicated, talented students sometimes go on to careers in the arts.

Self-enrichment teachers may have styles and methods of instruction that differ greatly. Most self-enrichment classes are relatively informal. Some classes, such as pottery or sewing, may be largely hands-on, with the instructor demonstrating methods or techniques for the class, observing students as they attempt to do it themselves, and pointing out mistakes to students and offering suggestions to improve techniques. Other classes, such as those involving financial planning or religion and spirituality, may center on lectures or might rely more heavily on group discussions. Self-enrichment teachers may also teach classes offered through religious institutions, such as marriage preparation or classes in religion for children.

Many of the classes that self-enrichment educators teach are shorter in duration than classes taken for academic credit; some finish in 1 or 2 days or several weeks. These brief classes tend to be introductory in nature and generally focus on only one topic—for example, a cooking class that teaches students how to make bread. Some self-enrichment classes introduce children and youth to activities, such as piano or drama, and may be designed to last anywhere from 1 week to several months.

Many self-enrichment teachers provide one-on-one lessons to students. The instructor may only work with the student for an hour or two a week, but tells the student what to practice in the interim until the next lesson. Many instructors work with the same students on a weekly basis for years and derive satisfaction from observing them mature and gain expertise. The most talented students may go on to paid careers as craft artists, painters, sculptors, dancers, singers, or musicians.

All self-enrichment teachers must prepare lessons beforehand and stay current in their fields. Many self-enrichment teachers are self employed and provide instruction as a business. As such, they must collect any fees or tuition and keep records of students whose accounts are prepaid or in arrears. Although not a requirement for most types of classes, teachers may use computers and other modern technologies in their instruction or to maintain business records.

*Work environment.* Few self-enrichment education teachers are full-time salaried workers. Most either work part time or are self-employed. Some have several part-time teaching assignments, but it is most common for teachers to have a full-time job in another occupation, often related to the subject that they teach, in addition to their part-time teaching job. Although jobs in this occupation are primarily part time and pay is low, most teachers enjoy their work because it gives them the opportunity to share a subject they enjoy with others.

Many classes for adults are held in the evenings and on weekends to accommodate students who have a job or family responsibilities. Similarly, self-enrichment classes for children are usually held after school, on weekends, or during school vacations.

Students in self-enrichment programs attend by choice so they tend to be highly motivated and eager to learn. Students also often bring their own unique experiences to class, which can make teaching them rewarding and satisfying. Self-enrichment teachers must have a great deal of patience, however, particularly when working with young children.

## Training, Other Qualifications, and Advancement

The main qualification for self-enrichment teachers is expertise in their subject area, but requirements vary greatly with the type of class taught and the place of employment.

*Education and training.* In general, there are few educational or training requirements for a job as a self-enrichment teacher beyond being an expert in the subject taught. To demonstrate expertise, however, self enrichment teachers may be required to have formal training in disciplines, such as art or music, where specific teacher training programs are available. Prospective dance teachers, for example, may complete programs that prepare them to teach many types of dance—from ballroom to ballet. Other employers may require a portfolio of a teacher's work. For example, to secure a job teaching a photography course, an applicant often needs to show examples of previous work. Some self-enrichment teachers are trained educators or other professionals who teach enrichment classes in their spare time. In many self-enrichment fields, however, instructors are simply experienced in the field, and want to share that experience with others.

*Other qualifications.* In addition to knowledge of their subject, self-enrichment teachers should have good speaking skills and a talent for making the subject interesting. Patience and the ability to explain and instruct students at a basic level are important as well, particularly for teachers who work with children.

Projections data from the National Employment Matrix

| Occupational Title | SOC Code | Employment, 2006 | Projected employment, 2016 | Change, 2006-2016 | |
|---|---|---|---|---|---|
| | | | | Number | Percent |
| Self-enrichment education teachers ................................................. | 25-3021 | 261,000 | 322,000 | 60,000 | 23 |

NOTE: Data in this table are rounded.

*Advancement.* Opportunities for advancement in this profession are limited. Some part-time teachers are able to move into full-time teaching positions or program administrator positions, such as coordinator or director. Experienced teachers may mentor new instructors.

## Employment

Teachers of self-enrichment education held about 261,000 jobs in 2006. The largest numbers of teachers were employed by public and private educational institutions, religious organizations, and providers of social assistance and amusement and recreation services. More than 20 percent of workers were self employed.

## Job Outlook

Employment of self-enrichment education teachers is expected to grow much faster than average, and job prospects should be favorable. A large number of job openings are expected due to job growth, the retirement of existing teachers, and because of those who leave their jobs for other reasons. New opportunities arise constantly because many jobs are short term and are often held as a second job.

*Employment change.* Employment of self-enrichment education teachers is expected to increase by 23 percent between 2006 and 2016, much faster than the average for all occupations. The need for self-enrichment teachers is expected to grow as more people embrace lifelong learning and as course offerings expand. Demand for self-enrichment education will also increase as a result of demographic changes. Retirees are one of the larger groups of participants in self-enrichment education because they have more time for classes. As members of the baby boom generation begin to retire, demand for self-enrichment education should grow. At the same time, the children of the baby boomers will be entering the age range of another large group of participants, young adults—who often are single and participate in self-enrichment classes for the social, as well as the educational, experience.

*Job prospects.* Job prospects should be favorable as increasing demand and high turnover creates many opportunities, but opportunities may vary as some fields have more prospective teachers than others. Opportunities should be best for teachers of subjects that are not easily researched on the Internet and those that benefit from hands-on experiences, such as cooking, crafts, and the arts. Classes on self-improvement, personal finance, and computer and Internet-related subjects are also expected to be popular.

## Earnings

Median hourly earnings of wage-and-salary self-enrichment teachers were $16.08 in May 2006. The middle 50 percent earned between $11.29 and $23.08. The lowest 10 percent earned less than $8.53, and the highest 10 percent earned more than $32.02. Self-

enrichment teachers are generally paid by the hour or for each class that they teach. Earnings may also be tied to the number of students enrolled in the class.

Part-time instructors are usually paid for each class that they teach, and receive few benefits. Full-time teachers are generally paid a salary and may receive health insurance and other benefits.

## Related Occupations

The work of self-enrichment teachers is closely related to that of other types of teachers, especially preschool, kindergarten, elementary school, middle school, and secondary school teachers. Self-enrichment teachers also teach a wide variety of subjects that may be related to the work done by those in many other occupations, such as dancers and choreographers; artists and related workers; musicians, singers, and related workers; recreation workers; and athletes, coaches, umpires, and related workers.

## Sources of Additional Information

For information on employment of self-enrichment teachers, contact local schools, colleges, or companies that offer self-enrichment programs.

## Teachers—Special Education

(O*NET 25-2041.00, 25-2042.00, and 25-2043.00)

## Significant Points

- All states require teachers to be licensed; traditional licensing requires the completion of a special education teacher training program and at least a bachelor's degree, though many states require a master's degree.

- Many states offer alternative licensure programs to attract college graduates who do not have training in education.

- Excellent job prospects are expected due to rising enrollments of special education students and reported shortages of qualified teachers.

## Nature of the Work

Special education teachers work with children and youths who have a variety of disabilities. A small number of special education teachers work with students with severe cases of mental retardation or autism, primarily teaching them life skills and basic literacy. However, the majority of special education teachers work with children with mild to moderate disabilities, using or modifying the general education curriculum to meet the child's individual needs. Most special education teachers instruct students at the elementary, middle, and secondary school level, although some work with infants and toddlers.

The various types of disabilities that may qualify individuals for special education programs include specific learning disabilities, speech or language impairments, mental retardation, emotional disturbance, multiple disabilities, hearing impairments, orthopedic impairments, visual impairments, autism, combined deafness and blindness, traumatic brain injury, and other health impairments. Students are classified under one of the categories, and special education teachers are prepared to work with specific groups. Early identification of a child with special needs is an important part of a special education teacher's job, because early intervention is essential in educating children with disabilities.

Special education teachers use various techniques to promote learning. Depending on the disability, teaching methods can include individualized instruction, problem-solving assignments, and small-group work. When students need special accommodations to take a test, special education teachers see that appropriate ones are provided, such as having the questions read orally or lengthening the time allowed to take the test.

Special education teachers help to develop an Individualized Education Program (IEP) for each student. The IEP sets personalized goals for the student and is tailored to that student's individual needs and ability. When appropriate, the program includes a transition plan outlining specific steps to prepare students with disabilities for middle school or high school or, in the case of older students, a job or postsecondary study. Teachers review the IEP with the student's parents, school administrators, and the student's general education teachers. Teachers work closely with parents to inform them of their child's progress and suggest techniques to promote learning at home.

Special education teachers design and teach appropriate curricula, assign work geared toward each student's needs and abilities, and grade papers and homework assignments. They are involved in the students' behavioral, social, and academic development, helping them develop emotionally, feel comfortable in social situations, and be aware of socially acceptable behavior. Preparing special education students for daily life after graduation also is an important aspect of the job. Teachers provide students with career counseling or help them learn routine skills, such as balancing a checkbook.

As schools become more inclusive, special education teachers and general education teachers increasingly work together in general education classrooms. Special education teachers help general educators adapt curriculum materials and teaching techniques to meet the needs of students with disabilities. They coordinate the work of teachers, teacher assistants, and related personnel, such as therapists and social workers, to meet the individualized needs of the student within inclusive special education programs. A large part of a special education teacher's job involves communicating and coordinating with others involved in the child's well being, including parents, social workers, school psychologists, occupational and physical therapists, school administrators, and other teachers.

Special education teachers work in a variety of settings. Some have their own classrooms and teach only special education students; others work as special education resource teachers and offer individualized help to students in general education classrooms; still others

teach together with general education teachers in classes including both general and special education students. Some teachers work with special education students for several hours a day in a resource room, separate from their general education classroom. Considerably fewer special education teachers work in residential facilities or tutor students in homebound or hospital environments.

Some special education teachers work with infants and usually travel to the child's home to work with the parents. Many of these infants have medical problems that slow or preclude normal development. Special education teachers show parents techniques and activities designed to stimulate the infant and encourage the growth and development of the child's skills. Toddlers usually receive their services at a preschool where special education teachers help them develop social, self-help, motor, language, and cognitive skills, often through the use of play.

Technology is becoming increasingly important in special education. Teachers use specialized equipment such as computers with synthesized speech, interactive educational software programs, and audiotapes to assist children.

*Work environment.* Special education teachers enjoy the challenge of working with students with disabilities and the opportunity to establish meaningful relationships with them. Although helping these students can be highly rewarding, the work also can be emotionally and physically draining. Many special education teachers are under considerable stress due to heavy workloads and administrative tasks. They must produce a substantial amount of paperwork documenting each student's progress and work under the threat of litigation against the school or district by parents if correct procedures are not followed or if they feel that their child is not receiving an adequate education. Recently passed legislation, however, is intended to reduce the burden of paperwork and the threat of litigation. The physical and emotional demands of the job cause some special education teachers to leave the occupation.

Some schools offer year round education for special education students, but most special education teachers work only the traditional 10-month school year.

## Training, Other Qualifications, and Advancement

All states require special education teachers to be licensed, which typically requires at least a bachelor's degree and completion of an approved training program in special education teaching. Many states require a master's degree. Most states have alternative methods for entry for bachelor's degree holders who do not have training in education.

*Education and training.* Many colleges and universities across the United States offer programs in special education at the undergraduate, master's, and doctoral degree levels. Special education teachers usually undergo longer periods of training than do general education teachers. Most bachelor's degree programs last years and include general and specialized courses in special education. However, an increasing number of institutions require a fifth year or other graduate-level preparation. Among the courses offered are educational psychology, legal issues of special education, child growth and development, and strategies for teaching students with

**Projections data from the National Employment Matrix**

| Occupational Title | SOC Code | Employment, 2006 | Projected employment, 2016 | Change, 2006-2016 | |
|---|---|---|---|---|---|
| | | | | Number | Percent |
| Special education teachers ................................................ | 25-2040 | 459,000 | 530,000 | 71,000 | 15 |
| Special education teachers, preschool, kindergarten, and elementary school ................................................ | 25-2041 | 219,000 | 262,000 | 43,000 | 20 |
| Special education teachers, middle school.................................. | 25-2042 | 102,000 | 118,000 | 16,000 | 16 |
| Special education teachers, secondary school ............................. | 25-2043 | 138,000 | 150,000 | 12,000 | 9 |

NOTE: Data in this table are rounded.

disabilities. Some programs require specialization, while others offer generalized special education degrees or a course of study in several specialized areas. The last year of the program usually is spent student teaching in a classroom supervised by a certified teacher.

*Licensure.* All 50 states and the District of Columbia require special education teachers to be licensed. The state board of education or a licensure advisory committee usually grants licenses, and licensure varies by state. In some states, special education teachers receive a general education credential to teach kindergarten through grade 12. These teachers then train in a specialty, such as learning disabilities or behavioral disorders. Many states offer general special education licenses across a variety of disability categories, while others license several different specialties within special education.

For traditional licensing, all states require a bachelor's degree and the completion of an approved teacher preparation program with a prescribed number of subject and education credits and supervised practice teaching. However, many states also require a master's degree in special education, involving at least one year of additional course work, including a specialization, beyond the bachelor's degree. Often a prospective teacher must pass a professional assessment test as well. Some states have reciprocity agreements allowing special education teachers to transfer their licenses from one state to another, but many others still require that experienced teachers reapply and pass licensing requirements to work in the state.

Most states also offer alternative routes to licensing which are intended to attract people into teaching who do not fulfill traditional licensing standards. Most alternative licensure programs are open to anyone with a bachelor's degree, although some are designed for recent college graduates or professionals in other education occupations. Programs typically require the successful completion of a period of supervised preparation and instruction and passing an assessment test. Individuals can then begin teaching under a provisional license and can obtain a regular license after teaching under the supervision of licensed teachers for a period of one to two years and completing required education courses through a local college or other provider.

*Other qualifications.* Special education teachers must be patient, able to motivate students, understanding of their students' special needs, and accepting of differences in others. Teachers must be creative and apply different types of teaching methods to reach students who are having difficulty learning. Communication and cooperation are essential skills because special education teachers spend a great deal of time interacting with others, including students, parents, and school faculty and administrators.

*Advancement.* Special education teachers can advance to become supervisors or administrators. They may also earn advanced degrees and become instructors in colleges that prepare others to teach special education. In some school systems, highly experienced teachers can become mentors to less experienced ones, providing guidance to those teachers while maintaining a light teaching load.

## Employment

Special education teachers held a total of about 459,000 jobs in 2006. Nearly all work in public and private educational institutions. A few worked for individual and social assistance agencies or residential facilities, or in homebound or hospital environments.

## Job Outlook

Employment of special education teachers is expected to increase faster than average. Job prospects should be excellent as many districts report problems finding adequate numbers of certified special education teachers.

*Employment change.* The number of special education teachers is expected to increase by 15 percent from 2006 to 2016, faster than the average for all occupations. Although student enrollments in general are expected to grow slowly, continued increases in the number of special education students needing services will generate a greater need for special education teachers.

The number of students requiring special education services has grown steadily in recent years due to improvements that have allowed learning disabilities to be diagnosed at earlier ages and medical advances that have resulted in more children surviving serious accidents or illnesses, but with impairments that require special accommodations. In addition, legislation emphasizing training and employment for individuals with disabilities and educational reforms requiring higher standards for graduation has increased demand for special education services. The percentage of foreign-born special education students also is expected to grow, as teachers become more adept in recognizing disabilities in that population. Finally, more parents are expected to seek special services for their children who have difficulty meeting the new, higher standards required of students.

*Job prospects.* In addition to job openings resulting from growth, a large number of openings will result from the need to replace special education teachers who switch to teaching general education, change careers altogether, or retire. At the same time, many school districts report difficulty finding sufficient numbers of qualified teachers. As a result, special education teachers should have excellent job prospects.

The job outlook does vary by geographic area and specialty. Although most areas of the country report difficulty finding qualified applicants, positions in inner cities and rural areas usually are more plentiful than job openings in suburban or wealthy urban areas. Student populations also are expected to increase more rapidly in certain parts of the country, such as the South and West, resulting in increased demand for special education teachers in those regions. In addition, job opportunities may be better in certain specialties—such as teachers who work with children with multiple disabilities or severe disabilities like autism—because of large increases in the enrollment of special education students classified under those categories. Legislation encouraging early intervention and special education for infants, toddlers, and preschoolers has created a need for early childhood special education teachers. Bilingual special education teachers and those with multicultural experience also are needed to work with an increasingly diverse student population.

## Earnings

Median annual earnings in May 2006 of wage-and-salary special education teachers who worked primarily in preschools, kindergartens, and elementary schools were $46,360. The middle 50 percent earned between $37,500 and $59,320. The lowest 10 percent earned less than $31,320, and the highest 10 percent earned more than $73,620.

Median annual earnings of wage-and-salary middle school special education teachers were $47,650. The middle 50 percent earned between $38,460 and $61,530. The lowest 10 percent earned less than $32,420, and the highest 10 percent earned more than $80,170.

Median annual earnings of wage-and-salary special education teachers who worked primarily in secondary schools were $48,330. The middle 50 percent earned between $38,910 and $62,640. The lowest 10 percent earned less than $32,760, and the highest 10 percent earned more than $78,020.

In 2006, about 58 percent of special education teachers belonged to unions—mainly the American Federation of Teachers and the National Education Association—that bargain with school systems over wages, hours, and the terms and conditions of employment.

In most schools, teachers receive extra pay for coaching sports and working with students in extracurricular activities. Some teachers earn extra income during the summer, working in the school system or in other jobs.

## Related Occupations

Special education teachers work with students who have disabilities and special needs. Other occupations involved with the identification, evaluation, and development of students with disabilities include psychologists, social workers, speech-language pathologists, audiologists, counselors, teacher assistants, occupational therapists, recreational therapists, and teachers—preschool, kindergarten, elementary, middle, and secondary.

## Sources of Additional Information

For information on professions related to early intervention and education for children with disabilities, listings of schools with special education training programs, information on teacher certification, and general information on related personnel issues, contact

▶ The Council for Exceptional Children, 1110 N. Glebe Rd., Suite 300, Arlington, VA 22201. Internet: http://www.cec.sped.org

▶ National Center for Special Education Personnel & Related Service Providers, National Association of State Directors of Special Education, 1800 Diagonal Rd., Suite 320, Alexandria, VA 22314. Internet: http://www.personnelcenter.org

To learn more about the special education teacher certification and licensing requirements in individual states, contact the state's department of education.

# Tellers

(O*NET 43-3071.00)

## Significant Points

■ Tellers should enjoy working with the public, feel comfortable handling large amounts of money, and be discreet and trustworthy

■ About 1 out of 4 tellers work part time.

■ Many job openings will arise from replacement needs because many tellers eventually leave for jobs in other occupations that offer higher pay or more responsibility.

■ Employment of tellers is projected to grow as fast as the average; good job prospects are expected.

## Nature of the Work

The teller is the worker most people associate with their bank. Among the responsibilities of tellers are cashing checks, accepting deposits and loan payments, and processing withdrawals. Tellers make up approximately one-fourth of bank employees and conduct most of a bank's routine transactions.

Prior to starting their shifts, tellers receive and count an amount of working cash for their drawers. A supervisor—usually the head teller—verifies this amount. Tellers disburse this cash during the day and are responsible for its safe and accurate handling. Before leaving, tellers count their cash on hand, list the currency received on a balance sheet making sure that the accounts balance, and sort checks and deposit slips. Over the course of a workday, tellers also may process numerous mail transactions. They also may sell savings bonds, accept payment for customers' utility bills and charge cards, process necessary paperwork for certificates of deposit, and sell travelers' checks. Some tellers specialize in handling foreign currencies or commercial or business accounts. Other tellers corroborate deposits and payments to automated teller machines (ATMs).

Being a teller requires a great deal of attention to detail. Before cashing a check, a teller must verify the date, the name of the bank, the identity of the person who is to receive payment, and the legality of the document. A teller also must make sure that the written and

**Projections data from the National Employment Matrix**

| Occupational Title | SOC Code | Employment, 2006 | Projected employment, 2016 | Change, 2006-16 | |
|---|---|---|---|---|---|
| | | | | Number | Percent |
| Tellers................................................................................ | 43-3071 | 608,000 | 689,000 | 82,000 | 13 |

NOTE: Data in this table are rounded.

numerical amounts agree and that the account has sufficient funds to cover the check. The teller then must carefully count cash to avoid errors. Sometimes a customer withdraws money in the form of a cashier's check, which the teller prepares and verifies. When accepting a deposit, tellers must check the accuracy of the deposit slip before processing the transaction.

As banks begin to offer more and increasingly complex financial services, tellers are being trained to identify customers who might want to buy these services. This task requires them to learn about the various financial products and services the bank offers so that they can explain them to customers and refer interested customers to appropriate specialized sales personnel. In addition, tellers in many banks are being cross-trained to perform some of the functions of customer service representatives.

Technology continues to play a large role in the job duties of all tellers. In most banks, for example, tellers use computer terminals to record deposits and withdrawals. These terminals often give them quick access to detailed information on customer accounts. Tellers can use this information to tailor the bank's services to fit a customer's needs or to recommend an appropriate bank product or service.

In most banks, head tellers manage teller operations. They set work schedules, ensure that the proper procedures are adhered to, and act as mentors to less experienced tellers. In addition, head tellers may perform the typical duties of a front-line teller, as needed, and may deal with the more difficult customer problems. They may access the vault, ensure that the correct cash balance is in the vault, and oversee large cash transactions.

*Work environment.* Tellers work in an office environment. They may experience eye and muscle strain, backaches, headaches, and repetitive motion injuries as a result of using computers every day. Tellers may have to sit for extended periods while reviewing detailed data.

Many tellers work regular business hours and a standard 40-hour week. Sometimes, they work evenings and weekends to accommodate extended bank hours. About 1 in 4 tellers worked part time.

## Training, Other Qualifications, and Advancement

Most teller jobs require a high school diploma or higher degree. Tellers are usually trained on the job.

*Education and training.* Most tellers are required to have at least a high school diploma, but some have completed some college training or even a bachelor's degree in business, accounting, or liberal arts. Although a college degree is rarely required, graduates sometimes accept teller positions to get started in banking or in a particular company with the hope of eventually being promoted to managerial or other positions.

Once hired, tellers usually receive on-the-job training. Under the guidance of a supervisor or other senior worker, new employees learn company procedures. Some formal classroom training also may be necessary, such as training in specific computer software.

*Other qualifications.* Experience working in an office environment or in customer service, and particularly in cash-handling can be important for tellers. Regardless of experience, employers prefer workers who have good communication and customer service skills. Knowledge of word processing and spreadsheet software is also valuable.

Tellers should enjoy contact with the public. They must have a strong aptitude for numbers and feel comfortable handling large amounts of money. They should be discreet and trustworthy because they frequently come in contact with confidential material. Tellers also must be careful, orderly, and detail-oriented to avoid making errors and to recognize errors made by others.

*Advancement.* Tellers usually advance by taking on more duties and being promoted to head teller or to another supervisory job. Many banks and other employers fill supervisory and managerial positions by promoting individuals from within their organizations, so outstanding tellers who acquire additional skills, experience, and training improve their advancement opportunities. Tellers can prepare for jobs with better pay or more responsibility by taking courses offered by banking and financial institutes, colleges and universities, and private training institutions.

## Employment

Tellers held about 608,000 jobs in 2006. The overwhelming majority of tellers worked in commercial banks, savings institutions, or credit unions. The remainder worked in a variety of other finance and other industries.

## Job Outlook

Employment of tellers is expected to grow about as fast as the average for all occupations. Overall job prospects should be favorable due to the need to replace workers who retire or otherwise leave the occupation.

*Employment change.* Employment is projected to grow by 13 percent between 2006 and 2016, which is about as fast as the average for all occupations. To attract customers, banks are opening new branch offices in a variety of locations, such as grocery stores and shopping malls. Banks are also keeping their branches open longer during the day and on weekends. Both of these trends are expected to increase job opportunities for tellers, particularly those who work part time.

Despite the improved outlook, automation and technology will continue to reduce the need for tellers who perform only routine transactions. For example, increased use of ATMs, debit cards, credit cards, and the direct deposit of pay and benefit checks have reduced the need for bank customers to interact with tellers for routine transactions. Electronic banking—conducted over the telephone or the Internet—also is spreading rapidly throughout the banking industry and will reduce the need for tellers in the long run.

Employment of tellers also is being affected by the increasing use of 24-hour telephone centers by many large banks. These centers allow a customer to interact with a bank representative at a distant location, either by telephone or by video terminal. Such centers usually are staffed by customer service representatives.

*Job prospects.* Job prospects for tellers are expected to be favorable. In addition to job openings expected from growth, most openings will arise from the need to replace the many tellers who transfer to other occupations—which is common for large occupations that normally require little formal education and offer relatively low pay. Prospects will be best for tellers with excellent customer service skills, knowledge about a variety of financial services, and the ability to sell those services.

## Earnings

Salaries of tellers vary with experience, region of the country, size of city, and type and size of establishment. Median annual earnings of tellers were $22,140 in May 2006. The middle 50 percent earned between $19,300 and $25,880 a year. The lowest 10 percent earned less than $16,770, and the highest 10 percent earned more than $30,020 a year in May 2006.

## Related Occupations

Tellers enter data into a computer, handle cash, and keep track of financial transactions. Other clerks who perform similar duties include bill and account collectors; billing and posting clerks and machine operators; bookkeeping, accounting, and auditing clerks; gaming cage workers; brokerage clerks; and credit authorizers, checkers, and clerks.

## Sources of Additional Information

Information on employment opportunities for tellers is available from banks and other employers, local offices of the state employment service, and from

▸ Bank Administration Institute, 1 North Franklin St., Suite 1000, Chicago, IL 60606. Internet: http://www.bai.org

# Truck Drivers and Driver/Sales Workers

(O*NET 53-3031.00, 53-3032.00, and 53-3033.00)

## Significant Points

■ Overall job opportunities should be favorable.

■ Competition is expected for jobs offering the highest earnings or most favorable work schedules.

■ A commercial driver's license is required to operate large trucks.

## Nature of the Work

Truck drivers are a constant presence on the nation's highways and interstates. They deliver everything from automobiles to canned food. Firms of all kinds rely on trucks to pick up and deliver goods because no other form of transportation can deliver goods door-to-door. Even though many goods travel at least part of their journey by ship, train, or airplane, almost everything is carried by trucks at some point.

Before leaving the terminal or warehouse, truck drivers check the fuel level and oil in their trucks. They also inspect the trucks to make sure that the brakes, windshield wipers, and lights are working and that a fire extinguisher, flares, and other safety equipment are aboard and in working order. Drivers make sure their cargo is secure and adjust the mirrors so that both sides of the truck are visible from the driver's seat. Drivers report equipment that is inoperable, missing, or loaded improperly to the dispatcher.

Drivers keep a log of their activities, as required by the U.S. Department of Transportation, to the condition of the truck, and the circumstances of any accidents.

*Heavy truck and tractor-trailer drivers* operate trucks or vans with a capacity of at least 26,000 pounds Gross Vehicle Weight (GVW). They transport goods including cars, livestock, and other materials in liquid, loose, or packaged form. Many routes are from city to city and cover long distances. Some companies use two drivers on very long runs—one drives while the other sleeps in a berth behind the cab. These "sleeper" runs can last for days or even weeks. Trucks on sleeper runs typically stop only for fuel, food, loading, and unloading.

Some heavy truck and tractor-trailer drivers who have regular runs transport freight to the same city on a regular basis. Other drivers perform ad hoc runs because shippers request varying service to different cities every day.

Long-distance heavy truck and tractor-trailer drivers spend most of their working time behind the wheel but also may have to load or unload their cargo. This is especially common when drivers haul specialty cargo because they may be the only ones at the destination familiar with procedures or certified to handle the materials. Auto-transport drivers, for example, position cars on the trailers at the manufacturing plant and remove them at the dealerships. When picking up or delivering furniture, drivers of long-distance moving vans hire local workers to help them load or unload.

*Light or delivery services truck drivers* operate vans and trucks weighing less than 26,000 pounds GVW. They pick up or deliver merchandise and packages within a specific area. This may include short "turnarounds" to deliver a shipment to a nearby city, pick up another loaded truck or van, and drive it back to their home base the same day. These services may require use of electronic delivery tracking systems to track the whereabouts of the merchandise or packages. Light or delivery services truck drivers usually load or unload the merchandise at the customer's place of business. They may have helpers if there are many deliveries to make during the day or if the load requires heavy moving. Typically, before the driver arrives for work, material handlers load the trucks and arrange items for ease of delivery. Customers must sign receipts for goods and pay drivers the balance due on the merchandise if there is a cash-on-delivery arrangement. At the end of the day, drivers turn in receipts, payments, records of deliveries made, and any reports on mechanical problems with their trucks.

A driver's responsibilities and assignments change according to the type of loads transported and their vehicle's size. The duration of runs depends on the types of cargo and the destinations. Local drivers may provide daily service for a specific route or region, while other drivers make longer, intercity and interstate deliveries. Interstate and intercity cargo tends to vary from job to job more than local cargo does.

Some local truck drivers have sales and customer service responsibilities. The primary responsibility of *driver/sales workers*, or *route drivers*, is to deliver and sell their firms' products over established routes or within an established territory. They sell goods such as food products, including restaurant takeout items, or pick up and deliver items such as laundry. Their response to customer complaints and requests can make the difference between a large order and a lost customer. Route drivers may also take orders and collect payments.

The duties of driver/sales workers vary according to their industry, the policies of their employer, and the emphasis placed on their sales responsibility. Most have wholesale routes that deliver to businesses and stores, rather than to homes. For example, wholesale bakery driver/sales workers deliver and arrange bread, cakes, rolls, and other baked goods on display racks in grocery stores. They estimate how many of each item to stock by paying close attention to what is selling. They may recommend changes in a store's order or encourage the manager to stock new bakery products. Laundries that rent linens, towels, work clothes, and other items employ driver/sales workers to visit businesses regularly to replace soiled laundry. Their duties also may include soliciting new customers along their sales route.

After completing their route, driver/sales workers place orders for their next deliveries based on product sales and customer requests.

Satellites and the Global Positioning System link many trucks with their company's headquarters. Troubleshooting information, directions, weather reports, and other important communications can be instantly relayed to the truck. Drivers can easily communicate with the dispatcher to discuss delivery schedules and what to do in the event of mechanical problems. The satellite link also allows the dispatcher to track the truck's location, fuel consumption, and engine performance. Some drivers also work with computerized inventory tracking equipment. It is important for the producer, warehouse, and customer to know their products' location at all times so they can maintain a high quality of service.

*Work environment.* Truck driving has become less physically demanding because most trucks now have more comfortable seats, better ventilation, and improved, ergonomically designed cabs. Although these changes make the work environment less taxing, driving for many hours at a stretch, loading and unloading cargo, and making many deliveries can be tiring. Local truck drivers, unlike long-distance drivers, usually return home in the evening. Some self-employed long-distance truck drivers who own and operate their trucks spend most of the year away from home.

The U.S. Department of Transportation governs work hours and other working conditions of truck drivers engaged in interstate commerce. A long-distance driver may drive for 11 hours and work for up to 14 hours—including driving and non-driving duties—after having 10 hours off-duty. A driver may not drive after having worked for 60 hours in the past 7 days or 70 hours in the past 8 days unless they have taken at least 34 consecutive hours off. Most drivers are required to document their time in a logbook. Many drivers, particularly on long runs, work close to the maximum time permitted because they typically are compensated according to the number of miles or hours they drive. Drivers on long runs face boredom, loneliness, and fatigue. Drivers often travel nights, holidays, and weekends to avoid traffic delays.

Local truck drivers frequently work 50 or more hours a week. Drivers who handle food for chain grocery stores, produce markets, or bakeries typically work long hours—starting late at night or early in the morning. Although most drivers have regular routes, some have different routes each day. Many local truck drivers, particularly driver/sales workers, load and unload their own trucks. This requires considerable lifting, carrying, and walking each day.

## Training, Other Qualifications, and Advancement

A commercial driver's license (CDL) is required to drive large trucks and a regular driver's license is required to drive all other trucks. Training for the CDL is offered by many private and public vocational-technical schools. Many jobs driving smaller trucks require only brief on-the-job training.

*Education and training.* Taking driver-training courses is a good way to prepare for truck driving jobs and to obtain a commercial drivers license (CDL). High school courses in driver training and automotive mechanics also may be helpful. Many private and public vocational-technical schools offer tractor-trailer driver training programs. Students learn to maneuver large vehicles on crowded streets and in highway traffic. They also learn to inspect trucks and freight for compliance with regulations. Some states require prospective drivers to complete a training course in basic truck driving before getting their CDL.

Completion of a program does not guarantee a job. Some programs provide only a limited amount of actual driving experience. People interested in attending a driving school should check with local trucking companies to make sure the school's training is acceptable. The Professional Truck Driver Institute (PTDI), a nonprofit organization established by the trucking industry, manufacturers, and others, certifies driver-training courses at truck driver training schools that meet industry standards and Federal Highway Administration guidelines for training tractor-trailer drivers.

Training given to new drivers by employers is usually informal and may consist of only a few hours of instruction from an experienced driver, sometimes on the new employee's own time. New drivers may also ride with and observe experienced drivers before getting their own assignments. Drivers receive additional training to drive special types of trucks or handle hazardous materials. Some companies give one to two days of classroom instruction covering general duties, the operation and loading of a truck, company policies, and the preparation of delivery forms and company records. Driver/sales workers also receive training on the various types of products their company carries so that they can effectively answer questions about the products and more easily market them to their customers.

New drivers sometimes start on panel trucks or other small straight trucks. As they gain experience and show competent driving skills, new drivers may advance to larger, heavier trucks and finally to tractor-trailers.

*Licensure.* State and federal regulations govern the qualifications and standards for truck drivers. All drivers must comply with federal regulations and any state regulations that are in excess of those federal requirements. Truck drivers must have a driver's license issued by the state in which they live, and most employers require a clean driving record. Drivers of trucks designed to carry 26,000 pounds or more—including most tractor-trailers, as well as bigger straight trucks—must obtain a commercial driver's license. All truck drivers who operate trucks transporting hazardous materials must obtain a CDL, regardless of truck size. In order to receive the hazardous materials endorsement, a driver must be fingerprinted and submit to a criminal background check by the Transportation Security Administration. In many states, a regular driver's license is sufficient for driving light trucks and vans.

To qualify for a CDL, an applicant must have a clean driving record, pass a written test on rules and regulations, and demonstrate that they can operate a commercial truck safely. A national database permanently records all driving violations committed by those with a CDL. A state will check these records and deny a CDL to those who already have a license suspended or revoked in another state. Licensed drivers must accompany trainees until they get their own CDL. A person may not hold more than one license at a time and must surrender any other licenses when a CDL is issued. Information on how to apply for a CDL may be obtained from state motor vehicle administrations.

Many states allow those who are as young as 18 years old to drive trucks within their borders. To drive a commercial vehicle between states one must be at least 21 years of age, according to the Federal Motor Carrier Safety Regulations published by the U.S. Department of Transportation (U. S. DOT). Regulations also require drivers to pass a physical examination once every two years. Physical qualifications include good hearing, at least 20/40 vision with glasses or corrective lenses, and a 70-degree field of vision in each eye. Drivers may not be colorblind. Drivers must also be able to hear a forced whisper in one ear at not less than 5 feet, with a hearing aid if needed. Drivers must have normal use of arms and legs and normal blood pressure. People with epilepsy or diabetes controlled by insulin are not permitted to be interstate truck drivers.

Federal regulations also require employers to test their drivers for alcohol and drug use as a condition of employment and require periodic random tests of the drivers while they are on duty. Drivers may not use any controlled substances, unless prescribed by a licensed physician. A driver must not have been convicted of a felony involving the use of a motor vehicle or a crime involving drugs, driving under the influence of drugs or alcohol, refusing to submit to an alcohol test required by a state or its implied consent laws or regulations, leaving the scene of a crime, or causing a fatality through negligent operation of a motor vehicle. All drivers must be able to read and speak English well enough to read road signs, prepare reports, and communicate with law enforcement officers and the public.

*Other qualifications.* Many trucking companies have higher standards than those described here. Many firms require that drivers be at least 22 years old, be able to lift heavy objects, and have driven trucks for three to five years. Many prefer to hire high school graduates and require annual physical examinations. Companies have an economic incentive to hire less risky drivers, as good drivers use less fuel and cost less to insure.

Drivers must get along well with people because they often deal directly with customers. Employers seek driver/sales workers who speak well and have self-confidence, initiative, tact, and a neat appearance. Employers also look for responsible, self-motivated individuals who are able to work well with little supervision.

*Advancement.* Although most new truck drivers are assigned to regular driving jobs immediately, some start as extra drivers—substituting for regular drivers who are ill or on vacation. Extra drivers receive a regular assignment when an opening occurs.

Truck drivers can advance to driving runs that provide higher earnings, preferred schedules, or better working conditions. Local truck drivers may advance to driving heavy or specialized trucks or transfer to long-distance truck driving. Working for companies that also employ long-distance drivers is the best way to advance to these positions. Few truck drivers become dispatchers or managers.

Many long-distance truck drivers purchase trucks and go into business for themselves. Although some of these owner-operators are successful, others fail to cover expenses and go out of business. Owner-operators should have good business sense as well as truck driving experience. Courses in accounting, business, and business mathematics are helpful. Knowledge of truck mechanics can enable owner-operators to perform their own routine maintenance and minor repairs.

## Employment

Truck drivers and driver/sales workers held about 3.4 million jobs in 2006. Of these workers, 445,000 were driver/sales workers and 2.9 million were truck drivers. Most truck drivers find employment in large metropolitan areas or along major interstate roadways where trucking, retail, and wholesale companies tend to have their distribution outlets. Some drivers work in rural areas, providing specialized services such as delivering newspapers to customers.

The truck transportation industry employed 26 percent of all truck drivers and driver/sales workers in the United States. Another 25 percent worked for companies engaged in wholesale or retail trade. The remaining truck drivers and driver/sales workers were distributed across many industries, including construction and manufacturing.

Around 9 percent of all truck drivers and driver/sales workers were self-employed. Of these, a significant number were owner-operators who either served a variety of businesses independently or leased their services and trucks to a trucking company.

**Projections data from the National Employment Matrix**

| Occupational Title | SOC Code | Employment, 2006 | Projected employment, 2016 | Change, 2006-16 | |
|---|---|---|---|---|---|
| | | | | Number | Percent |
| Driver/sales workers and truck drivers............................................ | 53-3030 | 3,356,000 | 3,614,000 | 258,000 | 8 |
| Driver/sales workers................................................................. | 53-3031 | 445,000 | 421,000 | -24,000 | -5 |
| Truck drivers, heavy and tractor-trailer....................................... | 53-3032 | 1,860,000 | 2,053,000 | 193,000 | 10 |
| Truck drivers, light or delivery services...................................... | 53-3033 | 1,051,000 | 1,140,000 | 89,000 | 8 |

NOTE: Data in this table are rounded.

## Job Outlook

Overall job opportunities should be favorable for truck drivers, although opportunities may vary greatly in terms of earnings, weekly work hours, number of nights spent on the road, and quality of equipment. Competition is expected for jobs offering the highest earnings or most favorable work schedules. Average growth is expected.

*Employment change.* Overall employment of truck drivers and driver/sales workers is expected to increase by 8 percent over the 2006–2016 decade, which is about as fast as the average for all occupations, due to growth in the economy and in the amount of freight carried by truck. Because it is such a large occupation, truck drivers will have a very large number of new jobs arise, over 258,000 over the 2006–2016 period. Competing forms of freight transportation—rail, air, and ship transportation—require trucks to move the goods between ports, depots, airports, warehouses, retailers, and final consumers who are not connected to these other modes of transportation. Demand for long-distance drivers will remain strong because they can transport perishable and time-sensitive goods more effectively than alternate modes of transportation.

*Job prospects.* Job opportunities should be favorable for truck drivers. In addition to growth in demand for truck drivers, numerous job openings will occur as experienced drivers leave this large occupation to transfer to other fields of work, retire, or leave the labor force for other reasons. Jobs vary greatly in terms of earnings, weekly work hours, the number of nights spent on the road, and quality of equipment. There may be competition for the jobs with the highest earnings and most favorable work schedules. There will be more competition for jobs with local carriers than for those with long-distance carriers because of the more desirable working conditions of local carriers.

Job opportunities may vary from year to year since the output of the economy dictates the amount of freight to be moved. Companies tend to hire more drivers when the economy is strong and their services are in high demand. When the economy slows, employers hire fewer drivers or may lay off some drivers. Independent owner-operators are particularly vulnerable to slowdowns. Industries least likely to be affected by economic fluctuation, such as grocery stores, tend to be the most stable employers of truck drivers and driver/sales workers.

## Earnings

Median hourly earnings of heavy truck and tractor-trailer drivers were $16.85 in May 2006. The middle 50 percent earned between $13.33 and $21.04 an hour. The lowest 10 percent earned less than $10.80, and the highest 10 percent earned more than $25.39 an hour.

Median hourly earnings in the industries employing the largest numbers of heavy truck and tractor-trailer drivers in May 2006 were

General freight trucking .......................................$18.38
Grocery and related product wholesalers ..................18.01
Specialized freight trucking ..................................16.40
Cement and concrete product manufacturing ...........15.26
Other specialty trade contractors............................14.94

Median hourly earnings of light or delivery services truck drivers were $12.17 in May 2006. The middle 50 percent earned between $9.31 and $16.16 an hour. The lowest 10 percent earned less than $7.47, and the highest 10 percent earned more than $21.23 an hour. Median hourly earnings in the industries employing the largest numbers of light or delivery services truck drivers in May 2006 were

Couriers .........................................................$17.80
General freight trucking .........................................15.33
Grocery and related product wholesalers ..................12.84
Building material and supplies dealers ....................11.54
Automotive parts, accessories, and tire stores............8.38

Median hourly earnings of driver/sales workers, including commissions, were $9.99 in May 2006. The middle 50 percent earned between $7.12 and $15.00 an hour. The lowest 10 percent earned less than $6.19, and the highest 10 percent earned more than $20.30 an hour. Median hourly earnings in the industries employing the largest numbers of driver/sales workers in May 2006 were

Drycleaning and laundry services ..........................$14.81
Direct selling establishments ................................13.72
Grocery and related product wholesalers ..................12.37
Full-service restaurants .........................................7.11
Limited-service eating places .................................7.02

Local truck drivers tend to be paid by the hour, with extra pay for working overtime. Employers pay long-distance drivers primarily by the mile. The per-mile rate can vary greatly from employer to employer and may even depend on the type of cargo being hauled. Some long-distance drivers are paid a percent of each load's revenue. Typically, earnings increase with mileage driven, seniority, and the size and type of truck driven. Most driver/sales workers receive commissions based on their sales in addition to their hourly wages.

Most self-employed truck drivers are primarily engaged in long-distance hauling. Many truck drivers are members of the International Brotherhood of Teamsters. Some truck drivers employed by companies outside the trucking industry are members of unions representing the plant workers of the companies for which they work.

## Related Occupations

Other driving occupations include ambulance drivers and attendants, except emergency medical technicians; bus drivers; and taxi drivers and chauffeurs. Another occupation involving sales duties is sales representatives, wholesale and manufacturing.

## Sources of Additional Information

Information on truck driver employment opportunities is available from local trucking companies and local offices of the state employment service.

Information on career opportunities in truck driving may be obtained from

▸ American Trucking Associations, Inc., 950 North Glebe Road, Suite 210, Arlington, VA 22203. Internet: http://www.trucking.org

A list of certified tractor-trailer driver training courses may be obtained from

▸ Professional Truck Driver Institute, 2200 Mill Rd., Alexandria, VA 22314. Internet: http://www.ptdi.org

Information on union truck driving can be obtained from

▸ The International Brotherhood of Teamsters, 25 Louisiana Ave. NW, Washington, DC 20001.

Information on becoming a truck driver may be obtained from: http://www.gettrucking.com

# Veterinary Technologists and Technicians

(O*NET 29-2056.00)

## Significant Points

■ Animal lovers get satisfaction from this occupation, but aspects of the work can be unpleasant, physically and emotionally demanding, and sometimes dangerous.

■ Entrants generally complete a 2-year or 4-year veterinary technology program and must pass a state examination.

■ Employment is expected to grow much faster than average.

■ Overall job opportunities should be excellent; however, keen competition is expected for jobs in zoos and aquariums.

## Nature of the Work

Owners of pets and other animals today expect state-of-the-art veterinary care. To provide this service, Veterinarians use the skills of veterinary technologists and technicians, who perform many of the same duties for a veterinarian that a nurse would for a physician, including routine laboratory and clinical procedures. Although specific job duties vary by employer, there often is little difference between the tasks carried out by technicians and by technologists, despite some differences in formal education and training. As a result, most workers in this occupation are called technicians.

Veterinary technologists and technicians typically conduct clinical work in a private practice under the supervision of a licensed veterinarian. They often perform various medical tests and treat and diagnose medical conditions and diseases in animals. For example, they may perform laboratory tests such as urinalysis and blood counts, assist with dental prophylaxis, prepare tissue samples, take blood samples, or assist Veterinarians in a variety of tests and analyses in which they often use various items of medical equipment, such as test tubes and diagnostic equipment. While most of these duties are performed in a laboratory setting, many are not. For example, some veterinary technicians obtain and record patients' case histories, expose and develop x rays and radiographs, and provide specialized nursing care. In addition, experienced veterinary technicians may discuss a pet's condition with its owners and train new clinic personnel. Veterinary technologists and technicians assisting small-animal practitioners usually care for companion animals, such as cats and dogs, but can perform a variety of duties with mice, rats, sheep, pigs, cattle, monkeys, birds, fish, and frogs. Very few veterinary technologists work in mixed animal practices where they care for both small companion animals and larger, nondomestic animals.

Besides working in private clinics and animal hospitals, veterinary technologists and technicians may work in research facilities, where they administer medications orally or topically, prepare samples for laboratory examinations, and record information on an animal's genealogy, diet, weight, medications, food intake, and clinical signs of pain and distress. Some may sterilize laboratory and surgical equipment and provide routine postoperative care. At research facilities, veterinary technologists typically work under the guidance of Veterinarians or physicians. Some veterinary technologists vaccinate newly admitted animals and occasionally may have to euthanize seriously ill, severely injured, or unwanted animals.

While the goal of most veterinary technologists and technicians is to promote animal health, some contribute to human health as well. Veterinary technologists occasionally assist Veterinarians in implementing research projects as they work with other scientists in medical-related fields such as gene therapy and cloning. Some find opportunities in biomedical research, wildlife medicine, the military, livestock management, or pharmaceutical sales.

*Work environment.* People who love animals get satisfaction from working with and helping them. However, some of the work may be unpleasant, physically and emotionally demanding, and sometimes dangerous. At times, veterinary technicians must clean cages and lift, hold, or restrain animals, risking exposure to bites or scratches. These workers must take precautions when treating animals with germicides or insecticides. The work setting can be noisy.

Veterinary technologists and technicians who witness abused animals or who euthanize unwanted, aged, or hopelessly injured animals may experience emotional stress. Those working for humane societies and animal shelters often deal with the public, some of whom might react with hostility to any implication that the owners are neglecting or abusing their pets. Such workers must maintain a calm and professional demeanor while they enforce the laws regarding animal care.

In some animal hospitals, research facilities, and animal shelters, a veterinary technician is on duty 24 hours a day, which means that some may work night shifts. Most full-time veterinary technologists and technicians work about 40 hours a week, although some work 50 or more hours a week.

# Training, Other Qualifications, and Advancement

There are primarily two levels of education and training for entry to this occupation: a two-year program for veterinary technicians and a four-year program for veterinary technologists.

*Education and training.* Most entry-level veterinary technicians have a two-year associate degree from an American Veterinary Medical Association (AVMA)-accredited community college program in veterinary technology in which courses are taught in clinical and laboratory settings using live animals. About 16 colleges offer veterinary technology programs that are longer and that culminate in a four-year bachelor's degree in veterinary technology. These four-year colleges, in addition to some vocational schools, also offer two-year programs in laboratory animal science. Several schools offer distance learning.

In 2006, 131 veterinary technology programs in 44 states were accredited by the American Veterinary Medical Association (AVMA). Graduation from an AVMA-accredited veterinary technology program allows students to take the credentialing exam in any state in the country.

Persons interested in careers as veterinary technologists and technicians should take as many high school science, biology, and math courses as possible. Science courses taken beyond high school, in an associate or bachelor's degree program, should emphasize practical skills in a clinical or laboratory setting.

Technologists and technicians usually begin work as trainees in routine positions under the direct supervision of a veterinarian. Entry-level workers whose training or educational background encompasses extensive hands-on experience with a variety of laboratory equipment, including diagnostic and medical equipment, usually require a shorter period of on-the-job training.

*Licensure and certification.* Each state regulates veterinary technicians and technologists differently; however, all states require them to pass a credentialing exam following coursework. Passing the state exam assures the public that the technician or technologist has sufficient knowledge to work in a veterinary clinic or hospital. Candidates are tested for competency through an examination that includes oral, written, and practical portions and that is regulated by the state Board of Veterinary Examiners or the appropriate state agency. Depending on the state, candidates may become registered, licensed, or certified. Most states, however, use the National Veterinary Technician (NVT) exam. Prospects usually can have their passing scores transferred from one state to another, so long as both states use the same exam.

Employers recommend American Association for Laboratory Animal Science (AALAS) certification for those seeking employment in a research facility. AALAS offers certification for three levels of technician competence, with a focus on three principal areas—animal husbandry, facility management, and animal health and welfare. Those who wish to become certified must satisfy a combination of education and experience requirements prior to taking the AALAS examination. Work experience must be directly related to the maintenance, health, and well-being of laboratory animals and must be gained in a laboratory animal facility as defined by AALAS. Candidates who meet the necessary criteria can begin pursuing the desired

certification on the basis of their qualifications. The lowest level of certification is Assistant Laboratory Animal Technician (ALAT), the second level is Laboratory Animal Technician (LAT), and the highest level of certification is Laboratory Animal Technologist (LATG). The AALAS examination consists of multiple-choice questions and is longer and more difficult for higher levels of certification, ranging from two hours and 120 multiple choice questions for the ALAT to three hours and 180 multiple choice questions for the LATG.

*Other qualifications.* As veterinary technologists and technicians often deal with pet owners, communication skills are very important. In addition, technologists and technicians should be able to work well with others, because teamwork with Veterinarians is common. Organizational ability and the ability to pay attention to detail also are important.

*Advancement.* As they gain experience, technologists and technicians take on more responsibility and carry out more assignments under only general veterinary supervision. Some eventually may become supervisors.

# Employment

Veterinary technologists and technicians held about 71,000 jobs in 2006. About 91 percent worked in veterinary services. The remainder worked in boarding kennels, animal shelters, stables, grooming salons, zoos, state and private educational institutions, and local, state, and federal agencies.

# Job Outlook

Excellent job opportunities will stem from the need to replace veterinary technologists and technicians who leave the occupation and from the limited output of qualified veterinary technicians from 2-year programs, which are not expected to meet the demand over the 2006–2016 period. Employment is expected to grow much faster than average.

*Employment change.* Employment of veterinary technologists and technicians is expected to grow 41 percent over the 2006–2016 projection period, which is much faster than the average for all occupations. Pet owners are becoming more affluent and more willing to pay for advanced veterinary care because many of them consider their pet to be part of the family. This growing affluence and view of pets will continue to increase the demand for veterinary care. The vast majority of veterinary technicians work at private clinical practice under Veterinarians. As the number of Veterinarians grows to meet the demand for veterinary care, so will the number of veterinary technicians needed to assist them.

The number of pet owners who take advantage of veterinary services for their pets—currently about 6 in 10—is expected to grow over the projection period, increasing employment opportunities. The availability of advanced veterinary services, such as preventive dental care and surgical procedures, also will provide opportunities for workers specializing in those areas as they will be needed to assist licensed Veterinarians. The rapidly growing number of cats kept as companion pets is expected to boost the demand for feline medicine and services. Further demand for these workers will stem from the desire to replace veterinary assistants with more highly

**Projections data from the National Employment Matrix**

| Occupational Title | SOC Code | Employment, 2006 | Projected employment, 2016 | Change, 2006-2016 | |
|---|---|---|---|---|---|
| | | | | Number | Percent |
| Veterinary technologists and technicians ........................................... | 29-2056 | 71,000 | 100,000 | 29,000 | 41 |

NOTE: Data in this table are rounded.

skilled technicians and technologists in animal clinics and hospitals, shelters, boarding kennels, and humane societies.

Biomedical facilities, diagnostic laboratories, wildlife facilities, humane societies, animal control facilities, drug or food manufacturing companies, and food safety inspection facilities will provide additional jobs for veterinary technologists and technicians. However, keen competition is expected for veterinary technologist and technician jobs in zoos and aquariums, due to expected slow growth in facility capacity, low turnover among workers, the limited number of positions, and the fact that the work in zoos and aquariums attracts many candidates.

*Job prospects.* Excellent job opportunities are expected because of the relatively few veterinary technology graduates each year. The number of 2-year programs has recently grown to 131, but due to small class sizes, fewer than 3,000 graduates are anticipated each year, which is not expected to meet demand. Additionally, many veterinary technicians remain in the field for only 7-8 years, so the need to replace workers who leave the occupation each year also will produce many job opportunities.

Employment of veterinary technicians and technologists is relatively stable during periods of economic recession. Layoffs are less likely to occur among veterinary technologists and technicians than in some other occupations because animals will continue to require medical care.

## Earnings

Median hourly earnings of veterinary technologists and technicians were $12.88 in May 2006. The middle 50 percent earned between $10.44 and $15.77. The bottom 10 percent earned less than $8.79, and the top 10 percent earned more than $18.68.

## Related Occupations

Others who work extensively with animals include animal care and service workers, and veterinary assistants and laboratory animal caretakers. Like veterinary technologists and technicians, they must have patience and feel comfortable with animals. However, the level of training required for these occupations is less than that needed by veterinary technologists and technicians. Veterinarians, who need much more formal education, also work extensively with animals, preventing, diagnosing, and treating their diseases, disorders, and injuries.

## Sources of Additional Information

For information on certification as a laboratory animal technician or technologist, contact

▶ American Association for Laboratory Animal Science, 9190 Crestwyn Hills Dr., Memphis, TN 38125. Internet: http://www.aalas.org

For information on careers in veterinary medicine and a listing of AVMA-accredited veterinary technology programs, contact

▶ American Veterinary Medical Association, 1931 N. Meacham Rd., Suite 100, Schaumburg, IL 60173-4360. Internet: http://www.avma.org

# QUICK
# JOB SEARCH

## Seven Steps to Getting a Good Job in Less Time

## The Complete Text of a Results-Oriented Minibook by Michael Farr

Millions of job seekers have found better jobs faster using the techniques in the *Quick Job Search*. So can you! The *Quick Job Search* covers the essential steps proven to cut job search time in half and is used widely by job search programs throughout North America. Topics include how to identify your key skills, define your ideal job, write a great resume quickly, use the most effective job search methods, get more interviews, and much more.

If you completed "Using the Job-Match Grid to Choose a Career" earlier in this book, the activities in this section will complement those efforts by helping you to define other skills you possess, focus your resume, and get a job quickly.

While it is a section in this book, the *Quick Job Search* is available from JIST Publishing as a separate booklet.

## *Quick Job Search* Is Short, But It May Be All You Need

While *Quick Job Search* is short, it covers the basics on how to explore career options and conduct an effective job search. While these topics can seem complex, I have found some simple truths about looking for a job:

- If you are going to work, you might as well look for what you really want to do and are good at.

- If you are looking for a job, you might as well use techniques that will reduce the time it takes to find one—and that help you get a better job than you might otherwise.

That's what I emphasize in *Quick Job Search*.

**Trust Me—Do the Worksheets.** I know you will resist completing the worksheets. But trust me. They are worth your time. Doing them will give you a better sense of what you are good at, what you want to do, and how to go about getting it. You will also most likely get more interviews and present yourself better. Is this worth giving up a night of TV? Yes, I think so.

Once you finish this minibook and its activities, you will have spent more time planning your career than most people do. And you will know more than the average job seeker about finding a job.

**Why Such a Short Book?** I've taught job seeking skills for many years, and I've written longer and more detailed books than this one. Yet I have often been asked to tell someone, in a few minutes or hours, the most important things they should do in their career planning or job search. Instructors and counselors also ask the same question because they have only a short time to spend with folks they're trying to help. I've given this a lot of thought, and the seven topics in this book are the ones I think are most important to know.

This minibook is short enough to scan in a morning and conduct a more effective job search that afternoon. Granted, doing all the activities would take more time, but they will prepare you far better than scanning the book. Of course, you can learn more about all the topics it covers, but this minibook, *Quick Job Search,* may be all you need.

---

You can't just read about getting a job. The best way to get a job is to go out and get interviews! And the best way to get interviews is to make a job out of getting a job.

After many years of experience, I have identified just seven basic things you need to do that make a big difference in your job search. Each will be covered and expanded on in this minibook.

1. Identify your key skills.

2. Define your ideal job.

3. Learn the two most effective job search methods.

4. Create a superior resume and a portfolio.

5. Organize your time to get two interviews a day.

6. Dramatically improve your interviewing skills.

7. Follow up on all leads.

So, without further delay, let's get started!

## STEP 1: Identify Your Key Skills and Develop a "Skills Language" to Describe Yourself

One survey of employers found that about 90 percent of the people they interviewed might have the required job skills, but they could not describe those skills and thereby prove that they could do the job they sought. They could not answer the basic question "Why should I hire you?"

Knowing and describing your skills are essential to doing well in interviews. This same knowledge is important to help you decide what type of job you will enjoy and do well. For these reasons, I consider identifying your skills a necessary part of a successful career plan or job search.

## The Three Types of Skills

Most people think of their skills as job-related skills, such as using a computer. But we all have other types of skills that are important for success on a job—and that are important to employers. The following triangle arranges skills in three groups, and I think that this is a very useful way to consider skills.

Let's look at these three types of skills—self-management, transferable, and job-related—and identify those that are most important to you.

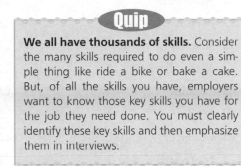

**Quip**

**We all have thousands of skills.** Consider the many skills required to do even a simple thing like ride a bike or bake a cake. But, of all the skills you have, employers want to know those key skills you have for the job they need done. You must clearly identify these key skills and then emphasize them in interviews.

## Self-Management Skills

To begin identifying your skills, answer the question in the box that follows.

---

### YOUR GOOD WORKER TRAITS

Write down three things about yourself that you think make you a good worker. Think about what an employer might like about you or the way you work.

1. _____

2. _____

3. _____

---

You just wrote down the most important things for an employer to know about you! They describe your basic personality and your ability to adapt to new environments. They are some of the most important skills to emphasize in interviews, yet most job seekers don't realize their importance—and don't mention them.

Review the Self-Management Skills Checklist that follows and put a check mark beside any skills you have. The key self-management skills listed first cover abilities that employers find particularly important. If one or more of the key self-management skills apply to you, mentioning them in interviews can help you greatly.

---

### SELF-MANAGEMENT SKILLS CHECKLIST

Following are the key self-management skills that employers value highly. Place a check by those you already have.

❏ Have good attendance                    ❏ Arrive on time

❏ Get work done on time                   ❏ Get along with co-workers

❏ Am honest                               ❏ Follow instructions

❏ Get along with supervisor               ❏ Am hard working/productive

---

*(continued)*

*(continued)*

Place a check by other self-management skills you have.

| | | |
|---|---|---|
| ❏ Ambitious | ❏ Discreet | ❏ Helpful |
| ❏ Mature | ❏ Physically strong | ❏ Sincere |
| ❏ Assertive | ❏ Eager | ❏ Humble |
| ❏ Methodical | ❏ Practical | ❏ Spontaneous |
| ❏ Capable | ❏ Efficient | ❏ Humorous |
| ❏ Modest | ❏ Problem-solving | ❏ Steady |
| ❏ Cheerful | ❏ Energetic | ❏ Imaginative |
| ❏ Motivated | ❏ Proud of work | ❏ Tactful |
| ❏ Competent | ❏ Enthusiastic | ❏ Independent |
| ❏ Natural | ❏ Quick to learn | ❏ Team player |
| ❏ Conscientious | ❏ Expressive | ❏ Industrious |
| ❏ Open-minded | ❏ Reliable | ❏ Tenacious |
| ❏ Creative | ❏ Flexible | ❏ Informal |
| ❏ Optimistic | ❏ Resourceful | ❏ Thrifty |
| ❏ Culturally tolerant | ❏ Formal | ❏ Intelligent |
| ❏ Original | ❏ Responsible | ❏ Trustworthy |
| ❏ Decisive | ❏ Friendly | ❏ Intuitive |
| ❏ Patient | ❏ Results-oriented | ❏ Versatile |
| ❏ Dependable | ❏ Good-natured | ❏ Loyal |
| ❏ Persistent | ❏ Self-confident | ❏ Well-organized |

List the other self-management skills you have that have not been mentioned but you think are important to include.

_____

_____

_____

After you finish checking the list, circle the five skills you feel are most important and write them in the box that follows.

## YOUR TOP FIVE SELF-MANAGEMENT SKILLS

1. _____

2. _____

3. _____

4. _____

5. _____

> *When thinking about their skills, some people find it helpful to complete the Essential Job Search Data Worksheet that starts on page 370. It organizes skills and accomplishments from previous jobs and other life experiences. Take a look at it and decide whether to complete it now or later.*

## Transferable Skills

We all have skills that can transfer from one job or career to another. For example, the ability to organize events could be used in a variety of jobs and may be essential for success in certain occupations. Your mission is to find a job that requires the skills you have and enjoy using.

> **Quip**
>
> **It's not bragging if it's true.** Using your new skills language may be uncomfortable at first, but employers need to learn about your skills. So practice saying positive things about the skills you have for the job. If you don't, who will?

---

### TRANSFERABLE SKILLS CHECKLIST

Following are the key transferable skills that employers value highly. Place a check by those you already have. You may have used them in a previous job or in some nonwork setting.

- ❏ Managing money/budgets
- ❏ Speaking in public
- ❏ Managing people
- ❏ Organizing/managing projects
- ❏ Meeting deadlines
- ❏ Using computers
- ❏ Meeting the public
- ❏ Writing well
- ❏ Negotiating

Place a check by the skills you have for working with data.

- ❏ Analyzing data
- ❏ Counting/taking inventory
- ❏ Auditing/checking for accuracy
- ❏ Investigating
- ❏ Budgeting
- ❏ Keeping financial records
- ❏ Calculating/computing
- ❏ Observing/inspecting
- ❏ Classifying data
- ❏ Paying attention to details
- ❏ Comparing/evaluating
- ❏ Researching/locating information
- ❏ Compiling/recording facts
- ❏ Synthesizing

Place a check by the skills you have for working with people.

- ❏ Administering
- ❏ Counseling people
- ❏ Being diplomatic
- ❏ Demonstrating
- ❏ Being kind
- ❏ Having insight
- ❏ Being outgoing
- ❏ Helping others
- ❏ Being patient
- ❏ Instructing others
- ❏ Being pleasant
- ❏ Interviewing people

*(continued)*

*(continued)*

❑ Being sensitive        ❑ Being tactful        ❑ Caring for others
❑ Listening              ❑ Supervising          ❑ Trusting
❑ Being sociable         ❑ Being tough          ❑ Coaching
❑ Persuading             ❑ Tolerating           ❑ Understanding
                                                ❑ Confronting others

Place a check by your skills in working with words and ideas.

❑ Being articulate           ❑ Being logical
❑ Creating new ideas         ❑ Remembering information
❑ Being ingenious            ❑ Communicating verbally
❑ Designing                  ❑ Speaking publicly
❑ Being inventive            ❑ Corresponding with others
❑ Editing                    ❑ Writing clearly

Place a check by the leadership skills you have.

❑ Being competitive          ❑ Having self-confidence
❑ Mediating problems         ❑ Planning events
❑ Delegating                 ❑ Influencing others
❑ Motivating people          ❑ Running meetings
❑ Directing others           ❑ Making decisions
❑ Motivating yourself        ❑ Solving problems
❑ Getting results            ❑ Making explanations
❑ Negotiating agreements     ❑ Taking risks

Place a check by your creative or artistic skills.

❑ Appreciating music         ❑ Dancing
❑ Expressing yourself        ❑ Playing instruments
❑ Being artistic             ❑ Drawing
❑ Performing/acting          ❑ Presenting artistic ideas

Place a check by your skills for working with things.

❑ Assembling things              ❑ Operating tools/machines
❑ Driving or operating vehicles  ❑ Constructing or repairing things
❑ Building things

Add the other transferable skills you have that have not been mentioned but you think are important to include.

_____

_____

_____

When you are finished, circle the five transferable skills you feel are most important for you to use in your next job and list them below.

---

### YOUR TOP FIVE TRANSFERABLE SKILLS

1. _____

2. _____

3. _____

4. _____

5. _____

---

## *Job-Related Skills*

Job content or job-related skills are those you need to do a particular occupation. A carpenter, for example, needs to know how to use various tools. Before you select job-related skills to emphasize, you must first have a clear idea of the jobs you want. So let's put off developing your job related skills list until you have defined the job you want—the topic that is covered next.

## STEP 2: Define Your Ideal Job

Too many people look for a job without clearly knowing what they are looking for. Before you go out seeking a job, I suggest that you first define exactly what you want—not *just a job* but *the job.*

Most people think that a job objective is the same as a job title, but it isn't. You need to consider other elements of what makes a job satisfying for you. Then, later, you can decide what that job is called and what industry it might be in. You can compromise on what you consider your ideal job later if you need to.

---

### EIGHT FACTORS TO CONSIDER IN DEFINING YOUR IDEAL JOB

As you try to define your ideal job, consider the following eight important questions. When you know what you want, your task then becomes finding a position that is as close to your ideal job as possible.

1. **What skills do you want to use?** From the skills lists in Step 1, select the top five skills that you enjoy using and most want to use in your next job.

   a._____

   b._____

   c._____

   d._____

   e._____

---

*(continued)*

*(continued)*

2. **What type of special knowledge do you have?** Perhaps you know how to fix radios, keep accounting records, or cook food. Write down the things you know from schooling, training, hobbies, family experiences, and other sources. One or more of these knowledge areas could make you a very special applicant in the right setting._____

   _____

   _____

3. **With what types of people do you prefer to work?** Do you like to work with competitive people, or do you prefer hardworking folks, creative personalities, relaxed people, or some other types?_____

   _____

   _____

4. **What type of work environment do you prefer?** Do you want to work inside, outside, in a quiet place, in a busy place, or in a clean or messy place; or do you want to have a window with a nice view? List the types of environments you prefer._____

   _____

   _____

5. **Where do you want your next job to be located—in what city or region?** If you are open to living and working anywhere, what would your ideal community be like? Near a bus line? Close to a childcare center?_____

   _____

   _____

6. **What benefits or income do you hope to have in your next job?** Many people will take less money or fewer benefits if they like a job in other ways—or if they need a job quickly to survive. Think about the minimum you would take as well as what you would eventually like to earn. Your next job will probably pay somewhere in between._____

   _____

   _____

7. **How much and what types of responsibility are you willing to accept?** Usually, the more money you want to make, the more responsibility you must accept. Do you want to work by yourself, be part of a group, or be in charge? If you want to be in charge, how many people are you willing to supervise?

   _____

   _____

   _____

8. **What values are important or have meaning to you?** Do you have important values you would prefer to include in considering the work you do? For example, some people want to work to help others, clean up the environment, build structures, make machines work, gain power or prestige, or care for animals or plants. Think about what is important to you and how you might include this in your next job. _____

_____

_____

_____

# Is It Possible to Find Your Ideal Job?

Can you find a job that meets all the criteria you just defined? Perhaps. Some people do. The harder you look, the more likely you are to find it. But you will likely need to compromise, so it is useful to know what is *most* important to include in your next job. Go back over your responses to the eight factors and mark a few of those that you would most like to have or include in your ideal job.

---

### FACTORS I WANT IN MY IDEAL JOB

Write a brief description of your ideal job. Don't worry about a job title, or whether you have the experience, or other practical matters yet. _____

_____

_____

_____

---

# How Can You Explore Specific Job Titles and Industries?

You might find your ideal job in an occupation you haven't considered yet. And, even if you are sure of the occupation you want, it may be in an industry that is unfamiliar to you. This combination of occupation and industry forms the basis for your job search, and you should consider a variety of options.

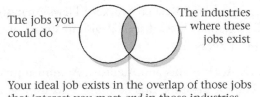

The jobs you could do — The industries where these jobs exist

Your ideal job exists in the overlap of those jobs that interest you most *and* in those industries that best meet your needs and interests!

There are thousands of job titles, and many jobs are highly specialized, employing just a few people. While one of these more specialized jobs may be just what you want, most work falls within more general job titles that employ large numbers of people.

## REVIEW THE TOP JOBS IN THE WORKFORCE

The list of job titles that follows was based on a list developed by the U.S. Department of Labor. It contains 270 major jobs that employ about 90 percent of the U.S. workforce.

The job titles are organized within 16 major groupings called interest areas, presented in bold type. These groupings will help you quickly identify fields most likely to interest you. Job titles are presented in regular type within these groupings.

Begin with the interest areas that appeal to you most, and underline any job title that interests you. (Don't worry for now about whether you have the experience or credentials to do these jobs.) Then quickly review the remaining interest areas, underlining any job titles there that interest you. Note that some job titles are listed more than once because they fit into more than one interest area. When you have gone through all 16 interest areas, go back and circle the 5 to 10 job titles that interest you most. These are the ones you will want to research in more detail.

1. **Agriculture and Natural Resources:** Agricultural and Food Scientists; Agricultural Workers; Biological Scientists; Conservation Scientists and Foresters; Engineers; Farmers, Ranchers, and Agricultural Managers; Fishers and Fishing Vessel Operators; Forest, Conservation, and Logging Workers; Grounds Maintenance Workers; Material Moving Occupations; Pest Control Workers; Purchasing Managers, Buyers, and Purchasing Agents; Science Technicians.

2. **Architecture and Construction:** Architects, except Landscape and Naval; Boilermakers; Brickmasons, Blockmasons, and Stonemasons; Carpenters; Carpet, Floor, and Tile Installers and Finishers; Cement Masons, Concrete Finishers, Segmental Pavers, and Terrazzo Workers; Construction and Building Inspectors; Construction Equipment Operators; Construction Laborers; Construction Managers; Drafters; Drywall Installers, Ceiling Tile Installers, and Tapers; Electrical and Electronics Installers and Repairers; Electricians; Elevator Installers and Repairers; Glaziers; Hazardous Materials Removal Workers; Heating, Air-Conditioning, and Refrigeration Mechanics and Installers; Insulation Workers; Landscape Architects; Line Installers and Repairers; Maintenance and Repair Workers, General; Material Moving Occupations; Painters and Paperhangers; Pipelayers, Plumbers, Pipefitters, and Steamfitters; Plasterers and Stucco Masons; Roofers; Sheet Metal Workers; Structural and Reinforcing Iron and Metal Workers; Surveyors, Cartographers, Photogrammetrists, and Surveying and Mapping Technicians.

3. **Arts and Communication:** Actors, Producers, and Directors; Advertising, Marketing, Promotions, Public Relations, and Sales Managers; Air Traffic Controllers; Announcers; Artists and Related Workers; Barbers, Cosmetologists, and Other Personal Appearance Workers; Broadcast and Sound Engineering Technicians and Radio Operators; Commercial and Industrial Designers; Dancers and Choreographers; Dispatchers; Fashion Designers; Floral Designers; Graphic Designers; Interior Designers; Interpreters and Translators; Musicians, Singers, and Related Workers; News Analysts, Reporters, and Correspondents; Photographers; Public Relations Specialists; Television, Video, and Motion Picture Camera Operators and Editors; Writers and Editors.

4. **Business and Administration:** Accountants and Auditors; Administrative Services Managers; Billing and Posting Clerks and Machine Operators; Bookkeeping, Accounting, and Auditing Clerks; Brokerage Clerks; Budget Analysts; Communications Equipment Operators; Data Entry and Information Processing Workers; Engineering Technicians; File Clerks; Gaming Cage Workers; Human Resources Assistants, except Payroll and Timekeeping; Human Resources, Training, and Labor Relations Managers and

Specialists; Management Analysts; Meeting and Convention Planners; Meter Readers, Utilities; Office and Administrative Support Worker Supervisors and Managers; Office Clerks, General; Operations Research Analysts; Payroll and Timekeeping Clerks; Postal Service Workers; Procurement Clerks; Production, Planning, and Expediting Clerks; Secretaries and Administrative Assistants; Shipping, Receiving, and Traffic Clerks; Stock Clerks and Order Fillers; Top Executives; Weighers, Measurers, Checkers, and Samplers, Recordkeeping.

5. **Education and Training:** Archivists, Curators, and Museum Technicians; Counselors; Education Administrators; Fitness Workers; Health Educators; Instructional Coordinators; Librarians; Library Assistants, Clerical; Library Technicians; Teacher Assistants; Teachers—Adult Literacy and Remedial Education; Teachers—Postsecondary; Teachers—Preschool, Kindergarten, Elementary, Middle, and Secondary; Teachers—Self-Enrichment Education; Teachers—Special Education.

6. **Finance and Insurance:** Advertising Sales Agents; Appraisers and Assessors of Real Estate; Bill and Account Collectors; Claims Adjusters, Appraisers, Examiners, and Investigators; Cost Estimators; Credit Authorizers, Checkers, and Clerks; Financial Analysts and Personal Financial Advisors; Financial Managers; Insurance Sales Agents; Insurance Underwriters; Interviewers; Loan Officers; Market and Survey Researchers; Securities, Commodities, and Financial Services Sales Agents; Tellers.

7. **Government and Public Administration:** Agricultural Workers; Court Reporters; Fire Fighting Occupations; Inspectors, Testers, Sorters, Samplers, and Weighers; Occupational Health and Safety Specialists and Technicians; Police and Detectives; Science Technicians; Tax Examiners, Collectors, and Revenue Agents; Top Executives; Urban and Regional Planners.

8. **Health Science:** Agricultural Workers; Animal Care and Service Workers; Athletic Trainers; Audiologists; Cardiovascular Technologists and Technicians; Chiropractors; Clinical Laboratory Technologists and Technicians; Dental Assistants; Dental Hygienists; Dentists; Diagnostic Medical Sonographers; Dietitians and Nutritionists; Licensed Practical and Licensed Vocational Nurses; Massage Therapists; Medical and Health Services Managers; Medical Assistants; Medical Records and Health Information Technicians; Medical Transcriptionists; Nuclear Medicine Technologists; Nursing, Psychiatric, and Home Health Aides; Occupational Therapist Assistants and Aides; Occupational Therapists; Opticians, Dispensing; Optometrists; Pharmacists; Pharmacy Aides; Pharmacy Technicians; Physical Therapist Assistants and Aides; Physical Therapists; Physician Assistants; Physicians and Surgeons; Podiatrists; Radiation Therapists; Radiologic Technologists and Technicians; Recreational Therapists; Registered Nurses; Respiratory Therapists; Science Technicians; Speech-Language Pathologists; Surgical Technologists; Veterinarians; Veterinary Technologists and Technicians.

9. **Hospitality, Tourism, and Recreation:** Athletes, Coaches, Umpires, and Related Workers; Barbers, Cosmetologists, and Other Personal Appearance Workers; Building Cleaning Workers; Chefs, Cooks, and Food Preparation Workers; Flight Attendants; Food and Beverage Serving and Related Workers; Food Processing Occupations; Food Service Managers; Gaming Services Occupations; Hotel, Motel, and Resort Desk Clerks; Lodging Managers; Recreation Workers; Reservation and Transportation Ticket Agents and Travel Clerks; Travel Agents.

10. **Human Service:** Child Care Workers; Counselors; Interviewers; Personal and Home Care Aides; Probation Officers and Correctional Treatment Specialists; Psychologists; Social and Human Service Assistants; Social Workers.

*(continued)*

*(continued)*

11. **Information Technology:** Coin, Vending, and Amusement Machine Servicers and Repairers; Computer and Information Systems Managers; Computer Operators; Computer Programmers; Computer Scientists and Database Administrators; Computer Software Engineers; Computer Support Specialists and Systems Administrators; Computer Systems Analysts; Computer, Automated Teller, and Office Machine Repairers.

12. **Law and Public Safety:** Correctional Officers; Emergency Medical Technicians and Paramedics; Fire Fighting Occupations; Job Opportunities in the Armed Forces; Judges, Magistrates, and Other Judicial Workers; Lawyers; Paralegals and Legal Assistants; Police and Detectives; Private Detectives and Investigators; Science Technicians; Security Guards and Gaming Surveillance Officers.

13. **Manufacturing:** Agricultural Workers; Aircraft and Avionics Equipment Mechanics and Service Technicians; Assemblers and Fabricators; Automotive Body and Related Repairers; Automotive Service Technicians and Mechanics; Bookbinders and Bindery Workers; Computer Control Programmers and Operators; Desktop Publishers; Diesel Service Technicians and Mechanics; Electrical and Electronics Installers and Repairers; Electronic Home Entertainment Equipment Installers and Repairers; Food Processing Occupations; Heavy Vehicle and Mobile Equipment Service Technicians and Mechanics; Home Appliance Repairers; Industrial Machinery Mechanics and Maintenance Workers; Industrial Production Managers; Inspectors, Testers, Sorters, Samplers, and Weighers; Jewelers and Precious Stone and Metal Workers; Machine Setters, Operators, and Tenders—Metal and Plastic; Machinists; Material Moving Occupations; Medical, Dental, and Ophthalmic Laboratory Technicians; Millwrights; Painting and Coating Workers, except Construction and Maintenance; Photographic Process Workers and Processing Machine Operators; Power Plant Operators, Distributors, and Dispatchers; Precision Instrument and Equipment Repairers; Prepress Technicians and Workers; Printing Machine Operators; Radio and Telecommunications Equipment Installers and Repairers; Semiconductor Processors; Small Engine Mechanics; Stationary Engineers and Boiler Operators; Textile, Apparel, and Furnishings Occupations; Tool and Die Makers; Water and Liquid Waste Treatment Plant and System Operators; Water Transportation Occupations; Welding, Soldering, and Brazing Workers; Woodworkers.

14. **Retail and Wholesale Sales and Service:** Advertising, Marketing, Promotions, Public Relations, and Sales Managers; Cashiers; Counter and Rental Clerks; Customer Service Representatives; Demonstrators, Product Promoters, and Models; Funeral Directors; Order Clerks; Property, Real Estate, and Community Association Managers; Purchasing Managers, Buyers, and Purchasing Agents; Real Estate Brokers and Sales Agents; Receptionists and Information Clerks; Retail Salespersons; Sales Engineers; Sales Representatives, Wholesale and Manufacturing; Sales Worker Supervisors.

15. **Scientific Research, Engineering, and Mathematics:** Actuaries; Atmospheric Scientists; Biological Scientists; Chemists and Materials Scientists; Drafters; Economists; Engineering and Natural Sciences Managers; Engineering Technicians; Engineers; Environmental Scientists and Hydrologists; Geoscientists; Mathematicians; Medical Scientists; Photographers; Physicists and Astronomers; Psychologists; Science Technicians; Social Scientists, Other; Statisticians; Surveyors, Cartographers, Photogrammetrists, and Surveying and Mapping Technicians.

16. **Transportation, Distribution, and Logistics:** Aircraft Pilots and Flight Engineers; Bus Drivers; Cargo and Freight Agents; Couriers and Messengers; Material Moving Occupations; Postal Service Workers; Rail Transportation Occupations; Taxi Drivers and Chauffeurs; Truck Drivers and Driver/Sales Workers; Water Transportation Occupations.

> You can find thorough descriptions for the job titles in the preceding list in the Occupational Outlook Handbook, *written by the U.S. Department of Labor. Its descriptions include information on earnings, training and education needed to hold specific jobs, work environment, advancement opportunities, projected growth, and sources for additional information. Most libraries have this book.*
>
> *You also can find descriptions of these jobs on the Internet. Go to www.bls.gov/oco/.*
>
> The *New Guide for Occupational Exploration, Fourth Edition, also provides more information on the interest areas used in this list. This book is published by JIST Works and describes about 1,000 major jobs, arranged within groupings of related jobs.*
>
> *Finally, "A Short List of Additional Resources" at the end of this minibook gives you resources for more job information.*

## CONSIDER MAJOR INDUSTRIES

What industry you work in is often as important as the career field. For example, some industries pay much better than others, and others may simply be more interesting to you. A book titled *10 Best Fields for Your Career* contains very helpful reviews for each of the major industries mentioned in the following list. Many libraries and bookstores carry this book, as well as the U.S. Department of Labor's *Career Guide to Industries*.

Underline industries that interest you, and then learn more about the opportunities they present. Jobs in most careers are available in a variety of industries, so consider what industries fit you best and focus your job search in these.

**Agriculture and natural resources:** Agriculture, forestry, and fishing; mining; oil and gas extraction.

**Manufacturing, construction, and utilities:** Aerospace product and parts manufacturing; chemical manufacturing, except drugs; computer and electronic product manufacturing; construction; food manufacturing; machinery manufacturing; motor vehicle and parts manufacturing; pharmaceutical and medicine manufacturing; printing; steel manufacturing; textile, textile products, and apparel manufacturing; utilities.

**Trade:** Automobile dealers, clothing, accessories, and general merchandise stores; grocery stores; wholesale trade.

**Transportation:** Air transportation; truck transportation and warehousing.

**Information:** Broadcasting; Internet service providers, Web search portals, and data processing services; motion picture and video industries; publishing, except software; software publishing; telecommunications.

**Financial activities:** Banking; insurance; securities, commodities, and other investments.

**Professional and business services:** Advertising and public relations; computer systems design and related services; employment services; management, scientific, and technical consulting services; scientific research and development services.

**Education, health care, and social services:** Child daycare services; educational services; health care; social assistance, except child care.

*(continued)*

*(continued)*

> **Leisure and hospitality:** Art, entertainment, and recreation; food services and drinking places; hotels and other accommodations.
>
> **Government and advocacy, grantmaking, and civic organizations:** Advocacy, grantmaking, and civic organizations; federal government; state and local government, except education and health care.

---

## THE TOP JOBS AND INDUSTRIES THAT INTEREST YOU

Go back over the lists of job titles and industries. For numbers 1 and 2 below, list the jobs that interest you most. Then select the industries that interest you most, and list them below in number 3. These are the jobs and industries you should research most carefully. Your ideal job is likely to be found in some combination of these jobs and industries, or in more specialized but related jobs and industries.

1. The five job titles that interest you most

   a._____

   b._____

   c._____

   d._____

   e._____

2. The five next most interesting job titles

   a._____

   b._____

   c._____

   d._____

   e._____

3. The industries that interest you most

   a._____

   b._____

   c._____

   d._____

   e._____

---

# Is Self-Employment or Starting a Business an Option?

More than one in 10 workers are self-employed or own their own businesses. If these options interest you, consider them as well. Talk to people in similar roles to gather information and look for books and Web sites that provide information on options that are similar to those that interest you. A book titled *Best Jobs for the 21st*

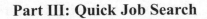

*Century* (JIST Works) includes lists and descriptions of jobs with high percentages of self-employed. Also, the Small Business Administration's Web site at www.sba.gov is a good source of basic information on related topics.

---

### SELF-EMPLOYMENT AREAS OF INTEREST

In the following space, write your current interest in self-employment or starting a business in an area related to your general job objective.

_____

_____

_____

---

## Can You Identify Your Job-Related Skills Now That You've Defined Your Ideal Job?

Earlier, I suggested that you should first define the job you want and then identify key job-related skills you have that support your ability to do that job. These are the job-related skills to emphasize in interviews.

So, now that you have determined your ideal job, you can pinpoint the job-related skills it requires. If you haven't done so, complete the Essential Job Search Data Worksheet starting on page 370. Completing it will give you specific skills and accomplishments to highlight.

Yes, completing that worksheet requires time, but doing so will help you clearly define key skills to emphasize in interviews—when what you say matters so much. People who complete that worksheet will do better in their interviews than those who don't. After you complete the Essential Job Search Data Worksheet, you are ready to list your top five job-related skills.

> **Quip**
>
> **It's a hassle, but...**Completing the Essential Job Search Data Worksheet that starts on page 370 will help you define what you are good at—and remember examples of when you did things well. This information will help you define your ideal job and will be of great value in interviews. Look at the worksheet now, and promise to do it later today.

---

### YOUR TOP FIVE JOB-RELATED SKILLS

List the top five job-related skills you think are most important. Include the job-related skills you have that you would most like to use in your next job.

1. _____

2. _____

3. _____

4. _____

5. _____

---

## STEP 3: Use the Most Effective Methods to Find a Job in Less Time

Employer surveys have found that most employers don't advertise their job openings. They most often hire people they already know, people who find out about the jobs through word of mouth, or people who happen to be in the right place at the right time. Although luck plays a part in finding job openings, you can use the tips in this step to increase your luck.

Most job seekers don't know how ineffective some traditional job-hunting techniques tend to be. For example, the chart below shows that fewer than 15 percent of all job seekers get jobs from the newspaper want ads, most of which also appear online. Other traditional techniques include using public and private employment agencies, filling out paper and electronic applications, and mailing or e-mailing unsolicited resumes.

*How people find jobs.*

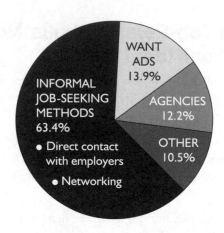

> **N o t e**
>
> *This step covers a number of job search methods. Most of the material is presented as information, with a few interactive activities. While each topic is short and reasonably interesting, taking a break now and then will help you absorb it all.*

Informal, nontraditional job-seeking methods have a much larger success rate. These methods are active rather than passive and include making direct contact with employers and networking.

**Quip**

**Your job search objective.** Almost everyone finds a job eventually, so your objective should be to find a good job in less time. The job search methods I emphasize in this minibook will help you do just that.

## Get the Most Out of Less Effective Job Search Methods

The truth is that every job search method works for someone. But experience and research show that some methods are more effective than others are. Your task in the job search is to spend more of your time using more effective methods—and increase the effectiveness of all the methods you use.

So let's start by looking at some traditional job search methods and how you can increase their effectiveness. Only about one-third of all job seekers get their jobs using one of these methods, but you should still consider using them to some extent in your search. Later in the step, you'll read about the most effective methods, the ones you should devote the most time to in your search.

## Newspaper and Internet Help Wanted Ads

Most jobs are never advertised, and fewer than 15 percent of all people get their jobs through the want ads. Everyone who reads the paper knows about these openings, so competition is fierce for the few advertised jobs.

The Internet also lists many job openings. But, as happens with newspaper ads, enormous numbers of people view these postings. Many job seekers make direct contact with employers via a company's Web site. Some people do get jobs through the bigger sites, so go ahead and apply. Just be sure to spend most of your time using more effective methods.

## Filling Out Applications

Most employers require job seekers to complete an application form or an application online. Applications are designed to collect negative information, and employers use applications to screen people out. If, for example, your training or work history is not the best, you will often never get an interview, even if you can do the job.

Completing applications is a more effective approach for young and entry-level job seekers. The reason is that there is a shortage of workers for the relatively low-paying jobs typically sought by less-experienced job seekers. As a result, when trying to fill those positions, employers are more willing to accept a lack of experience or fewer job skills. Even so, you will get better results by filling out the application, if asked to do so, and then requesting an interview with the person in charge.

When you complete an application, make it neat and error-free, and do not include anything that could get you screened out. If necessary, leave a problem section blank. You can always explain situations in an interview.

## Employment Agencies

There are three types of employment agencies. One is operated by the government and is free. The others, private employment agencies and temp agencies, are run as for-profit businesses and charge a fee to either you or an employer. Following are the advantages and disadvantages to using each.

**The government employment service and One-Stop centers.** Each state and province has a network of local offices to pay unemployment compensation, provide job leads, and offer other services—at no charge to you or to employers. The service's name varies by region. It may be called Job Service, Department of Labor, Unemployment Office, Workforce Development, or another name. Most of these offices are also online, and some require their users to sign up with a login and password to search for job leads and use other services on the Internet.

The Employment and Training Administration Web site at www.doleta.gov gives you information on the programs provided by the government employment service, plus links to other useful sites.

Visit your local office early in your job search. Find out whether you qualify for unemployment compensation and learn more about its services. Look into it—the price is right.

**Private employment agencies.** Private employment agencies are businesses that charge a fee either to you or to the employer who hires you. Fees can be from less than one month's pay to 15 percent or more of your annual salary. You will often see these agencies' ads in the help wanted section of the newspaper. Most have Web sites.

Be careful about using fee-based employment agencies. Recent research indicates that more people use and benefit from fee-based agencies than in the past. However, relatively few people who register with private agencies get a job through them.

If you use a private employment agency, ask for interviews with the employers who agree to pay the agency's fee. Do not sign an exclusive agreement or be pressured into accepting a job. Also, continue to actively look for your own leads. You can find these agencies in the phone book's yellow pages, and many state- or province-government Web sites offer lists of the private employment agencies in their states.

**Temporary agencies.** Temporary agencies offer jobs that last from several days to many months. They charge the employer an hourly fee, and then pay you a bit less and keep the difference. You pay no direct fee to the agency. Many private employment agencies now provide temporary jobs as well.

Temp agencies have grown rapidly for good reason. They provide employers with short-term help, and employers often use them to find people they might want to hire later. If the employers are dissatisfied, they can just ask the agency for different temp workers.

Temp agencies can help you survive between jobs and get experience in different work settings. Temp jobs provide a very good option while you look for long-term work, and you might get a job offer while working in a temp job. Holding a temporary job might even lead to a regular job with the same or a similar employer.

## School and Other Employment Services

Only a small percentage of job seekers use school and other special employment services, probably because few job seekers have the service available to them. If you are a student or graduate, find out about any employment services at your school. Some schools provide free career counseling, resume-writing help, referrals to job openings, career interest tests, reference materials, Web sites listing job openings, and other services. Special career programs work with veterans, people with disabilities, welfare recipients, union members, professional groups, and many others. So check out these services and consider using them.

## Mailing Versus Posting Resumes on the Internet

Many job search experts used to suggest that sending out lots of resumes was a great technique. That advice probably helped sell their resume books, but mailing resumes to people you do not know was never an effective approach. It very rarely works. A recent survey of 1,500 successful job seekers showed that only 2 percent found their positions through sending an unsolicited resume. The same is true for the Internet.

Although mailing your resume to strangers doesn't make much sense, posting it on the Internet might because

- It doesn't take much time.

- Many employers have the potential of finding your resume.

- You can post your resume on niche sites that attract only employers in your field.

- Your Internet resume is easily updated, allowing you to post your current accomplishments.

- You can easily link your resume to projects and Web sites that highlight your accomplishments.

Job searching on the Internet has its limitations, just like other methods. I'll cover resumes in more detail later and provide tips on using the Internet throughout this minibook.

## Use the Two Job Search Methods That Work Best

The fact is that most jobs are not advertised, so how do *you* find them? The same way that about two-thirds of all job seekers do: networking with people you know (which I call making warm contacts) and directly contacting employers (which I call making cold contacts). Both of these methods are based on the job search rule you should know above all:

> **The Most Important Job Search Rule:** Don't wait until the job opens before contacting the employer!

Employers fill most jobs with people they meet before a job is formally open. The trick is to meet people who can hire you before a job is formally available. Instead of asking whether the employer has any jobs open, I suggest that you say, *"I realize you may not have any openings now, but I would still like to talk to you about the possibility of future openings."*

## Most Effective Job Search Method 1: Develop a Network of Contacts in Five Easy Stages

Studies find that 40 percent of all people located their jobs through a lead provided by a friend, a relative, or an acquaintance. That makes the people you know your number one source of job leads—more effective than all the traditional methods combined! Developing and using your contacts is called *networking*, and here's how it works:

1.  **Make lists of people you know.** Make a thorough list of anyone you are friendly with. Then make a separate list of all your relatives. These two lists alone often add up to 25 to 100 people or more. Next, think of other groups of people that you have something in common with, such as former co-workers or classmates, members of your social or sports groups, members of your professional association, former employers, neighbors, and other groups. You might not know many of these people personally or well, but most will help you if you ask them. An easy way to find networking contacts is to join an online networking site such as LinkedIn (www.linkedin.com).

2.  **Contact each person in your list in a systematic way.** Obviously, some people will be more helpful than others, but any one of them might help you find a job lead.

3.  **Present yourself well.** Begin with your friends and relatives. Call and tell them you are looking for a job and need their help. Be as clear as possible about the type of employment you want and the skills and qualifications you have. Look at the sample JIST Card and phone script later in this step for good presentation ideas.

> **Most jobs are never advertised because employers don't need to advertise or don't want to.** Employers trust people referred to them by someone they know far more than they trust strangers. And most jobs are filled by referrals and people that the employer knows, eliminating the need to advertise. So, your job search must involve more than looking at ads.

4.  **Ask your contacts for leads.** It is possible that your contacts will know of a job opening that interests you. If so, get the details and get right on it! More likely, however, they will not, so you should ask each person the Three Magic Networking Questions.

### The Three Magic Networking Questions

- **Do you know of any openings for a person with my skills?**
  *If the answer is "No" (which it usually is), then ask...*

- **Do you know of someone else who might know of such an opening?** If your contact does, get that name and ask for another one.
  *If he or she doesn't, ask...*

*(continued)*

*(continued)*

- **Do you know of anyone who might know of someone else who might know of a job opening?**

    *Another good way to ask this is* "Do you know someone who knows lots of people?" *If all else fails, this will usually get you a name.*

5. **Contact these referrals and ask them the same questions.** From each person you contact, try to get two names of other people you might contact. Doing this consistently can extend your network of acquaintances by hundreds of people. Eventually, one of these people will hire you or refer you to someone who will!

If you are persistent in following these five steps, networking might be the only job search method you need. It works.

**Dialing for dollars.** The phone can get you more interviews per hour than any other job search tool. But it won't work unless you use it actively.

## *Most Effective Job Search Method 2: Contact Employers Directly*

It takes more courage, but making direct contact with employers is a very effective job search technique. I call these cold contacts because people you don't know in advance will need to warm up to your inquiries. Two basic techniques for making cold contacts follow.

**Use the yellow pages to find potential employers.** Begin by looking at the index in the front of your phone book's yellow pages. For each entry, ask yourself, *"Would an organization of this kind need a person with my skills?"* If you answer *"Yes,"* then that organization or business type is a possible target. You can also rate "Yes" entries based on your interest, writing a "1" next to those that seem very interesting, a "2" next to those that you are not sure of, and a "3" next to those that aren't interesting at all.

**Quip**

**The yellow pages in print and online provide the most complete, up-to-date listing of potential job search targets you can get.** It organizes them into categories that are very useful for job seekers. Just find a category that interests you, call each listing, and then contact employers listed there. All it takes is a 30-second phone call. Ask to speak with the hiring authority.

Next, select a type of organization that got a "Yes" response and turn to that section of the yellow pages. Call each organization listed there and ask to speak to the person who is most likely to hire or supervise you—typically the manager of the business or a department head—not the personnel or human resources manager. A sample telephone script is included later in this section to give you ideas about what to say.

You can easily adapt this approach for use on the Internet by using sites such as www.yellowpages.com to get contacts anywhere in the world, or you can find phone and e-mail contacts on an employer's own Web site.

**Drop in without an appointment.** Another effective cold contact method is to just walk into a business or organization that interests you and ask to speak to the person in charge. Although dropping in is particularly effective in small businesses, it also works surprisingly well in larger ones. Remember to ask for an interview even if there are no openings now. If your timing is inconvenient, ask for a better time to come back for an interview.

---

## Most Jobs Are with Small Employers

Businesses and organizations with fewer than 250 employees employ about 72 percent of all U.S. workers. Small organizations are also the source for around 75 percent of the new jobs created each year. They are simply too important to overlook in your job search! Many of them don't have personnel departments, which makes direct contacts even easier and more effective.

# Create a Powerful Job Search Tool—the JIST Card®

Look at the sample cards that follow—they are JIST Cards, and they get results. Computer printed or even neatly written on a 3-by-5–inch card, JIST Cards include the essential information employers want to know.

## A JIST Card Is a Mini Resume

JIST Cards have been used by thousands of job search programs and millions of people. Employers like their direct and timesaving format, and they have been proven as an effective tool to get job leads. Attach one to your resume. Give them to friends, relatives, and other contacts and ask them to pass them along to others who might know of an opening. Enclose them in thank-you notes after interviews. Leave one with employers as a business card. However you get them in circulation, you may be surprised at how well they work.

You can easily create JIST Cards on a computer and print them on card stock you can buy at any office supply store. Or have a few hundred printed cheaply by a local quick print shop. While they are often done as 3-by-5 cards, they can be printed in any size or format.

---

Sandy Nolan

Position: General Office/Clerical

Cell phone: (512) 232-9213

Email: snolan@aol.com

More than two years of work experience plus one year of training in office practices. Type 55 wpm, trained in word processing, post general ledger, have good interpersonal skills, and get along with most people. Can meet deadlines and handle pressure well.

Willing to work any hours.

Organized, honest, reliable, and hardworking.

---

**Richard Straightarrow**      **Home: (602) 253-9678**
**Message: (602) 257-6643**
**E-mail: RSS@email.cmm**

**Objective:** Electronics installation, maintenance, and sales

Four years of work experience plus a two-year A.S. degree in Electronics Engineering Technology. Managed a $360,000/year business while going to school full time, with grades in the top 25%. Familiar with all major electronic diagnostic and repair equipment. Hands-on experience with medical, consumer, communication, and industrial electronics equipment and applications. Good problem-solving and communication skills. Customer service oriented.

Willing to do what it takes to get the job done.

Self-motivated, dependable, learn quickly.

---

## *A JIST Card Can Lead to an Effective Phone Script*

The phone is an essential job search tool that can get you more interviews per hour than any other job search tool. But the technique won't work unless you use it actively throughout your search. After you have created your JIST Card, you can use it as the basis for a phone script to make warm or cold calls. Revise your JIST Card

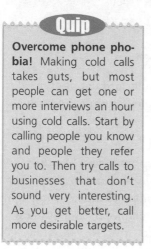

**Overcome phone phobia!** Making cold calls takes guts, but most people can get one or more interviews an hour using cold calls. Start by calling people you know and people they refer you to. Then try calls to businesses that don't sound very interesting. As you get better, call more desirable targets.

content so that it sounds natural when spoken, and then edit it until you can read it out loud in about 30 seconds. The sample phone script that follows is based on the content of a JIST Card. Use it to help you modify your own JIST Card into a phone script.

"Hello. My name is Pam Nykanen. I am interested in a position in hotel management. I have four years' experience in sales, catering, and accounting with a 300-room hotel. I also have an associate degree in hotel management, plus one year of experience with the Brady Culinary Institute. During my employment, I helped double revenues from meetings and conferences and increased bar revenues by 46 percent. I have good problem-solving skills and am good with people. I am also well-organized, hard working, and detail-oriented. When may I come in for an interview?"

With your script in hand, make some practice calls to warm or cold contacts. If making cold calls, contact the person most likely to supervise you. Then present your script just as you practiced it—without stopping.

Although the sample script assumes that you are calling someone you don't know, you can change it to address warm contacts and referrals. Making cold calls takes courage but works very well for many who are willing to do it.

# Use the Internet in Your Job Search

The Internet has limitations as a job search tool. While many have used it to get job leads, it has not worked well for far more. Too many assume they can simply add their resume to resume databases, and employers will line up to hire them. Just like the older approach of sending out lots of resumes, good things sometimes happen, but not often.

I recommend two points that apply to all job search methods, including using the Internet:

- It is unwise to rely on just one or two methods in conducting your job search.

- It is essential that you use an active rather than a passive approach in your job search.

## *Use More Than One Job Search Method*

I encourage you to use the Internet in your job search, but I suggest that you use it along with other techniques. Use the same sorts of job search techniques online as you do offline, including contacting employers directly and building up a network of personal contacts that can help you with your search.

### Tips to Increase Your Effectiveness in Internet Job Searches

The following tips can increase the effectiveness of using the Internet in your job search:

- **Be as specific as possible in the job you seek.** This is important in using any job search method, and it's even more important in using the Internet in your job search. The Internet is enormous, so it is essential to be as focused as possible in your search. Narrow your job title or titles to be as specific as possible. Limit your search to specific industries or areas of specialization. Locate and use specialized job banks in your area of interest.

- **Have reasonable expectations.** Success on the Internet is more likely if you understand its limitations and strengths. For example, employers trying to find someone with skills in high demand, such as nurses, are more likely to use the Internet to recruit job candidates.

- **Limit your geographic options.** If you don't want to move or would move only to certain areas, state this preference on your resume and restrict your search to those areas. Many Internet sites allow you to view or search for only those jobs that meet your location criteria.

- **Create an electronic resume.** With few exceptions, resumes submitted on the Internet end up as simple text files with no graphic elements. Employers search databases of many resumes for those that include key words or meet other searchable criteria. So create a simple text resume for Internet use and include words that are likely to be used by employers searching for someone with your abilities. (See Step 4 for more on creating an electronic resume.)

- **Get your resume into the major resume databases.** Most Internet employment sites let you add your resume for free and then charge employers to advertise openings or to search for candidates. Although adding your resume to these databases is not likely to result in job offers, doing so allows you to use your stored resume to easily apply for positions that are posted at these sites. These easy-to-use sites often provide all sorts of useful information for job seekers.

- **Make direct contacts.** Visit the Web sites of organizations that interest you and learn more about them. Many post openings, allow you to apply online, offer information on benefits and work environment, or even provide access to staff who can answer your questions. Even if they don't, you can always search the site or e-mail a request for the name of the person in charge of the work that interests you and then communicate with that person directly.

- **Network.** You can network online, too, finding names and e-mail addresses of potential employer contacts or of other people who might know someone with job openings. Look at and participate in interest groups, professional association sites, alumni sites, chat rooms, e-mail discussion lists, and employer sites—these are just some of the many creative ways to network and interact with people via the Internet.

## Check Out Career-Specific Sites First

Thousands of Internet sites provide lists of job openings and information on careers or education. Many have links to other sites that they recommend. Service providers such as Yahoo! (www.yahoo.com) and the Microsoft Network (www.msn.com) have partnered with sites such as Careerbuilder.com to include career information and job listings plus links to other sites. Also check out www.jist.com. Three additional career-related sites are Riley Guide at www.rileyguide.com, Monster at www.monster.com, and Indeed, a job aggregator, at www.indeed.com.

# STEP 4: Write a Simple Resume Now and a Better One Later

Sending out or e-mailing resumes and waiting for responses is not an effective job-seeking technique. But, many employers *will* ask you for a resume, and it can be a useful tool in your job search. I suggest that you begin with a simple resume you can complete quickly. I've seen too many people spend weeks working on a resume when they could have been out getting interviews instead. If you want a better resume, you can work on it on weekends and evenings. So let's begin with the basics.

## Tips for Creating a Superior Resume

The following tips make sense for any resume format:

- **Write it yourself.** It's okay to look at other resumes for ideas, but write yours yourself. Doing so will force you to organize your thoughts and background.

- **Make it error-free.** One spelling or grammar error will create a negative impressionist (see what I mean?). Get someone else to review your final draft for any errors. Then review it again because these rascals have a way of slipping in.

- **Make it look good.** Poor copy quality, cheap paper, bad type quality, or anything else that creates a poor appearance will turn off employers to even the best resume content. Get professional help with design and printing if necessary. Many professional resume writers and even print shops offer writing and desktop design services if you need help.

- **Be brief, be relevant.** Many good resumes fit on one page, and few justify more than two. Include only the most important points. Use short sentences and action words. If it doesn't relate to and support the job objective, cut it!

- **Be honest.** Don't overstate your qualifications. If you end up getting a job you can't handle, who does it help? And a lie can result in your being fired later.

- **Be positive.** Emphasize your accomplishments and results. A resume is no place to be too humble or to display your faults.

- **Be specific.** Instead of saying, "I am good with people," say, "I supervised four people in the warehouse and increased productivity by 30 percent." Use numbers whenever possible, such as the number of people served, percentage of sales increase, or amount of dollars saved.

You should also know that everyone feels that he or she is a resume expert. Whatever you do, someone will tell you that it's wrong. Remember that a resume is simply a job search tool.

You should never delay or slow down your job search because your resume is not good enough. The best approach is to create a simple and acceptable resume as quickly as possible and then use it. As time permits, create a better one if you feel you must.

**Avoid the resume pile.** Resume experts often suggest that a dynamite resume will jump out of the pile. This is old-fashioned advice. It assumes that you are applying to large organizations and for advertised jobs. Today most jobs are with small employers and are not advertised. To avoid joining that stack of resumes in the first place, look for job openings that others overlook.

# Writing Chronological Resumes

Most resumes use a chronological format where the most recent experience is listed first, followed by each previous job. This arrangement works fine for someone with work experience in several similar jobs, but not as well for those with limited experience or for career changers.

Look at the two resumes for Judith Jones that follow. Both use the chronological approach.

The first resume would work fine for most job search needs. It could be completed in about an hour.

Notice that the second one includes some improvements. The first resume is good, but most employers would like the additional positive information in the improved resume.

## *Basic Chronological Resume Example*

# Judith J. Jones

115 South Hawthorne Avenue
Chicago, Illinois 66204
tel: (312) 653-9217
email: jj@earthlink.com

### JOB OBJECTIVE

A position in the office management, accounting, or administrative assistant area that enables me to grow professionally.

### EDUCATION AND TRAINING

Acme Business College, Lincoln, IL
Graduate of a one-year business program.

John Adams High School, South Bend, IN
Diploma, business education.

U.S. Army
Financial procedures, accounting functions.

Other: Continuing-education classes and workshops in business communication, spreadsheet and database applications, scheduling systems, and customer relations.

### EXPERIENCE

2006–present—Claims Processor, Blue Spear Insurance Co., Wilmette, IL. Process customer medical claims, develop management reports based on created spreadsheets and develop management reports based on those forms, exceed productivity goals.

2005–2006—Returned to school to upgrade business and computer skills. Completed courses in advanced accounting, spreadsheet and database programs, office management, human relations, and new office techniques.

2002–2005—E4, U.S. Army. Assigned to various stations as a specialist in finance operations. Promoted prior to honorable discharge.

2001–2002—Sandy's Boutique, Wilmette, IL. Responsible for counter sales, display design, cash register, and other tasks.

1999–2001—Held part-time and summer jobs throughout high school.

### STRENGTHS AND SKILLS

Reliable, hardworking, and good with people. General ledger, accounts payable, and accounts receivable. Proficient in Microsoft Word, WordPerfect, Excel, and Outlook.

I give some tips you can use when you write your simple chronological resume. Use this resume as your guide.

## *Improved Chronological Resume Example*

# Judith J. Jones

115 South Hawthorne Avenue
Chicago, IL 66204

jj@earthlink.com
(312) 653-9217 (cell)

### JOB OBJECTIVE

A position requiring excellent business management expertise in an office environment. Position should require a variety of skills, including office management, word processing, and spreadsheet and database application use.

### EDUCATION AND TRAINING

Acme Business College, Lincoln, IL
Completed one-year program in **Professional Office Management.** Achieved GPA in top 30% of class. Courses included word processing, accounting theory and systems, advanced spreadsheet and database applications, graphics design, time management, and supervision.

John Adams High School, South Bend, IN
Graduated with emphasis on **business courses.** Earned excellent grades in all business topics and won top award for word-processing speed and accuracy.

Other: Continuing-education programs at own expense, including business communications, customer relations, computer applications, and sales techniques.

### EXPERIENCE

2006–present—**Claims Processor, Blue Spear Insurance Company,** Wilmette, IL. Process 50 complex medical insurance claims per day, almost 20% above department average. Created a spreadsheet report process that decreased department labor costs by more than $30,000 a year. Received two merit raises for performance.

2005–2006—**Returned to business school to gain advanced office skills.**

2002–2005—**Finance Specialist (E4), U.S. Army.** Systematically processed more than 200 invoices per day from commercial vendors. Trained and supervised eight employees. Devised internal system allowing 15% increase in invoices processed with a decrease in personnel. Managed department with a budget equivalent of more than $350,000 a year. Honorable discharge.

2001–2002—**Sales Associate promoted to Assistant Manager, Sandy's Boutique,** Wilmette, IL. Made direct sales and supervised four employees. Managed daily cash balances and deposits, made purchasing and inventory decisions, and handled all management functions during owner's absence. Sales increased 26% and profits doubled during tenure.

1999–2001—**Held various part-time and summer jobs through high school while maintaining GPA 3.0/4.0.** Earned enough to pay all personal expenses, including car insurance. Learned to deal with customers, meet deadlines, work hard, and handle multiple priorities.

### STRENGTHS AND SKILLS

Reliable, with strong work ethic. Excellent interpersonal, written, and oral communication and math skills. Accept supervision well, effectively supervise others, and work well as a team member. General ledger, accounts payable, and accounts receivable expertise. Proficient in Microsoft Word, Excel, PowerPoint, and Outlook; WordPerfect.

## Tips for Writing a Simple Chronological Resume

Follow these tips as you write a basic chronological resume:

- **Name.** Use your formal name (not a nickname).
- **Address and contact information.** Avoid abbreviations in your address and include your ZIP code. If you may move, use a friend's address or include a forwarding address. Most employers will not write to you, so provide reliable phone numbers and other contact options. Always include your area code in your phone number because you never know where your resume might travel. Make sure that you have an answering machine or voice mail, and record a professional-sounding message. Include alternative ways to reach you, such as a cell phone and e-mail address.
- **Job objective.** You should almost always have one, even if it is general. Notice how Judith Jones keeps her options open with her broad job objective in her basic resume on page 355. Writing "secretary" or "clerical" might limit her from being considered for other jobs.
- **Education and training.** Include any training or education you've had that supports your job objective. If you did not finish a formal degree or program, list what you did complete and emphasize accomplishments. If your experience is not strong, add details here such as related courses and extracurricular activities. In the two examples, Judith Jones puts her business schooling in both the education and experience sections. Doing this fills a job gap and allows her to present her training as equal to work experience.
- **Previous experience.** Include the basics such as employer name, job title, dates employed, and responsibilities—but emphasize specific skills, results, accomplishments, superior performance, and so on.
- **Personal data.** Do not include irrelevant details such as height, weight, and marital status or a photo. Current laws do not allow an employer to base hiring decisions on these points. Providing this information can cause some employers to toss your resume. You can include information about hobbies or leisure activities in a special section that directly supports your job objective.
- **References.** Make sure that each reference will make nice comments about you and ask each to write a letter of recommendation that you can give to employers. You do not need to list your references on your resume. List them on a separate page and give it to employers who ask. If your references are particularly good, however, you can mention this somewhere—the last section is often a good place.

When you have a simple, errorless, and eye-pleasing resume, get on with your job search. There is no reason to delay! If you want to create a better resume in your spare time (evenings or weekends), use the name and contact information you currently have and improve the other sections of the resume.

## Tips for an Improved Chronological Resume

Use these tips to improve your simple resume:

- **Job objective.** A poorly written job objective can limit the jobs an employer might consider you for. Think of the skills you have and the types of jobs you want to do; describe them in general terms. Instead of using a narrow job title such as "restaurant manager," you might write "manage a small to mid-sized business."
- **Education and training.** New graduates should emphasize their recent training and education more than those with a few years of related work experience would. A more detailed education and training section might include specific courses you took, and activities or accomplishments that support your job objective or reinforce your key skills. Include other details that reflect how hard you work, such as working your way through school or handling family responsibilities.
- **Skills and accomplishments.** Include those that support your ability to do well in the job you seek now. Even small details count. Maybe your attendance was perfect, you met a tight deadline, or you did the work of others during vacations. Be specific and include numbers—even if you have to estimate them. Judith's improved chronological resume example features more accomplishments and skills. Notice the impact of the numbers to reinforce results.
- **Job titles.** Past job titles may not accurately reflect what you did. For example, your job title may have been "cashier," but you also opened the store, trained new staff, and covered for the boss on vacations. Perhaps "head cashier and assistant manager" would be more accurate. Check with your previous employer if you are not sure.

*(continued)*

*(continued)*

- **Promotions.** If you were promoted or got good evaluations, say so—"cashier, promoted to assistant manager," for example. You can list a promotion to a more responsible job as a separate job if doing so results in a stronger resume.
- **Gaps in employment and other problem areas.** Employee turnover is expensive, so few employers want to hire people who won't stay or who won't work out. Gaps in employment, jobs held for short periods, or a lack of direction in the jobs you've held are all concerns for employers. So consider your situation and try to give an explanation of a problem area. Here are a few examples:

2007—Continued my education at...

2007—Traveled extensively throughout...

2006 to present—Self-employed as barn painter and...

2006—Took year off to have first child

Use entire years to avoid displaying employment gaps you can't explain easily. If you had a few months of unemployment at the beginning of 2007 and then began a job in mid-2007, for example, you can list the job as "2007 to present."

# Writing Skills and Combination Resumes

**Skip the negatives.** Remember that a resume can get you screened out, but it is up to you to get the interview and the job. Cut out anything negative in your resume!

The skills resume emphasizes your most important skills, supported by specific examples of how you have used them. This type of resume allows you to use any part of your life history to support your ability to do the job you want.

While skills resumes can be very effective, creating them requires more work. And some employers don't like them because they can hide a job seeker's faults (such as job gaps, lack of formal education, or little related work experience) better than can a chronological resume. Still, a skills resume may make sense for you.

Look over the sample resumes that follow for ideas. Notice that one resume includes elements of a skills *and* a chronological resume. This so-called combination resume makes sense if your previous job history or education and training are positive.

## *More Resume Examples*

**A resume is not the most effective tool for getting interviews.** A better approach is to make direct contact with those who hire or supervise people with your skills and ask them for an interview, even if no openings exist now. Then send a resume.

Find resume layout and presentation ideas in the four samples that follow.

The **chronological resume sample on page 359** focuses on accomplishments through the use of numbers. While Jon's resume does not say so, it is obvious that he works hard and that he gets results.

The **skills resume on page 360** is for a recent high school graduate whose only work experience was at a school office!

The **combination resume on page 361** emphasizes Grant's relevant education and transferable skills because he has little work experience in the field.

The **electronic resume on page 362** is appropriate for scanning or e-mail submission. It has a plain format that is easily read by scanners. It also has lots of key words that increase its chances of being selected when an employer searches a database.

*Use the information from your completed Essential Job Search Data Worksheet to write your resume.*

## The Chronological Resume to Emphasize Results

*This simple chronological resume has few but carefully chosen words. It has an effective summary at the beginning, and every word supports his job objective.*

### Jon Feder

2140 Beach Road
Pompano Beach, Florida 20000

Phone: (222) 333-4444
E-mail: jfeder@com.com

**Objective:**  Management position in a major hotel

*He emphasizes results!*

**Summary of Experience:**  Three years of experience in sales, catering banquet services, and guest relations in a 75-room hotel. Doubled sales revenues from conferences and meetings. Increased dining room and bar revenues by 40%. Won prestigious national and local awards for increased productivity and services.

**Experience:**  Beachcomber Hotel, Pompano Beach, Florida
Assistant Manager
20XX to Present

*Notice his use of numbers to increase the impact of the statements.*

- Oversee a staff of 24, including dining room and bar, housekeeping, and public relations operations.
- Introduced new menus and increased dining room revenues by 40%. Awarded *Saveur* magazine's prestigious first place Hotel Cuisine award as a result of my selection of chefs.
- Attracted 58% more bar patrons by implementing Friday night Jazz at the Beach.

Beachcombers' Suites, Hollywood Beach, Florida
Sales and Public Relations
20XX to 20XX

*Bullets here and above improve readability and emphasize key points.*

- Doubled venues per month from weddings, conferences, and meetings.
- Chosen Chamber of Commerce Newcomer of the Year 20XX for the increase in business within the community.

**Education:**  Associate Degree in Hotel Management from Sullivan Technical Institute
Certificate in Travel Management from Phoenix University

*While Jon had only a few years of related work experience, he used this resume to help him land a very responsible job in a large resort hotel.*

## The Skills Resume for Those with Limited Work Experience

*In this skills resume, each skill directly supports the job objective of this recent high school graduate with very limited work experience.*

### Catalina A. Garcia
2340 N. Delaware Street · Denver, Colorado 81613
Home: (413) 643-2173 (Leave Message)
Cell phone: (413) 345-2189
E-mail: cagarcia@net.net

### Position Desired
Office assistant in a fast-paced business

*Support for her key skills comes from her activities: school, clubs, and volunteer work.*

### Skills and Abilities

*Note her key skills.*

**Communications**    Excellent written and verbal presentation skills. Use proper grammar and have a good speaking voice.

**Interpersonal**    Able to get along well with all types of people. Accept supervision. Received positive evaluation from previous supervisors.

**Flexible**    Willing to try new things and am interested in improving efficiency on assigned tasks.

*Notice the emphasis on adaptive skills.*

**Attention to Detail**    Maintained confidential student records accurately and efficiently. Uploaded 500 student records in one day without errors.

**Hard Working**    Worked 30 hours per week throughout high school and maintained above-average grades.

*She makes good use of numbers.*

*This statement is very strong.*

**Student Contact**    Cordially dealt with as many as 150 students a day in Dean's office.

**Dependable**    Never absent or tardy in four years.

**Awards**    English Department Student of the Year, April 20XX
20XX Outstanding Student Newspaper, Newspaper Association of America

### Education
Denver North High School. Took advanced English and communication classes. Member of student newspaper staff and FCCLA for four years. Graduated in top 30% of class.

### Other
Girls' basketball team for four years. This taught me discipline, teamwork, how to follow instructions, and hard work. I am ambitious, outgoing, reliable, and willing to work.

*Catalina's resume makes it clear that she is talented and hard working.*

## *The Combination Resume*

Grant just finished computer programming school and has no work experience in the field. After listing the topics covered in the course, he summarized his employment experience, specifying that he earned promotions quickly. This would be attractive to any employer.

### Grant Thomas

717 Carlin Court • Mendelein, IL 60000 • (555) 555-3333
E-mail: gthomas@com.com

#### Profile

- Outstanding student and tutor
- Winner of international computer software design competition three years
- Capable of being self-directed and independent, but also a team player
- Effective communicator, both orally and written
- Creative problem solver

#### Education and Training

M.S. in Software Engineering, Massachusetts Institute of Technology, Cambridge, MA
B.S. in Computer Engineering, California State University, Fullerton, CA
A rigorous education that focuses on topics such as

He includes important information that specifies topics he studied.

- Structure and interpretation of computer programs
- Circuits and electronics
- Signals and systems
- Computation structures
- Microelectronic devices and circuits
- Computer system engineering
- Computer language engineering
- Mathematics for computer science
  Analog olootronics laboratory
- Digital systems laboratory

The work experiences support the job objective.

#### Highlights of Experience and Abilities

- Develop, create, and modify general computer applications software.
- Analyze user needs and develop software solutions.
- Confer with system analysts, computer programmers, and others.
- Modify existing software to correct errors.
- Coordinate software system installation and monitor equipment functioning to ensure specifications are met.
- Supervise work of programmers and technicians.
- Train customers and employees to use new and modified software.

#### Employment History

Software Specialist, First Rate Computers, Mendelein, IL 20XX – Present
- Technician and Customer and Employee Trainer throughout high school
- Promoted to software specialist and worked as a full-time telecommuting employee while completing the B.S. and M.S. degrees

References available on request

## The Electronic Resume

```
William Brown
409 S. Maish Road
Phoenix, AZ 50000

Phone message: (300) 444-5567

E-mail: wbrown@email.com

OBJECTIVE

Store management career track in car audio store

================================================================
SUMMARY OF SKILLS

Strategic planning, time management, team building,
leadership, problem solving, quality customer service,
conflict resolution, increasing productivity, confident,
outgoing, high performing, aggressive sales

================================================================
EXPERIENCE

Total of three years in sales

* SHIFT SUPERVISOR, Tech World, Audio Department, Phoenix,
AZ, April 20XX to present: Promoted to Shift Supervisor of
nine salespeople in three months. Responsible for strategic
planning, time management, team building, leadership,
problem solving, quality customer service, conflict
resolution, and increasing productivity. Highest-selling
team for three years.

* AUDIO SALESPERSON, Tech World, Audio Department, Phoenix,
AZ, January 20XX to April 20XX: Arranged display, organized
stockroom, sales to customers, and tracked inventory.
Highest-selling staff member for three months.

================================================================
EDUCATION AND TRAINING

Phoenix High School, top 40% of class

Additional training: Team Building, Franklin Time Management
seminar, Team Building seminar

================================================================
OTHER

* Installed audio systems in 10 cars: family, friends, and
my own.

* Member of United States Autosound Association (USAA)
```

*Because this electronic format is to be scanned or e-mailed, it has no bold, bullets, or italics.*

*The many key words ensure that the employers' computer searches will select this resume.*

*Note the results statements and numbers used below.*

# Use a Career Portfolio to Support Your Resume

Your resume is impressive, but there is another way that you can show prospective employers evidence of who you are and what you can do—a career portfolio.

## What Is a Career Portfolio?

Unlike a resume, a career portfolio is a collection of documents that can include a variety of items. Here are some items you may want to place in your portfolio:

- Resume
- School transcripts
- Summary of skills
- Credentials, such as diplomas and certificates of recognition
- Reference letters from school officials and instructors, former employers, or co-workers
- List of accomplishments: Describe hobbies and interests that are not directly related to your job objective and are not included on your resume.
- Examples of your work: Depending on your situation, you can include samples of your art, photographs of a project, audiotapes, videotapes, images of Web pages you developed, and other media that can provide examples of your work.

Place each item on a separate page when you assemble your career portfolio.

## Create a Digital Portfolio

A digital portfolio, also known as an electronic portfolio, contains all the information from your career portfolio in an electronic format. This material is then copied onto a CD-ROM or published on a Web site. With a digital portfolio, you can present your skills to a greater number of people than you can your paper career portfolio.

---

### YOUR CAREER PORTFOLIO

On the following lines, list the items you want to include in your career portfolio. Think specifically of those items that show your skills, education, and personal accomplishments.

_____

_____

_____

_____

_____

_____

_____

_____

_____

_____

---

## STEP 5: Redefine What Counts as an Interview, and Then Get Two a Day

The average job seeker gets about five interviews a month—fewer than two a week. Yet many job seekers use the methods in this *Quick Job Search* to get two interviews a day. Getting two interviews a day equals 10 a week and 40 a month. That's 800 percent more interviews than the average job seeker gets. Who do you think will get a job offer quicker?

However, getting two interviews a day is nearly impossible unless you redefine what counts as an interview. If you define an interview in a different way, getting two a day is quite possible.

**The New Definition of an Interview:** Any face-to-face contact with someone who has the authority to hire or supervise a person with your skills—even if no opening exists at the time you talk with him or her.

If you use this new definition, it becomes *much* easier to get interviews. You can now interview with all sorts of potential employers, not just those who have job openings now. While most other job seekers look for advertised or actual openings, you can get interviews before a job opens up or before it is advertised and widely known. You will be considered for jobs that may soon be created but that others will not know about. And, of course, you can also interview for existing openings just as everyone else does.

Spending as much time as possible on your job search and setting a job search schedule are important parts of this step.

## Make Your Search a Full-Time Job

Job seekers average fewer than 15 hours a week looking for work. On average, unemployment lasts three or more months, with some people out of work far longer (for example, older workers and higher earners). My many years of experience researching job seeking indicate that the more time you spend on your job search each week, the less time you will likely remain unemployed.

Of course, using the more effective job search methods presented in this minibook also helps. Many job search programs that teach job seekers my basic approach of using more effective methods and spending more time looking have proven that these seekers often find a job in half the average time. More importantly, many job seekers also find better jobs using these methods.

So, if you are unemployed and looking for a full-time job, you should plan to look on a full-time basis. It just makes sense to do so, although many do not, or they start out well but quickly get discouraged. Most job seekers simply don't have a structured plan—they have no idea what they are going to do next Thursday. The plan that follows will show you how to structure your job search like a job.

## Decide How Much Time You Will Spend Looking for Work Each Week and Day

First and most importantly, decide how many hours you are willing to spend each week on your job search. You should spend a minimum of 25 hours a week on hard-core job search activities with no goofing around. The following worksheet walks you through a simple but effective process to set a job search schedule for each week.

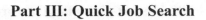

---

### PLAN YOUR JOB SEARCH WEEK

1. How many hours are you willing to spend each week looking for a job?_____

2. Which days of the week will you spend looking for a job?_____

3. How many hours will you look each day?_____

4. At what times will you begin and end your job search on each of these days?_____

_____

---

## Create a Specific Daily Job Search Schedule

Having a specific daily schedule is essential because most job seekers find it hard to stay productive each day. The sample daily schedule that follows is the result of years of research into what schedule gets the best results. I tested many schedules in job search programs I ran, and this particular schedule worked best.

Consider using a schedule like this sample daily schedule. Why? Because it works.

### A Sample Daily Schedule That Works

| Time | Activity |
|---|---|
| 7–8 a.m. | Get up, shower, dress, eat breakfast |
| 8–8:15 a.m. | Organize work space, review schedule for today's interviews and promised follow-ups, check e-mail, update schedule as needed |
| 8:15–9 a.m. | Review old leads for follow-up needed today; develop new leads from want ads, yellow pages, the Internet, warm contact lists, and other sources; complete daily contact list |
| 9–10 a.m. | Make phone calls and set up interviews |
| 10–10:15 a.m. | Take a break |
| 10:15–11 a.m. | Make more phone calls, set up more interviews |
| 11 a.m.–Noon | Send follow-up notes and do other office activities as needed |
| Noon–1 p.m. | Lunch break, relax |
| 1–3 p.m. | Go on interviews, make cold contacts in the field |
| Evening | Read job search books, make calls to warm contacts not reachable during the day, work on a better resume, spend time with friends and family, exercise, relax |

If you are not accustomed to using a daily schedule book or electronic planner, promise yourself to get a good one tomorrow. Choose one that allows for each day's plan on an hourly basis, plus daily to-do lists. Record your daily schedule in advance, and then add interviews as they come. Get used to carrying your planner with you and use it!

You can find a variety of computer programs or pocket-sized electronic schedulers to help organize your job search. If you don't use electronic tools, a simple schedule book and other paper systems will work just fine.

# STEP 6: Dramatically Improve Your Interviewing Skills

Interviews are where the job search action is. You have to get them; then you have to do well in them. According to surveys of employers, most job seekers do not effectively present the skills they have to do the job. Even worse, most job seekers can't answer one or more problem questions.

This lack of performance in interviews is one reason why employers will often hire a job seeker who does well in the interview over someone with better credentials. The good news is that you can do simple things to dramatically improve your interviewing skills. This section will emphasize interviewing tips and techniques that make the most difference.

## Your First Impression May Be the Only One You Make

Some research suggests that if the interviewer forms a negative impression in the first five minutes of an interview, your chances of getting a job offer approach zero. I know from experience that many job seekers can create a lasting negative impression within seconds.

### Tips for Interviewing

Because a positive first impression is so important, I share these suggestions to help you get off to a good start:

- **Make a good impression before you arrive.** Your resume, e-mails, applications, and other written correspondence create an impression before the interview, so make them professional and error-free.

- **Do some homework on the organization before you go.** You can often get information on a business and on industry trends from the Internet or a library.

- **Dress and groom the same way the interviewer is likely to be dressed—but cleaner!** Employer surveys find that almost half of all people's dress or grooming creates an initial negative impression. So this is a big problem. If necessary, get advice on your interviewing outfits from someone who dresses well. Pay close attention to your grooming, too—little things do count.

- **Be early.** Leave in plenty of time to be a few minutes early to an interview.

- **Be friendly and respectful with the receptionist.** Doing otherwise will often get back to the interviewer and result in a quick rejection.

- **Follow the interviewer's lead in the first few minutes.** It's often informal small talk but very important for that person to see how you interact. This is a good time to make a positive comment on the organization or even something you see in the office.

- **Understand that a traditional interview is not a friendly exchange.** In a traditional interview situation, there is a job opening, and you will be one of several applicants for it. In this setting, the employer's task is to eliminate all applicants but one. The interviewer's questions are designed to elicit information that can be used to screen you out. And your objective is to avoid getting screened out. It's hardly an open and honest interaction, is it?

  Setting up interviews before an opening exists eliminates the stress of a traditional interview. In pre-interviews, employers are not trying to screen you out, and you are not trying to keep them from finding out stuff about you. Having said that, knowing how to answer questions that might be asked in a traditional interview is good preparation for any interview you face.

- **Be prepared to answer the tough interview questions.** Your answers to a few key problem questions may determine whether you get a job offer. There are simply too many possible interview questions to cover one by one. Instead, 10 basic questions cover variations of most other interview questions. So, if you can learn to answer the Top 10 Problem Interview Questions well, you will know how to answer most others.

- **Be prepared for the most important interview question of all.** "Why should I hire you?" is the most important question of all to answer well. Do you have a convincing argument why someone should hire you over someone else? If you don't, you probably won't get that job you really want. So think carefully about why someone should hire you and practice your response. Then make sure you communicate this in the interview, even if the interviewer never asks the question in a clear way.

## Top 10 Problem Interview Questions

1. Why should I hire you?
2. Why don't you tell me about yourself?
3. What are your major strengths?
4. What are your major weaknesses?
5. What sort of pay do you expect to receive?
6. How does your previous experience relate to the jobs we have here?
7. What are your plans for the future?
8. What will your former employer (or references) say about you?
9. Why are you looking for this type of position, and why here?
10. Why don't you tell me about your personal situation?

# Follow the Three-Step Process for Answering Interview Questions

I've developed a three-step process for answering interview questions. I know this might seem too simple, but the three-step process is easy to remember and can help you create a good answer to most interview questions. The technique has worked for thousands of people, so consider trying it.

1. **Understand what is really being asked.**

   Most questions are designed to find out about your self-management skills and personality, but interviewers are rarely this blunt. The employer's *real* question is often one or more of the following:

   - Can I depend on you?

   - Are you easy to get along with?

   - Are you a good worker?

   - Do you have the experience and training to do the job if we hire you?

   - Are you likely to stay on the job for a reasonable period of time and be productive?

   Ultimately, if you don't convince the employer that you will stay and be a good worker, it won't matter if you have the best credentials—he or she won't hire you.

2. **Answer the question briefly in a nondamaging way.** Present the facts of your particular work experience as advantages, not disadvantages. Many interview questions encourage you to provide negative information. One classic question I included in my list of Top 10 Problem Interview Questions was "What are your major weaknesses?" This is obviously a trick question, and many people are just not prepared for it.

   A good response is to mention something that is not very damaging, such as *"I have been told that I am a perfectionist, sometimes not delegating as effectively as I might."*

   But your answer is not complete until you continue with the next step.

3. **Answer the real question by presenting your related skills.** Base your answer on the key skills you have that support the job, and give examples to support these skills. For example, an employer might say to a recent graduate, *"We were looking for someone with more experience in this field. Why should we consider you?"* Here is one possible answer:

*"I'm sure there are people who have more experience, but I do have more than six years of work experience, including three years of advanced training and hands-on experience using the latest methods and techniques. Because my training is recent, I am open to new ideas and am used to working hard and learning quickly."*

In the previous example (about your need to delegate), a good skills statement might be

*"I've been working on this problem and have learned to let my staff do more, making sure that they have good training and supervision. I've found that their performance improves, and it frees me up to do other things."*

Whatever your situation, learn to answer questions that present you well. It's essential to communicate your skills during an interview, and the three-step process can help you answer problem questions and dramatically improve your responses. It works!

## How to Earn a Thousand Dollars a Minute

What do you do when the employer asks, "How much money would it take to get you to join our company?"

---

### Tips on Negotiating Pay

Remember these few essential tips when it comes time to negotiate your pay:

- **The Number 1 Salary Negotiation Rule: The person who names a specific amount first loses.**

- **The only time to negotiate is after you have been offered the job.** Employers want to know how much you want to be paid so that they can eliminate you from consideration. They figure if you want too much, you won't be happy with their job and won't stay. And if you will take too little, they may think you don't have enough experience. So never discuss your salary expectations until an employer offers you the job.

- **If pressed, speak in terms of wide pay ranges.** If you are pushed to reveal your pay expectations early in an interview, ask the interviewer what the normal pay range is for this job. Interviewers will often tell you, and you can say that you would consider offers in this range.

  If you are forced to be more specific, speak in terms of a wide pay range. If you figure that the company will likely pay from $25,000 to $29,000 a year, for example, say that you would consider "any fair offer in the mid- to upper-twenties." This statement covers the employer's range and goes a bit higher. If all else fails, tell the interviewer that you would consider any reasonable offer.

  For this tip to work, you must know in advance what the job is likely to pay. You can get this information by asking people who do similar work, or from a variety of books and Internet sources of career information.

- **If you want the job, you should say so.** This is no time to be playing games.

- **Don't say "no" too quickly.** Never, ever turn down a job offer during an interview! Instead, thank the interviewer for the offer and ask to consider the offer overnight. You can turn it down tomorrow, saying how much you appreciate the offer and asking to be considered for other jobs that pay better or whatever. And it is okay to ask for additional pay or other concessions. But if you simply can't accept the offer, say why and ask the interviewer to keep you in mind for future opportunities. You just never know.

---

## STEP 7: Follow Up on All Job Leads

It's a fact: People who follow up with potential employers and with others in their network get jobs more quickly than those who do not.

## Rules for Effective Follow-Up

Here are four rules to guide you in your job search:

- **Send a thank-you note or e-mail to every person who helps you in your job search.**
- **Send the note within 24 hours after speaking with the person.**
- **Enclose JIST Cards with thank-you notes and all other correspondence.**
- **Develop a system to keep following up with good contacts.**

# Thank-You Notes Make a Difference

Although thank-you notes can be e-mailed, most people appreciate and are more impressed by a mailed note. Here are some tips about mailed thank-you notes that you can easily adapt to e-mail use:

- You can handwrite or type thank-you notes on quality paper and matching envelopes.

- Keep the notes simple, neat, and error-free.

- Make sure to include a few copies of your JIST Card in the envelope.

Here is an example of a simple thank-you note.

---

*April 5, XXXX*

*Mr. Kijek,*

*Thanks so much for your willingness to see me next Wednesday at 9 a.m. I know that I am one of many who are interested in working with your organization. I appreciate the opportunity to meet you and learn more about the position.*

*I've enclosed a JIST Card that presents the basics of my skills for this job and will bring my resume to the interview. Please call me if you have any questions at all.*

*Sincerely,*

*Bruce Vernon*

---

# Use Job Lead Cards to Follow Up

If you use contact management software, use it to schedule follow-up activities. But the simple paper system I describe here can work very well or can be adapted for setting up your contact management software.

- Use a simple 3-by-5–inch card to record essential information about each person in your network.

- Buy a 3-by-5–inch card file box and tabs for each day of the month.

- File the cards under the date you want to contact the person.

- Follow through by contacting the person on that date.

**Quip**

The JibberJobber Web site (www.jibberjobber.com) provides online tools for tracking your contacts.

I've found that staying in touch with a good contact every other week can pay off big. Here's a sample card to give you ideas about creating your own.

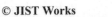

```
ORGANIZATION: ___Mutual Health Insurance_____
CONTACT PERSON: __Anna Tomey_____   PHONE: __317-355-0216__
SOURCE OF LEAD: ___Aunt Ruth_____
NOTES: __4/10 Called. Anna on vacation. Call back 4/15. 4/15 Interview set
____4/20 at 1:30. 4/20 Anna showed me around. They use the same computers
____we used in school! (Friendly people.) Sent thank-you note and JIST
____Card, call back 5/1. 5/1 Second interview 5/8 at 9 a.m.!
```

# In Closing

This is a short book, but it may be all you need to get a better job in less time. I hope this will be true for you, and I wish you well in your search. Remember this: You won't get a job offer because someone knocks on your door and offers one. Job seeking does involve luck, but you are more likely to have good luck if you are out getting interviews.

I'll close this minibook with a few final tips:

- **Approach your job search as if it were a job itself.** Create and stick to a daily schedule, and spend at least 25 hours a week looking.

- **Follow up on each lead you generate and ask each contact for referrals.**

- **Set out each day to schedule at least two interviews.** Remember the new definition of an interview—an interview includes talking to potential employers who don't have an opening now.

- **Send out lots of thank-you notes and JIST Cards.**

- **When you want the job, tell the employer that you want it and why you should be hired over everyone else.**

Don't get discouraged. There are lots of jobs out there, and someone needs an employee with your skills—your job is to find that someone.

I wish you luck in your job search and in your life.

## ESSENTIAL JOB SEARCH DATA WORKSHEET

Take some time to complete this worksheet carefully. It will help you write your resume and answer interview questions. You can also photocopy it and take it with you to help complete applications and as a reference throughout your job search. Use an erasable pen or pencil to allow for corrections. Whenever possible, emphasize skills and accomplishments that support your ability to do the job you want. Use extra sheets as needed.

Your name_____

Date completed_____

Job objective_____

## Key Accomplishments

List three accomplishments that best prove your ability to do the kind of job you want.

  1. _____

  2. _____

  3. _____

## Education and Training

**Name of high school(s) and specific years attended**_____

Subjects related to job objective_____

_____

Related extracurricular activities/hobbies/leisure activities _____

_____

Accomplishments/things you did well_____

_____

Specific things you can do as a result_____

_____

**Schools you attended after high school, specific years attended, and degrees/certificates earned**_____

_____

Courses related to job objective_____

_____

Related extracurricular activities/hobbies/leisure activities_____

_____

Accomplishments/things you did well_____

_____

Specific things you can do as a result_____

_____

## Other Training

Include formal or informal learning, workshops, military training, skills you learned on the job or from hobbies—anything that will help support your job objective. Include specific dates, certificates earned, or other details as needed._____

_____

*(continued)*

*(continued)*

---

### Work and Volunteer History

List your most recent job first, followed by each previous job. Military experience, unpaid or volunteer work, and work in a family business should be included here, too. If needed, use additional sheets to cover *all* significant paid or unpaid work experiences. Emphasize details that will help support your new job objective. Include numbers to support what you did: the number of people served over one or more years, number of transactions processed, percentage of sales increased, total inventory value you were responsible for, payroll of the staff you supervised, total budget responsible for, and so on. Emphasize results you achieved, using numbers to support them whenever possible. Mentioning these things on your resume and in an interview will help you get the job you want.

#### *Job 1*

Dates employed _____

Name of organization _____

Supervisor's name and job title _____

Address _____

Phone number/e-mail address/Web site _____

What did you accomplish and do well? _____

_____

Things you learned; skills you developed or used _____

_____

Raises, promotions, positive evaluations, awards _____

_____

Computer software, hardware, and other equipment you used _____

_____

Other details that might support your job objective _____

_____

#### *Job 2*

Dates employed _____

Name of organization _____

Supervisor's name and job title _____

Address _____

Phone number/e-mail address/Web site _____

What did you accomplish and do well? _____

_____

Things you learned; skills you developed or used _____

_____

---

Raises, promotions, positive evaluations, awards _____

_____

Computer software, hardware, and other equipment you used _____

_____

Other details that might support your job objective _____

_____

### *Job 3*

Dates employed _____

Name of organization _____

Supervisor's name and job title _____

Address _____

Phone number/e-mail address/Web site _____

What did you accomplish and do well? _____

_____

Things you learned; skills you developed or used _____

_____

Raises, promotions, positive evaluations, awards _____

_____

Computer software, hardware, and other equipment you used _____

_____

Other details that might support your job objective _____

_____

### References

Think of people who know your work well and will be positive about your work and character. Past supervisors are best. Contact them and tell them what type of job you want and your qualifications, and ask what they will say about you if contacted by a potential employer. Some employers will not provide references by phone, so ask them for a letter of reference in advance. If a past employer may say negative things, negotiate what he or she will say or get written references from others you worked with there.

**Reference name** _____

Position or title _____

Relationship to you _____

Contact information (complete address, phone number, e-mail address) _____

_____

*(continued)*

*(continued)*

Reference name_____

Position or title_____

Relationship to you_____

Contact information (complete address, phone number, e-mail address)_____

_____

Reference name_____

Position or title_____

Relationship to you_____

Contact information (complete address, phone number, e-mail address)_____

_____

# A Short List of Additional Resources

Thousands of books and countless Internet sites provide information on career subjects. Space limitations do not permit me to describe the many good resources available, so I list here some of the most useful ones. Because this is my list, I've included books I've written or that JIST publishes. You should be able to find these and many other resources at libraries, bookstores, and Web bookselling sites.

## Resume and Cover Letter Books

**My books.** *The Quick Resume & Cover Letter Book* is one of the top-selling resume books at various large bookstore chains. It is very simple to follow, is inexpensive, has good design, and has good sample resumes written by professional resume writers. For more in-depth but still quick help, check out my two books in the *Help in a Hurry* series: *Same-Day Resume* (with advice on creating a simple resume in an hour and a better one later) and *15-Minute Cover Letter,* co-authored with Louise Kursmark (offering sample cover letters and tips for writing them fast and effectively).

**Other books published by JIST.** The following titles include many sample resumes written by professional resume writers, as well as good advice: *Amazing Resumes* by Jim Bright and Joanne Earl; *Cover Letter Magic* by Wendy S. Enelow and Louise M. Kursmark; the entire *Expert Resumes* series by Enelow and Kursmark; *Federal Resume Guidebook* by Kathryn Kraemer Troutman; *Gallery of Best Resumes, Gallery of Best Cover Letters,* and other books by David F. Noble; and *Résumé Magic* by Susan Britton Whitcomb.

## Job Search and Interviewing Books

**My books.** In addition to the books mentioned above, check out *Next-Day Job Interview* (quick tips for preparing for a job interview at the last minute). *The Very Quick Job Search* is a thorough book with detailed advice and a "quick" section of key tips you can finish in a few hours. *Getting the Job You Really Want* includes many activities and good career decision-making and job search advice.

**Other books published by JIST.** Titles include *Inside Secrets of Finding a Teaching Job* by Warner, Bryan, and Warner; *Insider's Guide to Finding a Job* by Wendy S. Enelow and Shelly Goldman; *Job Search Handbook for People with Disabilities* by Daniel J. Ryan; *Job Search Magic* and *Interview Magic* by Susan Britton Whitcomb; *Ultimate Job Search* by Richard H. Beatty; and *Over-40 Job Search Guide* by Gail Geary.

## Books with Information on Jobs

**The primary reference books.** The *Occupational Outlook Handbook* is the source of job titles listed in this book. Published by the U.S. Department of Labor and updated every other year, the *OOH* covers about 90 percent of the workforce. The *O\*NET Dictionary of Occupational Titles* book has descriptions for almost 1,000 jobs based on the O\*NET (Occupational Information Network) database developed by the Department of Labor. The *Enhanced Occupational Outlook Handbook* includes the *OOH* descriptions plus more than 7,000 additional descriptions of related jobs from the O\*NET and other sources. The *New Guide for Occupational Exploration* allows you to explore major jobs based on your interests.

**Other books published by JIST.** Here are a few good books that include job descriptions and helpful details on career options: *Overnight Career Choice, Best Jobs for the 21st Century, 50 Best Jobs for Your Personality, 200 Best Jobs for College Graduates, 300 Best Jobs Without a Four-Year Degree, Salary Facts Handbook,* and *Health-Care CareerVision.*

## Internet Resources

There are too many Web sites to list, but here are a few places you can start. A book by Anne Wolfinger titled *Best Career and Education Web Sites* gives unbiased reviews of the most helpful sites and ideas on how to use them. *Job Seeker's Online Goldmine,* by Janet Wall, lists the extensive free online job search tools from government and other sources. This book's job descriptions also include Internet addresses for related organizations. Be aware that some Web sites provide poor advice, so ask your librarian, instructor, or counselor for suggestions on those best for your needs.

## Other Resources

**Libraries.** Most libraries have the books mentioned here, as well as many other resources. Most provide Internet access so that you can research online information. Ask the librarian for help finding what you need.

**People.** People who hold the jobs that interest you are one of the best career information sources. Ask them what they like and don't like about their work, how they got started, and the education or training needed. Most people are helpful and will give advice you can't get any other way.

**Career Counseling.** A good vocational counselor can help you explore career options. Take advantage of this service if it is available to you! Also consider a career-planning course or program, which will encourage you to be more thorough in your thinking.

# Sample Resumes for Some of the Fastest-Growing Careers

If you read the previous information, you know that I believe you should not depend on a resume alone in your job search. Even so, you will most likely need one, and you should have a good one.

Unlike some career authors, I do not preach that there is only one right way to do a resume. I encourage you to be an individual and to do what you think will work well for you. But I also know that some resumes are clearly better than others. The following pages contain some resumes that you can use as examples when preparing your own resume.

Each resume was written by a professional resume writer who is a member of one or more professional associations. These writers are highly qualified and hold various credentials. Most will provide help (for a fee) and welcome your contacting them (although this is not a personal endorsement).

The resumes appear in books published by JIST Works, including the following:

- *Expert Resumes for Computer and Web Jobs* by Wendy S. Enelow and Louise M. Kursmark

- *Expert Resumes for Engineers* by Wendy S. Enelow and Louise M. Kursmark

- *Expert Resumes for Teachers and Educators* by Wendy S. Enelow and Louise M. Kursmark

- *Gallery of Best Resumes* by David F. Noble

- *Gallery of Best Resumes for People Without a Four-Year Degree* by David F. Noble

# Contact Information for Resume Contributors

The following professional resume writers contributed resumes to this section. Their names are listed in alphabetical order. Each entry indicates which resume(s) that person contributed.

**Carol A. Altomare**
World Class Resumes
P.O. Box 483
Three Bridges, NJ 08887-0483
Phone: (908) 237-1883
Toll-free: (877) 771-6170
Fax: (908) 237-2069
E-mail: caa@worldclassresumes.com
Web site: www. worldclassresumes.com
Member: PARW/CC
Certification: CPRW
Resume on pages 392–393

**Ann Baehr**
Best Resumes of New York
East Islip, NY 11730
Phone: (631) 224-9300
Fax: (631) 314-6871
E-mail: resumesbest@earthlink.net
Web site: www.ebestresumes.com or
www.nyresumewriter.com
Member: CMI, NRWA, PARW/CC
Certification: CPRW
Resume on page 388

**Karen Bartell**
Best-in-Class Resumes
4940 Merrick Rd., Ste. 160
Massapequa Park, NY 11762
Phone: (631) 704-3220
Toll-free: (800) 234-3569
E-mail: kbartell@bestclassresumes.com
Web site: www.bestclassresumes.com
Certification: CPRW
Resume on pages 383–384

**Rosie Bixel**
A Personal Scribe Resume Writing &
Design (a division of BHH Group)
4800 SW Macadam Ave., Suite 105
Portland, OR 97239
Phone: (503) 254-8262
Fax: (503) 255-3012
E-mail: aps@bhhgroup.com
Web site: www.bhhgroup.com/resume/ap
Member: NRWA
Resume on page 385

**Patricia Chapman**
CareerPro-Naperville, Inc.
520 E. Ogden Ave., Suite 3
Naperville, IL 60563

Phone: (630) 983-8882
Toll-free: (866) 661-2269
Fax: (630) 983-9021
E-mail: pat@career2day.com
Web site: www.career2day.com
Member: CMI, PRWRA, NAFE
Certification: CRW
Resume on page 381

**Darlene M. Dassy**
Dynamic Resume Solutions
602 Monroe Dr.
Harleysville, PA 19438
Phone and fax: (215) 368-2316
E-mail: darlene@attractiveresumes.com
Web site: www.attractiveresumes.com
Certification: CRW
Resume on pages 394–395

**MJ Feld**
Careers by Choice, Inc.
205 E. Main St., Ste. 2–4
Huntington, NY 11743
Phone: (631) 673-5432
Fax: (631) 673-5824
E-mail: mj@careersbychoice.com
Web site: www.careersbychoice.com
Member: PARW/CC
Certifications: MS, CPRW
Resume on pages 386–387

**Michele Haffner**
Advanced Resume Services
1314 W. Paradise Ct.
Glendale, WI 53209
Phone: (414) 247-1677
Fax: (414) 247-1808
E-mail: michele@resumeservices.com
Web site: www.resumeservices.com
Certifications: CPRW, JCTC
Resume on page 380

**Don Orlando**
The McLean Group
640 S. McDonough St.
Montgomery, AL 36104
Phone: (334) 264-2020
Fax: (334) 264-9227
E-mail: yourcareercoach@
charterinternet.com
Member: CMI, PARW/CC, Phoenix
Career Group

Certifications: MBA, CPRW, JCTC,
CCM, CCMC
Resume on pages 390–391

**Diana Ramirez**
Ramirez Consulting Services
Seatac, WA 98198
Phone: (206) 870-7366
Mobile: (253) 332-5521
E-mail: ramirezconsulting@yahoo.com
Web site: www.ramirezconsulting.us
Member: NRWA, NCDA, NAWW
Certifications: NCDA; Registered Counselor, Project Management, Human
Resources Management
Resume on page 382

**MeLisa Rogers**
Ultimate Career/Insyte Solutions
16 Linda Ct.
Scroggins, TX 75480
Phone: (903) 717-1027
Fax: (903) 860-3963
E-mail: success@ultimatecareer.biz
Web site: www.ultimatecareer.biz
Member: PARW/CC, SHRM, ASTD
Certifications: Ed.D., CPRW, CPBA,
DDI, Achieve Global, VLST
Resumes on pages 377–378, 396

**Deanna Verbouwens**
Ace in the Hole Resume Writing and
Career Services
14 Mitchell Court
Hicksville, NY 11801
Phone: (516) 942-5986
E-mail: verbouwens@yahoo.com and
info@aceinthehole.net
Member: PARW/CC
Resume on page 389

**Jeremy Worthington**
Buckeye Resumes
2092 Atterbury St.
Columbus, OH 43229
Phone: (614) 861-6606
Fax: (614) 737-6166
E-mail: Jeremy@buckeyeresumes.com
Web site: www.buckeyeresumes.com
Member: CDI
Resume on page 379

## Accountants and Auditors

# Mary W. Kingston—CPA, MBA

*178 Stanton Drive*          *Cedar Park, Texas 78795*          *512-785-6857*          *mkingston@aol.com*

## PROFFESSIONAL SUMMARY

**Degreed Accounting Professional** with over 25 years of progressively responsible experience in a detail-oriented, multi-functional setting. Key accomplishments include

*Led the audit of a multimillion-dollar* construction project.
*Developed and implemented* multiple *accounting training programs.*
*Implemented* the concepts and procedures for multiple computerized systems.
*Reduced processing time by 70%* of raw material contracts, receipts and payments.

| | |
|---|---|
| Accounts payable | Collections |
| Payroll | Financial reports |
| General ledger | System debugging |
| Financial statement preparation | Legal compliance examination |

## PROFESSIONAL ACHIEVEMENTS

- Implemented payroll upgrades resulting in *increased payroll processing efficiency and accountability* by allowing department managers to input hours.
- *Corrected $3 million in errors* through identifying and debugging problems with the purchasing and accounts payable invoice matching system.
- *Improved accuracy, efficiency and overall effectiveness* of accounting month-end journals by implementing computerized systems combined with complex Excel workbooks.
- *Enhanced interdepartmental communications* through the development and implementation of training guides and programs in support of non-accounting personnel, including engineers, planning/schedulers, clerks and managers. Topics included sales tax issues, construction in progress, fixed-asset additions and disposals.
- *Strengthened the auditing division* by applying procedures and experience gained in national accounting firms and various small businesses.

## PROFESSIONAL EXPERIENCE

*University of Texas, Austin, Texas*                                        *2003–Present*
**ADJUNCT INSTRUCTOR**
- ❖ Teach college-level accounting classes: Intermediate II, Cost and Budget.
- ❖ Research, document and implement strategies for increased learning retention.
- ❖ Draft and present class content outline for College Dean approval.
- ❖ Lead students to master accounting concepts through formal and informal review/grading sessions.
- ❖ Incorporate "hands-on" industry application examples from professional experience.
- ❖ Mentor, counsel and guide students in career options that include the accounting profession.

*(continued)*

*(continued)*

## MARY W. KINGSTON—CPA, MBA
—Page Two—

*Brackenridge Hospital, Austin, Texas*                                          2000–2002
**DIRECTOR OF ACCOUNTING**
- ❖ Managed a staff of seven direct reports, including an accounting supervisor and six administrative personnel.
- ❖ Planned, organized and directed the functions of the accounting department, including accounts payable, payroll, general ledger and financial statement preparation; set goals and objectives for the department at all levels; partnered with the Assistant Administrator of Finance and Administration on special projects; managed outside vendors and auditors.
- ❖ Converted all accounting worksheets from Lotus to Excel and implemented improvements.

*Hays County Community Hospital, San Marcos, Texas*                             2000–2000
**ACCOUNTANT and CFO**
- ❖ Developed procedures to track business office collections, posting and balancing.
- ❖ Trained and coached staff in procedures designed to improve accuracy and efficiency.
- ❖ Prepared financial statements by developing Excel spreadsheets to document work.

*TP Chemicals, San Marcos, Texas*                                               1988–1999
**ACOUNTANT III**
- ❖ Maintained financial books, prepared financial reports, mentored and coached accounting department personnel, provided support to Controller and enhanced the effectiveness and efficiency of the department.
- ❖ Supported, mentored, trained and delegated accounting activities to clerical help to expand their skills/abilities and to improve their self worth and value to the company.
- ❖ Developed concepts and procedures; analyzed, debugged and resolved general ledger interfaces with computerized work order/purchasing system and project accounting system.
- ❖ Prepared timely monthly accruals and reversals; posted interfaces, including inventories, work orders, construction in progress, fixed assets; closed timely the financial books, prepared and issued monthly financial reports for efficient and effective operation of the plant.

*State of Colorado, Denver, Colorado*                                           1986–1988
**EXAMINER OF PUBLIC ACCOUNTS**
- ❖ Performed financial audits and prepared financial statements for county school boards and county commissioners. Performed legal compliance examination for judges of probate, tax assessors and tax collectors.

## EDUCATION and TRAINING

Masters of Business Administration, University of Texas, Austin, Texas, 1993
Bachelor of Science in Accounting, Cum Laude, University of Colorado, Denver, Colorado, 1974

Microsoft Word/Excel * WordPerfect * Lotus Quicken * Quick Books Pro * AS400 Query

## AFFILIATES AND MEMBERSHIPS

Professional Association of Certified Public Accountants (PACPA)
CPA—Colorado and Texas
Texas Association of CPAs
Treasurer, Mission of Hope Recovery Outreach, Inc.

## Barbers, Cosmetologists, and Other Personal Appearance Workers

### EVA RAMIREZ

7704 Greenland Place • Powell, Ohio 43065
Home: 614-237-9671 • Cellular: 614-294-4544
Email: eva@sevilla.com

### COSMETIC SUPPLY TERRITORY MANAGEMENT • COSMETIC ARTISTRY

Cosmetology Techniques/Methods • Mask Applications • Facial Spa Equipment • Maneuvers • Manipulations

**Customer-oriented cosmetology professional** with valuable blend of business ownership and management experience combined with noticeable talent in esthetic skin care leading to customers' enhanced appearance and well-being. Utilize history as licensed **Cosmetologist, Manager and Instructor** to propel all facets of client care, organizational management and strategic planning agendas. Extremely well organized, dedicated and resourceful, with ability to guide operations and associates to **technique improvements, maximized productivity and bottom-line increase.**

### AREAS OF STRENGTH

- Relationship Building • Customer Service •
- Time Management • Creative/Strategic Selling •
- Follow-Up • Merchandising/Promotion •
- Relationship Management •
- Product Introduction • Inventory Management •
- Expense Control • Vendor Negotiations •
- Client Needs Analysis •

### EDUCATION

TIFFIN ACADEMY OF COSMETOLOGY ... Tiffin, Ohio
• Cosmetology • Manager • Instructor •
Licenses

TIFFIN ACADEMY OF HAIR DESIGN ... Tiffin, Ohio
Graduate in Hair Design

### SEMINARS & SPECIALIZED TRAINING

Continuing Education Units
(to meet requirements of 8 credits annually)

Certificate of Achievement for Advanced Basic
Esthetics and Spa Therapies, August 2004

Several seminars held by various cosmetic
associations

### ADDITIONAL BACKGROUND

**The Hair Place** ... Dublin, Ohio
Manager of Licensed Cosmetologists
(1993–1996)

**Beverly Hills Salons** ... Worthington, Ohio
Licensed Cosmetologist
(1990–1993)

### PROFESSIONAL CAREER

**PRINCESS SALONS** ... Powell, Ohio (1996 to Present)
*Full-service and independent customized hair, nails and tanning boutique positioned in strip mall (suburban locale) setting; operations staffed by 5 employees, contractors and technicians.*

**Owner/General Manager**
**Administered entire scope of operations while simultaneously contributing as cosmetologist in one station of four-station salon.** As single owner of small business, administered profits and losses, undertook all facets of decision making, strategically guiding salon operations and productivity, and assumed complete responsibility for revenue performance.

Management responsibilities included cosmetic/accessories sales, customer service and client management, accounting and finance, associate development/management, regulation compliance, business/operations legal requisites, retail merchandising and advertising, inventory procurement and control, vendor relationships, contract negotiations, booth rental contracts and leases to licensed cosmetologists and nail technicians.

→ **Successfully conceived and launched full scale of operations** and guided business to strong reputation for quality output of product and services; consistently met challenges of market conditions and business atmosphere to persevere throughout 8 years of ownership.

→ **Maintained operating costs at lowest possible point by reducing inventory and labor hours during seasonal periods.** Also negotiated with vendors to secure better pricing for goods and services.

→ **Facilitated revenue increase by bringing in cosmetic line to enhance product offering to clients.**

→ **Recognized opportunity to supplement revenue** and spearheaded remodel of existing tanning space to provide for salon.

→ **Expanded market visibility by becoming member of Powell Chamber of Commerce.**

→ **Modified policies and procedures to ensure employee compliance with changing licensing regulations.**

→ **Worked in concert with American Cancer Society to provide styling services to cancer patients** with aim of improving appearance, outlook, confidence and self-esteem.

## Computer Scientists and Database Administrators

# DAVID SUZUKI

Email: davidsuzuki@yahoo.com

145 West Rosecliff Court
Saukville, WI 53080

Office: (414) 629-3676
Res: (262) 344-3449

## TECHNICAL PROFILE

A dedicated and loyal systems professional with 20+ years of hands-on experience as a **database administrator and application developer.** Solid understanding of relational databases. Excellent design, coding, and testing skills. Strong oral and written communication abilities.

| | |
|---|---|
| Databases: | DB2, Oracle, SQL |
| Languages: | COBOL, IBM/AS, Visual Basic |
| Operating Systems: | VM, UNIX, DOS, Windows 98 and XP |
| Third-Party Software: | COGNOS, Impromptu, Informatica, Microsoft Access |

## PROFESSIONAL EXPERIENCE

**Midwest Staffing Inc.,** Milwaukee, WI                                     1984 to Present
   *(A global employment services organization with annual sales in excess of $10 billion.)*

**LEAD DATABASE ADMINISTRATOR AND DEVELOPER**
Lead mainframe and Oracle database administrator with 24/7 responsibility for performance, tuning, recovery, and planning. Use various utilities to transfer data to other platforms and build tables/indexes. Respond to end users' requests for information and resolve discrepancies in data reports. Research and interact with vendors in the purchase of third-party software. Train and supervise assistant DBAs. Write user manuals, operating procedures, and internal documentation.

Selected Database Development Projects and Achievements:

- Administer mission-critical payroll and billing database that bills $5+ million per week.
- Designed, developed, and implemented Oracle databank—a duplicate of the mainframe databank. End users now have greater access to data using desktop tools.
- Developed and maintain franchise fee billing application.
- Developed Central Billing consolidation application that bills $5 million per month.
- Researched and recommended purchase of ETL Informatica PowerMart utility. Data movement to the data repository, the Internet, and databases is now accomplished in one step. Previously, data movement involved large amounts of development time.
- Developed mainframe processes using the ESSCON Channel (high-speed data transfer) to move data from the mainframe to the AIX platform. Compared to the old method using Outbound, this has reduced data transfer time by at least 50%.
- Selected by management to train assistant database administrator. Assistant is now a reliable backup on mainframe-related database issues.

## EDUCATION

**Oracle and Oracle Tuning,** Certificate Courses, University of Wisconsin—Milwaukee, 2003

## Construction Laborers

# Mark A. Benton

520 E. Ogden Avenue • Naperville, Illinois 06060 • 000–983–8882

### PROFILE

#### Focus: Laborer position in the construction industry

Excel in troubleshooting and problem solving, readily understand instructions of a complicated nature, and respond to challenges with a "get the job done" attitude. Grasp client's requirements and management's needs quickly and apply appropriate actions to complete tasks in a timely manner. Constantly seeking new and more effective methods for performing professional duties. Working knowledge of Microsoft Windows and Word. Focused on personal and professional growth.

### EXPERIENCE SUMMARY

- **Tradesman/Warehouseman/Laborer:** Light carpentry, painting, window preparations, frame building, shipping and receiving, loading of building supplies, use of various power tools and forklift operator.
- **Housekeeping Technician:** General housekeeping for one of the largest hotels in Chicago. Responsible for servicing up to 20 floors.
- **Building Services Technician:** General office cleaning, horizontal and vertical dusting, stripping/buffing of floors and restroom maintenance. Provided office security.
- **Security:** Ensured safe, clean and proper order of facility.
- **Administrative Support Technician:** Setup and maintenance of administrative files; answering and routing of phone calls; typing file labels, memos and letters using Microsoft Word. Copying and faxing documents, sorting incoming mail and preparing outgoing mail.

### RELATED SKILLS

- Forklift Operator—Certified
- Computer Training and Enhancement
- Building Maintenance Services
- Equipment Maintenance Training

### EMPLOYMENT HISTORY

**Inventory/Receiving/Laborer,** M&P Construction, Chicago, IL (02/01–Present)

**Quality Control Coordinator,** Teracotta Data Systems, Inc., Chicago, IL (04/99–02/01)

**Laborer,** Western and Block Construction, Chicago, IL (04/92–04/99)

**Laborer,** Buillion Construction/Cook County Hospital, Chicago, IL (01/89–04/92)

**Housekeeper,** Holiday Inn, Chicago, IL (03/86–01/89)

**Warehouseman/Mover/Loader/Driver,** We Move You, Chicago, IL (05/83–03/86)

**Security,** Your Answering Service, Bedford Park, IL (08/80–05/83)

### EDUCATION

New Cycle Ministries, Inc., Chicago, Illinois. **Computer Training & Enhancement. 2004 Graduate**
Chicago High School, Chicago, Illinois. **1980 Graduate**

## Dental Assistants

# Carol A. Weiss
DENTAL ASSISTANT

62482 110<sup>th</sup> Avenue S., Federal Way, WA 99999     (000) 000-0000     email: cweiss@resume.com

## PROFILE:

More than 25 years of Dental Assistant experience in meeting high infection-control standards, sterilizing and disinfecting instruments and equipment, preparing tray setup for dental procedures, and instructing patients on postoperative and general oral health care.

- ➤ **Supervised** two Dental Assistants.
- ➤ Trained in **product knowledge** (bonding, impression materials, and more).
- ➤ Experienced in working with all ages of people, from small children to senior citizens.
- ➤ **Managed office,** ensuring that it was organized, clean, fully stocked, and prepared daily.
- ➤ Worked in a **lab** within the same facility, making any shade changes or polishing of dentures, crowns, and bridge work.
- ➤ Caring, detailed-oriented, hard worker who has learned different state-of-the-art dentistry styles, **procedures, and techniques.** Always seeks ways to keep skills current.

## SUMMARY OF QUALIFICATIONS:

- ▶ Root canal treatment
- ▶ Air particle machines
- ▶ Polishing of all fillings
- ▶ Soft and hard relines
- ▶ Rubber dam replacement
- ▶ Crown and bridge preparation and delivery
- ▶ Composite and amalgam fillings
- ▶ Denture and partial procedures
- ▶ Assisted with multiple extractions
- ▶ Took full-series radiographs and panolipse radiographs

## OFFICE SKILLS:

- ▶ Windows, DOS, MS Office (Word, Excel, PowerPoint), word processing, spreadsheets, databases, Ex-Change+, Internet (Netscape, Explorer), email.
- ▶ Typewriter, word processor, copier, calculator, fax machine, printers, multiline phone systems
- ▶ Records management, medical terminology, healthcare plan knowledge, billing codes

## PROFESSIONAL EXPERIENCE:

| | |
|---|---|
| Dr. Ronald McPherson, DDS—Federal Way, WA<br>Dental Assistant | 2001–Current |
| Dr. D. Maynard Debus, DDS—Federal Way, WA<br>Dental Assistant | 1999–2001 |
| Dr. Larry W. Howard, DDS—Federal Way, WA<br>Dental Assistant | 1999 (temp) |
| Dr. Abel D. Sanchez, DDS—Federal Way, WA<br>Dental Assistant | 1979–1989 |

**Engineers**

# JILL KEATING

51 Gibbs Lane • Farmingville, NY 11738
631.555.5555 (H) • 631.555.5555 (C) • jkeating@yahoo.com

## ENGINEERING PROFILE

*Track record of success in the design and delivery of advanced technology solutions.*

Accomplished, technically sophisticated Engineer with extensive experience in the oversight, planning, design, and delivery of diverse mechanical systems and devices. Offer special expertise in the manufacture and design of industrial automation solutions. Possess track record of waste and cost reductions, cycle time and process improvements, and system enhancements arising from effective use of Lean Manufacturing and related techniques. Manage, coordinate, train, and evaluate performance of cross-functional and multidisciplinary teams. Maintain high standards and promote team participation for the attainment of company goals. *Highlights of Expertise:*

- Project/Program Management
- Lean Manufacturing Principles
- Supply Chain Administration
- Customer/Vendor Relationships

- Product Lifecycle Management
- Pneumatic & Electromechanical Devices
- Business Management Systems
- Multidisciplinary Team Management

- Production Planning
- ISO & UL Compliance
- Staff Management
- HR Administration

*Technical Proficiencies:*

Certifications: ISO Auditor Certification, UL Certification

Tools: Visual Basic, Tour de Force (TDF), Siemens S7 300, Allen Bradley RS Logix 500, PanelBuilder 32, PanelView, Automation Direct (Koyo), Device Net, UltraWare, Festo SPC200, FST4.02, AB 6200, ICOM PLC2/PLC5, Wonderware MMI, SAP R/3, WinTelligent, AutoCAD 2005, RS Logix 500, Device Net/EthernetIP, Uniop Designer, UltraWare, AutoQuoter, Deflection Calculator, Wmermoc, MS Office Suite/MS Project

## PROFESSIONAL EXPERIENCE

AUTOMATION CENTRAL, INC., Amherst, MA                    2006–Present

**Sales Engineer**

Sell industrial automation solutions, including pneumatics, machine and motion control devices, sensors, air compressors, vacuum pumps, and associated products. Evaluate and suggest product and service solutions in line with client needs and requirements. Orchestrate conferences to assess and implement product and service enhancements. Utilize MS Outlook-based Tour de Force (TDF) and associated software to manage client relationships and for enterprise-wide reporting. Generate and submit weekly project status and progress reports to senior-level management to support business directives.

**Key Contribution:**

- Boosted potentiality of securing high-value client account through superior sales and relationship-building skills, greatly advancing organizational objectives.

PETRI CORPORATION, Smithtown, NY                    1995–2006

**Engineering & Project Supervisor, Automated Systems Division** (2002–2006)

Directed 8-member engineering and drafting team in the design and manufacture of industrial automation solutions. Provided full product lifecycle administration, including resource, material, and time management; created and maintained production and engineering Master Schedules to execute directives. Administered department-wide ISO procedural compliance, providing instruction to

*…continued…*

*(continued)*

*(continued)*

## JILL KEATING • Page 2

engineering and drafting teams on relevant standards and protocols. Coordinated with clients, vendors, and cross-functional teams to optimize communications in support of project directives. Negotiated and consulted with clients on project design, specifications, pricing, and delivery.

**Key Contributions:**

- Successfully managed multimillion-dollar projects, regularly exceeding customer expectations through on-time, within-budget project delivery of high-quality products and services.
- Utilized Lean Manufacturing principles to reduce costs and improve on-time delivery by 20%.
- Enhanced design review process by improving interdepartmental communications through the standardization of blueprints and related documentation.
- Improved output by effectively coordinating manufacturing production and documentation processes, as well as enhancing test fixture design.
- Effectively reconciled competing cross-functional team interests to accelerate production time by hundreds of hours.
- Provided full project lifecycle management of one of the company's largest projects in ten years, motivating staff for enhanced efficiency and a 300% increase in output.

**Senior Project Engineer, Integrated Systems Unit** (1995–2002)

Conceptualized and designed electrical and electro/pneumatic control panels and servo control systems for automation and handling equipment, utilizing in-house and vendor-based PLC controls and programming features. Used ERP, Excel, and related software systems to administer product lifecycle production schedules and operational sequences. Communicated with cross-functional teams to facilitate smooth operations. Produced client instruction manuals providing/describing BOM, schematics, testing procedures, and operational cycles.

**Key Contributions:**

- Developed and implemented valuable product-line improvements.
- Successfully launched and administered ISO and UL safety compliance standards and procedures, instructing and monitoring cross-functional teams on relevant standards and protocols.

** ** **

*Prior Experience as Senior Engineer for Shimada Corporation of Manorville, NY*

### EDUCATION AND TRAINING

**Master of Science Degree in Technological Systems Management**
STONY BROOK UNIVERSITY, Stony Brook, NY

**Bachelor of Science Degree in Mechanical Engineering**
NEW YORK INSTITUTE OF TECHNOLOGY, Old Westbury, NY

*Professional Development*
Signature Training Program for Supervisors / Certificate of Achievement

## Food and Beverage Serving and Related Workers

---

# *Valerie W. Butler*

333 S.E. Riveredge Drive • Vancouver, Washington 33333

222-222-2222 *cell*                                                          *home* 555-555-5555

---

### *Server*

---

### *Professional Profile*

Energetic and highly motivated *Food Server* with extensive experience in the food service industry. Expertise lies in working with the fine dining restaurant, providing top quality service, and maintaining a professional demeanor. Solid knowledge of the restaurant business, with strengths in excellent customer service and food and wine recommendations.

Get along well with management, coworkers, and customers. Well-developed communication skills. Known as a caring and intuitive "people person," with an upbeat and positive attitude. Highly flexible, honest, and punctual, with the ability to stay calm and focused in stressful situations. Committed to a job well done and a long-term career.

---

### *Outstanding Achievements & Recommendations*

• Served notable VIP clientele, including clients associated with Murdock Charitable Trust.
• History of repeat and new customers requesting my service as their waitress.
• Known for creating an atmosphere of enjoyment and pleasure for the customer.

*"...Valerie was warm, friendly, kind, and very efficient.*
*We didn't feel rushed. She handled our requests, and*
*we appreciated her genuine 'May I please you' attitude...."*

---

### *Related Work History*

**Waitress • Banquets** • Heathman Lodge • Vancouver, Washington • *2002–present*
*Northwest seasonal cuisine.*

**Banquets** • Dolce Skamania Lodge • Stevenson, Washington • *2001–2002*
*Casual fine-dining restaurant.*

**Waitress** • Hidden House • Vancouver, Washington • *1993–2001*
*Exclusive fine-dining restaurant.*

**Waitress** • Multnomah Falls Lodge Restaurant • Corbett, Oregon • *1992–1993*
*Historic Columbia Gorge Falls restaurant serving authentic Northwestern cuisine.*

**Waitress** • The Ahwahnee at Yosemite National Park • California • *1 year*
*World-renowned, award-winning fine-dining restaurant—sister lodge to Timberline Lodge.*

## Human Resources, Training, and Labor Relations Managers and Specialists

# AARON WALKER
5 Linden Avenue, Roslyn, NY 11576 ▪ aaronwalker00@aol.com
*residence* 555-555-5555 ▪ *cellular* 555-555-5555

## HUMAN RESOURCES PROFESSIONAL
### PHR CERTIFICATE
*Seeking a Generalist Role*

*Emphasis on:*

Recruitment & Staffing • HRIS • Training & Development

Compensation • Salary Structures • Benefits Administration

Workforce Reengineering & Change Management • Job Task Analysis

Performance Appraisals • Employee Retention • Employee Communications

## PROFESSIONAL EXPERIENCE

COMPUTER ASSOCIATES, Islandia, NY                                         2002–Present
**Human Resources Specialist** (2003–Present)
**Human Resources Generalist**\* (2003)
**Human Resources Associate** (2002–2003)

\**Selected for rotational assignments as a leave replacement for other HR staff members.*

▪▪▪

### HR Generalist Responsibilities and Achievements

Supported and provided HR-related guidance to general-management teams at two newly acquired facilities with a combined staff of approximately 130 employees.

- Contributed to a five-person team charged with establishing and implementing yearly **salary increases.**
- Managed a **job-reclassification project.** Conducted occupational research to determine if job titles were in sync with workplace norms.
- Assisted with **employee-performance** issues. Wrote disciplinary reports and developed a strategy for resolution.
- Reviewed **applicant résumés** and collaborated on **new-hire offers.**
- Tackled the **I-9 recertification** of approximately 2800 employees at 12 locations. Through research, identified all employees whose paperwork was deficient. Trained support staff and line managers in proper documentation, which rectified oversights expediently and improved I-9 administration going forward.
- Articulated **corporate policies and procedures** to employees seeking clarification regarding payroll, disability, terminations, leaves of absence, and COBRA coverage issues.
- Authored a policies and procedures document to address the sometimes-confusing hiring categories of "rehires" and "reinstatements." Created and delivered **PowerPoint presentations** to the HR community, which, together with the written document, served as clarification on this issue.
- Regularly conducted the "benefits" portion of **new-hire orientations.** In one-hour sessions, provided information to 50+ employees.
- Participated in the **campus recruitment** program. Attended college fairs and **interviewed candidates** for internships and entry-level positions.
- Processed **employee data** for new hires and terminations.

*Continued...*

**AARON WALKER**

Page Two

## HRIS Responsibilities and Achievements

- Identified a significant administrative challenge regarding the inaccuracy of employee time-off accrual plans. Rectified the problem by creating an Access database linked to Lawson HRIS, which accurately provided the needed data.
- Designed, developed, and brought to fruition approximately 30 HRIS audits to ensure the accuracy of employee records. Defined audit parameters for compliance with federal, state, and company policies. Created numerous HRIS ad hoc reports as requested by the HR community and line managers.
- Improved the administration of employee sabbaticals by creating HRIS automation tools. In so doing, decreased processing time by approximately 50%.
- Represented HR Services during a company wide Lawson system upgrade. As project manager, identified and advocated for the unique needs of the HR Services function. During implementation, served as trainer to the department's staff.

**DEVELOPMENTAL DISABILITIES INSTITUTE,** Brookville, NY                    1999–2002
**Residential Manager** (2001–2002)
**Assistant Residential Manager** (2000–2001)
**Direct Care Counselor** (1999–2000)

- As residential manager, oversaw 20 direct-care counselors and one assistant supervisor.
- Hired approximately 15 direct-care counselors, all of whom became good employees. More than half were rated "exceptional."
- Developed and implemented a staff-training program that provided enhanced quality of care to residents and contributed to a reduction in employee attrition.
- Conducted in-depth analyses of residents' skills and abilities. Set appropriate skill goals based on present functional status. Instilled motivation to reach objectives.

### EDUCATIONAL CREDENTIALS

**Master of Business Administration,** 2005. Hofstra University, Uniondale, NY

**Bachelor of Arts,** Psychology, 1999. Muhlenberg College, Allentown, PA

**Professional in Human Resources (PHR) Certificate,** 2003. Pace University, New York, NY
Workforce Planning & Employment, Performance Management, Compensation & Benefits,
Employee & Labor Relations, Occupational Health, Safety & Security,
Organizational Structure, Ethical & Legislative Issues

### TECHNICAL SKILLS

Lawson HRIS System, Windows, Word, Excel, PowerPoint, Outlook, and Access

### PROFESSIONAL AFFILIATION

Member, Society for Human Resource Management (SHRM)

∎∎∎

## Paralegals and Legal Assistants

# PATRICIA JUHASZ

555 Riddle Avenue • Smithtown, NY 55555 • (888) 999-0000 • Pjuhasz@telcomm.net

## *Legal Assistant/Paralegal Assistant*

Experienced Legal Assistant with excellent office management and client-attorney relation skills seeking an entry-level Paralegal Assistant position where a working knowledge of legal terminology, general law, and legal proceedings, and continuing education in Paralegal Studies will be utilized and expanded. Bring experience working within a Legal Department/Collection Agency environment in the following select areas:

*Civil Litigation...Collections...Settlements...Affidavits...Skip Tracing...Attorney Sourcing & Selection Bankruptcies...Judgments...Liens...Summons & Complaint...Estate Searches...Statute of Limitations*

## PROFESSIONAL EXPERIENCE

**Legal Assistant,** Legal Recoveries, Inc., Lake Grove, NY                                     1998–present

Joined this Collection Agency's legal department at a time of unit-wide staffing changes. Responsible for managing a high volume of civil litigation case files for major accounts that partially included Century Detection, Credit Union of New York, AB Bank National Association, and St. Mary's Hospital.

- Collaborate extensively with internal departments including collections, medical billing, finance, production, special projects, and clerical to obtain, verify, and process documentation pertaining to the status of more than 50 weekly referred collections cases forwarded to the legal department.
- Carefully source and select nationally based bonded attorneys utilizing the *American Lawyers Quarterly, Commercial Bar Directory, National Directory List,* and *Columbia Directory List;* determine the appropriate choice upon obtainment and review of résumés, copies of insurance policies, and court filing fees.
- Perform estate searches and integrate traditional investigative methods and the DAKCS database system to gather account histories and case-sensitive documentation for attorneys including *debtors and guarantors, credit bureau reports, court affidavits, judgments, skip-tracing records, bankruptcy notices, banking statements, proof of statute of limitations, proof of assets, and trial letters.*
- Maintain communications with attorneys and clients from point of referral/discovery to trial phase to facilitate and expedite case settlements that historically award clients a minimum of 80% in recovered funds.

## EDUCATION

**Bachelor of Science in Paralegal Studies, 1998**
ST. JOSEPH'S COLLEGE, Brentwood, NY

## COMPUTER SKILLS

DOS/Windows 2000; WordPerfect and Microsoft Word; DAKCS

## EARLIER WORK HISTORY

| | |
|---|---|
| **Administrative Assistant,** State Insurance, Patchogue, NY | 1997–1998 |
| **Office Support Assistant,** Financial Association of America, Inc., Islip, NY | 1995–1997 |
| **Appointment Coordinator,** Phlebotomy Services, Huntington, NY | 1991–1996 |
| **Senior Office Support Assistant,** AB National Bank, Hicksville, NY | 1986–1991 |

*Professional References Provided upon Request*

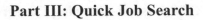

## Loan Officers

# Simon K. Pastor

21 George Drive
Syosset, New York 11791
**516.555.5555**
skp@optonline.net

Strong communication and interpersonal abilities, effective marketing and presentation skills;
goal-oriented individual with a history of proven results.

## Experience:

**Direct Mortgage Corporation, Hicksville, New York**
**Mortgage Division Loan Officer,** November 2003 through Present

- Manage loan process from prequalification through closing; research, create and distribute loan proposals for all clients, including but not limited to analyzing financial and risk assessments, satisfaction of loan requirements and sufficient payment schedule.
- Ensure that all loan documentation is submitted in a timely manner to guarantee efficient closings for all clients.
- Responsible for soliciting prospective clients via cold calling, networking with Realtors and implementing unique marketing programs/promotions.
- Develop and manage solid working relationships with Realtors, processors, underwriters and closers.
- Expert knowledge of principles of credit, income and appraisal guidelines.
- Order titles, appraisals, credit, payoff letters, insurance certificates and subordination agreements.

**Colonial Corporation, Manhasset, New York**
**Mortgage Loan Consultant,** August 2002 through November 2003

- Researched and developed loan proposals through a variety of third-party vendors for purchase or refinance of residential and commercial properties.
- Evaluated client's risk assessment; analyzed if prospective client met the lending institution requirements.
- Responsible for the solicitation of residential first and second mortgages through networking with Realtors, builders and developers.
- Cultivated and maintained exemplary relationships with third-party vendors, processors and underwriters.

**GMZ Company, Flushing, New York**
**Operations Officer,** March 1980 through July 2002

- Strategically enhanced customer service and company profitability through the effective management of all operational functions for a small chain of wholesale/retail footwear/sportswear establishments.
- Ordered and distributed merchandise for both wholesale and retail operations.
- Developed inventory control and quality assurance procedures and implemented shrinkage reduction strategies.
- Managed accounts receivable, accounts payable, payroll, banking and financial and tax reporting.
- Responsible for managing all phases of human resources, including interviewing potential candidates for hire, selecting employees for promotion or dismissal and implementing company health care plan.
- Successfully fostered solid working relationships with vendors, sales representatives and wholesale customers.

## Computer Skills:

Microsoft Windows, Excel, PowerPoint, Access; Microsoft Works; Microsoft Money; Lotus 123; expert knowledge of Internet Explorer and Netscape Navigator browsers

## Education:

**Adelphi University, Garden City, New York**
Course work completed in Sociology, 1980

---

## Sales Representatives, Wholesale and Manufacturing

*READY TO RELOCATE TO THE **SEATTLE** AREA*

### Charles W. Broadway

4200 Centre Street   Montgomery, Alabama 36100   cbroad555@aol.com   ☎ 334.555.5555

### WHAT I CAN OFFER **TopLine** AS YOUR NEWEST **SALES PROFESSIONAL**

- ○ Penetrating and holding **new markets,**

- ○ Gathering and leveraging **sales intelligence** faster than our competition,

- ○ Mastering our customers' business so well we **anticipate** their **needs,**

- ○ Putting together "win-win" sales deals that yield **enduring profits,**

- ○ Communicating so powerfully that **sales** are **closed** — at every level from shop floor to boardroom, and

- ○ **Managing risk** prudently.

### RECENT WORK HISTORY WITH EXAMPLES OF PROBLEMS SOLVED

- ○ *Hired away by the CEO to be* **Sales Development Manager** *and then promoted over four more experienced eligibles to be* **Sales Director,** Arista Corporation, Montgomery, Alabama                                                                     Oct 04 to Present
  *Arista is the world's largest auto transmission manufacturer.*

  Supervise three regional sales managers directly. Lead a territory that covers all of America east of the Mississippi River and portions of Canada. Build and defend a travel budget of $400K. My district generates $45M in annual sales.

  Chosen by the President to **guide us into a new market** dominated by four tough competitors. Found, and really listened to, all potential customers. Identified our market niche. Then made the calls that led to **20 presentations nationwide,** many at presidential levels. *Payoffs:* **From $0 sales to $3.5M** in sales in just 16 months.

  **Moved faster than our competition** to discover an RFP before it hit the street. When none of our products met this customer's needs, **put together a win-win deal** that shared both risks and profits. *Payoffs:* When I showed our customer's CEO how I could **save him $2M** over the life of the contract, I **won a $4M contract for us.**

  Used polite persistence to **"steal" a customer from a competitor** who had served them for a decade. Soon uncovered our competitor's weakness. **Carefully timed and executed "cold calls"** on the right people. *Payoffs:* By appealing right to their specific needs, brought in **$8M** in the last two years alone.

  Saw opportunity a potential customer missed — even after he awarded his contract to another company. Tracked our competitor's performance right up until contract renewal. *Payoffs:* My presentation, made on the same day as other firms, carried the **sale: $4M** over several years — even though we weren't the lowest bidder.

*More indicators of performance* **TopLine** *can use ☞*

Charles Broadway      **Sales Professional**      334.555.5555

Uncovered an unmet need in a major market. Worked with the customer and a manufacturer to design a new product. Persuaded our leadership to invest $200K in the prototype I knew we would need for the competition. *Payoffs:* **Won a $14M sale and took away our competitor's dominance** in this market.

Picked up the signs that a competitor's customer wasn't happy, and then found out why. Got a 100-percent response to our needs-analysis survey to define the best new product for the market. *Payoffs:* **Profit margin up** four percent—**double the industry average.** My methods became the **corporate standard** for customer analysis.

○  Plant Manager, Plantar Corporation, Montgomery, Alabama      May 98 to Sep 04

○  **Sales Manager for Business Products,** Mylar Corporation, Montgomery, Alabama
Mar 96 to May 98

## EDUCATION & PROFESSIONAL DEVELOPMENT

○  MPA, Auburn University—Montgomery, Montgomery, Alabama      00

○  BS, Troy State University, Troy, Alabama      96
*Earned this degree working 10 hours a week.*

○  Instructed classes in Value Analysis for Product Improvement and Cost of Sales
96 to 98

*Selected from five more experienced professionals to teach these six-week courses, preparing 100 sales professionals to represent up to ten different products.*

## IT SKILLS

○  Expert in proprietary **sales, billing, and customer contact software** suite; proficient in Outlook, Word, Excel, PowerPoint, and Internet search methods

## Secretaries and Administrative Assistants

# CARA WAVERLY

58 Chelsea Way  •  Bridgeport, CT 22222  •  (333) 333-3333  •  cara@aol.com

*Executive-level administrative support professional whose accomplishments reflect excellent administrative skills and a demonstrated commitment to providing exemplary service*

### SUMMARY OF QUALIFICATIONS

- Capable executive assistant with extensive experience in administrative roles.
- Organized and detail-oriented with demonstrated project coordination skills. Practiced in prioritizing and managing tasks. Effective at balancing the competing demands of multiple projects.
- Excellent interpersonal skills. Able to develop easy rapport with others while building trust.
- Versatile and resourceful team player who is willing to do whatever is necessary to complete goals and meet deadlines. Polished and professional, yet warm and accommodating.
- Recognized "go-to" person for a broad range of issues and concerns.
- Committed to providing the highest levels of customer service.

### PROFESSIONAL EXPERIENCE

PETPHARMA CORP., Bridgeport, Connecticut                          2001 to present

**Administrative Assistant**

As lead administrative assistant, provide effective support to VP of Global Marketing, VP of International Operations, and three other managers. Handle administrative details such as maintaining calendars, making travel arrangements, scheduling meetings, and coordinating conferences.

#### Administrative Leadership

- Established strong record in developing best practices for administrative support. Proactively provide support, looking beyond immediate need to maximize effectiveness.
- Hired as first administrative assistant in newly relocated group; developed and documented group processes and procedures. Trained and mentored new administrative assistants.
- Developed administrative checklist for new hires, ensuring smooth transition for more than 20 new employees.
- Implemented filing system for all product-related literature, creating easy-to-use resource for customer inquiries. Also developed individual product binders for each sales rep.
- Effectively support group training efforts by developing manuals and presentations, and scheduling and facilitating training sessions.
- Consistently explore lower-cost options in keeping with company's "Smart Initiatives."

#### Project Coordination

- Successfully arranged numerous domestic and international conferences, effectively planning and coordinating events for groups of more than 100 people.
- Oversaw all administrative details to ensure flawless events. Booked all facilities, negotiating favorable pricing. Made travel arrangements and scheduled ground transportation for all attendees. Generated handouts and purchased gifts and awards. Shipped materials to site, meeting all project timetables.
- Implemented effective follow-up system to ensure all projects and tasks remain on schedule.
- Effectively supported Transition Team, collecting and collating staff résumés for timely presentation to management.

CARA WAVERLY                                                                                    PAGE 2

PETPHARMA CORP., Westport, Connecticut                                          1998 to 2001

**Administrative Assistant**

Provided effective administrative support for Customer Development, Sales Training, and Sales Operations groups following relocation. Maintained all personnel and customer files.

- Developed guidelines and procedures for administrative assistants. Documented procedures for new hires.
- Established and managed system to track broker payments.
- Developed process for customer scorecarding, following up with clients to determine satisfaction with products, delivery times, and customer service. Developed spreadsheet to record and track response.
- Maintained divisional "dashboard"—a prominent display that tracked key performance measures and staff awards.
- Successfully planned and coordinated large-scale conferences and sales meetings.

BOYD, INC., Mullica Hill, New Jersey                                             1992 to 1998

**Executive Secretary**

Assisted president and controller in managing International Division. Prepared all correspondence and assisted in preparing all confidential salary reviews, business plans, budgets, and presentations.

- Organized office, setting up effective filing systems and archiving old files.
- Developed and implemented more efficient procedures for office operations.
- Effectively organized numerous conferences and sales meetings.
- Served as Board Member for Boyd's Federal Credit Union in addition to regular duties.

**Corporate Flight Coordinator**

Assisted Manager of Flight Operations and scheduled flights for corporate executives.

- As first full-time coordinator, set up effective scheduling system to accommodate increasing demand for flight services.

UNITED CHEMICALS, Clifton, New Jersey                                           1985 to 1992

**Administrative Assistant**

Assisted Region Administrative Manager, providing support in the area of marketing, administration, office services, information systems, and annual planning activities.

- Gathered background information for reports and special projects.
- Coordinated and scheduled system usage, enforcing region guidelines. Mobilized system specialists to handle problems and requests.
- Provided instruction for all software packages.

## COMPUTER SKILLS

Word ◆ Excel ◆ PowerPoint ◆ Outlook ◆ Internet ◆ E-mail
DCIS (database for sales reporting)

*References Available Upon Request*

## Teachers—Preschool, Kindergarten, Elementary, Middle, and Secondary

# JUDY CASSIDY

724 West South Street
Philadelphia, PA 19110
215-745-3372 ▪ judyc@aol.com

## PROFILE

ELEMENTARY EDUCATOR with more than 20 years of experience fostering academic learning and enhancing critical-thinking abilities. Incorporate effective cooperative learning techniques and unique classroom management style to establish creative and stimulating classroom environment. Dedicated, resourceful teacher skilled in building rapport and respect with students and student teachers.

Honored with **New Teacher Mentor Award** for Outstanding Service (2004).

*"Miss Cassidy is an exceptional teacher. She is respectful to and of her students, and that respect is reciprocated. Using a variety of materials and techniques, Miss Cassidy challenges her students to excel. Her classroom is a warm, nurturing atmosphere where children are called to be their best selves."* A.F., School Administrator

## EDUCATION AND CERTIFICATIONS

Instructional II—Permanent Certification, **State of Pennsylvania** (2002)

Master of Arts—**LaSalle University** (1994)

Bachelor of Science, Elementary Education—**Chestnut Hill College** (1988)

## CAREER HIGHLIGHTS

- Developed and executed **Everyday Math Program** at John Smith Elementary School (1999). Program resulted in 180-point improvement in overall math grades in 2002 (versus previous year's scores). Participated in ongoing staff development and district training sessions to ensure utilization of hands-on, cooperative learning approach along with reinforcement and assessment techniques.

- Served as **Middle States Team Evaluator** for Brooklyn Diocese School System (1998). Collaborated with four colleagues in accreditation process that included interviewing teachers/committee, writing evaluation report, and creating recommended action plan. Conducted comprehensive academic assessment in similar capacity as Catholic Elementary School Evaluator for Diocese of Camden (1995).

- Achieved 90% passing rate in students graduating to fifth grade by directing and facilitating promotional requirements for **Multidisciplinary Learning Project** at John Smith Elementary School (1999–2002). Through intensive interaction, students developed research, writing, and computer skills to accomplish long-term school project with City Year members. Initiative strengthened student knowledge, pride, and enthusiasm for learning.

## TEACHING EXPERIENCE

**Philadelphia Public School District**                                                         1999–Present
**John Smith Elementary School**
**Elementary Teacher**, Fourth Grade

Plan, implement, and evaluate various curriculum areas. Encourage cooperative learning, peer interaction, and increased achievement levels among disadvantaged and challenged students.

Appointed by principal as **Grade Chairman and Mentor** (2000–2003).

**Judy Cassidy**
**Page Two**

### TEACHING EXPERIENCE (continued)

**St. Agnes–Sacred Heart School**                                              1995–1998
<u>ELEMENTARY TEACHER</u>, Third Grade

Instructed students in Reading, Integrated Language Arts, Religion, and Social Studies. Coordinated and implemented Language Arts Program for first- to fourth-grade students.

**New Jersey Area Parochial School System**                                    1989–1995
<u>ELEMENTARY TEACHER</u>, Third and Fourth Grade

- Saint Joseph Regional School
- Blessed Sacrament School
- Our Lady of Perpetual Help

**Philadelphia Parochial School System**                                       1978–1988
<u>ELEMENTARY TEACHER</u>, First and Second Grade

- Immaculate Heart of Mary School
- Our Lady of the Holy Souls School
- Saint Timothy School

### TEACHING TESTIMONIALS

*"Judith has, from the outset, displayed a level of professional competence and a striving for professional development that has benefited her students, our staff, and the entire school community in concrete ways. She introduced and implemented a variety of innovative classroom management strategies, such as Workshop Way and Integrated Language Arts, having been the first to pilot such a program in our school. She has challenged and motivated students to achievement and activities that have not only developed each child's personal gifts and talents, but also developed cooperative learning strategies to foster collaboration and interaction among her students." G.S., Principal*

*"Judy's professionalism, enthusiasm, and talent as a teacher are evident on a daily basis. Judy employs a thematic approach, and the varied learning experiences the children have to showcase their talents are not just one-time activities but are related to all curriculum areas. Judy is comfortable with and flexible in following many different styles of administration and has been recommended to assume leadership roles many times during her career." F.B., School Administrator*

### PROFESSIONAL DEVELOPMENT COURSES

<u>Attended and participated in various courses from 1998–2004, including</u>

- The Middle Years Literacy Framework
- Middle Years Balanced Literacy
- Academy of Reading Program
- Bringing Curriculum to Life
- Accelerated Reading Program
- Professional Education for Central-East AAO
- Rigby Guided Reading and Literature Circles
- Improving Decision-Making/Values Clarification
- Improving Ability to Communicate Mathematically
- Everyday Math Program and PowerPoint for Educators

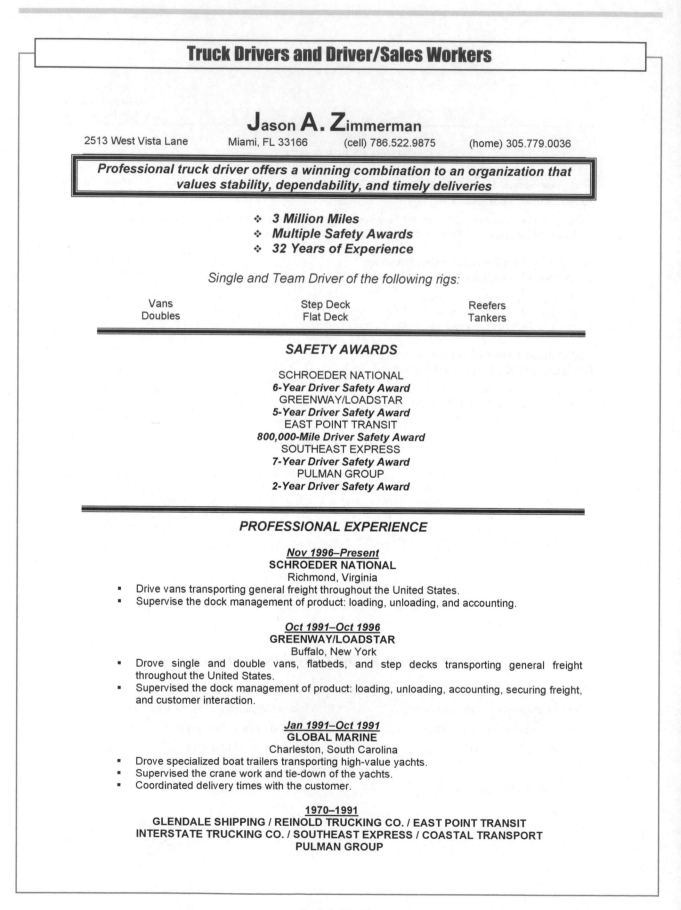

## Truck Drivers and Driver/Sales Workers

# Jason A. Zimmerman

2513 West Vista Lane        Miami, FL 33166        (cell) 786.522.9875        (home) 305.779.0036

> *Professional truck driver offers a winning combination to an organization that values stability, dependability, and timely deliveries*

- ❖ *3 Million Miles*
- ❖ *Multiple Safety Awards*
- ❖ *32 Years of Experience*

*Single and Team Driver of the following rigs:*

| Vans | Step Deck | Reefers |
|------|-----------|---------|
| Doubles | Flat Deck | Tankers |

### SAFETY AWARDS

SCHROEDER NATIONAL
*6-Year Driver Safety Award*
GREENWAY/LOADSTAR
*5-Year Driver Safety Award*
EAST POINT TRANSIT
*800,000-Mile Driver Safety Award*
SOUTHEAST EXPRESS
*7-Year Driver Safety Award*
PULMAN GROUP
*2-Year Driver Safety Award*

### PROFESSIONAL EXPERIENCE

#### Nov 1996–Present
**SCHROEDER NATIONAL**
Richmond, Virginia
- Drive vans transporting general freight throughout the United States.
- Supervise the dock management of product: loading, unloading, and accounting.

#### Oct 1991–Oct 1996
**GREENWAY/LOADSTAR**
Buffalo, New York
- Drove single and double vans, flatbeds, and step decks transporting general freight throughout the United States.
- Supervised the dock management of product: loading, unloading, accounting, securing freight, and customer interaction.

#### Jan 1991–Oct 1991
**GLOBAL MARINE**
Charleston, South Carolina
- Drove specialized boat trailers transporting high-value yachts.
- Supervised the crane work and tie-down of the yachts.
- Coordinated delivery times with the customer.

#### 1970–1991
**GLENDALE SHIPPING / REINOLD TRUCKING CO. / EAST POINT TRANSIT
INTERSTATE TRUCKING CO. / SOUTHEAST EXPRESS / COASTAL TRANSPORT
PULMAN GROUP**

# Important Trends in Jobs and Industries

In putting this section together, my objective was to give you a quick review of major labor market trends. To accomplish this, I included three excellent articles that originally appeared in U.S. Department of Labor publications.

The first article is "Tomorrow's Jobs." It provides a superb—and short—review of the major trends that will affect your career in the years to come. Read it for ideas on selecting a career path for the long term.

The second article is "Employment Trends in Major Industries." While you may not have thought much about it, the industry you work in is just as important as your occupational choice. This great article will help you learn about major trends affecting various industries.

The first chart, "High-Paying Occupations with Many Openings, Projected 2006–2016," shows median earnings for high-paying occupations that also have a large number of openings.

The second chart, "Large Metropolitan Areas That Had the Fastest Employment Growth, 2006," lists areas of the U.S. that experienced a high rate of growth.

# Tomorrow's Jobs

Making informed career decisions requires reliable information about opportunities in the future. Opportunities result from the relationships between the population, the labor force, and the demand for goods and services.

Population ultimately limits the size of the labor force—individuals working or looking for work—which limits the goods and services that can be produced. Demand for various goods and services is largely responsible for employment in the industries providing them. Employment opportunities, in turn, result from demand for skills needed within specific industries. Opportunities for medical assistants and other healthcare occupations, for example, have surged in response to rapid growth in demand for health services.

Examining the past and present and projecting changes in these relationships are the foundation of the Occupational Outlook Program. This chapter presents highlights of the Bureau of Labor Statistics' projections of the labor force and occupational and industry employment that can help guide your career plans.

## Population

Population trends affect employment opportunities in a number of ways. Changes in population influence the demand for goods and services. For example, a growing and aging population has increased the demand for health services. Equally important, population changes produce corresponding changes in the size and demographic composition of the labor force.

The U.S. civilian noninstitutional population is expected to increase by 21.8 million over the 2006–2016 period (Chart 1). The 2006–2016 rate of growth is slower than the growth rate over the 1986–1996 and 1996–2006 periods—9 percent, 11 percent, and 13 percent, respectively. Continued growth, however, will mean more consumers of goods and services, spurring demand for workers in a wide range of occupations and industries. The effects of population growth on various occupations will differ. The differences are partially accounted for by the age distribution of the future population.

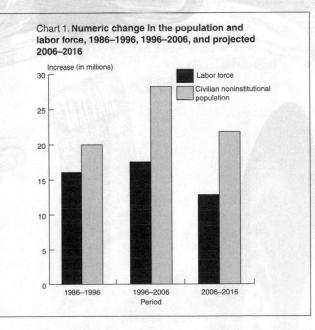

Chart 1. **Numeric change in the population and labor force, 1986–1996, 1996–2006, and projected 2006–2016**

As the baby boomers continue to age, the 55-to-64 age group will increase by 30.3 percent or 9.5 million persons, more than any other group. The 35-to-44 age group will decrease by 5.5 percent, reflecting a slowed birth rate following the baby boom generation, while the youth population, aged 16 to 24, will decline 1.1 percent over the 2006–2016 period.

Minorities and immigrants will constitute a larger share of the U.S. population in 2016. The numbers of Asians and people of Hispanic origin are projected to continue to grow much faster than other racial and ethnic groups.

# Labor Force

Population is the single most important factor in determining the size and composition of the labor force—people either working or looking for work. The civilian labor force is projected to increase by 12.8 million, or 8.5 percent, to 164.2 million over the 2006–2016 period.

The U.S. workforce will become more diverse by 2016. White, non-Hispanic persons will continue to make up a decreasing share of the labor force, falling from 69.1 percent in 2006 to 64.6 percent in 2016 (Chart 2). However, despite relatively slow growth, white non-Hispanics will remain the overwhelming majority of the labor force. Hispanics are projected to be the fastest-growing ethnic group, growing by 29.9 percent. By 2016, Hispanics will continue to constitute an increasing proportion of the labor force, growing from 13.7 percent to 16.4 percent. Asians are projected to account for an increasing share of the labor force by 2016, growing from 4.4 to 5.3 percent. Blacks will also increase their share of the labor force, growing from 11.4 percent to 12.3 percent.

The numbers of men and women in the labor force will grow, but the number of women will grow at a slightly faster rate than the number of men. The male labor force is projected to grow by 8.0 percent from 2006 to 2016, compared with 8.9 percent for women, down from 12.7 and 13.4 percent, respectively, from 1996 to 2006. As a result, men's share of the labor force is expected to decrease from 53.7 to 53.4 percent, while women's share is expected to increase from 46.3 to 46.6 percent.

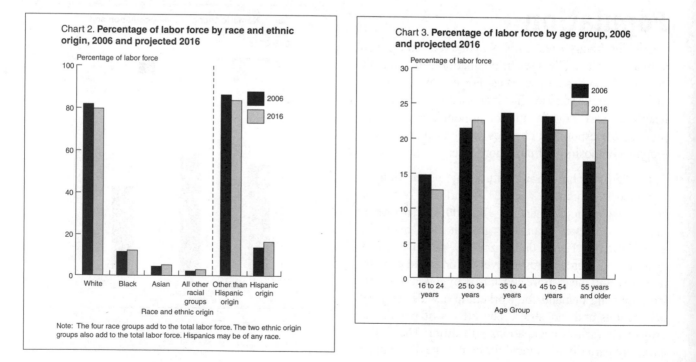

Chart 2. **Percentage of labor force by race and ethnic origin, 2006 and projected 2016**

Note: The four race groups add to the total labor force. The two ethnic origin groups also add to the total labor force. Hispanics may be of any race.

Chart 3. **Percentage of labor force by age group, 2006 and projected 2016**

The youth labor force, aged 16 to 24, is expected to decrease its share of the labor force to 12.7 percent by 2016. The primary working age group, between 25 and 54 years old, is projected to decline from 68.4 percent of the labor force in 2006 to 64.6 percent by 2016. Workers 55 and older, on the other hand, are projected to leap from 16.8 percent to 22.7 percent of the labor force between 2006 and 2016 (Chart 3). The aging of the baby boom generation will cause not only an increase in the percentage of workers in the oldest age category, but a decrease in the percentage of younger workers.

# Employment

Total employment is expected to increase from 150.6 million in 2006 to 166.2 million in 2016, or by 10 percent. The 15.6 million jobs that will be added by 2016 will not be evenly distributed across major industrial and occupational groups. Changes in consumer demand, technology, and many other factors will contribute to the continually changing employment structure in the U.S. economy.

The following two sections examine projected employment change from industrial and occupational perspectives. The industrial profile is discussed in terms of primary wage and salary employment. Primary employment excludes secondary jobs for those who hold multiple jobs. The exception is employment in agriculture, which includes self-employed and unpaid family workers in addition to wage and salary workers.

The occupational profile is viewed in terms of total employment—including primary and secondary jobs for wage and salary, self-employed, and unpaid family workers. Of the roughly 150 million jobs in the U.S. economy in 2006, wage and salary workers accounted for 138.3 million, self-employed workers accounted for 12.2 million, and unpaid family workers accounted for about 130,000. Secondary employment accounted for 1.8 million jobs. Self employed workers held nearly 9 out of 10 secondary jobs and wage and salary workers held most of the remainder.

# Industry

**Service-providing industries.** The long-term shift from goods-producing to service-providing employment is expected to continue. Service-providing industries are expected to account for approximately 15.7 million new wage and salary jobs generated over the 2006–2016 period (Chart 4), while goods-producing industries will see overall job loss.

*Education and health services.* This industry supersector is projected to grow by 18.8 percent and add more jobs, nearly 5.5 million, than any other industry supersector. More than 3 out of every 10 new jobs created in the U.S. economy will be in either the healthcare and social assistance or public and private educational services sectors.

Health care and social assistance—including public and private hospitals, nursing and residential care facilities, and individual and family services—will grow by 25.4 percent and add 4 million new jobs. Employment growth will be driven by increasing demand for health care and social assistance because of an aging population and longer life expectancies. Also, as more women enter the labor force, demand for childcare services is expected to grow.

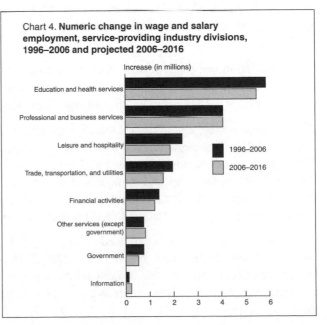

Chart 4. **Numeric change in wage and salary employment, service-providing industry divisions, 1996–2006 and projected 2006–2016**

Public and private educational services will grow by 10.7 percent and add 1.4 million new jobs through 2016. Rising student enrollments at all levels of education will create demand for educational services.

*Professional and business services.* This industry supersector, which includes some of the fastest-growing industries in the U.S. economy, will grow by 23.3 percent and add 4.1 million new jobs.

Employment in administrative and support and waste management and remediation services will grow by 20.3 percent and add 1.7 million new jobs to the economy by 2016. The largest industry growth in this sector will be enjoyed by employment services, which will be responsible for 692,000 new jobs, or more than 40 percent of all new jobs in administrative and support and waste management and remediation services. Employment services ranks second among industries with the most new employment opportunities in the nation and is expected to have a growth rate that is faster than the average for all industries. This will be due to the need for seasonal and temporary workers and for highly specialized human resources services.

Employment in professional, scientific, and technical services will grow by 28.8 percent and add 2.1 million new jobs by 2016. Employment in computer systems design and related services will grow by 38.3 percent and add nearly one-fourth of all new jobs in professional, scientific, and technical services. Employment growth will be driven by the increasing reliance of businesses on information technology and the continuing importance of maintaining system and network security. Management, scientific, and technical consulting services also will grow at a staggering 78 percent and account for another third of growth in this supersector. Demand for these services will be spurred by the increased use of new technology and computer software and the growing complexity of business.

Management of companies and enterprises will grow by 14.9 percent and add 270,000 new jobs.

*Information.* Employment in the information supersector is expected to increase by 6.9 percent, adding 212,000 jobs by 2016. Information contains some of the fast-growing computer-related industries such as software publishing, Internet publishing and broadcasting, and wireless telecommunication carriers. Employment in these industries is expected to grow by 32 percent, 44.1 percent, and 40.9 percent, respectively. The information supersector also includes motion picture production; broadcasting; and newspaper, periodical, book, and directory publishing. Increased demand for telecommunications services, cable service, high-speed Internet connections, and software will fuel job growth among these industries.

*Leisure and hospitality.* Overall employment will grow by 14.3 percent. Arts, entertainment, and recreation will grow by 30.9 percent and add 595,000 new jobs by 2016. Most of these new job openings, 79 percent, will be in the amusement, gambling, and recreation sector. Job growth will stem from public participation in arts, entertainment, and recreation activities, reflecting increasing incomes, leisure time, and awareness of the health benefits of physical fitness.

Accommodation and food services is expected to grow by 11.4 percent and add 1.3 million new jobs through 2016. Job growth will be concentrated in food services and drinking places, reflecting increases in population, dual-income families, and the convenience of many new food establishments.

*Trade, transportation, and utilities.* Overall employment in this industry supersector will grow by 6 percent between 2006 and 2016. Transportation and warehousing is expected to increase by 496,000 jobs, or by 11.1 percent, through 2016. Truck transportation will grow by 11 percent, adding 158,000 new jobs, while rail transportation is projected to decline. The warehousing and storage sector is projected to grow rapidly at 23.5 percent, adding 150,000 jobs. Demand for truck transportation and warehousing services will expand as many manufacturers concentrate on their core competencies and contract out their product transportation and storage functions.

Employment in retail trade is expected to increase by 4.5 percent. Despite slower-than-average growth, this industry will add almost 700,000 new jobs over the 2006–2016 period, growing from 15.3 million employees to 16 million. While consumers will continue to demand more goods, consolidation among grocery stores and department stores will temper growth. Wholesale trade is expected to increase by 7.3 percent, growing from 5.9 million to 6.3 million jobs.

Employment in utilities is projected to decrease by 5.7 percent through 2016. Despite increased output, employment in electric power generation, transmission, and distribution and natural gas distribution is expected to decline through 2016 because of improved technology that increases worker productivity. However, employment in water, sewage, and other systems is expected to increase 18.7 percent by 2016. Jobs are not easily eliminated by technological gains in this industry because water treatment and waste disposal are very labor-intensive activities.

*Financial activities.* Employment is projected to grow 14.4 percent over the 2006–2016 period. Real estate and rental and leasing is expected to grow by 18 percent and add 392,000 jobs by 2016. Growth will be due, in part, to increased demand for housing as the population grows. The fastest-growing industry in the real estate and rental and leasing services sector will be activities related to real estate, such as property management and real estate appraisal, which will grow by 29 percent—remnants of the housing boom that pervaded much of the first half of the decade.

Finance and insurance are expected to add 815,000 jobs, an increase of 13.2 percent, by 2016. Employment in securities, commodity contracts, and other financial investments and related activities is expected to grow 46 percent by 2016, reflecting the increased number of baby boomers in their peak savings years, the growth of tax-favorable retirement plans, and the globalization of the securities markets. Employment in credit intermediation and related services, including banks, will grow by 8.2 percent and add almost one-third of all new jobs within finance and insurance. Insurance carriers and related activities are expected to grow by 7.4 percent and add 172,000 new jobs by 2016. The number of jobs within agencies, brokerages, and other insurance-related activities is expected to grow about 15.4 percent. Growth will stem from the needs of an increasing population and new insurance products on the market.

*Government.* Between 2006 and 2016, government employment, not including employment in public education and hospitals, is expected to increase by 4.8 percent, from 10.8 million to 11.3 million jobs. Growth in government employment will be fueled by an increased demand for pubic safety, but dampened by budgetary constraints and outsourcing of government jobs to the private sector. State and local governments, excluding education and hospitals, are expected to grow by 7.7 percent as a result of the continued shift of responsibilities from the federal government to state and local governments. Federal government employment, including the Postal Service, is expected to decrease by 3.8 percent.

*Other services (except government and private households).* Employment will grow by 14.9 percent. About 2 out of every 5 new jobs in this supersector will be in religious organizations, which are expected to grow by 18.9 percent. Automotive repair and maintenance (as opposed to mechanical/electrical and body repair and maintenance) will be the fastest-growing industry at 40.7 percent, reflecting demand for quick maintenance services for the increasing number of automobiles on the nation's roads. Also included among other services are business, professional, labor, political, and similar organizations, which are expected to increase by 13.6 percent and add 68,000 new jobs. This industry includes homeowner, tenant, and property owner associations.

**Goods-producing industries.** Employment in the goods-producing industries has been relatively stagnant since the early 1980s. Overall, this sector is expected to decline 3.3 percent over the 2006–2016 period. Although employment is expected to decline overall, projected growth among goods-producing industries varies considerably (Chart 5).

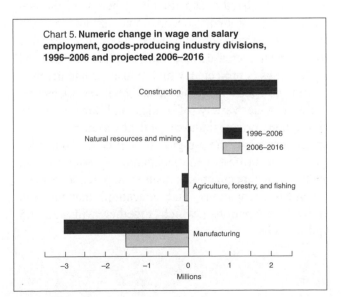

Chart 5. **Numeric change in wage and salary employment, goods-producing industry divisions, 1996–2006 and projected 2006–2016**

*Construction.* Employment in construction is expected to increase by 10.2 percent, from 7.7 million to 8.5 million. Demand for commercial construction and an increase in road, bridge, and tunnel construction will account for the bulk of job growth in this supersector.

*Manufacturing.* While overall employment in this supersector will decline by 10.6 percent or 1.5 million jobs, employment in a few detailed manufacturing industries will increase. For example, employment in pharmaceutical and medicine manufacturing is expected to grow by 23.8 percent and add 69,000 new jobs by 2016. However, productivity gains, job automation, and international competition will adversely affect employment in most manufacturing industries. Employment in household appliance manufacturing is expected to decline by 25.8 percent and lose 21,000 jobs over the decade. Similarly, employment in machinery manufacturing, apparel manufacturing, and computer and electronic product manufacturing will decline by 146,000, 129,000, and 157,000 jobs, respectively.

*Agriculture, forestry, fishing, and hunting.* Overall employment in agriculture, forestry, fishing, and hunting is expected to decrease by 2.8 percent. Employment is expected to continue to decline due to rising costs of production, increasing consolidation, and more imports of food and lumber. The only industry within this supersector expected to grow is support activities for agriculture and forestry, which includes farm labor contractors and farm management services. This industry is expected to grow by 10.5 percent and add 12,000 new jobs. Crop production will see the largest job loss, with 98,000 fewer jobs in 2016 than in 2006.

*Mining.* Employment in mining is expected to decrease 1.6 percent, or by some 10,000 jobs, by 2016. Employment in support activities for mining will be responsible for most of the employment decline in this industry, seeing a loss of 17,000 jobs. Other mining industries, such as coal mining and metal ore mining, are expected to see little or no change or a small increase in employment. Employment stagnation in these industries is attributable mainly to technology gains that boost worker productivity and strict environmental regulations.

# Occupation

Expansion of service-providing industries is expected to continue, creating demand for many occupations. However, projected job growth varies among major occupational groups (Chart 6).

*Professional and related occupations.* These occupations include a wide variety of skilled professions. Professional and related occupations will be one of the two fastest-growing major occupational groups and will add the most new jobs. Over the 2006–2016 period, a 16.7 percent increase in the number of professional and related jobs is projected, which translates into nearly 5 million new jobs. Professional and related workers perform a wide variety of duties and are employed throughout private industry and government. Almost three-quarters of the job growth will come from three groups of professional occupations—computer and mathematical occupations; healthcare practitioners and technical occupations; and education, training, and library occupations—which together will add 3.5 million jobs.

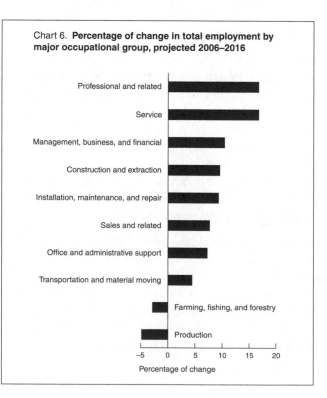

Chart 6. **Percentage of change in total employment by major occupational group, projected 2006–2016**

*Service occupations.* Duties of service workers range from fighting fires to cooking meals. Employment in service occupations is projected to increase by 4.8 million, or 16.7 percent, the second-largest numerical gain and tied with professional and related occupations for the fastest rate of growth among the major occupational groups. Food preparation and serving related occupations are expected to add the most jobs among the service occupations, 1.4 million, by 2016. However, healthcare support occupations and personal care and service occupations are expected to grow the fastest, at 26.8 percent and 22 percent, respectively. Combined, these two occupational groups will account for 2.1 million new jobs.

*Management, business, and financial occupations.* Workers in management, business, and financial occupations plan and direct the activities of business, government, and other organizations. Their employment is expected to increase by 1.6 million, or 10.4 percent, by 2016. Among management occupations, the numbers of social and community service managers and gaming managers will grow the fastest, by 24.7 percent and 24.4 percent, respectively. Construction managers will add the most new jobs—77,000—by 2016. Farmers and ranchers are the only workers whose numbers are expected to see a large decline, losing 90,000 jobs. Among business and financial occupations, accountants and auditors and all other business operation specialists will add the most jobs, 444,000 combined. Financial analysts and personal financial advisors will be the fastest-growing occupations in this group, with growth rates of 33.8 percent and 41 percent, respectively.

*Construction and extraction occupations.* Construction and extraction workers build new residential and commercial buildings and also work in mines, quarries, and oil and gas fields. Employment of these workers is expected to grow 9.5 percent, adding 785,000 new jobs. Construction trades and related workers will account for nearly 4 out of 5 of these new jobs, or 622,000, by 2016. Minor declines in extraction occupations will reflect overall employment stagnation in the mining and oil and gas extraction industries.

*Installation, maintenance, and repair occupations.* Workers in installation, maintenance, and repair occupations install new equipment and maintain and repair older equipment. These occupations will add 550,000 jobs by 2016, growing by 9.3 percent. Automotive service technicians and mechanics and general maintenance and repair workers will account for close to half of all new installation, maintenance, and repair jobs. The fastest growth rate will be among locksmiths and safe repairers, an occupation that is expected to grow 22.1 percent over the 2006–2016 period.

*Transportation and material moving occupations.* Transportation and material moving workers transport people and materials by land, sea, or air. Employment of these workers should increase by 4.5 percent, accounting for 462,000 new jobs by 2016. Among transportation occupations, motor vehicle operators will add the most jobs, 368,000. Material moving occupations will decline slightly, 0.5 percent, losing 25,000 jobs.

*Sales and related occupations.* Sales and related workers solicit goods and services to businesses and consumers. Sales and related occupations are expected to add 1.2 million new jobs by 2016, growing by 7.6 percent. Retail salespersons will contribute the most to this growth by adding 557,000 new jobs.

*Office and administrative support occupations.* Office and administrative support workers perform the day-to-day activities of the office, such as preparing and filing documents, dealing with the public, and distributing information. Employment in these occupations is expected to grow by 7.2 percent, adding 1.7 million new jobs by 2016. Customer service representatives will add the most new jobs, 545,000, while stock clerks and order fillers are expected to see the largest employment decline among all occupations, losing 131,000 jobs.

*Farming, fishing, and forestry occupations.* Farming, fishing, and forestry workers cultivate plants, breed and raise livestock, and catch animals. These occupations will decline 2.8 percent and lose 29,000 jobs by 2016. Agricultural workers, including farmworkers and laborers, will account for nearly three out of four lost jobs in this group. The number of fishing and hunting workers is expected to decline by 16.2 percent, while the number of forest, conservation, and logging workers is expected to decline by 1.4 percent.

*Production occupations.* Production workers are employed mainly in manufacturing, where they assemble goods and operate plants. Production occupations are expected to decline by 4.9 percent, losing 528,000 jobs by 2016. Some jobs will be created in production occupations, mostly in food processing and woodworking. Metal workers and plastic workers; assemblers and fabricators; textile, apparel, and furnishings occupations; and other production workers will account for most of the job loss among production occupations.

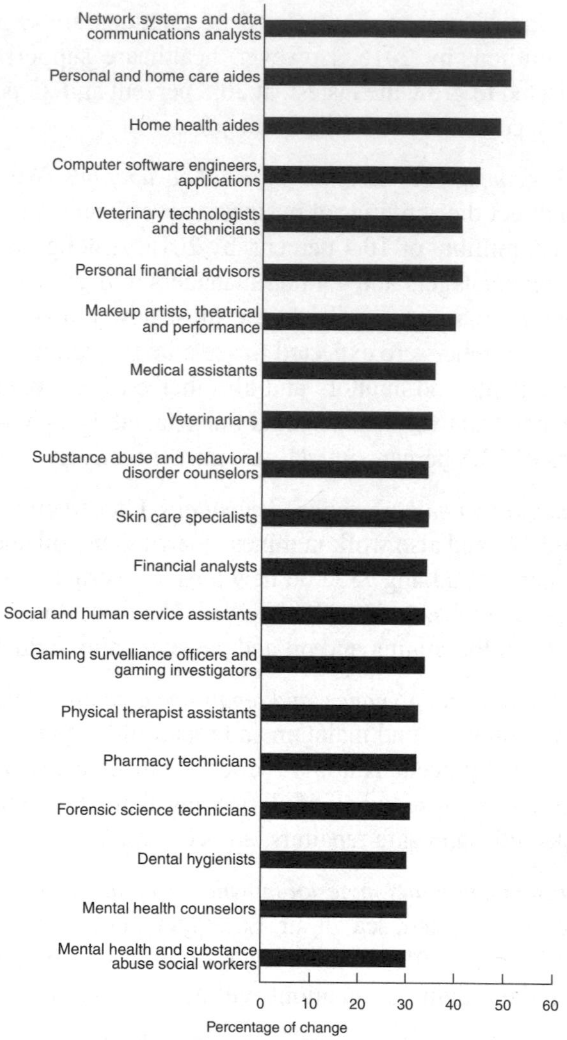

Among all occupations in the economy, healthcare occupations are expected to make up 7 of the 20 fastest-growing occupations, the largest proportion of any occupational group (Chart 7). These seven healthcare occupations, in addition to exhibiting high growth rates, will add nearly 750,000 new jobs between 2006 and 2016. Other occupational groups that have more than one occupation in the 20 fastest-growing occupations are computer occupations, personal care and service occupations, community and social services occupations, and business and financial operations occupations. High growth rates among occupations in the top 20 fastest-growing occupations reflect projected rapid growth in the healthcare and social assistance industries and the professional, scientific, and technical services industries.

The 20 occupations listed in Chart 8 will account for more than one-third of all new jobs, 6.6 million combined, over the 2006–2016 period. The occupations with the largest numerical increases cover a wider range of occupational categories than do those occupations with the fastest growth rates. Health occupations will account for some of these increases in employment, as will occupations in education, sales, and food service. Occupations in office and administrative services will grow by 1.7 million jobs, one-fourth of the job growth among the 20 occupations with the largest job growth. Many of the occupations listed below are very large and will create more new jobs than will those with high growth rates. Only 3 out of the 20 fastest-growing occupations—home health aides, personal and home care aides, and computer software application engineers—also are projected to be among the 20 occupations with the largest numerical increases in employment.

Declining occupational employment stems from declining industry employment, technological advances, changes in business practices, and other factors. For example, installation of self-checkouts and other forms of automation will increase productivity and are expected to contribute to a decline of 118,000 cashiers over the 2006–2016 period (Chart 9). Fourteen of the 20 occupations with the largest numerical decreases are either production occupations or office and administrative support occupations, which are affected by increasing plant and factory automation and the implementation of office technology that reduces the need for these workers. The difference between the office and administrative occupations that are expected to experience the largest declines and those that are expected to see the largest increases is the extent to which job functions can be easily automated or performed by other work-

Chart 7. **Percentage of change in employment in occupations projected to grow fastest, 2006–2016**

ers. For instance, the duties of executive secretaries and administrative assistants involve a great deal of personal interaction that cannot be automated, while the duties of file clerks—adding, locating, and removing business records—can be automated or performed by other workers.

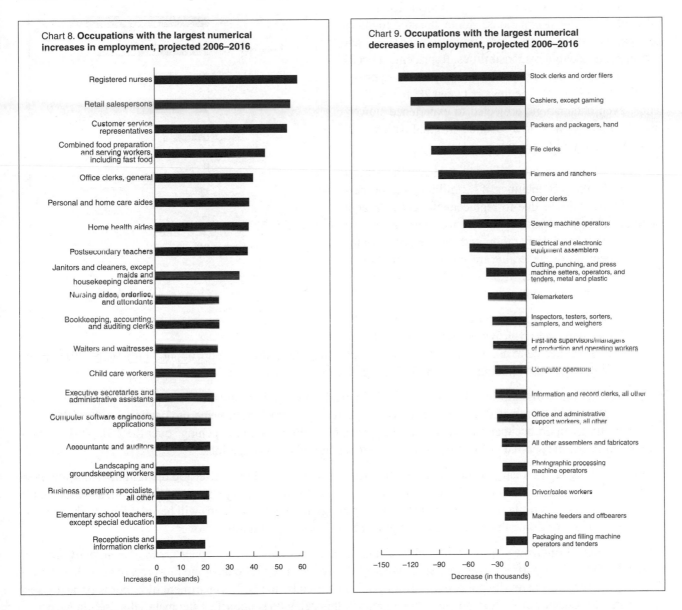

**Chart 8. Occupations with the largest numerical increases in employment, projected 2006–2016**

Registered nurses
Retail salespersons
Customer service representatives
Combined food preparation and serving workers, including fast food
Office clerks, general
Personal and home care aides
Home health aides
Postsecondary teachers
Janitors and cleaners, except maids and housekeeping cleaners
Nursing aides, orderlies, and attendants
Bookkeeping, accounting, and auditing clerks
Waiters and waitresses
Child care workers
Executive secretaries and administrative assistants
Computer software engineers, applications
Accountants and auditors
Landscaping and groundskeeping workers
Business operation specialists, all other
Elementary school teachers, except special education
Receptionists and information clerks

Increase (in thousands) 0 10 20 30 40 50 60

**Chart 9. Occupations with the largest numerical decreases in employment, projected 2006–2016**

Stock clerks and order filers
Cashiers, except gaming
Packers and packagers, hand
File clerks
Farmers and ranchers
Order clerks
Sewing machine operators
Electrical and electronic equipment assemblers
Cutting, punching, and press machine setters, operators, and tenders, metal and plastic
Telemarketers
Inspectors, testers, sorters, samplers, and weighers
First-line supervisors/managers of production and operating workers
Computer operators
Information and record clerks, all other
Office and administrative support workers, all other
All other assemblers and fabricators
Photographic processing machine operators
Driver/sales workers
Machine feeders and offbearers
Packaging and filling machine operators and tenders

Decrease (in thousands) −150 −120 −90 −60 −30 0

# Education and Training

For 12 of the 20 fastest-growing occupations, an associate degree or higher is the most significant level of postsecondary education or training. On-the-job training is the most significant level of postsecondary education or training for another 6 of the 20 fastest-growing occupations. In contrast, on-the-job training is the most significant level of postsecondary education or training for 12 of the 20 occupations with the largest numerical increases, while 6 of these 20 occupations have an associate degree or higher as the most significant level of postsecondary education or training. On-the-job training is the most significant level of postsecondary education or training for 19 of the 20 occupations with the largest numerical decreases.

# Total Job Openings

Job openings stem from both employment growth and replacement needs (Chart 10). Replacement needs arise as workers leave occupations. Some transfer to other occupations while others retire, return to school, or quit to assume household responsibilities. Replacement needs are projected to account for 68 percent of the approximately 50 million job openings between 2006 and 2016. Thus, even occupations projected to experience slower-than-average growth or to decline in employment still may offer many job openings.

Service occupations are projected to have the largest number of total job openings, 12.2 million, and 60 percent of those will be due to replacement needs. A large number of replacements will be necessary as young workers leave food preparation and service occupations. Replacement needs generally are greatest in the largest occupations and in those with relatively low pay or limited training requirements.

Professional and related occupations are projected to be one of the two fastest-growing major occupational

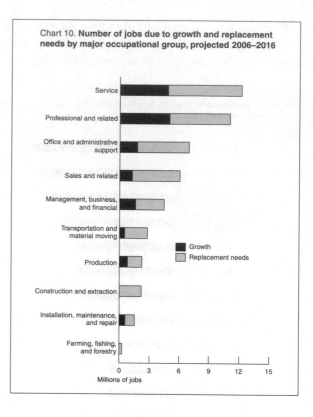

Chart 10. **Number of jobs due to growth and replacement needs by major occupational group, projected 2006–2016**

groups and are expected to add more jobs than any other major occupational group, about 5 million, by 2016. However, the majority of job openings are expected to come from more than 6 million replacements.

Office automation will significantly affect many individual office and administrative support occupations. While these occupations are projected to grow about as fast as average, some are projected to decline rapidly. Office and administrative support occupations are projected to create 6.9 million total job openings over the 2006–2016 period, ranking third behind service occupations and professional and related occupations.

Farming, fishing, and forestry occupations and production occupations should offer job opportunities despite overall declines in employment. These occupations will lose 29,000 and 528,000 jobs, respectively, but are expected to provide more than 2.4 million total job openings. Job openings among these groups will be solely due to the replacement needs of a workforce that is exhibiting high levels of retirement and job turnover.

Editor's Note: "Tomorrow's Jobs," with minor changes, came from the *Occupational Outlook Handbook* and was written by the U.S. Department of Labor staff. Much of this section uses 2006 data, the most recent available at press time. By the time it is carefully collected and analyzed, data used by the U.S. Department of Labor is typically several years old. Because market trends tend to be gradual, this delay does not affect the material's usefulness.

# Employment Trends in Major Industries

The U.S. economy can be broken down into numerous industries, each with its own set of characteristics. The Department of Labor has identified 45 industries that account for three-quarters of all workers. This section provides an overview of these industries and the economy as a whole.

## Nature of the Industry

Industries are defined by the processes they use to produce goods and services. Workers in the United States produce and provide a wide variety of products and services and, as a result, the types of industries in the U.S. economy range widely—from agriculture, forestry, and fishing to aerospace manufacturing. Each industry has a unique combination of occupations, production techniques, inputs and outputs, and business characteristics. Understanding the nature of industries that interest you is important because it is this unique combination that determines working conditions, educational requirements, and the job outlook.

Industries consist of many different places of work, called establishments. Establishments are physical locations in which people work, such as the branch office of a bank, a gasoline service station, a school, a department store, or a plant that manufactures machinery. Establishments range from large factories and corporate office complexes employing thousands of workers to small community stores, restaurants, professional offices, and service businesses employing only a few workers. Establishments should not be confused with companies or corporations, which are legal entities. Thus, a company or corporation may have a single establishment or more than one establishment. Establishments that use the same or similar processes to produce goods or services are organized together into industries. Industries are, in turn, organized together into industry groups such as Information and Trade. These are further organized into industry subsectors and then ultimately into industry sectors. For the purposes of labor market analysis, the Bureau of Labor Statistics organizes industry sectors into industry supersectors. A company or corporation could own establishments classified in more than one industry, industry sector, or even industry supersector.

Each industry subsector is made up of a number of industry groups, which are, as mentioned, determined by differences in production processes. An easily recognized example of these distinctions is in the food manufacturing subsector, which is made up of industry groups that produce meat products, preserved fruits and vegetables, bakery items, and dairy products, among others. Each of these industry groups requires workers with varying skills and employs unique production techniques. Another example of these distinctions is found in utilities, which employs workers in establishments that provide electricity, natural gas, and water.

There were almost 8.8 million private business establishments in the United States in 2006. Business establishments in the United States are predominantly small; 60.4 percent of all establishments employed fewer than 5 workers in

March 2006. However, the medium-sized to large establishments employ a greater proportion of all workers. For example, establishments that employed 50 or more workers accounted for only 4.7 percent of all establishments, yet employed 56.5 percent of all workers. The large establishments—those with more than 500 workers—accounted for only 0.2 percent of all establishments, but employed 17.1 percent of all workers. Table 1 presents the percent distribution of employment according to establishment size.

The average size of these establishments varies widely across industries. Most establishments in the construction, wholesale trade, retail trade, finance and insurance, real estate and rental and leasing, and professional, scientific, and technical services industries are small, averaging fewer than 20 employees per establishment. However, wide differences within industries can exist. Hospitals, for example, employ an average of 542.7 workers, while physicians' offices employ an average of 10.3. Similarly, although there is an average of 14.7 employees per establishment for all of retail trade, department stores employ an average of 130.3 people but jewelry stores employ an average of only 5.9.

Establishment size can play a role in the characteristics of each job. Large establishments generally offer workers greater occupational mobility and advancement potential, whereas small establishments may provide their employees with broader experience by requiring them to assume a wider range of responsibilities. Also, small establishments are distributed throughout the nation—every locality has a few small businesses. Large establishments, in contrast, employ more workers and are less common, but they play a much more prominent role in the economies of the areas in which they are located.

**Table 1. Percent distribution of establishments and employment in all private industries by establishment size, March 2006**

| Establishment size (number of workers) | Percent of establishments | Percent of employment |
|---|---|---|
| Total | 100.0 | 100.0 |
| 1 to 4 | 60.4 | 6.8 |
| 5 to 9 | 16.5 | 8.3 |
| 10 to 19 | 10.9 | 11.2 |
| 20 to 49 | 7.6 | 17.3 |
| 50 to 99 | 2.6 | 13.4 |
| 100 to 249 | 1.5 | 16.6 |
| 250 to 499 | 0.4 | 9.4 |
| 500 to 999 | 0.1 | 6.7 |
| 1,000 or more | 0.1 | 10.4 |

# Working Conditions

Just as the goods and services produced in each industry are different, working conditions vary significantly among industries. In some industries, the work setting is quiet, temperature-controlled, and virtually hazard-free, while other industries are characterized by noisy, uncomfortable, and sometimes dangerous work environments. Some industries require long workweeks and shift work, but standard 40-hour workweeks are common in many other industries. In still other industries, a lot of the jobs can be seasonal, requiring long hours during busy periods and abbreviated schedules during slower months. Production processes, establishment size, and the physical location of work usually determine these varying conditions.

One of the most telling indicators of working conditions is an industry's injury and illness rate. Overexertion, being struck by an object, and falls on the same level, are among the most common incidents causing work-related injury or illness. In 2006, approximately 4.1 million nonfatal injuries and illnesses were reported throughout private industry. Among major industry divisions, manufacturing had the highest rate of injury and illness—6.0 cases for every 100 full time workers—while financial activities had the lowest rate—1.5 cases. About 5,703 work-related fatalities were reported in 2006; the most common events resulting in fatal injuries were transportation incidents, contact with objects and equipment, assaults and violent acts, and falls.

Work schedules are another important reflection of working conditions, and the operational requirements of each industry lead to large differences in hours worked and in part-time versus full-time status. In food services and drinking places, for example, fully 36.5 percent of employees worked part time in 2006 compared with only 2.0 percent in motor vehicles and motor vehicle equipment manufacturing. Table 2 presents industries having relatively high and low percentages of part-time workers.

**Table 2. Part-time workers as a percent of total employment, selected industries, 2006**

| Industry | Percent part-time |
| --- | --- |
| All industries | 15.4 |
| **Many part-time workers** | |
| Food services and drinking places | 36.5 |
| Grocery stores | 31.9 |
| Clothing, accessories, and general merchandise stores | 36.4 |
| Arts, entertainment, and recreation | 27.2 |
| Child day care services | 26.1 |
| Motion picture and video industries | 23.6 |
| Social assistance, except child day care | 23.6 |
| **Few part-time workers** | |
| Mining | 2.6 |
| Computer and electronic product manufacturing | 2.4 |
| Pharmaceutical and medicine manufacturing | 2.4 |
| Steel manufacturing | 2.1 |
| Motor vehicle and parts manufacturing | 2.0 |
| Utilities | 1.8 |
| Aerospace product and parts manufacturing | 1.8 |

The low proportion of part-time workers in some manufacturing industries often reflects the continuous nature of the production processes that makes it difficult to adapt the volume of production to short-term fluctuations in product demand. Once these processes are begun, it is costly to halt them; machinery must be tended and materials must be moved continuously. For example, the chemical manufacturing industry produces many different chemical products through controlled chemical reactions. These processes require chemical operators to monitor and adjust the flow of materials into and out of the line of production. Because production may continue 24 hours a day, 7 days a week under the watchful eyes of chemical operators who work in shifts, full-time workers are more likely to be employed. Retail trade and service industries, on the other hand, have seasonal cycles marked by various events that affect the hours worked, such as school openings or important holidays. During busy times of the year, longer hours are common, whereas slack periods lead to cutbacks in work hours and shorter workweeks. Jobs in these industries are generally appealing to students and others who desire flexible, part-time schedules.

# Employment

The total number of jobs in the United States in 2006 was 150.6 million. This included 12.2 million self-employed workers, 130,000 unpaid workers in family businesses, and 138.3 million wage and salary jobs—including primary and secondary job holders. The total number of jobs is projected to increase to 166.2 million by 2016, and wage and salary jobs are projected to account for almost 153.3 million of them.

As shown in table 3, wage and salary jobs are the vast majority of all jobs, but they are not evenly divided among the various industries. Education, health, and social services had the largest number of jobs in 2006 with almost 29.1 million. The trade supersector was the second largest, with about 21.2 million jobs, followed by professional and business services with 17.6 million jobs in 2006. Manufacturing accounted for roughly 14.2 million jobs in the United States in 2006. Among the industries covered in the *Career Guide*, wage and salary employment ranged from only 154,300 in steel manufacturing to more than 13.6 million in health care. The three largest industries—education services, health care, and food services and drinking places—together accounted for 38.5 million jobs, more than one-quarter of the nation's wage and salary employment.

**Table 3. Wage and salary employment in industries covered in the *Career Guide*, 2006 and projected change, 2006–2016 (Employment in thousands)**

| Industry | 2006 | | 2016 | | 2006–2016 | |
|---|---|---|---|---|---|---|
| | Employment | Percent distribution | Employment | Percent distribution | Percent change | Employment change |
| All industries | 138,310 | 100.0 | 153,262 | 100.0 | 10.8 | 14,951 |
| **Natural resources, construction, and utilities** | 10,076 | 7.3 | 10,710 | 7.0 | 6.3 | 634 |
| Agriculture, forestry, and fishing | 1,220 | 0.9 | 1,114 | 0.7 | -8.6 | -105 |
| Construction | 7,689 | 5.6 | 8,470 | 5.5 | 10.2 | 781 |
| Mining | 619 | 0.4 | 609 | 0.4 | -1.6 | -10 |
| Utilities | 548 | 0.4 | 518 | 0.3 | -5.7 | -31 |
| **Manufacturing** | 14,197 | 10.3 | 12,695 | 8.3 | -10.6 | -1,503 |
| Aerospace product and parts manufacturing | 472 | 0.3 | 497 | 0.3 | 5.4 | 25 |
| Chemical manufacturing, except drugs | 576 | 0.4 | 486 | 0.3 | -15.7 | -90 |
| Computer and electronic product manufacturing | 1,316 | 1.0 | 1,159 | 0.8 | -12.0 | -157 |
| Food manufacturing | 1,484 | 1.1 | 1,489 | 1.0 | 0.3 | 5 |
| Machinery manufacturing | 1,192 | 0.9 | 1,045 | 0.7 | -12.3 | -146 |
| Motor vehicle and parts manufacturing | 1,070 | 0.8 | 918 | 0.6 | -14.3 | -153 |
| Pharmaceutical and medicine manufacturing | 292 | 0.2 | 362 | 0.2 | 23.7 | 69 |
| Printing | 636 | 0.5 | 497 | 0.3 | -21.8 | -138 |
| Steel manufacturing | 154 | 0.1 | 116 | 0.1 | -25.1 | -39 |
| Textile, textile product, and apparel manufacturing | 595 | 0.4 | 385 | 0.3 | -35.4 | -211 |
| **Trade** | 21,217 | 15.3 | 22,332 | 14.6 | 5.3 | 1,115 |
| Automobile dealers | 1,247 | 0.9 | 1,388 | 0.9 | 11.3 | 141 |
| Clothing, accessory, and general merchandise stores | 4,352 | 3.1 | 4,676 | 3.1 | 7.5 | 324 |
| Grocery stores | 2,463 | 1.8 | 2,479 | 1.6 | 0.7 | 16 |
| Wholesale trade | 5,898 | 4.3 | 6,326 | 4.1 | 7.3 | 428 |
| **Transportation and warehousing** | 4,466 | 3.2 | 4,962 | 3.2 | 11.1 | 496 |
| Air transportation | 486 | 0.4 | 522 | 0.3 | 7.3 | 35 |
| Truck transportation and warehousing | 2,074 | 1.5 | 2,381 | 1.6 | 14.8 | 307 |

| Industry | 2006 | | 2016 | | 2006–2016 | |
|---|---|---|---|---|---|---|
| | Employment | Percent distribution | Employment | Percent distribution | Percent change | Employment change |
| **Information** | 3,055 | 2.2 | 3,267 | 2.1 | 6.9 | 212 |
| Broadcasting | 331 | 0.2 | 362 | 0.2 | 9.3 | 31 |
| Motion picture and video industries | 357 | 0.3 | 396 | 0.3 | 10.9 | 39 |
| Publishing, except software | 660 | 0.5 | 611 | 0.4 | -7.5 | -49 |
| Software publishers | 243 | 0.2 | 321 | 0.2 | 32.0 | 78 |
| Telecommunications | 973 | 0.7 | 1,022 | 0.7 | 5.0 | 48 |
| Internet services providers, web search portals, and data processing services | 383 | 0.3 | 437 | 0.3 | 14.0 | 54 |
| **Financial activities** | 8,363 | 6.0 | 9,570 | 6.2 | 14.4 | 1,207 |
| Banking | 1,825 | 1.3 | 1,898 | 1.2 | 4.0 | 74 |
| Insurance | 2,316 | 1.7 | 2,488 | 1.6 | 7.4 | 172 |
| Securities, commodities, and other investments | 816 | 0.6 | 1,192 | 0.8 | 46.1 | 376 |
| **Professional and business services** | 17,552 | 12.7 | 21,644 | 14.1 | 23.3 | 4,092 |
| Advertising and public relations services | 458 | 0.3 | 520 | 0.3 | 13.6 | 62 |
| Computer systems design and related services | 1,278 | 0.9 | 1,768 | 1.2 | 38.3 | 489 |
| Employment services | 3,657 | 2.6 | 4,348 | 2.8 | 18.9 | 692 |
| Management, scientific, and technical consulting services | 921 | 0.7 | 1,639 | 1.1 | 77.9 | 718 |
| Scientific research and development services | 593 | 0.4 | 649 | 0.4 | 9.4 | 56 |
| **Education, health, and social services** | 29,082 | 21.0 | 34,543 | 22.5 | 18.8 | 5,461 |
| Child day care services | 807 | 0.6 | 1,078 | 0.7 | 33.7 | 272 |
| Educational services | 13,152 | 9.5 | 14,564 | 9.5 | 10.7 | 1,412 |
| Health services | 13,621 | 9.8 | 16,576 | 10.8 | 21.7 | 2,954 |
| Social assistance, except child day care | 1,502 | 1.1 | 2,326 | 1.5 | 54.8 | 823 |
| **Leisure and hospitality** | 13,143 | 9.5 | 15,016 | 9.8 | 14.2 | 1,873 |
| Arts, entertainment, and recreation | 1,927 | 1.4 | 2,522 | 1.6 | 30.9 | 595 |
| Food services and drinking places | 9,383 | 6.8 | 10,407 | 6.8 | 10.9 | 1,024 |
| Hotels and other accommodations | 1,833 | 1.3 | 2,088 | 1.4 | 13.9 | 254 |
| **Government and advocacy, grantmaking, and civic organizations** | 11,210 | 8.1 | 11,895 | 7.8 | 6.1 | 685 |
| Advocacy, grantmaking, and civic organizations | 1,234 | 0.9 | 1,392 | 0.9 | 12.8 | 158 |
| Federal Government | 1,958 | 1.4 | 1,868 | 1.2 | -4.6 | -90 |
| State and local government, except education and health | 8,018 | 5.8 | 8,634 | 5.6 | 7.7 | 617 |

*NOTE: May not add to totals due to omission of industries not covered.*

Although workers of all ages are employed in each industry, certain industries tend to possess workers of distinct age groups. For the previously mentioned reasons, retail trade employs a relatively high proportion of younger workers to fill part-time and temporary positions. The manufacturing sector, on the other hand, has a relatively high median age because many jobs in the sector require a number of years to learn and perfect specialized skills that do not easily transfer to other industries. Also, manufacturing employment has been declining, providing fewer opportunities for younger workers to get jobs. As a result, more than one-fourth of the workers in retail trade were 24 years of age or younger in 2006, compared with only 8.1 percent of workers in manufacturing. Table 4 contrasts the age distribution of workers in all industries with the distributions in five very different industries.

**Table 4. Percent distribution of wage and salary workers by age group, selected industries, 2006**

| Industry | Age group | | | |
|---|---|---|---|---|
| | 16 to 24 | 25 to 44 | 45 to 64 | 65 and older |
| All industries | 14 | 45 | 37 | 4 |
| Computer systems design and related services | 5 | 63 | 30 | 2 |
| Educational services | 9 | 42 | 45 | 4 |
| Food services and drinking places | 43 | 38 | 17 | 2 |
| Telecommunications | 8 | 53 | 37 | 2 |
| Utilities | 4 | 42 | 54 | 1 |

Employment in some industries is concentrated in one region of the country. Such industries often are located near a source of raw or unfinished materials upon which the industry relies. For example, oil and gas extraction jobs are concentrated in Texas, Louisiana, and Oklahoma; many textile mills and products manufacturing jobs are found in North Carolina, South Carolina, and Georgia; and a significant proportion of motor vehicle manufacturing jobs are located in Michigan and Ohio. On the other hand, some industries—such as grocery stores and educational services—have jobs distributed throughout the nation, reflecting the general population density.

# Occupations in the Industry

The occupations found in each industry depend on the types of services provided or goods produced. For example, because construction companies require skilled trades workers to build and renovate buildings, these companies employ large numbers of carpenters, electricians, plumbers, painters, and sheet metal workers. Other occupations common to construction include construction equipment operators and mechanics, installers, and repairers. Retail trade, on the other hand, displays and sells manufactured goods to consumers. As a result, retail trade employs numerous retail salespersons and other workers, including more than three-fourths of all cashiers. Table 5 shows the industry sectors and the occupational groups that predominate in each.

**Table 5. Industry sectors and their largest occupational group, 2006**

| Industry sector | Largest occupational group | Percent of industry wage and salary jobs |
|---|---|---|
| Agriculture, forestry, fishing, and hunting | Farming, fishing, and forestry occupations | 58.3 |
| Mining | Construction and extraction occupations | 37.8 |
| Construction | Construction and extraction occupations | 66.8 |
| Manufacturing | Production occupations | 52.5 |
| Wholesale trade | Sales and related occupations | 26.3 |
| Retail trade | Sales and related occupations | 54.1 |
| Transportation and warehousing | Transportation and material moving occupations | 59.8 |
| Utilities | Installation, maintenance, and repair occupations | 27.1 |
| Information | Professional and related occupations | 33.3 |
| Finance and insurance | Office and administrative support occupations | 49.8 |
| Real estate and rental and leasing | Sales and related occupations | 24.5 |
| Professional, scientific, and technical services | Professional and related occupations | 45.0 |

| Industry sector | Largest occupational group | Percent of industry wage and salary jobs |
|---|---|---|
| Management of companies and enterprises | Management, business, and financial occupations | 33.1 |
| Administrative and support and waste management and remediation services | Service occupations | 31.4 |
| Educational services, public and private | Professional and related occupations | 67.4 |
| Health care and social assistance | Professional and related occupations | 43.3 |
| Arts, entertainment, and recreation | Service occupations | 58.8 |
| Accommodation and food services | Service occupations | 86.6 |
| Government | Service occupations | 25.0 |

The occupational distribution clearly is influenced by the structure of its industries, yet there are many occupations, such as general managers or secretaries, that are found in all industries. In fact, some of the largest occupations in the U.S. economy are dispersed across many industries. For example, the group of professional and related occupations is among the largest in the nation while also experiencing the fastest growth rate. (See table 6.) Other large occupational groups include service occupations; office and administrative support occupations; sales and related occupations; and management, business, and financial occupations.

**Table 6. Total employment and projected change by broad occupational group, 2006–2016 (Employment in thousands)**

| Occupational group | Employment, 2006 | Percent change, 2006–2016 |
|---|---|---|
| Total, all occupations | 150,620 | 10.4 |
| Professional and related occupations | 29,819 | 16.7 |
| Service occupations | 28,950 | 16.7 |
| Office and administrative support occupations | 24,344 | 7.2 |
| Sales and related occupations | 15,985 | 7.6 |
| Management, business, and financial occupations | 15,397 | 10.4 |
| Production occupations | 10,675 | -4.9 |
| Transportation and material moving occupations | 10,233 | 4.5 |
| Construction and extraction occupations | 8,295 | 9.5 |
| Installation, maintenance, and repair occupations | 5,883 | 9.3 |
| Farming, fishing, and forestry occupations | 1,039 | -2.8 |

# Training and Advancement

Workers prepare for employment in many ways, but the most fundamental form of job training in the United States is a high school education. Better than 88 percent of the nation's workforce possessed a high school diploma or its equivalent in 2006. However, many occupations require more training, so growing numbers of workers pursue additional training or education after high school. In 2006, 28.7 percent of the nation's workforce reported having completed some college or an associate degree as their highest level of education, while an additional 30.2 percent continued in their studies and attained a bachelor's or higher degree. In addition to these types of formal education, other sources of qualifying training include formal company-provided training, apprenticeships, informal on-the-job training, correspondence courses, Armed Forces vocational training, and non–work-related training.

The unique combination of training required to succeed in each industry is determined largely by the industry's production process and the mix of occupations it requires. For example, manufacturing employs many machine operators who generally need little formal education after high school, but sometimes complete considerable on-the-job training. In contrast, educational services employs many types of teachers, most of whom require a bachelor's or higher degree. Training requirements by industry sector are shown in table 7.

Table 7. Percent distribution of workers by highest grade completed or degree received, by industry sector, 2006

| Industy sector | High school diploma or less | Some college or associate degree | Bachelor's or higher degree |
|---|---|---|---|
| All industries | 41.1 | 28.7 | 30.2 |
| Agriculture, forestry, fishing, and hunting | 62.3 | 22.0 | 15.8 |
| Mining | 58.8 | 24.9 | 16.3 |
| Construction | 64.5 | 24.2 | 11.3 |
| Manufacturing | 50.7 | 25.6 | 23.6 |
| Wholesale trade | 43.0 | 29.3 | 27.8 |
| Retail trade | 50.8 | 32.1 | 17.1 |
| Transportation and warehousing | 52.3 | 32.1 | 15.7 |
| Utilities | 39.3 | 34.4 | 26.3 |
| Information | 25.6 | 31.6 | 42.8 |
| Finance and insurance | 22.7 | 31.0 | 46.3 |
| Real estate and rental and leasing | 33.6 | 32.5 | 33.9 |
| Professional, scientific, and technical services | 13.4 | 24.6 | 61.9 |
| Administrative and support and waste management services | 53.9 | 28.3 | 17.9 |
| Educational services | 17.3 | 19.2 | 63.5 |
| Health care and social assistance | 29.8 | 34.6 | 35.5 |
| Arts, entertainment, and recreation | 39.5 | 32.1 | 28.3 |
| Accommodation and food services | 61.3 | 27.8 | 10.9 |

Persons with no more than a high school diploma accounted for about 64.5 percent of all workers in construction; 62.3 percent in agriculture, forestry, fishing, and hunting; 61.3 percent in accommodation and food services; 58.8 percent in mining; 53.9 percent in administrative and support and waste management services; and 52.3 in transportation and warehousing. On the other hand, those who had acquired a bachelor's or higher degree accounted for 63.6 percent of all workers in private educational services; 61.9 percent in professional, scientific, and technical services; 46.3 percent in finance and insurance; and 42.8 percent in information.

Education and training also are important factors in the variety of advancement paths found in different industries. Each industry has some unique advancement paths, but workers who complete additional on-the-job training or education generally help their chances of being promoted. In much of the manufacturing sector, for example, production workers who receive training in management and computer skills increase their likelihood of being promoted to supervisory positions. Other factors that impact advancement and that may figure prominently in industries include the size of the establishments, institutionalized career tracks, and the mix of occupations. As a result, persons who seek jobs in particular industries should be aware of how these advancement paths and other factors may later shape their careers.

# Earnings

Like other characteristics, earnings differ by industry, the result of a highly complicated process that reflects a number of factors. For example, earnings may vary due to the nature of occupations in the industry, average hours worked, geographical location, workers' average age, educational requirements, profits, and the degree of union representation of the workforce. In general, wages are highest in metropolitan areas to compensate for the higher cost of living. Also, as would be expected, industries that employ a large proportion of unskilled minimum-wage or part-time workers tend to have lower earnings.

The difference in earnings between software publishers and the food services and drinking places industries illustrates how various characteristics of industries can result in great differences in earnings. In software publishers, earnings of all wage and salary workers averaged $1,444 a week in 2006, while in food services and drinking places, earnings of all wage and salary workers averaged only $215 weekly. The difference is large primarily because software publishing establishments employ more highly skilled, full-time workers, while food services and drinking places employ many lower skilled workers on a part-time basis. In addition, most workers in software publishing are paid an annual salary, while many workers in food services and drinking places are paid an hourly wage, but many are able to supplement their low hourly wage rate with money they receive as tips. Table 8 highlights the industries with the highest and lowest average weekly earnings.

### Table 8. Average weekly earnings of production or nonsupervisory workers on private nonfarm payrolls, selected industries, 2006

| Industry | Earnings |
| --- | --- |
| All industries | $568 |
| **Industries with high earnings** | |
| Software publishers | 1,444 |
| Computer systems design and related services | 1,265 |
| Scientific research and development services | 1,136 |
| Utilities | 1,136 |
| Aerospace product and parts manufacturing | 1,153 |
| Securities, commodities, and other investments | 1,055 |
| **Industries with low earnings** | |
| Employment services | 453 |
| Grocery stores | 328 |
| Arts, entertainment, and recreation | 332 |
| Hotels and other accommodations | 353 |
| Child day care services | 316 |
| Food services and drinking places | 215 |

Employee benefits, once a minor addition to wages and salaries, continue to grow in diversity and cost. In addition to traditional benefits—paid vacations, life and health insurance, and pensions—many employers now offer various benefits to accommodate the needs of a changing labor force. Such benefits sometimes include childcare, employee assistance programs that provide counseling for personal problems, and wellness programs that encourage exercise, stress management, and self-improvement. Benefits vary among occupational groups, full- and part-time workers, public and private sector workers, regions, unionized and nonunionized workers, and small and large establishments. Data indicate that full-time workers and those in medium-sized and large establishments—those with 100 or more workers—usually receive better benefits than do part-time workers and those in smaller establishments.

Union representation of the workforce varies widely by industry, and it also may play a role in determining earnings and benefits. In 2006, about 13.2 percent of workers throughout the nation were union members or covered by union contracts. As table 9 demonstrates, union affiliation of workers varies widely by industry. 51.6 percent of the workers in air transportation were union members, the highest rate of all the industries, followed by 37.6 percent in educational services, and 34.4 percent in public administration. Industries with the lowest unionization rate include computer systems design and related services, 1.7 percent; food services and drinking places, 1.5 percent; and Internet service providers, web search portals, and data processing services and software publishing, both with virtually no union workers.

**Table 9. Union members and other workers covered by union contracts as a percent of total employment, selected industries, 2006**

| Industry | Percent union members or covered by union contract |
|---|---|
| All industries ......................................................................13.2 | |
| **Industries with high unionization rates** | |
| Air transportation ...............................................................51.6 | |
| Educational services ..........................................................37.6 | |
| Public administration .........................................................34.4 | |
| Utilities...............................................................................31.9 | |
| **Industries with low unionization rates** | |
| Computer systems design and related services ......................1.7 | |
| Food services and drinking places.........................................1.5 | |
| Internet service providers, web search portals, and data processing services....................................................................0.0 | |
| Software publishing ..............................................................0.0 | |

# Outlook

Total wage and salary employment in the United States is projected to increase by about 10.8 percent over the 2006–2016 period. Employment growth, however, is only one source of job openings. The total number of openings in any industry also depends on the industry's current employment level and its need to replace workers who leave their jobs. Throughout the economy, replacement needs will create more job openings than will employment growth. Employment size is a major determinant of job openings—larger industries generally have larger numbers of workers who must be replaced and provide more openings. The occupational composition of an industry is another factor. Industries with high concentrations of professional, technical, and other jobs that require more formal education—occupations in which workers tend to leave their jobs less frequently—generally have fewer openings resulting from replacement needs. On the other hand, more replacement openings generally occur in industries with high concentrations of service, laborer, and other jobs that require little formal education and have lower wages because workers in these jobs are more likely to leave their occupations.

Employment growth is determined largely by changes in the demand for the goods and services provided by an industry, worker productivity, and foreign competition. Each industry is affected by a different set of variables that determines the number and composition of jobs that will be available. Even within an industry, employment may grow at different rates in different occupations. For example, changes in technology, production methods, and business practices in an industry might eliminate some jobs, while creating others. Some industries may be growing rapidly overall, yet opportunities for workers in occupations within those industries could be stagnant or even declining because they are adversely affected by technological change. Similarly, employment of some occupations may be declining in the economy as a whole, yet may be increasing in a rapidly growing industry.

As shown earlier in table 3, employment growth rates over the next decade will vary widely among industries. Natural resources, construction, and utilities are primarily expected to grow due to growth in construction, offsetting job declines in agriculture, mining, and utilities. Growth in construction employment will stem from new factory construction as existing facilities are modernized; from new school construction, reflecting growth in the school-age population; and from infrastructure improvements, such as road and bridge construction. Employment in agriculture, forestry, and fishing should continue to decrease with consolidation of farm land, increasing worker productivity, and depletion of wild fish stocks. Employment in mining is expected to decline due to the use of new laborsaving technology and with the continued reliance on foreign sources of energy.

Employment in manufacturing is expected to decline overall with some growth in selected manufacturing industries. Employment declines are expected in chemical manufacturing, except drugs; computer and electronic product manufacturing; machinery manufacturing; motor vehicle and parts manufacturing; printing; steel manufacturing; and textile, textile product, and apparel manufacturing. Textile, textile product, and apparel manufacturing is projected to lose about 211,000 jobs over the 2006–2016 period—more than any other manufacturing industry—due primarily to increasing imports replacing domestic products.

Employment gains are expected in some manufacturing industries. Small employment gains in food manufacturing are expected, as a growing and ever more diverse population increases the demand for manufactured food products. Employment growth in pharmaceutical and medicine manufacturing is expected as sales of pharmaceuticals increase with growth in the population, particularly among the elderly, and with the introduction of new medicines to the market. Both food and pharmaceutical and medicine manufacturing also have growing export markets. Aerospace product and parts manufacturing is expected to have modest employment increases as well.

Growth in overall employment will result primarily from growth in service-providing industries over the 2006–2016 period, almost all of which are expected to have increasing employment. Job growth is expected to be led by health care and educational services, with large numbers of new jobs also in food services and drinking places; social assistance, except child day care; management, scientific, and technical consulting services; employment services, state and local government, except education and health care; arts entertainment, and recreation; computer systems design and related services; and wholesale trade. When combined, these sectors will account for nearly two-thirds of all new wage and salary jobs across the nation. Employment growth is expected in many other service-providing industries, but they will result in far fewer numbers of new jobs.

Health care will account for the most new wage and salary jobs, almost 3.0 million over the 2006–2016 period. Population growth, advances in medical technologies that increase the number of treatable diseases, and a growing share of the population in older age groups will drive employment growth. General medical and surgical hospitals, public and private—the largest health care industry group—is expected to account for about 691,000 of these new jobs.

Educational services is expected to grow by 10.7 percent over the 2006–2016 period, adding about 1.4 million new jobs. A growing emphasis on improving education and making it available to more children and young adults will be the primary factors contributing to employment growth. Employment growth is expected at all levels of education, particularly at the postsecondary level, as children of the baby boomers continue to reach college age, and as more adults pursue continuing education to enhance or update their skills.

Employment in the nation's fastest growing industry—management, scientific, and technical consulting services is expected to increase by almost 78 percent, adding another 718,000 jobs over the 2006–2016 period. Projected job growth can be attributed primarily to economic growth and to the continuing complexity of business. A growing number of businesses means increased demand for advice in all areas of business operations and planning.

The food services and drinking places industry is expected to add more than 1.0 million new jobs over the 2006–2016 projection period. Increases in population, dual-income families, and dining sophistication will contribute to job growth. In addition, the increasing diversity of the population will contribute to job growth in food services and drinking places that offer a wider variety of ethnic foods and drinks.

Almost 617,000 new jobs are expected to arise in state and local government, except education and health care, growth of almost 8 percent over the 2006–2016 period. Job growth will result primarily from growth in the population and its demand for public services. Additional job growth will result as state and local governments continue to receive greater responsibility from the federal government for administering federally funded programs.

Wholesale trade is expected to add more than 428,000 new jobs over the coming decade, reflecting growth both in trade and in the overall economy. Most new jobs will be for sales representatives at the wholesale and manufacturing levels. However, industry consolidation and the growth of electronic commerce using the Internet are expected to limit job growth to 7.3 percent over the 2006–2016 period, less than the 10.8 percent projected for all industries.

Continual changes in the economy have far-reaching and complex effects on employment in industries. Job seekers should be aware of these changes, keeping alert for developments that can affect job opportunities in industries and the variety of occupations that are found in each industry.

*Editor's Note: The preceding article was adapted from the* Career Guide to Industries, *a publication of the U.S. Department of Labor. A book titled* 40 Best Fields for Your Career *(JIST Publishing) includes information from the* Career Guide to Industries *plus useful "best fields" lists and other helpful insights.*

# High-Paying Occupations with Many Openings, Projected 2006–2016

Over the 2006–2016 decade, career choices abound for those seeking high earnings and lots of opportunities. High-paying occupations that are projected to have many openings are varied. This diverse group includes teachers, managers, and construction trades workers.

The job openings shown in the chart on the next page represent the total that are expected each year for workers who are either entering for the first time or moving from job to job within the occupation. The job openings result from each occupation's growth and from the need to replace workers who retire or leave the occupation permanently for some other reason.

Median earnings, such as those listed in the chart, indicate that half of the workers in an occupation made more than that amount, and half made less. The occupations in the chart ranked in the highest or second-highest earnings quartiles for 2006 median earnings. This means that median earnings for workers in these occupations were higher than the earnings for at least 50 percent of all occupations in 2006.

Most of these occupations had another thing going for them in 2006: low or very low unemployment. Workers in occupations that had higher levels of unemployment—carpenters and truck drivers—were more dependent on a strong economy or seasonal employment.

# High-Paying Occupations with Many Openings, Projected 2006–2016

| Occupation | Annual average job openings due to growth and total replacement needs, projected 2006–2016 | Median annual earnings 2006 |
|---|---|---|
| Truck drivers, heavy and tractor-trailer | 279,032 | $35,040 |
| Postsecondary teachers | 237,478 | 57,770 |
| Executive secretaries and administrative assistants | 235,314 | 37,240 |
| Registered nurses | 233,499 | 57,280 |
| Carpenters | 223,225 | 36,550 |
| First-line supervisors/managers of retail sales workers | 221,241 | 33,960 |
| Elementary school teachers, except special education | 181,612 | 45,570 |
| Maintenance and repair workers, general | 165,502 | 31,910 |
| Sales representatives, wholesale and manufacturing, except technical and scientific products | 156,215 | 49,610 |
| Business operation specialists, all other | 150,806 | 55,650 |
| First-line supervisors/managers of office and administrative support workers | 138,420 | 43,510 |
| Accountants and auditors | 134,463 | 54,630 |
| Farmers and ranchers | 129,552 | 37,130 |
| Management analysts | 125,669 | 68,050 |
| General and operations managers | 112,072 | 85,230 |
| Managers, all other | 103,838 | 82,490 |
| Painters, construction and maintenance | 101,140 | 31,190 |
| Automotive service technicians and mechanics | 97,350 | 33,780 |
| Computer support specialists | 97,334 | 41,470 |
| Secondary school teachers, except special and vocational education | 93,166 | 47,740 |

*Source: U.S. Department of Labor, Office of Occupational Statistics and Employment Projections.*

# Large Metropolitan Areas That Had the Fastest Employment Growth, 2006

The Sun Belt beamed for employment growth from 2005 to 2006, according to data from the Bureau of Labor Statistics. Between May 2005 and May 2006, the Sun Belt was home to almost all the large metropolitan areas in the United States in which employment growth was highest. Total U.S. nonfarm payroll employment increased 1.8 percent over his period as the nation experienced a lukewarm economy. As the chart on the next page shows, employment in 10 of the metropolitan areas with at least 300,000 jobs in May 2005 grew by at least two times the national rate over the same period—and one of them increased at more than three times the national rate.

But before packing your bags for one of these metropolitan areas, remember that these data do not show the variation in the kinds of jobs added.

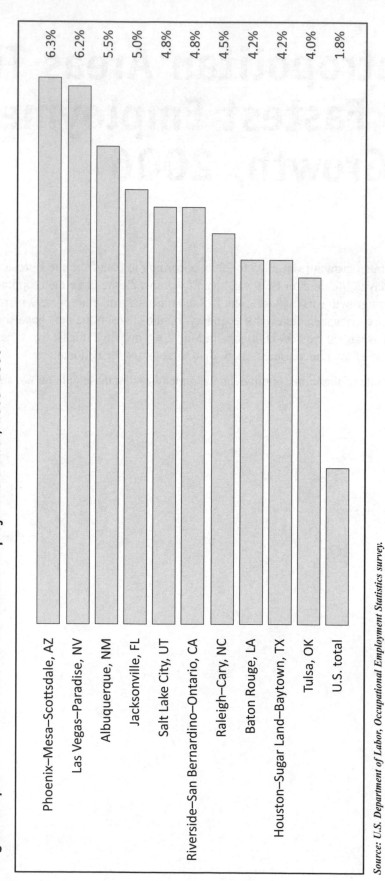

**Large Metropolitan Areas That Had the Fastest Employment Growth, 2005–2006**

| Metropolitan Area | Percent |
|---|---|
| Phoenix–Mesa–Scottsdale, AZ | 6.3% |
| Las Vegas–Paradise, NV | 6.2% |
| Albuquerque, NM | 5.5% |
| Jacksonville, FL | 5.0% |
| Salt Lake City, UT | 4.8% |
| Riverside–San Bernardino–Ontario, CA | 4.8% |
| Raleigh–Cary, NC | 4.5% |
| Baton Rouge, LA | 4.2% |
| Houston–Sugar Land–Baytown, TX | 4.2% |
| Tulsa, OK | 4.0% |
| U.S. total | 1.8% |

*Source: U.S. Department of Labor, Occupational Employment Statistics survey.*

# Index